Groundwater problems in coastal areas

A contribution to the
International Hydrological
Programme

Publication of the IHP Working Group
on Changes in the salt-fresh water
balance in deltas, estuaries and coastal
zones due to structural works and
groundwater exploitation

Prepared by E. Custodio, Chairman,
with the collaboration of
G. A. Bruggeman
and the contribution of case histories
by other experts

Unesco

In this work, countries or parts of countries are referred to as geographical areas and not as political entities. The designations employed and the presentation of the material herein do not imply the expression of any opinion whatsoever on the part of Unesco concerning the legal status of any country or territory, or its authorities, or concerning the frontiers of any country or territory.

Published in 1987 by the United Nations
Educational, Scientific and Cultural Organization,
7, place de Fontenoy, 75700 Paris
Printed by
Imprimerie Bietlot Frères, Fleurus, Belgique

ISBN 92-3-102415-9

Preface

Although the total amount of water on earth is generally assumed to have remained virtually constant, the rapid growth of population, together with the extension of irrigated agriculture and industrial development, are stressing the quantity and quality aspects of the natural system. Because of the increasing problems, man has begun to realize that he can no longer follow a 'use and discard' philosophy - either with water resources or any other natural resources. As a result, the need for a consistent policy of rational management of water resources has become evident.

Rational water management, however, should be founded upon a thorough understanding of water availability and movement. Thus, as a contribution to the solution of the world's water problems, Unesco, in 1965, began the first world-wide programme of studies of the hydrological cycle - the International Hydrological Decade (IHD). The research programme was complemented by a major effort in the field of hydrological education and training. The activities undertaken during the Decade proved to be of great interest and value to Member Stated. By the end of that period, a majority of Unesco's Member States had formed IHD National Committees to carry out relevant national activities and to participate in regional and international co-operation within the IHD programme. The knowledge of the world's water resources had substantially improved. Hydrology became widely recognized as an independent professional option and facilities for the training of hydrologists had been developed.

Conscious of the need to expand upon the effort initiated during the International Hydrological Decade and following the recommendations of Member States, Unesco, in 1975, launched a new long-term intergovernmental programme, the International Hydrological Programme (IHP), to follow the Decade.

Although the IHP is basically a scientific and educational programme, Unesco has been aware from the beginning of a need to direct its activities toward the practical solutions of the world's very real water resources problems. Accordingly, and in line with the recommendations of the 1977 United Nations Water Conference, the objectives of the International Hydroloical Programme have been gradually expanded in order to cover not only hydroloical processes considered in interrelationship with the environment and human activities, but also the scientific aspects of multipurpose utilization and conservation of water resources to meet the needs of economic and social development. Thus, while maintaining IHP's scientific concept, the objectives have shifted perceptibly towards multidisciplinary approach to the assessment, planning, and rational management of water resources.

As part of Unesco's contribution to the objectives of the IHP, two publication series are issued: 'Studies and Reports in Hydrology' and 'Technical Papers in Hydrology'. In addition to these publications, and in order to expedite exchange of information in the areas in which it is most needed, works of a preliminary nature are issued in the form of Technical Documents.

The purpose of the continuing series 'Studies and Reports in Hydrology' to which this volume belongs, is to present data collected and the main results of hydrological studies, as well as to provide information on hydrological research techniques. The proceedings of symposia are also sometimes included. It is hoped that these volumes will furnish material of both practical and theoretical interest to water resources scientists and also to those involved in water resources assessment and the planning for rational water resources management.

Contents

Introduction

<u>General scope</u>

This monograph began with the first session (9-17 April 1975) of the International Hydrological Programme Intergovernmental Council, after considering the guidelines for the 1975-1980 period approved by the Unesco General Conference at its 18th Session. Project 5 was established to deal with the evaluation of hydrological and ecological effects of man's activities. Point 6 refers to the estimation of changes in the salt water-fresh water balance in coastal areas due to hydraulic works and groundwater exploitation. A special focus is put on the study of hydrological studies related to new energy sources.

At the second meeting of the Intergovernmental Council, held in Paris on 20-27 June 1977, it was decided to re-establish the Working Group on evaluation of the changes on salt water-fresh water balance (surface and underground) in deltas, estuaries and coastal zones, due to the construction of structures and to groundwater exploitation (1977-1979) to prepare a technical note (1975-1977) to include a general description of the problems, studies and methods to be used to evaluate and foresee the changes in the salt water-fresh water balancees in coastal zones as a consequence of human activities, with a deadline of 1978. Subsequent delays prevented finishing part of the work until 1982.

At the third meeting of the Working Group, it was decided that the paper to be written was to be a monograph with wider coverage to deal with the different aspects needed to understand coastal water resources. The title 'Costal water problems' was adopted, but the contents still follow the main scope set by the Unesco Council.

<u>Constitution and task of the Working Group</u>

The Working Group was initially formed by A. Al-Mugrin (Riyadh, Saudi Arabia, groundwater); E. Custodio (Barcelona, Spain, groundwater); K.G. Lubomirova (Moscow, USSR, surface water); and K. Sannuganathan (Reading, U.K., surface water). Later G.A. Bruggeman was added (the Netherlands, groundwater).

Only E. Custodio was able to attend the first meeting in Paris, and was entrusted with the Chairmanship of the group. Due to unforeseen circumstances K.G. Lubomirova and A. Al-Mugrin could not actively participate in the Working Group, and it was thus reduced to three people, plus the technical sectretariat. V. Cotecchia (Bari, Italy, groundwater) was called upon to help the group as an observer, and performed a part of the task. Some aid was also received from R. Dijon (United Nations, New York) and J.C. van Dam (Delft, the Netherlands) acting as advisors mainly on the groundwater aspects. The technical secretariat and the Chairman looked for a wide spectrum of case histories and information, writing to IHP National Committees and to a broad list of world experts. The answers received are analysed in chapter 10, and have also been used as background material for the other chapters.

At the second meeting in Wallingford, and later the third in Paris, the Working Group established a detailed outline and shared among its members the task of writing the different chapters. This task was only partially accomplished due to difficulties and delays, and in the fall of 1981, since the surface water part proved to be the most incomplete and difficult to finish, it was decided to handle only the groundwater part.

For this volume, the Chairman took the task of modifying the outline, reorganizing the existing material, updating it, and writing the parts not yet contributed by one of the groundwater experts.

Acknowledgements

The Chairman of the Working Group is highly indebted for the help received from the Comisaria de Aguas del Pirineo Oriental (Eastern Pyrenees Water Authority) of the General Directorship of Public Works, the Industrial Engineers High Technical School of Barcelona, and Barcelona's Polytechnic University, and for permission to devote much time to the task of writing and reviewing the present monograph. Also he is indebted to the organizations above and the International Groundwater Hydrology Course of Barcelona for the manpower and financial help in typing much of the draft and drawing half of the figures, and also for providing the required secretariat facilities and the expenses involved.

Thanks are also due to the Civil Engineering Faculty of the Bari University for the aid received from Mr. Vincenzo Cotecchia, and to the Dutch Rijksinstituut voor Dinkwater Vorziening for the collaboration of Mr. G.A. Bruggeman.

Acknowledgements must also be made to those who have contributed case histories, whether appearing in chapter 10 or not, and to those who have contributed other material, especially Mr. Robert Dijon of the United Nations (New York), Mr. J.C. van Dam of the Delft Technical University (the Netherlands), Mr. José-Ignacio Garcia-Bengochea of Florida, Francis A. Kohout of the U.S. Geological Survey (Washington), and Arthur Bruigton of the Los Angeles County Flood Control District (California).

The Spanish, Dutch and Italian National Committees for the International Hydrological Programme have helped in solving various problems, and have all encouraged the work. All contributors are mentioned in the contents.

Most of the first typing of the manuscript was accomplished by Ms. Maria Felisa Zurbano, and the drawings done by Ms. Charo Alaiz, both of them working for the Eastern Pyrenees Water Authority and the International Groundwater Hydrology course. The final editing was carried out by Prof. Neil Grigg with the aid of Ms. Verdia Johnson and Mr. Gabriel Sabadell of Colorado State University.

Emilio Custodio
Chairman of the Working Group
Barcelona, August 1982

1. General considerations

E. Custodio

Coastal zones often contain some of the most densely populated areas in the world. The availability of flat land, communications arteries, easy sea transportation, good soils, and high productivity of organic matter explains this fact. The areas close to rivers or deltas generally present the best conditions.

The demand for fresh water resources easily exceed available resources in areas not directly fed by rivers, and water supply shortages are common.

Man's activities interfere with natural processes and many physical and biological changes are produced or expected, such as sea water intrusion, the destruction of the natural habitat or shore modification through erosion and sedimentation.

Also common is the progressive occupation of periodically flooded lands, as well as the desiccation or drainage of wetlands. In order to protect these settlements, many types of civil works are constructed. These easily alter natural processes and have a wide spectrum of indirect effects. Many of these effects are not considered or anticipated when the civil works or modifications are done, and in many instances they produce unexpected changes that need new corrective measures or impair existing uses of natural resources.

The coastal zone is subject to more severe and complex issues than most other land and water resources, and must be viewed as an important component of a water resources system. The coastal zone, as the transition area from land to sea, and from fresh water to salt water, contains some of the world's most biologically productive units, the estuaries being the key element, as shown by the following data (Teal and Teal, 1971):

Source	Production rate t/km^2/year
Arid agriculture	0.5 – 3.5
Moist agriculture	3.5 – 12
Estuarine zone	12 – 24
Coastal water	2.5 – 3.5
Open ocean	~ 1.0

Fresh water flow, both surface and underground, has an important impact upon the characteristics and quality of the productive estuarine, coastal lagoon and wetlands waters, and upon sedimentary deposits along the coast.

Associated with man's activities are his uses, and in many instances abuses, of coastal resources. These will continue to grow since man will concentrate his activities and urban establishments along the coasts. By the year 2000 it is assumed that more than three quarters of the world's population will be at or near the coast, and will draw heavily on the already stressed coastal environment.

The main uses of coastal areas, including dry lands, marshes, submerged land, the surrounding waters and the natural resources, may be classified (USGPO, 1969) as:

- urbanization and development (industry, housing, port and harbor)

- water supply (municipal, agricultural, recreational and industrial)

- waste disposal (municipal, domestic, industrial, agricultural)

- transportation (land, sea, air)

- extraction of mineral resources (oil, gas, sand and gravel)

- biological resources (fisheries, aquaculture)

- recreation (beaches, swimming, boating, fishing, scenery, hunting)

- wildlife, estuarine and wetland preservation.

By far, the major impact comes from urbanization and development. The present monograph covers only water resources and the effects of their exploitation, but the other aspects must be borne in mind.

Estuarine and groundwater outflow areas have a dilution effect of sea water salinity that affects aquatic life. River use, groundwater exploitation, urbanization impact on surface runoff and groundwater recharge modify the dilution pattern and affect aquatic life accordingly. Surface-groundwater relationships cannot be neglected. Also marshes pose interesting problems of soils, cultivation, wildlife, and disease control where groundwater outflow may have a dominant role.

Not only is water a major component of the coastal zone, but sand and gravel are also important elements. Dam construction, reforestation and deforestation, agricultural development, urbanization, land erosion control programs, water transportation, river channelization, sand and gravel extraction, etc., have a great effect on the solid transport and equilibrium in coastal areas, especially in beaches. Sedimentology is as important as hydrology and hydraulics.

Since uses are varied and often conflicting, it is necessary to have coastal zone planning and management in order to have a rational way to manage multiple coastal resources. Fresh water resources conservation and exploitation need well established planning so future generations can use them.

The outline of a rational public policy for a coastal zone must consider different factors:

- physical, chemical and biological characteristics

- urbanization, agriculture, transportation, industry and development

- governmental capacity for adequate policy development and implementation.

After Dzurik (1973), one must consider that neither complete exploitation nor total preservation is appropriate or feasible. A balance is needed and must be maintained in order to maximize long-term as well as immediate benefits through correct and adequate management of coastal resources within the framework of water resource systems.

Management of coastal resources cannot be separated from the management of inland water resources, and the converse is also true. Although a narrow scope is frequently necessary in dealing with resource and water problems, the subsystem should be understood within the framework of the larger resource system. The Aswan High Dam is now a classic example of the great changes and damages which can occur to coastal resources through disregard or insufficient consideration of the interaction of river and coastal waters. But unfortunately it is not the only example, and a long list of failures, total or partial, can be easily gathered both in developed high technology countries and in developing countries under colonial or national rule.

Not all changes in inland waters are damaging to coastal resources or the whole system. When changes and uses are necessary, they should include the evaluation of the total possible effects and the correction of the negative aspects, without impairing others.

Pollutants generated by man's activities gather in the oceans as a final receptacle, and they are frequently trapped and physically or biologically concentrated in estuarine zones. The long-term effects can be serious and irreversible. Along many urban centers, coastal waters are used as a sump for industrial and domestic waste disposal, and thus has been ruined for most other uses. Prime ecological systems, recreation areas, natural surface and underground storage systems have been eliminated needlessly through lack of adequate planning and management. The Mediterranean area has been subjected to many such negative aspects.

Acute problems may appear in developing countries, especially in those subject to tropical climates, in islands and when the population density and birth rate are very high. The recent acquisition of independence or broad autonomy has generated great hopes among the populations for the improvement of living conditions, especially as regards water supply (Dijon, 1978). Water demand for irrigation, port installations and related industries, and water uses -- especially tourism -- have also increased dramatically, as a result of the drive of the countries towards economic self-sufficiency.

As a summary, Unesco's Man and the Biosphere Programme (MAB, 1974) enumerated the following characteristics of the coastal environment that make it vulnerable to human impact:

- land-sea interactions, both cyclical and unidirectional;

- productivity and the nutrient trap effect. Nutrient levels are usually enhanced due to intensive recycling processes, but those factors are also responsible for their conversion to pollution sinks;

- food-web structure;

- vulnerability of coastal zone organisms;

- sedimentation control in the environment;

- importance of freshwater inflow;

- epidemiological characteristics. Human and animal pathogens find favorable conditions for their multiplication in deltaic coastal areas, such as malaria, noxious mosquitoes, arboviroses, amebiosis, choleria, enterobacterioses, leptospiroses, schistosomioses, oncocercoses, etc.

These aspects are beyond the scope of the present monograph and will not be considered further.

Only fresh groundwater resources will be considered from the hydrologic point of view.

Sea water encroachment problems in coastal aquifers have been recognized since the first quantitative studies at the turn of the century, and have not been considered an important separate aspect of groundwater hydrology until recently. A good historical discussion on what is known about salt water intrusion can be found in Kashef (1972), and some aspects of the development will be given in section 3.1.

Probably the first classical book to include a chapter on quantitative aspects of sea water encroachment in coastal aquifers is that of Todd (1958). The U.S. Geological Survey Water-Supply Paper 1613-C (Cooper et al. 1964) was also an important benchmark.

Perhaps one of the first international meetings to include sea water intrusion problems expressly was the Haifa Symposium organized by the International Association of Scientific Hydrology (Pub 92).

In Europe, initially restricted to Nordic European Countries, the Sea Water Intrusion Meetings (SWIM) have been convened every two years, each time with a wide coverage of problems, areas and countries. The most recent meetings have been:

1975 IV   - Ghent, Belgium
1977 V   - Medmenham, U.K.
1979 VI   - Hannover, Federal Republic of Germany
1981 VII   - Uppsala, Sweden
1983 VIII - Bari, Italy

There is no formal organization for these meetings, but an agreement of a national organization to invite experts to discuss their achievements, the publication of the proceedings being handled by the host organization.

1.1   References

Cooper, H.H. Jr.; Kohout, F.A.; Henry, H.R.; Glober, R.E. (1964). Sea water in coastal aquifers. U.S. Geol. Survey, Water-Supply Paper 163-C, 84 pp.

Dijon, R. (1978). A review of United Nations water resources activities in coastal areas and islands. Selected Water Problems in Islands and Coastal Areas. Seminar of Malta, 1978, United Nations Economic Commission for Europe. Pergamon, 1979, pp.87-98.

Dzurik, A.A. (1973). The coastal zone as an integral element of water-resource systems. Water Resources Bulletin, AWRA. Vol. 9, No.4, pp.733-745.

Kashef, A.A.I. (1972). What do we know about salt water intrusion? Water Resources Bull. AWRA. Vol. 8, No. 2, April, pp. 282-293.

MAB (1974). Ecological effects of human activities on the value and resources of lakes, marshes, rivers, deltas, estuaries and coastal zones: final report. Programme on Man and the Biosphere (MAB): Unesco. MAB Report Series No. 21, 80 pp.

Teal, J.M.; Teal, M. (1971). Man in the living environment. Report of the Workshop on Global Ecological Problems. The Institute of Ecology. USA.

Todd, D.K. (1958). Groundwater hydrology. John Wiley and Sons, New York.

USGPO (1969). Science and environment (1969). Panel Reports of the Commission of Marine Science, Engineering and Resources. USGPO. Washington, 340 pp.

2. Coastal aquifers

E. Custodio

2.1   General

The great length of coasts requires that a small but significant part of the
continental water discharged to the oceans outflows directly from the ground.
A much greater part discharges to the lower tracts of rivers, in areas where
coastal conditions prevail.

The total direct discharge of groundwater into the oceans is a
speculative figure since no direct measures can be made. Frequently the
discharge in a given coastal area is obtained from the residual term in the
groundwater balance, and it accumulates all the errors. The resulting figure,
generally small relative to other terms in the balance, is not reliable.

Since the hydrogeological and hydrodynamical data along the coast
are generally inaccurate, Zekster and Dzhamalov (1981b) made an estimate by
applying to the discharge along the coast the same specific figures obtained
for the lower tracts of the rivers. Most of the fresh groundwater discharge
corresponds to the shallow aquifers. The values, in $l/s/km^2$ of surface contributing to the coast, vary from as high as 14 $l/s/km^2$ in very permeable
materials in areas with normal-to-high rainfall, to as low as less than 0.2
$l/s/km^2$ in cold or warm arid areas. The results are reproduced in table 2.1.
The total figure is close to 2460 x 10^9 m^3/year (about 15 mm/year), similar to
that obtained from other methods by the same authors. It must be compared
with the total river outflow of about 45000 x 10^9 m^3/year (300 mm/year) (Sokolov et al., 1974).

Direct groundwater outflow is thus about 5% of the total continental
fresh water outflow, although due to its greater salinity, it contributes
about 1/3 of total continental salts transported by water from the continent
to the oceans, and thus it has a significant effect on the sea salt balances
and on many geochemical process leading to rock and mineral formation.

The importance of that apparently small 5% appears when considering
its distribution along the coast, thus being more directly susceptible to the
intense human activities in those areas. Also their susceptibility to easy
degradation by sea water intrusion poses delicate problems for the use of the
sometimes great groundwater reserves in highly porous coastal formations.

Table 2.1 - Groundwater discharge to the World Ocean. Modified from Zekster and Dzhamalov (1981a).

Ocean	Continent	Contributing area 10^3 km^2	Groundwater discharge	
			10^9 m^3/year	l/s/km^2
Atlantic	Europe	541	71	4.2
	North America	1932	229	3.8
	South America	1940	186	3.0
	Africa	1713	216	4.0
	Main islands	555	77	4.4
			779	
Mediterranean	Europe	294	49	5.3
	Asia	108	8	2.4
	Africa	404	5	0.4
	Main islands	65	6	2.8
			68	
Pacific	Asia	1683	254	4.7 (2–11)[*]
	North America	936	163	5.5 (1–13)
	South America	553	201	11.5 (11–15)
	Australia	200	7	1.1
	Main islands	1693	713	11.4 (4–33)
			1338	
Indian	Asia	1227	65	1.7
	Africa	1266	22	0.5
	Australia	2350	16	0.2
	Main islands	733	117	5.1
			220	
Arctic	Europe	461	51	3.5
			51	

Total general   2456 x 10^9 m^3/year   * Range

A 3% sea water percentage can render the water too salty for many uses, and 5% practically renders it useless, except if very expensive desalting processes are used.

2.2   Types of coast

The measurement and classification of coasts and shores can help in the understanding of their importance. The total length of the perimeter of the entire World Ocean has been calculated to be about 777,000 km (Luk'yanova and Kholodilin, 1975). This figure must be used with caution. Due to the shapes of fiord and ria shores and coasts, the length of their shoreline increases sharply, but in fact they do not occur frequently by comparison with other types of shores.

The above figure refers to the shoreline, which has a macroscopic aspect given by the initial type of dissection, and a microscopic aspect that depends on the sinuosity, produced mainly by wave action. The number of micro and macro elements of the shoreline is described by a ruggedness or sinuosity index (Auphan, 1971), that relates the length of the shoreline to the length of the corresponding segments of the shore and coast.

The shore can be considered as the zone bounded by the seaward and the landward water limiting lines. The length is measured by the smoothed median curve. An allowance is made for the microelements in plan, mainly due to wave action.

The coast is defined similarly, but the definition must consider the macroelements, such as heads of fiords and rias, open lagoons and continental islands.

When considering the shore and the coast lengths, the perimeter of the World Ocean is reduced to 469,000 and 413,000 km, respectively. Tables 2.2 and 2.3 show the importance and ruggedness of the different types of shores (according to the abrasion-accretion process) and coast (according to their morphological origin), given by the work of Luk'yanova and Kholodilin (1975).

Table 2.2 – Length percentage and ruggedness of the shore types along the World Ocean. Modified from Luk'yanova and Kholodilin (1975).

Shore types	% length	Ruggedness
1. Unchanged or slightly changed by the sea		
1a. Ingressional, deeply dissected (fiord)	15	3
1b. Flat	7	1
2. Denuational-abrasional		
2a. Ingressional, deeply dissected (ria)	3	4
2b. Ingressional bay	0.5	1
2c. Flat	0.5	1.5
3. Abrasional		
3a. Ingressional abrasional (bay)	16	1
3b. Planate	6	1
3c. Dead cliff and accretion terrace	1	1
4. Abrasional-accretional		
4a. Ingressional, deeply dissected (low ria)	2	1
4b. Ingressional, secondarily dissected	15	1
4c. Planate	4	1
5. Accretional		
5a. Ingressional	2	2
5b. Secondarily dissected	7	2
5c. Planate lagoon	10	1.5
5d. Planate with accretional terrace	11	1

Total length of shores   469,000 km

Table 2.3 - Length percentage and ruggedness of the coast types along the World Ocean. Modified from Luk'yanova and Kholodilin (1975).

Coast types	% length	Ruggedness
1. Mountains		
1a. Techtonically and erosionally dissected		
- subject to glaciation (fiords)	12	4
- others (including rias)	6	4
1b. Mainly block-techtonic dissection	2.5	3
1c. Dissection of volcanic forms	2	2
2. Tablelands and plateau		
2a. Strongly dissected relief	5	2
2b. Slightly dissected relief	9	1
3. Glaciated		
3a. Present ice sheets (ice coasts)	10	1
3b. Glacial aggradational and denudational (plains, elevations)	7	3
3c. Fluvioglacial and glacial-lacustrine aggradational plains	2	2
4. Alluvial		
4a. Plains with permafrost or vein ice (also marine)	1.5	1.5
4b. Plains	8	1
4c. Alluvial-marine plains	21	1
5. Marine		
5a. Aggradational and abrasional-aggradational	8	2
5b. Abrasional	1	1.5
6. Others		
6a. Eolian and eolian-marine plains	3	1
6b. Plains of varying origin	2	1

Total length of coasts   413,000 km

The coast classification is more adapted to the description of the different relationships between fresh and salt groundwaters in coastal areas. However it is necessary also to consider hydrodynamic conditions (water table, confined systems, semiconfining layers, low lands, etc.), that can greatly influence relationships. Sea bottom sediments also can play an important role.

From the hydrogeological point of view not all coast types have the same importance, since those of hard, low fractured rocks (granites, gneiss) are almost improductive, while terrace deposits and great recent sedimentary basins have a clearly overwhelming interest.

The following classification is adopted:

(a) Unconsolidated materials (glaciated, alluvial, marine and eolian), mainly accretional, about 25% of total coast.
(a1) water table
(a2) small islands
(a3) confined
(a4) semiconfined
(a5) multilayered
(a6) young deltas

(b) Consolidated materials (some mountains, tablelands and plateau), mainly abrasional or denudational, about 20% of total coast.
b1) fissured hard rocks
b2) karstified rocks

Other factors to be considered in subclassifications are:

- sea behavior (tidal regime, storm surges, wave action, sea bottom sediments)

- climate (wet tropical, semi-arid, temperate, mediterranean; predominant winds; rain intensity)

- recharge regime

- man interventions (desiccation, poldering, river basin modification, agriculture, urbanization)

- long-term evolution (sea water transgressions or regressions, subsidence).

2.3   Sources of salt

The main source of salt in coastal areas is sea water. Sea water has a rather constant chemical composition except for small changes due to the variable evaporation rates (higher in the tropics and the Mediterranean) or great continental fresh water contributions (Caribbean). Greater differences can be found in closed or half-closed seas such as the Baltic, the Caspian, the Black Sea, etc.

Typical sea water analyses are (from Custodio and Llamas, 1976, p. 1080) (g/l):

	Oceanic	Mediterranean
HCO_3	0.07 - 0.14	0.07 - 0.17
SO_4	2.4 - 2.7	2.9 - 3.2
Cl	17.5 - 19.0	20.5 - 21.5
Na	9.7 - 10.5	11.7 - 11.8
K	0.36	0.27 - 0.50
Ca	0.38 - 0.40	0.4 - 0.5
Mg	1.0 - 1.3	1.1 - 1.4
TDS	33 - 35	36 - 43

The density (specific mass) varies with salinity and temperature as shown in figure 2.1. It can be calculated by the formula:

$$\rho = 1000 + 0.8054S - 0.0065 \, (\theta - 4 + 0.2214S)^2$$

in which

ρ = density in kg/m^3
S = salinity in ppt (parts per thousand $\simeq$ g/l)
θ = temperature (^oC)

Other sources of salt can be found in coastal areas and must be taken into account when considering the different processes that lead to fresh water salinization.

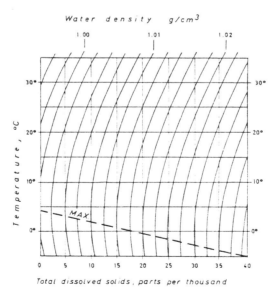

Fig. 2.1 - Relationship among total dissolved solids in water (abscissae), water temperature (ordinates) and water density (curves).

Old sea water with different degrees of chemical changes, dilution, or concentration, can be found in sediments, especially in low permeability formations (clay and silt lenses and strata), confined aquifers and the bottom of coastal sediments presenting a very flat surface. The origin of old sea water is not always known in detail, but can be related to sea transgressions and regressions (well studied in the Netherlands, see Meinardi, 1975) and entrapped (connate) sea water in the sediments deposited in estuaries, coastal lagoons, advancing coasts, etc. (well known in the Llobregat area, see Custodio, 1981). Chemical reactions with the sediments (ion exchange, calcite and dolomite precipitation and dissolution, intense reducing conditions), dilution by fresh water (diffusion and dispersion), or evaporation while on the surface (lagoons) lead to salinity and chemical changes. The complexity of sedimentation in deltas and coastal basins, and the movement of pore-water due to load and compactation gradients, complicate even more the entrapped salt water distribution. In some areas fresh brackish or salt water may be under geopressurized conditions.

Old sea water only means salt water not in a direct relationship with present ocean water, and can be as young as a few hundred years old, or older than many ten thousands of years, even many hundred thousand years. For old sea water the name 'relict' salt water was proposed in the Uppsala 1981 SWIM meeting.

Evaporation from surface water bodies or directly from the ground when the phreatic table is at a shallow depth produce saline water, even from fresh continental water without any previous mixing with sea water. It appears in very flat and low lying coastal areas in dry climates (e.g. the coast north of Mar del Plata in Argentina).

Since the sea is the lowest drainage area of many great continental basins, regional flow systems with very low flow and very long residence time can discharge brackish and even salty water near the coast. This situation is not related to the sea water salinity and must not be confused with an oceanic influence.

Other sources of salt such as the dissolution of evaporite deposits are less important and only of very local importance. They are only significant in special situations, generally localized ones.

2.4   References

Auphan, E. (1971). *La mesure de la découpure des cotes.* Norois, Vol. 18, No. 71.

Custodio, E. (1981). *Sea water encroachment in the Llobregat and Besós areas, near Barcelona (Catalonia, Spain).* Intruded and Relict Groundwater of Marine Origin. VII Salt Water Intrusion Meeting. SWIM-81. Uppsala. Sveriges Geologiska Undersökning, repporter och meddelanden 27, pp. 120-152.

Custodio, E., Llamas, M.R. (1976). *Hidrología Subterránea* (Groundwater hydrology). Ediciones Omega, Barcelona, 2 vols, 2350 pp.

Luk'yanova, S.A., Kholodilin, N.A. (1975). *Length of the shoreline of the World Ocean and of various types of shores and coasts.* Soviet Hydrology: Selected Papers. No. 2. Am. Geophysical Union, Washington.

Meinardi, C.R. (1975). *Brackish groundwater bodies as a result of geological history and hydrological conditions.* R.I.D. Mededeling 75-1, Rijksinstituut voor Drinkwatervoorziening. The Hague. Also in, Symp. on Brackish Water as a factor in Development. Beer-Sheva, Israel.

Sokolov, A.A. et al. (1974). *World water balance.* Studies and Reports on Hydrology 25-Unesco. Paris.

Zekster, I.S., Dzhamalov, R.G. (1981a). *Groundwater discharge into the World Oceans.* Unesco. Nature and Resources. vol. XVII, 3, pp. 20-22.

Zekster, I.S., Dzhamalov, R.G. (1981b). *Groundwater discharge to the Pacific Ocean.* Hydrological Sciences Bull. Vol. 26, No. 3, September, 1981, pp. 271-279.

3. Salt-fresh water interrelationships under natural conditions

E. Custodio

Contents

3.0 Introduction

The main characteristics of the fresh water flow, head, mixing zone and salt water wedge, will be discussed qualitatively in the following paragraphs. The calculation methods will be presented in full in chapter 5. Permeability and hydraulic characteristics under natural conditions must be taken into account.

The discussion focuses on porous unconsolidated media, since they are the best known, but a discussion on hard rock and half consolidated formations is also included. Case studies are presented in chapter 10.

3.1 Basic concepts

3.1.1 The salt groundwater wedge, the interface and the mixing zone

In an aquifer with a sea front there is direct contact between continental fresh water and marine salt water. Besides differences in viscosity between the two fluids, there exists a density change that depends mainly on salinity differences. In a stable system the fresh water floats on the salt water and a landward sloping <u>interface</u> exists between them. The salt groundwater body adopts the form of a <u>wedge</u> resting on the aquifer floor. The fresh water thickness decreases from the wedge toe towards the sea (fig. 3.1).

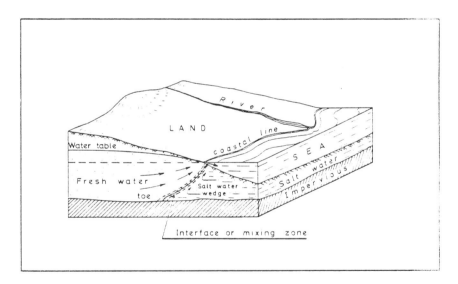

Fig. 3.1 - Salt water wedge in a water table coastal aquifer. Landward penetration increases with increasing aquifer thickness and permeability and with decreasing fresh water flow. Depending on the aquifer dispersivity, the fresh and sea water fluctuations and the fresh water flow, a mixing zone develops between fresh and salt groundwater. When the mixing zone is thin relative to the aquifer thickness, it can be considered as a sharp interface between the two miscible fluids. It is a realistic situation in many circumstances, but in others the mixing zone cannot be neglected and in some instances represents a significant portion of the aquifer thickness.

-15-

The <u>interface</u> separates two fully immiscible fluids. Since mixing, diffusion and hydrodynamic dispersion occurs, the interface is a <u>transition</u> or <u>mixing</u> zone where thickness depends on the hydrodynamic characteristics of the aquifer. A sharp interface exists only when this zone represents a few percent of the saturated thickness.

Since the fresh water flow thickness decreases seaward, the slope of the piezometric head or the water table must increase towards the coast. Thus the interface is concave upwards.

The mixing zone limits can be defined as the surfaces of 1% and 95% sea water content, based on total dissolved solids or chloride ion content. Otherwise, the lower value may be chosen equal to the maximum total dissolved solids or chloride content for drinking water or when the fresh water natural background value begins to increase. The upper one depends on analytical sensitivity. In some highly dispersive situations the mixing zone occupies a significant part of the saturated thickness and its upper limit is close to the upper aquifer boundary. In other situations the mixing zone thickness is small when compared with the aquifer thickness, and for practical and calculation purposes can be considered as a sharp transition (interface plane).

Kohout (1980) disagrees with use of the term <u>interface</u> in place of <u>zone of diffusion</u>, <u>zone of dispersion</u> or <u>transition zone</u>, since he mentions the lack of data supporting the contention of an immiscible sharp fluid <u>interface</u> in a coastal aquifer. <u>Zone of diffusion</u> was used by the early Dutch investigators and is a chemical term, as is <u>zone of dispersion</u> used by more recent investigators. Dispersion is the more precise term, in that both mechanical mixing and chemical diffusion are operative in a groundwater environment. <u>Transition zone</u> is a general term that could apply equally well to a geologic transition, a geographic transition, a paleontologic transition, etc.

3.1.2 The hydrostatic approach: Badon Ghyben-Herzberg principle. Applicability and limitations

The first quantitative observations of the salt water depth in coastal porous aquifers were done independently by Badon Ghyben (also written Ghijben, 1889) in Holland, and Herzberg (1901) in Northern Germany. They lead to a hydrostatic approach that applies the U-tube equilibrium of two stationary immiscible fluids of different density (fig. 3.2). At any one point of the sharp interface, the water pressure on both sides must be the same, and this pressure is given by the water depth times the water specific weight.

Fresh water pressure at point A = $(h_f + z)\gamma_f$

Salt water pressure at point A' = $z\gamma_s$

$$(h_f + z)\gamma_f = z\gamma_s; \quad z = \frac{\gamma_f}{\gamma_s - \gamma_f} h_f = \alpha h_f \qquad (3.1.1)$$

h_f = fresh water head (water table elevation over mean sea level)

z = depth of the interface below mean sea level

γ_f = fresh water specific weight $\simeq$ 1000 kg/m^3

γ_s = salt water specific weight $\simeq$ 1025 kg/m^3 (generally between 1020 and 1030, depending on salinity and temperature, see fig. 2.1)

α = $\gamma_f/(\gamma_s - \gamma_f) \simeq$ 40 (between 33 and 50).

      Formula (3.1.1) is known as the <u>Badon Ghyben-Herzberg formula</u>, that will be shortened to the BGH formula or principle.

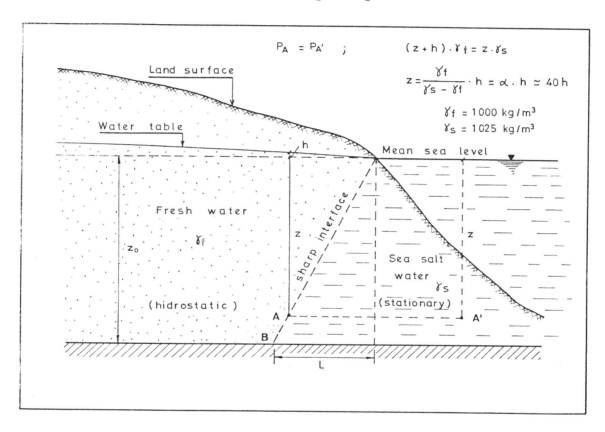

Fig. 3.2 – Explanation of the Badon Ghyben-Herzberg principle in an idealized hydrostatic fresh-salt groundwater system. γ is the specific weight, z the depth below mean sea level and h the fresh water head over mean sea level. Applying usual γ values results in z = 40 h, although other values can be obtained for other γ values. A sharp interface is assumed, really such a system cannot be hydrostatic, and then the formula is not exact, especially near the fresh water outlet, but is very useful in first calculations, and reasonably accurate when applied far from the shoreline in aquifers with a narrow mixing zone.

This means that, in a first approach, the interface depth below mean sea level in every place is about 40 times the fresh water head (water table elevation) over mean sea level, and the wedge toe is below the water head contour line $h_f = z_o/\alpha$, z_o being the depth of the aquifer floor below mean sea level (fig. 3.2). In a thick highly permeable aquifer, with a reduced fresh water flow, since the fresh water slope is very small, the salt water wedge penetrates far inland. In a thin low permeability water table aquifer, having a significant fresh water flow, the salt water wedge is almost nonexistent and the interface is steep, due to a sloping fresh water table.

It must be taken into account that in many schematic figures such as 3.1 and 3.2, to clarify the representation, the vertical scale is distorted and the fresh water heads or water table position are exaggerated when compared with the interface and aquifer thickness, and both are exaggerated with respect to horizontal dimensions.

The BGH formula is a crude approximation and has significant limitations:

- If the groundwater body is not under hydrostatic conditions, the pressure on the interface does not correspond with the water depth, especially in the fresh water body near the coast, as shown in section 3.1.3. Except in special situations, the interface under equilibrium conditions is deeper than calculated. This is especially true near the sea coast to allow for a fresh water outflow gap. The strict BGH formula leads to a vanishing fresh water thickness near the coast, and this is impossible if a finite value for the water table slope is maintained.

- If the sea is at rest, then only steady state situations are taken into account.

- If the mixing zone thickness is not negligible, the BGH formula can only predict an interface inside the mixing zone, the sea water being deeper and the brackish water upper boundary being much higher.

Notwithstanding these limitations, the BGH formula is used with success in simple calculations if correctly applied, using some corrections when necessary, and avoiding some extreme situations.

Some authors (Chidley and Lloyd, 1977) adopt an empirical α factor, according to local observations and situations, with some success, in order to calculate the top position of the mixing zone, but subsequent calculations must be used with great care, and possibly cannot be extrapolated.

3.1.3   Dynamic fresh water flow on a stationary salt water wedge

If a sharp equilibrium interface exists between a stationary salt water body and a dynamic fresh water body, the interface is a boundary for the fresh water body similar to a water table. On the interface, the salt water head is constant and equal to the mean sea level, and acts as a surface of fresh water flow lines. This allows the use of potential

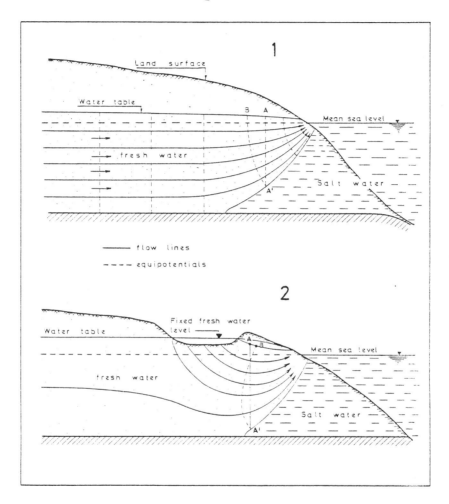

Fig. 3.3 - Schematic flow net in a water table coastal aquifer showing the vertical variation of fresh water head. A sharp interface and a stationary salt water body is assumed. The pressure at point A' is given by the water table elevation at point B. It can be different from the water table elevation at point A, on the same vertical as A'. Situation one is the most common situation and because the water table elevation at point B is higher than at point A, the interface depth is higher than predicted using the Badon Ghyben-Herzberg formula. In some instances, the interface can be shallower than predicted, as in areas of great recharge, as shown in situation two.

theory (see chapter 5) to define flow nets in vertical two-dimensional situations, as shown schematically in figure 3.3, to calculate the true fresh water head on the interface, h'_f (Hubbert, 1940; 1953). Then, the corrected BGH formula (Hubbert's correction), $z = \alpha h'_f$, avoids the first limitation.

3.1.4   True dynamic equilibrium

In the contact between the immiscible fresh and salt water, some mixing exists, mainly through microscopic and macroscopic dispersion. Then, salt water is dragged along with the fresh water flow towards the sea. To conserve the salt balance, this implies a small landward salt water flow in a coastal groundwater aquifer under equilibrium, as shown schematically in figure 3.4, and then a _dynamic equilibrium_ is the true situation. The situation is similar to that existing in a stratified estuary.

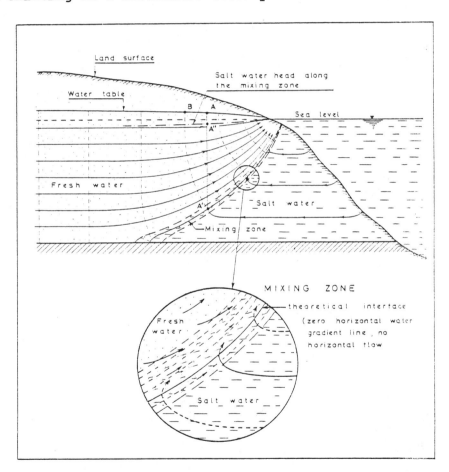

Fig. 3.4 – Development of mixing zone between the fresh and the salt water bodies. In the mixing zone exists a seaward flow of salt exists. To maintain the salt balance a landward salt water flow is needed, thus decreasing salt water head along the mixing zone, and lowering the predicted interface depth according to the Badon Ghyben-Herzberg formula or the Hubbert's correction to it.

The landward flow of salt water produces a head loss, and then the pressure on the salt water side of a thin interface is smaller than that corresponding to the depth under mean sea level. The effect is magnified when the sea water penetration is hindered by sea bottom fine, low permeability sediments.

These qualitative conclusions, presented the first time by Nomitsu, Toyohara and Kamimoto (1927), can be derived from a simplified study of the water velocities in the interface zone, assuming that it is divided into a number of slipping bands of homogeneous salinity (Santing, 1963), and much more rigorously obtained through an analysis of the continuity and mass transport equations (Wooding, 1972). See chapter 5.

Consider a situation in which the mixing zone is thin. At a point on the interface at depth z, with a fresh water head h_f and a salt water head h_s, (the same reference datum must be used, not necessarily coinciding with the mean sea level), the pressure equilibrium leads to (see figure 3.5 for definitions):

$$(z + h_f)\gamma_f = (z + h_s)\gamma_s$$

$$z = \frac{\gamma_f}{\gamma_s - \gamma_f} h_f - \frac{\gamma_s}{\gamma_s - \gamma_f} h_s = \alpha h_f - (1 + \alpha) h_s$$

$$= \alpha(h_f - h_s) - h_s \qquad\qquad (3.1.3)$$

This relationship is known as the <u>Hubbert's formula</u>.

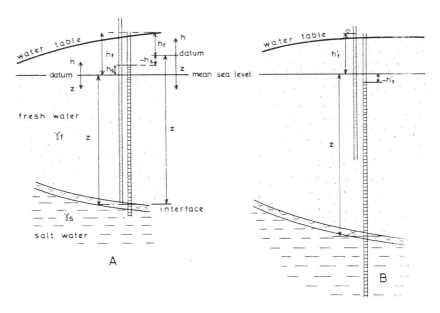

Fig. 3.5 - Equilibrium of the interface. Figure A shows the conditions to establish the Hubbert's formula, and figure B shows a real situation. When the vertical components of water velocity can be neglected, $h'_f \simeq h_f$ and $h'_s \simeq h_s$, and then the depth to the interface, z, can be calculated.

Note that h_f and h_s are positive above the datum and z below the datum. The landward sea water flow implies a decrease in h_s, and then z is higher (the interface is deeper) than predicted with the BGH formula ($h_s = 0$ if the datum is mean sea level), inclusive if h_f is measured on the interface (Hubbert's correction).

Hubbert's formula can also be applied in non-equilibrium conditions if h_f and h_s can be measured. If vertical velocity components are negligible in practice, h_f and h_s can be determined with two piezometers, one in the fresh water and the other in the salt water body. When the mixing zone is thick, the above consideration does not hold, and z corresponds to a virtual interface inside the mixing zone.

After Kohout (1964), a zero horizontal hydraulic gradient surface can be defined inside the mixing zone (fig. 3.4), and represents a kind of virtual interface. Figures 10.97 and 10.98, corresponding to an example in Florida, show the trend and situation of such a surface.

At the salt water wedge toe, the isosalinity surfaces must finish perpendicular to the aquifer bottom, because the lower impervious boundary is not a salt source. It does not hold for a sharp interface in equilibrium conditions. At the sea outlet, the sharp interface is vertical.

3.1.5 The differential equations of groundwater flow in a coastal aquifer

Darcy's law is generally expressed in a homogeneous medium and fluid as:

$$q = - k\nabla h; \quad h = \frac{P}{\gamma} + \varsigma; \quad k = k_0 \, \gamma/\mu,$$

where:

q = volume flow or flow velocity (vector) (L/T)

m = porosity (dynamic or effective porosity of flow) (nondimensional)

∇ = gradient operator = $i \frac{\partial}{\partial x} + j \frac{\partial}{\partial y} + k \frac{\partial}{\partial \varsigma}$ (1/L)

i, j, k = unit vectors in the x, y, ς directions

ρ = density or specific mass = γ/g (M/L^3)

γ = specific weight (F/L^3)

g = acceleration of gravity (L/T^2)

P = pressure (F/L^2)

ς = elevation over a datum (L) (positive upwards)

k_0 = intrinsic permeability

k = permeability or hydraulic conductivity

μ = dynamic viscosity (FT/L^2)

h = hydraulic head (L)

In a nonhomogeneous medium, k is a tensor quantity.

The intergranular or real water velocity has a mean value $v = q/m$ (L/T).

In a coastal aquifer, γ and μ are space and time dependent and then a more generalized form of Darcy's law is needed (Yih, 1960), using a force-potential (the true driving force) instead of the water head. The force-potential is:

$$\phi = \frac{k_o}{\mu} (P + \gamma \zeta) = \frac{k_o}{\mu} \gamma h$$

and Darcy's law is now (k_o and μ are assumed constant in space):

$$q = -\nabla\phi = -\nabla(\frac{k_o}{\mu} \gamma h) = -\frac{k_o}{\mu} [\gamma\nabla h + h\nabla\gamma] \qquad (3.1.4)$$

The vector q is parallel to ∇h only if γ is constant, that is to say, inside the fresh or the salt water body, but not in the mixing zone. Inside the mixing zone, if $\nabla\gamma$ is dominant, q is parallel to the isoconcentration surfaces. It is true in mixing zones of small thickness. A more detailed treatment will be presented in chapter 5.

The continuity or **water mass conservation** equation is:

$$-\nabla(\rho q) + F\rho_F = S_S \frac{\partial}{\partial t} (\frac{P}{g} + \rho\zeta) \qquad (3.1.5)$$

F = generation of water volume of density ρ_F, per unit aquifer volume and time (1/T)

t = time (T)

S_S = specific storage coefficient (per unit aquifer thickness (1/L)

F = 0 in many practical circumstances, but it can represent the recharge through the upper or lower aquifer boundaries, when vertical flow components are negligible; since F = W/b, W = water volume input per unit surface, and time (L/T), and b = aquifer thickness (L).

Since chemical interactions do not change significantly the salinity or slow the salinity movement, the salt **transport equation** is:

$$m\nabla(D\nabla c) - \nabla(cq) + Fc_f = \frac{\partial(cm)}{\partial t} \qquad (3.1.6)$$
$$\quad (1) \qquad\qquad (2) \qquad (3) \qquad (4)$$

c = salt concentration in the water (M/L^3)

$\underline{D}$ = dispersion coefficient (tensor) (L^2/T). It must be a macroscopic value

m = porosity

c_f = salinity of generated water.

Term (1) takes into account the salinity dispersion (diffusion + hydrodynamic dispersion); term (2) the convective transport of salinity; term (3) is a source which may involve many different origins and reactions.

Since in a non-compressible medium, $\nabla q = 0$, if m is constant:

$$\nabla(\underline{D}\nabla c) - \frac{q}{m}\nabla c + \frac{F}{m}c_f = \frac{\partial c}{\partial t} \qquad (3.1.6)$$

When (i) $F = 0$, (ii) the system is stationary, (iii) the dispersion is negligible relative to convective transport, (iv) there is a linear relationship between salt concentration and density, then:

$$q\nabla\rho = 0 \qquad (3.1.7)$$

This means that in such a situation, the density (ρ) is constant along any streamline. This is not exactly true if dispersion is not negligible compared with convection. Dispersion must be considered if the Péclet number, $P\acute{e} = qd/D \geq 10$; d is the pore size; D is essentially a longitudinal macroscopic dispersion coefficient depending on the flow velocity, q, and the medium macroscopic characteristics, including stratification and nonhomogeneities. Tidal oscillations increase $P\acute{e}$ and favor a thicker mixing zone.

The simultaneous solution of equations (3.1.4, 3.1.5 and 3.1.6) is a very difficult task, and many simplifications must be introduced, including numerical treatment. The reader is referred to specific references such as De Josseling De Jong (1969), Wooding (1972), Yih (1960), Segol, Pinder and Gray (1975), Pinder and Bredehoeft (1974), etc., and chapter 5 of this monograph.

D must include molecular diffusion, but for most practical situations with water in movement it can be neglected. Thus, D (L^2/T) generally depends only on the pore geometry, represented by an intrinsic dispersivity, D_o (L), and on the intergranular flow velocity, v. In normal circumstances, $D = D_o v$. Taking into account the aquifer nonhomogeneities, D_o may range from a few centimeters for homogeneous fine sands to several hundred meters for highly dispersive fissured aquifers (see Custodio and Llamas, 1976, chap. 12.1). In stratified nonhomogeneous media, D_o increases with the traveled distance until a maximum value is reached (Mercado, 1967). Recently the increase of D_o and its possible asymptotic value have been questioned. A time-increase model has been proposed (Dieulin, Matheron and de Marsily, 1981; Matheron and de Marsily, 1980).

3.1.6 Water heads in water of variable density. Movement inside the mixing zone

In a variable density groundwater body, the heads measured with point piezometers based on local water (density γ_p) are _point water heads_. These heads are not directly useful to the study of the groundwater flow in the transition zone by means of isopiezometric maps. Their use can lead to clearly anomalous situations such as flow apparently converging to areas inside the aquifers since the measured head decreases when the fluid becomes heavier (fig. 3.6).

It is possible to adopt a reference fluid of specific weight γ_r, and transform the point water heads, h_p (measured with a water of specific weight γ_p) into _reference fluid water heads_, h_r, establishing the pressure equilibrium at the bore-hole open end, at depth z(positive downwards):

$$(z + h_p) \, \gamma_p = (z + h_r) \, \gamma_r; \qquad h_r = \frac{\gamma_p - \gamma_r}{\gamma_r} \, z + \frac{\gamma_p}{\gamma_r} \, h_p \qquad (3.1.8)$$

The h values are measured from a datum upwards, and z from the same datum downwards, and then (z+h) represents the water column. If $\gamma_r = \gamma_s$ (salt water), the _salt water head_ is obtained. Used more frequently is the conversion to a _fresh water head_ taking $\gamma_r = \gamma_f$ (fresh water). When $\gamma_f \leq \gamma_r \leq \gamma_s$, then $h_f \geq h_r \geq h_s$.

This conversion allows for the calculation of the true horizontal gradients and horizontal components of water flow only if the heads refer to the same depth (fig. 3.6). The fresh water heads in a brackish or salt water area can lead to highly erroneous results if they do not correspond to the same depth. It is basic to show that in a steady salt water body, with constant salt water head, fresh water head increases with depth, thus arising nonexistent hydraulic gradients. It is clearly shown in figure 3.6.

Assume a homogeneous medium of permeability $k = k_o \, \gamma/\mu$. If h and γ are the point water head at depth z and point water specific weight; $h = z + P/\gamma$; P = pressure at depth z. When the water heads are measured with a new fluid of specific weight γ_o, the new heads are $h_o = z + P/\gamma_o$.

$$P = (h_o - z) \, \gamma_o = (h - z)\gamma$$

$$h = z + (h_o - z) \, \gamma_o/\gamma = \frac{1}{\gamma} \, [\gamma_o h_o - z \, (\gamma_o - \gamma)]$$

Then, Darcy's law in a homogeneous fluid $\underline{q} = - \, k_o \frac{\gamma}{\mu} \, \nabla h$ transforms into: $- \frac{\mu}{k_o} \, \underline{q}_o = \gamma_o \, \nabla h_o - (\gamma_o - \gamma) \, \nabla z$. Since $(\gamma_o - \gamma) \, \nabla z$ is a vertical vector, $\underline{q}_o$ is not parallel to ∇h_o. In a horizontal-flow system, the transformation of h into h_o creates apparent nonexistent vertical flows except if $\nabla z = 0$, where the points are at the same depth, z.

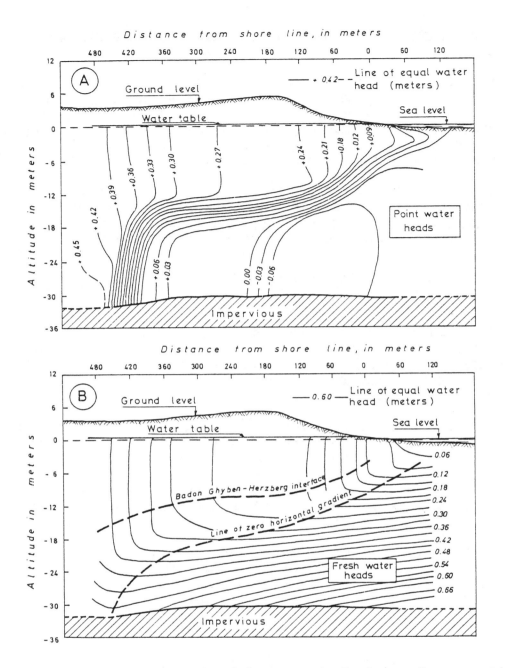

Fig. 3.6 – Lines of equal water head in a vertical plane, for mean tidal conditions in a low fresh water head period, in the Cutler area, in the
Biscayne Bay (Miami, Florida). A – point water heads have been
used; a closed area appears, without any physical meaning. B – the
same situation when freshwater heads have been used; the closed area
disappears, but apparently a high vertical gradient occurs; vertical
gradients cannot be calculated and only horizontal gradients can be
obtained; the line of zero horizontal gradient can be drawn and
represents a hydrodynamical interface since it is a boundary between
the freshwater flow and the salt water flow. It is placed in that
case inside the mixing zone. The BGH interface is much higher due
to the effect of the upward vertical components of groundwater flow
(after Kohout, 1964).

In a hydrostatic fluid of variable density, the change of water pressure with depth is $\partial_p / \partial_z = \rho g$, when z is positive downward. If the pressure P_1 at depth z_1 (point 1) is known, the pressure P_2 at depth z_2 (point 2) can be easily calculated if the vertical distribution of water density $\rho(z)$ is also known.

$$P_2 = P_1 + g \int_{z_1}^{z_2} \rho(z)dz$$

The respective water heads are, in terms of local water at a point, h_p, and expressed in terms of fresh water, h_f:

(a) $\quad h_{p2} = \dfrac{P_2}{\rho_2 g} + z_2; \quad h_{p1} = \dfrac{P_1}{\rho_1 g} + z_1$

(b) $\quad h_{f2} = \dfrac{P_2}{\rho_f g} + z_2; \quad h_{f1} = \dfrac{P_1}{\rho_f g} + z_1$.

When the true head at point 2, h_2^*, is measured (in point water or fresh water terms), then:

$h_2^* = h_2$ when the flow is hydrostatic (only horizontal flow)

$h_2^* < h_2$ when there is a downward flow

$\quad$ (when pt. 2 is below pt. 1)

$h_2^* > h_2$ when there is an upward flow.

If $\Delta h = h_2^* - h_2$, in fresh water terms, $\Delta h_f = h_{f2}^* - h_{f2}$

$$\Delta h_f = (h_{f2}^* - h_{f1}) - (z_2 - z_1) - \frac{1}{\rho f} \int_{z_1}^{z_2} \rho(z)dz \qquad (3.1.9)$$

The mean upward vertical velocity is

$$q_z = k_v \frac{\Delta h_f}{z_2 - z_1}$$

where k_v = vertical velocity.

h_{f1} can be assumed equal to the water table elevation. $\rho(z)$ can be obtained by direct sampling from bore-hole cores (difficult, unusual and expensive), or indirectly by means of geoelectrical logs. Salinity logs of the water inside a fully screened bore-hole do not necessarily represent the salinity stratification in the bore-hole. When there are several bore-holes opened at different depths it is possible to draw an approximate salinity distribution.

In a vertical cross-section normal to the coast, when enough data on the vertical distribution of water heads are available (point piezometers at different depths with known water density), the horizontal hydraulic gradient can be obtained, for a reference fluid, i.e. fresh water. It is the difference in fresh water head between two points on the same horizontal line divided by the horizontal distance between them. When these horizontal fresh water gradients are determined, it is possible to draw the flow tubes in a homogeneous medium, because in a flow tube the product of the vertical thickness times the horizontal flow must be constant (Kohout, 1964; see also section 10.6) according to the law of mass conservation. The horizontal flow is the horizontal permeability times the horizontal gradient. Figure 3.7 shows an application to the Cutler area, near Miami(USA).

Since in many practical situations horizontal flows dominate the vertical ones, and isoconcentration lines are close to the horizontal, it is possible to calculate the water heads on a given isoconcentration surface when two or more bore-holes exist, opened to a certain depth (van Dam, 1977). Let point 1 be a bore-hole at depth z_1 in which the head h_1 is known, measured with water of density ρ_1, and point 2 be the point on the isoconcentration surface of density ρ_2 and depth z_2. The pressure P_2 and point water head h_2, are:

$$P_2 = P_1 + g \int_{z_1}^{z_2} \rho(z)dz = g \left[\rho_1 (h_1 + z_1) + \int_{z_1}^{z_2} \rho(z)dz \right]$$

$$h_2 = -z_2 + \frac{\rho_1}{\rho_2} (h_1 + z_1) + \frac{1}{\rho_2} \rho(z)dz$$

When h_2 is calculated at two points, A and B, the horizontal flow velocity is $q_x = k_h \dfrac{h_{2A} - h_{2B}}{\overline{AB}}$. Then, in a cross-section with the isoconcentration lines, the point water heads can be calculated on these lines and the direction of flow can be deduced.

The concept of water heads of variable density was introduced in a study of Long Island (Perlmutter, Geraghty and Upson, 1959; Perlmutter and Geraghty, 1963). Lusczynski (1961) introduced the concept of environmental head. It can be defined as the head in a tube opened to a given depth, z, filled with water having the same density distribution as the water in the surrounding aquifer (environmental) plus or minus the necessary fresh water on top to exactly equalize the pressure at depth z. It is clear that this theoretical value measures Δh, as discussed before, when one of the control values is the water table. Later on, de Wiest (1965) introduced the true environmental head, that is the head measure in a piezometer screened along the whole length. The concepts of water heads of variable density were introduced in order to simplify the study of water flow in aquifers with variable water density, as in Long Island (New York) (Perlmutter, Geraghty and Upson, 1959; Perlmutter and Geraghty, 1963; Lusczynski, 1961; Lusczynski and Swarzenski, 1962, 1966). However, they do not solve the problem in a clear way.

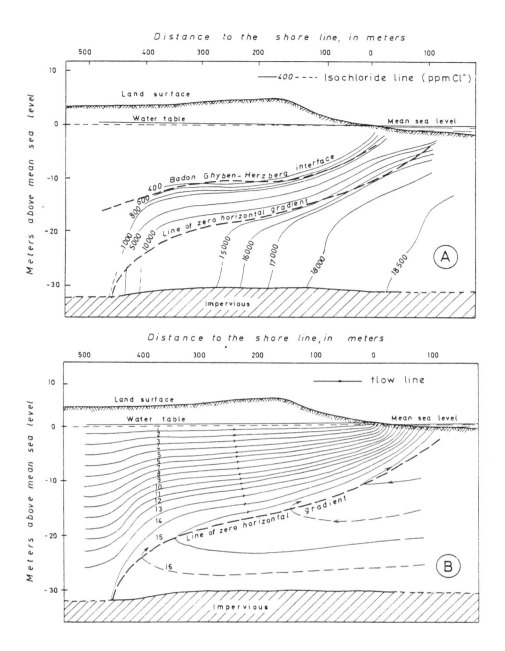

Fig. 3.7 - Isochloride lines (a) in a normal to the coast vertical cross section, showing that the lower end must be normal to the aquifer bottom impervious boundary. In this case the Ghyben-Herzberg interface
is near the top of the mixing zone. The line of zero horizontal
gradient is shown, and may be interpreted as a virtual interface.
The figure corresponds to Kohout's (1964) study of the Cutler area,
in the Biscayne Bay (Miami, Florida). B shows the flow lines. In
this case (a very permeable nonhomogeneous calcareous aquifer),
representing a mean situation, 7/8 of total water discharging in the
sea is fresh water and 1/8 is salt water.

3.1.7   Response of the fresh-salt groundwater body and the interface to water head changes and tidal oscillations

A change in water head in a salt groundwater body offsets the dynamic equilibrium, and the interface or the mixing zone moves to a new equilibrium position if the change persists. It takes a long time to reach a new dynamic equilibrium since the groundwater must be physically displaced, and this movement is generally very slow. Thus, after a rapid head change, the salt-fresh groundwater body reacts initially as a single fluid body. Afterwards it slowly modifies the interface position to adapt to the new situation if the change lasts.

When a sharp interface is present, equation 3.1.3 holds. Differentiating it, and since $dz/dt \simeq 0$,

$$\frac{dh_f}{dt} = \frac{1 + \alpha}{\alpha} \frac{dh_s}{dt} \simeq \frac{dh_s}{dt}$$

That means that the change in head in one of the water bodies is entirely transmitted to the other.

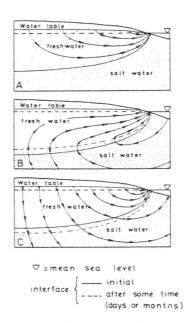

Fig. 3.8 - Effect of changes in the groundwater recharge in a coastal aquifer, after Visher (1960). A - constant recharge. The system is dynamically stationary B - situation during a dry period (or a high sea water level stage). Salt water increases its landward flow, but the fresh water flow towards the sea outlet continues (only in very high sea water level stages can temporarily be stopped). The interface initiates an upward and landward movement. C - situation during a wet period (or a low sea water level stage). Both the fresh and the salt water flow seaward. The interface initiates a downward and seaward movement. The interface or mixing zone movement is very slow, and the landward movement needs some time (days or months) to be noticeable.

A rapid recharge of fresh water increases the fresh water head; consequently it also increases the salt water head, as shown in the detailed classical study of the Biscayne Bay, in Florida (Kohout, 1964; Kohout and Klein, 1967). Both fresh and salt water flow towards the sea and the mixing zone moves slowly seaward and downwards, increasing its slope. The reverse is true in a dry period (fig. 3.8 and 3.9).

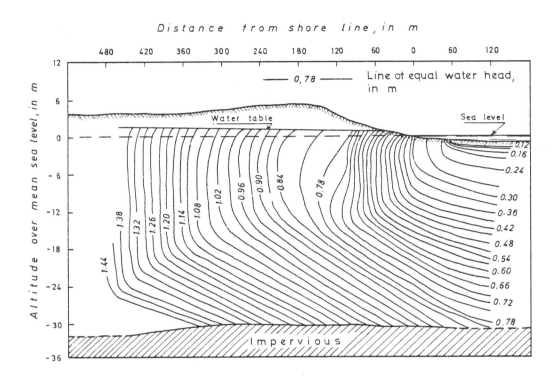

Fig. 3.9 - Lines of equal water head in a vertical plane in the Cutler area, in the Biscayne Bay (Miami, Florida), in a period of high fresh water head. Both fresh water and salt water flow towards the sea. No zero horizontal gradient line develops (after Kohout, 1964).

Sea tides produce the same effect. The sea level change is transmitted through the aquifer as it has only one fluid, with only a small distortion caused by the small oscillations of the interface about a central position (fig. 3.10).

Assuming a one-dimensional situation (horizontal flow normal to a rectilinear sea shore), the water mass balance equation, if density variations are not taken into account, reduces to:

(3.1.10)
$$\frac{\partial^2 h}{\partial x^2} = \frac{S}{T} \frac{\partial h}{\partial t}$$

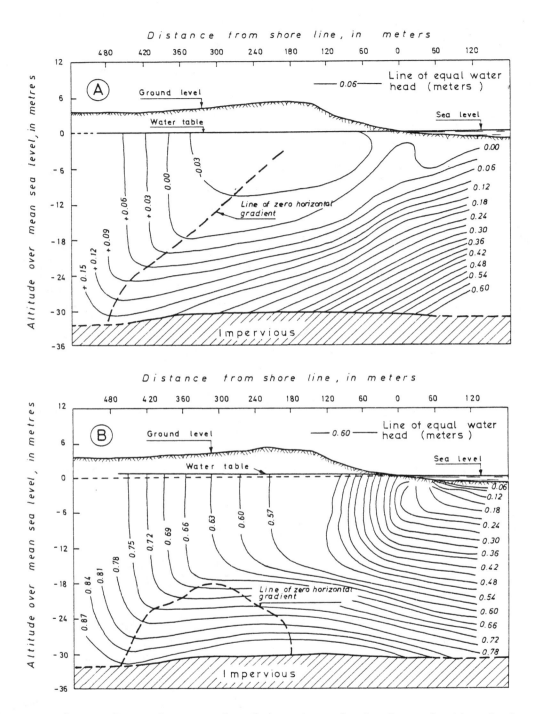

Fig. 3.10 – Lines of equal water head in a vertical plane in the Cutler area, in the Biscayne Bay (Miami, Florida), in a period of low fresh water head. A – in high tide conditions; there is a clear landward salt water flow, though some fresh and mixed water continue to flow towards the sea. B – in low tide conditions; there is a clear flow of fresh and salt water towards the sea, except in a small bottom area, where mixing effects increase (after Kohout, 1964).

where:

h = $h(x, t)$, groundwater head (L)

x = distance normal to the coast. The origin is generally placed at the sea shore, and x is positive landwards (L)

t = time (T)

T = transmissivity (assumed constant) (L^2/T)

S = storage coefficient (nondimensional)

T/S = hydraulic diffusivity (assumed constant) (L^2/T).

For a steady system in which $h = 0$ for $t \leq 0$, the water head variation according to a function $h = h(0, t)$ in $x = 0$, creates a response at a distance x and at time t, given by the convolution equation:

$$h(x,t) = \int_0^t h(0,\tau) \cdot P(x, t - \tau) \, d\tau = \int_0^t h(0, t - \tau) \cdot P(x, \tau) \, d\tau$$

in which P is the water head response velocity after a unit step change, and τ is a dummy variable of integration. Putting $A = \frac{x}{2} \sqrt{\frac{S}{T}}$ and using well known heat conduction solutions for a semi-infinite medium (Jaeger, 1963; Carslaw and Jaeger, 1959; see also Venetis, 1968; Custodio and Llamas, 1976, Vol. I p. 869; Cotecchia, 1977a):

$$P(x, t - \tau) = \frac{A}{\sqrt{\pi} \, (t - \tau)^{3/2}} \exp \left(- \frac{A^2}{t - \tau} \right)$$

and then, the water head change is:

$$h(x,t) = \frac{A}{\sqrt{\pi}} \int_0^t (t - \tau)^{-3/2} \exp \left(- \frac{A^2}{t - \tau} \right) h(0,\tau) d\tau$$

$$= \frac{2}{\sqrt{\pi}} \int_0^t h(0,\tau) \exp \left(- \frac{A^2}{t - \tau} \right) d \left(\frac{A^2}{t - \tau} \right)$$

For a steady head change, $h(0,\tau) = h_0 = $ constant, and

$h(x,t) = h_0 \, \mathrm{erfc} \left(\frac{A}{\sqrt{t}} \right)$, where $\mathrm{erfc} \left(\frac{A}{\sqrt{t}} \right) = i - \frac{2}{\sqrt{\pi}} \int_0^{A/\sqrt{T}} e^{-\xi^2} d\xi$.

For a sinusoidal sea tide component of half-range Σ_0 and period t_0, in a confined aquifer or in a water table aquifer with small changes in the saturation thickness:

$$h(x,t) = \Sigma_o \exp(-x \cdot \eta) \cdot \sin(2\pi t/t_o - x \cdot \eta)$$

in which $\eta^2 = \pi S/(t_o T)$. There is a damping effect of $\exp(-x \cdot \eta)$, and a time-lag of $x \cdot \eta \cdot t_o/2\pi = 1/2x \sqrt{\dfrac{t_o S}{T}}$.

For a leaky aquifer (de Cazenove, 1971):

$$h(x, t) = \Sigma_o \exp(-\xi x \eta) \sin(2\pi t/t_o - x\eta/\xi)$$

in which ξ must be deduced from $\xi^2 - 1/\xi^2 = Tt_o/(\eta S B^2)$, where B^2 = the leakage coefficient of the aquitard.

In an aquifer open to the sea, Σ_o is the tide half-range, the origin of distances being placed at an effective sea outlet, but if it is a confined aquifer not sea connected, Σ_o must be multiplied by the tide efficiency, TE < 1. TE depends on the elastic properties of the aquifer materials and water (Jacob, 1950), and it is thus related with the elastic storage coefficient, S, by

$$S = \frac{\gamma \cdot m \cdot \beta \cdot b}{1 - TE} \, ,$$

where:

γ = water specific weight

m = porosity

β = volumetric compressibility of water

b = aquifer thickness

In figure 3.11 the different situations are shown schematically, and in figures 3.12 and 3.13 the tide induced oscillations are represented.

The horizontal oscillation half-range of the interface is (Cooper, 1959):

$$a = \frac{k}{m} \exp(-x \cdot \eta) \sqrt{\frac{t_o s}{2\pi T}} \, ,$$

where:

k = permeability (L/T)

m = porosity (nondimensional)

The to and fro movement of the interface is well illustrated in some well studied cases in Florida (Kohout, 1961; Kohout and Klein, 1967).

The damping effect and the time-lag depend on the period t_o, and the different components of the tide are modified differently. Generally, the semidiurnal (sometimes the diurnal) effect dominates and it is the most conspicuous, but when considering long records, longer periods are also interesting, since the shorter ones damp out landward. When the tidal effect is determined, other causes of fluctuations must be taken into account, such as the barometric effect and the effect of periodical pumpages (see Custodio and Llamas, 1976, section 8.6).

In order to know the true water level fluctuations in a coastal aquifer the tidal and barometric effects must be filtered out. See figures 3.14, 3.15 and 3.16.

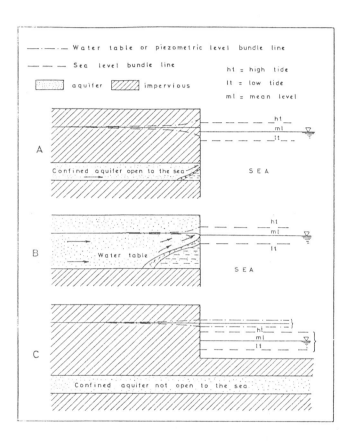

Fig. 3.11 - Effect of the sea tides on groundwater oscillations in a coastal aquifer. Mean and extreme situations are shown. The extreme situations are not simultaneous since there exists a time lag. In a confined aquifer, open to the sea (A), the oscillation is measurable far inland since the hydraulic diffusivity (T/S) is high, but in a water table aquifer of the same transmissivity the oscillation is restricted to the coastal zone (lower hydraulic diffusivity). In case A the difference between extreme tide positions and extreme piezometric levels at the submarine outlet is the fresh water head needed to overcome the salt water column there. In case C the confined aquifer is not open to the sea and then the tidal oscillations must be reduced according to the tidal efficiency.

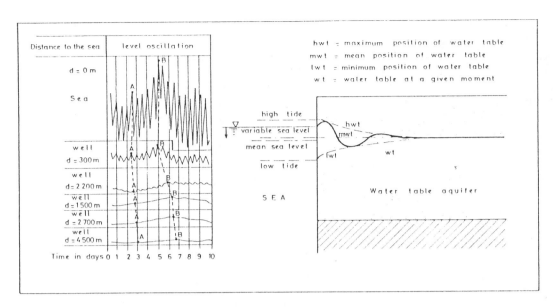

Fig 3.12 – The damping effect and the lag of the groundwater level oscillations due to the sea tides increase with distance to the coast and with the period of the sinusoidal component. In the left hand figure (modified from Werner and Noren, 1951) the semidiurnal oscillation (point A) is less damped and the lag is smaller than the fortnightly oscillation (point B). The right hand figure shows the form of the water table at a given moment when sea level is changing from high tide to mean position.

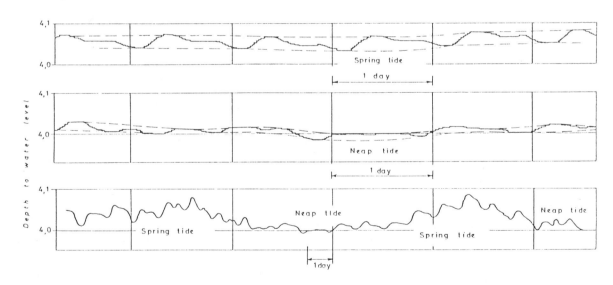

Fig. 3.13 – Tidal oscillations in a leaky aquifer (piezometer A.2.b) near the shore of the Llobregat delta (Barcelona) in the Mediterranean coast, where the sea tide range is between 0.2 and 0.4 meters. The diurnal effect dominates over the semidiurnal effect. The 24 hours 52 minutes period is clearly visible since in one day the maximum and minimum positions are somewhat later than in the preceeding one. This is the best way to differentiate the tidal effect from the effect of pumping walls, which shows a 24 hour period (after Custodio and Llamas, 1976, chapter 8.6).

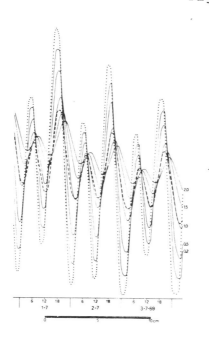

Fig. 3.14 - Example of how attenuation A is determined. The dotted line indicates the fluctuations of the Ionian Sea as recorded at Porto Cesareo (Apulia) tide gauge between 1 and 4 July 1969. Continuous lines show five of the fourteen curves calculated (number reduced for clarity) by introducing various attentuation values A (0.2, 0.5, 1.0, 1.5 and 2.0) in eq. 1. The dashed line illustrates the fluctuations in groundwater level recorded during the same period in a well. This line approximates well to the curve for A^2 = 1.0 hour (Magri and Troisi, 1969).

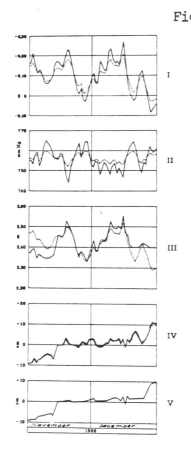

Fig. 3.15 - Example of processing procedure adopted. I: Original sea-level trends (continuous line) and attenuated fluctuation curve considered (dotted line); II: Original atmospheric pressure trends (continuous line) and attenuated pressure curve considered (dotted line); III: Trend of groundwater level fluctuations recorded in a well (continuous line) and of attenuated sea levels; IV: Trend of differences (continuous line) between the two curves in Diagram III, with the attenuated pressure curve superimposed (dotted line); V: Trend of groundwater levels obtained by eliminating the pressure effect by graphical methods. Measurements for 1966 (Tadolini and Zanframundo, 1974).

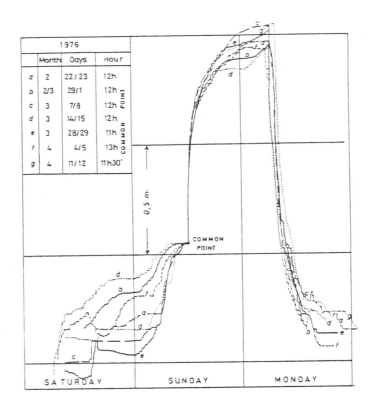

1976			
	Month	Days	Hour
a	2	22/23	12h
b	2/3	29/1	12h
c	3	7/8	12h
d	3	14/15	12h
e	3	28/29	11h
f	4	4/5	13h
g	4	11/12	11h30'

Fig. 3.16 - The water head in the confined aquifer of the Besós Delta is continuously fluctuating due to numerous industrial wells with a variable schedule. It masks the tidal effect. But at the end of the
Sunday recovery these effects have almost disappeared and the tidal
effects can be seen during a few hours, in a different phase from
one week to another (ascending or horizontal trend just before Mon-
day draw-down). It results in a tidal efficiency estimate of about
0.22 (Custodio, Suárez and Galofré, 1976).

3.1.8   Unstable situations

In open water, fresh water overlain by salt water is an unstable situation.
Due to the difference in density, the fresh water moves upward and is replaced
by salt water. The only counteracting force is the internal friction of the
fluids.

    In the ground a different situation exists. Beside the internal
friction of the fluids, there is friction between the fluids and the soil particles. According to Bear (1972) and Wooding (1972), the flow velocity of the
fluid with the lowest density (q) in an isotropic medium is governed by the
following equation of movement:

$$q = - \frac{k_o \rho_f g}{\mu} \left[\frac{1}{\rho_f g} \frac{\partial P}{\partial s} + \frac{\partial \zeta}{\partial s} - \frac{\rho_s - \rho_f}{\rho_f} \right]$$

-38-

where:

k_o = the intrinsic permeability

ρ_s = the density of the heaviest fluid

ρ_f = the density of the lightest fluid

g = acceleration of gravity

m = ground porosity

μ = dynamic viscosity

P = internal pressure of the fluid

ς = distance in the vertical direction

s = distance in the flow direction

In the case of free convection, there are no external forces and groundwater flow is governed only by forces due to the difference in densities. The vertical flow velocity is:

$$q_z = - \frac{k_o (\rho_s - \rho_f) g}{\mu}$$

Free convection occurs only under conditions where the so called Rayleigh Number (R_a) exceeds a fixed critical value:

$$R_a = - \frac{gb^3 (\rho_s - \rho_f)}{D_m \mu}$$

where:

b = the height of the fresh water layer

D_m = molecular diffusivity

There is a critical Rayleigh Number to spontaneously start free convection, but there is a lack of data. Nield (1968) gives a value of 40, but this figure must be used with caution since he uses a different definition of R_a. It is defined by Wooding (1972) as $R_a = k_o g \dfrac{b (\rho_s - \rho_f)}{D_m \mu}$, where k_o substitutes for b^2.

An alternative approach is possible by applying thermodynamical principles, translated in density differences (Horton and Rogers, 1945; Pomper, 1979). There is a critical density gradient under which free convection flow is possible:

$$\frac{\rho_a - \rho_b}{H} = \frac{4\pi^2 D_h}{kb^2}$$

where D_h is the thermal diffusion coefficient (0.0864 m^2/day) and b is the thickness of the layer considered. From it the following critical relationship between the difference in density ($\rho_a - \rho_b$) and the transmissivity of the layer with water of the lowest density (kb) can be obtained, $\rho_1 - \rho_2 = C/kb$ in which the constant C is 3.4 kg/m/day.

Stability under free flow is only possible when a combination of a small difference in density and a low value for the transmissibility (kH) occurs. The latter can be caused by a low value for the hydraulic conductivity k or by a small thickness b. When there is a stable salinity inversion in a free flow unstable situation, there must be forces to compensate for the buoyancy force, such as upward vertical components in the groundwater flow, given by:

$$q_z = - \frac{k_o}{\mu} \left[\frac{\partial P}{\partial s} - g\,(\rho_s - \rho_f) \right].$$

3.2   Coastal conditions

3.2.1   Saline wedge penetration

In conditions close to equilibrium the length of the saline wedge penetration can be measured as a first approximation by (see Custodio and Llamas, 1976, pp 1358; and also section 5.2.5):

$$L = \frac{1}{2\alpha} \frac{kb^2}{q_o}$$

in which:

L = length of the salt water wedge when there is a sharp interface and the aquifer is homogeneous and isotopic

α = BGH factor = $\rho_f / (\rho_s - \rho_f)$

k = aquifer permeability

b = aquifer thickness

q_o = fresh groundwater flow per unit of coast length.

Then, sea water wedge penetration depends on the following:

(a) Directly on aquifer permeability. The most permeable tracts are more affected by the saline water. The occurrence of highly permeable formations or layers, or rock discontinuities (big fractures, karstic channels) is an extreme situation that generally arises from a great salt water wedge penetration. In wide karstic channels or in wide highly permeable formations, the situation is closer to that occurring in surface water systems.

(b) Directly on the square of the aquifer thickness. This is a major factor in many circumstances, since deep gravel channels, deep vertical discontinuities or the presence of thick pervious formations lead to localized great salt water penetrations, sometimes unexpected.

(c) Inversely on the fresh water flow. Then salt water penetration increases when:

- the climate is more arid

- the groundwater basins are smaller

- groundwater recharge is more reduced

- the surface drainage is more dense or the evaporation is greater, since it reduces the water that arrives at the coast for underground discharge. This is especially important in very flat coastal areas.

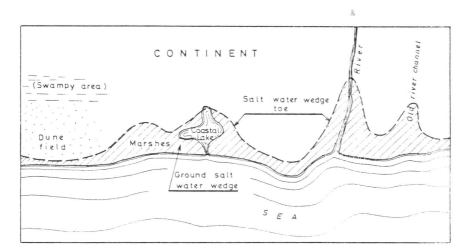

Fig. 3.17 - Changes in ground salt water wedge penetration along a recent coast. The presence of marshes, a sea connected coastal lake, a river channel and an old river channel filled with coarse sediments, originate areas of low water table and correspondingly the salt water wedge is more penetrant, especially where the aquifer is thicker. In the dune field exists a higher groundwater recharge that increases the local water table, thus reducing the salt water wedge penetration. The high water table in the dune area may create a swampy area in the landward side. In warm arid climates the intense evaporation in these swamps originates non sea related brackish or salty waters. The figure is an oversimplified sketch of the situation in the upper aquifer of the Llobregat Delta (Barcelona).

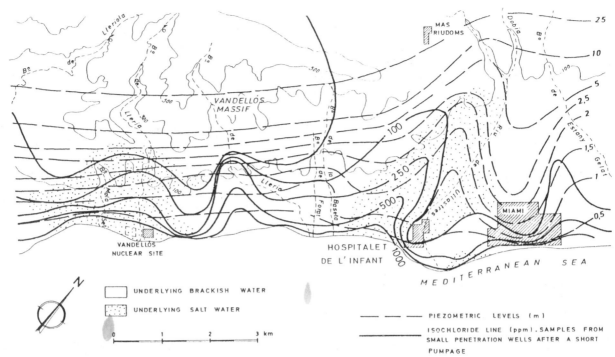

Fig. 3.18 - Natural sea water intrusion along the coast of the Vandellós Massif in Tarragona (Catalonia, Spain). The presence of brackish and salt water at shallow depths is indicated.

3.2.2 Nonhomogeneity effects

As deduced from the preceding paragraph, a nonhomogeneous coast presents a variable penetration of the sea water wedge (figs. 3.17 and 3.18). The penetration can be negligible in shallow, low permeability formations and very great in thick very permeable formations or discontinuities, in spite of the fact that these zones act as preferential discharge locations in which the fresh groundwater flow is greatly increased. It is reflected in concentrated outflows or coastal springs.

The aquifer transmissivity, T, does not describe the coastal conditions well since $T = kb$ and the relevant factor in the salt water penetration is kb^2.

In stratified aquifers, the presence of an upper layer of high permeability favors the presence of salt water in the aquifer profile, while when the upper layer is of low permeability it favors a thicker fresh water body.

In thick low permeability aquifers, an important upward fresh water flow exists near the coast. If they are covered by a layer of highly permeable materials (recent coarse sediments, highly fractured rock, young lavas or breccias), an extreme situation of the stratified aquifers appears, and a salt or brackish water body may develop in the upper layer, especially in dry climates, floating on fresh water. This is an unstable situation maintained by the upward fresh water flow. A thick mixing zone develops, penetrating irregularly in the lower materials, according to the flow nonhomogeneities or the presence of vertical descending branches of the convective cells that try to overturn the situation.

3.2.3   Anisotropy effects

The aquifer anisotropy influences the flow pattern and the interface position. The mathematical treatment cannot be done with a simple transformation for isotropy, because the interface is a boundary condition depending on the flow potential. It can be qualitatively said that for a given fresh water flow, the horizontal permeability being the same, a lower vertical permeability deepens the interface and shortens the salt water wedge, and a higher vertical permeability reduces the fresh water thickness over the interface and extends the salt water wedge landward. When the upward vertical flow components are reduced, the water head on the interface increases. The same is true for the presence of horizontal layers of reduced permeability (similar to a lower vertical permeability), or the presence of vertical fissures or joints (similar to a higher vertical permeability), that are frequent in hard roks and karstic formations.

3.2.4   Sea bottom conditions

Sea bottom conditions can alter the fresh-salt water relationships in coastal aquifers. A cover of low permeability materials renders difficult the fresh water discharge into the sea and especially the sea water infiltration. The result is a fresh water head increase and a salt water head decrease, thus reducing the salt water wedge penetration.

The fresh water outflow or the effect of the tides and waves may hamper the formation of this cover in the proximity of the shore.

When the coastal sediments clog fissures, fractures and channels, there is a smaller salt and brackish water penetration, except in singular areas, where the outflow hinders the sedimentation around these areas.

When sea bottom sediments are more permeable, the effect is of little importance. The same applies if the rock permeability increases in the sea bottom by fissure opening, though the mixing zone width can be increased.

3.2.5   The thickness of the mixing zone

Theoretically it can be shown that (Wooding, 1972) the thickness of the mixing zone is approximately proportional to the square root of the interface radius of curvature. Thus, the thickness should tend to decrease towards the coast. But this cannot be the case since the influence of tidal variations increases towards the sea outlet, thus increasing the mixing effect. The same is true when fissure permeability increases towards the sea due to decompression effects or the aggressive effect of brackish water on carbonate rocks.

In general, the thickness of the mixing zone increases when:

- Tidal range increases. The effect is more severe near the coast.

- The tidal zone increases (the strip land width between high and low tide). This effect is limited to the environs of this tidal zone.

- Permeability increases, because then the wedge penetration increases and also the dispersivity, especially in confined conditions (greater groundwater oscillations).

- The interface or mixing zone length increases.

- The frequency and size of the nonhomogeneities in or near the mixing zone increases, because then the macroscopic dispersivity increases.

- The fresh water flow decreases. The thickness is greater the more arid the climate and smaller the groundwater basin.

- The seasonal groundwater variations increase.

In some instances the mixing zone is very thin, a few meters or less, but in other situations it can attain more than a hundred meters, especially in highly nonhomogeneous formations (young volcanics, classic reef limestones, coarse coastal piedmont deposits, karstic carbonate massifs). See figure 3.7. In nonhomogeneous highly permeable materials, especially when fresh water flow is small, the top of the mixing zone can reach the water table and no fresh water is found, or it is reduced to a very thin layer.

The existence of an old salt water body in the lower part of the aquifer favors the existence of a thicker transition zone if upward diffusion or dispersion of the salt is possible (Meinardi, 1975).

The thickness of the transition zone can be increased until the fresh water body disappears in a part of the aquifer, when this part is periodically sea flooded. Also, a geothermal warming of the deep water in a very thick aquifer can destabilize the salinity stratification and increase the mixing effect through vertical pure convective currents (Kohout, 1965).

The thickness of the mixing zone is not constant and in a cross section normal to the coast can vary towards the sea. In a normal situation the thickness can be a minimum in an intermediate part and increase landward and seaward. The last effect is related to increasing dispersion near the coast, and the first is due to the small flow rate near and inside the mixing zone; towards the sea, the flow rate increases, especially in the fresh water side, and thus the thickness decreases. In fissured and karstic formations the minimum of the mixing zone thickness may be close to the coast (Cotecchia, 1977b). Along a flow tube the concentration cannot decrease, but an acceleration of the flow allows for a smaller cross-section.

The mixing zone thickness expands and contracts according to the succession of low and high tides and to dry and wet periods. A thickness decrease necessarily implies an increase in the flow towards the sea inside the mixing zone in order to conserve the salt balance. This flow is effective in transporting salts to the sea. Usually there is a lag between the effective rainy period and the mixing zone modification. Cotecchia (1977a) has observed greater movements of the mixing zone far inland. It seems that the movement increases towards the base of the mixing zone (fig. 3.19), being greater inland, and that it is also greater than the water table changes, in agreement with the BGH principle. The same was observed in Miami (fig. 3.20).

The fresh water flow domain decreases in thickness from the wet to the dry period, and it is accomplished mainly through an adjustment of the interface depth.

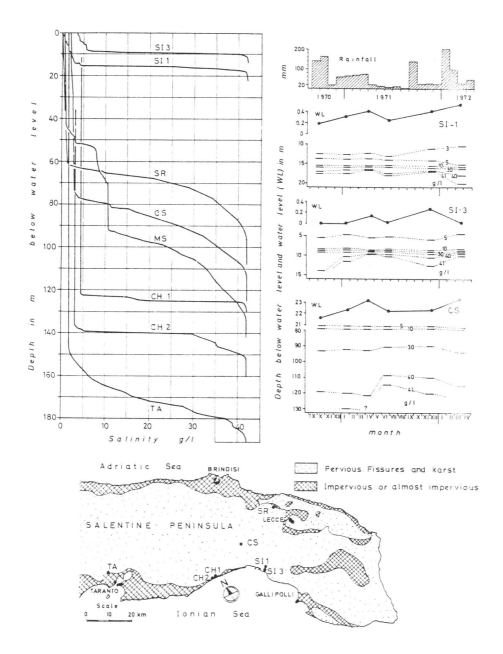

Fig. 3.19 - Natural sea water encroachment in the Salentine Peninsula (Southern Italy), after Cotecchia (1977 a). In the left side the salinity logs of some bore-holes are shown; the mixing zone is well defined. The changes in the mixing zone thickness in three bore-holes is represented; there is a contraction after a wet period and an expansion after a dry period, the movement being greater at the base. It is the response to changes in flow velocity inside the mixing zone.

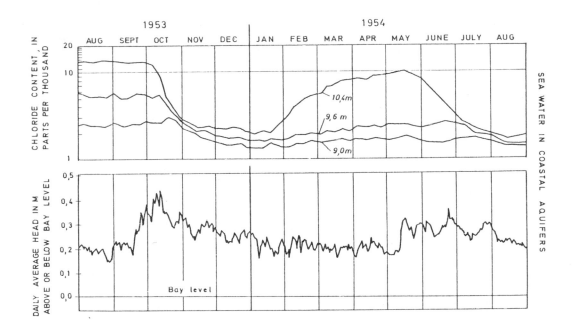

Fig 3.20 – Fluctuations of chloride content and water level in a well in the Silver Bluff area, near Miami, Florida (Kohout, 1964). The well is cased until 8.9 m below sea level and reaches 10.7 m. The chloride changes at 9.0, 9.6 and 10.4 m below mean sea level are shown. The mixing zone contracts after recharge events and expands in dry periods, mainly changing the depth to the bottom of the mixing zone.

In a pumped aquifer, the expansion and contraction of the mixing zone do not necessarily follow the same pattern. Thus, in the Honolulu aquifer (Hawaian Islands), the greatest movement corresponds to the top of the mixing zone, while the base is almost stationary (Todd and Meyer, 1971).

In some cases, especially in fissured rocks, the interface depth in an observation bore-hole can fluctuate widely and rapidly, sometimes several tens of meters from high to low tide (Monkhouse and Fleet, 1975; Mather and Buckley, 1973). This does not represent the true situation in the aquifer, in which the oscillations are much less, but the changes in water head between different subaquifers or fissures short-circuited by the bore-hole.

In nonhomogeneous formations with only horizontal flow, the vertical salinity profile determined in a bore-hole can show some irregularities representing the changes in permeability (fig. 3.21). The log is steeper in the more permeable tracts than in the low permeability ones.

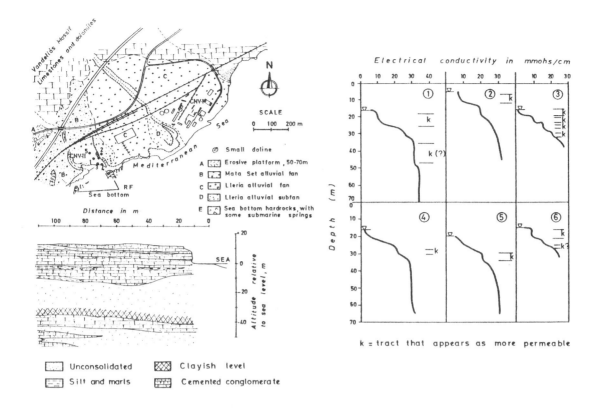

Fig. 3.21 - Water salinity logs of some bore-holes in the Lleria-Mala Set alluvial fans, bordering the Vandellós limestone massif (Tarragona, Spain). The alluvial fans form a cliff at the shore due to the erosive effect of the sea; several highly cemented and fissured (sometimes karstified) levels alternate with almost unconsolidated levels. The salinity logs show some irregularities related to permeability variations along the fully slotted bore-holes; the K indicates the more permeable tracts. Artificial radioisotope tests show that the flow is fully horizontal. RF in the situation map indicates the presence of a rocky sea floor, in which the sand cover has been eliminated by submarine water outflows (after Custodio, 1978).

3.2.6   Unstable situations

The most frequent situations that can lead to an unstable condition are those in which saline water lies on fresh water. Such situations can be encountered:

        - near the shoreline, in the fresh water discharge strip under the sea (see figs. 3.3, 3.4);

        - below the tidal zone, when this is wide (fig. 3.22 and 3.23);

        - in coastal zones affected by sea storms or saline spray;

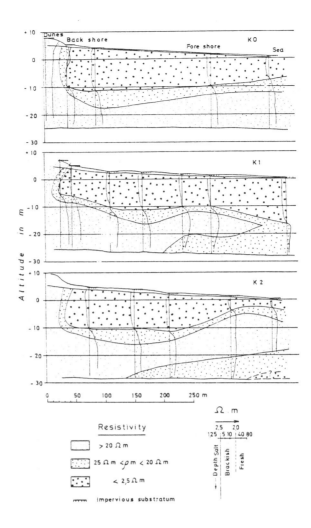

Fig. 3.22 - Resistivity profiles perpendicular to the shore line of the Westhoek area, in southern Belgium (after Lebbe, 1981). The ground resistivity profiles, obtained with a long normal device (AM = 1 m) are shown. The upper saline water infiltration during high tides and stormy events. Fresh water mixes with saline water and can penetrate below the sea.

- below estuaries with salt water in the bottom, when they act as fresh water drainages;

- below very flat badly drained areas, where there is high evaporation rates of the discharging groundwater; (Salt water is not of direct sea origin)

- in sea flooded areas where vertical flow of underlying fresh water is retarded by the presence of a low permeability cover (clays, clay loams, silty clay, peat), such as in the Dutch polder area (fig. 3.24);

- in multi-layer aquifers, a very frequent situation.

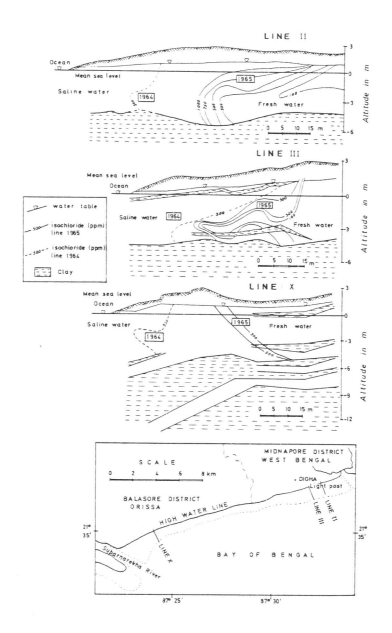

Fig. 3.23 – Cross-sections perpendicular to the sea coast near Digha (India) showing the saline water-fresh water contact in 1964 and a year later, after a dry period. The contact migrates landward until some ten meters (after Goswami, 1968). Nonhomogeneity of aquifer permeability and the introduction of salty water through the ground surface after heavy storms, produce an unusual form of the mixing zone, with an upper layer of salt water. The storms produce a retrogradation of the shore line.

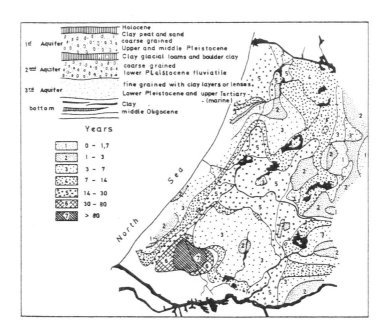

Fig. 3.24 - Vertical resistence of the Holocene layers in the Netherlands. These Holocene layers, shown in the stratigraphical inset, retard the vertical outflow of groundwater (after Pomper and Wesseling, 1978). The vertical resistence is the value of the aquitard thickness over its vertical permeability.

The flow of fresh groundwater serves to expel the salt water penetrating through possible convective flows. Other possible situations leading to unstable conditions have been mentioned in the preceding paragraph, and are created by thermal changes in the water density. They are more frequent in tectonically active areas in which shallow-seated magmatic intrusions can be found (see section 3.3.6).

3.2.7   Sea level conditions

Sea level is the coastal reference level that controls continental fresh water discharge. Most of the effects are related to mean sea level, the tides only producing oscillations that damp out landward (see section 3.1.7). This means sea level must be known with precision and varies along the coast due to currents, preferential winds, non-sphericity of the Earth, rotation forces, etc. Then the zero datum of a country is not necessarily the mean sea level in a certain place, and small corrections must be introduced from observations in local tide-recorders.

In some areas or islands the zero datum is taken at the lowest spring ebb tide. Attention must be given to that circumstance.

In flat coasts, where the tidal width is great, there is a tendency to maintain a mean salt groundwater level under that area that is higher than the local mean sea level, since sea water goes up easily in flood-tide, but recedes with difficulty in ebb-tide. In bays and sounds, with only a narrow connection with the sea, in spite of showing a certain tidal effect, the mean local elevation can be slightly different from that in the ocean, since the evaporation, continental runoff (both surface and subterranean) and tide deformation through the inlet must be considered (Urish, 1980).

3.2.8   Water table coastal aquifers

In water table aquifers, direct recharge by rainfall infiltration is possible, and also recharge by irrigation return flows, floods, river channels, etc. Also losses to the atmosphere are possible when the water table is high enough to allow for direct uptake by plants or direct evaporation. The water can be easily drained toward topographical depressions.

The sea water wedge penetration is variable according to the different hydrogeological and hydrological circumstances, according to section 3.2.1. The salt water wedge starts practically at the shore line and often small fresh or brackish water leakages are found near the shore, easy to identify in fine sand beaches (especially in ebb-tide) due to the quick condition of the sand or to the formation of small elongated depressions. In highly nonhomogeneous formations the outlet may be concentrated in conspicuous springs. The water salinity decreases landward. Near the shore, when the fresh groundwater flow is high, the upward flow components are important. Then, in flat coastal areas or in low lying beaches, boreholes open in the lower part of the fresh water body can flow naturally, discharging fresh or slightly salty water. The freshness and head or discharge tend to increase in high tide stage, though a time lag exists. In some cases this effect is highly noticeable, but in others the changes are not appreciable.

In thin low permeability coastal water table aquifers, having a high fresh water flow, the salt water wedge is very short and its penetration is limited to the shore-line environs.

In very thick and highly permeable coastal water table aquifers, especially when the fresh water flow is small, the salt water wedge naturally penetrates deeply inland. A penetration of a few or many kilometers is not unusual, depending on the depth of the lower impervious boundary of the aquifer.

3.2.9   Confined coastal aquifers

The salt water-fresh water relationships in a confined coastal aquifer, open to the sea bottom at some distance seaward, are the same as in a water table aquifer and the Badon Ghyben-Herzberg (BGH) formula or its improvements also apply when piezometric levels are used.

In the submarine outlet, the salt water column must be forced by enough fresh water pressure. Then, if the top of the confined aquifer intersects the sea bottom at a depth z, the minimum piezometric level over mean sea level h, needed to overcome the salt water column is (fig. 3.25)(see section 3.1.2 for definitions):

$$(h + z) \cdot \gamma_f = z \cdot \gamma_s; \qquad h = \frac{\gamma_s - \gamma_f}{\gamma_f} = z/\gamma$$

This can be obtained directly from the BGH formula; h increases as z increases. Then, it is not surprising in flat coastal areas that the boreholes drilled in fresh water confined aquifers under natural steady conditions are flowing ones, with a higher head corresponding to deeper aquifers. Since the fresh water body extends seaward, fresh water wells can be drilled offshore (fig. 3.25).

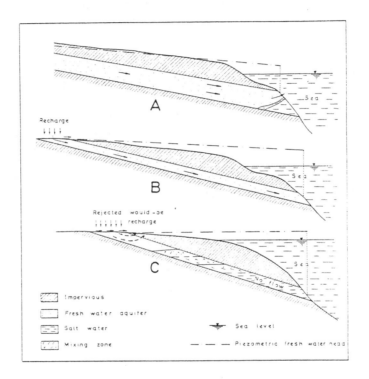

Fig. 3.25 - Confined coastal aquifers. In case A the fresh water piezometric head at the outlet counterbalances the salt water column and a normal salt water wedge develops. In case B the piezometric head is high enough to counterbalance the salt water column corresponding to the lower edge of the aquifer submarine outlet. In case C the recharge area is at an altitude lower than that needed to create a piezometric head that overcomes the salt water column at the aquifer submarine outlet, and then the sea water is like a plug and water is stationary. The recharge at the continental outcrop is rejected and the aquifer contains brackish and salt water.

A deep confined aquifer having a piezometric level close to sea level cannot contain fresh water in a steady state. If it yields fresh water, an unsteady situation is present, probably related to groundwater abstraction.

The variations in the outcrop depth of the aquifer at the sea bottom concentrate the outflow in the shallowest zones. Thus, irregularities in piezometric level, wedge penetration and salinity distribution develop.

In areas where the fresh water head is not enough to produce outflow, the sea water invades part of the aquifer and an extensive mixing zone develops. If the piezometric level of the fresh water is less than the minimum value along the shallowest aquifer submarine outcrop, the sea acts as a plug. No fresh water circulation exists and salt or brackish water fill the aquifer, since the dispersed salt cannot be washed out, except if some upward leakage is possible through semipervious cover or outlets through fissures or wells. Some small coastal springs discharging brackish water represent such outlets.

If the fresh water head at the outlet is higher than z'/γ (z' = depth of the lower part of aquifer outlet) no salt water wedge develops.

In confined coastal aquifers not open to the sea, water is stagnant, or very slowly flowing if the confining bed allows for a small leakage. Though brackish or salty water is common, generally the origin of salinity is not directly related to modern sea water, and other phenomena can be present such as diffusion and osmotic effects, which proceed at a very slow pace, and they do not have a direct bearing on water resources studies. In some circumstances these aquifers must be geopressurized, and may be an energy source.

3.2.10   Semiconfined coastal aquifers

The situation in a semiconfined (leaky) coastal aquifer is similar to that in a confined aquifer, but generally water leaks upward and then the piezometric level diminishes seawards (fig. 3.26 and 3.27), following a decreasing function.

If there is a submarine aquifer outcrop and there the residual head is enough to overcome the salt water column, it exists an outflow and the aquifer is filled with fresh water, except in the area occupied by the salt water wedge.

When the head is not enough to overcome the salt water column, there is no fresh water outflow in the aquifer outcrop and salt and brackish water fill the aquifer until the zone where the piezometric head counterbalances a sea water column equal to the local aquifer depth below sea level.

The same applies when there is no submarine outcrop and the only outlet is the upward leakage.

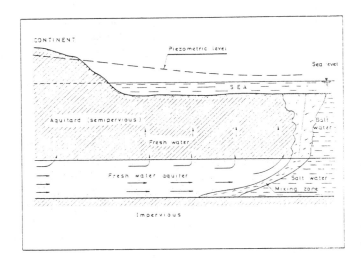

Fig. 3.26 - Submarine semiconfined (leaky) aquifer. Fresh water leaks upward until the remaining fresh water head cannot counterbalance the salt water column. The existence of a fresh water flow does not necessarily imply that the aquifer is open to the sea.

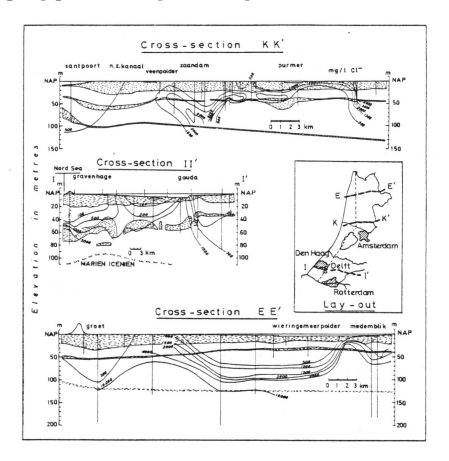

Fig. 3.27 - Upward flow in the Dutch coastal semiconfined aquifers in response to the different aquitard resistance and the surface water levels (after Pomper, 1981).

3.2.11   Multilayered coastal aquifers

The fresh-salt water relationships in multilayered aquifers depend on the vertical distribution of permeabilities. Two extreme cases can be considered: a) the whole thickness is permeable; and b) there are impervious or semipervious interlayerings and thus a multiaquifer system is present.

In a multiaquifer system, a particular fresh-salt water relationship develops in every one of the aquifers, according to the general concepts presented before (fig. 3.28). The situation can be complex if leakage between adjacent aquifers occurs. Depending on depth, recharge, thickness and permeability of the individual layers, the salt water wedge penetration is variable. The piezometric level generally increases, the deeper the aquifer, since the coast is the lowest outflow line of continental systems.

When the whole thickness is permeable, the interface is affected by the permeability distribution along a vertical, as described in section 3.2.2. In a two layer coastal aquifer, the most permeable layer dominates the flow. If it is the upper one, the salt water wedge reaches further inland. If it is the lower one, the salt water wedge is shorter than in a homogeneous case presenting the mean permeability (Fetter, 1972).

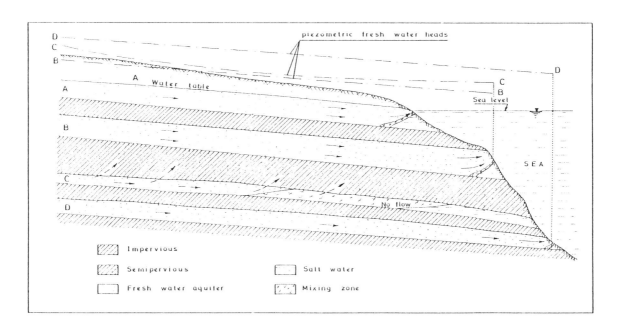

Fig. 3.28 - Coastal multiaquifer system. Aquifer A is a water table one. Aquifers B and D are confined and discharge into the sea; piezometric head is above land surface near the coast. Aquifer C leaks to aquifer B and does not have enough head to counterbalance the salt water column; near the coast is filled with brackish and salt water. Fresh groundwater exists beyond the shore line in confined aquifers when there is a water flow.

3.2.12 Natural unsteady situations

A natural system is not always in dynamic equilibrium. The dynamic equilibrium is offset by the tides and the variations of recharge, but since they are almost cyclic phenomena and there is an oscillation about a central position, a mean dynamic equilibrium can develop.

Notwithstanding, some noncyclic or long term natural actions occur, such as:

- changes in the sea level relative to the continent (eustatic or tectonic); (Figure 3.29 shows the recent eustatic sea level changes. Other data can be found in Cronin et al. (1981))

- changes in the shore-line position by accretion (delta expansion, coastal sedimentation) or abrasion (coast retrogradation);

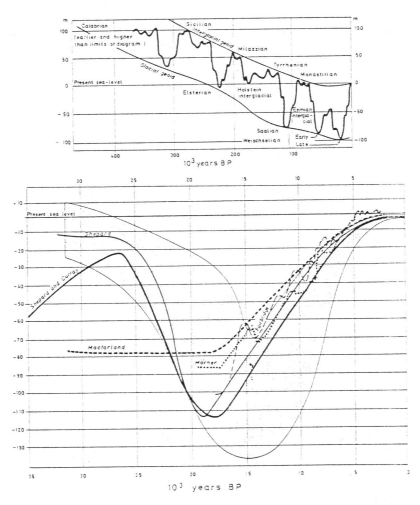

Fig 3.29 - Eustatic sea level changes. The upper figure refers to the traditional Mediterranean sequence during the Pleistocene (after Fairbridge, 1961) and the lower one gives the band of changes deduced by different authors (Rice, 1977).

- changes in recharge, related with slow climate modifications or hydrographic alterations;

- changes in the sea-aquifer contact surface by sedimentation or erosion.

All these changes offset or impede a true equilibrium to develop. Since the movement or replacement of big quantities of salt or fresh water is needed, the dynamic equilibrium sometimes takes a long time to be established after the modification ceases. In certain natural situations the new equilibrium cannot be attained since the leading change is continuously going on. These changes cannot be observed easily, but the disequilibrium can be measured if it is important.

The existence of salt or brackish water in certain aquifers and formations can be explained as natural non-steady situations. In chapter 10 some case histories deal with this problem.

Also as described in section 3.2.6, coastal areas that are sea flooded during extraordinary storms, or as a consequence of the retrogradation of the coast, or the weakening of some natural barriers (dunes), are under long-term unsteady conditions. The density inversion is an unstable situation with overturnings that lead to an increased mixing and some complicated transient situations, more acute in nonhomogeneous environments.

3.2.13   Entrapped old sea water

Frequently in coastal areas an extensive deep salt water body exists. This is a direct consequence of the BGH principle in very flat areas or in very permeable thick formations, and cannot be interpreted as a consequence of lateral sea water movement after the exploitation.

In some other circumstances the fresh water head is enough to avoid the existence of sea water, according to the BGH principle, but salt or brackish water exists in some deep formations. This can be explained as follows:

(a) In deep lenticular or discontinuous permeable formations, not open to the sea, salt water penetrated in earlier times (connate or infiltrated), cannot be expelled, and only disappears by upward diffusion towards the fresh water body. This is a very slow process, that can last for centuries or millenia as observed in the Netherlands (Meinardi, 1975, 1976), in some areas of Catalonia (Custodio, Bayó and Batista, 1977) or in Japan (Okutsu, 1972). Details of the successive Pleistocene and Holocene sea transgressions and regressions, and the lay-out of the involved sediments are needed. Figure 3.30 shows an example from the Federal Republic 0f Germany.

(b) In low permeability recent formations, such as clay and silt deltaic lenses, salty connate water remains for a long time, between fresh water bodies. This salty water generally does not appear in wells (except for some sandy interlayerings), but must be taken into account in geoelectrical prospecting (Custodio et al., 1976; see also the Llobregat example in section 10.1).

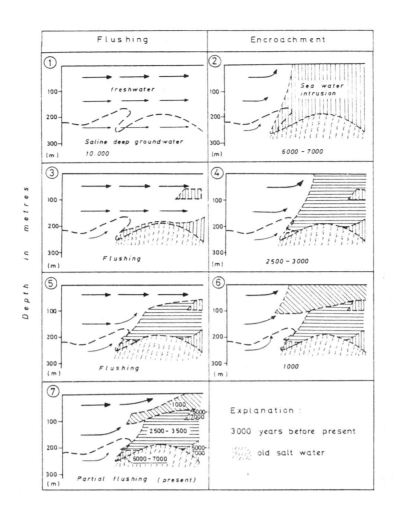

Fig 3.30 – Different successive phases of flushing and sea water encroachment during the Holocene in the region of Wittmund, Federal Republic of Germany (after Hahn, 1975, with some changes). The figures indicate years before present. A complicated old sea water distribution is thus originated.

3.3   Application to several types of coastal areas

3.3.1   Importance of geologic conditions

Fresh-salt water relationships in coastal areas depend on local circumstances in a more detailed way than groundwater heads. A more complete description of the physical environments is needed, in three dimensions. Such information cannot generally be gathered except in very special circumstances or in research studies.

Then, there is certain lack of accuracy in the interpretation of the observations. A better understanding can be reached when the stratigraphy and structure of the sediments can be explained by the sequence of events that led to the present situation.

According to Hansen (1971) in sedimentary coastal plains the existence of conformities and nonconformities, truncations, paraconformities, stratigraphical lagoons, pinch-out and overlayerings must be considered. Palaeochannels are nonconformities of two types:

- Closed: from rivers rich in suspended matter and from swampy areas. Fine and distributed sandy areas are formed, with low permeability, separated by finer sediments.

- Open: from rivers in which bottom transport dominates. Thick, continuous, sometimes extensive permeable formations develop, with irregular less frequent impervious boundaries, interconnected and with an easy recharge.

Changes in facies can appear:

- Parallel to the deep: they are formed under sea conditions, parallel to the coast, by current and wave processes. They do not act as true permeability barriers and the change is gradational.

- Following the deep: they are formed under continental fluvial conditions, and give way to more nonhomogeneous formations that can act as a permeability barrier.

Under deltaic conditions the complexity of the sediment built up must be understood.

In hard rocks the tectonic circumstances that create the secondary permeability (joints and faults) may play a dominant role. In carbonate rocks, the solubility of the carbonate minerals play an important role in the present permeability distribution, jointly with the sea level changes. Karstification and diagenetic processes (dolomitization and dedolomitization) must be considered, since they greatly effect permeability and porosity distribution. The presence of clay-rich and other less soluble materials must be known in order to interpret the secondary permeability evolution.

3.3.2   Deltas and coastal alluvial formations

Two examples are considered in section 10.2.

Many young deltas have been forming after the last ice-age, so they are typically less than 10,000 years old, and reflect man's effect on the environment. In many situations, that are typical on the Mediterranean coast, there occur sand and gravel deposits in the lower part of the deltaic formations, occupying an old estuary, laterally extended through buried beach and dune deposits. These bottom formations are covered by deposits of fine sand, silt and clay, sometimes with peat and methane gas, forming an impervious or semipervious, continuous or discontinuous lens, that present lateral facies variations in agreement with the complicated sequence of filling with sand bars, dune ridges, river banks, flood fine sediments, alluvium and lagoon deposits. In the top, recent formations of gravels, sand and silt occur (see figs. 3.31, 3.32 and 3.33).

The intermediate lens, formed in a salty or brackish water environment, still may contain connate water (see case history no. 1 in section 10.2).

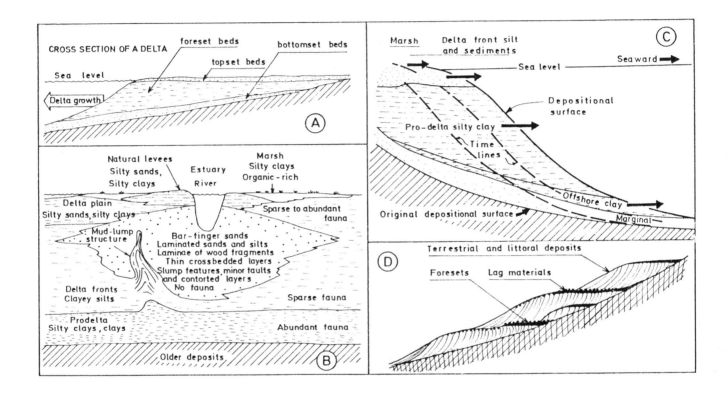

Fig. 3.31 - Simplified structures and formation of deltas (after Reineck and Singh, 1973). A - schematic illustration of the construction of a delta body (see section 10.2). B - characteristic features of bar-finger sands and associated facies. C - seaward progradation of a depositional deltaic environment, in which different environments migrate toward the sea during the growth of the delta. D - hypothetical section showing how deltaic deposits form during a rapid rising of the sea level.

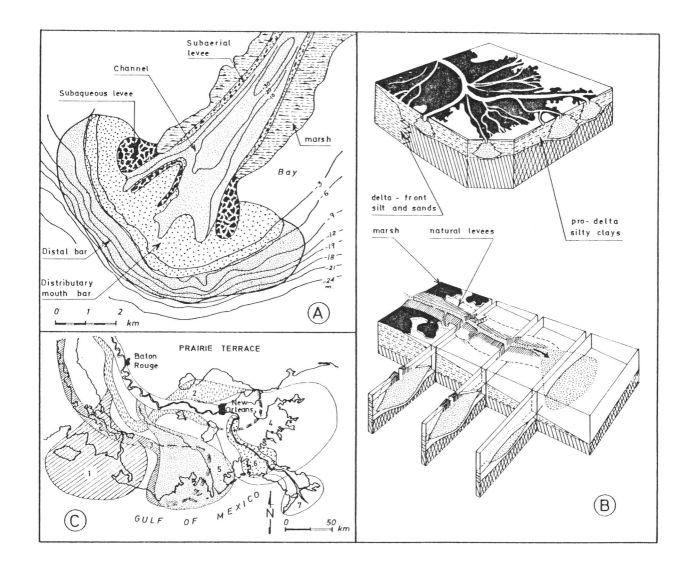

Fig. 3.32 – Delta sedimentation, after Reineck and Singh (1973). A – diagrammatic representation of the various sedimentation zones in a delta front environment, based on the mouth of the Southwest Pass, in the Mississippi Delta. B – schematic diagram of bar-finger sands in the Mississippi Delta. C – the seven deltaic lobes in the imbricating delta of the Mississippi river, formed during the last 5000 years, after Kolb and Van Lopik (1958) in Reineck and Singh (1973). Figures indicate the sequence of lobe formation.

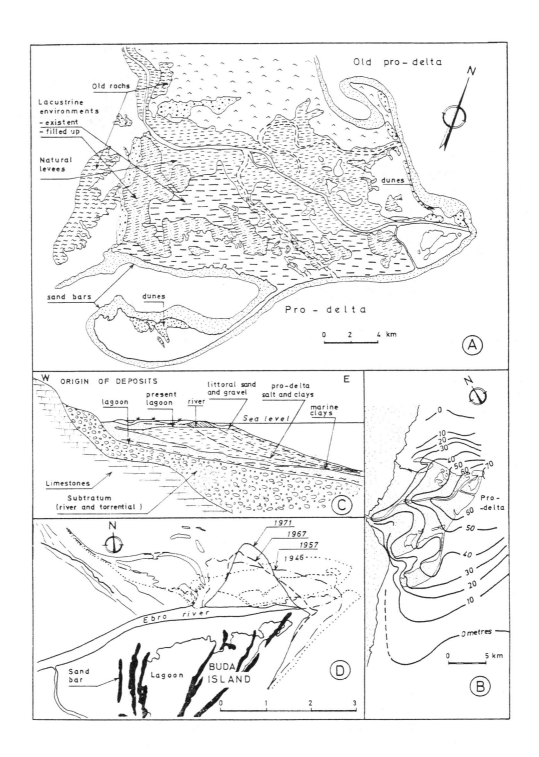

Fig. 3.33 - The Ebro river delta (Catalonia, Spain), after Maldonado (1977). A - main sedimentary environments. B - map showing the thickness of the delta deposits and the different macroenvironments. C - longitudinal cross-section showing the different materials. Present delta contour is the result of fast changes that involve abrasion and accretion, that can reach 100 m/year, especially at the main month (D).

The deep aquifer contains fresh or salt water depending on the existence of an outlet to the sea and enough fresh water head to allow for a fresh water outflow. Figure 3.34 shows schematically two typical situations in the Mediterranean coast. In one of them there is enough fresh water head (the recharge area is generally controlled by the river, upstream) to maintain a water flow, but in the other one this fresh water head is not enough to establish a seaward water flow because the area and the river bed have insufficient elevation.

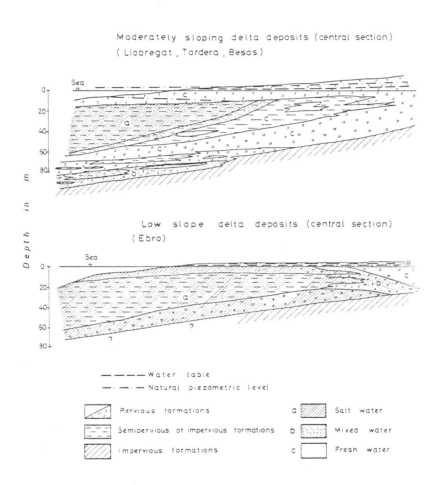

Fig. 3.34 - Existence of salt and brackish water in young deltas, based on the experience in several deltas along the Mediterranean coast of Catalonia (Spain). The deep aquifer contains fresh water when it is open to the sea and enough fresh water head can develop in a well recharged area with enough altitude (after Custodio, Bayó and Batista, 1977).

Figure 3.35 represents schematically the morphologic evolution of the Dutch coastal area in the Rhine delta, showing how this evolution conditions the salt-fresh water relationships. Figure 3.36 shows the detailed structure and figure 3.37 the formation of the ice built ridges.

Badly drained, swampy areas occur frequently, with many sea inlets and salt or brackish lagoons.

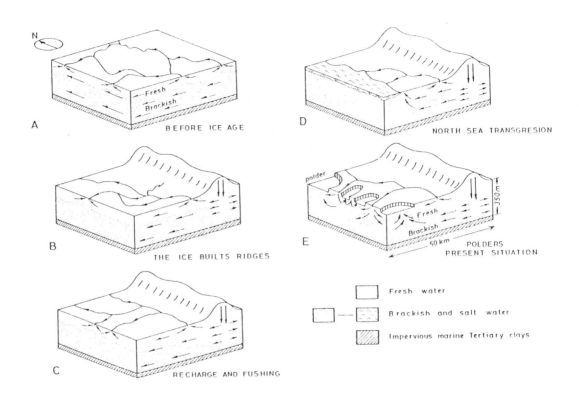

Fig. 3.35 - Explanation of the existence of brackish groundwater bodies in the course of the geological time in the Central-Western part of the Netherlands (after Meinardi, 1974). A - situation before the Saale Ice Age; it was a flat country with draining rivers; the weak groundwater flow implied a shallow interface. B - situation shortly after the Saale Ice Age; a fresh water body was formed under the recently built ice-pushed ridges, in which increased groundwater recharge existed. C - situation at the beginning of the Holocene Age; recharge in the ice-pushed ridges favors the flushing-out of the salt water. D - situation shortly before the creation of the polders; the Holocene North sea invades the land and the rivers drain the aquifer; salt water encroachment at the coast. E - situation after the creation of the polders, with coastal dunes (not shown); intensive groundwater flow with infiltrating rivers; the North Sea retreats; the groundwater bodies change.

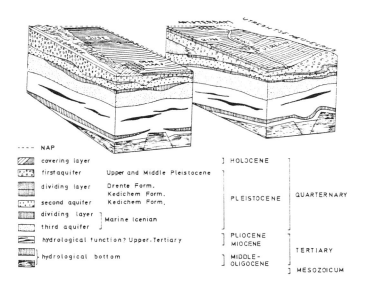

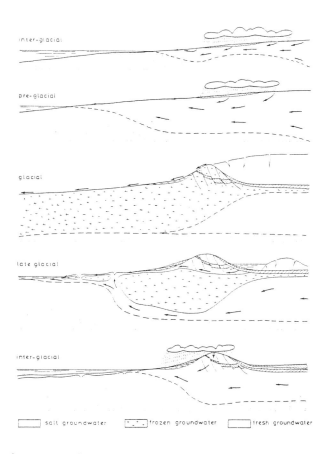

Fig. 3.36 - Schematic block-diagrams of the ground in the mid-western part of the Netherlands (after ICW, 1976), showing the sequence of aquifers and aquitards.

Fig. 3.37 - Changes in groundwater flow during a glacial cycle, inspired in the observations in the Netherlands (after Pomper, 1977). At present the ice-pushed ridges play an important role in groundwater recharge and in the salt groundwater depth.

3.3.3 Coastal plains

Coastal plains have many different origins and some of them are considered in the case histories of section 10.3. Figure 3.38 shows some typical simplified situations.

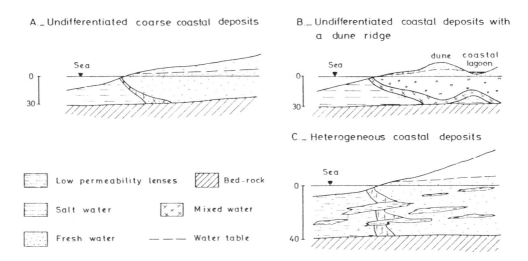

Fig. 3.38 – Salt-fresh water relationships in coastal unconsolidated deposits, in several different situations observed along the coast of Catalonia, Spain (after Custodio, Bayó and Batista, 1977). A is a common situation in quasi-homogeneous materials. B represents a situation in which the good recharge along a dune belt limits the salt water wedge penetration; in many instances a back lagoon exists, with fresh or salty water (sea salinity or evaporation salinity); when the lagoon is salty, the fresh water body may be limited to the dune ridge environs. C represents the situation when discontinuous low permeability lenses occur, creating local subaquifers with different water levels.

The ground/sea water configuration may be complicated due to the many nonhomogeneities present, both in formations of glacial and fluvioglacial origin (eastern United States, Western Europe, see figs. 3.39 and 3.40), and in those originated under arid conditions (piedmonts along the Mediterranean coast).

Sometimes the aquifer thickness reduces to a few meters, as in Belgium or in the NE of the Federal Republic of Germany (fig. 3.41), but in other instances thicker sequences of quaternary deposits can be found. These thick deposits usually contain low permeability interlayerings, corresponding to sea transgressions, that create local confined and semiconfined conditions. In many instances these interlayerings do not outcrop and are difficult to anticipate, except for morphological features that indicate a change in the sedimentation. Then, the regional permeable formation gets partially confined near the coast.

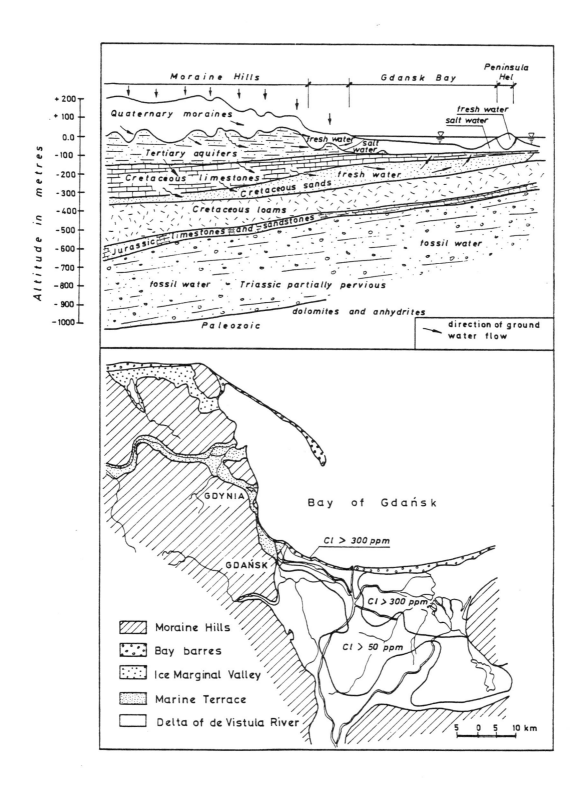

Fig. 3.39 – Hydrogeological cross-section of the Gdansk plain and delta (Poland) showing the fresh water movement and the existence of deep seated brackish fossil water (after Kozerski, 1981).

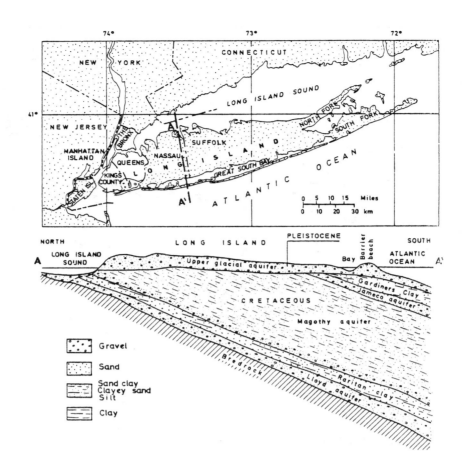

Fig. 3.40 – Simplified cross-section of Long Island, showing the geologic features of the groundwater reservoir (after Franke and McClymonds, 1972).

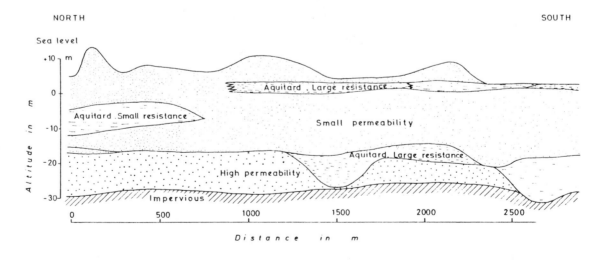

Fig. 3.41 – North-south hydrogeological cross-section through the Westhock area (Southern Belgium) showing the changes of permeability along the coast (after Lebbe, 1979).

Conditions along the sea become very important since the accumulation of low permeability materials (facies change or tectonical elevation of the bottom) favors a short salt water wedge. The interlayering of low permeability materials affect the groundwater movement and sea water penetration (fig. 3.42, 3.43 and 3.44).

In coastal areas formed by torrential deposits, such as a sequence of alluvial fans, the connection with the sea and the thickness are important in order to predict the salt water wedge penetration (fig. 3.45). The actual sea-aquifer relationship depends also on the dominant coastal process, accretion by new sediments, and coastal erosion.

In many circumstances coastal dune belts form and separate the shore from the flat low-lying continent, where lagoons are frequent and much water is lost by evaporation. Below these flat areas, saline water, and possibly brackish shallow water, may be found at low depths, while the dunes contain a continuous or discontinuous underground lenticular ridge of fresh water.

3.3.4   Hard rocks

The main difference between hardrock aquifers and unconsolidated porous aquifers is the possibility of rock discontinuities such as fissures, fractures, open joints, and solution-enlarged fissures and cavities (karst). In some dense hard-rocks, pore permeability is negligible (compact limestones, granites), but in others the primary pore porosity remains dominant (chalk, volcanics), although permeability may be dominated by the discontinuities.

The fresh water-salt water relationships in the discontinuities follows the basic general principles, especially if they are narrow or sediment filled, but they represent a macroscopic nonhomogeneity of the medium. Furthermore, in coastal areas and near the surface, the weathering effect, rock decompression and sea action opens and enlarges the discontinuities, thus increasing the nonhomogeneities in the permeability. It produces an irregular sea water wedge and increases the mixing zone width. The length, depth and orientation of the discontinuities influence the fresh-salt water relationships. The degree and form of linkage between the discontinuities and the rock pores is also an important factor. A densely fractured rock is macroscopically similar to a porous medium, generally anisotropic, and the dispersivity is much greater.

When discontinuities are widely spaced and their presence alters noticeably the groundwater flow, a fresh-salt water anomaly appears in their surroundings. It is different for a long vertical discontinuity and for a horizontal discontinuity. In the vertical discontinuity, the fresh water flows over salt water and a mixing zone develops between them. The geometrical distribution depends on the water flow and the discontinuity penetration depth and width.

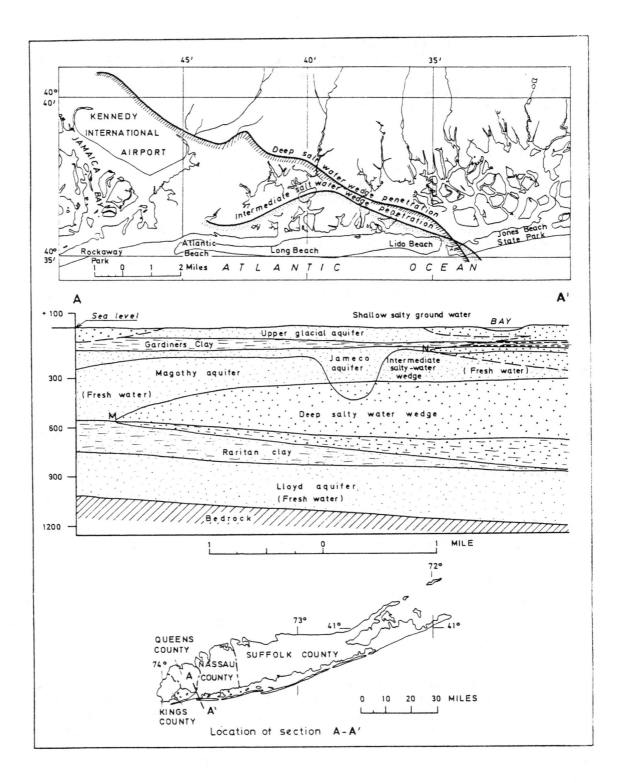

Fig. 3.42 - Penetration of the two main salt water wedges in the SW part of Long Island (New York). The semipervious layers act as lower boundaries for the salt water wedges, and fresh water can be found below (Franke and McClymonds, 1972; Lusczynski and Swarzenski, 1966).

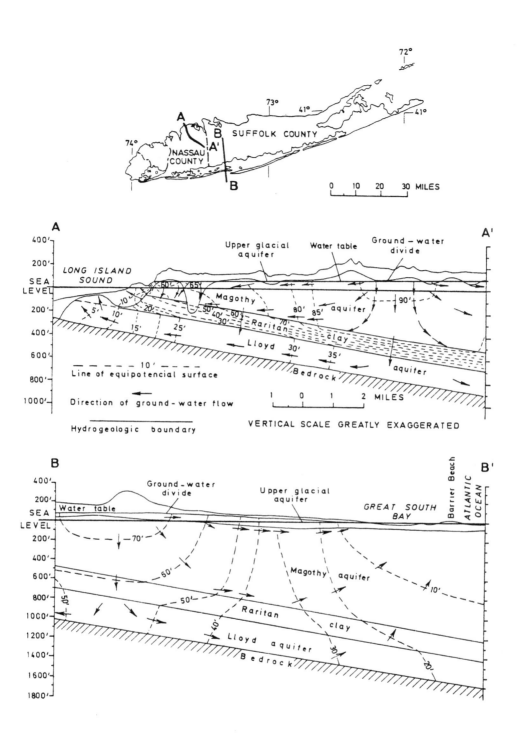

Fig. 3.43 - Cross-sections of the Western part of Long Island, New York, in which the fresh water movement is indicated. The Raritan formation is an aquitard which conditions the groundwater movement in the coastal aquifer (Lusczynski and Swarzenski, 1962, 1966).

-71-

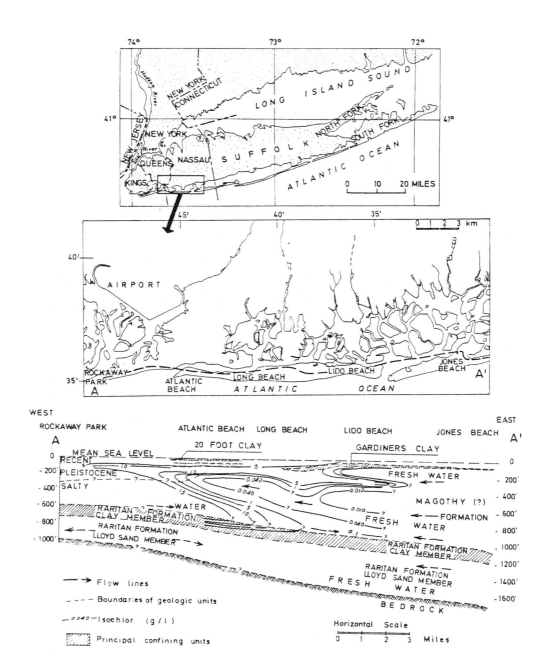

Fig. 3.44 - Isochloride lines along the SW coast of Long Island (New York) in an area of bays and sand bars. The complicated pattern is due to the existence of flows normal to the drawing and the presence of less pervious interlayerings. The arrow indicates the groundwater flow component on the draining plane (Lusczynski and Swarzenski, 1962).

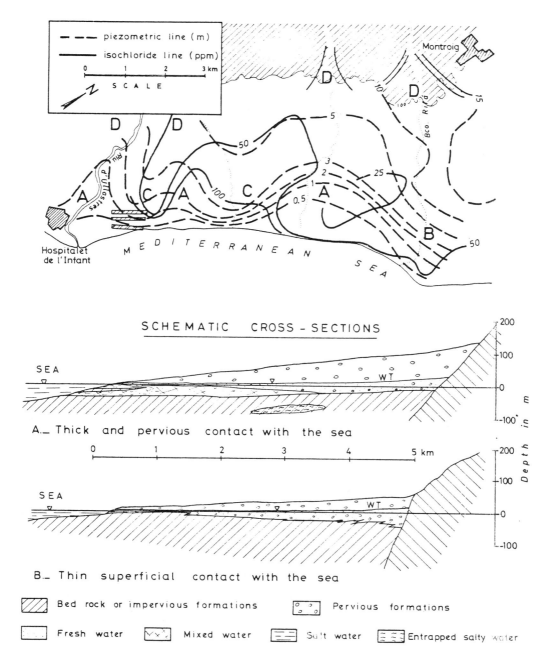

Fig. 3.45 – Sea-fresh water relationships in coastal torrential deposits, representing typical situations in the South Tarragona Plain (Spain), with a fresh water flow about 1 million m³/year/km of coastline (after Custodio, Bayó and Batista, 1977). A – thick and pervious contact with the sea; the salt water penetrates far inland and the mixing zone is thick. B – thin superficial contact with the sea, with less permeable sediments in the contact; the salt water penetration is limited to the environments of the coastal line. C – low-permeability deposits between the different alluvial fans (D), in which sea penetration is small.

In a wide vertical discontinuity the situation is similar to that in a surface water channel. In many situations the small water gradient produces a fresh water layer flowing on a nearly flat deeply penetrating salt water wedge, with a mixing zone generally well developed. Salt or brackish water can reach several kilometers inland. These large discontinuities are generally intersected by other less important discontinuities, some of them in connection with the sea. In a horizontal discontinuity, the depth below sea level and the fresh water head determine the possibility of water flow, in a similar way as in a confined aquifer. Thus, a borehole may intersect discontinuities containing water of different salinity, generally increasing downwards, each situation uniquely determining the water salinity.

The orientation of the fissure sets in respect with the coast is of utmost importance. A set of fissures intersecting the coast at about right angles favors a much greater salt water wedge penetration due to a greater permeability in that direction. The effect increases if they are of tectonic origin since their penetration is greater. But the degree of filling of the fissures is also very important, because it reduces the fissure permeability. Figure 3.46 shows an example.

Dykes have a similar effect. Since there are generally vertical fissures parallel to the dykes, when they are normal to the coast they favor the salt water penetration.

When dealing with hard rocks, the effect of the weathered zones and the associated sediment must be taken into account. Figure 3.47 shows some examples.

Moderately old volcanics are very similar to other hard fissured rocks, but present a higher effective porosity. Near surface enlargement of fissures is an important factor. High local nonhomogeneities are common, such as dykes, sills, almagre (red) layers, cooling joints, etc., thus creating a very irregular penetration of the salt water wedge and a thick transition zone. Except for the upper younger or decompressed part and some large fissures, these materials are generally poorly permeable, and then high water gradients are common in zones with a high relief, including arid areas. Some permeability can be maintained until great depths, and a high fresh water head is generally present. Near the coast the fresh groundwater can be covered with an irregular mixed salty water layer, in response to the much higher upper permeability. It is not rare to find in a borehole an alternation of fresh, brackish and salt water.

Young basic lavas and loose lapillis and ejecta are highly permeable, especially in the top and bottom lava flow breccias. When they reach the coast, they form a highly permeable upper layer. Since the water table slope is very small, only in areas with a high fresh water flow and shallow formations is there a layer of fresh water. In general, since dispersivity is very high and the fresh water head is close to mean sea level, the top of the mixing zone reaches the water table. Below these young formations, fresh water sometimes can be found in deeper less permeable materials, although some mixing with the upper salty water can be very difficult to avoid. Sometimes recent low permeability sediments cover the more permeable volcanics (the caprock in Hawaii) and confined conditions develop. The flow discharge is through the caprock discontinuities, originating springs which salinity increases toward the shore.

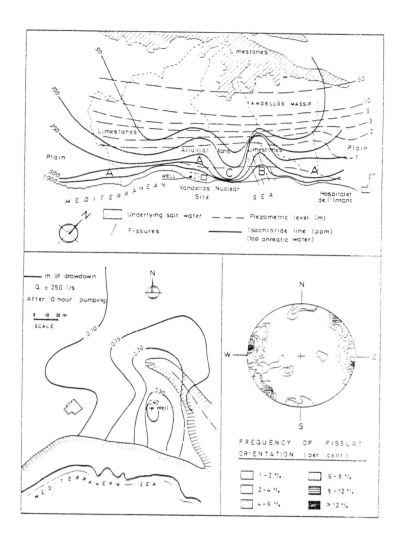

Fig. 3.46 - Different penetration of the salt and brackish water wedge in the Vandellós coastal limestone massif (Tarragona, Spain). The penetration increases with the thickness and permeability of coastal formations, and when the dominant set of fissures are normal to the coast. A - thick highly pervious piedmont and alluvial fan deposits, half-consolidated and fissured; the two bottom figures show the fissure orientation frequency (mainly vertical fissures normal to the coast) and the effect of the anisotropy on the drawdown cone during a pumping test is the Lleria-Malaset alluvial fan, at the Vandellós Nuclear Site. B - normal to the coast fissured limestones. C - non-fissured low permeability limestones (after Custodio, 1978; frequency of fissures after Risueño, personal communication).

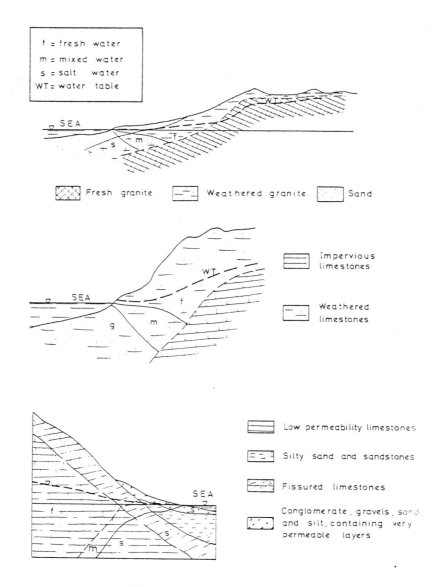

Fig. 3.47 – Schematic salt-fresh water relationships in hard-rock aquifers. The more permeable weathered zones and the highly permeable covering sediments allow for a well developed and penetrant sea water wedge and a thick mixing zone. The situation can be different from one fissure to another.

3.3.5   Special situations in karstic formations

Solution enlarged joints or solution channels are common in many limestone formations, and they pose difficult problems when they reach the sea. They represent highly permeable discontinuities if not filled by sediments or clay.

In a carbonate (limestone and dolomite) massif, the solution channels adopt irregular patterns, with imposed orientations both by local and regional geological patterns. There exist great differences from one formation to another from the point of view of the ability to be karstified. It depends on the lithology, characteristics of preexisting fissures, such as opening, slope and orientation, groundwater flow pattern and changes in the water level, now and in the past. Many coastal karstic systems were formed under sea levels different from the present one, leading to one or several karstic systems at different depths.

The solution process is more active the greater the water flow and the more aggressive the water is (when it contains an excess of CO_2 over the equilibrium value), especially in vegetation covered massifs. As will be described in chapter 6, the water aggressivity increases in the mixing zone due to the change in ionic strength, and thus these parts of the formation have greater opportunities to become karstified.

In karstic formations, diagrams of local and regional tectonic directions are important tools in explaining the karstic orientations, and consequently in the explanation of the sea water penetration.

Sometimes the principal faults of horizontal displacement (decrochement faults) are very prone to the development of karstic channels, that constitute submarine springs. Solution is not the only active process in a limestone massif. The fissures and solution discontinuities can be also clogged by calcite or by residual clay (terra rossa), and sometimes by aloctone sediments, that tend to reduce water circulation.

3.3.6   Littoral and submarine springs

The solution discontinuities in karstic formations and other big discontinuities in other formations (big crevices, volcanic tubes, etc.) may produce littoral and submarine springs near the coast.

Submarine openings having a fresh-water head enough to outflow are not uncommon, especially in carbonate karstic areas, and are related with eustatic or epirogenic sea water changes. Generally they do not exceed about 100 m below sea level, and submarine springs deeper than 30 or 40 m are very scarce. Some sources yield more than one m^3/s and are well known since olden times, and have been used to obtain small quantities of fresh water under special circumstances. Kohout (1966) reviews the old literature, and Schwerdtfeger(1979) comments on some of the best known coastal springs.

A special case of submarine springs corresponds to the outflow in the sea bottom when an impervious cover has been dismantled locally and the permeable formation, generally a karstic formation, outcrops (see section 10.4). The lack of sea bottom sediments in certain places points to these outlets, as can be seen in aerial photographs when the depth is small (see figure 3.21).

A submarine spring only flows when the fresh water head in it is enough to overcome the weight of the sea water column. When not, the fresh water is stopped and the channel is filled with salt water. Some of these springs only flow in low tide and sometimes in high tide they act as a sea water sump. Such a spring-sump system is known as an 'estavelle'.

When fresh water flow cannot leave, the sea bottom outlet and the channel become sediment clogged and the fresh water develops other less deep outlets, generally enlarging a coastal vertical fissure, giving a vertical shaft discharging at the sea shore (fig. 3.48). The flowing water may be fresh until the littoral exit, but in most instances these waters become progressively brackish towards the outlet. It is the effect of the small discontinuities, mainly microfissure networks, that connect the main channel with

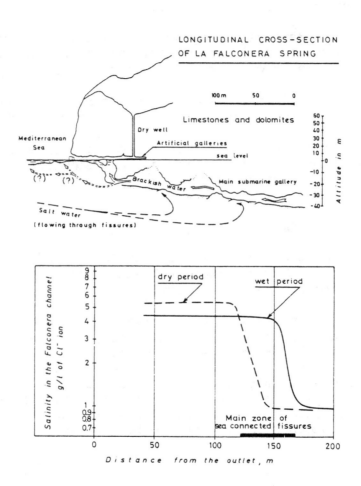

Fig. 3.48 – Cross-section of the Falconera submarine spring, in the karstic carbonate Garraf massif, 30 km south of Barcelona. The salinity in the submarine gallery increases seaward due to the effect of some fissures carrying salt water. In a wet period, the higher fresh water head decreases or stops the small salt water flow in some fissures, and salt water contamination diminishes. The landward salt water flow through the sea connected fissures initiates at the sea bottom, where the water potential or equivalent fresh water head is greater than near the channel (after Custodio and Galofré, 1977).

the sea bottom. Since the fresh water head in the main channel is not enough to overcome the salt water column in the deeper parts, a small flow of salt water penetrates continuously through these fissures, only limited by the flow head loss, and modified to some extent by head changes in the main channel, according to the sequence of dry and wet periods or the tides. These fissures can be concentrated in certain tracts (fig. 3.48).

Littoral springs are common in coastal aquifers, including unconsolidated formations, when local depressions in the ground surface appear. In hard-rock they are sometimes very conspicuous and correspond to the extreme of fissures reaching the sea or when littoral sediments separate the sea from the formation.

Some openings near the shore can be flooded periodically at high tide or during storms, thus facilitating the entry of salt water and increasing the width of the mixing zone, especially if they act as an 'estavelle'.

A very special situation occurs at the Greek Ionian island of Kaphallinia, in the Argostili peninsula (Maurin and Zölt, 1965; Bourdon and Papakis, 1963; Llopis, 1970), where sea water sumps in a littoral cavity, moving an old mill (fig. 3.49). It can probably be explained by a thermal induced flow (Geze, 1953) or less probably by some Venturi-tube effects maintained by flowing fresh water in nearly underground channels (Thombe, 1952). Unfortunately, such an abnormal situation was observed by the Ancient Greek philosophers and inevitably led to erroneous conceptions about groundwater flow, especially in the coast, that have lasted until recently.

Geothermal induced flows are also mentioned in other areas, such as Florida (Kohout, 1965, 1967).

In that case (fig. 3.50) the driving flow force is the geothermal flow from deep, impervious anhydrites acting on a very thick highly cavernous carbonate formation (boulder zone or limestones and dolomites partially dissolved by circulating water in a selective calcite solution and dolomitization process). The deep straits of Florida (on the other side, the Gulf of Mexico is shallow and does not intervene) supplies cold sea water that after infiltrating is heated and returned to the sea by convection, dragging along with it the downward infiltrating fresh water. The entry of sea bottom cold water produces a temperature anomaly.

Oceanic atolls frequently overlay a recent volcano whose top is a few hundred meters below present sea level. The sides are generally very steep. The increased geothermal flow below the reef, in pervious material, starts a corrective cell (fig. 3.51) that allows for the cold sea water entry in depth and the upward vertical circulation, until it discharges anew in the sea at a shallow depth, mixed with fresh water. This enhanced sea water flow explains alteration in the volcanics, but especially the dolomitization of the atoll limestones.

In the Yugoslavian dinaric karst, Javremović (1963) observed the existence of different behaviors of coastal springs. The salinity of some were affected by sea level changes and others were not. The salinity was almost constant in a group of springs, while in others it was inversely proportional to the discharge, but in a few the chloride content increased with discharge, being more brackish in the wet season. It can be explained by an increase in the movement of the mixing zone due to the augmented flow.

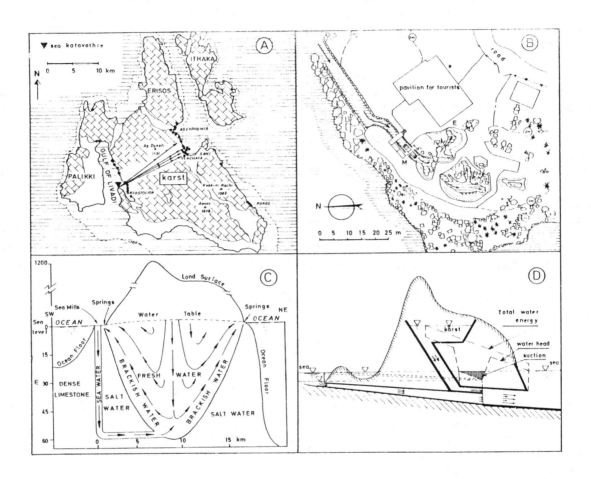

Fig. 3.49 – The Kathavothe of Argostitolion, in Kephallinia (Greece), where sea water sumps. A – location of the kathavothe, and results of some dye-tracer tests that indicate the probable movement direction of the sea water. B – detailed map of the kathavothe, in 1963; there are different sumps. C – explanation by means of the transport along the mixing zone (Stringfield and LeGrand, 1969). D – explanation of Maurin and Zoelt (1963) through a Venturi effect; this explanation is less plausible since very high flow velocities are required.

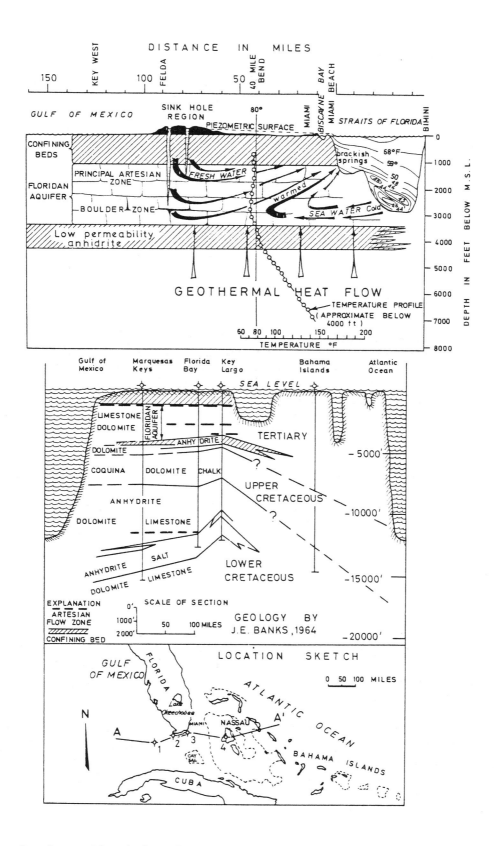

Fig. 3.50 - Geothermally induced flow under the Floridian platform through the highly pervious Floridian aquifer (after Kohout, 1965).

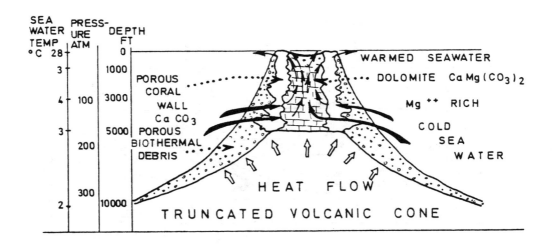

Fig. 3.51 - Idealized diagram of a coraline atoll (modified from Fairbridge, 1961, and Kohout, 1966) showing that magnesium-rich sea water can be expected to circulate through an atoll by thermal convection resulting from upward volcanic heat flow. The conditions for conversion of permeable limestone, $CaCO_3$, to dolomite, $CaMg(CO_3)_2$, should exist somewhere within the internal core of the atoll.

3.3.7   Small pervious islands

Some examples will be given in section 10.5. In small permeable islands the fresh water body takes the form of a lens floating on salt water (fig. 3.52). This is a common situation in sand bars, coral reef islands, small volcanic islands, etc. Sometimes these islands have a circular form, but in other instances they are long strips. It applies to close to the coast islands and to oceanic islands.

The spatial distribution of permeability is a dominant factor in the fresh water lens configuration, both in horizontal and in vertical directions. The theoretical interface is at a depth roughly about 40 times the water table elevation over mean sea level, and in areas of low permeability and/or high recharge rate, the salt water body may not be present if impervious materials occur at a certain depth.

Most of the considerations referring to coastal water table aquifers apply to permeable islands. In a small circular island or in a strip sand bar the ratio of shore line length to island surface is rather high and the water table is flatter than in a bigger island or in a long linear continental coast, with similar materials and recharge rate. The fresh water thickness is smaller and the mixing zone thicker.

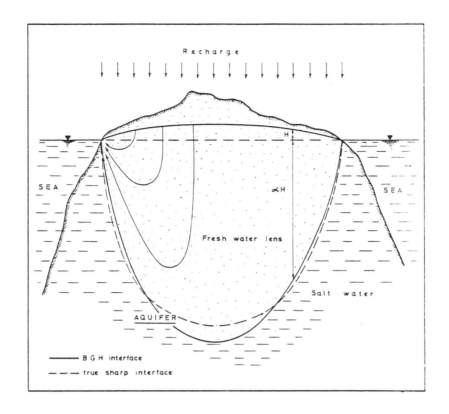

Fig. 3.52 - Fresh-salt water relationships in an homogeneous permeable oceanic
island. A fresh water lens is formed. Vertical dimensions are
highly exaggerated. Near the center of the island and near the
coast, the vertical flow components of water velocity can be important and consequently the depth to the interface is less in the central part and greater near the coast, than the values obtained
through the BGH formula. The mixing zone can be also well developed
in the central part and near the coast. In some cases a reduced α
value for the BGH formula can be used to define the top of the mixing zone.

In figure 3.53 some of these real situations are shown in a
schematic form. Figure 3.54 shows the complicated sediment lay-out in frange
reefs.

In many circumstances the sea-tide effect has a great importance and
it is really very difficult to get a reliable water table map. In such circumstances it is better to map the interface by means of bore-holes (if they
exist) or more commonly by surface geoelectrical means (see chapter 7). A
further complication is the relatively important thickness of the mixing zone.
Sometimes the depth of the upper part of the mixing zone can be related with
water table elevation over mean sea level by an empirical α value, smaller
than that obtained from the BGH principle, e.g. 20 to 30 (Chidley and Lloyd,
1977).

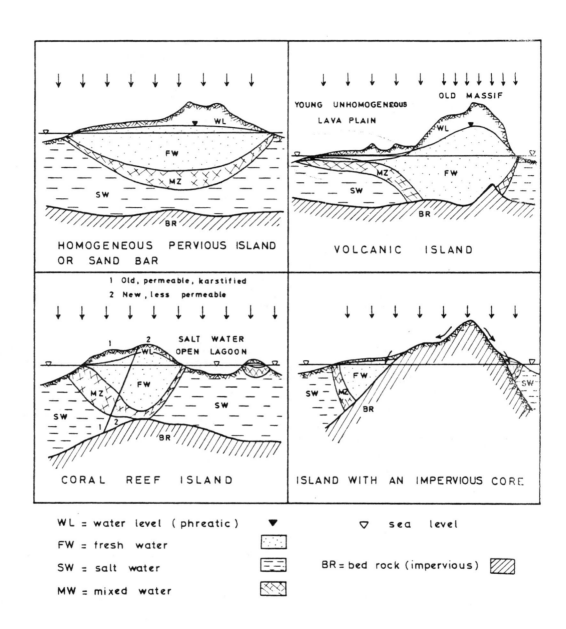

Fig. 3.53 – Different salt-fresh water situations in islands, taking into account the rock permeability and the depth to the bed-rock.

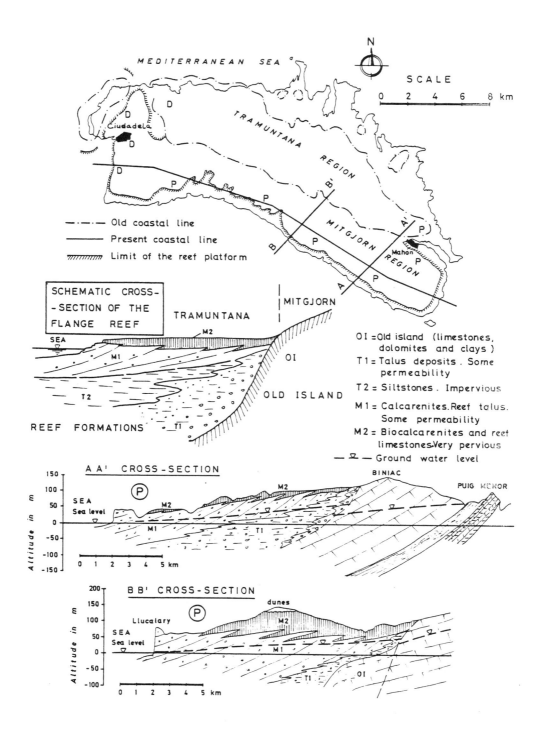

Fig. 3.54 - Permeability distribution in the recent coastal sediments of the Isle of Menorca (Spanish Mediterranean area). Sea water intrusion depends on the topographic position of the very pervious reef formations. Area D is in danger of easy sea water contamination, as it occurs near Ciudadella. Area P is protected by low permeability sediments and the reef is over sea level. The old limestones (OI) can be a source of sea water intrusion (after Bayó and Barón, personal communication).

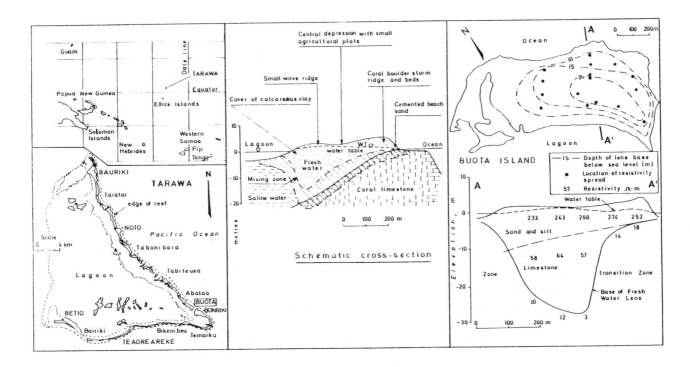

Fig. 3.55 - Fresh water lens in the Tarawa ocean atoll (Gilbert Islands) show-
          ing the asymmetry due to differences in permeability. Sediments in
          the lagoon side are less permeable than those in the ocean side
          (after Lloyd et al., 1980).

        Asymmetrical fresh water lenses may develop due to changes in per-
meability (e.g. the inner part of an atoll is generally less pervious than the
outer part) or to differences in effective sea level on two sides of the
island (sand bars, atolls with a half opened central lagoon). Figures 3.55
and 3.56 show two examples.

        In small islands (oceanic sand bars or delta islands) fresh water
lenses are frequently very tiny or do not form at all. When they exist, fresh
water in storage is small relative to the outflow; then, the water table position and the depth to the top of the mixing zone changes conspicuously from
wet to dry periods, and the fresh water lens may almost disappear in dry
years. The fresh water lens is frequently the source of water for local vegetation and its lowering or salinization greatly affects the existing trees.

        Some reef islands, such as the Bahamian archipelago (Mather and
Buckley, 1973) can present deep sink-holes, both in the land and in the sea,
with water of variable density. Some of those having fresh or salt water may
become springs in certain moments. The water level is affected not only by
the tidal effect, but also by the salinity changes.

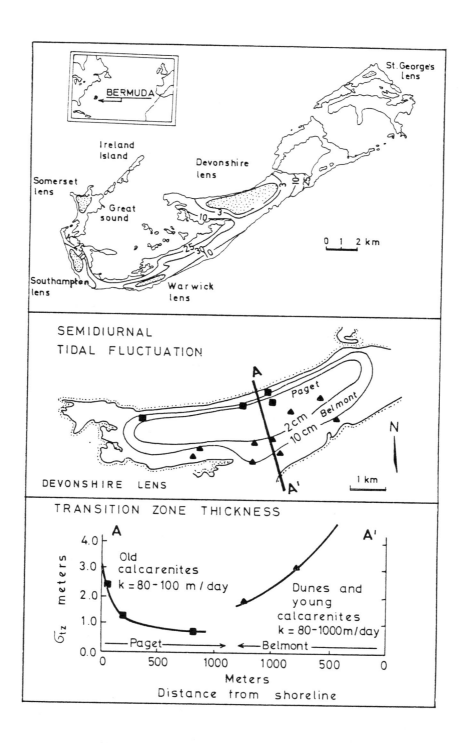

Fig. 3.56 – Fresh water lenses in Bermuda, where they can be formed (after Vacher, 1978; Vather and Ayers, 1980). The Devonshire lens is considered in the case history of section 10.4.

3.4   Mixed ground-surface water conditions

3.4.1   Effects in coastal sea water

In table 2.1 typical values of groundwater discharge into the sea are given, varying between 1 and 14 $l/s/km^2$. For typical widths of the coastal basins (the part directly contributing to the sea) from 1 to 10 km, values between 0.03 and 4.4 million $m^3/year/km$ of coastal length are obtained. Most frequently values in Mediterranean areas are 0.5 to 2×10^6 $m^3/year/km$, such as those determined for the piedmont and littoral plain of Tarragona (Custodio and Martín Arnáiz, 1976; Custodio, 1980). A typical case is presented in section 10.6.

The discharge of fresh groundwater produces changes in the sea water salinity and temperature near the coast, in sea inlets and in localized areas, reflected in special chemical and biological zonation. In some areas typical flora and fauna develop, and they are well known by local fishermen.

These effects of submarine springs are described by Kohout (1966) as a 'neglected phenomenon of coastal hydrology,' although recently there has been some important progress, such as that in the Yucatan Peninsula (Mexico) by Back and his coworkers. A clear biological zonation has been described for the Cutler area (near Miami, Florida) as due mainly to groundwater induced salinity gradients (Kohout and Kolipinski, 1967).

Though the most conspicuous effects correspond to karstic carbonate areas, similar effects can be found in other areas such as deltas and volcanic islands.

3.4.2   Estuaries

Estuaries drain fresh groundwater from the boundaries since the mean water level is close to that in the sea. In a strafied estuary, the bottom salt water may have enough potential to infiltrate the local aquifers and then a salt water wedge may develop landward, that continues the marine coastal salt water wedge.

The estuary bottom fine sediments may play the role of decreasing the salt water potential after infiltration and thus limit the salt water wedge landwards, but when currents, mainly tidal currents in the estuary, prevent the fine bottom sediments from accumulating, that effect is greatly reduced.

When the estuary depth is less than the aquifer thickness, fresh groundwater flows from the estuary bottom and then the salt water penetration is wholly or partially prevented by the increasing fresh water head, in terms of mean sea level. Tides produce periodical increases in the salt water head that can produce a sea water penetration, that mixes with the outflowing fresh groundwater, and a certain mixing zone develops.

In well mixed estuaries the brackish water penetration depends on the density differences, but is highly reduced; the estuary water is more diluted.

3.4.3   Low lands

Low lands are very frequent in some areas such as Virginia, the coast of NE Brazil, E. Argentina, etc., and especially the Netherlands and part of the coast of Belgium. A dune ridge is a common feature between the sea and the areas just inland, that frequently have complicated patterns of lakes and swampy areas. The open water salinity is the complex result of continental flows, sea tides and evaporation, in a network of channels, straits and flat areas, with the bottom reaching several meters below mean sea level.

Generally, local and regional groundwater discharges in the area where salt water underlays fresh water. The mixing zone can reach the ground surface thus contributing to surface water salinity, but that contribution depends highly on the possibility of salt water being replaced according to the rate of consumption in the mixing zone.

The top formations are influenced by surface water quality, but when they are impervious and water is saline, the inverse saline stratification can be stable with no overturning produced.

3.5   References

Badon Ghijben (Ghyben), W. (1889). Nota in verband met de voorgenomen putboring nabij Amsterdam. (Notes on the probable results of the proposed well drilling near Amsterdam). Tijdschrift het koninklijk Instituut voor Ingenieurs, The Hague, pp. 8-22.

Bear, J. (1972). Dynamics of fluids in porous media. American Elsevier, 764 pp.

Bear, J. (1979). Hydraulics of groundwater. McGraw-Hill, New York, 567 pp.

Bourdon, D.J., Papakis, N. (1963). Handbook of karst hydrology. FAO, Rome, 270 pp.

Carslaw, H.S., Jaeger, J.C. (1959). Conduction of heat in solids. Oxford University Press. 510 pp.

de Cazenove, J. (1971). Ondes phrétiques sinusoidales. L'Houille Blanche, 264, 601-616 pp. Paris.

Chidley, T.R.E., Lloyd, J.W. (1977). A mathematical model study of freshwater lenses. Ground Water, Vol. 15, No. 3, May-June, pp. 215-222.

Cooper, H.H. Jr. (1959). A hypothesis concerning the dynamic balance of fresh water and salt water in a coastal aquifer. Jour. Geophysical Research, Vol. 64, No. 4, pp 461-467. Also in Sea Water in Coastal Aquifers. U.S. Geological Survey, Water Supply Paper 1613-C, 1964, Washington, pp C1-C12.

Cotecchia, V. (1977 a). Studies and investigations on Apullian groundwaters and intruding sea waters (Salento Peninsula). Quaderni dell Instituto di Recerche, Rome. 462 pp.

Cotecchia, V. (1977 b). Direct and laboratory observations of the mixing phenomena of fresh and salt water in coastal groundwater: particular case of fractured media. Symp. Hydrodynamic Diffusion and Dispersion in Porous Media. Pavia. Inst. Assoc. Hydraulic Research, Committee on Flow through Porous Media. Istituto di Hidraulica dell'Universitá di Pavia, pp. 489-524.

Cronin, Szabo, Ager, Hazel, Owens (1981). Quaternary climates and sea levels of the U.S. Atlantic Coastal Plain. Science, Vol. 211, No. 4479, pp. 233-240.

Custodio, E. (1978). Ensayos para determinar la viabilidad de una excavación profunda en el litoral del Macizo de Vandellós (Tàrragona, España). (Tests to determine the flexibility of a deep excavation in the coast of the Vandellós Massif, Tarragona, Spain). Symposium on Water in Mining and Underground Works. Granada. Nat. Assoc. Mining Eng. pp. 85-109.

Custodio, E. (1980). Els recursos hidraulics a les comarques meridionals de Catalunya. (Water resources at the Southern areas of Catalonia). Obra Agrícola de 'La Caixa.' Barcelona.

Custodio, E., Llamas, M.R. editors (1976). Hidrología Subterránea (Groundwater hydrology). Ediciones Omega, Barcelona, 2 Vols. 2375 pp.

Custodio, E., Galofré, A. (1977). Basin recharge in Sitges plain (Barcelona, Spain) to eliminate temporarily municipal water. Int. Assoc. Hydrogeologists. Birmingham Meeting. Vol. XIII-1, pp. F. 41-57.

Custodio, E., Suárez, M., Galofré, A. (1976). Ensayos para el análisis de la recarga de aguas residuales en el Delta del Besós (Tests for the study of waste water recharge in the Besós Delta). Second National Assembly of Geodesy and Geophysics. Barcelona Meeting, Instituto Geográfico y Catastral. pp. 1893-1936.

Custodio, E., Bayó, A., Batista, E. (1977). Sea water encroachment in Catalonia coastal aquifers. Int. Assoc. Hydrogeologists. General Assembly of Birmingham. Vol. XIIII, 1, pp. F. 1-14.

Custodio, E., Cacho, F., Peláez, M.D., García, J.L. (1976). Problemática de la intrusión marina en los acuíferos del Delta del Llobregat (Sea water encroachment problems in the Llobregat Delta aquifers). Second National Assembly of Geodesy and Geophysics. Barcelona. Instituto Geográfico y Catastral. Madrid. pp. 2103-2129.

Custodio, E., Martín Arnáiz, M. (1976). Métodos de balance de agua subterránea en el área de Vandellós. (Groundwater balance methods in the Vandellós area). Actas del Simposio Nacional de Hidrogeología. Valencia. pp. 1262-1290.

van Dam, J.C. (1977). <u>Determination of horizontal and vertical ground-water flow from piezometric levels observed in groundwater of varied densities.</u> International Hydrological Programme. 5th Salt Water Intrusion Meeting. Medmenham, England. pp 1-19. Also in Delft Progress Report. Civil Engineering, vol 3, pp. 19-34.

Dieulin, S., Matheron, G., de Marsily, G. (1981). <u>Growth of the dispersion coefficient with the mean travelled distance in porous media.</u> The Science of the Total Environment. Elsevier, Amsterdam. No. 21, pp. 319-329.

Fairbridge, R.W. (1961). <u>Eustatic changes in sea level.</u> Physics and Chemistry of the Earth. Vol. 4, pp. 99-185.

Fetter, C.W. Jr. (1972). <u>Saline water interface beneath oceanic islands.</u> Water Resources Research, Vol. 8, No. 5.

Franke, O.L., McClymonds, N.E. (1972). <u>Hydrology and some effects of urbanization on Long Island, New York: summary of the hydrologic situation on Long Island, New York, as a guide to water-management alternatives.</u> U.S. Geological Survey; Prof. Paper, 627 F. pp. F1-F59. Washington.

Geze, B. (1953). <u>La Genese de gouffres</u> (The origin of sumps. Premier Congres Int. de Speleologie. Paris 1953. Sec. 1.

Ghyben, Ghijben (see Badon Ghijben).

Goswami, A.B. (1968). <u>A study of salt water encroachment in the coastal aquifer at Digha, Midnapore District, West Bengal, India.</u> Bull. Int. Assoc. Scientific Hydrology, XIII, No. 3, pp. 77-87.

Hahn, J. (1975). <u>Das Erscheinungsbild dar Künstenversalzung in Raume Wittmund, Ostfriesland</u> (The phenomenon of seawater intrusion on the region of Wittmund-Ostfriesland). Proc. IV Salt Water Intrusion Meeting Ghent. 1974. Ed. W. de Breuck. IHD. pp. 40-58.

Hansen, H. (1971). <u>Common stratigraphic boundaries associated with coastal plain aquifers.</u> Ground Water, Vol. 9, No. 1, pp. 5-12.

Herzberg, A. (1901). <u>Die Wasserversorgung einiger Nordseebäder</u> (The water supply on parts of the North Sea coast). Jour. für Gasbeleuchtung und Wasserversorgung, München, No. 44, pp. 815-819; No. 45, pp. 842-844.

Horton, C.W., Rogers, F.T. (1945). <u>Convection currents in a porous medium.</u> J. Applied Physics, Vol. 16.

Hubbert, M.K. (1940). <u>The theory of groundwater motion.</u> Journal of Geology, Vol. 48, No. 8, pp. 785-944.

Hubbert, M.K. (1953). <u>Entrapment of petroleum under hydrodynamic conditions.</u> Am. Assoc. Petroleum Geologists Bull., Vol. 37, No. 8, pp. 1954-2026.

ICW (1976). <u>Hydrologie en waterkwaliteit van Midden West-Nederland.</u> Regionale Studies, Instituut voor Cultuurtechniek en Waterhuishouding. No. 9. The Netherlands. 100 pp.

Jacob, E.C. (1950). <u>Flow of groundwater.</u> Engineering Hydraulics, H. Rouse Ed. John Wiley and Sons, New York, Chapter 5, pp. 321-386.

Jaeger, J.C. (1963). <u>Application of the theory of heat conduction to geothermal measurements.</u> Geophysical Monograph Series, No. 8. W.H.K. Lee, editor. Am. Geophysical Union.

Jevremović, M. (1963). <u>Hydraulic characteristics and classification of brackish springs in the Adriatic area of the Dinaric Karst.</u> Int. Assoc. Hydrogeologists. Belgrade Congress. pp. 293-297.

de Josseling de Jong (1969). <u>Generating formations in the theory of flow through porous media.</u> Flow through porous media. De Wiest, Ed. Academic Press, New York, pp. 377-400.

Kohout, F.A. (1961). <u>Case history of salt water encroachment caused by a storm sewer in Miami.</u> Journal American Water Works Assoc., Vol. 53, No. 11, Nov. pp. 1406-1416.

Kohout, F.A. (1964). <u>The flow of fresh water and salt water in the Biscayne aquifer of the Miami Area, Florida.</u> Sea Water in Coastal Aquifers. U.S. Geological Survey, Water Supply Paper No. 1613-C. Washington, pp. C12-C32. Also in Journal of Geophysical Research, Vol. 53, No. 7, July 1960, pp. 2133-2141, under a different title.

Kohout, F.A. (1965). <u>A hypothesis concerning cyclic flow of salt water related to geothermal heating in the Floridian aquifer.</u> Trans. New York Academy of Sciences, Series II, Vol. 28, No. 2, pp. 249-271.

Kohout, F.A. (1966). <u>Submarine springs: a neglected phenomenon of coastal hydrology;.</u> Central Treaty Organization's Symposium on Hydrology and Water Resources. Development U.S. Dep. Interior. Geological Survey. Washington. pp. 390-413.

Kohout, F.A., Klein, H. (1967). <u>Effect of pulse recharge on the zone of diffusion in the Biscayne aquifer.</u> Int. Assoc. Scientific Hydrology, Publ. No. 72, Symp of Haifa, pp. 252-270.

Kohout, F.A. (1967). <u>Groundwater flow and the geothermal regime of the Floridian Plateau.</u> Trans. Gulf Coast Assoc. of Geological Sciences. Vol. XVII, pp. 339-354.

Kohout, F.A. (1980). <u>Differing positions of saline interfaces in aquifers and observation boreholes: comments.</u> Journal of Hydrology No. 48 (1980), pp. 191-195. Elsevier.

Kohout, F.A., Kolipinsky, M. (1967). <u>Biological zonation related to groundwater discharge along the shore of Biscayne Bay, Miami, Florida.</u> Estuaries, Am. Assoc. Advancement of Science. pp. 488-499.

Kozerski, B. (1981). <u>Salt water intrusions into coastal aquifers of Gdansk region.</u> Proc. VII Salt Water Intrusion Meeting, SWIM-81, Uppsala. Sveriges Geologiska Undersokwing, Reporter och Meddelandan No. 28, pp. 83-90.

Lebbe, L. (1979). <u>Hydrogeological study of the dune area of De Pane (Belgium).</u> Proc. VI Sea Water Intrusion Meeting, SWIM-79, Hannover. Geologisches Jahrbuch. Reihe C. Heft 29 (1981), pp. 115-132.

Lebbe, L. (1981). <u>The subterranean flow of fresh and salt water underneath the Western Belgium beach.</u> Proc. VII Salt Water Intrusion Meeting, SWIM-81, Uppsala. Sveriges Geologiska Undersöhning, Reporter och Meddelanden No. 27, pp. 193-219.

Llopis, N. (1970). <u>Fundamentos de hidrología karstica</u> (Fundamentals of karstick hydrogeology). Ed. Blume, Madrid, pp. 92-93.

Lloyd, J.W., Miles, J.C., Chessman, G.R., Bugg, S.F. (1980). <u>A groundwater resources study of a Pacific ocean atoll: Tarawa, Gilbert Islands.</u> Water Resources Bull., Vol. 16, No. 4, pp. 646-653.

Lusczynski, N.J. (1961). <u>Head and flow of groundwater of variable density.</u> Jour. Geophysical Research, Vol. 66, No. 12, pp. 4247-4256.

Lusczynski, N.S., Swarzenski, W.V. (1962). <u>Fresh and salty groundwater in Long Island, N.Y.</u> Proc. Am. Soc. Civil Engineers, J. Hydraulics Division, H 4.4. pp. 173-184. Washington.

Lusczynski, N.S., Swarzenski, W.V. (1966). <u>Salt water encroachment in Southern Nassau and Southeastern Queens Counties, Long Island, New York.</u> U.S. Geological Survey, Water Supply Paper 1613-F. Washington, 76 pp.

Magri, G., Tadolini, T. (1966). <u>Influenza della pressione atmosférica su livelli della falda profonda della Penisola Salentina</u> (On the influence of the water level table fluctuations on the coastal groundwater levels: applications to the study of the groundwater flow in the Salentine Peninsula). Geologia Applicata e Idrogeologia, Vol. IV, pp. 25-42. Bari.

Magri, G., Troisi, S. (1969). <u>Sull' influenza delle fluttuazioni di specchi d'acqua sui livelli delle falde costiere: applicazioni allo studio della circolazione idrica sotteranea nella Penisola Salentina.</u> Geología Applicata e Idrogeologia. Vol. IV, pp. 25-42. Bari.

Maldonado, A. (1977). <u>Introducción geológica al delta del Ebro</u> (Geological introduction to the Ebro delta). Treballs de la Institució Catalana de'Historia Natural: El sistemes naturals del delta de l'Ebre. Barcelona, pp. 7-45.

Mather, J.D., Buckley, D.K. (1973). <u>Tidal fluctuations and groundwater conditions in the Bahamian Archipelago.</u> First Int. Conf. on Ground Water Planning. Palermo.

Matheron, G., de Marsily, G. (1980). <u>Is transport in porous media always diffusive? A counter-example.</u> Water Resources Research, 16 (5), pp. 901-917.

Maurin, V., Zoelt, J. (1965). <u>Salt water encroachment in the low karst water horizons of the island of Kephallinia (Ionian Islands).</u> Dubrovnik Symp. on Hydrology of Fractured Rocks. Int. Assoc. Scientific Hydrology-Unesco. pp. 423-438.

Meinardi, C.R. (1974). <u>The origin of brackish groundwater in the lower parts of the Netherlands.</u> Rijksinstituut voor drinkwatervoorziening. Mededeling 74-6. The Netherlands. 16 pp.

Meinardi, C.R. (1975). <u>Brackish groundwater bodies as a result of geological history and hydrological conditions.</u> Int. Symp. on Brackish Water as a Factor in Development. Beer-Sheva. Ben-Gurion University of the Negev, Institute for Desert Research. Israel. pp. 25-39.

Meinardi, C.R. (1976). <u>Characteristic examples of the natural groundwater composition in the Netherlands.</u> Rijkinstitut voor drinkwatervoorziening. Mededeling 76.1, 28 pp.

Mercado, A. (1967). <u>The spreading pattern of injected water in a permeable stratified aquifer.</u> Int. Assoc. Scientific Hydrology-UNESCO, Haifa Symposium. Pub. 72, pp. 26-36.

Monkhouse, R.A., Fleet, M. (1975). <u>A geophysical investigation of saline water in the chalk of the South coast of England.</u> Quarterly Journal of Engineering Geology, London, UK, Vol. 8, pp. 291-302.

Nield, D.A. (1968). <u>Onset of thermohaline convection in a porous medium.</u> Water Resources Research, Vol. 3.

Nomitsu, I.I., Toyohara, Y., Kamimoto, R. (1927). <u>On the contact surface of fresh and salt water near a sandy sea shore.</u> Kyoto Imperial University, Mem. Coll. Sciences, Series A, Vol. 10, No. 7, pp. 279-302.

Okutsu, H. (1972). <u>On some aspects of fossil water on hydrological map.</u> Mem. Int. Assoc. Hydrogeologists, Vol. IX, Conress Tokyo, 1971. Pub. Japan Nat. Com. pp. 164-170.

Perlmutter, N.M., Geraghty, J.L., Upson, J.E. (1959). <u>The relation between fresh and salty groundwater in Southern Nassau and Southeastern Queens Counties, Long Island, New York.</u> Economic Geology, Vol. 54, No. 3, pp. 426-435.

Perlmutter, N.M., Geraghty, J.L. (1963). <u>Geology and groundwater conditions in Southern Nassau and Southeastern Queens Counties, Long Island, New York.</u> U.S. Geological Survey Water-Supply Paper 1613-A. Washington. 205 pp.

Pinder, G.F., Bredehoeft, J.D. (1974). <u>Groundwater chemistry and the transport equations.</u> Int. Symp. on Mathematical Models in Hydrology, Warsaw, 1971. Int. Assoc. Scientific Hydrology-Unesco. Paper 615, 13 pp.

Pomper, A.B. (1977). An estimation of chloride intrusion in the Midwest Netherlands during the Pleistocene epoch. Proc. V Sea Water Intrusion Meeting. Medmenhan, UK. IHP-Unesco. pp. 114-125,

Pomper, A.B., Wesseling, J. (1978). Chloride content of surface water as a result of geologic processes and groundwater flow in a coastal area in the Netherlands. Seminar on Selected Water Problems in Islands and Coastal Areas, with special regard to Desalination and Groundwater. Economic Commission for Europe. United Nations. Malta.

Pomper, A.B. (1979). A possible explanation of the occurrence of inversions in the chloride content of groundwater in the Western Netherlands. VI Sea Water Intrusion Meeting, Hannover 1979. Geologisches Jahrbuch, Hannover, 1981. pp. 205-215.

Pomper, A.B. (1981). Hydrochemical observations in the subsoil of the Western part of the Netherlands. Proc. VII Seventh Salt Water Intrusion Meeting, SWIM-81, Uppsala. Sveriges Geologiska Unttersökning, Reporter och Meddelanden No. 27, pp. 101-119.

Reineck, H.E., Singh, I.B. (1973). Depositional sedimentary environments with reference to terrigenous clastics. Springer-Verlag. pp. 264-279.

Rice, R.J. (1977). Fundamentals of geomorphology. Longman, London. 387 pp.

Santing, G. (1963). Salt water-fresh water relationships. The Development of Groundwater Resources with Special Reference to Deltaic Areas. ECAFE-Unesco. Water Resources Series No. 24, pp. 52-63.

Schwerdtfeger, B.C. (1979). On the occurrence of submarine fresh water discharges. VI Salt Water Intrusion Meeting. Hanover 1979. Geologisches Jahrbuch, 1981. Hannover. pp. 231-240.

Segol, G., Pinder, G.F., Gray, W.G. (1975). A Galerkin-finite element technique for calculating the transient position of the saltwater front. Water Resources Research Vol. 11, No. 2, pp. 343-347.

Stringfield, V., Le Grand, H.E. (1969). Relation of sea water to fresh water in carbonate rocks in coastal areas, with special reference to Florida, USA, and Cephalonia (Kephallinia), Greece. Journal of Hydrology, Vol. 9 (1969, pp. 387-404. Elsevier.

Tadolini, T., Zanframundo, P. (1974). Studio sulle oscillazioni della superficie della falda profonda della Penisola Salentina (Study on the water table oscillations of the Salentine Peninsula deep aquifer). Geological Applicata e Idrogeologia, Vol. IX, pp. 1-11. Bari.

Thombe, F. (1952). Traité d'spéléologie (Speleology treatise). Ed. Payot. Paris. 376 pp.

Todd, D.K., Meyer, C.F. (1971). Hydrology and geology of the Honolulu aquifer. Proc. American Society Civil Engineers, Journal Hydraulics Division, HY2, February. Washington. pp. 233-356.

Urish, D.W. (1980). <u>Asymmetric variation of Ghyben-Herzberg lens.</u>   Am.   Soc. Civil Engineers, J. Hydraulics Division, HY7.   pp. 1149-1158.   Washington.

Vacher, H.L. (1978).   <u>Hydrology of small oceanic islands: influence of atmospheric pressure on the water table.</u> Ground Water, Vol. 16, No. 6, pp. 417-423.

Vacher, H.L., Ayers, J.F. (1980).   <u>Hydrology of small oceanic islands: utility of an estimate of recharge inferred from the chloride concentration of the fresh water lenses.</u> Journal of Hydrology, Vol. 45 (1980), pp. 21-37.

Venetis, C. (1968).   <u>On the impulse response of an aquifer.</u> Bull. Int. Assoc. Scientific Hydrology, Vol. XIII, No. 3, pp. 136-139.

Visher, F.N. (1960).   <u>Qualitative hydrodynamics within an oceanic island.</u> Int. Assoc. Scientific Hydrology, General Assembly of Helsinky, Pub. 52, pp. 470-477.

Werner, P.W., Noren, D. (1951).   <u>Progressive waves in non-artesian aquifers.</u> Trans. Am. Geophysical Union. Vol. 32, pp. 238-244.

de Wiest, R.J.M. (1965).   <u>Geohydrology.</u> Ed. John Wiley and Sons, New York. 366 pp. (See pp. 304-315.)

Wooding, R.A. (1972).   <u>Groundwater problems of the interaction of saline and fresh water.</u> Salinity and Water Use. Ed. T. Talsma and J.R. Philip. Australian Academy of Sciences, MacMillan, Dorking. pp. 125-139.

Yih, C.S. (1960).   <u>Flow of a nonhomogeneous fluid in a porous medium.</u> Journal of Fluid Mechanics, Vol. 10, pp. 133-141.

4. Effects of human activities on salt-fresh water relationships in coastal aquifers

E. Custodio

Contents

4.0   Introduction

Man's activities may interfere with groundwater flow and cause complex changes in the salt-fresh water relationships in coastal aquifers. Usually the freshwater discharge into the sea is decreased. The effects, both favorable or unfavorable, are caused by as man's direct and indirect influence on groundwater flow. Mixed surface-groundwater situations will be considered later.

Most of the effects develop very slowly so that it is often difficult to relate cause to effect, or to be aware of the effects. Sometimes effects arrive years or tens of years after an activity started. For ordinary people, an action with no short-term adverse effects can frequently be ignored. To have a realistic evaluation of the effects of man's activities on a coastal aquifer, a good understanding of the salt-fresh water relationships and information on the pace of change are necessary, as well as continuous data collection programs and opportunities to correct problems.

The discussion will be presented in a descriptive form to outline the main problems. Quantitative methods of calculation and evaluation will be given mostly in chapter 5.

Water retention in half-closed pores and pockets, mixing by diffusion with the aquifer flowing water, has two practical aspects. When fresh water is displaced by salt water, it is diluted by the remaining fresh water, but the water continues to be salty. When fresh water displaces salt water, the slow diffusion of retained salt water can contaminate the new fresh water for a long time. An aquifer contaminated with salt water must be carefully washed before it can contain only fresh water again.

Economic damage as a consequence of sea water intrusion can easily be identified. Sometimes it is tremendous and even threatens to impair the living conditions of future generations. Sometimes social consequences can be of great political importance, and if an area loses its sources of income and water supplies are greatly impaired people must be relocated or water from other areas must be imported, sometimes with resulting conflict. The Hermosillo situation, in Sonora, Mexico, is an example; after fresh groundwater was exhausted no other water was available in that arid area.

4.1   Direct effects

4.1.1   Effects related to groundwater abstraction

Groundwater abstraction reduces coastal fresh water discharge and alters the dynamic equilibrium. The perturbed system changes to a new equilibrium position if any outflow to the sea continues. The final result is a deeper and more penetrating sea water wedge, with a thicker transition zone (fig. 4.1). When abstraction is greater than actual recharge, no final equilibrium position can be attained, but the aquifer has sea water intruded very deeply.

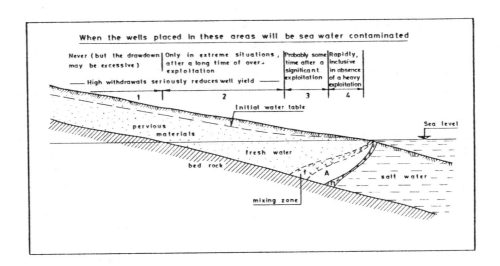

Fig. 4.1 – Degree of salt water contamination to be expected in a coastal aquifer. Wells placed in areas 3 and 4 can easily get some sea or mixed water, but careful construction and exploitation can avoid most of the problem, especially when less permeable interlayerings exist. A represents the one-time reserve of fresh water, most of it consumed during the movement of the mixing zone from situation n to f, in order to maintain the necessary fresh water flow to the sea over the salt water body. The quantity n is the mixing zone in the natural situation and f is the mixing zone after a new equilibrium is attained (abstraction is less than recharge).

If the salt water wedge penetration must be limited in order to protect existing wells or abstraction works, a fresh groundwater discharge must be maintained, and the fraction of the recharge that can be exploited is reduced.

Different initial and final conditions must be considered, according to figure 4.1.

(a) Wells are far from the coast, where the aquifer bottom is above sea level. No direct salt water intrusion can happen, but the abstraction of a high fraction of total recharge reduces dramatically the saturated thickness and the yield of the wells;

(b) Wells are far from the coast and from the natural sea water wedge, but the aquifer bottom is below sea level. Sea water intrusion will reach the wells only when total abstraction is close to or greater than total recharge, and after a relatively long time. The situation is aggravated for deeper aquifer bottoms, and when there are layers of preferential permeability. Abstractions of salt or brackish water in areas close to the coast reduce the danger;

(c) Wells are close to the coast, but in areas not reached by the initial salt water wedge. There is an eventual danger of salt water contamination when a fraction of total recharge is abstracted;

(d) Wells are drilled over the salt water wedge. There is a danger of salinization by salt water upconing, including for shallow low yield wells.

Figure 4.2 shows a confined aquifer which has been fully intruded by seawater, caused by a sustained overdraft.

The movement of the salt water body requires the displacement of large volumes of salt and fresh water, and is necessarily slow. The fresh water in the zone between the initial and the final position of the interface is lost to the sea and compensates for the reduction in fresh water flow supply from landward, during the transient situation, which may last several years or decades (figs. 4.3 and 4.4). Only in small and pervious coastal aquifers can the salt water wedge encroach much in a short time after exploitation starts.

In confined aquifers open to the sea or in semiconfined aquifers extending landward it is easy to produce overexploitation, with an excessive drawdown of piezometric levels. The undesirable effects can appear many years after the start (see sections 10.2 and 10.3), especially when the sea water enters far off shore.

Many references in the hydrogeological literature mention coastal aquifers protected from sea water intrusion by the presence of low permeability barriers such as facies changes, overlaying or faulting (Thauvin, 1982; Zebidi, 1978; Zeryouhi, 1982). However, since a small sea water penetration is enough to seriously impair water quality, these barriers must not be

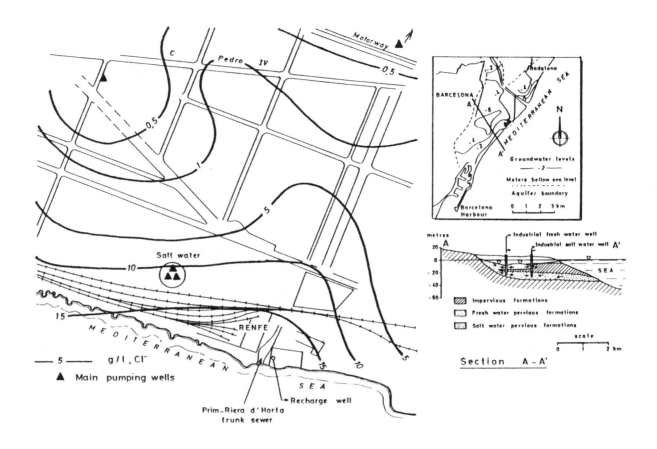

Fig. 4.2 - Sea water intrusion near the Riera d'Horta area in Besós delta
(Barcelona). The abstraction of salt water in an industrial settlement protects inland wells (after Vilaró, Custodio and Bruington,
1970; Custodio, Suarez and Galofré, 1976).

trusted unless a detailed study is accomplished and a good network of observation wells is maintained to follow the response to the abstractions (Custodio,
Ganoulis and Potié, 1982). The Llobregat case (see case history no. 1 in
chapter 10) is a clear example of an apparently well protected deep aquifer
that after 10 to 12 years showed a clear sea water intrusion. Arad, Kafri and
Fleisher (1975) report on the salinization of the confined aquifer in Judea's
plain by means of faults perpendicular to the coast in the Gulf of Tel-Aviv.

During the transient phase, mixing can be very important, especially
when the aquifer is nonhomogeneous. The salt water advances more rapidly
through the most permeable layers or discontinuities, and salinization by horizontal salt water movement can occur progressively, instead of suddenly.

Fresh water abstractions create local water head drawdowns, and when
the well or drain is located over the salt water wedge, according to the Badon
Ghyben-Herzberg principle, a salt water upconing (below a well) or a salt
water ridge (below a drain or gallery) develops. Three situations can develop
(fig. 4.5):

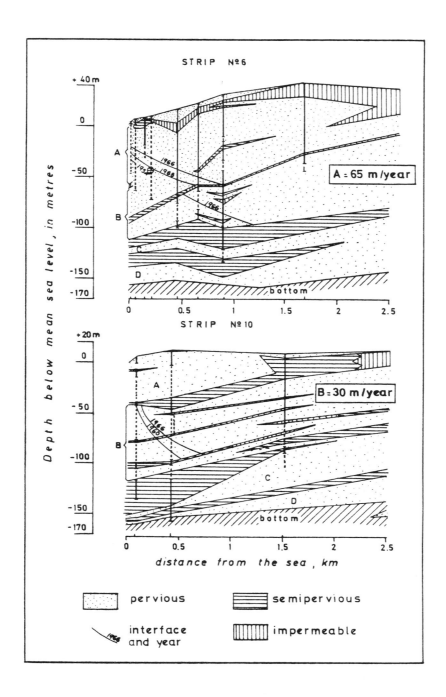

Fig. 4.3 – Sea water encroachment in the Coastal Plain of Israel (Schmorak, 1967). The successive interfaces in 1954, 1962 and 1966 are shown, when there is enough data. There are four aquifers designated A, B, C and D. The interface velocity penetration in the main aquifers of each of the two strips shown (normal to the sea) is included. More recent data has shown that the encroachment process is more complicated than that shown.

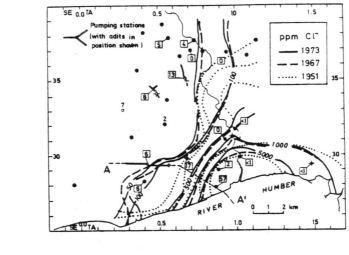

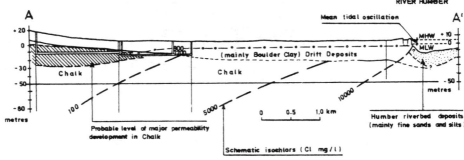

Fig. 4.4 - Sea water encroachment in the chalk aquifer on North Humberside (UK). The different penetration in 1951, 1967 and 1973 is shown, and also a schematic cross section (Foster, Parry and Chilton, 1976). Advancement is very low.

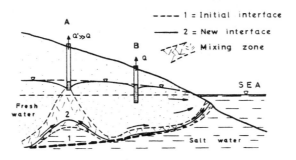

Fig. 4.5 - Upconing under groundwater abstraction works. Well A is not directly affected by the salt water since it does not reach sea level, but around it there is no net fresh water flow towards the coast; then, the mixing zone expands and after some time some brackish water, less dense than sea water, can reach the well bottom. Well B, in spite of its penetrating below sea level, is operated with a small water level drawdown, and no long-term impairment of the water quality appears when fresh water flow towards the sea is maintained below it. If wells A and B are on a same flow path, the expansion of the mixing zone created by well A will propagate downstream and can affect well B, especially when exploitation is intermittent.

(a) the salt water reaches the well bottom and a direct mixture of fresh and salt water results;

(b) the salt water, being heavier than the fresh water, does not reach the well or drain, but since there is a flow over or inside the interface zone toward the abstraction work, the mixed water accumulates under the stagnation point or line, and is captured by it, with some salinization produced;

(c) the effect on the interface zone is very slight and the flow along it toward the sea is not interrupted. The abstraction work does not receive mixed water, but in general the yield must be very small to maintain such a situation.

Figures 4.6, 4.7 and 4.8 show some actual situations.

It can be shown (see chapter 5) that the upconing elevation under a well is directly proportional to the well discharge; and inversely proportional to the aquifer horizontal permeability, and to the distance from the well bottom to the initial interface.

The upconing velocity decreases with vertical permeability. Then the presence of horizontal low permeability layers delays the negative effects of the salt water upconing.

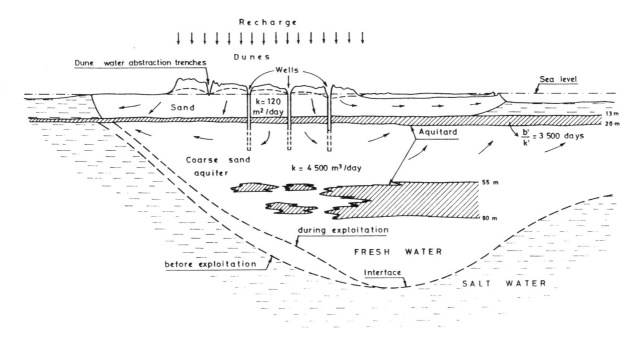

Fig. 4.6 - Simplified representation of the groundwater exploitation near Amsterdam, in the Dutch coastal dune areas. The groundwater abstraction has depressed the water table, thus decreasing the depth to the interface. No important upconing effects appear, since the clay lenses (aquitards) avoid the presence of local drawdowns under the wells at the interface situation (modified from Huisman, 1957).

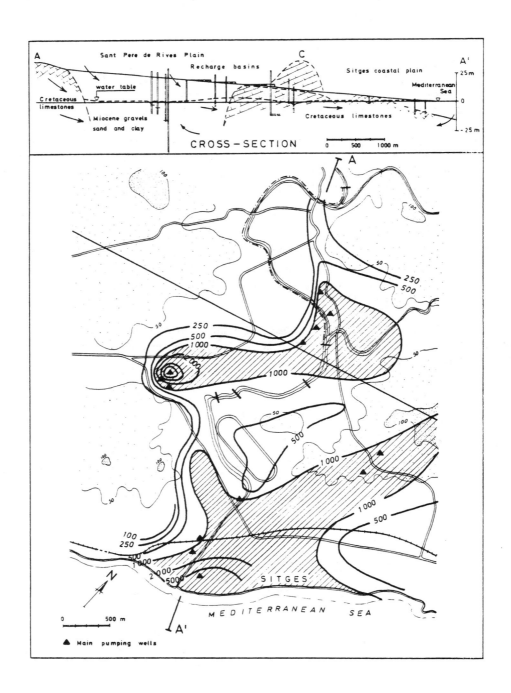

Fig. 4.7 – Upconing of ground saline water in the Sant Pere de Ribes-Sitges coastal plain (south of Barcelona, Spain) as a consequence of local abstractions. The values are in ppm Cl⁻. The dashed areas are those having more than 1000 ppm Cl⁻. The unconsolidated sediments lie on permeable limestones that outcrop at the boundary and in the hills in the middle of the plain. The limestones are the path for salt water penetration (after Custodio and Galofré, 1977).

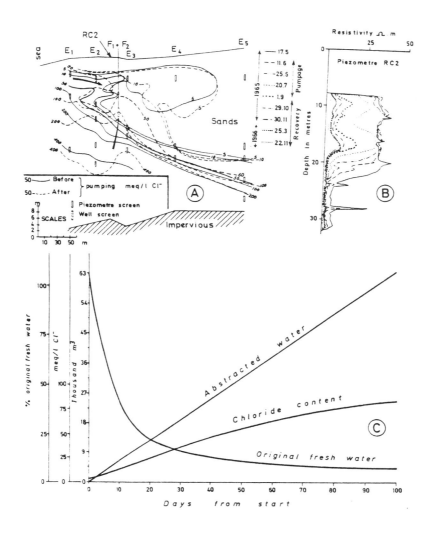

Fig. 4.8 - Effect of pumping on a sand aquifer with sea water in the bottom.
It corresponds to the Atlantic coast of Malika, near Dakar, Senegal
(Debuisson, 1967, 1970). A shows the deformation of isochloride
lines, and B the changes in ground resistivity along a PVC screened
piezometer; there is a clear upconing. Figure C shows that the
chloride content in pumped water tends to be an equilibrium value.

There is a critical cone elevation, for a critical pumping value,
about 1/4 to 1/3 of the distance from the well bottom to the initial interface, above which the cone becomes unstable; gravity segregation of salt water
is no longer maintained, and well salinization is unavoidable.

Upconing is a relatively short phenomenon, except for very low vertical permeabilities. Consequently the main effect disappears shortly after
the action ceases, but the expansion of the mixing zone, especially the top,
remains. It moves downstream, where it may produce some salinity effects,
especially for intermittently operated wells.

The landward movement of the salt water wedge caused by the ground-water abstraction increases existing upconing problems and creates new ones, requiring the abandonment of some wells or water works, or the reduction of discharge or penetration.

The situation in fissured rocks is similar to that in porous materials. When most of the easily mobile water is in the fissures, and since the water volume in storage is low, the salt water movement induced by the fresh water abstraction can proceed at a much faster pace, especially when karstic cavities and channels are involved. Since local vertical permeability may be high, salt water upconing is generally ubiquitous, and fresh water replacement for salt water or mixed water in a fissure or channel takes place in a short time, from hours to a few days in many cases. Only small abstractions of fresh water can be allowed if other costly measures are not applied. This sea water encroachment through the major discontinuities does not necessarily reach the less permeable parts of the formations, and fresh water pockets develop. Since this water is generally abstracted through the discontinuity system, it mixes with salt or brackish water.

In very thick coastal aquifers with a deep salt water layer separated from the upper fresh water by a thick mixing zone, distributed fresh water abstraction causes an expansion of the mixing zone, the top reacting faster than the bottom (Todd and Meyer, 1971). Conversely, a decrease in groundwater exploitation or an increase in groundwater recharge produces a positive effect since salt water penetration can be reduced and the mixing zone is flushed, but fresh water losses to the sea are increased.

4.1.2 Secondary effects related to wells and other groundwater abstraction works

When a well is drilled in a multilayered aquifer or multiaquifer system, easier connections or short circuits between the different layers or aquifers can be established when:

    (a)   the well has different screened zones;

    (b)   a long gravel-pack is placed;

    (c)   permeability between the casing and the drill-hole exists;

    (d)   corrosion perforates the casing at the non-exploited levels (generally in the more saline ones).

If some levels contain salt water or are sea water intruded, and the piezometric heads in the saline levels are higher than in the fresh ones, continuous salt water pollution takes place when the well or bore-hole is not operated or is abandoned without suitable backfilling (fig. 4.9). When the well is pumped, generally all the pervious layers produce water and the abstracted water becomes salt water contaminated to some extent.

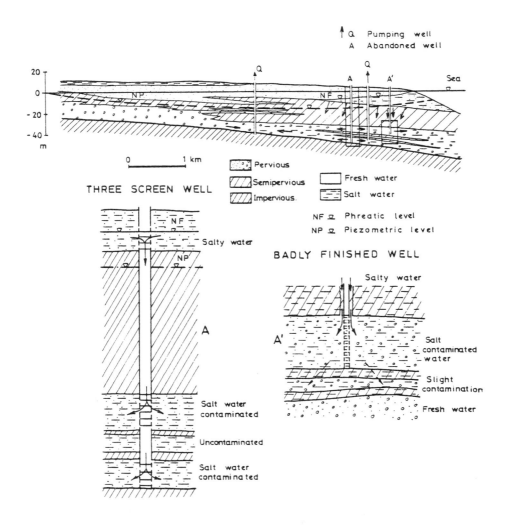

Fig. 4.9 - Salt water pollution through wells. It represents the present situation in some wells in the Besós delta, near Barcelona (Custo-dio, 1975). The intense exploitation of the deep aquifers create a downward gradient that allows for the salt, brackish or polluted water in the upper aquifer to penetrate the deep aquifers through the multiscreened wells or through the annulus between the hole and the tube in badly drilled or badly finished wells.

In some areas, salt groundwater is pumped for cooling or other industrial purposes, thus creating a sea water head decrease that protects inland areas. Abstracted water is generally a mixture of salt and fresh water, though the salt water may dominate. In some instances, the shutdown of these salt water wells is undesirable for other groundwater pumping centers inland, which dominate the flow, because sea water intrusion to them can accelerate or increase (see the Llobregat example in chapter 10.) Such a positive effect may produce some undesirable results when the salty or brack-ish water is not properly discharged.

4.2 Indirect effects

4.2.1 Actions which affect groundwater recharge

An increase in recharge has positive effects since it reduces salt water encroachment. It can be derived from:

- development, improvement or extension of an irrigated area, applying imported surface water (canal losses play an important role in many situations);

- increase in imported or surface water losses to the ground through extensive water distribution networks, sewers and sanitary collector systems, and through diffusion wells, trenches, pits or cesspools;

- improvement in runoff and river infiltration, when there are favorable natural or artificial conditions such as a deep water table;

- establishment of artificial recharge works, such as recharge basins, ponds, trenches and pits, and injection wells.

Many other activities can lead to an increase in the potential for sea water encroachment. Some of these activities are:

- urbanization, industrialization and paving of former agricultural or wild areas. The paving, roofing, soil compaction, vegetation eradication, etc., leads to a reduction in recharge and an increase in non-useful surface runoff.

- suppression of irrigated areas or decrease in irrigation excess water through improvement in irrigation practices, when surface or imported water is used. The same applies when canal losses are reduced;

- suppression of cesspools, diffusion wells and similar underground disposal works after a sanitary sewer network is established;

- channeling of rivers and creeks in order to avoid or reduce floods, thus decreasing runoff infiltration in the river bed and in the formerly flooded areas;

- river regulation with upstream dams, when the river recharges the coastal aquifer, naturally or through induced recharge. Regulation by means of surface reservoirs reduces the importance and frequency of floods that scour the river bed and restore the infiltration capacity. Upstream water diversion or consumption increases this effect. An impairment of the physical and biological river water quality has the same effect since the river bed is more easily clogged. When sedimentation in the reservoir produces cleaner water downstream, recharge in the river bed and canals can increase, but erosion also increases, thus producing an increased aquifer drainage to lowered river beds;

- deforestation or vegetation cover impairment that reduces infiltration and increases non-useful surface runoff.

As previously described, these positive or negative effects influence the fresh-salt water relationships and upset the dynamic equilibrium. The change rate to a new equilibrium is slow and may need years to complete, so some effects are not clear, and an understanding of the phenomena involved is needed to foresee future problems.

4.2.2 Actions to reclaim or improve the utilization of coastal areas

Some effects related to land management have already been described, including those related to agriculture, urbanization and river management. Other effects that generally can change the sea water encroachment situation are:

- desiccation and reclamation of coastal marshes and swamps. If they are filled up, some improvement can be attained. More frequently, the reclamation is done by drainage in order to lower the water table, thus increasing salinity problems. The drained water may be fresh, but it generally becomes brackish and sometimes salty. The salinity impairment is not always important nor immediate, and in flat coastal piedmonts, some swampy areas have enough elevation to allow for a water table lowering without important effects on sea water encroachment. In low areas, the reclamation of swamps and lakes by pumped drainage or by preferential water discharge at low tide (such as is done in the Dutch polders) may create some salt water upconing (fig. 4.10), that can be reduced to a small value when the bottom of such areas is of low permeability;

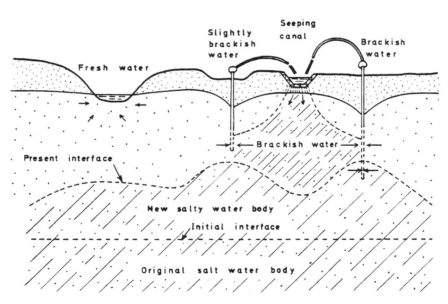

Fig. 4.10 - Changes in the depth to the ground salt water caused by drainage works. The reinfiltration or abstracted brackish or salty water can cause a serious pollution problem.

- excavation of channels to link the coast with inland areas. When there is insufficient fresh water flow in these channels, as frequently occurs during the year or dry season, a salt or brackish water tongue penetrates inland through the channel (Kohout, 1961). Wells close to it can become salt water polluted. In situations where the water table is at sea level, salt water can encroach through the lower part of the channel, until the salt water wedge is balanced by the fresh water flow. When the channel intersect areas of heavy pumpage, having a water table below sea level, massive salt water contamination can develop. The same considerations apply to the deepening of river channels for navigation or other uses, and the excavation of inland harbors;

- modification of the shore line caused by accretion or abrasion. In the first case improvements develop slowly and changes for the worse in the second. These can be related to the establishment of new harbors; enlargement or dredging of existing ones; coastal drift correction through piers; gravel and sand extraction in the beach and in river channels; river impoundments that intercept solid transportation, etc.

4.2.3   Effects derived from civil works and building activities

The effects derived from civil works and building activities stem from changes in the groundwater recharge, in the permeability or in the aquifer water balance. Examples are:

- temporal or permanent drainages of the underground part of buildings, cellars, tunnels, subways, etc., or excavations for new buildings or civil works. The water abstraction lowers the water table and reduces the fresh water flow, thus favoring a salinity increase. A further problem is the drainage water disposal when it is saline or brackish. Improper disposal can cause salinization problems through infiltration;

- blocking up of groundwater flow by underground works such as tunnels, sewers, pipes, foundations, etc., in such a way to produce a decrease in fresh water flow towards the coast. It occurs when the damming effect creates aquifer overflow, increases drainage or evapotranspiration, or reduces recharge from surface water;

- removal of impervious or semipervious covers during the excavations for building foundations or for gravel and sand mining or for agricultural purposes. In low laying areas (polders) it accelerates the upward flow of saline water.

4.3   Other effects related to groundwater exploitation

Vegetation in low elevation coastal areas can be affected by the lowering of the water table and the increase in the salinity near it. The plants and trees on the dune belts and sand bars are sensitive to these effects. In coral reef oceanic islands or in sandy flat deltaic islands, groundwater exploitation, though small, may lead to the decline of dense vegetation cover, since it depends highly on the existing tiny fresh water lenses.

In agricultural areas undesirable effects arise when irrigation water is too salty and excessively high in sodium (see chapter 6). The soil clay fraction is deflocculated and the permeability decreases, thus impairing the drainage and the soil aeration, and increasing the soil salinity problems.

Undesirable effects related to clay deflocculation on aquifer permeability reduction, or increase in surface runoff, do not seem of major importance. The same may be true for water chemical changes in the mixing zone (increased hardness due to ion exchange or calcite subsaturation).

A further secondary effect is related to land subsidence, generally caused by heavy groundwater abstraction (as in Venice), or when young unconsolidated land is loaded with buildings, dockyards, parking lots, etc. In very flat areas this produces a landward movement of the coastal line and salt water penetration through channels and other coastal forms.

Some secondary effects in urban or industrial coastal areas are related to the shutdown of the pumping wells when they become excessively salty, or when due to land use changes. The wells maintained an artificially depressed water table that in flat coastal areas was equivalent to an effective land drainage. In such circumstances, building foundations, cellars, underground excavations and parking lots, subway tunnels, etc., constructed when the water table was depressed, without taking into account the natural water table level, may be in trouble when the pumping ceases and the water table rises, creating underpressure flotation and inundation problems. The Besós area (Barcelona, Spain) and the southwestern part of New York Long Island (Cohen, Franke and Foxworthy, 1969) are typical examples. See figure 4.11.

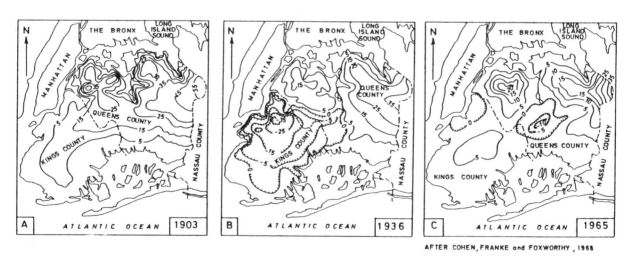

Fig. 4.11 - Groundwater levels in Kings and Queens Counties in 1903, 1936 and 1965, showing the creation of a big drawdown cone and the recovery after reduction in groundwater abstraction (after Cohen, Franke and Foxworthy, 1969a, 1969b).

The depletion of the water table also can be detrimental to foundations resting on wood piers. When permanently wet, including under salt
water, they are well preserved, but when the ground dries or is periodically
wet and dry (especially under saline water) they weaken and finally collapse.

4.4   Mixed surface-groundwater situations

The exploitation of groundwater near tidal estuaries and saline coastal
lagoons has problems similar to coastal aquifers, due to the presence of the
permanent or variable salty water in the open water bodies.

Generally the lagoons and estuaries, and also other surface water
channels, are effluent streams (discharge groundwater). But groundwater
abstraction reduces the outflow and it can be reversed, creating conditions of
induced recharge. When surface water is brackish the waters are of about the
same density, and normal dispersive displacement can be assumed. Abstracted
water may become contaminated with salt in the same way a well near a polluted
stream does.

Man's influence on surface water salinity has an effect on groundwater when there are conditions of induced recharge. When the channel bottom
contains a salt water wedge, conditions are the same as in the coast, but with
salt water at a somewhat lower head. Saline water wedge penetration and
upconing problems may develop. A typical example is the sea water encroachment in Miami due to canals (Kohout, 1961).

Littoral lagoons may present large salinity variations during the
year according to the inflow-outflow conditions, evaporation being one of the
main factors. Groundwater outflow can yield significant salt quantities that
are concentrated by evaporation. Man may change the conditions dramatically
by the construction of levees, outlets and surface flow diversions (Jean and
Toni, 1974), and groundwater quality may be greatly affected.

One special case is that of the polders or internal depressions in
low coastal areas, desiccated for land reclamation, leaving the bottom at a
level some meters below mean sea level. The Netherlands is a country in which
polder reclamation was initiated several centuries ago, and is still underway
(Wesseling, 1980). These polders are desiccated by means of shallow ditches,
and the water discharged to the sea at low tide, generally by pumping (wind
machines or motor pumps). Soil desalting is accomplished by means of surface
water (Rivers Rhine and Meuse) diverted by means of canals.

A polder is like a large diameter well that produces salt or brackish water upconing, and the upward groundwater flow must be collected and
disposed of. The presence of a silt, clay or peat polder bottom greatly and
effectively reduces this upward flow, if not disturbed by man's activities
such as deep foundations, leaky wells, deep trenches or sand pits. Drained
water is first fresh, but then, depending on the areas, it becomes progressively brackish or salty over a long time span. It is expected that in many
tens of years or in a few centuries the salinity may decrease anew from the
reduction in salt water head due to its consumption (the replacement needs an

increased flow from the sea), especially at second line polders, when first
line polders reduce the salt water head. Figure 4.12 is a schematic representation of the groundwater flow to a polderland. Figure 4.13 gives the upward
and downward flows, and figure 4.14 shows the salt loads from seepage.

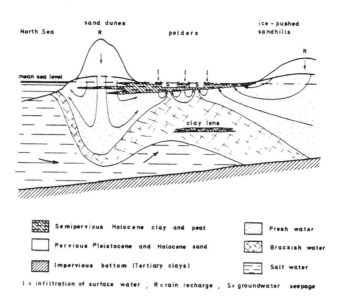

Fig. 4.12 – Geohydrologic profile of the western part of the Netherlands
(after van Dam, 1976). The upconing effects below the polders are
shown.

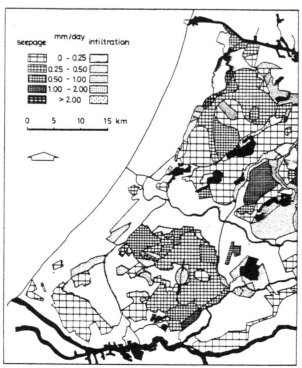

Fig. 4.13 – Values of seepage and infiltration in the Netherlands (after ICW,
1976).

The discharge to drains in a low land is a function of the aquifer recharge and the flow pattern affects the salinity of the outflow water. Recharge increases the outflow to the drain, but after a slow salinity decrease due to the total reaction of the water body, salinity increases due to the increased washout of the mixing zone (fig. 4.15).

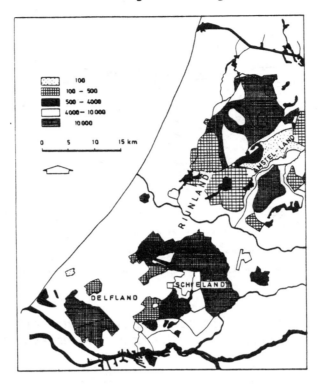

Fig. 4.14 - Salt loads from upward saline seepage, in kg/ha/year (after Pomper and Wesseling, 1978).

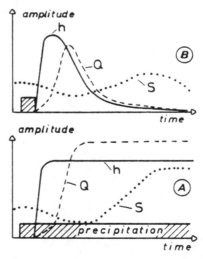

Fig. 4.15 - Changes in drain discharge and outflow water salinity in a low land for a prolonged recharge period and for a short recharge period (after Mania and Meens, 1981). The time span is of a few days. Q = drain discharge; h = piezometric head; s = salinity.

-114-

4.5 References

Arad, A., Kafri, U., Fleisher, E. (1975). The Na'Aman springs, Northern Israel: salinization mechanism of an irregular fresh water-sea water interface. Journal of Hydrology, Vol. 25 (1975), pp. 81-104.

Cohen; Franke; Foxworthy (1969). An atlas of Long Island's water resources. New York Water Resources Commission Bulletin No. 62. State of New York. 59 pp.

Custodio, E. (1975). Les nappes cotieres (coastal aquifers). Committee on Porous Media, Int. Water Resources Assoc. Rapperswil meeting. Institut de Hydroméchanique at D'Aménagement des Eaux de l'École Polytechnique Féderale de Zürich. Vol. 1, Sec. D, pp. 1-31.

Custodio, E., Suárez, M., Galofré, A. (1976). Ensayos para el análisis de la recarga de aguas residuales en el delta del Besós (Tests to study the feasibility of recharge with treated sewage water in the Besós delta). II Asemblea Nacional de Geodesia y Geofísica. Barcelona. Instituto Geográfico y Catastral. Madrid. pp. 1893-1936.

Custodio, E., Ganoulis, A., Potié, L. (1982). Utilisation rationelle des ressources en eau dans les zones cotieres (Rational use of water resources in coastal areas). IV International Conference on Water Resources Planning and Management. Marseille. Bulletin BRGM (2) III: 3/4, 1982, pp. 305-315. Paris.

Custodio, E., Galofré, A. (1977). Basin recharge in the Sitges Plain (Barcelona, Spain) used for the temporary disposal of municipal waste water. Memories Birmingham Congress, U.K. Int. Assoc. Hydrogeologists. Vol. XIII, pp. F41-F57.

van Dam, J.C. (1976a). Partial depletion of saline water by seepage. Journal of Hydrology. Vol. 29, No. 3/4, pp. 315-339. Elsevier.

van Dam, J.C. (1976b). Possibilities and limitations of the resistivity method of geoelectrical prospecting in the solution of geohydrological problems. Geoexploration. 14 (1976), pp. 179-183. Elsevier.

Debuisson, J. (1970). La nappe aquifere du cordon dunaire de Malika (Sénégal) (The dune belt aquifer of Malika, Senegal). Bull. BR M, 2nd Serie. Sec. III, No. 3, pp. 149-161. Paris.

Debuisson, J., Mousu, H. (1976) Une étude experimentale de l'intrusion des eaux marines dans une nappe cotiere du Sénégal sous l'effect de l'exploitiation. (An experimental study of the marine water intrusion in a coastal aquifer of the Senegal under exploitation effect). Artificial Recharge and Management of Aquifers. Haifa Symposium. International Association Scientific Hydrology. Pub. 72, pp. 15-44.

Dijon, R. (1978). <u>A review of United Nations water resources activities in coastal areas and islands.</u> Seminar on Selected Water Problems in Islands and Coastal Areas with special regard to Desalination and Groundwater. Malta. U.N. Economic Commission for Europe. WATER/SEM. 5/R.52. 13 pp.

Foster, S.S.D., Parry, E.L., Chilton, P.J. (1976). <u>Groundwater resource development and saline water intrusion in the Chalk aquifer of North Humberside.</u> Natural Environment Research Council, Institute of Geological Science. U.K., rep. 76/4. 34 pp. London.

Huisman, L. (1957). <u>The determination of the geohydrological contacts for the dune-water catchment area of Amsterdam.</u> General Assembly of Toronto, Int. Assoc. Scientific Hydrology, Pub. 44, pp. 168-182. Gentbrugge.

ICW (1976). <u>Hydrologie en waterkwaliteit van Midden West-Netherland.</u> Regionale Studies, Instituut voor Culturtechnick en Waterhuishouding No. 9. The Netherlands. 100 pp.

Jean, A.M., Toni, C.C. (1974). <u>Influence des irrigations et drainages sur le régime des eaux superficielles et souterraines dans le delta de la Camargue</u> (Irrigations and drainage influence on the surface and groundwater regime in the Camargue delta). Soc. Hydrotechnique de France. XIII Journees de l'Hydraulique. Paris. Q III, R. 8, pp. 1-11.

Kohout, F.A. (1961). <u>Case history of salt water encroachment caused by a storm sewer in Miami.</u> Journal Am. Water Works Assoc. Vol. 53, No. 11, November 1961, pp. 1406-1416.

Mania, J., Meens, V. (1981). <u>Dewatering influence on the stability of the fresh and salt water interface in Flanders (France).</u> Quality of Groundwater Ed. W. van Duijvenbooden, P. Glasbergen, H. van Lelyveld. Studies in Environmental Science 17. Elsevier. pp. 973-978.

Pomper, A.B., Wesseling, J. (1978). <u>Chloride content of surface water as a result of geologic processes and groundwater flow in a coastal area in the Netherlands.</u> Seminar on Selected Water Problems in Islands and Coastal Areas with special regard to Desalination and Groundwater, U.N. Economic Commission for Europe. Malta.

Schmorak, S. (1967). <u>Salt water encroachment in the Coastal Plain of Israel.</u> Inter. Assoc. Scientific Hydrology, Haifa. Pub. 72. pp. 305-318.

Thauvin, J.P. (1982). <u>Surexploitation d'aquiferes cotiers en zone semi-aride (Almerie, Espagne): essai d'utilisation rationelle des resources globales de la région</u> (Overdevelopment of coastal aquifers in a semi-arid area (Almeria, Spain): attempts at rational utilization of the regional global resources). IV International Conference on Water Resources Planning and Management. Marseille. CEMPE. Vol. 1, 8 pp.

Todd, D.K., Meyer, C.F. (1971). <u>Hydrology and geology of the Honolulu aquifer.</u> Proc. Am. Society of Civil Engineers, Journal of the Hydraulic Division, HY 2, 1971. pp. 233-256.

Vilaró, F., Custodio, E., Bruington, A. (1970). <u>Sea water intrusion and water pollution in the Pirineo Oriental (Spain).</u> American Soc. Civil Engineers, National Water Resources Meeting, Memphis, Tenn. January, 42 pp.

Wesseling, J. (1980). <u>Saline seepage in the Netherlands, occurrence and magnitude.</u> Research on Possible Changes in the Distribution of Saline Seepage in the Netherlands. Committee for Hydrological Research TNO. Proc. and Information No. 26, pp. 17-33.

Zebidi, H. (1978). <u>L'exploitation des nappes cotieres en Tunisie: problemes et perspectives</u> (Exploitation of coastal aquifers in Tunisia: problems and perspectives). Seminar on Selected Water Problems in Islands and Coastal Areas, with special regard to Desalination and Groundwater. Malta. U.N. Economic Commission for Europe. WATER. 5/R. 10 pp.

Zeryouhi, I. (1982). <u>Les nappes cotieres du Maroc: gestion de leurs ressources</u> (The coastal aquifers of Morocco: management of its resources). IV International Conference on Water Resources Planning and Management. Marseille. CEMPE. Vol. 1, 10 pp.

5. Methods of calculation

G. A. Bruggeman - E. Custodio

Contents

5.0   Introduction

Methods of calculation for salt-fresh water relationships in coastal aquifers vary from very simple ones, useful for first calculations and to obtain coarse evaluations, to very sophisticated ones, that are usually too difficult to be applied on a regular basis or that lead to solutions that are too complicated. The need for accuracy and the right conceptual model of the geohydrological setup must guide the selection and application of the most appropriate method, that which fits best the real problem to be solved.

After a short discussion of parameters and variables, the different analytical methods are presented. Afterwards, analog models are introduced and then mathematical (digital or numerical) ones. Analytical methods are considered in detail and examples are given in order to clarify the text. The reader must go to the other references for details common to other groundwater situations, as the presentation is focused on the special problems that arise in coastal areas.

Practical formulae will be given in chapter 8.

5.1   Parameters and variables

Prepared by G.A. Bruggeman

5.1.1   Differential form of Darcy's law

In describing flow through porous media we may distinguish between variables of state of fluid motion, such as velocity, head, and pressure, and the variables related to the properties of the porous medium and the fluid, such as permeability, porosity, density, viscosity, etc., the so-called parameters of the soil-water medium.

A basic relationship between a number of variables and parameters in groundwater flow forms Darcy's law, derived in the following general way. Generally groundwater flows very slowly and the variations of the velocity are very small so that the inertial forces that are associated with changes of flow can be neglected in comparison with the other forces acting on the flow. This means that acceleration is assumed to be absent and the other forces must be in equilibrium with each other.

Consider an elemental volume, $\Delta V = \Delta A \cdot \Delta s$, of the aquifer arbitrarily oriented in the field flow, where ΔA and Δs are, respectively, the elemental area and the elemental length normal to the area (see fig. 5.1).

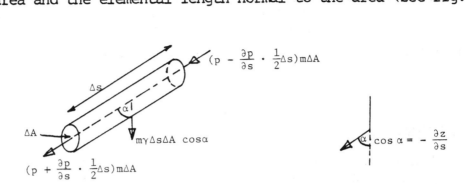

Fig. 5.1

The forces acting on the water in this elemental volume, are the **pressure force** F_p, the **weight** F_W and the **shear force** F_S that is the force exerted on the water by the solid skeleton.

(a) **Pressure force**

$$F_p = (p - \frac{\partial p}{\partial s} \cdot \frac{1}{2}\Delta s)\, m\Delta A - (p + \frac{\partial p}{\partial s} \cdot \frac{1}{2}\Delta s)\, m\Delta A$$

or

$$F_p = - m\Delta A\Delta s\, \frac{\partial p}{\partial s} \qquad\qquad (1)$$

in which m = porosity i.e. that part of the soil which is filled with groundwater.

(b) **Weight** F_W

In general the **density** ρ of the groundwater varies with place and a density gradient in the s-direction will be present. As for the **specific weight** $\gamma = \rho g$, its gradient will be $\partial\gamma$. Along Δs the average specific weight equals γ as can be seen from:

$$\gamma_{av} = \frac{\gamma - \frac{\partial\gamma}{\partial s} \cdot \frac{1}{2}\Delta s + \gamma + \frac{\partial\gamma}{\partial s} \cdot \frac{1}{2}\Delta s}{2} = \gamma$$

from which

$$F_w = m\gamma\Delta A\Delta s\, \frac{\partial z}{\partial s} . \qquad\qquad (2)$$

(c) Shear force

It is assumed that the total surface ΔO_g of the grains within ΔV is proportional to ΔV: $\Delta O_g = C_1 \Delta V$ ($C_1 [L^{-1}]$). The parameter τ $[ML^{-1}T^{-2}]$ represents the shear stress between the grains and the flowing water, opposite to the velocity of the groundwater, then:

$$F_S = - C_1 \tau \Delta A \Delta s \ . \tag{3}$$

From physical considerations it may be concluded that τ is dependent on the velocity of the groundwater, the viscosity of the fluid and the geometry of the pores and the grains.

By means of the Π-theorem in dimensional analysis the relation between these parameters can be found:

$$\Pi = \tau \mu^x v_r^y a^z$$

in which

Π = dimensionless number $\qquad$ [0]

τ = shear stress $\qquad$ $[ML^{-1}T^{-2}]$

μ = dynamic viscosity of the groundwater $\qquad$ $[ML^{-1}T^{-1}]$

a = arbitrary length $\qquad$ [L]

v_r = real average velocity of the water $\qquad$ $[LT^{-1}]$

$$\Pi = M^0 L^0 T^0 = [ML^{-1}T^{-2}] \ [ML^{-1}T^{-1}]^x \ [LT^{-1}]^y \ [L]^z$$

$$\begin{array}{l} M \to \\ L \to \\ T \to \end{array} \begin{bmatrix} x & +1 = 0 \\ -x+y+z-1 = 0 \\ -x-y & -2 = 0 \end{bmatrix} \quad \to \quad x = -1 \qquad y = -1 \qquad z = 1 \ .$$

So

$$\Pi = C_2 = \frac{\tau a}{\mu v_r} \ \text{or} \ \tau = C_2 \ \frac{\mu v_r}{a} = C_2 \ \frac{\mu m_e v_s}{a}$$

in which

m_e = effective porosity

v_s = bulk velocity in s-direction.

If $C_1 C_2 = C_3 [L^{-1}]$, then from (3) follows:

$$F_S = - C_3 \ \frac{\mu m_e v_s}{a} \ \Delta A \Delta s \ . \tag{4}$$

The equilibrium equation of the three forces $F_p + F_w + F_s = 0$ gives:

$$- \Delta A \Delta S \left(m \frac{\partial p}{\partial s} + m \gamma \frac{\partial z}{\partial s} + C_3 \frac{\mu m_e v_s}{a} \right) = 0$$

and

$$V_s = - \frac{am}{C_3 m_e \mu} \left(\frac{\partial p}{\partial s} + \gamma \frac{\partial z}{\partial s} \right) .$$

If

$$k_{os} = \frac{am}{C_3 m_e} \quad [L^2] \tag{5}$$

is introduced as the coefficient of _intrinsic permeability_ of the porous matrix, the expression for V_s becomes:

$$V_s = - \frac{k_{os}}{\mu} \left(\frac{\partial p}{\partial s} + \gamma \frac{\partial z}{\partial s} \right) .$$

As the s-direction was arbitrary this equation may be generalized to all directions and then becomes in vector notation:

$$\vec{V} = - \frac{k_o}{\mu} (\nabla p + \gamma \nabla z)$$

or

$$V_x = \frac{k_{ox}}{\mu} \frac{\partial p}{\partial x} , \qquad V_y = \frac{k_{oy}}{\mu} \frac{\partial p}{\partial y} , \qquad V_z = - \frac{k_{oz}}{\mu} \left(\frac{\partial p}{\partial z} + \gamma \right) \tag{6}$$

where k_o = intrinsic permeability.

Equation (6) represents the _general differential form of Darcy's law_. The parameters k_o, μ and $\gamma = \rho g$ are generally variables and functions of x, y and z, whereas the coefficient of permeability may be not only a function of space (heterogeneous soils), but also of the direction (anisotropic soils), for instance k_{ox}, k_{oy}, k_{oz}, k_s etc.

If, and only if the _density_ of the water (and thus also the specific weight) is _constant_ equation (6) may be written as:

$$\vec{V} = - \frac{k_o}{\mu} \nabla (p + \gamma z)$$

or

$$\vec{V} = \frac{k_o \gamma}{\mu_o} \nabla \left(\frac{p}{\gamma} + z \right)$$

$\frac{p}{\gamma} + z$ is the _head_ ϕ if $z = 0$ is the plane of reference;

$$\frac{k_o \gamma}{\mu} = k [LT^{-1}] = \underline{Darcy\ permeability}. \tag{7}$$

So in the case of constant density equation (6) is simplified to Darcy's law in its well-known form:

$$\vec{V} = - k\nabla\phi$$

$$V_x = - k_x \frac{\partial\phi}{\partial x} \, , \qquad V_y = - k_y \frac{\partial\phi}{\partial y} \, , \qquad V_z = - k \frac{\partial\phi}{\partial z} \, .$$

(8)

If k is also a constant, then the velocity vector is _proportional to the gradient of a scalar function_ which is characteristic for _potential_ flow or _irrotational_ flow and ϕ is called the _potential function_.

From the general form of Darcy's law (equation 6), where γ is variable, such a potential function cannot be derived; for instance if we put again $\phi = \frac{p}{\gamma} + z$ then $\frac{\partial\phi}{\partial x} = \frac{1}{\gamma}\frac{\partial p}{\partial x} - \frac{p}{\gamma^2}\frac{\partial\gamma}{\partial x}$ etc., and as $V_x = - \frac{k_o}{\mu}\frac{\partial p}{\partial x}$ it follows that V_x is not proportional to $\frac{\partial\phi}{\partial x}$ and a real potential function does not exist.

All attempts to introduce substitute 'potentials' (point-water head, fresh water head, environmental head, true environmental head, force potential, etc.) in case of variable densities, have little sense and lead to unnecessary complications in calculations with regard, for instance, to fresh-salt water problems, because of the fact that the velocities cannot be derived directly from those 'potentials.' In these cases it is much more convenient to use _pressures_ and if possible _stream functions_ (see section 5.2).

In the general equation (6) for Darcy's law, a number of parameters and variables occur which will be treated separately in the next paragraphs.

5.1.2   Permeability

The coefficient of proportionality, k, appearing in the expression for Darcy's law (equation 8) is called the _hydraulic conductivity_ or _Darcy permeability_ or _coefficient of permeability_. It is a scalar with dimension $[LT^{-1}]$ that expresses the ease with which a fluid is transported through a porous matrix. It is, therefore, a coefficient that depends on both soil and fluid properties, as can be seen from equation (7):

$$k = \frac{k_o\gamma}{\mu} = \frac{k_o\rho g}{\mu} \, .$$

The fluid properties in this relation are the density ρ $[ML^{-3}]$ and the viscosity μ $[ML^{-1}T^{-1}]$. In this paragraph brief attention will be paid to the _intrinsic permeability_ k_o $[L^2]$, which is only dependent on the properties of the soil, such as the dimensions and the size distribution of the grains and the pores. In section 5.1.1 was found (equation 5):

$$k_o = \frac{am}{C_3 m_e} \, .$$

As C_3 has the dimension $[L^{-1}]$ one may write $C_4 = lC_3$ in which l is an arbitrary length (L) and the constant C_4 is dimensionless. So

$$k_0 = \frac{alm}{C_4 m_e} = C_5 al$$

with $C_5 = \frac{m}{C_4 m_e}$ [dimensionless].

If $al = d^2$, the square of mean diameter of the grains results in:

$$k_0 = Cd^2 \qquad\qquad [L^2] . \qquad\qquad (9)$$

Usually d is taken as d_{10}, that is a diameter such that 10% (by weight) of the soil consists of grains smaller than d. Experimental values of C lie between 10^{-4} and 10^{-3}.

When k_0 is space dependent, i.e. $k_0 = k_0 (x, y, z)$, the porous medium is __nonhomogeneous__ or __heterogeneous__. When, at some point, k_0 varies with direction, the medium at that point is __anisotropic__.

In case of constant fluid properties ρ and μ, the most general form of Darcy's law for anisotropic soils is:

$$-V_x = k_{xx} \frac{\partial \phi}{\partial x} + k_{xy} \frac{\partial \phi}{\partial y} + k_{xz} \frac{\partial \phi}{\partial z} \qquad\qquad (10)$$

$$-V_y = k_{xy} \frac{\partial \phi}{\partial x} + k_{yy} \frac{\partial \phi}{\partial y} + k_{yz} \frac{\partial \phi}{\partial z}$$

$$-V_z = k_{zx} \frac{\partial \phi}{\partial x} + k_{zy} \frac{\partial \phi}{\partial y} + k_{zz} \frac{\partial \phi}{\partial z} .$$

If $k_{xy} = k_{yx} = k_{xz} = k_{zx} = k_{yz} = k_{zy} = 0$, then the x, y and z directions are said to be the __principal directions of the permeability__ and the equations reduce to:

$$V_x = - k_{xx} \frac{\partial \phi}{\partial x} = - k_x \frac{\partial \phi}{\partial x} \qquad\qquad (11)$$

$$V_y = - k_{yy} \frac{\partial \phi}{\partial y} = - k_y \frac{\partial \phi}{\partial y}$$

$$V_z = - k_{zz} \frac{\partial \phi}{\partial z} = - k_z \frac{\partial \phi}{\partial z} .$$

It can be shown that in the general anistropic case represented by equations (10) there always exist three mutually orthogonal directions (x', y', z') for which the equations (11) hold, if (x, y, z) are transformed into (x', y', z'). It follows that in anisotropic soils the vector $\vec{V}$ and $\nabla\phi$ are no longer parallel to each other, that means that __in anisotropic soils the direction of flow in a point in the field is no longer always perpendicular to the equipotential surface or line through that point__.

The directional derivative $\frac{\partial \phi}{\partial s}$ in the direction of the flow is according to its definition equal to the scalar product of the potential gradient and the unit vector in the flow direction:

$$\frac{\partial \phi}{\partial s} = \frac{\vec{V}}{V} \cdot \nabla \phi \qquad\qquad (12)$$

where

$$V = \left| \vec{V} \right| .$$

If starting from (11) one defines a _directional hydraulic conductivity_, analog to the conductivity in Darcy's law, as the ratio between the specific discharge V at a point and the component of the potential gradient in the direction of $\vec{V}$, then:

$$V = - k_s \cdot \frac{\partial \phi}{\partial s}$$

and with (12):

$$k_s = \frac{V^2}{\vec{V} \cdot \nabla \phi} = \frac{-V^2}{V_x \frac{\partial \phi}{\partial x} + V_y \frac{\partial \phi}{\partial y} + V_z \frac{\partial \phi}{\partial z}} .$$

As $V_x = - k_x \frac{\partial \phi}{\partial x}$ or $\frac{\partial \phi}{\partial x} = - \frac{V_x}{k_x}$ etc., then:

$$\frac{V^2}{k_s} = \frac{V_x^2}{k_x} + \frac{V_y^2}{k_y} + \frac{V_z^2}{k_z} . \qquad\qquad (13)$$

Consider a position vector $\vec{r}$, parallel to $\vec{V}$, with components x, y and z and magnitude $\left| \vec{r} \right| = \sqrt{k_s}$. Equation (13) then becomes:

$$\frac{x^2}{k_x} + \frac{y^2}{k_y} + \frac{z^2}{k_z} = 1 , \qquad\qquad (14)$$

the equation of an ellipsoid with semi-axes $\sqrt{k_x}$, $\sqrt{k_y}$ and $\sqrt{k_z}$.

In two dimensions (14) becomes the ellipse $\frac{x^2}{k_x} + \frac{z^2}{k_z} = 1$, shown in figure 5.2. A horizontal and a vertical (z) direction is chosen because in many practical cases, especially in sediments, the horizontal permeability may differ considerably from the vertical one, the latter being smaller as a consequence of the layered soil structure.

The ellipsoid (or ellipse in two dimensions) gives in every direction the magnitude of the root of the directional conductivity. It also enables the construction of the direction of the flow in a point if the tangent to the equipotential line through that point is given, and conversely. This is based on the fact that equipotential planes (lines) and streamlines are adjoint to each other in the ellipsoid (ellipse), that means that the tangential line to the ellipsoid at the intersection point with the line through the origin in the flow direction is parallel to the tangential plane to the equipotential surface through the point under consideration. This can be proved as follows:

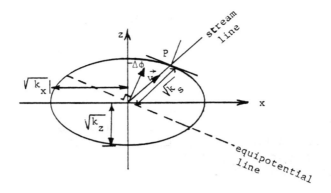

Fig. 5.2

Assume the point of intersection of the line through the origin in the direction of the vector $\vec{V} = (V_x, V_y, V_z)$ with the ellipsoid: $P_2(x_o, y_o, z_o)$.

Then

$$\frac{x_o^2}{k_x} + \frac{y_o^2}{k_y} + \frac{z_o^2}{k_z} = 1$$

and also

$$\frac{V_x}{x_o} = \frac{V_y}{y_o} = \frac{V_z}{z_o} . \tag{15}$$

From the equation of the ellipsoid, written in the form

$$f(x,y,z) = \frac{x^2}{k_x} + \frac{y^2}{k_y} + \frac{z^2}{k_z} - 1 = 0$$

the vector perpendicular to the surface of the ellipsoid at the point $P(x_o, y_o, z_o)$ can be derived as the gradient of the function f at that point:

$$\nabla f(P) = \nabla f = (\frac{2x_o}{k_x}, \frac{2y_o}{k_y}, \frac{2z_o}{k_z}) .$$

The vector representing the potential gradient can be written as

$$\nabla \phi = (\frac{\partial \phi}{\partial x}, \frac{\partial \phi}{\partial y}, \frac{\partial \phi}{\partial z}) = \nabla \phi = (-\frac{V_x}{k_x}, -\frac{V_y}{k_y}, -\frac{V_z}{k_z}) .$$

So $\nabla \phi$ and ∇f are parallel, from equations (15) and also the planes to which they are perpendicular, i.e. the tangential planes to the equipotential surface and the ellipsoid successively.

The foregoing considerations about directional conductivities in anisotropic soils refer in the first place to the intrinsic permeabilities, k_{ox} etc.; only for constant viscosity and density of the fluid will they also hold for the Darcy permeabilities.

5.2   Methods of calculation

Prepared by G.A. Bruggeman

5.2.1   Introduction

In groundwater flow, the ground is the medium through which water particles
are transported. In general, this transport will influence groundwater quality. If a water particle, which at a certain time has a known concentration of
dissolved solids, is followed along its path through time, the concentration
of dissolved solids will change. This change results from chemical and physical processes such as mixing of particles of different compositions, decomposition of dissolved solids, diffusion, absorption, etc. If the moving water
particles are observed at a fixed point in a ground water body, the concentration of dissolved solids will vary in time. This variation in concentration is
due to differences in travel time of the passing particles and the different
starting points of the particles.

          An example of flow in brackish water is given in fig. 5.3. Particles
that originally found themselves at P_1 and P_2, will successively arrive at P.
Because of the longer travelling time of the particle originating from P_2,
there is more opportunity for decomposition of the dissolved solids in that
particle, apart from the differences in concentration that originally were
present at P_1 and P_2. This example assumes steady flow. If the boundary
values are varied and also in non-steady flow, the streamlines will change,
which will lead to a much more complicated relation between groundwater flow
and groundwater quality.

          In general one may say that flow of groundwater, either under
natural conditions or generated artificially, will be accompanied by changes
in water quality.

          In particular cases, determination of groundwater quality as a func-
tion of time, can even lead to conclusions about the origin of the groundwater.

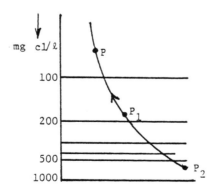

Fig. 5.3

Changes in the quality of groundwater need not always be accompanied by groundwater flow, as can be seen on the phenomenon of diffusion. On the other hand, differences in water quality of neighboring particles even may lead to groundwater flow, if these differences are coupled with differences in density. This is called density flow.

In practice, the relationships between groundwater flow and quality play an important role, which will increase in the future because of the increasing complexity of society, environmental pollution and increasing demand for drinking water of good quality.

Among practical groundwater quality problems, salt-fresh water problems are very important, especially salt water intrusion in coastal areas under natural conditions, or caused by human activities such as groundwater abstraction, both subjects of this monograph.

In general, solution of this kind of problem involves the determination of the variation of the groundwater quality, that means the chlorine content with time and place in the relevant flow field. If, for example, a water company operating near a coast wants to enlarge the pumping capacities, the question arises to what extent the abstraction of fresh groundwater can go on without attracting water of inferior quality (saline water), and if this happens, how long before water with an unacceptable Cl-content will reach the wells?

To obtain numerical results for such a problem and determine the Cl-concentrations quantitatively as a function of time and place, a good insight is required of the groundwater flow in the case under consideration. A calculation of the flow picture is necessary, and the basis of solving salt-fresh water problems must be a good knowledge of the calculation methods for groundwater flow problems in general.

If water quality plays an important role in groundwater flow, we must distinguish between a number of categories of flow, each of which requires a different calculation method. In the next section several kinds of groundwater flow in relation to groundwater quality, with methods of numerical calculation, will be described, while later in this chapter some calculation methods will be described in detail, laying emphasis on those methods which will be most applicable in practice.

5.2.2   Calculation possibilities

Groundwater flow can be divided into two main categories: Darcy flow and non-Darcy flow. The latter may occur, for example, in karstic areas, although in most natural situations and also under man's influence Darcy's flow is a good approximation.

In Darcy flow for salt-fresh water problems, one may distinguish between single-phase flow and multiple-phase flow.

A. Single phase flow

Here the assumption is made that the differences in concentration of the dissolved solids do not influence the flow picture; differences in density are neglected and only one single fluid with different contents of solids is taken into account.

B. Multiple phase flow, mostly two phases. Here two kinds of flow may take place:

1. Flow of miscible liquids. In this case the fluids are completely soluble in each other and will mix together. There is no abrupt interface between the liquids and the phenomenon of dispersion occurs.

2. Flow of immiscible liquids. The fluids are not soluble in each other and they do not mix. There is a distinct interface between the fluids on a microscopic scale, that means in every pore of the medium where both liquids are present.

Examples of two-phase flow of immiscible fluids are oil and water or water and air. In the case of oil-water flow, simultaneous flow of two liquids must be considered.

Flow of water and air takes place in the unsaturated zone. It requires the same calculation method as for water-oil flow with the only difference that the flow of air is neglected in many instances.

As flow of immiscible fluids is not relevant for fresh-salt water problems, it will not be discussed in this chapter.

Salt, brackish and fresh water are completely soluble in each other, for that reason salt-fresh water problems belong to the category of two-phase flow of miscible liquids. In theory an abrupt interface between fresh and salt water is not possible and the hydrodynamic dispersion (and diffusion as a part of it) creates a transition zone (mixing zone), in which the chlorine content gradually changes from that of salt water via brackish water to that of fresh water.

Theoretically, problems concerning miscible fluids may be worked out by solving the differential equation with boundary values for the dispersion, together with the solution of the flow problem. This will be discussed in section 5.2.9.

Only for very simplified cases are analytical solutions available, and the application of numerical methods encounters great difficulties if the dispersion phenomenon is taken into account. It is therefore not amazing that one tries to solve salt-fresh water problems without dispersion. The dispersion may be neglected if the transition zone is small and a more or less abrupt interface of macroscopic scale can be introduced. Then the assumption is made that if the hydrological regime changes, for instance due to human activities, such as groundwater abstraction, a new equilibrium of the interface will be obtained without an appreciable transition zone as well.

Calculations of these problems with an assumed sharp interface are based on simultaneous flow of two liquids of different densities, which will be discussed in section 5.2.7.

Mostly, if two fluids with much difference in density present themselves, then the flow in the heaviest fluid can be neglected when dealing with salt-fresh water problems with a sharp interface. Only the fresh water moves, while the salt water is immobile. Then the interface is a stream surface.

In some of these cases exact analytical solutions can be found; some examples will be given in section 5.2.3.

A frequent simplification is the assumption of only horizontal flow of the fresh water, while the salt water remains immobile. This calculation method is based on the Badon Ghyben-Herzberg (BGH) principle (see chapter 3).

A further simplification is obtained if the differences in density that originate from the differences in Cl-contents can also be neglected. Then the flow problem is reduced to a simple phase system with one single fluid with different concentrations of dissolved solids (the ideal tracer). The method of moving fronts can be applied in these cases, as will be seen in section 5.2.4.

The two methods, the BGH and moving fronts methods, are best suited for practical use and will be treated extensively. For both methods it holds that a good knowledge of the calculation methods for groundwater flow in general must exist. In the next paragraph an overall view of mathematical analysis of steady and non-steady two- and three-dimensional flow is therefore given.

5.2.3   Analytical calculation methods for groundwater flow in general

A. Importance of vertical flow

In general, most problems concerning groundwater flow, are dealt with in a one-dimensional way; that means that only horizontal flow in the aquifer towards wells, drains, canals, reservoirs, etc., is considered and if possible they are treated as stationary problems. This is in a way understandable, because, if the problem is treated one-dimensionally and stationary, it is governed by a one-dimensional or ordinary differential equation, which in most cases can be solved easily. In fact, in many geohydrological problems, when a steady state presents itself and where for instance the magnitudes of the seepage through a dam or the discharge of a series of pumping wells are the unknowns to be solved, neglecting the vertical flow is acceptable. Even in problems of partial penetrating wells, canals, etc., difficulties can be avoided by application of the rule that at a distance of

$$\sim 1.5b \ \sqrt{\frac{k_v}{k_h}}$$

the effect of the partial penetration will have vanished, in which b   = thickness of the aquifer

k_v, k_h = coefficients of vertical and horizontal permeability respectively.

However, as soon as groundwater flow computation must be performed in order to get a better insight into the attracting and especially into the raising of deeper groundwater with a higher Cl-content, the vertical components of the groundwater velocity must be taken into account. When dealing with one aquifer, or, in case of more aquifers separated by semipermeable layers, the problem must be treated as with horizontal flow in the aquifers and vertical flow through the semi-permeable layers (fig. 5.4).

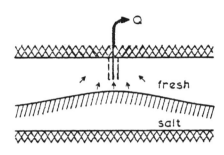

Fig.   5.4

Thus one arrives at a basic rule: In most cases, salt water intrusion problems in groundwater flow can only be treated adequately by means of two- or three-dimensional analysis with even an extra dimension, the time, in non-steady cases.

The main consequence of this rule is that, if exact solutions are desired, methods must be available to solve partial differential equations, or in the case of multi-layer systems, to solve simultaneous differential equations, with boundary values.

Of course, in most cases only numerical or analog solutions can be found. In fact, for complicated problems only these devices may lead to an acceptable result, but exact solutions, if practical, are always preferable.

A second consequence of the given rule is that if vertical flow presents itself, the anisotropy may also play a role. Anisotropy of the underground means that unlike isotropic ground, the permeability coefficient of the ground varies with the direction, in a homogeneous anisotropic aquifer this variation being the same in every point of the aquifer.

In practice, in sediments, anisotropy occurs more frequently than isotropy; especially the difference in vertical and horizontal permeability plays an important role. This difference can be considerable, and a horizontal permeability of over 50 times the vertical permeability is not unusual. For this reason the following rule holds: With regard to sediment layers with salt water intrusion problems, the anisotropy of the underground always should be taken into account.

If anisotropy is neglected and the horizontal permeability is chosen to represent the whole aquifer, the results of the calculation of, for instance, an upconing of a salt water body will be inaccurate, as the calculated vertical groundwater velocities will be too high in comparison to the real velocities.

In analytical computations the anisotropy does not cause much trouble if the directions of the main permeabilities coincide with the directions of the coordinate axes, as will usually be the case. Then, by means of a skillful substitution, the difference in the permeabilities can be eliminated in the differential equation without affecting its character.

For example, consider the differential equation for two-dimensional non-steady flow:

$$k_h \frac{\partial^2 \phi}{\partial x^2} + k_v \frac{\partial^2 \phi}{\partial z^2} = S_s \frac{\partial \phi}{\partial t}$$

ϕ = water head (L)

k_h, k_v = horizontal, vertical permeability (L/T)

x, z = horizontal, vertical coordinates (L)

t = time (T)

S_s = specific storage coefficient (1/L).

Divide by k_h and put $\dfrac{k_v}{k_h} = a^2$

$$\frac{\partial^2 \phi}{\partial x^2} + a^2 \frac{\partial^2 \phi}{\partial z^2} = \frac{S_s}{k_h} \cdot \frac{\partial \phi}{\partial t} \ .$$

Substitute $Z = az_1$, then:

$$\frac{\partial^2 \phi}{\partial z^2} = \frac{1}{a^2} \frac{\partial^2 \phi}{\partial z_1^2}$$

and the differential equation becomes:

$$\frac{\partial^2 \phi}{\partial x^2} + \frac{\partial^2 \phi}{\partial z_1^2} = \frac{S_s}{k_h} \frac{\partial \phi}{\partial t}$$

and this is again the 'normal' differential equation for isotropic ground with one permeability (the horizontal one) for all directions: the groundwater body has been expanded figuratively in the z-direction with a factor $\frac{1}{a}$ (> 1 if $k_v < k_h$).

In this connection it must be pointed out that in anisotropic ground the stream and equipotential lines are not perpendicular to each other (except at points where a streamline has the direction of one of the main permeabilities).

-132-

By means of special non-steady pumping tests with partial penetrating pumping wells and observation wells at several depths, the values of the horizontal as well as of the vertical permeability may be determined.

B. Differential equations

The general differential equation for three-dimensional non-steady groundwater flow in the saturated zone in homogeneous, isotropic ground, is as follows:

$$\frac{\partial^2 \varphi}{\partial x^2} + \frac{\partial^2 \varphi}{\partial y^2} + \frac{\partial^2 \varphi}{\partial z^2} + F(x,y,z,t) = \frac{S_s}{k} \frac{\partial \varphi}{\partial t}$$

in which

φ = the potential head of the groundwater

x,y,z = space variables

t = time variable

S_s = specific storage coefficient

$F(x,y,z,t)$ = a function that denotes the way in which water is generated or abstracted into or from the groundwater body under consideration.

In dealing with steady flow the term with $\frac{\partial \varphi}{\partial t}$ must be cancelled out. Without injection or abstraction the term F can also be deleted. In that case the differential equation for steady flow through homogeneous isotropic ground reduces to the three-dimensional differential equation of Laplace:

$$\frac{\partial^2 \varphi}{\partial x^2} + \frac{\partial^2 \varphi}{\partial y^2} + \frac{\partial^2 \varphi}{\partial z^2} = 0 \ .$$

If there is axial symmetry, the use of cylindrical coordinates is obvious; the differential equation then becomes:

$$\frac{\partial^2 \varphi}{\partial r^2} + \frac{1}{r} \frac{\partial \varphi}{\partial r} + \frac{\partial^2 \varphi}{\partial z^2} = 0 \ .$$

The greater number of salt water intrusion problems will be governed by the two following differential equations and this paper is restricted to these:

1^e $\dfrac{\partial^2 \varphi}{\partial x^2} + \dfrac{\partial^2 \varphi}{\partial y^2} = \dfrac{S_s}{k} \dfrac{\partial \varphi}{\partial t}$ (two-dimensional flow)

2^c $\dfrac{\partial^2 \varphi}{\partial r^2} + \dfrac{1}{r} \dfrac{\partial \varphi}{\partial r} + \dfrac{\partial^2 \varphi}{\partial z^2} = \dfrac{S_s}{k} \dfrac{\partial \varphi}{\partial t}$ (three-dimensional axial symmetric flow)

and to the analog equations for steady flow (without $\frac{\partial \varphi}{\partial t}$).

All these equations are partial differential equations and the main problem with them is that unlike ordinary differential equations, a general solution with some constants cannot be found. A partial differential equation has to be solved with the initial and boundary values. There are adequate methods to solve partial differential equations and some of them will be treated below.

C. Conformal mapping

In the first place the very elegant method of conformal mapping must be mentioned. This method may be used if the problem is a so-called potential flow problem, governed by the differential equation:

$$\frac{\partial^2 \phi}{\partial x^2} + \frac{\partial^2 \phi}{\partial z^2} = 0$$

or

$$\frac{\partial^2 \phi}{\partial x^2} + \frac{\partial^2 \phi}{\partial y^2} = 0 \; ,$$

the last one not being of interest for upcoming problems (only horizontal flow in two directions).

This method is treated in many handbooks on hydrology, and for the time being please refer to these books (for a thorough treatment see Polubarinova-Kochina, 1962). Almost every potential flow problem in homogeneous confined aquifers with constant thickness and straight boundaries, and a number of phreatic water or a salt-fresh water interface problems can be solved exactly by means of this complex plane method, especially with the Schwarz-Christoffel and hodograph version of it (see also section 5.2.6.).

D. Integral transformations

A disadvantage of the method of conformal mapping is that only steady two-dimensional problems can be solved and as soon as time or a third dimension or seepage through a semi-permeable layer present themselves, it cannot be used and other methods have to be applied. Among them, the integral transformation methods are very powerful tools for obtaining exact solutions, but they are surprisingly little known or at least scarcely applied in geohydrology.

The integral transformation techniques are based on the fact that by means of a skillful substitution in integral form, one of the dimensions of the differential equation can be eliminated, and by continuing this procedure, the partial differential equation can be reduced to an ordinary differential equation or even to a common algebraic equation, which usually can be solved with help of the transformed boundary values.

The solution obtained in this way must undergo reverse transformations in order to obtain the desired solution of the problem.

(a)   Laplace transformation

The Laplace transformation is generally used to eliminate the time variable; so it is most frequently applied to non-steady problems. The following example will show us the procedure.

Consider a confined aquifer of thickness b, infinitely extended in the y-direction and semi-infinitely in the x-direction (o < x < ∞) while the aquifer at x = 0 is openly connected to an infinite, fully penetrating canal.

By means of a sudden lowering of the canal level, which then is kept constant, a drawdown of the piezometric head, dependent on time and place, is introduced. The initial drawdown is assumed to be zero (fig. 5.5).

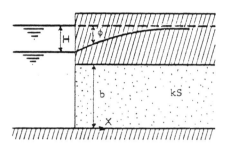

Fig.   5.5

The problem is non-steady and one-dimensional in space (only x-coordinate). The drawdown ϕ must be determined as a function of x and t:

$$\phi = \phi(x,t) \ .$$

The boundary value problem becomes:

$$\frac{\partial^2 \phi}{\partial x^2} = \frac{S}{kD} \cdot \frac{\partial \phi}{\partial t}$$

$\phi(x,o) = 0$, $\phi(o,t) = H$, $\phi(\infty,t) = 0$

in which k and S represent the permeability and the storage coefficient of the aquifer respectively.

Now the unknown function $\phi(x,t)$ is multiplied by the factor e^{-st} and integrated with respect to t from zero to infinity, thus obtaining a new function, independent of t:

$$L\{\phi(x,t)\} = \int_o^\infty e^{-st} \cdot \phi(x,t)dt = \bar{\phi}(x,s) \text{ (s an arbitrary positive value)}.$$

This operation on the function $\phi(x,t)$ is called the Laplace transformation of $\phi(x,t)$ and the new function is called the Laplace_transform which will usually be indicated by L{ϕ} or by means of a bar: $\bar{\phi}(x,s)$ or shortly $\bar{\phi}$.

The same operation applying to the differential equation gives:

$$L\left\{\frac{\partial\phi}{\partial t}\right\} = \int_0^\infty \frac{\partial\phi}{\partial t}\cdot e^{-st}\, dt = \int_0^\infty e^{-st}\, d\phi = \left[\phi e^{-st}\right]_0^\infty - \int_0^\infty d(e^{-st}) =$$

$$- \phi(x,o) + s\int_0^\infty e^{-st}\,\phi(x,t)dt = s\bar\phi - \phi(x,o)$$

and

$$L\left\{\frac{\partial^2\phi}{\partial x^2}\right\} = \int_0^\infty \frac{\partial^2\phi}{\partial x^2} e^{-st}\, dt = \frac{\partial^2}{\partial x^2}\int_0^\infty \phi e^{-st}\, dt = \frac{\partial^2\bar\phi}{\partial x^2}\ .$$

The transformed differential equation becomes:

$$\frac{\partial^2\bar\phi}{\partial x^2} = \beta^2\, s\bar\phi - \beta^2\bar\phi(x,o)\ ;$$

as $\phi(x,o) = 0$ (initial value):

$$\frac{\partial^2\phi}{\partial x^2} - \beta^2\, s\bar\phi = 0 \qquad\text{with}\qquad \beta^2 = \frac{S}{kb}\ .$$

This differential equation is an ordinary one, with only one variable x and the device of the transformation is obvious: to eliminate the differential quotient $\frac{\partial\phi}{\partial t}$ and to reduce it to the transformed function $\bar\phi$. A further advantage of the transformation is that the initial value at the same time is incorporated.

Now the two remaining boundary values still have to be transformed:

$$\bar\phi\,(\infty,s) = o \qquad\text{and}\qquad \bar\phi\,(o,s) = \int_0^\infty H.e^{-st}dt = \left[-\frac{H}{s}\,e^{-st}\right]_0^\infty = \frac{H}{s}\ .$$

The transformed boundary value problem thus becomes:

$$\frac{\partial^2\bar\phi}{\partial x^2} - \beta^2\, s\phi = 0\ , \qquad \bar\phi\,(\infty,s) = 0\ , \qquad \bar\phi\,(o,s) = \frac{H}{s}$$

with the transformed solution:

$$\bar\phi(x,s) = \frac{H}{s}\,e^{-\beta x\sqrt{s}}\ .$$

From tables of Laplace transforms the reverse transform can be found as:

$$\phi(x,t) = H\,\text{erfc}\left(\frac{\beta x}{2\sqrt{t}}\right) = H\,\text{erfc}\left(\frac{x}{2}\sqrt{\frac{S}{kbt}}\right)$$

and this is the desired exact solution, in which erfc(z) = complementary error function $= 1 - \text{erf}(z) = 1 - \frac{2}{\sqrt{\pi}}\int_0^z e^{-\lambda^2}\, d\lambda$ and indeed, the Laplace transform of this solution is:

$$L\left[H\int_0^\infty e^{-st}\, \text{erfc}\left(\frac{\beta x}{2\sqrt{t}}\right) dt\right] = \frac{H}{s}\, e^{-\beta x\sqrt{s}}\;.$$

Similar problems with varying water table in the canal and even variations according to an arbitrary function of the time f(t) can be solved easily by means of the Laplace transformation technique. Besides this, numerous other examples could have been given, but from this simple example, the importance of the Laplace transformation method for solution of non-steady problems will have become clear.

The case presented represents the fluctuations of the groundwater head in a coastal aquifer due to sea tides or canal operation when density differences can be neglected.

(b)   Hankel transformations

The Hankel transformations can be divided into finite and infinite Hankel transformations. Both transformations are applied to axial-symmetric problems, that is in all problems where the independent variable r plays a role.

The _infinite Hankel transformation_ is the operation in which the unknown function $\varphi(r)$ is multiplied by the factor $r\, J_0(\alpha r)$ and the product is integrated with respect to r from zero to infinity, thus obtaining a new function, denoted as $H\{\varphi(r)\}$ or $\varphi(r)$, _independent of r_:

$$\varphi(\alpha) = \int_0^\infty r\, \varphi(r)\, J_0(\alpha r)dr$$

in which $J_0(\alpha r)$ is the Bessel function of the first kind and of zero order and α has an arbitrary positive value.

For instance, the transform of $f(r) = \frac{1}{r}\, e^{-cr}$ becomes:

$$f(\alpha) = \int_0^\infty \frac{1}{r}\, e^{-cr} \cdot r\, J_0(\alpha r)dr = \int_0^\infty e^{-cr}\, J_0(\alpha r)dr = \frac{1}{\sqrt{\alpha^2 + c^2}}$$

$$\text{(Laplace integral)}.$$

The main property from which the infinite Hankel transformation derives its value is that it reduces the terms $\dfrac{d^2\varphi}{dr^2} + \dfrac{1}{r}\dfrac{d\varphi}{dr}$, which always occur in the differential equations of axial-symmetric problems, to the transformed function itself, as can be shown as follows:

$$\int_0^\infty \left(\frac{d^2\varphi}{dr^2} + \frac{1}{r}\frac{d\varphi}{dr}\right) r\, J_0(\alpha r)dr = \int_0^\infty \left\{\frac{1}{r}\frac{d}{dr}\left(r\frac{d\varphi}{dr}\right)\right\} r\, J_0(\alpha r)dr$$

$$= \int_0^\infty J_0(\alpha r)\, d\left(r\frac{d\varphi}{dr}\right) = J_0(\alpha r)\, r\frac{d\varphi}{dr} - \int_0^\infty r\frac{d\varphi}{dr}\, d\,\{J_0(\alpha r)\}$$

$$= J_0(\alpha r)\, r\frac{d\varphi}{dr} + \alpha \int_0^\infty r\, J_1(\alpha r)\, d\varphi$$

$$= J_0(\alpha r) \, r \, \frac{d\phi}{dr} + \alpha r \, J_1(\alpha r) \cdot \phi - \alpha \int_0^\infty \phi \, d \, \{r \, J_1(\alpha r)\}$$

$$= r \, J_0(\alpha r) \, \frac{d\phi}{dr} + \alpha r \, J_1(\alpha r) \, \phi - \alpha^2 \int_0^\infty \phi \, r \, J_0(\alpha r) \, dr$$

$$= \left[r \, J_0(\alpha r) \, \frac{d\phi}{dr} + \alpha r \, J_1(\alpha r) \, \phi \right]_0^\infty - \alpha^2 \phi \, (\alpha),$$

in which $J_1(\alpha r)$ = Bessel function of the first kind and first order.

So, if the function $\phi(r)$ satisfies the condition that both ϕ and $\frac{d\phi}{dr}$ vanish for $r = \infty$, we obtain:

$$H \left\{ \frac{d^2\phi}{dr^2} + \frac{1}{r} \frac{d\phi}{dr} \right\} = - \lim_{r \to 0} \, (r \, \frac{d\phi}{dr}) - \alpha^2 \phi \, (\alpha) \ .$$

Hence, application of the infinite Hankel transformation is possible for an axial-symmetric problem for which the horizontal velocity at $r = 0$ is given and the potential drawdown or elevation and the groundwater velocity at infinity can be assumed zero.

From the theory of Bessel functions it is known that an arbitrary function $f(r)$ under certain conditions can be represented by the Hankel integral, as follows:

$$f(r) = \int_0^\infty \alpha \, A(\alpha) \, J_0(r\alpha) \, d\alpha$$

in which

$$A(\alpha) = \int_0^\infty r \, f(r) \, J_0(\alpha r) \, dr \ .$$

As $A(\alpha)$ is the Hankel transform of $f(r)$ or $A(\alpha) = f(\alpha)$, the inverse Hankel transformation turns out to be very simple:

$$\phi(r) = \int_0^\infty \alpha \, \phi \, (\alpha) \, J_0(r\alpha) \, d\alpha \ .$$

As an example, consider infiltration with a constant velocity q from a circular pond into an assumed infinitely thick aquifer, which will yield a steady curved phreatic surface (fig. 5.6).

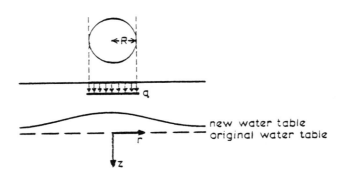

Fig. 5.6

For simplification the water table aquifer may be approximated by a confined aquifer in such a way that the original horizontal water table coincides with the bottom of the impermeable layer that covers the aquifer, while water supply takes place at the rate q per unit time per unit area over a circular disc. The boundary conditions of the curved unknown phreatic surface are thus reduced to boundary conditions in a fixed plane. Now the elevation ϕ of the original piezometric head has to be determined as a function of r and z: $\phi = \phi(r,z)$ (fig. 5.7).

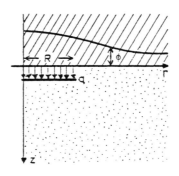

Fig. 5.7

The boundary value problem can be translated mathematically as follows:

$$\frac{\partial^2 \phi}{\partial r^2} + \frac{1}{r} \frac{\partial \phi}{\partial r} + \frac{\partial^2 \phi}{\partial z^2} = 0$$

$$\phi (\infty,z) = 0 \qquad \frac{\partial \phi}{\partial r} (o,z) = 0$$

$$\phi (r,\infty) = 0 \qquad \frac{\partial \phi}{\partial z} (r,o) = -\frac{q}{k} \text{ for } o < r < R$$

$$= o \text{ for } r > R .$$

The Hankel transformation with respect to r of the discontinuous boundary condition for z = 0 yields:

$$\frac{\partial \phi}{\partial z} (\alpha,0) = \int_0^\infty \frac{\partial \phi}{\partial z} (r,o) \, r \, J_0(\alpha r) \, dr = -\frac{q}{k} \int_0^R r \, J_0(\alpha r) \, dr$$

$$= -\frac{qR}{k\alpha} J_1(\alpha R)$$

whereupon the transformed boundary value problem becomes:

$$\frac{\partial^2 \phi}{\partial z^2} - \alpha^2 \phi = 0, \qquad \phi (\alpha,\infty) = 0, \qquad \frac{\partial \phi}{\partial z} (\alpha,o) = -\frac{qR}{k\alpha} J_1 (\alpha R) .$$

The solution of this ordinary differential equation is:

$$\phi (\alpha,z) = \frac{qR}{k\alpha^2} J_1(\alpha R) e^{-\alpha z} .$$

Inverse infinite Hankel transformation gives the desired solution:

$$\phi(r,z) = \frac{qR}{k} \int_0^\infty \frac{1}{a} J_1(Ra) J_0(ra) e^{-za} \, da$$

which expression can be evaluated in infinite series and thus calculated for every value of r and z. Along the coordinate axes the integral function reduces to transcendental functions.

For example, along the z-axis:

$$\phi(o,z) = \frac{qR}{k} \int_0^\infty \frac{1}{a} J_1(Ra) e^{-za} \, da = \frac{q}{k} \left[-z + \sqrt{R^2 + z^2} \right] \quad \text{(Laplace integral)}$$

and along the r-axis:

$$\phi(r,o) = \frac{qR}{k} \int_0^\infty \frac{1}{a} J_1(Ra) J_0(ra) \, da \quad \text{(Weber-Schaftheitlin integral)} ,$$

i) for r < R; $\phi(r,o) = \dfrac{2qr}{\pi k} E\left(\dfrac{r^2}{R^2}\right)$;

ii) for R > r; $\phi(r,o) = \dfrac{2q \, (R^2 - r^2)}{\pi k r} K\left(\dfrac{R^2}{r^2}\right) + \dfrac{2qr}{\pi k} E\left(\dfrac{R^2}{r^2}\right)$

in which K(z) and E(z) represent complete elliptic integrals of the first and second kinds, respectively.

From the theory of Bessel function it is known that under certain conditions an arbitrary function can be represented by a so called Fourier-Bessel series:

$$f(x) = \sum_{n=1}^\infty c_n J_0\left(\frac{a_n x}{a}\right) = c_1 J_0\left(\frac{a_1 x}{a}\right) + c_2 J_0\left(\frac{a_2 x}{a}\right) + \cdots \text{ ad infinitum}$$

with

$$c_n = \frac{2}{a^2 J_1^2(a_n)} \int_0^a x \, f(x) J_0\left(\frac{a_n x}{a}\right) dx$$

and in which a_n (n = 1, 2, ...) are the successive roots of the equation $J_0(a) = 0$.

Now we can consider the integral in this expression as an operation performed on the function f(x). This operation is called the finite Hankel transformation. For instance:

$$H_n \{\phi(r)\} = \int_0^R r\phi(r) J_0\left(\frac{a_n r}{R}\right) dr = \phi(n) .$$

The inverse transform can be determined immediately:

$$c_n = \frac{2}{R^2 J_1^2(a_n)} \phi(n)$$

and so:

$$\phi(r) = \frac{2}{R^2} \sum_{n=1}^{\infty} \phi(n) \frac{J_0 \frac{\alpha_n r}{R}}{J_1^2(\alpha_n)} \; .$$

Like the infinite Hankel transformation, the finite transformation also reduces the terms

$$\frac{d^2\phi}{dr^2} + \frac{1}{r} \frac{d\phi}{dr}$$

to the transformed function itself as follows:

$$H_n \left\{ \frac{d^2\phi}{dr^2} + \frac{1}{r} \frac{d\phi}{dr} \right\} = \alpha_n J_1(\alpha_n) \phi(R) - \lim_{r \to o} \left(r\frac{d\phi}{dr} \right) - \frac{\alpha_n^2}{R^2} \phi(n) \; .$$

Hence, application of the finite Hankel transformation is useful in axial-symmetric problems with given horizontal velocity at r = 0 and given potential distribution at a fixed distance from the center.

For example, calculate the unsteady drawdown distribution caused by abstracting a discharge Q from a fully penetrating well at the center of a circular island. The aquifer is assumed to be confined (fig. 5.8).

$$\phi = \phi(r,t)$$

$$\left[\begin{array}{ll} \dfrac{\partial^2\phi}{\partial r^2} + \dfrac{1}{r}\dfrac{\partial\phi}{\partial r} = \dfrac{\partial\phi}{\partial t} & \beta^2 = \dfrac{S}{kb} \\[2ex] \phi(r,o) = 0 & \phi(R,t) = 0 \\[2ex] \lim_{r \to o} r\dfrac{\partial\phi}{\partial r} = -\dfrac{Q}{2\pi kb} & \text{for } t > 0 \end{array} \right] \; .$$

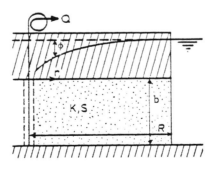

Fig. 5.8

The finite Hankel transformation with respect to n gives:

$$\left[\frac{Q}{2\pi kb} - \frac{\alpha_n^2}{R^2} \, \varphi = \beta^2 \, \frac{\partial \varphi}{\partial t} \qquad \varphi(n,o) = 0 \right]$$

an ordinary differential equation with solution:

$$\varphi(n,t) = \frac{Q}{2\pi kb} \cdot \frac{R^2}{\alpha_n^2} \left\{ 1 - \exp\left(\frac{-\alpha_n^2 t}{\beta^2 R^2} \right) \right\} .$$

The reverse Hankel transformation yields immediately:

$$\varphi(r,t) = \frac{Q}{\pi kb} \sum_{n=1}^{\infty} \frac{J_0\left(\frac{\alpha_n r}{R}\right)}{\alpha_n^2 J_1^2(\alpha_n)} \left\{ 1 - \exp\left(- \frac{\alpha_n^2 t}{\beta^2 R^2} \right) \right\} .$$

As $\displaystyle\sum_{n=1}^{\infty} \frac{J_0\left(\frac{\alpha_n r}{R}\right)}{\alpha_n^2 J_1^2(\alpha_n)}$ is the Fourier-Bessel representation on the interval $a \leq r \leq R$ of the function: $\frac{1}{2} \ln \frac{R}{r}$, we get:

$$\varphi(r,t) = \frac{Q}{2\pi kb} \ln \frac{R}{r} - \frac{Q}{\pi kb} \sum_{n=1}^{\infty} \frac{J_0\left(\frac{\alpha_n r}{R}\right)}{\alpha_n J_1^2(\alpha_n)} \exp\left(\frac{-\alpha_n^2 kbt}{R^2 S} \right) .$$

If t tends to infinity the series vanishes, and the well known solution for the steady state is obtained:

$$\varphi(r) = \frac{Q}{2\pi kb} \ln \frac{R}{r} .$$

(c)   Fourier transformations

The Fourier transformations can be divided into the:

(1)   Infinite sine transformation

(2)   Infinite cosine transformation

(3)   Finite sine transformation

(4)   Finite cosine transformation

These transformations are useful in solving problems which are two-dimensional, as they all eliminate the second differential quotient of a variable, e.g., $\dfrac{\partial^2 \varphi}{\partial x^2}$ or $\dfrac{\partial^2 \varphi}{\partial z^2}$.

The operations necessary for these transformations are similar to those of the Hankel transforms and it will suffice to refer to the survey of integral transforms of table 5.1.

Table 5.1 - Survey of integral transformations.

	Transformation	Main property	Inverse transform
Laplace	$L\{\phi(t)\} = \bar{\phi}(s)$ $= \int_0^\infty \phi(t)e^{-st}dt$	$L\left\{\dfrac{\partial\phi}{\partial t}\right\} = s\bar{\phi} - \phi(o)$	a. by means of operations and from tables b. by integration in the complex plane
Fourier A. Finite 1. sine	$S_n\{\phi(x)\} = \breve{\phi}(n)$ $= \int_0^a \phi(x)\sin\dfrac{n\pi x}{a}\,dx$	$S_n\left\{\dfrac{\partial^2\phi}{\partial x^2}\right\}$ $= -\left(\dfrac{n\pi}{a}\right)^2\breve{\phi} + \dfrac{n\pi}{a}\{\phi(o) - (-1)^n\phi(a)\}$	$S_n^{-1}\{\breve{\phi}(n)\} = \phi(x)$ $= \dfrac{2}{a}\sum_{n=1}^\infty \breve{\phi}(n)\sin\dfrac{n\pi x}{a}$
2. cosine	$C_n\{\phi(x)\} = \breve{\phi}(n)$ $= \int_0^a \phi(x)\cos\dfrac{n\pi x}{a}\,dx$	$C_n\left\{\dfrac{\partial^2\phi}{\partial x^2}\right\}$ $= -\left(\dfrac{n\pi}{a}\right)^2\breve{\phi} + (-1)^h\dfrac{\partial\phi}{\partial x}(a) - \dfrac{\partial\phi}{\partial x}(o)$	$C_n^{-1}\{\breve{\phi}(n)\} = \phi(x)$ $= \dfrac{1}{a}\phi(o) + \dfrac{2}{a}\sum_{n=1}^\infty \breve{\phi}\cos\dfrac{n\pi x}{a}$
B. Infinite 1. sine	$S\{\phi(x)\} = \hat{\phi}(\alpha)$ $\int_0^\infty \phi(x)\sin(\alpha x)dx$	$S\left\{\dfrac{\partial^2\phi}{\partial x^2}\right\}$ $= -\alpha^2\hat{\phi} + \alpha\phi(o)$ with $\phi(\infty) = \dfrac{\partial\phi}{\partial x}(\infty) = 0$	$S^{-1}\{\hat{\phi}(\alpha)\} = \phi(x)$ $= \dfrac{2}{\pi}\int_0^\infty \hat{\phi}(\alpha)\sin(x\alpha)d\alpha$

Table 5.1 (continued)

Transformation	Main property	Inverse transform
2. cosine $C\{\phi(x)\} = \hat{\phi}(\alpha)$ $$= \int_0^\infty \phi(x)\cos(\alpha x)dx$$	$C\left\{\dfrac{\partial^2 \phi}{\partial x^2}\right\}$ $$= -\alpha^2 \hat{\phi} - \frac{\partial \phi}{\partial x}(o)$$ with $$\phi(\infty) = \frac{\partial \phi}{\partial x}(\infty) = 0$$	$C^{-1}\{\hat{\phi}(\alpha)\} = \phi(\alpha)$ $$= \frac{2}{\pi}\int_0^\infty \phi(\alpha)\cos(x\alpha)d\alpha$$
Hankel A. Finite $H_n\{\phi(r)\} = \hat{\phi}(n)$ $$\int_0^R r\phi(r) J_0\,\frac{a_n r}{R}\,dr$$ with a_n the roots of $$J_0(a) = 0$$	$H_n\left\{\dfrac{\partial^2 \phi}{\partial r^2} + \dfrac{1}{r}\dfrac{\partial \phi}{\partial r}\right\}$ $$= a_n J_1(a_n)\phi(R) - \lim_{r\to o} r\,\frac{\partial \phi}{\partial r}$$ $$- \frac{a_n^2}{R^2}\hat{\phi}(n)$$	$H_n^{-1}\{\hat{\phi}(n)\} = \phi(r)$ $$= \frac{2}{R^2}\sum_{n=1}^\infty \hat{\phi}(n)\,\frac{J_0\left(\dfrac{a_n r}{R}\right)}{J_1^2(a_n)}$$
B. Infinite $H\{\phi(r)\} = \phi(\alpha)$ $$= \int_0^\infty r\phi(r) J_0(\alpha r)dr$$	$H\left\{\dfrac{\partial^2 \phi}{\partial r^2} + \dfrac{1}{r}\dfrac{\partial \phi}{\partial r}\right\}$ $$= -\lim_{r\to o}\left(r\,\frac{\partial \phi}{\partial r}\right) - \alpha^2 \phi$$ with $$\phi(\infty) = \frac{\partial \phi}{\partial r}(\infty) = 0$$	$H^{-1}\{\phi(\alpha)\} = \phi(r)$ $$= \int_0^\infty \alpha\,\phi\, J_0(r\alpha)d\alpha$$

5.2.4   Method of moving fronts

This method is based on the assumption that the differences in density, caused by the differences in Cl⁻ contents of the various parts of the fluid, may be neglected. There is only one fluid with different Cl⁻ concentrations, and these do not influence the flow pattern. An interface between two different concentrations, when compared with a two phase flow, is no longer a stream surface; the streamlines pass right across it.

The consequence is that each particle of an interface, or a front as it is called under these circumstances, follows along its own streamline, so that at each time step after the beginning of the (steady) flow, the front possesses another shape and has been preceded in the flow direction. This process ends only if the groundwater at one side of the front has been completely replaced by the groundwater at the other side. No equilibrium of the front or interface will be reached.

As an illustration of this method of moving fronts in comparison with a stationary interface, the following example may serve: A difference of level of surface water between both sides of a long barrier causes a two-dimensional groundwater flow in a thick aquifer in which at a certain depth a horizontal interface between fresh and salt (brackish) water exists, as shown in figure 5.9. In A it is assumed that the density differences between fresh and salt water are such that the flow of the salt water may be neglected. The interface is a streamline (stream surface) and after some time a new equilibrium of this interface will be reached.

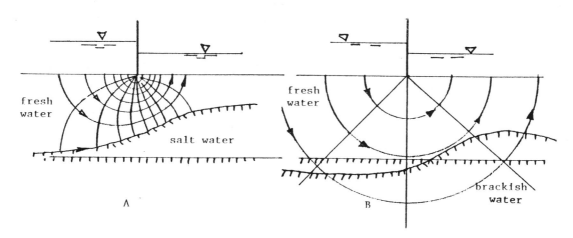

Fig.   5.9

On the contrary, in B it is assumed that brackish water is present beneath the horizontal interface and that the Cl⁻ content of that water is such that the difference in density with that of the overlying fresh water can be neglected. The interface in this case is not a stream surface, but behaves as a moving front which position is dependent on time. A feature of a front is that it always is composed of the same group of particles.

Neglecting the density differences is possibly allowable up to 4000 to 5000 mg/l Cl⁻. It will be clear that the neglecting of the density differences and the dispersion simplifies the mathematical calculations considerably, compared with a two-phase system. In this case only flow of one fluid has to be considered and the solution can be realized analytically by means of the methods described in section 5.2.3, even for rather complicated problems.

As soon as the groundwater head or the drawdown is known as a function of location, the velocity components in the directions of the coordinate axes can be derived, after which the equations of movement for the water particles can be written down as follows:

$$v_x = k_x \frac{\partial \phi}{\partial x} = m_e \frac{dx}{dt} \qquad v_y = k_y \frac{\partial \phi}{\partial y} = m_e \frac{dy}{dt} \qquad v_z = k_z \frac{\partial \phi}{\partial z} = m_e \frac{dz}{dt}$$

in which ϕ and its derivatives to x, y and z are functions of x, y and z, while m_e = effective porosity. This system of three simultaneous differential equations can be solved numerically and can be plotted digitally in the form of lines of equal travelling times or as moving fronts.

Besides the advantage of the relatively simple calculations that are required, a very useful characteristic of the method of moving fronts originates from the fact that the movement of the various particles along the streamlines is known. For that reason one can start with an arbitrary three-dimensional distribution of Cl⁻ contents and at any place calculate the Cl⁻ concentration as a function of time. In this way the assumption of a sharp interface between fresh and salt (brackish) water is no longer necessary and the complete mixing zone between fresh and brackish water can be taken into account, which will influence the reliability of the results positively.

Also the effect of neglecting the dispersion is weakened in this way, because of the less abrupt concentration differences that occur, which will diminish the magnitude of the diffusion and thus of the dispersion.

The moving front method is a combination of an analytical method (the solution of the equations of movement and the time-dependent chloride distribution in the flow field).

5.2.5   Badon Ghyben–Herzberg Method

The Badon Ghyben–Herzberg Method (abbreviated to BGH Method, see also chapter 3), is based on the following assumptions:

1.   A sharp interface between the fresh and salt water is present.

2.   There is no flow of the fluid with the highest density; so the salt or brackish water is assumed immobile.

3.   There is only horizontal flow of the fresh water and along verticals are hydrostatic conditions.

-146-

It was shown in chapter 3 that (fig. 5.10):

$$z = \alpha h$$

in which

$$\alpha = \frac{\rho_f}{\rho_s - \rho_f}$$

ρ_f = fresh water density

ρ_s = salt water density.

The law of Darcy gives the specific discharge in x- and y-directions for an isotropic medium:

$$v_x = - k \frac{\partial h}{\partial x} \qquad v_y = - \frac{\partial h}{\partial y} .$$

We may now distinguish in calculations for phreatic, confined, semi-iconfined, non steady and multilayer conditions.

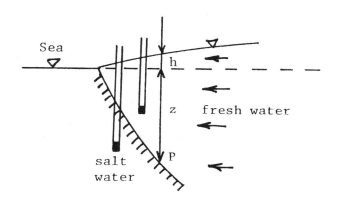

Fig. 5.10

A. Phreatic conditions

The total discharge over a vertical becomes (fig. 5.10):

$$q_x = - k \frac{\partial h}{\partial x} (z + h) = - k(1 + \alpha) h \frac{\partial h}{\partial x}$$

$$q_y = - k \frac{\partial h}{\partial y} (z + h) = - k(1 + \alpha) h \frac{\partial h}{\partial y}$$

If we assume an equivalent permeability $k^* = (1 + \alpha) k = \dfrac{\rho_s}{\rho_s - \rho_f} k$ and a new potential function $\phi = \frac{1}{2} h^2$, the equations for the discharges become:

$$q_x = - k^* \frac{\partial \phi}{\partial x} \quad \text{and} \quad q_y = - k^* \frac{\partial \phi}{\partial y} \; .$$

According to paragraph 5.4.3(B) the differential equation for two-dimensional steady flow will be:

$$\frac{\partial^2 \phi}{\partial x^2} + \frac{\partial^2 \phi}{\partial y^2} + \frac{F(x,y)}{k^*} = 0$$

and for radial steady flow:

$$\frac{\partial^2 \phi}{\partial r^2} + \frac{1}{r} \frac{\partial \phi}{\partial r} + \frac{F(x,y)}{k^*} = 0$$

in which $F(x,y)$ is a function that denotes the way in which water is generated or abstracted into or from the groundwater body under consideration. In most cases the function F represents that part of the rainfall that joins with the groundwater stock and is then equal to a constant W (recharge) or to zero. The differential equations for two-dimensional flow (radial and non-radial) then become:

$$\frac{\partial^2 \phi}{\partial x^2} + \frac{\partial^2 \phi}{\partial y^2} + \frac{W}{k^*} = 0 \quad \text{and} \quad \frac{\partial^2 \phi}{\partial r^2} + \frac{1}{r} \frac{\partial \phi}{\partial r} + \frac{W}{k^*} = 0 \; .$$

These equations are linear and identical with the differential equations for problems in steady flow in confined aquifers with one kind of fluid. The solution for phreatic fresh-salt water problems of the BGH-character thus can directly be derived from those for steady confined single phase flow by replacing k by an equivalent k* with $k^* = (1 + \alpha)k$ and the groundwater head ϕ by $\phi = \frac{1}{2}h^2$.

From the solution for the fresh water head h, the shape and the position of the interface can directly be derived by putting $z = \alpha h$.

B. Confined aquifer

In case of fully confined groundwater it is easier to work with the depth of the interface below the confining layer instead of the fresh water head (fig. 5.11).

$$v_x = - k \frac{\partial h}{\partial x} \qquad v_y = - k \frac{\partial h}{\partial y}$$
$$q_x = - kz \frac{\partial h}{\partial x} \qquad q_y = - kz \frac{\partial h}{\partial y}$$

$z + \alpha = \alpha h$ from which

$$\frac{\partial h}{\partial x} = \frac{1}{\alpha} \frac{\partial z}{\partial x} \qquad \text{and} \qquad \frac{\partial h}{\partial y} = \frac{1}{\alpha} \frac{\partial z}{\partial y},$$

$$q_x = -\frac{k}{a}\frac{\partial(\frac{1}{2}z^2)}{\partial x} \qquad q_y = -\frac{k}{a}\frac{\partial(\frac{1}{2}z^2)}{\partial y}$$

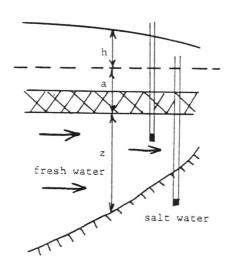

Fig. 5.11

and so the differential equations for two-dimensional radial and non-radial steady confined flow under BGH conditions become:

$$\frac{\partial^2\phi}{\partial x^2} + \frac{\partial^2\phi}{\partial y^2} + \frac{F(x,y)}{k^*} = 0 \qquad \text{and} \qquad \frac{\partial^2\phi}{\partial r^2} + \frac{1}{r}\frac{\partial\phi}{\partial r} + \frac{F(x,y)}{k^*} = 0$$

the same as for phreatic water, however with

$$k^* = \frac{k}{a} \qquad \text{and} \qquad \phi = \frac{1}{2}z^2.$$

From the solution for z, the fresh groundwater head h can be determined by means of the relation

$$ah = z + a$$

in which a = constant.

Also for fully confined fresh-salt water problems of the BGH character the statement holds that their solutions directly can be derived from those for steady confined single phase flow, in this case by replacing k by $\frac{k}{a}$ and ϕ by $\frac{1}{2}z^2$ and assuming F(x,y) constant or zero.

C. Semiconfined aquifer

Under semiconfined conditions (fig. 5.12) an exchange of water through the semipermeable layer with resistance c (in days) takes place.

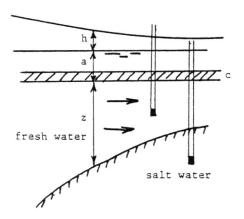

Fig.   5.12

Darcy's Law gives, like in the previous example for confined water:

$$q_x = -\frac{k}{a}\frac{\partial(\frac{1}{2}z^2)}{\partial x} \qquad q_y = -\frac{k}{a}\frac{\partial(\frac{1}{2}z^2)}{\partial y} \ .$$

The continuity equation yields:

$$\frac{\partial q_x}{\partial x} + \frac{\partial q_y}{\partial y} = -\frac{h}{c} = -\frac{z+a}{ac}$$

assuming that the salt water head equals the constant level in the upper aquifer.

The differential equation thus becomes:

$$\frac{\partial^2(\frac{1}{2}z^2)}{\partial x^2} + \frac{\partial^2(\frac{1}{2}z^2)}{\partial y^2} - \frac{z+a}{kc} = 0 \ .$$

This is a non-linear differential equation which differs from that for confined flow by the function $F(x,y)$, which is here not a constant but equal to $-\frac{z+a}{c}$.

By means of linearization of this differential equation, approximate solutions can be obtained, and also by numerical integration.

D.   <u>Non-steady conditions</u>

In a <u>water-table aquifer</u> (phreatic aquifer) the continuity equation becomes (fig. 5.10):

$$\frac{\partial q_x}{\partial x} + \frac{\partial q_y}{\partial y} + \varepsilon\frac{\partial h}{\partial t} + m_e\frac{\partial z}{\partial t} = P$$

in which ε is the specific yield of the water-table aquifer and m_e is the effective porosity.

-150-

The term $\varepsilon \frac{\partial h}{\partial t}$ describes the amount of water that will be taken into storage if the phreatic level rises, and the term $m_e \frac{\partial z}{\partial t}$ describes the amount of fresh water that replaces the salt water if the interface goes down.

With

$$q_x = - k (1 + \alpha) h \frac{\partial h}{\partial x} \qquad q_y = - k (1 + \alpha) h \frac{\partial h}{\partial y}$$

and $z = \alpha h$ the differential equation becomes:

$$\frac{\partial^2 (\frac{1}{2}h^2)}{\partial x^2} + \frac{\partial^2 (\frac{1}{2}h^2)}{\partial y^2} + \frac{W}{k(1 + \alpha)} = \frac{\varepsilon + \alpha m_e}{k(1 + \alpha)} \frac{\partial h}{\partial t} .$$

This is a non-linear equation which may be solved numerically or by linearization.

Under <u>confined conditions</u> (see Fig. 5.11) the continuity equation becomes:

$$\frac{\partial q_x}{\partial x} + \frac{\partial q_y}{\partial y} + S_s z \frac{\partial h}{\partial t} + m_e \frac{\partial z}{\partial t} = 0$$

in which S_s = specific elastic storage coefficient.

With $q_x = - \frac{k}{\alpha} \frac{\partial (\frac{1}{2}z^2)}{\partial x}$ and $q_y = - \frac{k}{\alpha} \frac{\partial (\frac{1}{2}z^2)}{\partial y}$ and $\frac{\partial h}{\partial t} = \frac{\partial}{\partial t} (z + d) \frac{1}{\alpha}$ $= \frac{1}{\alpha} \frac{\partial z}{\partial t}$, the differential equation can be derived:

$$\frac{\partial^2 (\frac{1}{2}z^2)}{\partial x^2} + \frac{\partial^2 (\frac{1}{2}z^2)}{\partial y^2} = \frac{S_s z + \alpha m_e}{k} \frac{\partial z}{\partial t} .$$

In general the elastic storage may be neglected compared with the storage due to the movement of the interface and thus the differential equation for non-steady confined flow in salt-fresh water problems under BGH conditions becomes:

$$\frac{\partial^2 (\frac{1}{2}z^2)}{\partial x^2} + \frac{\partial^2 (\frac{1}{2}z^2)}{\partial y^2} = \frac{\alpha m_e}{k} \frac{\partial z}{\partial t} .$$

Whereas for <u>semi-confined</u> flow (fig. 5.12) the differential equation:

$$\frac{\partial^2 (\frac{1}{2}z^2)}{\partial x^2} + \frac{\partial^2 (\frac{1}{2}z^2)}{\partial y^2} - \frac{z + d}{kc} = \frac{\alpha m_e}{k} \frac{\partial z}{\partial t}$$

holds, as easily may be verified.

Both differential equations are non-linear and numerical integration or linearization methods will lead to solutions.

E. Multilayers

If the geological formation under consideration consists of several aquifers separated by semi-confined layers in which groundwater flow takes place, while in the deeper aquifer a fresh-salt water interface is present, a so-called multilayer problem has to be solved.

In a similar way as has been shown in the previous cases, Darcy's law and the continuity equations now lead to a set of simultaneous non-linear differential equations which may be solved numerically.

5.2.6 Hodograph method

The hodograph method for solving fresh-salt water problems is applied to steady two dimensional potential flow in which a sharp interface exists between the moving fresh water and the immobile salt water. Then vertical flow of the fresh water is considered. The interface thus becomes a stream-line in two dimensional or a streamsurface in three dimensional flow (see fig. 5.9A).

In general a streamsurface in steady three dimensional flow can be represented by z_s as a function of x and y:

$$z_s = z_s(x,y)$$

and

$$\frac{dz_s}{dt} = \frac{\partial z_s}{\partial x} \cdot \frac{dx}{dt} + \frac{\partial z_s}{\partial y} \cdot \frac{dy}{dt}$$

holds at every point on the stream surface. In this equation, $\frac{dx}{dt}$, $\frac{dy}{dt}$ and $\frac{dz}{dt}$ are the components in the three coordinate directions of the real velocity of a groundwater particle which direction is tangent to the stream surface.

As $\frac{dx}{dt} = \frac{V_x}{m_e} = -\frac{k}{m_e} \frac{\partial \phi}{\partial x}$ etc., the differential equation for a stream surface $z_s = z_s(x,y)$ becomes:

$$\frac{\partial \phi_s}{\partial x} \cdot \frac{\partial z_s}{\partial x} + \frac{\partial \phi_s}{\partial y} \cdot \frac{\partial z_s}{\partial y} - \frac{\partial \phi_s}{\partial z} = 0$$

and in particular for the interface $z_i = z_i(x,y)$:

$$\frac{\partial \phi_i}{\partial x} \frac{\partial z_i}{\partial x} + \frac{\partial \phi_i}{\partial y} \cdot \frac{\partial z_i}{\partial y} - \frac{\partial \phi_i}{\partial z} = 0 \ . \tag{1}$$

In general the fresh water head in an arbitrary point of a steady flow field is:

$$\varphi(x,y,z) = z + \frac{p}{\rho_f g}$$

in which p is the pressure and g the acceleration of gravity. In particular, the fresh water head at a point of the interface:

$$\phi_i(x,y,z_i) = z_i + \frac{p_i}{\rho_f g} \; .$$

The salt water head at that point is:

$$\phi_{is} = z_i + \frac{p_i}{\rho_s g}$$

from which $\dfrac{p_i}{g} = \rho_s \, (\phi_{is} - z_i)$ and so the fresh water head becomes

$$\phi_i = z_i + \frac{\rho_s}{\rho_f} \, (\phi_{is} - z_i)$$

or, as the salt water is assumed to be in rest from which $\dfrac{\rho_s}{\rho_f} \phi_{is}$ is a constant = c:

$$\phi_i(x,y,z_i) = c - \frac{1}{\alpha} \, z_i(x,y) \tag{2}$$

with $\alpha = \dfrac{\rho_f}{\rho_s - \rho_f}$. This relation between the fresh water head for points on the interface and the equation of the interface itself may be compared with a similar property of the phreatic surface (line):

$$\phi_{ph}(x,y,z_{ph}) = z_{ph}(x,y) \; .$$

Differentiation of equation (2) with respect to x and y respectively yields:

$$\frac{\partial \phi_i}{\partial x} + \frac{\partial \phi_i}{\partial z_i} \cdot \frac{\partial z_i}{\partial x} = -\frac{1}{\alpha} \frac{\partial z_i}{\partial x}$$

$$\frac{\partial \phi_i}{\partial y} + \frac{\partial \phi_i}{\partial z_i} \cdot \frac{\partial z_i}{\partial y} = -\frac{1}{\alpha} \frac{\partial z_i}{\partial y}$$

from which:

$$\frac{\partial z_i}{\partial x} = -\frac{\dfrac{\partial \phi_i}{\partial x}}{\dfrac{1}{\alpha} + \dfrac{\partial \phi_i}{\partial z}} \qquad \text{and} \qquad \frac{\partial z_i}{\partial y} = -\frac{\dfrac{\partial \phi_i}{\partial y}}{\dfrac{1}{\alpha} + \dfrac{\partial \phi_i}{\partial z}} \; .$$

Replacing $\dfrac{\partial z_i}{\partial x}$ and $\dfrac{\partial z_i}{\partial y}$ in equation (1) by these expressions gives the differential equation for the salt-fresh water interface in three dimensional flow under the conditions mentioned before:

$$\left(\frac{\partial \phi_i}{\partial x}\right)^2 + \left(\frac{\partial \phi_i}{\partial y}\right)^2 + \left(\frac{\partial \phi_i}{\partial z}\right)^2 + \frac{1}{\alpha} \frac{\partial \phi_i}{\partial z} = 0 \; . \tag{3}$$

This expression can be understood as the boundary condition along the interface, which shape however is unknown before.

For a steady state, the relation between the components in the three coordinate directions of the specific discharge along the interface can be derived from equation (3) by means of $v_x = - k \frac{\partial \varphi}{\partial x}$ etc.:

$$v_x^2 + v_y^2 + v_z^2 - \frac{k}{a} v_z = 0 . \tag{4}$$

From this equation it follows that if the specific discharge vector at every point of the surface that represents the interface is plotted from an origin with coordinate axes v_x, v_y and v_z, the endpoints form a sphere with center M $(0, 0, \frac{k}{2a})$ and radius R $= \frac{k}{2a}$.

In general the vector representation of the specific discharges in points of the physical space is called the hodograph representation and we see that an abrupt interface that separates stagnant salt water from moving fresh water in three dimensional steady flow is represented by a sphere in the hodograph space. Otherwise, by hodograph representation of the specific discharge along the boundaries of the physical flow domain, a hodograph domain with its bonding hodograph surfaces is obtained. In two dimensional steady flow the physical plane is mapped onto the hodograph plane and as the a priori unknown interface line in the physical plane is transformed into a boundary of known form, that is the circle

$$v_x^2 + v_z^2 - \frac{k}{a} v_z = 0$$

in the hodograph plane, it is obvious that this property yields a method to obtain an exact solution for the flow net and for the shape of the interface by means of conformal mapping.

5.2.7   Simultaneous flow of two fluids (shearflow)

Simultaneous flow of two fluids occurs if two fluids of different density, separated by a sharp interface, move simultaneously. In this case, unlike the assumptions made in the BGH and hodograph methods, the heaviest fluid also flows, which results in a movement of the interface, and the shape and position of the interface are functions of time, which does not necessarily mean that the flow must be unsteady.

The main feature of the calculation model is that the interface completely separates the two liquids and that within each region Darcy's law is applicable, which yields, together with the continuity principle for each region separately, the Laplace differential equation (see fig. 5.13):

$$\frac{\partial^2 \varphi_j}{\partial x^2} + \frac{\partial^2 \varphi_j}{\partial y^2} + \frac{\partial^2 \varphi_j}{\partial x^2} = \frac{S_s}{k_j} \frac{\partial \varphi_j}{\partial t} \quad (j = 1,2) .$$

S_s may be the same for both regions but as:

$$k_1 = \frac{k_o \rho_1 g}{\mu_1} \text{ and } k_2 = \frac{k_o \rho_2 g}{\mu_2}$$

k_o = intrinsic permeability

μ = viscosity

the permeability coefficients differ.

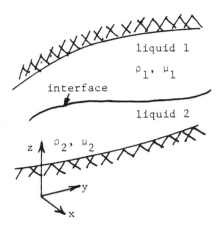

Fig. 5.13

The boundary conditions along the interface can be obtained by means of a similar procedure as in the previous paragraph; however, instead of a steady stream surface the interface here is a moving front represented by:

$$z_i = z_i(x,y,t) \ .$$

At every point of the moving front the following expression holds:

$$\frac{dz_i}{dt} = \frac{\partial z_i}{\partial x}\frac{dx}{dt} + \frac{\partial z_i}{\partial y}\frac{dy}{dt} + \frac{\partial z_i}{\partial t} \ .$$

As $\frac{dx}{dt} = \frac{v_x}{m_e} = -\frac{k_f}{m_e}\frac{\partial \phi_f}{\partial x}$ as well as $= -\frac{k_s}{m_e}\frac{\partial \phi_s}{\partial x}$, etc.

Along the interface, assuming fresh water (liquid 1) overlying salt water (liquid 2), the differential equations for the moving interface become:

$$\frac{\partial \phi_{if}}{\partial x} \cdot \frac{\partial z_i}{\partial x} + \frac{\partial \phi_{if}}{\partial y} \cdot \frac{\partial z_i}{\partial y} - \frac{\partial \phi_{if}}{\partial z} = \frac{m_e}{k_f}\frac{\partial z_i}{\partial t}$$

$$\frac{\partial \phi_{is}}{\partial x} \cdot \frac{\partial z_i}{\partial x} + \frac{\partial \phi_{is}}{\partial y} \cdot \frac{\partial z_i}{\partial y} - \frac{\partial \phi_{is}}{\partial z} = \frac{m_e}{k_f}\frac{\partial z_i}{\partial t}$$

(5)

or in terms of Darcy velocities:

$$\frac{\partial z_i}{\partial x} V_{xf} + \frac{\partial z_i}{\partial y} V_{yf} - V_{zf} + \frac{\partial z_i}{\partial t} = 0$$

$$\frac{\partial z_i}{\partial x} V_{xs} + \frac{\partial z_i}{\partial y} V_{ys} - V_{zs} + \frac{\partial z_i}{\partial t} = 0 \ .$$

Subtraction of these two equations gives at the interface a first relation between the differences of the velocities in the three coordinate directions on both sides of the interface:

$$(V_{xf} - V_{xs}) \frac{\partial z_i}{\partial x} + (V_{yf} - V_{ys}) \frac{\partial z_i}{\partial y} - (V_{zf} - V_{zs}) = 0 \ . \tag{6}$$

At a point of the interface is $\varphi_{if} = \dfrac{p_i}{\rho_f g} + z_i$ and $\phi_{is} = \dfrac{p_i}{\rho_f g} + z_i$. Elimination of p_i gives:

$$\rho_f(\phi_{if} - z_i) = \rho_s g(\phi_{is} - z_i) \tag{7}$$

at the interface.

Differentiation of (7) with respect to x yields:

$$\rho_f \left(\frac{\partial \phi_{if}}{\partial x} + \frac{\partial \phi_{if}}{\partial z} \cdot \frac{\partial z_i}{\partial x} - \frac{\partial z_i}{\partial x} \right) = \rho_s \left(\frac{\partial \phi_{is}}{\partial x} + \frac{\partial \phi_{is}}{\partial z} \cdot \frac{\partial z_i}{\partial x} - \frac{\partial z_i}{\partial x} \right)$$

and with $V_{xf} = - \dfrac{k_o \rho_f g}{\mu} \dfrac{\partial \phi_{if}}{\partial x}$, $V_{xs} = \dfrac{k_o \rho_s g}{\mu} \dfrac{\partial \phi_{is}}{\partial x}$ etc., assuming $\mu_f = \mu_s$ (equal viscosities) we arrive at a second relation between the differences of the Darcy velocities on both sides of the interface:

$$V_{xf} - V_{xs} + (V_{zf} - V_{zs}) \frac{\partial z_i}{\partial x} = \frac{k_o g}{\mu} (\rho_s - \rho_f) \frac{\partial z_i}{\partial x} \ . \tag{8}$$

In the same way, differentiating (7) with respect to y we find the third relation:

$$V_{yf} - V_{ys} + (V_{zf} - V_{zs}) \frac{\partial z_i}{\partial y} = \frac{k_o g}{\mu} (\rho_s - \rho_f) \frac{\partial z_i}{\partial y} \ . \tag{9}$$

From the three equations 6, 8 and 9 the three velocity differences can easily be solved:

$$V_{xf} - V_{xs} = \frac{\dfrac{k_o}{\mu} g (\rho_s - \rho_f) \dfrac{\partial z_i}{\partial x}}{\left(\dfrac{\partial z_i}{\partial x}\right)^2 + \left(\dfrac{\partial z_i}{\partial y}\right)^2 + 1}$$

$$V_{yf} - V_{ys} = \frac{\dfrac{k_o}{\mu} g (\rho_s - \rho_f) \dfrac{\partial z_i}{\partial y}}{\left(\dfrac{\partial z_i}{\partial x}\right)^2 + \left(\dfrac{\partial z_i}{\partial y}\right)^2 + 1}$$

$$V_{zf} - V_{zs} = \frac{\dfrac{k_o}{\mu} g (\rho_s - \rho_f) \left[\left(\dfrac{\partial z_i}{\partial x}\right)^2 + \left(\dfrac{\partial z_i}{\partial y}\right)^2 \right]}{\left(\dfrac{\partial z_i}{\partial x}\right)^2 + \left(\dfrac{\partial z_i}{\partial y}\right)^2 + 1} . \tag{10}$$

For the sake of simplicity and in order to require a better under-standing of the flow mechanism in the immediate neighborhood of the interface, we continue with the two dimensional case (no flow in y direction). Equations (10) then become with $\dfrac{\partial z_i}{\partial y} = 0$ and $\dfrac{\partial z_i}{\partial x} = tg\ \theta$ (see fig. 5.14):

$$V_{xf} - V_{xs} = \frac{k_o}{\mu} g (\rho_s - \rho_f) \sin\theta \cos\theta$$

$$V_{zf} - V_{zs} = \frac{k_o}{\mu} g (\rho_s - \rho_f) \sin^2\theta . \tag{11}$$

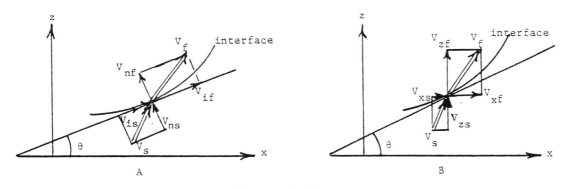

Fig. 5.14

These equations can be derived directly from the two conditions, the continuity and the equilibrium condition at the interface, as follows.

The continuity requires that V_n, the component perpendicular to the interface, is continuous. So (fig. 5.14A):

$$V_{nf} = V_{ns} . \tag{12}$$

Equilibrium requires that at the interface the pressures p_f and p_s for the fresh and the salt water are equal:

$$p_{if} = p_{is} \, . \tag{13}$$

To find a relation between the discharge components along the interface V_{if} and V_{is} we express them in terms of pressure gradients:

$$V_{if} = - \frac{k_o}{\mu} \left(\frac{\partial p_{if}}{\partial i} + g\rho_f \frac{\partial z_i}{\partial i} \right) \qquad V_{is} = - \frac{k_o}{\mu} \left(\frac{\partial p_{is}}{\partial i} + g\rho_f \frac{\partial z_i}{\partial i} \right).$$

Eliminating $\frac{\partial p_{if}}{\partial i} = \frac{\partial p_{is}}{\partial i}$ we find with $\frac{\partial z_i}{\partial i} = \sin\theta$:

$$V_{if} - V_{is} = \frac{k_o}{\mu} g \, (\rho_2 - \rho_1) \sin\theta \, . \tag{14}$$

The expressions (12) and (14) describe the behaviors of the Darcy velocity at an interface. Equation (12) says that the normal velocity component has no jump whereas equation (14) shows the magnitude of a jump parallel to the interface. This jump in the parallel flow is called shearflow, as the fluids glide over each other, such that the interface has the character of a shear plane.

With the relations $V_n = - V_x\sin\theta + V_z\cos\theta$ and $V_i = V_x\cos\theta + V_z\sin\theta$ (compare A with B in fig. 5.14), we find from (12):

$$- V_{xf}\sin\theta + V_{zf}\cos\theta = - V_{xs}\sin\theta + V_{zs}\cos\theta$$

or

$$(V_{xf} - V_{xs})\sin\theta = (V_{zf} - V_{zs})\cos\theta \tag{15}$$

and from (14):

$$V_{xf}\cos\theta + V_{zf}\sin\theta - V_{xs}\cos\theta - v_{zs}\sin\theta = \frac{k_o}{\mu} g \, (\rho_2 - \rho_1)\sin\theta \, .$$

or

$$(V_{xf} - V_{xs})\cos\theta + (V_{zf} - V_{zs})\sin\theta = \frac{k_o}{\mu} g \, (\rho_2 - \rho_1)\sin\theta \, . \tag{16}$$

Equations (15) and (16) combined give again the equations (11), which were found in a more general way.

As can be concluded from the equations (10) or (11), the differences of the velocities of the two fluids immediately on both sides of the separating interface in the three coordinate directions are dependent, apart from the physical properties of the fluids, on the slope of the interface at the point of consideration and independent of the character of the flow system.

Putting

$$d_x = V_{xf} - V_{xs} \qquad d_y = V_{yf} - V_{ys} \qquad d_z = V_{zf} - V_{zs}$$

the following mutual relations between the velocity differences at the interface may be derived from equations (10):

$$d_x : d_y : d_z = \frac{\partial z_i}{\partial x} : \frac{\partial z_i}{\partial y} : \left[\left(\frac{\partial z_i}{\partial x} \right)^2 + \left(\frac{\partial z_i}{\partial y} \right)^2 \right] \qquad (17)$$

$$d_x^2 + d_y^2 + d_z^2 = \frac{k_o}{\mu} g \, (\rho_s - \rho_f) \, d_z \; . \qquad (18)$$

In the steady state of the interface and if the heaviest fluid has become immobile, in which case $V_{xs} = V_{ys} = V_{zs} = 0$ and $d_x = V_x$ etc., equation (18) transforms into equation (4), the 'sphere' equation for the velocities, under conditions mentioned under the hodograph method.

Of course the separate values of the velocities on both sides of the interface are unknown in general and have to be determined by solving simultaneously the differential equations with initial and boundary values for the heads or pressures in the fresh and salt water regions, making use of the common boundary conditions along the interface, which shape and position as a function of time, is a priori unknown.

In general this problem is analytically unsolvable and without rigorous assumptions numerical methods also give difficulties. Nevertheless, for certain cases, with help of some practical assumptions, it is possible to derive and solve a differential equation for the motion of the interface. Some examples will be given in section 7.3.

5.2.8   Rotational flow

If instead of two kinds of water with different densities, separated by a sharp interface, a fluid in which the density gradually changes with place is considered, we may speak of rotational flow. This flow may be treated by the so called vortex theory. The following will make this clear.

Consider an element of cubical form in the soil (fig. 5.15) having small but finite sides dx, dy and dz. At the point (x, y, z) the velocity vector $\vec{V}$ has the three components V_x, V_y and V_z. Since the flow varies with distance with each of the three coordinates, at every corner of the cube it will vary by amounts which depend upon the length of the sides and the gradients of each velocity component. For the sake of simplicity we shall follow the changes in one face of the cube, later extending the relationships to the other faces. For instance, in figure 5.16 the velocity components in the x and y directions will be considered.

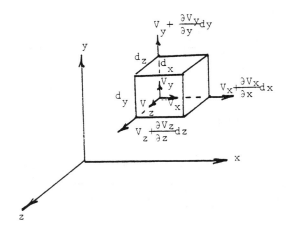

Fig. 5.15

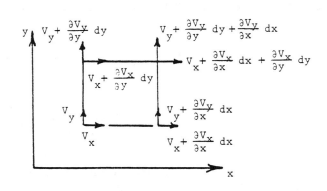

Fig. 5.16

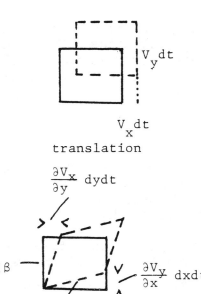

translation

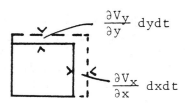

linear deformation

angular deformation

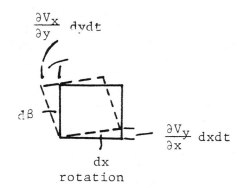

rotation

Fig. 5.17

Neglecting for a moment the change with time at a fixed point in space (steady flow) and omitting derivatives of the second order, it is seen from the illustration that during a small time increment dt the actual motions of the several corners of the face must be different. Hence, not only will the face be moved through space, but it must at the same time suffer a change in its original form. There are four essential types of movement which the face may undergo: a translation of the square in the x and y directions; a change in the length of each pair of parallel sides (linear deformation); a change in each of the four corner angles (angular deformation); and a turning movement in one direction or the other (rotation). Each of these four essential types of displacement is shown schematically in figure 5.17.

During the time increment dt the magnitude of the translation in the two directions will be represented by the equations $V_x dt$ and $V_y dt$. The magnitude of the linear deformation will be given by the difference between the distances moved by each pair of opposite sides: $\frac{\partial V_x}{\partial x} dx\, dt$ and $\frac{\partial V_y}{\partial y} dy\, dt$. The change in the right angle at the point (x, y) will depend upon the angular movements $d\alpha$ and $d\beta$ of the two sides dx and dy. Since over a very short time these angular increments will be small, they may be put equal to their respective tangents; selecting the counterclockwise direction as positive:

$$d\alpha = \frac{\frac{\partial V_y}{\partial x} dx\, dt}{dx} = \frac{\partial V_y}{\partial x} dt \qquad d\beta = -\frac{\frac{\partial V_x}{\partial y} dy\, dt}{dy} = -\frac{\partial V_x}{\partial y} dt \; .$$

In general the angular changes are composed of two types of movement: rotation and angular deformation. The rotation of the face is defined as the total angle through which the face is rotated; this will be the average value of $d\alpha$ and $d\beta$.

In figure 5.18 the distinction between rotation and angular deformation is shown for $d\beta$ positive (A), as well as $d\beta$ negative (B). For both cases the results are:

$$\text{Angular deformation} = 2\,\frac{d\alpha - d\beta}{2} = \left(\frac{\partial V_y}{\partial x} + \frac{\partial V_x}{\partial y}\right) dt$$

$$\text{Rotation} = \frac{d\alpha + d\beta}{2} = \frac{1}{2}\left(\frac{\partial V_y}{\partial x} - \frac{\partial V_x}{\partial y}\right) dt \; .$$

Owing to the finite dimensions of the original cube, the values just given for each type of displacement are not exact, derivatives of second order and higher having been omitted. But if the sides of the cube are now assumed to become infinitesimal, all corners then approaching the point (x, y, z) as a limit, each type of movement may be expressed as a rate of change with time. At the given point the rate of translation in the three coordinate directions will be simply the three velocity components V_x, V_y and V_z, or in vector notation:

$$\text{Rate of translation} = \vec{V} \; .$$

The rate of linear deformation in each of the coordinate directions will be:

$$\frac{\partial V_x}{\partial x} \, dx \ , \qquad \frac{\partial V_y}{\partial y} \, dy \qquad \text{and} \qquad \frac{\partial V_z}{\partial z} \, dz \ .$$

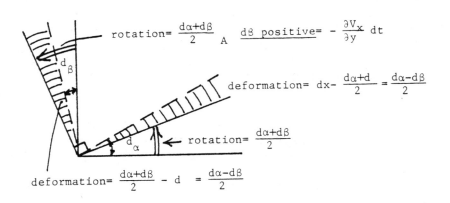

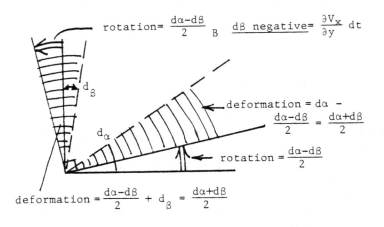

Fig. 5.18

Applying the continuity principle for a constant volume of the cube it will be clear that:

$$\text{div } \overrightarrow{V} = \frac{\partial V_x}{\partial x} + \frac{\partial V_y}{\partial y} + \frac{\partial V_z}{\partial z} = 0 \ .$$

The rate of angular deformation at a given point in planes normal to each of the three coordinate directions will be:

$$\frac{\partial V_z}{\partial y} + \frac{\partial V_y}{\partial z} \ , \qquad \frac{\partial V_x}{\partial z} + \frac{\partial V_z}{\partial x} \qquad \text{and} \qquad \frac{\partial V_y}{\partial x} + \frac{\partial V_x}{\partial y} \ .$$

Special attention in this paragraph will be given to the rotation of the groundwater which is a type of displacement, allied to translation, since both denote movement of the water particle without changing its form. So the <u>rate of rotation</u> will also be a vector with components in the three coordinate directions and is equal to the <u>angular velocity</u> $\overrightarrow{\omega}$ or <u>vorticity</u> (usually = $2\overrightarrow{\omega}$) .

$$\omega_x = \frac{1}{2}\left(\frac{\partial V_x}{\partial y} - \frac{\partial V_y}{\partial z}\right) \qquad \omega_y = \frac{1}{2}\left(\frac{\partial V_x}{\partial z} - \frac{\partial V_z}{\partial x}\right) \qquad \omega_z = \frac{1}{2}\left(\frac{\partial V_y}{\partial x} - \frac{\partial V_x}{\partial y}\right)$$

or in vector notation:

$$\vec{\omega} = \frac{1}{2}\,\text{curl}\,\vec{V} = \frac{1}{2}\begin{vmatrix} \bar{i} & \bar{j} & \bar{k} \\ \frac{\partial}{\partial x} & \frac{\partial}{\partial y} & \frac{\partial}{\partial z} \\ V_x & V_y & V_z \end{vmatrix}. \qquad (18a)$$

So long as the rotation vector $\vec{\omega}$ has a finite value, the flow is characterized as <u>rotational flow</u>. If each component of this vector is reduced to zero, the flow will become <u>irrotational</u>. If the flow is a so called <u>potential</u> flow, which means that the velocity vector is the gradient of a scalar quantity, the potential $k\phi$, the the flow is irrotational, which can be seen immediately when applying the values for the velocities

$$V_x = -k\,\frac{\partial\phi}{\partial x} \qquad V_y = -k\,\frac{\partial\phi}{\partial y} \qquad V_z = -k\,\frac{\partial\phi}{\partial z}$$

to the equations (18a), for instance:

$$\frac{\partial V_y}{\partial x} = -k\,\frac{\partial^2\phi}{\partial y\partial x} = \frac{\partial V_x}{\partial y} = -k\,\frac{\partial^2\phi}{\partial x\partial y} \quad \text{etc.}$$

If k is not a constant, as is the case in anisotropic and/or heterogeneous soils, the flow becomes rotational.

We shall restrict ourselves here to rotational two dimensional steady flow with variable density in a homogeneous isotropic medium, which means that in the expression for the Darcy permeability

$$k = \frac{k_o \rho g}{\mu}$$

k, g and μ are constants, whereas ρ is a function of x and z. As usual in salt-fresh water problems a vertical cross section with x in the horizontal and z in the vertical direction is considered here. The velocity vector becomes (see 5.1, equation 6):

$$\vec{V} = -\frac{k_o}{\mu}(\gamma\nabla z + \nabla p)$$

or

$$V_x = -\frac{k_o}{\mu}\frac{\partial p}{\partial x} \qquad V_z = -\frac{k_o}{\mu}\left(\gamma + \frac{\partial p}{\partial z}\right)$$

with $\gamma = \rho g = $ specific weight $= \gamma(x,z)$.

The vorticity 2ω becomes:

$$2\omega = \frac{\partial V_z}{\partial x} - \frac{\partial V_x}{\partial z} = -\frac{k_o}{\mu}\left(\frac{\partial \gamma}{\partial x} + \frac{\partial^2 \rho}{\partial z \partial x} - \frac{\partial^2 \rho}{\partial x \partial z}\right)$$

or

$$2\omega = -\frac{k_o}{\mu}\frac{\partial \gamma}{\partial x} \, . \tag{18b}$$

If the density ρ (and thus the specific weight $\gamma = \rho g$) is a function of space in such a way that it is independent of the pressure (incompressible water) but for instance a function of the concentration of a solute, it is assumed that a certain volume (the control volume) remains the same with changing concentration. In that case the principle of conservation of volume may be applied. Thus for steady flow:

$$\text{div } \vec{V} = 0 \qquad \text{or} \qquad \frac{\partial V_x}{\partial x} + \frac{\partial V_z}{\partial z} = 0 \, .$$

From this equation it can be seen that a function ψ may be defined, such that:

$$V_x = -\frac{\partial \psi}{\partial z} \qquad\qquad V_z = \frac{\partial \psi}{\partial x} \, . \tag{18c}$$

The vorticity, expressed by the function ψ becomes:

$$2\omega = \frac{\partial V_z}{\partial x} - \frac{\partial V_x}{\partial x} = \frac{\partial^2 \psi}{\partial x^2} + \frac{\partial^2 \psi}{\partial z^2} = \nabla^2 \psi$$

and thus we get the important relation between the function $\psi(x,z)$ and the rotation of the flow:

$$\frac{\partial^2 \psi}{\partial x^2} + \frac{\partial^2 \psi}{\partial z^2} = 2\omega = -\frac{k_o}{\mu}\frac{\partial \gamma}{\partial x} \, . \tag{18d}$$

The function ψ is very similar (but not identical!) to the stream function in potential flow (for $\omega = 0$, $\nabla^2 \psi = 0$ as in potential flow).

The differential equation (18d) is a so called Poisson equation; it says that in every point (x_0, y_0) of the flow field, where the gradient of the fluid density has a horizontal component, the flow contains a vorticity $2\omega(x_0, z_0)$.

The vorticity in general is defined as the limit of the circulation around the enclosing curve of a region, divided by the area of that region, if that area approaches zero. For circulation Γ should be understood the line integral of the tangential velocity component around any closed curve (see fig. 5.19):

$$\Gamma = \oint^{\lambda} V_{\lambda} \, d\lambda$$

and

$$\lim_{A \to o} \frac{\Gamma_A}{A} = 2\omega \; . \tag{18e}$$

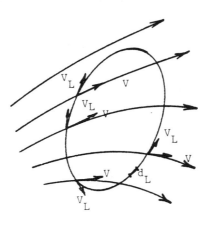

Fig.   5.19

This relationship will be apparent after considering the circulation around the rectangle in the xy-plane shown in fig. 5.19. If the elementary rectangle is sufficiently small, the line integral of tangential velocity along each side will equal the average velocity between the two corners times the length of the side. Writing the circulation in counterclockwise direction:

$$\Delta \Gamma_{xy} = (V_x + \tfrac{1}{2} \frac{\partial V_x}{\partial x} dx) dx + (V_y + \frac{\partial V_y}{\partial x} dx + \tfrac{1}{2} \frac{\partial V_y}{\partial y} dy) dy$$

$$- (V_x + \frac{\partial V_x}{\partial y} dy + \tfrac{1}{2} \frac{\partial V_x}{\partial x} dx) dx - (V_y + \tfrac{1}{2} \frac{\partial V_y}{\partial y} dy) dy$$

$$= \frac{\partial V_y}{\partial x} dxdy - \frac{\partial V_x}{\partial y} dydx = 2\omega_z dxdy \; .$$

As the area of the surface approaches zero in the limit, the resulting expression for circulation per unit area will be the component of the vorticity vector perpendicular to that area:

$$\lim_{dxdy \to o} \frac{\Delta \Gamma_{xy}}{dxdy} = 2\omega_z = \frac{\partial V_y}{\partial x} - \frac{\partial V_x}{\partial y} \; .$$

In order to solve the differential equation (18d), the flow is considered as a potential flow for which $\frac{\partial^2 \psi}{\partial x^2} + \frac{\partial^2 \psi}{\partial z^2} = 0$ holds, while at each point where $\frac{\partial \gamma}{\partial x} \neq 0$, a vortex is introduced, with an intensity that equals the value of $-\frac{k_o}{\mu} \frac{\partial \gamma}{\partial x}$ at that point.

Such a vortex at a point causes a change in the value of the streamfunction ψ everywhere in the field, similar to the change in head in a field, due to abstraction of water from a well. That change of ψ is, naturally, dependent on the boundary values of the flow problem, as well as on the intensity of the vortex.

The total contribution of all vortices in the field, where $\frac{\partial \gamma}{\partial x} \neq 0$, to the value of ψ at an arbitrary point (x, z) of the field, gives the solution to the problem.

First the effect on ψ of a <u>single vortex</u> with <u>constant velocity</u>, located at the origin of an <u>infinite field</u>, will be determined. Partly following de Josselin de Jong (1977), consider a small circular area A with radius R around the origin with a vorticity 2ω, such that inside A the Poisson equation

$$\frac{\partial^2 \psi_1}{\partial x^2} + \frac{\partial^2 \psi_1}{\partial z^2} = 2\omega$$

and outside A the Laplace equation

$$\frac{\partial^2 \psi_2}{\partial x^2} + \frac{\partial^2 \psi_2}{\partial z^2} = 0$$

hold (fig. 5.20). As the problem is purely radial, these may be written as

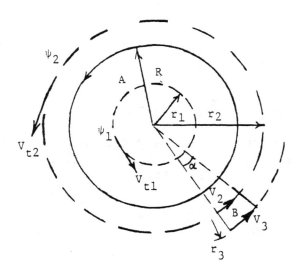

Fig. 5.20

-166-

$$\frac{1}{r_1} \frac{d}{dr_1} \left(r_1 \frac{d\psi_1}{dr_1} \right) = 2\omega$$

and

$$\frac{d}{dr_2} \left(r_2 \frac{d\psi_2}{dr_2} \right) = 0$$

successively.

Inside A $(r_1 \leq R)$ we can derive $\frac{d}{dr_1} \left(r_1 \frac{d\psi_1}{dr_1} \right) = 2\omega r_1$; $r_1 \frac{d\psi_1}{dr_1} = \omega r_1^2$ + constant. As the total velocity at a point at a distance r from the origin is equal to the tangential velocity V_t along the circle with radius r, which is represented by $\frac{d\psi}{dr}$, we find if we assume that $V_t = 0$ for $r = 0$:

$$V_{t1} = \frac{d\psi_1}{dr_1} = \omega r_1 . \tag{18f}$$

The circulation becomes

$$\Gamma_1 = 2\pi r_1 \, V_{t1} = 2\pi \omega r_1^2 \tag{18g}$$

and is a function of r_1.

Equation (18g) could have been derived directly from equation (18e) which holds for rotational flow:

$$\Gamma_1 = 2\omega \cdot A_1 = 2\omega \pi r_1^2 .$$

Outside the area A $(r_2 \geq R)$, $\frac{d}{dr_2} \left(r_2 \frac{d\psi_2}{dr_2} \right) = 0$; and $\frac{d\psi_2}{dr_2} = \frac{C}{r_2}$ with C a constant, which follows from the continuity of the tangential velocity $V_t = \frac{d\psi}{dr}$ along the circle r = R. Equation (18f) gives:

$$\frac{d\psi_1}{dr_1} (R) = \omega R = \frac{d\psi_2}{dr_2} (R) = \frac{C}{R}$$

from which

$$C = \omega R^2$$

and so

$$V_{t2} = \frac{d\psi_2}{dr_2} = \frac{\omega R^2}{r_2} \tag{18h}$$

The circulation $\Gamma_2 = 2\pi r_2 \, V_{t2} = 2\pi r_2 \, \dfrac{\omega R^2}{r_2} = 2\pi\omega R^2$ is independent of r_2 and can be written as:

$$\Gamma_2 = 2\omega \cdot A \quad . \tag{18i}$$

Although the flow outside the area A is a potential flow we find a constant value for a circulation which includes the point where the vortex is situated. A circulation which does not include a vortex area must be equal to zero, as can be seen from the circulation around the area B in figure 5.2.18 which lies outside A:

$$\Gamma_B = V_3 \, ar_2 - V_2 \, ar_2 = 0$$

as $Vr = C$.

According to (18i) and with $\Gamma = 2\pi r \, V_t = 2\pi r \, \dfrac{d\psi'}{dr}$ we find:

$$\frac{d\psi'}{dr} = \frac{\omega A}{\pi r} = V_t \quad .$$

The magnitude of the area A is not decisive for the analysis; so we may choose this area of vorticity with strength ωA as small as we like, such that A becomes dA. The vortex area then becomes a vortex around a point which creates everywhere in the field a tangential velocity:

$$dV_t = \frac{\omega dA}{\pi r} \quad .$$

If a small region of the size $dA = dx_0 dz_0$ around the point $P(x_0, z_0)$ contains vorticity 2ω, the tangential velocity at a point Q at a distance r from P becomes:

$$dV_t = \frac{\omega dx_0 dz_0}{\pi \sqrt{(x - x_0)^2 + (z - z_0)^2}} \quad .$$

If ω is a function of place $\omega = \omega(x,z)$ the total distribution of the velocity is given by:

$$V_t = \frac{d\psi'}{dr} = \frac{1}{\pi} \iint \frac{\omega(x_0, z_0) \, dx_0 dz_0}{\sqrt{(x - x_0)^2 + (z - z_0)^2}}$$

or

$$\psi = \frac{1}{\pi} \iint \omega(x_0, z_0)\ln r \, dx_0 dz_0 + C \quad .$$

According to (18d) $2\omega = -\dfrac{k_0}{\mu} \dfrac{\partial \gamma}{\partial x}$.

The way of solving the Poisson differential equation (18d) now starts with introducing vortices in all points of the flow field where the specific weight γ varies in the x-direction, with vorticity that equals the value of $-\frac{k_o}{\mu}\frac{\partial\gamma}{\partial x}$ at that point. The total value of Ψ_1, caused by these vortices in an <u>infinite field</u> is:

$$\Psi_1 = -\frac{k_o}{2\pi\mu}\iint\limits_S \frac{\partial\gamma}{\partial x}(x_o, z_o)\ln(r)dx_o dz_o \qquad (18j)$$

where $r = \sqrt{(x - x_o)^2 + (z - z_o)^2}$.

The integration has to be performed over the area S where $\frac{\partial\gamma}{\partial x} \neq 0$.

As Ψ_1 is a solution in an infinite field, a second solution Ψ_2 has to be found, such that $\nabla^2\Psi_2 = 0$ and $\Psi_1 + \Psi_2$ satisfies the boundary conditions of the problem. The final solution is $\Psi = \Psi_1 + \Psi_2$.

This solution for Ψ describes only an instantaneous flow situation, as the flow is essentially non-steady because of the variation of γ with time. This becomes clear if we develop the basic continuity equation for incompressible fluid with variable density, flowing through a nondeformable porous medium:

$$\text{div }(\rho\vec{V}) + \Theta\frac{\partial\rho}{\partial t} = 0$$

or

$$\rho\text{ div}\vec{V} + \vec{V}\cdot\nabla\rho + \Theta\frac{\partial\rho}{\partial t} = 0 \ .$$

As div $\vec{V} = 0$ there remains:

$$V_x\frac{\partial\gamma}{\partial x} + V_z\frac{\partial\gamma}{\partial z} + \Theta\frac{\partial\gamma}{\partial t} = 0 \ . \qquad (18k)$$

A complete description of the nonsteady flow problem consists of the two equations

$$\text{div }\vec{V} = 0$$

and

$$\vec{V}\ \nabla\gamma + \Theta\frac{\partial\gamma}{\partial t} = 0$$

together with the initial and boundary conditions. Instead of a potential function, another generating function Ψ now has been introduced here, such that the equations (18c) are valid. The two differential equations then also can be written as:

$$\frac{\partial^2\Psi}{\partial x^2} + \frac{\partial^2\Psi}{\partial z^2} + \frac{k_o}{\mu}\frac{\partial\gamma}{\partial x} = 0 \qquad (18l)$$

$$\frac{\partial\Psi}{\partial x}\cdot\frac{\partial\gamma}{\partial z} - \frac{\partial\Psi}{\partial z}\cdot\frac{\partial\gamma}{\partial x} + \Theta\frac{\partial\gamma}{\partial t} = 0$$

where $\Psi = \Psi(x,z,t)$ and $\gamma = \gamma(x,z,t)$.

A direct solution of these simultaneous equations is not available in general; so numerical methods have to be applied. With the aid of the foregoing analysis it is possible to solve the first equation of (181) for the initial situation if the density distribution is known at that moment. It is then possible to determine from the function Ψ the displacement of fluid particles during a small time interval. Taking into account the change in specific weight by this displacement during that time interval according to the second equation of (181), the new density distribution can be calculated, from which again a new function Ψ can be derived.

5.2.9 Dispersion

A. Homogeneous soils

In theory a sharp interface between salt and fresh water cannot exist and also in practice a more or less extended transition zone (mixing zone) is present between the fresh and salt water, with gradually increasing chloride content from fresh to salt. This transition zone is due to dispersion and may be of such importance that it should not be neglected.

A differential equation will be derived by means of which, together with initial and boundary values, dispersion problems for homogeneous soils may be solved. Moreover, in the next paragraph attention will be paid to the very important concept of macrodispersion, which is related to heterogeneous soils.

For soils with little heterogeneity on macroscopic scale (in microscopic scale all soils are very heterogeneous) it is assumed that Fick's Law of diffusion can be applied to describe the transport of a solute in groundwater with the aid of a coefficient, the dispersion coefficient, that has the same character as the normal diffusion coefficient, but is much larger than the latter as a result of the intensified process of diffusion caused by the flow of the groundwater through the heterogeneous pore system.

In this case only steady flow is considered whereas the concentration C (x, y, z, t) of a solute in the groundwater in general is a function of space and time, and is expressed in solute mass per unit volume of the fluid $[ML^{-3}]$. There will take place mass transport per unit time or mass flux of the solute due to fluid convection, advection and to a process like diffusion, the dispersion. The flux F of the solute or tracer can be expressed as mass per time $[MT^{-1}]$, and the specific flux f is defined as flux per unit area in a cross section $[ML^{-2}T^{-1}]$. The relation between both is:

$$f = \frac{F}{m_e \sigma} \qquad (19)$$

in which m_e = effective porosity and σ = total area of the cross section.

Consider a cubic element in three dimensional Cartesian space, as represented in figure 5.21. The mass transport per unit time or the mass flux by convection in the x-direction per unit fluid area in the cross section dydz

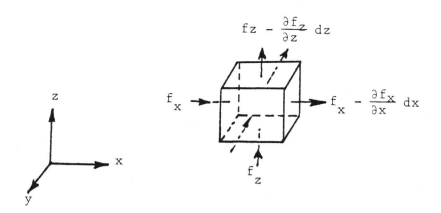

Fig. 5.21

is u (where u = real average velocity in x-direction), that is $u = \dfrac{V_x}{m_e}$ if V_x = Darcy velocity in x direction.

The specific mass flux caused by dispersion in x-direction is proportional to the concentration gradient = $D_x \dfrac{\partial C}{\partial x}$ where D_x = dispersion coefficient in x direction $[L^2 T^{-1}]$. The total specific flux therefore will be:

$$f_x = uC - D_x \frac{\partial C}{\partial x} \qquad (20)$$
$$f_y = vC - D_y \frac{\partial C}{\partial y}$$
$$f_z = wC - D_z \frac{\partial C}{\partial z}$$

where u, v and w are the real average velocities in the three coordinate directions.

$$u = \frac{V_x}{m_e} \qquad v = \frac{V_y}{m_e} \qquad \text{and} \qquad w = \frac{V_z}{m_e} .$$

The negative signs before the dispersive terms indicate that the solute moves toward the zone of lower concentration.

In general the concentration C, and the concentration gradients $\dfrac{\partial C}{\partial x}$, $\dfrac{\partial C}{\partial y}$ and $\dfrac{\partial C}{\partial z}$ are functions of x, y, z and t and the real velocities u, v and w functions of x, y and z (steady flow assumed) whereas D_x, D_y and D_z for the time being will be considered as constants.

From figure 5.21 it can be seen that the difference of the amount of mass of the solute that enters and leaves the cubic element is

$$- \left(\frac{\partial f_x}{\partial x} + \frac{\partial f_y}{\partial y} + \frac{\partial f_z}{\partial z} \right) m_e \, dxdydzdt .$$

The mass conservation principle says that this amount must be equal to the amount of mass accumulated within the element. This rate of mass change is represented mathematically by the expression

$$\frac{\partial C}{\partial t} m_e \, dxdydzdt \ .$$

So this relationship holds:

$$\frac{\partial_{fx}}{\partial x} + \frac{\partial_{fy}}{\partial y} + \frac{\partial_{fz}}{\partial z} = -\frac{\partial C}{\partial t} \qquad \text{or} \qquad \text{div } \vec{f} = -\frac{\partial C}{\partial t} \ . \tag{21}$$

In combination with equation (20) this can be evaluated as follows:

$$u\frac{\partial C}{\partial x} + C\frac{\partial u}{\partial x} - D_x\frac{\partial^2 C}{\partial x^2} + v\frac{\partial C}{\partial y} + C\frac{\partial v}{\partial y} - D_y\frac{\partial^2 C}{\partial y^2} + w\frac{\partial C}{\partial z} + C\frac{\partial w}{\partial z} - D_z\frac{\partial^2 C}{\partial z^2} + \frac{\partial C}{\partial t} = 0 \ .$$

We are dealing with steady incompressible flow so div $\vec{V}$ $= \frac{\partial v_x}{\partial x} + \frac{\partial v_y}{\partial y} + \frac{\partial v_z}{\partial z} = 0$ everywhere in the fluid and also $\frac{\partial u}{\partial x} + \frac{\partial v}{\partial y} + \frac{\partial w}{\partial z} = 0$.

These terms disappear in the equation so that the general differential equation for the dispersion becomes:

$$D_x\frac{\partial^2 C}{\partial x^2} + D_y\frac{\partial^2 C}{\partial y^2} + D_z\frac{\partial^2 C}{\partial z^2} = u\frac{\partial C}{\partial x} + v\frac{\partial C}{\partial y} + w\frac{\partial C}{\partial z} + \frac{\partial C}{\partial t} \tag{22}$$

where C is a function of space and time and u, v and w are functions of space only.

In the development of equation (22) it was assumed that the density of the fluid is not influenced by the variation of the solute concentration. In cases where high concentrations of a contaminant occur, as in coastal aquifers, this assumption is no longer valid in general. The density ρ then will be a function of the concentration of the solute: $\rho = \rho(C)$.

Although the density ρ is now a function of space and time, it is assumed that a certain volume (the control volume) remains the same with changing concentration because ρ is independent of pressure. For that reason div $\vec{V}$ remains equal to zero but the flow is no longer independent of the variation of ρ as can be seen with the aid of the general form of Darcy's Law (see section 5.1 equation 1):

$$\frac{\partial V_x}{\partial x} + \frac{\partial V_y}{\partial y} + \frac{\partial V_z}{\partial z} = 0$$

$$= -\frac{k_o}{\mu}\frac{\partial^2 p}{\partial x^2} - \frac{k_o}{\mu}\frac{\partial^2 p}{\partial y^2} - \frac{k_o}{\mu}\frac{\partial^2 p}{\partial z^2} - \frac{k_o}{\mu}\frac{\partial(\rho g)}{\partial z} = *$$

$$\frac{\partial^2 p}{\partial x^2} + \frac{\partial^2 p}{\partial y^2} + \frac{\partial^2 p}{\partial z^2} + \frac{\partial(\rho g)}{\partial z} = 0 \ . \tag{23}$$

As in (23) ρ is a function of C, it will be clear that the groundwater flow in this case depends on the concentration distribution too and the differential equations for both the dispersion and the fluid motion must be solved simultaneously.

For salinity problems with considerable differences in density of the various kinds of water one may use equation (22) only in combination with equation (23), bearing in mind that V_x, V_y and V_z can be expressed in ρ and ρg. Although the fluid is assumed incompressible and the soil nondeformable, the flow is nonsteady because C is a function of time and so are ρ and p.

For uniform flow the terms with v and w disappear in equation (22), and if dispersion only occurs in the direction of the flow, for instance lateral dispersion caused by a contamination equally spread over a plane perpendicular to the flow direction, the differential equation becomes:

$$D \frac{\partial^2 C}{\partial x^2} - u \frac{\partial C}{\partial x} = \frac{\partial C}{\partial t} . \qquad (24)$$

An instantaneous or continuous point injection or point contamination in uniform flow has to be handled with a differential equation in which the dispersion coefficient in the flow direction (lateral dispersion coefficient $D_L = D_x$) differs from that perpendicular to the flow direction (transversal dispersion coefficient $D_T = D_y = D_z$:

$$D_L \frac{\partial^2 C}{\partial x^2} + D_T \left(\frac{\partial^2 C}{\partial y^2} + \frac{\partial^2 C}{\partial z^2} \right) - u \frac{\partial C}{\partial x} = \frac{\partial C}{\partial t} . \qquad (25)$$

If $D_x = D_y = D_z = D$ it can be shown that for pure radial flow the following differential equation holds:

$$D \left(\frac{\partial^2 C}{\partial r^2} + \frac{1}{r} \frac{\partial C}{\partial r} \right) - u_r \frac{\partial C}{\partial r} = \frac{\partial C}{\partial t} \qquad (26)$$

with $u_r = \dfrac{V_r}{m_e}$ = radial flow component.

B. Heterogeneous soils

The previous derivation of a differential equation for the dispersion is based on the assumption of macroscopic homogeneity of the porous medium while the microscopic heterogeneity of the pore system causes, together with diffusion, the dispersion, which we may call micro-dispersion. This concept is important because of the fact that besides the micro-dispersion, also the phenomenon of the macro-dispersion exists. Similar to micro-dispersion, macro-dispersion can be described as a phenomenon that is caused by the heterogeneity on a microscopic scale. For instance, an aquifer may consist of several geological formations with different permeabilities, in which case the aquifer is not homogeneous on macroscopic scale. In practice a homogeneous soil is an exception rather than a rule; so macro-dispersion is in general in practical problems of more importance than micro-dispersion.

Often the similarity between micro- and macro-dispersion is extended
by describing the macro-dispersive flux by means of an equation of the diffusion character like the equations (20) in which then D_x, D_y and D_z are macro-dispersion coefficients that are related somehow to the macroscopic structures
of the soil. These coefficients have a different meaning and are of another
order of magnitude than the micro-dispersion coefficients.

It is questionable if it is allowable to apply the differential
equation of the microscopic scale and for macro-dispersion in heterogeneous
soils and this question is discussed in the geohydrological literature frequently.

An analytical approach of the macro-dispersion without using dispersion coefficients and which gives better insight into the phenomenon will be
given in this paragraph.

Consider a confined aquifer which consists of several horizontal
layers of different thickness b_i and permeability k_i (fig. 5.22).

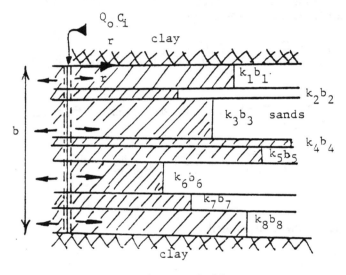

Fig.   5.22

In an injection well, that completely penetrates the aquifer, a constant discharge Q $[L^3T^{-1}]$ of water that contains a tracer solution with a constant concentration C_i $[ML^{-3}]$ is injected. This injection causes 'fingering'
due to the nonhomogeneous structure of the aquifer. That means that the movement of the front of the tracer will not be the same at all depths, but
differs according to the relative magnitudes of the permeabilities of the
various layers. Some time t_0 after the beginning of the injection, the
injected water in the example of figure 5.22 may have taken the shaded position. In this approach the spreading of the tracer caused by lateral micro-dispersion in horizontal directions and transversal micro-dispersion in the
vertical direction is supposed to be negligible compared with the macro-dispersive influence. The dispersion here is considered as a consequence only
of the different velocities of the groundwater in the various layers.

After some time (in the sequel denoted with <u>critical time</u> = t_{cr}) at a distance R of the injection well, a tracer concentration starts, which over a distinct period of time, the <u>break-through time</u> = t_f, increases from zero to the tracer concentration C_i of the injected water. This increase can be represented by means of a <u>break-through curve</u> that is a graph of the concentration at a certain distance from the injection point or well as a function of time (see figs. 5.23 and 5.24) where C_i = concentration of the injected water and C = the concentration of the tracer in the groundwater as a function of time (originally assumed to be zero).

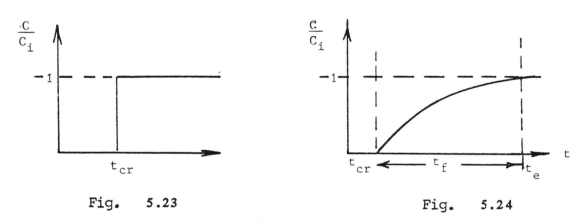

Fig.　5.23　　　　　　　　　　　　Fig.　5.24

Figure 5.23 shows the theoretical break-through curve for a homogeneous nonlayered aquifer with thickness b. It is a stepfunction as could be expected. We shall denote the critical time for this hypothetical case with a capital T_{cr}.

As $Q = 2\pi r\, b\, V_r$, where $V_r = \dfrac{Q}{2\pi rb} = m_e \dfrac{dr}{dt}$ from which $dt = \dfrac{2\pi m_e\, b}{Q}\, r\, dr$

and so

$$T_{cr} = \frac{2\pi m_e\, b}{Q} \int_0^R r\, dr = \frac{\pi R^2 m_e\, b}{Q} \,. \qquad (26a)$$

In this case $t_{cr} = t_e$ and $t_f = 0$, while T_{cr} is independent of the permeability.

For a layered aquifer with varying permeability the break-through curve may look like the curve in figure 5.24. Starting with an arbitrary distribution of the permeability values over the depth of the aquifer, it is possible to derive an analytical expression for the break-through curve, measured in an observation well at a fixed distance from the injection well, which will be shown in the following.

We assume the various layers of the aquifer to be arranged in such a way that the k-value per layer decreases with increasing z (fig. 5.25 with positive z downwards). This new arrangement makes no difference for the shape of the break-through curve. The required discrete k-distribution now is approximated by a continuous distribution as shown in fig 5.25. The permeability k is presented here as a continuous function that decreases with increasing z:

$$k = k(z) \qquad \text{for} \qquad 0 \le z \le b \,.$$

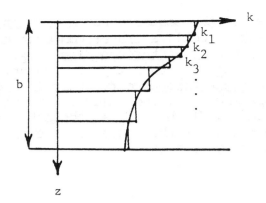

Fig. 5.25

As we assume pure horizontal flow, the increase of groundwater head $\emptyset$ is independent of z

$$V_r = k(z) \frac{d\emptyset}{dr}$$

in which $k(z)$ is a function of z only and $\frac{d\emptyset}{dr}$ of r only, while V_r is a function of both z and r. At a distance r of the injection well is

$$Q = 2\pi r \int_o^b V_r dz = 2\pi r \frac{d\emptyset}{dr} \int_o^b k(z) dz \ .$$

If we put the average value of k:

$$\bar{k} = \frac{1}{b} \int_o^b k(z) dz$$

then $\frac{d\emptyset}{dr} = \frac{Q}{2\pi r \bar{k} b}$; $V_r = \frac{Q k(z)}{2\pi r \bar{k} b} = m_e \frac{dr}{dt}$ and so the equation of motion along a horizontal streamline becomes:

$$t = \frac{\pi r^2 m_e \bar{k} b}{Q k(z)} + C \ .$$

If we take $t = 0$ for the beginning of the injection, the detention time t_d (travelling time, residence time) of a particle that flows along a horizontal streamline at depth z is a function of r and z:

$$t_d = \frac{\pi r^2 m_e \bar{k} b}{Q k(z)} \ . \tag{27}$$

This equation expresses at the same time the front position $f(r, z, t) = 0$ of the injected water at any time, if the newly arranged position of the k-values is kept in mind.

In a vertical at a distance R, the first injected particle will arrive along the streamline with the highest k-value, k_o, that is along the streamline $z = 0$. The critical time becomes according to equation (27):

$$t_d = \frac{\pi r^2 m_e \bar{k} b}{k_o Q} \ . \tag{28}$$

If the smallest value of k is assumed to be αk_o ($\alpha < 1$), along $z = b$, the time t_e, when the original concentration C_i will be reached all over the depth of the aquifer, becomes:

$$t_e = \frac{\pi R^2 m_e \bar{k} b}{\alpha k_o Q} \qquad (29)$$

and the break-through time:

$$t_b = t_e - t_{cr} = \frac{1 - \alpha}{\alpha} t_{cr} \cdot \qquad (30)$$

Compared with the critical time T_{cr} for a homogeneous aquifer (equation (26a)) it appears that:

$$t_{cr} = \frac{\bar{k}}{k_o} T_{cr} \qquad \text{and} \qquad t_e = \frac{\bar{k}}{\alpha k_o} T_{cr} \cdot \qquad (31)$$

After a certain period $t_o > t_{cr}$, the injected particle that moves along the streamline $z = z_o$ arrives at the observation well at a distance R, if the relationship $t_o = \frac{\pi R^2 m_e \bar{k} b}{Q k(z_o)}$ or $k(z_o) = \frac{\pi r^2 m_e \bar{k} b}{Q t_o}$ holds.

Water with a tracer concentration C_i has already arrived over a depth z_o at the time t_o, whereas from $z = z_o$ until $z = b$ still water with the original concentration zero is present. So the mixed concentration along the vertical at a distance R is: $C = \frac{z_o}{b} C_i$. Elimination of z_o from the two last equations and replacing t_o by t gives the tracer concentration as a function of the time at a distance R:

$$k(b \frac{C}{C_i}) = \frac{\pi R^2 m_e \bar{k} b}{Q t} = k_o \frac{t_{cr}}{t} \qquad (32)$$

and in which $k(b \frac{C}{C_i})$ is the same function as $k(z)$ but with the argument $b \frac{C}{C_i}$ instead of z.

Equation (32) is a general formula for the break-through curve at a fixed distance from the injection well if the permeability distribution over the depth of the aquifer is known. Inversely, from this formula the permeability distribution can be derived if the break-through curve has been of a Gaussian normal distribution of the permeabilities and its impact on the break-through curve has a special interest.

It can easily be shown that for <u>uniform flow</u> the same equations (27) to (32) hold if $\frac{\pi r^2}{Q}$ and $\frac{\pi R^2}{Q}$ are replaced by $\frac{x}{q}$ and $\frac{X}{q}$ respectively, in which q is the discharge $[L^2 T^{-1}]$ of an injection gallery or infinitely extended well screen, and X a fixed distance from the gallery.

5.3   Models

Prepared by E. Custodio

5.3.1   Introduction

Models are simplifications and schematizations of real systems given as an ordered set of assumptions, in order to be able to apply to them solution techniques in order to understand the flow system and the relationships with other systems and to get answers to different exploitation or perturbation actions.

The real system is called the prototype and always needs a set of assumptions to be simplified. The validity of those assumptions condition the validity of the model, its ability to answer acceptable responses and the actual usefulness. The simplification process needs the best available data and a good knowledge of the system. Calibration is the process to adjust the parameters to get answers comparable to the observed reality, if the model structure is well conceived. Validation refers to the solution tool itself, because it must be correct and with bounded errors. In some instances the solution tool can yield unstable results in the sense that it does not give the right solution or the errors grow continuously. Validation is usually performed on very simple cases, not necessarily real, with known solutions obtained by other means.

Models can be roughly divided into three categories:

- analytical models, which directly solve the equations, after the necessary manipulation to eliminate or obviate the difficulties;

- physical models and analogs which try to solve the equations by comparing the model of the prototype with other physical phenomenon responding to the same mathematical principles;

- numerical (mathematical or digital) models, which solve the mathematical equations by approximate methods, such as the finite differences or the finite elements. They are the ones most used for practical purposes.

5.3.2   Analytical models

Using several simplified assumptions, most analytical models lead to an exact closed form solution of the governing differential equations. However, this is not always possible. Among the more common simplifying assumptions are: simple geometry, homogeneity and isotropy of aquifer properties, steady state conditions, and linearization of the equations or boundary conditions. Solutions to analytical models usually require only pencil, paper and tables of common functions. Sometimes numerical integration is necessary, utilizing the services of a computer, but the numerical burden is slight.

Most of section 5.2 is devoted to solution methods for analytical models. Some of them are very simple, as the Badon Ghyben-Herzberg principle presented in section 3.1, which is the basis for many later developments. The Dupuit-Forchheimer horizontal flow model is also a very simple one that leads to the solution of many more complicated or insoluble problems.

Table 5.2 is a summary of some of the main analytical models existing until 1979. Recently some others have appeared, though the main efforts are on numerical models. The Dutch school at Delft is now very active in analytical models.

The first sophisticated analytical models are those of Glover (1959), Henry (1964a), Bear and Dagan (1964a), from which many others are derived. Glover (1959), Henry (1964a), Bear and Dagan (1964b), Rumer and Shiau (1968), Verruijt (1968) and Van der Veer (1979), accounting for vertical flow and using conformal mapping and/or hodograph techniques, calculated several solutions for the steady state position of a sharp interface in coastal aquifers, subject to different boundary conditions; they examined a vertical cross section of a homogeneous and isotropic aquifer. Glover (1959), Rumer and Shiau (1968) and Van der Veer (1979) looked at infinitely deep aquifers, in which fresh water is a _lens_ on a continuous salt water body. Although Bear and Dagan (1964b) also looked at a lens model, they and Henry (1964b) examined seawater intrusion in finite depth confined aquifers, in which the salt water wedge finish at a _toe_. Rumer and Shiau (1968) included the effects of anisotropy and layered nonhomogeneities. Henry (1964b) also solved the steady state problem of seawater intrusion in a confined aquifer, considering vertical flow and dispersion. His work is the only analytical study of seawater intrusion examining the effect of mixing on the location and extent of the mixing zone.

Bear and Dagan (1964b) analytically applied the hydraulic approach (no vertical flow) to study a confined aquifer with a sharp interface with changing fresh water flow. Other basic applications of the sharp interface/hydraulic approach are given in Rumer and Harleman (1963) and Fetter (1972), as well as the reviews by Bear (1970, 1972 and 1979).

Using the hydraulic approach and the Ghyben-Herzberg sharp interface approximation, Hantush (1968) established and analytically solved differential equations that approximate different situations of the unsteady movement of a freshwater lens in infinitely deep, homogeneous and isotropic phreatic aquifers, under BGH conditions.

Other authors have examined the steady state shape and position of the interface in leaky aquifers, using the sharp interface/hydraulic approach:

(a) Collins and Gelhar (1971) -- Seawater intrusion in a leaky aquifer. They solve the governing equations analytically inland of the seawater wedge and by numerical integration over the wedge.

(b) Mualem and Bear (1974) -- Steady state flow in an aquifer where a thin semipervious zone divides the aquifer into two layers, using the Dupuit approximation and only vertical flow in the semipervious zone.

Table 5.2 - Classification of analytical models (Sá da Costa and Wilson, 1979).

Type of model		Author	Independent variables	Type of aquifer	Method of solution	Field equation	Salt water
Fully mixed		Henry (1964b)	$h_f(x,z); C(x,z)$	confined	Fourier/Galerkin	hydrodynamic	---
	Lens	Glover (1959)	$h_f(x,z)$	confined	conformal mapping	hydrodynamic ssw	static
		Van der Veer (1979)	$h_f(x,z)$	phreatic	potential flow	hydrodynamic ssw	static
		Rumer+Shiau (1968)	$h_f(x,z)$	confined anisotropic or layered	conformal mapping	hydrodynamic ssw	static
		Hantush (1968)	$\bar{h}_f(x,y,t)$	phreatic	approximated PDE	hydraulic ssw	static
Deep interface		Henry (1964a)	$h_f(x,z)$	confined/phreatic	conformal mapping	hydrodynamic ssw	static
		Bear+Dagan (1964a)	$h_f(x,z)$	confined	hodograph method	hydrodynamic ssw	static
		Bear+Dagan (1964b)	$\bar{h}_f(x,t); \zeta(x,t)$	confined	approximated PDE	hydraulic dsw	dynamic
	Toe	Collins+Gelhar (1971)	$\bar{h}_f(x)$	leaky confined	approximated PDE	hydraulic ssw	static
		Mualem+Bear (1974)	$\bar{h}_f(x)$	multi-layered leaky	approximated PDE	hydraulic ssw	static
		Verou (1978)	$\bar{h}_f(x)$	leaky confined	approximated PDE	hydraulic ssw	static
		Hashish et al. (1979)					
		Strack (1976)	$\bar{h}_f(x,y)$	confined/phreatic	potential flow	hydraulic ssw	static
		Kishi+Fukuo (1977)	$\bar{h}_f(r,\theta)$	confined	approximated PDE	hydraulic ssw	static
		Kashef (1975,1976)	$\bar{h}_f(x,y,t)$	confined	superposition	hydraulic ssw	static
		Kashef+Smith (1975)					

C - concentration of salt
h_f - freshwater piezometric head
$\bar{h}_f$ - depth averaged freshwater piezometric head
ζ - interface depth

x,y,z - Cartesian coordinates (z vertical)
r,θ - cylindrical coordinates
t - time
PDE - partial differential equation
ssw - steady sea water
dsw - dynamic sea water

(c)   Verou (1978), Hashish et al. (1979) -- Leaky layer at the top of the aquifer; steady state position of the interface for several types of leakage and inland boundary conditions.

Several other authors, also using the sharp interface/hydraulic approach, have examined the effects of pumping and/or recharge wells on coastal seawater intrusion in finite depth aquifers. Strack (1976) found the steady state solution for confined and phreatic aquifers, using Girinskii potential flow theory. Kishi and Fukuo (1977) looked at steady flow in confined aquifers, by linearizing the freshwater equations above the interface and using Green's functions. Kashef (1975, 1976) and Kashef and Smith (1975) used the Ghyben-Herzberg approximation and the principle of superposition to estimate the transient effect of recharge wells on piezometric head and interface position in a confined aquifer.

With the exception of Henry (1964b), all these analytical models take a sharp interface approach. Among these, only one (Bear and Dagan, 1964b) considered dynamics of the seawater. However, almost all of these models are based on simple assumptions about geometry (infinitely deep or of constant thickness), properties (homogeneous and isotropic) and boundary conditions. If these assumptions were not made, it would be difficult, if not impossible, to solve the governing equations analytically. Since in practical problems the aquifer geometry and parameters vary in space, and natural recharge and pumping vary in both time and space, numerical models are required.

5.3.3   Physical models

A.   General comments

Since direct analytical solutions are frequently impossible, or inadequate, or impractical for engineering purposes, or are difficult to be interpreted in a given physical context, model and analog methods are frequently employed.

The analog may be considered as a single purpose computer which has been designed and built for a given problem. Modeling is the technique of reproducing the behavior of a phenomenon on a different and more convenient scale.

In modeling, two systems are considered: the prototype, or system under investigation, and the analog system. These systems are analogous if the characteristic equations describing their dynamic and kinematic behavior are similar in form. This occurs only if there is a one-to-one correspondence between elements of the two systems. A direct analogy is a relationship between two systems in which corresponding elements are related to each other in a similar manner.

A model is an analog which has the same dimensions as the prototype, and in which every prototype element is reproduced, differing only in size. An analog is based on the analogy between systems belonging to entirely different physical categories. Similarity is recognized in an analog by two characteristics: (a) for each dependent variable and its derivatives in the equations describing one system, there corresponds a variable with corresponding derivatives in the second system's equations; (b) independent variables and associated derivatives are related to each other in the same manner in the two sets of equations. The analogy stems from the fact that the characteristic equations in both systems represent the same principles of conservation and transport that govern physical phenomena. It is possible to develop analogs without referring to the mathematical formulation, an approach which is particularly advantageous when the mathematical expressions are excessively complicated or are unknown.

Analogs may be classed as either discrete or continuous with respect to space variables. In both cases, time remains a continuous independent variable.

The need for complete information concerning the flow field of a prototype system is obvious, and no method of solution can bypass this requirement. However, in many practical cases involving complicated geology and boundary conditions, it is usually sufficient to base the initial construction of the analog on available data and on rough estimates of missing data. The analog is then calibrated by reproducing in it the known past history of the prototype. This is done by adjusting various analog components until a satisfactory fit is obtained between the analog's response and the response actually observed in the prototype. Once the analog reproduces past history reliably, and within a required range of accuracy, it may be used to predict the prototype's response to planned future operations.

Physical models, except the electrical ones, are mostly laboratory devices and experimental apparatus, though they have also been used for the solution of practical situations. In general they furnish data to prepare computational tables and formulae.

Among the different possible models and analogs (see de Wiest, 1965; Anguita et al., 1972; Custodio and Llamas, 1976, sect. 16) only a few are useful to study problems directly related to coastal aquifers. Hele-Shaw analogs, especially the vertical ones, are the best suited. The ion-motion analog is also useful and the sandbox model is only approximately applicable. Electric analogs of the resistance-capacity or of the electrolytic types are not useful but for stationary interface using a trial and error method to adjust the boundaries.

B.   Sandbox or seepage tank model

It is a reduced scale representation of a natural porous medium domain. It is composed of a rigid, watertight container, a porous matrix filler (sand, glass beads or crushed glass), one or several fluids, a fluid supply system and measuring devices. The box geometry corresponds to that of the investigated flow domain, the most common shapes being rectangular, radial and columnar. For one-dimensional flow problems, the sand column is the most common experimental tool. Transparent material is preferred for the box construction, especially when more than one liquid may be present and a dye tracer is to be used. Porosity and permeability variations in the prototype may be simulated by varying the corresponding properties of the material used as a porous matrix in the model according to the appropriate scaling rules. The porous matrix may be anisotropic. In order to measure piezometric heads and underpressures, piezometers and tensiometers may be inserted into the flow domain of the model.

Well effects are often eliminated by gluing sand grains to the walls of the box. This effect can also be reduced by making the porous matrix sufficiently large in the direction normal to the wall. Inlets and outlets in the walls connected to fixed-level reservoirs or to pumps are used to simulate the proper boundary and initial conditions of the prototype.

Water is usually used in models which simulate groundwater aquifers, although liquids of a higher viscosity may be used to achieve a more suitable time scale.

The sandbox model is used extensively because of its special features which permit studies of phenomena related to the microscopic structure of the medium such as: hydrodynamic dispersion, unsaturated flow, miscible and immiscible displacement, simultaneous flow of two or more liquids at different relative saturations, fingering, wettability and capillary pressure. The capillary fringe in a sandbox model is disproportionately larger than the corresponding capillary rise in the prototype, and for this reason the sandbox model is usually used to simulate flow under confined rather than phreatic conditions.

Rumer and Harleman (1963) used a sandbox model to confirm their analytical models, and Jeanson and Dufort (1970) to aid in the prediction of salt water pollution problems.

C. Ion-motion analog

This analog uses the fact that the velocity of ions in an electrolytic solution under the action of a DC voltage gradient is analogous to the average velocity of fluid particles under imposed potential gradients in a porous medium. In this case, both electric and elastic storativities are neglected. The primary advantage of the ion motion analogy is that, in addition to the usual potential distribution, it permits a direct visual observation of the movement of an interface separating two immiscible fluids. In groundwater interface problems where gravity is involved, this analog cannot be used. Scaling for the analog is based on the similarity between Darcy's Law and Ohm's Law governing the ion motion in an electrolytic solution.

Physically the analog consists of an electrolytic tank having the same geometry as the investigated flow domain. Inflow and outflow boundaries are simulated by positive and negative electrodes, and two- and three-dimensional flow domains may be investigated.

D. Hele-Shaw (viscous flow) analog

The Hele-Shaw or viscous flow analog is based on the similarity between the differential equations governing two-dimensional, saturated flow in a porous medium and those describing the flow of a viscous liquid in a narrow space between two parallel planes. In practice, the planes are transparent plates, and the plates are usually mounted in a vertical or horizontal orientation.

-183-

The vertical Hele-Shaw analog is the most appropriate. It is not possible to model a free groundwater table or percolation in a horizontal model.

The Hele-Shaw analog has been widely used in studies and experiences on fresh-salt water relationships, and it has been a common tool to validate numerical models. They have been used by many investigators (Bear and Dagan, 1964a; Collins and Gelhar, 1971; Gelhar, Wilson and Miller, 1972; Mualem and Bear, 1974; Columbus, 1965).

Under certain circumstances an analog may be preferred to a digital solution, when the accuracy and/or amount of field data is small. In many simple cases, the analog is likely to be less expensive than a digital computer; whereas, for large regions or unsteady three-dimensional problems, the computer may be less expensive.

The Hele-Shaw model also has definite advantages when demonstrations of the salt-water intrusion phenomenon to a public body, or other laymen involved in political decision-making, is considered. This type of model allows for direct observation of the phenomenon without the numerical interpretations used in the computer models.

(a) Equations of the Hele-Shaw vertical model

The viscous flow analog, more commonly referred to as a parallel-plate or Hele-Shaw model, was first used by Hele Shaw (1897, 1899) to demonstrate two-dimensional potential flow of fluid around a ship's hull and other variously shaped objects. The analog is based on the similarity of the differential equations which describe two-dimensional laminar flow, or potential flow for that matter, of a viscous fluid between two closely spaced parallel plates; and those equations which describe the field of flow below the phreatic surface of groundwater, namely Darcy's Law:

$$q_x = - k_x \frac{\partial h}{\partial x} ; \qquad q_z = - k_z \frac{\partial h}{\partial z}$$

where

q_x, q_z = Darcy velocity of specific discharge in the x-direction and z-direction, respectively

k_x, k_z = hydraulic conductivity in the x-direction and z-direction, respectively

x = horizontal direction (major flow direction)

z = vertical direction

h = potentiometric head

and, by use of the conservation of mass principle, the Laplace equation:

$$\frac{\partial^2 h}{\partial x^2} + \frac{\partial^2 h}{\partial z^2} = 0 \; .$$

To demonstrate the analogy of model and prototype, the equations of motion and continuity for laminar flow of a viscous fluid between two closely spaced parallel plates will be developed and then compared to the preceding equations.

In a viscous incompressible fluid flowing ever slowly enough between two parallel plates which are spaced such that the Reynolds' number R_e, based on the interspace width is less than 500 (Aravin and Numerov, 1965) the general Navier-Stokes equations can be applied (Bear, 1972; Christensen and Evans, 1974, 1975; de Wiest, 1965; Maasland and Bittinger, 1967). The y-dimension is perpendicular to the plates.

If no slip conditions (adherence to the walls) of the fluid particles are assumed for the molecules closest to the walls of the parallel plates, it is easily seen that the velocity gradient in the y-direction is much larger than the velocity gradient in either the x- or y-directions. Also, because of the very low velocities, the inertia terms are very small when compared to the viscous terms.

Since the velocity in the y-direction is zero, the only noncancelable body force acting on the fluid is gravity. Then, after some calculation it is possible to find that the specific discharges q, along the x and z axis, parallel to the plates, are:

$$q_x = -\frac{b^2}{12}\frac{\gamma}{\mu}\frac{\partial h}{\partial x} \qquad\qquad q_z = -\frac{b^2}{12}\frac{\gamma}{\mu}\frac{\partial h}{\partial z}$$

b = plate interspace thickness

h = potentiometric head = $z + \dfrac{p}{\gamma}$

p = pressure

γ = specific weight

μ = viscosity.

The equivalent permeabilities are:

$$k_x = -\frac{b^2}{12}\frac{\gamma}{\mu} \qquad\qquad k_z = -\frac{b^2}{12}\frac{\gamma}{\mu} \; .$$

It is obvious that for a model of constant spacing b, the quantity $\frac{b^2}{12}\frac{\gamma}{\mu}$ does not vary in either the x- or z-direction. Defining the model hydraulic conductivity as $k_{xm} = k_{zm} = \frac{b^2}{12}\frac{\gamma}{\mu}$:

$$q_x = -k_{xm} \frac{\partial h}{\partial x} \; ; \qquad q_z = -k_{zm} \frac{\partial h}{\partial z}$$

which, of course, is analogous to groundwater flow equations.

The two-dimensional continuity equation for flow between parallel plates is:

$$\frac{\partial V_x}{\partial x} + \frac{\partial V_z}{\partial z} = 0 \; .$$

The specific discharge or Darcy velocity is related to the velocity by the vector equation $m\vec{q} = \vec{V}$, where m is the effective porosity of the flow media. In the model, m equals 1. From the analogy $V_x = q_x$; $V_z = q_z$; then:

$$-k_{xm} \frac{\partial}{\partial x} (\frac{\partial h}{\partial x}) - k_{zm} \frac{\partial}{\partial z} (\frac{\partial h}{\partial z}) = 0$$

or dividing by $-k_m$ and recalling that for a model $k_m = k_{xm} = k_{zm}$:

$$\frac{\partial^2 \varphi}{\partial x^2} + \frac{\partial^2 \varphi}{\partial z^2} = 0$$

which is clearly analogous to the mass conservation equation.

(b) Scaling

The two-dimensional equation along the free surface, or water table, of an anisotropic porous media given by Bear (1972) is:

$$k_{xp} \left(\frac{\partial h_p}{\partial x_p} \right)^2 + k_{zp} \left[\left(\frac{\partial h_p}{\partial z_p} \right)^2 - \frac{\partial h_p}{\partial z_p} \right] = m_p \frac{\partial h_p}{\partial t_p} \qquad (1)$$

where the subscript p denotes the prototype. For a Hele-Shaw model, using the subscript m, the equation can be written as:

$$k_{xm} \left(\frac{\partial h_m}{\partial x_m} \right)^2 + k_{zm} \left[\left(-\frac{\partial h_m}{\partial z_m} \right)^2 - \frac{\partial h_m}{\partial z_m} \right] = m_m \frac{\partial h_m}{\partial t_m} \; . \qquad (2)$$

Introducing the similitude ratios, denoted by the subscript r, of the corresponding parameter of model and prototype:

$$k_{xr} = \frac{k_{xm}}{k_{xp}} \; ; \qquad k_{zr} = \frac{k_{zm}}{k_{zp}}$$

$$x_r = \frac{x_m}{x_p} \; ; \qquad z_r = \frac{z_m}{z_p}$$

$$h_r = \frac{h_m}{h_p} \; ; \qquad m_r = \frac{m_m}{m_p}$$

$$x_r = \frac{x_m}{x_p} \; ; \qquad z_r = \frac{z_m}{z_p}$$

$$t_r = \frac{t_m}{t_p}$$

and substituting these relationships into equation (1), the following is obtained:

$$\frac{k_{xm}}{k_{xr}} \left(\frac{\partial (h_m/h_r)}{\partial (x_m/x_r)} \right)^2 + \frac{k_{zm}}{k_{zr}} \left(\left(\frac{\partial (h_m/h_r)}{\partial (z_m/z_r)} \right)^2 - \frac{\partial (h_m/h_r)}{\partial (z_m/z_r)} \right)$$
$$= \frac{m_m}{m_r} \cdot \frac{\partial (h_m/h_r)}{\partial (t_m/t_r)} \; . \tag{3}$$

The ratios of model to prototype quantities are constant and can be removed from behind the differential; therefore, equation (3) can be rearranged to give:

$$\frac{x_r^2}{k_{xr} h_r^2} k_{xm} \left(\frac{\partial h_m}{\partial x_m} \right)^2 + k_{zm} \left[\frac{z_r^2}{k_{zr} h_r^2} \left(\frac{\partial h_m}{\partial z_m} \right)^2 - \frac{z_r}{k_{zr} h_r} \frac{\partial h_m}{\partial z_m} \right]$$
$$= \frac{t_r}{m_r h_r} m_m \frac{\partial h_m}{\partial t_m} \; . \tag{4}$$

Comparing the equations (2) and (4), it is evident that, if the equations are identical, the following must be true:

$$1 = \frac{x_r^2}{k_{xr} h_r^2} = \frac{z_r^2}{k_{zr} h_r^2} = \frac{z_r}{k_{zr} h_r} = \frac{t_r}{m_r h_r} \; . \tag{5}$$

Solving the third equality for z_r, it is found:

$$z_r = h_r \; . \tag{6}$$

The second equality, after cross-multiplying, yields:

$$\left(\frac{x_r}{z_r} \right)^2 = \frac{k_{xr}}{k_{zr}} \; . \tag{7}$$

Recalling the definitions of k_{xr} and k_{zr} and remembering that $k_{xm} = k_{zm}$ in an isotropic model, the above equation can be rewritten:

$$\left(\frac{x_r}{z_r}\right)^2 = \frac{k_{xm}/k_{xp}}{k_{zm}/k_{zp}} = \frac{k_{zp}}{k_{xp}} . \tag{8}$$

The ratio of $\dfrac{k_{zp}}{k_{xp}}$ is called the ratio or degree of anisotropy of the prototype.

Using the fourth equality of equation (5), the *time ratio* of the model and prototype is established:

$$t_r = \frac{m_r \, z_r}{k_{zr}} ; \qquad t_r = \frac{m_r \, x_r^2}{k_{xr} \, h_r} . \tag{9}$$

Substituting the vertical ratio z_r, for the potentiometric head established by equation (5) and the similitude ratios of time, hydraulic conductivity and porosity into equation (9):

$$\frac{t_m}{t_p} = \frac{m_m}{m_p} = \frac{k_{xp}}{k_{xm}} \frac{x_r^2}{z_r} . \tag{10}$$

The effective porosity of an isotropic model (m_m) is unity. The hydraulic conductivity of the model was defined previously as $\frac{b^2 \gamma}{12}\mu$, thus the time scale for the model is finally written as:

$$t_m = \frac{12}{\gamma} \frac{\mu}{m_p} \frac{k_{xp}}{b^2} \frac{x_r}{z_r} t_p . \tag{11}$$

(c)   Anisotropy

The Hele-Shaw model is normally isotropic. This is because of the non-variance of the spacing of the parallel plates. There are, however, two methods for *simulating anisotropy* in a model, derived from equation (8).

Since $k_{xm} = k_{zm}$, the x or z ratio can be adjusted so that the model's hydraulic conductivities are kept equal. This is usually done by choosing a suitable horizontal ratio. Knowing the prototype parameters, a vertical scale for the model is computed so that the aforementioned conductivities are kept equal:

$$z_r = \frac{z_m}{z_p} = \frac{x_m}{x_p} \cdot \sqrt{\frac{k_{xp}}{k_{zp}}} .$$

The geometric distortion method is adequate for modeling only one ratio of anisotropy. If there is a second aquifer, within the prototype which has a different vertical or horizontal hydraulic conductivity, the second aquifer cannot be correctly simulated, unless the second aquifer's ratio of anisotropy is the same as the ratio of the first. This restriction would severely limit the use of the Hele-Shaw analog in modeling of regional ground-water problems unless another method were available to correct the ratio of anisotropy.

Polubarinova-Kochina (1962) suggested using some kind of grooved plate within the model to correct the ratio of anisotropy of the second flow zone. The degree of anisotropy of the second aquifer and the amount of geometric distortion used to model the first flow zone determines the directions the grooves or bars are placed; however, the grooves are normally placed horizontally or vertically. Collins and Gelhar (1970) have developed the conductivity equations for the flow zone in which Polubarinova-Kochina's grooved plate is used. The analysis assumes one-dimensional flow and can be used equally well with either vertical or horizontal orientation of the grooves.

Assuming vertical grooves (in the z-direction) Collins and Gelhar (1970) found:

$$k_{xm} = \frac{b^2 \gamma}{12\mu (1 - \lambda)} \qquad k_{zm} = \frac{b^2 \gamma}{12\mu} (a^3 \lambda \xi + 1 - \lambda)$$

$$\xi \simeq 1 - \frac{192}{\pi^5} \left(\frac{ab}{\lambda L} \text{ Th } \frac{\pi \lambda L}{2ab} \right).$$

b, λ and a are defined in figure 5.26.

(d)   Interaquifer leakage

Since it is generally assumed that in the aquitards the direction of flow is only vertical, $k_{xp} = 0$.

Bear, Zaslavsky and Irmay (1968) suggested the use of vertical slots to model such a semi-pervious layer. To accomplish this, the spacing between the parallel plates of the Hele-Shaw analog is filled with a slotted middle plate.

The analysis to determine the effective vertical hydraulic conductivity of a model's leaky layer closely parallels that for an anisotropic grooved zone. After Collins (1976):

$$k_{zm} = \frac{\gamma}{\mu} a^3 \lambda \xi \frac{b^2}{12} .$$

b and a are defined in figure 5.26; ξ is the same as above.

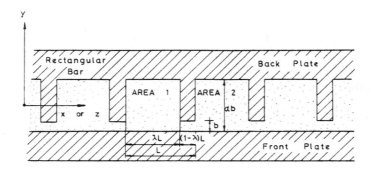

A._ SECTION OF ANISOTROPIC GROOVED ZONE

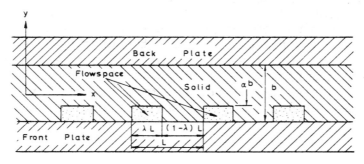

B._ SECTION OF LEAKY ZONE

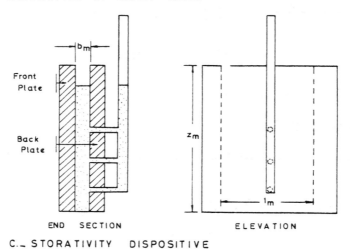

END SECTION   ELEVATION

C._ STORATIVITY DISPOSITIVE

Fig. 5.26 – Methods to solve anisotropy, vertical leakage and storage in vertical Hele-Shaw models. The dotted part represents the fluid and the
cross-hatched part the solid.

(e)   Storage

        The problem of storage has not been completely solved. In many
instances it has been neglected. Discrete tubes attached to either the front
or back plate and connected to the aquifer can be used to model the specific
storage of a confined aquifer in the same way it is done in horizontal Hele-
Shaw models (de Wiest, 1965).

        For a non-isotropic aquifer, the prototype and model mass-
conservation equations must be rewritten:

$$k_{xp} \frac{\partial^2 h_p}{\partial x_p^2} + k_{zp} \frac{\partial^2 h_p}{\partial z_p^2} = S_{op} \frac{\partial h_p}{\partial t_p}$$

$$k_{xm} \frac{\partial^2 h_m}{\partial x_m^2} + k_{zm} \frac{\partial^2 h_m}{\partial z_m^2} = S_{om} \frac{\partial h_m}{\partial t_m}$$

S_o = specific storage.

Defining a ratio of storativity

$$S_{or} = \frac{S_{om}}{S_{op}}$$

it follows that:

$$k_{xr} \frac{z_r}{x_r^2} = \frac{k_{zr}}{z_r} = S_{or} \frac{z_r}{t_r} .$$

Referring to figure 5.26, the storage represented by the model in the discrete length 1_m is equal to:

$$S_{om} = \frac{A_m}{b_m 1_m z_m}$$

where A_m is the cross-sectional area of the storativity tube.

(f) Discharge

The discharge scales are obtained from Darcy's Law.

These are in the x-direction:

$$Q_{xp} = - k_{xp} \frac{\partial h_p}{\partial x_p} b_p z_p$$

$$Q_{xm} = - k_{xm} \frac{\partial h_m}{\partial x_m} b_m z_m .$$

Dividing the two equations and recalling the definitions for the various parameters' ratios, it follows that:

$$Q_{xr} = k_{xr} h_r b_r \frac{z_r}{x_r} = k_{xr} b_r \frac{z_r^2}{x_r} .$$

Similarly, in the z-direction:

$$Q_{zr} = k_{zr} h_r b_r \frac{x_r}{z_r} = k_{zr} b_r x_r .$$

Since $(x_r/z_r)^2 = k_{xr}/k_{zr}$, it follows that:

$$Q_{xr} = k_{zr} \left(\frac{x_r}{z_r}\right)^2 b_r \left(\frac{z_r^2}{x_r}\right) = k_{zr}\, b_r\, x_r \; ; \qquad Q_{xr} = Q_{zr} = Q_r \; .$$

(g)   Recharge

Recharge is measured as a volume per unit horizontal area per unit time:

$$R_r = \frac{Q_r}{b_r\, x_r}$$

and then it follows that:

$$R_r = \frac{k_{xr}\, z_r^2}{x_r^2} = k_{zr} \; .$$

(h)   Water volume

If V represents water volume:

$$V_r = Q_r \cdot t_r = k_{zr}\, b_r\, x_r\, m_r\, \frac{z_r}{k_{zr}} = b_r\, m_r\, x_r\, z_r \; .$$

The volume scale is usually neglected. However, in the case of free surface water bodies, lakes, rivers, etc., if the volume exchange of liquid between the aquifer water and the free water is of interest and has to be modeled, the volume scale requires an additional restriction. The bar above the width dimension will indicate the free water surface of a river, lake, ocean, or such.

In the portion of the model simulating the body of free water, the spacing of the model is increased to maintain hydrostatic pressure distributions within the model.   In the model the narrower spacing of the model is the less permeable and corresponds to the aquifer.   In the prototype, however, the width of the open water and the aquifer are equal. For the model and prototype it leads to:

$$U_r = m_r\, b_r\, x_r\, z_r$$
$$\bar{U}_r = \bar{m}_r\, \bar{b}_r\, x_r\, z_r \; .$$

The same volume ratio must be applicable to both the narrow and the enlarged interspace; therefore, $\bar{U}_r = U_r$. It follows that:

$$\bar{m}_r\, \bar{b}_r = m_r\, b_r$$

but,

$$\bar{m}_r = \frac{\bar{m}_m}{\bar{m}_p} = 1$$

so,

$$\bar{b}_r = m_r\, b_r \; .$$

It must be taken into account that for an anisotropic media, m_m does not necessarily equal one.

5.3.4 Numerical models

A. Introduction

Numerical models (also called mathematical or digital models) are at present powerful tools with which to study and solve groundwater problems. Generally the available solution methods, which need fast computing machines and computer codes, are far superior to the available hydrological data and parameters, and also to the ability to define correctly boundary conditions.

Solution methods use space discretizations on which finite differences and finite elements are the main ways to transform the differential equations and the boundary conditions into a set of algebraic equations. Time discretization is accomplished by finite difference methods (backward, forward or mixed Crank-Nicholson methods).

Non-linear equations are common, such as those resulting from water table aquifers with variable transmissivity according to variable saturated thickness, semiconfined conditions, direct ground evapotranspiration, etc., and are generally solved by iterative methods, with some safeguards to avoid instabilities.

Standard publications must be consulted for further details (Prickett and Lonnquist, 1971; Pinder and Gray, 1977; Remson, Hornberger and Molz, 1971; Custodio and Llamas, sect. 16, 1976; Anguita et al., 1972).

Generally two-dimensional models are applied since most practical situations can be reasonably described assuming horizontal flow, or a multilayer aquifer can be treated as a set of horizontal flow layers connected by vertical flows through the aquitards, real or assumed.

In some instances a better understanding of the situation can be obtained through the use of models for a cross-section, assuming no flow normal to the section.

True three-dimensional models are used less due to the difficulty of preparing the data, and especially to the inability to obtain reliable data. Some years ago computation capacity was also a great difficulty and it is still now in some situations, but generally this is not now a limiting factor.

Numerical models always rely on a simplification of the real system -- the prototype -- and they use a mix of parameters and values obtained by different methods, with different accuracies, and sometimes they are just assumed data. Then, models must be calibrated against the observed real behavior of the system, and this need enough accurate and complete observations to be gathered. A non calibrated model is only an imperfect tool that must be used with caution and it is better called a pre-model.

B. Coastal mathematical models

Different kinds of coastal groundwater mathematical models can be envisaged:

- models to study the interface, considered as a sharp transition zone, and its movement

- models to study the behavior of the mixing zone

- models to simulate the behavior of the whole aquifer, in which the salt water wedge or the sea outlet conditions are considered only as a simplified or oversimplified boundary condition

- models to simulate the behavior of the whole aquifer, incorporating some ways to consider the changes in the salt water body, and if possible, of the mixing zone.

The objectives cover a wide spectrum, such as:

- obtaining a tool to study the behavior of the salt-fresh water zone from an academic point of view or to derive other calculation methods

- evaluating the actual and present behavior of the aquifer

- making predictions of the aquifer behavior under different exploitation or intervention situations.

There is a difference between models that only consider one fluid with some restricted conditions and models that separate fresh water from salt water. The first ones are useful for transient situations in which a fast movement of groundwater is produced; the water body reacts close to the behavior of a homogeneous water body, and displacement calculations can be applied.

In the second ones, since the depth to the interface is considered, the interface movements greatly effect the fresh and salt water storage. The changes in the fresh water reserve cannot be calculated only through the fresh water head change; a method to calculate the actual interface movement is needed.

In general, in order to simplify the mathematical treatment, the solution methods and the boundary conditions, the Badon Ghyben-Herzberg or Hubbert principles are applied, jointly with the Dupuit-Forchheiner approximation, e.g.:

- horizontal flow

- constant velocity along a vertical

- head gradient measured by the water table slope.

It is implicit that a sharp interface is assumed. The salt water can be assumed static (static or pure BGH type) or in movement (dynamic type). In order to solve the problem with two fluids, fresh and salt groundwater, an equation is written down of each one. The problems can be solved when in the whole water domain there are present the two waters (lens type), such as in small pervious islands or in sand bars (fig. 5.27). But when the interface intersects the aquifer bottom (toe type) there is the transition from a two fluid system to a single fluid system, and that changing transition line must be known every time the calculation is performed. That moving boundary condition must be considered carefully. When there is not a sharp interface but a wide mixing zone, the salt transport equation must be considered and solved, jointly with the flow equation.

C.   Available numerical models and its evolution

With the advent of high speed digital computers, numerical models have become an attractive solution method for problems that are too complicated to solve analytically. Table 5.3 presents the various seawater intrusion numerical models found in the literature, taken from the work of Sá da Costa and Wilson (1979). They are classified, according with the above comments in:

- sharp interface models, both of the lens (two fluids in the whole domain) and of the toe (one or two fluids in the problem domain, separated by the toe line) type.

- fully mixed models, in which a density homogeneous or nonhomogeneous fluid is considered.

The lack of well documented coastal aquifer studies do not allow for the application of existing models to complex real situations. Some exceptions are the Miami area (Florida), Long Island (New York), the Netherlands, and the coastal plain of Israel.

(a)   Sharp interface models

Most of the existing sharp interface models are based on the Dupuit-Forchheimer approach (horizontal flow or hydraulic approach) in two-dimensions, and allow for transient flow conditions. Such are those of Fetter (1972) and Rofail (1977) for a lens situation, or some other used by private or research centers (Water Resources Centre, Medmenham, UK.; BURGEAP, France; Bonnet and Sauty, 1975; Mercer, Larson and Faust, 1981). Pinder and Page (1976) formulated the transient lens problem in a Galerkin finite element model using linear triangular elements; the interface extends under the entire investigated region: South Fork, Long Island. These models do not consider the tracking of the toe problem.

Table 5.3 - Classification of numerical models (after Sá da Costa and Wilson, 1979).

Type of model		Author	Space variables	Type of equation Flow	Mass transport	Method of solution
Fully mixed		Pinder and Cooper (1970)	x,z	steady*	transient	FD/MC**
		Lee and Cheng (1974)	x,z	steady*	steady	FE
		Segol et al. (1975)	x,z	steady*	transient	FE
		Desai and Contractor (1977)	x,y	steady*	transient	FE
		INTERCOMP (1976)	x,y,z	steady*	transient	FD
				Freshwater flow	Seawater flow	
Sharp interface	Lens	Kono (1974)	x,z	steady	static	FE
		Liu and Liggett (1978)	x,z	steady	static	BIEM
		Cheng and Hu (1975)	x,z	steady	steady	FE
		Fetter (1972)	x,y	steady	static	FD
		BURGEAP (France)	x,y	transient	static	FD
		Rofail (1977)	x,y	transient	transient	FD
		W.R.C. (UK.)	x,y	transient	transient	FD
		Pinder and Page (1976)	x,y	transient	transient	FE
	Toe	Shamir and Dagan (1971)	x	transient	transient	FD
	Lens/toe	SWIM, Sá da Costa+Wilson (1979)	x,y	transient	transient	FE

x,y,z - Cartesian coordinates (z vertical)
FD   - finite differences
FE   - finite elements
MC   - method of characteristics
BIEM - boundary integral equation method
*   - Does not account for time varying boundary conditions; only accounts for time vary-
        ing flow due to changes in the density of the fluid
**   - FD for flow and dispersion and MC for advection

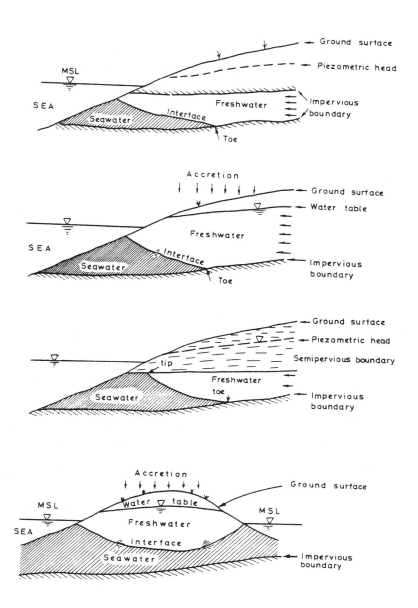

Fig. 5.27 - Seawater intrusion in different types of aquifers.

The one-dimensional transient toe problem was modeled by Shamir and Dagan (1971) using the sharp interface/hydraulic approach and finite difference techniques. Particular attention was given to the toe of the interface, which was represented by a moving node; that is, a new finite difference mesh was generated at each time step. The general two-dimensional sharp interface/hydraulic numerical code to solve the toe problem, under steady or unsteady conditions, was considered by Bear and Kapuler (1981) using finite differences, and by Sá da Costa and Wilson (1979), using Galerkin finite elements in order to get a better representation of geometric boundaries, allow for a more flexible spatial discretization, permit a better handling of non-homogeneities and anisotropies, and reduce storage requirements for data sets due to the smaller number of node points required. It uses a toe tracking algorithm based on a fixed mesh and the Gauss quadrature points which are necessary for performing spatial finite element integration over the elements.

For solving the hydrodynamical flow (considering vertical flows), in 1974 Kono used the finite element method, applying a variational formulation and linear triangular elements, to solve the steady state flow for freshwater above a sharp interface, considering the effects of vertical flow; the problem of interface upconing under a pumping well in the zone above the intruding wedge was examined. In 1978, Liu and Liggett used the boundary integral equation method to study the interface in an infinitely deep confined aquifer, also considering the effects of vertical flow. All of them compared their numerical solutions to analytical solutions (Henry, 1964a; Bear and Dagan, 1964a), with good success.

Cheng and Hu (1975) examined the flow of a density stratified liquid through an embankment by looking at a vertical cross section, solving simultaneous equations for the freshwater and seawater zones by means of quadratic quadrilateral finite elements.

(b)   Fully mixed models

The fully mixed models all use a hydrodynamic flow equation and a steady state flow solution not allowing for time varying boundary conditions, which are very common in groundwater problems.

Pinder and Cooper (1970) studied the movement of the transition zone in coastal aquifers by analyzing a vertical cross section of the aquifer using flow and mass transport equations. While the flow equation is a parabolic equation which is accurately approximated by finite difference or finite element methods, the mass transport equation has hyperbolic and parabolic terms. Approximation of the hyperbolic advective forced convection terms by these methods is usually not very satisfactory, unless the advective terms are less important than the dispersive ones (see Pinder and Gray, 1977), and numerical dispersion arises, or the method results diverge. Examining a vertical cross-sectional view of a homogeneous, isotropic confined coastal aquifer, Pinder and Cooper (1970) solved the steady state flow problem using a finite difference scheme with an iterative alternating direction procedure, and the transient solute transport problem by the method of characteristics for advection and finite differences for dispersion. They have considered variations in time in the flow equations due only to variations in the density of the fluid at a particular position in space, and then it is a kind of 'steady state' equation.

All of the fully mixed models mentioned below use the same approach. Lee and Cheng (1974) solved the steady state version of this problem using the finite element method with linear triangular elements and a Raleigh-Ritz procedure. Segol et al. (1975) analyzed the general problem posed by Pinder and Cooper (1970) using the Galerkin formulation and quadrilateral elements, with linear or quadratic sides. Time integration was handled with an iterative implicit finite difference scheme. This model was applied to the Biscayne aquifer, Florida (Segol and Pinder, 1976). Desai and Contractor (1977) present a similar finite element model for coastal aquifers.

INTERCOMP (1976) developed a three-dimensional finite difference transient model for the U.S. Geological Survey, to evaluate the effects of liquid waste disposal in aquifers. This model has also been used to examine seawater intrusion in aquifers, but the solutions show slow convergence and lengthy computations.

D.   Simplified governing equations and the solutions

(a)   Sharp interface method

Most treatments make the following assumptions:

- only horizontal flow (vertically integrated flow)

- Dupuit-Forchheimer assumptions are valid

- sharp salt-fresh water interface

- hydrostatic salt-fresh water equilibrium (Badon Ghyben-Herzberg)

- permeability and storage properties constant along a vertical (layered system needs special treatment)

- when there is leakage, it is under steady state (no storage form the aquitard is used).

For the symbols to be used see figure 5.28.

f   = fresh water

s   = salt water

I   = interface

ρ = density

μ = viscosity

m   = porosity

h   = water head

h'   = constant head at the other side of an aquitard

S'   = specific storage coefficient (per unit thickness)

k_O = intrinsic permeability in the x and y directions

k'   = aquitard vertical permeability

x,y = horizontal coordinates

b   = water thickness

b' = aquitard thickness

z = altitude over the datum

Q = discharge (exposed in distributed form)

R = recharge (distributed from the surface).

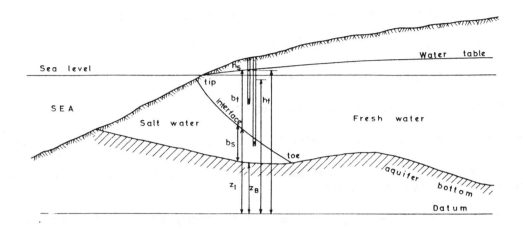

Fig. 5.28 - Definition of the different terms used to derive the simplified governing equation.

The conservation of mass balance, jointly with Darcy's Law, yields the change in storage, including the water table and interface movement.

To include both confined and water table conditions, a factor a is introduced, a = 1 for water table conditions and a = 0 for confined conditions.

Fresh yield through change in the water table elevation =

$$m \frac{\partial h_f}{\partial t} = \sigma_f \; .$$

Fresh water yield through change in the interface elevation =

$$m \frac{\partial z_I}{\partial t} = \sigma_s$$

but

$$(h_f - z_I) \, \rho_f = (h_s - z_I) \, \rho_s$$

$$z_I = \frac{\rho_f}{\rho_s - \rho_f} \, h_f - \frac{\rho_s}{\rho_s - \rho_f} \, h_s$$

-200-

$$\sigma_s = m \left(\frac{\rho_f}{\rho_s - \rho_f} \frac{\partial h_f}{\partial t} - \frac{\rho_s}{\rho_s - \rho_f} \frac{\partial h_s}{\partial t} \right).$$

Fresh water body:

$$S_f \, b_f \, \frac{\partial h_f}{\partial t} + \alpha \, m \, \frac{\partial h_f}{\partial t} - m \left(\frac{\rho_f}{\rho_s - \rho_f} \frac{\partial h_f}{\partial t} - \frac{\rho_s}{\rho_s - \rho_f} \frac{\partial h_s}{\partial t} \right)$$

$$= \frac{\partial}{\partial x} \left(b_f \, k_o^x \, \frac{\rho_f}{\mu f} \, \partial \frac{h_f}{\partial x} \right) + \frac{\partial}{\partial y} \left(b_f \, k_o^y \, \frac{\rho_f}{\mu f} \, \frac{\partial h_f}{\partial y} \right)$$

$$+ \, Q_f - \alpha R - (1 - \alpha) \, \frac{k'}{b'} \, (h' - h_f) \, .$$

Salt water body:

$$\frac{\rho_s}{\rho_f} \, S_f \, b_s \, \frac{\partial h_s}{\partial t} + m \left(\frac{\rho_f}{\rho_s - \rho_f} \frac{\partial h_f}{\partial t} - \frac{\rho_s}{\rho_s - \rho_f} \frac{\partial h_s}{\partial t} \right)$$

$$= \frac{\partial}{\partial x} \left(b_s \, k_o^x \, \frac{\rho_s}{\mu_s} \, \frac{\partial h_s}{\partial x} \right) + \frac{\partial}{\partial y} \left(b_s \, k_o^y \, \frac{\rho_s}{\mu_s} \, \frac{\partial h_s}{\partial y} \right) - Q_s = 0 \, .$$

The net withdrawal of fresh and salt water is considered. When a well mixes salt and fresh water, the two components must be separated.

For multilayered aquifers a set of equations must be established for each one of the layers. Bear and Kapuler (1981) have done this for a two layered aquifer with an impervious separation extending from the coast inland, but without reaching the upstream aquifer boundary.

The b values are a function of the heads:

$$b_f = \alpha h_f + (1 - \alpha) \, z_I - z_I = \alpha h_f + (1 - \alpha) \, z_I - \frac{\rho_f}{\rho_s - \rho_f} \, h_f$$

$$+ \frac{\rho_s}{\rho_s - \rho_f} \, h_s$$

z_I = elevation of the aquifer top

$$b_s = z_I - z_B = \frac{\rho_f}{\rho_s - \rho_f} \, h_f - \frac{\rho_s}{\rho_s - h_f} \, h_s - z_B \, .$$

This introduces non-linearities in the equations. A convenient transformation gives to the fresh water and the salt water equations the same form (Ferrer and Ramos, 1981).

To solve the equations, after some kind of linearization is adopted, finite difference methods (Pinder and Cooper, 1970; Abbott, Ashamalla and Rodenhuis, 1972; Layla, 1980; Mercer, Larson and Faust, 1980, 1981; Bear and Kapuler, 1979, 1981.) or finite element methods (Sá da Costa and Wilson, 1979) can be applied, using permeability and water thickness values in the cell boundaries given by the arithmetic or the weighed harmonic mean. For the non-linearities, iterative calculations are applied.

To solve the set of equations, different methods are available. Mercer, Larson and Faust (1981) presented a discussion of the advantages and disadvantages of some of them.

When dealing with two fluid systems, such as small pervious islands, two fluids are present in the whole flow domain. Only the tip fresh-water flow domain appear, but it has a small influence when the aquifer is open to the sea and can be neglected. It refers to the variable exit gap of fresh water at the sea bottom. Strictly it has a zero width according to the BGH hydrostatic principle, but it can be approximated with the Glover or Henry formula. When the freshwater discharge is through a semipervious cover, the tip position can vary widely (fig. 5.29). When there is a salt water wedge toe, a region of two fluids converts into a region of only one fluid. This is the toe problem. If a fixed mesh is used, the method used to evaluate inter-model flow coefficients can produce difficulties in those nodes along the salt-water toe (also along the fresh-water tip, but, as said, they are much less important). The equations describing the behavior at these modes may contain non-zero flow terms for both fluids, but indicate an interface position below the aquifer bottom (or above the aquifer top for the tip problem).

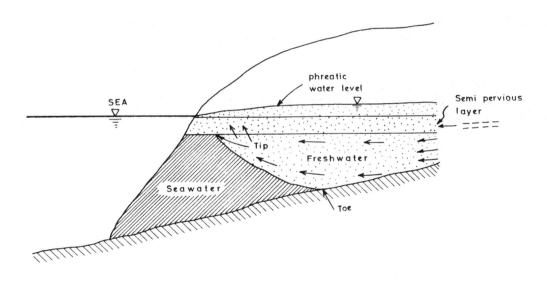

Fig. 5.29 - Coastal aquifer with a fresh-water tip and a salt-water toe.

Thus, changes in interface position that are necessary to balance mass flow residuals may produce an artificial increase or decrease of mass within the considered cell.

It is possible to apply explicit corrections to prevent these ficti-tious accumulations of mass (positive or negative), but they do not seem suc-cessful in salt-water advancing problems. Fortunately the errors in the computation in the interface position are not so serious as the mass balance difference would indicate. After Mercer, Larson and Faust (1980, 1981), simulations without correction that produce mass balance errors of about 5% resulted in interface displacements that were essentially the same as those with corrections, and thus the approach is used by these authors and others (Bonnet and Sauty, 1975; Bonnet and Carlier, 1974; Ferrer and Ramos, 1981). By recognizing the source of the errors and by making proper evaluations of their impact, this approach will probably be feasible for most problems.

Shamir and Dagan (1971) circumvent the toe problem in a one-dimensional problem, by tracking it. A finite difference grid is regenerated each time step such that the toe coincides with the edge of a grid cell. Two equations are used on one side of the toe and only one equation is used in the freshwater area beyond the toe. After each time-step, the position of the toe is recomputed and a new mesh is constructed. It eliminates or at least minimizes the above mentioned mass balance problem. This method is also used by Bear and Kapuler (1981), who divide the flow domain into several parts, and also by Sá da Costa and Wilson (1979), who use finite elements instead of finite differences.

For two-dimensional flow in a horizontal plane, the tracking method involves great computational difficulties.

Some simplified models only solve the fresh water equation. Chidley and Lloyd (1977), for the case of small islands, use a similar equation with a fresh water thickness:

$$b_f = h_f - z_I = h + \alpha h = (1 + \alpha) h$$

in which

h = fresh water head over mean sea level

$\alpha = \rho_f / (\rho_s - \rho_f)$ or some adjusted value to simulate the thickness of the fresh water body over the mixing zone.

$$(1 + \alpha) \left[\frac{\partial}{\partial x} k_x h \frac{\partial h}{\partial x} + \frac{\partial}{\partial y} k_y h \frac{\partial h}{\partial y} \right] - (1 + \alpha) S \frac{\partial h}{\partial t} + R = 0$$

R = net recharge

S = specific yield.

If the equation is transformed into:

$$\frac{\partial}{\partial x} k_x h \frac{\partial h}{\partial x} + \frac{\partial}{\partial y} k_y h \frac{\partial h}{\partial y} - S \frac{\partial h}{\partial t} + \frac{R}{1 + \alpha} = 0$$

or for isotropic ground:

$$\frac{\partial^2 h^2}{\partial x^2} + \frac{\partial^2 h^2}{\partial y^2} - \frac{2S}{k} \frac{\partial h}{\partial t} + \frac{2R}{1 + \alpha} = 0$$

which are the common groundwater flow equations in which the recharge R is changed by $R/(1 + \alpha)$.

It is assumed that a change in h, Δh, produces a parallel and simultaneous change in the interface depth of $\alpha \Delta h$. In order to maintain the assumption of essentially horizontal flow, since that change needs great vertical permeability, horizontal flow in the salt water body must be intense, i.e., great transmissivity (the salt water body must be very thick). Anderson (1976), when solving the problem of an oceanic island with two pervious levels, in order to circumvent the parallel and simultaneous change above mentioned, uses the so called delayed interface response in which the correction:

$$\frac{\partial}{\partial x}\left[k \ (h + B) \ \frac{\partial h}{\partial x}\right] - S \ \frac{\partial h}{\partial t} + R = 0$$

is used. It does not consider the movement of the interface in the _storage term and B = fresh water thickness below sea level is taken as $B = \alpha h(t)$, $h(t)$ being the fresh water head over mean sea level in the former computation time (e.g. 30 days). In spite of the error in the mass balance, it performs well.

(b)   Fully mixed (salt transport) methods

In fully mixed or salt transport methods, only one fluid is considered, but nonhomogeneous in density. The transient position of the salt-water front, defined by a set of isoconcentration (or isochloride) surfaces, and the flow pattern must be determined considering the existence of dispersion.

The solution of the problem requires the simultaneous solution of the following two equations:

- groundwater flow equation

- dissolved salt transport equation.

It is generally assumed that:

(a) the solid medium is incompressible and then the release of water from storage has a negligible effect on the movement of the salt water front

(b) porosity is constant = m

(c) dynamic viscosity is constant = μ

(d) dispersion :

(i) proportional to the flow velocity, $D = d_0 \cdot v$; d_0 = intrinsic permeability with a longitudinal d_{0L} and transverse d_{0T} values, and

(ii) is constant = D. This assumption is only valid when small variations in v are expected.

The Darcy equation is formulated:

$$\text{mass average flux} \quad \underline{q} = - \frac{\bar{\bar{k}}_o}{\mu} (\nabla p + \rho \underline{g})$$

$\bar{\bar{k}}_o$ = intrinsic permeability tensor

p = pressure

$\underline{g}$ = vertical gravity vector.

The flow velocity is $\underline{v} = \underline{q}/m$.

The continuity equation of incompressible flow: $\nabla (\rho \cdot \underline{q}) = 0$ (propagation of pressure is very fast relative to salt transport). These two equations combined yield:

$$\nabla \left[\frac{\bar{\bar{k}}_o}{\mu} (\nabla p + \rho \underline{g}) \right] = 0 \ .$$

The salt transport equation:

$$\nabla (\bar{\bar{D}} \nabla C) - \nabla (\underline{v} \cdot C) - \frac{\partial C}{\partial t} = 0$$

C = salt concentration (mass/fluid volume)

assuming no interaction with the solid matrix nor chemical reactions, nor salt sources or sumps.

Concentration C, and density ρ, can be related by the simple approximate formula:

$$\rho = \rho_f (1 - E \frac{C}{C_s})$$

ρ_f = density of fresh water

E = coefficient $\simeq$ 0.025 (dimensionless)

C_s = salinity of sea water.

This dispersive-convective (advective) equation is very difficult to solve by means of finite difference methods, due to numerical dispersion, except when dispersion effects are dominant. Usually the advective term is dominant. Numerical dispersion not only produces a greater spread of the mixing zone, but for too long time steps may yield even negative values for C in the high pressure gradient areas.

The method of characteristics (fluid particles are moved along the flow lines at a given time step, while being dispersed) can yield good results, and has been used (Konikow and Bredehoeft, 1978; Pinder and Cooper, 1970; Reddell and Sunada, 1970; Green and Cox, 1966; Bredehoeft and Pinder, 1973) but it is too heavy and tedious in most circumstances. Recently, methods similar to that of Montecarlo seem to yield good results with a reasonable computer effort.

The Galerkin-finite element approach (Pinder and Gray, 1977) is an alternative solution method, but in coastal aquifers, the direct application poses great problems.

Cheng (1974) and Lee and Cheng (1974) have obtained a steady state solution to the saltwater intrusion problem by using a discontinuous velocity formulation, that uses a stream function and a concentration function. It is satisfactory for small Péclet numbers. Numerical instability is encountered when convective transport is dominant, as is also demonstrated by Volker and Rushton (1982). Segol, Pinder and Gray (1975) obtain a continuous velocity field through the Galerkin-finite element method and it is iteratively improved after the subsequent solution of the separate transport equation. Tyagi (1975) studied the solution of the transition zone under changing recharge conditions.

Boundary conditions, moreover that are necessary for the flow equation, include those needed for the salt transport equation. On an impervious boundary $dC/dn = 0$, where n is the outward-pointing normal direction to the boundary. On the outlet section of the aquifer, where it is exposed to open sea, it can be assumed that seepage velocity is perpendicular to the outlet surface (Henry, 1964b; Pinder and Cooper, 1970). The transport equation can be written in it, in its simple finite difference form with respect to local coordinates:

$$ q_n \left[\frac{C_g - C_s}{\nabla n} \right] = \left(D \frac{\partial C}{\partial n} \right)_g = - \left(D \frac{\partial C}{n} \right)_s \frac{1}{\nabla n} $$

∇n = differential increment in the direction perpendicular to the seepage surface

g   = ground side

s   = sea side.

Therefore, the exact boundary condition of C depends not only on the salt concentration of sea water, but also on the salt concentration gradient, $(\partial C/\partial n)_s$, in the immediate vicinity of the seepage surface, that is to say, on the circulation and mixing process near the seabed. It is a difficult condition and then it is generally assumed that $C_g = C_s$ and consequently $(\partial C/\partial n)_g = 0$.

Lee and Cheng (1974) and Segol and Pinder (1976) have applied their solution methods to the well known Cutler area limestone aquifer (Biscayne Bay, Miami, Florida), with reasonable results.

Another simulation model, resolved numerically by the finite differences method, was found to be accurate when applied to the aquifer on North Haven Island, near Long Island (Pinder, 1973).

5.4   References

Abbott, M.B., Ashamalla, A.F., Rodenhuis, G.S. (1972). On the numerical computation of stratified groundwater flow. Bull. Int. Assoc. Scientific Hydrology, Vol. XVII, 17/1972, pp. 177-182.

Anderson, M.P. (1976). Unsteady groundwater flow beneath strip oceanic islands. Water Resources Research, Vol. 12, No. 4, pp. 640-644.

Anguita, F., et al. (1972). Seminario sobre modelos analógicos y digitales para la explotación y administración de recursos hidráulicos subterráneos (Seminar on analogical and digital models for groundwater resources exploitation and evaluation). Servicio Geológico de Obras Públicas, Informaciones y Estudios, Bull. 37. Madrid, 178 pp.

Aravin, V.I., Numerov, S.N. (1965). Theory of motion of liquids and gases in undeformable porous media. Trans. A. Moscona. Jerusalem: Israel Program for Scientific Translation, 1965.

Bear, J. (1970). Two liquid flows in porous media. Advances in Hydroscience, Vol. 6. Ven T. Chow, ed., Academic Press, New York.

Bear, J. (1972). Dynamics of fluids in porous media. New York: American Elsevier Publishing Company, Inc.

Bear, J. (1979). Hydraulics of groundwater. McGraw-Hill, New York, 567 pp.

Bear, J., Dagan, G. (1964). Some exact solutions of interface problems by means of the hodograph method. Journal of Geophysical Research, Vol. 69, No. 8, pp. 1563-1572.

Bear, J., Dagan, G. (1964). Moving interface in coastal aquifers. Journal of Hydraulics Division of ASCE, 90 (HY4), 193-216 pp.

Bear, J., Zaslavsky, D., Irmay, S. (1968). Physical principles of water percolation and seepage. Paris: Unesco.

Bear, J., Kapuler, I. (1981). A numerical solution for the movement of an interface in a layered coastal aquifer. Journal of Hydrology, 50 (1981). Elsevier, pp. 273-298.

Bonnet, M., Carlier, P. (1974). Étude par modeles du dispositive de captage et consignes d'exploitation optimales d'une nappe littorale en comunication avec la mer, le bassin du Dradere-Soueive (Model study of the abstraction works and optimal exploitation rules of a coastal aquifer communicating with the sea: the Dradere-Soueive Bassin). Bull BRGM, 3rd Series, Sec. III, No. 1. Paris, pp. 125-135.

Bonnet, M., Sauty, J.P. (1975). Un modele simplifié pour la simulation des nappes avec intrusion saline (A simplified model for sea water intruded aquifer simulation). Proc. Bratislava Symposium on Mathematical Models in Hydrology and Water Resources Systems. AIHS, Pub. 115, pp. 45-56.

Cheng, R.T. (1974). _On the study of convective dispersion equation._ Finite Elements in Flow Problems. University of Alabama Press, Tuscaloosa, pp. 29-47.

Cheng, R.T., Hu, M.H. (1975). _Study of fluid movements through causeway._ J. of Hydraulics Division of ASCE, 101 (HY1), pp. 155-165.

Chidley, T.R.E., Lloyd, J.W. (1977). _A mathematical model study of freshwater lenses._ Ground Water, 15 (3), pp. 215-222.

Christensen, B.A., Evans, A.J., Jr. (1974). _A physical model for prediction and control of saltwater intrusion in the Floridian aquifer._ Water Resources Research Center, University of Florida, Gainesville. Pub. 27, 88 pp.

Christensen, B.A., Evans, A.J., Jr. (1975). _Salt water encroachment in coastal aquifers evaluated by physical models._ Water for Human Needs. Proc. II World Congress on Water Resources. Vol. III. New Dehli. Int. Water Resources Assoc. pp. 259-312.

Collins, M.A., Gelhar, L.W. (1970). _Ground water hydrology of the Long Island aquifer system._ Hydrodynamics Laboratory, Report No. 122. MIT, Cambridge, Massachusetts.

Collins, M.A., Gelhar, L.W. (1971). _Seawater intrusion in layered aquifers._ Water Resources Research, 7 (4), pp. 971-979.

Columbus, N. (1965). _Viscous model study of sea water intrusion in water table aquifers._ Water Resources Research. Vol. 1, No. 2, second quarter, pp. 313-323.

Custodio, E., Llamas, M.R. (1976). _Hidrología Subterránea_ (Groundwater hydrology). Ed. Omega, Barcelona, 2375 pp.

van Dam, J.C. (1976). _Partial depletion of saline groundwater by seepage._ J. of Hydrology, 29 (3/4), pp. 315-339.

Desai, C.S., Contractor, D.N. (1977). _Finite element analysis of flow, diffusion and salt water intrusion in porous media._ Formulation and Computational Algorithms in Finite Element Analysis. Ed. by K.J. Bathe et al., MIT Press, pp. 958-983.

Ferrer Polo, J., Ramos Ramis, J. (1981). _Un modelo quasi-tridimensional para el estudio de la intrusió salina en acuíferos costeros_ (A quasi-tridimensional model for the study of saltwater intrusion in coastal aquifer). Jornadas sobre el Análisis y Evolución de la Contaminación de Aguas Subterráneas en España. Barcelona. Sec. 4. Curso Internacional de Hidrología Subterránea. Barcelona. 12 pp.

Gelhar, L.W., Wilson, J.L., Miller, J.S. (1972). _Gravitational and dispersive mixing in aquifers._ J. of the Hydraulics Division. ASCE (HY12), pp. 2135-2153.

Glover, R.E. (1959). <u>The pattern of fresh-water flow in a coastal aquifer.</u> Journal of Geophysical Research. Vol. 64, No. 4, pp. 457-459.

Green, D.W., Cox, R.L. (1966). <u>Storage of fresh water in underground reservoirs containing saline water.</u> Phase 1, Completion Report 3, 24 pp. Kansas Water Resources Research Institute. Manhattan.

Hantush, M.S. (1968). <u>Unsteady movement of fresh water in thick unconfined saline aquifers.</u> Bulletin of International Association of Scientific Hydrology, XII (2), 40-60 pp.

Hashish, M.A., Rasmy, M.E., Amer, A.M. (1979). <u>One dimensional steady state sea water intrusion in leaky aquifers.</u> Conference on Water Resources Planning in Egypt, Cairo.

Hele-Shaw, H.S. (1897). <u>Experiments on the nature of surface resistance in pipes and on ships.</u> Transactions Institute Naval Architects. Vol. 39, pp. 145-146. London.

Hele-Shaw, H.S. (1899). <u>Streamline motion of a viscous film.</u> British Association for the Advancement of Science, 68th Meeting. Vol 136, pp. 136-142.

Henry, H.R. (1964). <u>Interfaces between salt water and fresh water in coastal aquifers.</u> Sea Water in Coastal Aquifers, ed. H.H. Cooper, et al., Geological Survey Water Supply Paper 1613-C, Washington, D.C., pp. 35-69.

Henry, H.R. (1964). <u>Effects of dispersion on salt encroachment in coastal aquifers.</u> Sea Water in Coastal Aquifers, ed. H.H. Cooper et al., Geological Survey Water Supply Paper 1613-C, Washington, D.C., pp. 70-83. 1964.

INTERCOMP (1976). <u>A model for calculation effects of liquid waste disposal in deep saline aquifers.</u> Intercomp Resource Development and Engineering, Inc., prepared for USGS, NTIS PB256-203.

Jeanson, B., Dufort, J. (1970). <u>Etude sur modele physique des conditions de pollution des nappes cotieres par l'eau salée lors de la production.</u> Bull. BRGM, 2nd Series, Sec. III, No. 3, pp. 98-148.

de Jossselin de Jong, G. (1977). <u>Review of vortex theory for multiple fluid flow.</u> Delft Progress Report, Vol. 2, pp. 225-236.

Kashef, A.A.I. (1975). <u>Management of retardation of salt water intrusion in coastal aquifers.</u> Office of Water Research and Technology, Washington, D.C.

Kashef, A.A.I. (1976). <u>Control of salt-water intrusion by recharge wells.</u> J. of the Irrigation and Drainage Division. ASCE, 102 (IR4), pp. 445-457.

Kashef, A.A.I., Smith, J.C. (1975). Expansion of salt-water zone due to well discharge. Water Resources Bulletin, J. AWRA, 11 (6), pp. 1107-1120.

Kishi, Y., Fukuo, Y. (1977). Studies on salinization of groundwater, I: theoretical considerations on the three-dimensional movement of salt water interface caused by pumpage of a confined groundwater in fanshiped alluvium. J. of Hydrology, 35 (1/2), pp. 1-29.

Konikow, L.F., Bredehoeft, J.D. (1978). Computer model of two dimensional transport and dispersion in groundwater. Techniques of Water Resources Investigation, Book 7, Ch. C.2. U.S. Geological Survey.

Kono, I. (1974). Analysis of interface problems in groundwater flow by finite element method. Finite Elements in Fluids, Vol. 1. Ed. R.H. Gallagher et al., John Wiley and Sons, U.K. Also in Delft University of Technology, Delft, Rep. Soil Mech. Lab. (1972).

Layla, R. (1980). Numerical analysis of transient salt-frsh water interface in coastal aquifers. Ph.D. Thesis, Colorado State University.

Lee, C., Cheng, R.T. '1974). On sea water encroachment in coastal aquifers. Water Resources Research, Vol. 10, No. 5, pp. 1039-1043.

Liu, P.L.F., Liggett, J.A. (1978). An efficient numerical method of two-dimensional steady groundwater problems. Water Resources Research, 14 (3), pp. 385-390.

Maasland, D.E.L., Bittinger, M.W. (1967). Drainage of a saline-water aquifer recharged by fresh water. Haifa Symp. on Artificial Recharge and Management of Aquifers. Int. Assoc. Scientific Hydrology. Pub. 72, pp. 350-359.

Mercer, J.W., Larwon, S.P., Faust, C.R. (1980). Simulation of salt-water interface motion. Ground Water, Vol. 18, No. 4, pp. 374-385.

Mercer, J.W., Larson, S.P., Faust, C.R. (1980). Finite-difference model to simulate the annual flow of salt water and fresh water separated by an interface. U.S. Geological Survey, open-file report 80-407, 58 pp.

Mualem, Y., Bear, J. (1974). The shape of the interface in steady flow in a stratified aquifer. Water Resources Research, 10 (6), pp. 1207-1215.

Pinder, G.F. (1973). A Galerkin-finite element simulation of groundwater contamination on Long Island, New York. Water Resources Research, Vol. 9, No. 6, pp. 1657-1669.

Pinder, G.F., Cooper, H.H. (1970). A numerical technique for calculating the transient position of the saltwater front. Water Resources Research, 6 (3), pp. 875-882.

Pinder, G.F., Gray, W.G. (1977). *Finite element simulation in surface and subsurface hydrology.* Academic Press, New York.

Pinder, G.F., Page, R.H. (1976). *Finite element simulation of salt water intrusion on the South Fork of Long Island.* International Conference in Finite Elements in Water Resources, Princeton, N.J. July, Part II, 18 pp.

Polubarinova-Kochina, Y. (1962). *Theory of ground water movement.* Trans. J.M.R. de Weist. Princeton: Princeton University Press, 613 pp.

Prickett, T.A., Lonnquist, C.G. (1971). *Selected digital computer techniques for ground water resource evaluation.* Illinois State Water Survey, Bull. 55. Urbana.

Reddell, D.L., Sunada, D.K. (1970). *Numerical simulation of dispersion in groundwater aquifers.* Hydrology Papers 41, 79 pp. Colorado State University, Fort Collins.

Remson, I., Hornberger, G.M., Molz, F.J. (1971). *Numerical methods in subsurface hydrology.* Wiley-Interscience, New York. 389 pp.

Rofail, N. (1977). *A mathematical model of stratified groundwater flow.* Hydrological Sciences Bulletin, XII (4), pp. 503-512.

Rumer, R.R., Harleman, D.R.F. (1963). *Intruded salt-water wedge in porous media.* J. of Hydraulics Division. ASCE, 89 (HY6), pp. 193-220.

Rumer, R.R., Shiau, J.C. (1968). *Saltwater interface in a layered coastal aquifer.* Water Resources Research, 4 (6), pp. 1235-1247.

Sá da Costa, A.A.G., Wilson, J. (1979). *A numerical model of sea-water intrusion in aquifers.* Ralph M. Parsons Laboratory for Water Resources and Hydrodynamics. Dept. Civil Engineering. Massachusetts. Report No. 247, R79-41, 245 pp.

Segol, G., Pinder, G.F. (1970). *Transient simulation of saltwater intrusion in Southeastern Florida.* Water Resources Research, 12 (1), pp. 65-70.

Segol, G., Pinder, G.F., Gray, W.C. (1975). *A Galerkin-finite element technique for calculating the transient position of the salt-water front.* Water Resources Research, 11 (2), pp. 343-347.

Shamir, V., Dagan, G. (1971). *Motion of the sea water interface in coastal aquifers: a numerical solution.* Water Resources Research, Vol. 7, No. 3, pp. 644-657.

Strack, O.D.L. (1976). *Single-potential solution for regional interface problems in coastal aquifers.* Water Resources Research, 12 (6), pp. 1165-1174.

Tyagi, A.K. (1975). <u>Finite element modeling of sea water intrusion in coastal ground water systems.</u> Water for Human Needs. Proc. II World Congress on Water Resources. Vol. III, New Dehli. Int. Water Resources Assoc., pp. 325-338.

van der Veer, P. (1979). <u>Analytical solution of steady interface flow in a coastal aquifer involving a phreatic surface with precipitation.</u> Journal of Hydrology, 34 (1/2), pp. 1-11. Elsevier.

Verou, M. (1978). <u>Seawater intrusion in a leaky coastal aquifer.</u> M.Sc. Thesis, Massachusetts Institute of Technology. Cambridge, Massachusetts.

Verruijt, A. (1968). <u>A note on the Ghyben-Herzberg formula.</u> Bulletin International Association of Scientific Hydrology, 13 (4), pp. 43-46.

Volker, R.E., Rushton, K.R. (1982). <u>An assessment of the importance of some parameters for seawater intrusion in aquifers and a comparison of dispersive and sharp interface modeling approaches.</u> Journal of Hydrology, 56 (1962), pp. 239-250. Elsevier.

de Wiest, J.R.M. (1965). <u>Geohydrology.</u> John Wiley Sons.

6. Hydrogeochemistry and tracers

E. Custodio

Contents

6.0   Introduction

Chemical aspects of groundwater, including environmental isotopes and tracers, are key factors in the understanding and evaluation of the flow pattern, in spite of the lack of easy quantitative methods and the complexity of the processes involved. In coastal areas those chemical aspects are still more important due to the rapidly changing hydrochemical facies and the special role of ion exchange. Furthermore the great impairing of groundwater quality when small quantities of sea water are mixed, as described in chapter 2, highlights the interest in reviewing the water quality criteria under the chemical point of view.

6.1   Salinity and water quality

Sea water contains large amounts of dissolved salts, mainly sodium chloride, but also significant quantities of alkaline-earth sulphates are present, transmitting high hardness. Total dissolved solids in sea water are about 35 g/l, and the chloride ion content is close to 20 g/l.

Such a saline water cannot be used in most human activities, and is certainly not potable. Mixtures of fresh and sea water result also in a generally nonusable water, even if sea water is only a small portion. According to potable water standards (table 6.1) three parts of sea water to 100 parts of fresh water communicates a saline taste and the water is no longer useful for drinking purposes under normal conditions.

Table 6.1 - Maximum allowable concentrations in drinking water for some dissolved salts and ions frequent in sea water (WHO, 1971).

| Substances | Values in mg/l | | | | |
| | Maximum concentration in drinking water | | Concentration in standard sea water | Dilution factor of sea water in fresh water to meet standards | |
	Acceptable	Allowable		Acceptable	Allowable
TDS (1)	500	1500	35000	70	23
Ca^{++}	75	200	400	5	2
Mg^{++}	50	150	1272	25	8
$SO_4^{=}$	200	400	2649	13	7
Cl^{-}	200	600	19000	95	32
$MgSO_4+Na_2SO_4$	500	1000	3300	7	3
Na^{+} (2)					

(1) TDS = total dissolved solids
(2) High sodium concentrations is today a great concern since it is blamed for high blood pressure disorders.

Without attempting to cover in detail the effects of salinity on the uses of water, a short comment will follow on the main impairing effects that the mixture with sea water has in fresh water. The discussion will consider only the effects related to total salinity, chloride content, hardness and sodium ion concentration. More details can be found in Unesco (1978) or in other standard books.

A. Use for drinking purposes.

According to the World Health Organization (WHO,1971), a convenient chloride ion concentration limit is 200 mg/l. Many national standards are more limited in the admissible upper limit, although higher values are tolerated in severe drought periods or under special circumstances, when no other water is available. The chloride ion is not a serious toxic or a poison, but a permanent overdose may result in some human body malfunctions or negative effects. Some of the dangers are probably related to the sodium ion, closely related to high blood overtension. A total dose (water and food) of 20 g/day Na^+ seems a tolerable upper limit, and about 6 g/day NaCl is a recommended limit, although there is a tendency to lower this figure further. There is no general medical agreement on the influence of water hardness on heart diseases.

In some coastal urban areas, during the summer time, tap water reaches one or two g/l in Cl^-, without known side effects apart from taste complaints, but in part it is due to generalized bottled water consumption for drinking purposes, and sometimes also for cooking.

Generally, a salty water taste produces complaints about the water supply. Such a taste develops clearly when the chloride content reaches one g/l and sometimes with only 0.5 g/l.

B. Use for domestic and urban purposes, other than potable ones.

Brackish or salty water impairs cooking. Washing is impaired through higher consumption of soap or other washing substances. Hardness is the main offender. When water evaporates, scale easily deposits. The high conductivity of the water favors electrolytic processes, and pipes, vessels and other metallic installations or objects, including those of stainless steel, easily corrode unless special and costly protections are applied. The salt residue after water evaporation is also highly corrosive because it remains wet due to its hygroscopicity. It is also abrasive.

A total dissolved solids content of 0.5 g/l is the desirable upper limit, but upto 1.5 g/l can be tolerated without serious problems.

C. Use for irrigation and farming purposes.

Plants, including those in house gardens have an upper tolerance to water salinity that varies with the type of plant, the water chemical composition, the soil nature and the climate, among other factors. Total irrigation water salinity is related to pore water salinity, and the greater the salinity, the more difficult it is for the plant roots to perform their task, since the available osmotic pressure difference decreases. Predominantly sodium waters, such as those contaminated with sea water, produce a decrease in soil permeability through ion exchange, thus reducing the drainage properties. This effect may result in soil logging, that reduces soil aeration, increases salinity problems and may result in soil salinization, especially in arid and semiarid areas. This is a frequent process in fertile coastal areas, after several years of irrigation with brackish water without taking the necessary corrective measures.

The suitability of a water for irrigation purposes, according to the U.S. Salinity Laboratory Staff, depends on the total dissolved solids content and on the relative concentration of Na^+ with respect to the alkaline-earth ions, measured by the sodium absorption ratio, SAR = rNa/$\sqrt{1/2(rCa + rMg)}$ in which the r indicates that the concentration is measured in milli-equivalents per liter. The SAR value for sea water is 7.3, which exceeds several times the recommended values. A corrected SAR value takes into account possible Ca dissolution or precipitation. Other criteria, such as the exchangeable sodium ratio, that can be found in water quality publications, lead to the same conclusions.

Sea water also contains about 5 mg/l of boron, mainly in the form of borate ion. Boron is highly detrimental to crops, a value of one mg/l being the maximum allowable for semitolerant plants.

Cattle are generally more salinity tolerant than humans, but also an upper limit must be established, generally of a few g/l total salinity. Greater values may impair the market quality of the cattle and the reproduction rate. The same is true for poultry.

D. Use for cooling purposes.

Cooling is less dependent on water quality since water is only used for extracting and transporting heat. Notwithstanding, brackish or salty water is more corrosive and encrustant than fresh water and thus the installation life is shorter or protective measures must be applied, producing a cost increase. Moreover, leakages and the discharge of these waters can produce some difficulties or complaints. When brackish water is used in closed cooling loops with wet cooling towers, evaporation produces a rapid salt increase in the water, thus augmenting the cost in scale and corrosion protective chemicals and also the frequency or the percentage of blow-down.

Notwithstanding, some industrial installations near the shoreline, mainly power plants, now use sea water for cooling, but they are especially designed for it and must correct fouling problems created by living organisms and corrosivity.

E. Industrial use.

Although water use in industry is highly variable, brackish and salty water generally induce more corrosion problems, scaling and encrustation, more consumption of chemicals and some disposal problems. Installations and equipment life are shorter, thus increasing production and maintenance costs. Sometimes, a separate water supply or special treatment facilities are needed in order to meet potability (drinking, food processing, beverages preparation, etc.), steam generator minimum qualities, etc.

In coastal areas, not only brackish or salt water are problems; but also salinity variations, which may cause corrosion problems in distribution networks and pipes and impair industrial processes that need a constant water quality. In estuaries, wells and abstraction works influenced by salt water upconing, salinity changes can be rapid and frequent, with undesirable effects.

The above considerations suggest that an upper limit of the transition zone between fresh and sea water can be defined from the tolerable salinity limit; a 0.5 or 1.0 g/l Cl⁻ is usually considered as the limit between fresh and salt water.

6.2 Fresh water, sea water and mixtures

Natural water has a highly variable chemical composition, but a few fundamental or principal ions represent in most cases more than the 99 per cent of total ionic content.

The fundamental anions are: chloride (Cl^-), sulphate ($SO_4^=$) and bicarbonate (HCO_3^-), and in some circumstances carbonate ($CO_3^=$), when the pH is high. A high nitrate (NO_3^-) generally indicates a non-natural contribution.

The fundamental cations are the alkaline-earth ions: calcium (Ca^{++}) and magnesium (Mg^{++}) both determining the major part of water hardness; and the alkaline ions, represented mainly by sodium (Na^+) and secondarily by potassium (K^+). Sometimes the ammonium ion (NH_4^+) must be considered as well.

Some dissolved gases must be considered, mainly carbon dioxide (CO_2) that hydrolyzes to the bicarbonate ion, and also the main air components, oxygen (O_2) and nitrogen (N_2). Also the silica compounds, mainly silicic acid, are fundamental constituents in natural water, mostly in a non-ionic form, in soluble or colloidal state.

In a natural water many other ions and substances can be found, but in most cases they are only a small fraction of the total dissolved solids content. In some circumstances, the metallic ions Fe^{++}, Mn^{++}, Sr^{++}, and the anions F^-, Br^- and boric acid compounds can be found in amounts exceeding one part per million. They are minor ions or compounds, although their effects can be highly undesirable. Other substances present in smaller quantities are generally called trace elements.

Fundamental components are generally easy to sample and measure, and most chemical laboratories can determine them accurately. They are essential to study the relationships between the natural medium and the water flow. The role of minor and trace elements will be discussed below, in section 6.6.

Continental fresh water, if not severely polluted by human activities, is generally of the earth-alkaline bicarbonate type (these ions dominate), and in many situations the calcium ion exceeds the magnesium ion content. Exceptions to this rule are frequent, especially in deep water, but in most circumstances the ions mentioned are always an important fraction of total ionic content, the alkaline-earth to alkaline ions ratio being greater than in sea water.

Total salinity and chemical composition is a complex function of lithology, soil characteristics and vegetation, climate and water flow pattern. Some of these relations can be shown or characterized by means of chemical ratios (between the concentration of selected ions) or chemical diagrams, as will be discussed in section 6.7.

Sea water is characterized by a net predominance of chloride and sodium ions, although the absolute concentration of the other fundamental and some minor ions is also important, since total dissolved solids content is very high, close to 35 g/l.

Mean sea salinity is naturally between 34 and 35 g/l, the 35 g/l figure taken as a standard value. Actual values may be different according to local circumstances, such as continental influence, degree of evaporation, oceanic currents, etc. Salinity of the Mediterranean sea water is higher than that of the Atlantic Ocean, and the salinity is some areas of the Mediterranean and the Red Sea may reach 45 g/l. Continental outflow reduces the salinity of the Black Sea to 18 to 22 g/l and that of the Baltic Sea to 3 to 8 g/l. In the Atlantic Ocean, salinity is higher than in the Pacific Ocean, 36.9 g/l at latitude 25^ON versus 33.6 g/l at latitude 40^ON in the Pacific Ocean. After Gilcher (1965), in an open sea, total water salinity S, can be calculated according to:

$$S(g/l) = 34.6 + 0.0175 \ (E - P)$$

E and P being respectively the evaporation rate and the rainfall, both in mm/year, but sea currents alter the results somewhat.

As shown in chapter 2, corresponding density changes can be calculated with the formula (van Dam, 1977):

$$\rho = 1000 + 0.80545 - 0.0065 \ (\theta - 4 + 0.2214S)^2$$

in which:

ρ = water density, in g/l

S = salinity in parts per thousand ($^O/oo$)

θ = water temperature in degrees C.

Chloride ion content is generally taken at about 19 g/l, but figures as high as 21 g/l can be found in the Mediterranean Sea. There is always a slight excess of chloride over alkaline ($Na^+ + K^+$) ions in terms of chemical equivalents, and magnesium is greatly in excess over calcium. Chemical ratios in sea water can be taken as fairly constant. Some of the most representative values are shown in table 6.2. Some of the chemical ratios (ionic ratios) are highly characteristic of sea water and different from those of the continental waters, especially Mg/Ca and Cl/HCO_3, but the small variability of other ratios is also an important fact.

The chemical mixtures of fresh and salt water can be calculated easily. If x is the fraction of fresh water of concentration F, and 1-x is the fraction of sea water of concentration S, the fresh water concentration in the mixture M, is:

$$M = x \cdot F + (1 - x) \ S \ .$$

This formula is applicable to total salinity or to the individual components.

Table 6.2 - Representative values of sea water chemical composition, including the Mediterranean Sea.

Anion	HCO_3^-	$SO_4^=$	Cl^-	Br^-	Borates (B)
mg/l	70-150	2500-2900	18000-21000	60-120	~ 5
Cation	Na^+	K^+	Ca^{++}	Mg^{++}	Sr^{++}
mg/l	10000-11800	350-400	380-440	1100-1400	~ 13

General data	pH	Electrical conductivity	Total dissolved solids	Total cations or anions
	~ 8	45-55 mS/cm, 25°C	34.5-43 g/l	580-660 meq/l

Ratios	rMg/rCa	rNa/rK	rSO_4/rCl	rCl/$rHCO_3$	rAlk/rCl
	4.5-5.2	42-47	0.10-0.11	200-500	0.871-0.885

r   = concentration in milliequivalents per liter (meq/l)
rAlk = alkaline ions = $rNa^+ + rK^+$
~   = close to the shown figure

The mixtures can be taken as chemically stable (no precipitate forms) in most situations, but the above mentioned calculations give theoretical concentrations since the mixture interacts with solid matter in several forms that will be discussed in the next paragraphs.

6.3   Ion exchange phenomena and alkaline ion/chloride ratio

Minerals, mainly those of clay, have free negative chemical valences on the surface, which are saturated with water cations in proportion to its relative abundance and sorption characteristics. This is applicable to the ionic chemical equilibrium between river water and its solid transport, and to that established between ground water and the porous or fissured porous media. Thus, the solid surfaces have sorbed cations, according to the ion exchange capacity and the water chemical composition, following relationships expressed by exchange isotherms. Typical calcic continental fresh water saturates the free valences on the clay and mineral particules, mainly with calcium ions. Typical sodium marine water saturates the free valences on clay particules, mainly with sodium ions.

When the cationic ratios in the water change, the sorbed ionic part also is modified in order to adjust to the new environment, that is to say, sorbed cations are freed and replaced by the new dominant ones. Thus, the solid phase tends to oppose the chemical change in the water. These reactions are very rapid and in most circumstances can be regarded as instantaneous.

When marine water is changed for fresh water, the solid phase gives up the sorbed calcium and also part of the magnesium, and replaces them by sodium. In this way, marine water loses sodium and gains calcium and magnesium. Since the chloride ion remains unchanged, it can be taken as a reference. Thus, in marine water the ratio rNa/rCl decreases and the ratio $(rCa + rMg)/rCl$ increases, where $\Delta(rCa + rMg) = -\Delta rNa$ (Δ means the variation in the cation concentration; r indicates that the concentrations must be given in meq/l). Accordingly, the increase in $(rCa + rMg)/rCl$ balances the decrease in rNa/rCl. In other words, when fresh water is replaced by marine water, marine water hardens.

When fresh water is changed for marine water, the solid phase gives up the sorbed sodium, and is replaced by calcium and magnesium. Thus, fresh water loses calcium and magnesium (is said to be softened), the ratio rNa/rCl increases and the ratio $(rCa + rMg)/rCl$ decreases in the same amount that the previous ratio has increased.

The same is true for the mixtures of sea and continental waters.

The importance of the above-mentioned phenomena depends on the cation exchange capacity of the ground. All minerals have some exchange capacity, but it is maximum in clay minerals especially those of the smectite and montmorillonite types. Until final exchange equilibrium is attained, important water modifications can be expected in sediments with a significant clay fraction or clayish interbeddings, and only slight modifications in pure silica sands or pure limestones. In fissured hardrocks, exchange capacity can be noticeable if enough exposed surface exists, as in volcanics, highly fissured limestones, etc. When a few large fractures represent the transmissive properties of the rock, small changes, if any, can be expected, because the mineral surface is very small. Such is the case of highly karstic areas, inside ground water channels. In zones away from them, modification may take place more clearly.

All the discussion supposes that the ratio between alkaline and alkaline-earth cations in fresh water is always smaller than in sea water. This is the general situation, inclusive in granite derived waters of the sodium dominant type.

There is also an ionic exchange between calcium and magnesium ions, and remembering that the ratio rMg/rCa in sea water is usually much greater than in continental waters, the ratio increases when fresh water invades formations previously saturated with sea water and decreases when salt water invades terrains previously saturated with fresh water. Other phenomena may obscure such a behavior, such as carbonate solution or precipitation.

The fate of potassium ions with respect to sodium ions is not so simple because K$^+$ tends to be highly retained by the structure of clay minerals, but a similar trend of evolution exists. The rNa/rK ratio depends on the species existing and on the environmental temperature.

In the ground, the ionic exchange processes only appear when the salt-fresh water interface is in movement, or there is a continuous evolution towards aquifer salinization or desalinization through salt water displacement and washout of the entrapped salts. The processes are present mainly in mixed water. Once the change is established, the exchange ceases since the capacity is exhausted. The percentage of fresh and sea water in a mixture can be easily calculated through the chloride content, since this ion is neither affected by ion exchange nor by other modifying processes.

If:

x   = fraction of fresh water in the mixture

1-x = fraction of sea water in the mixture

Cl_m = chloride concentration in the mixture

Cl_s = chloride concentration in the marine water

Cl_f = chloride concentration in the original fresh water, then

$$Cl_m = x \cdot Cl_f + (1 - x)Cl_s; \qquad x = \frac{Cl_s - Cl_m}{Cl_s - Cl_f} \, .$$

x can also be determined graphically as shown in figure 6.1.

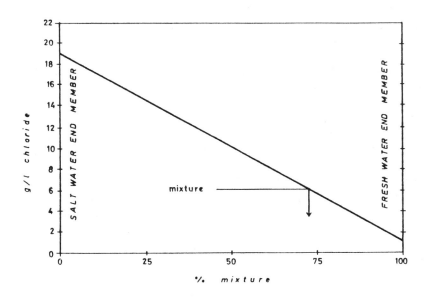

Fig. 6.1 – Graphical calculation of salt-fresh water mixtures. Theoretical mixtures plot on the straight line connecting the two end members.

The theoretical concentrations, A_m^t of Ca^{++}, Mg^{++} and Na^+ or $(Na^+ + K^+)$ in the mixture can be easily calculated when x is known:

$$A_m^t = x \cdot A_f + (1 - x)A_s,$$

A being the concentration of one of those cations and the subscripts meaning the same as in the previous formula.

If there is some cation exchange, the actual concentration, A_m^a, will be different from A_m^t, if no other modifying phenomena dominates, according to previous comments. The difference in alkaline-earth cations in the mixture between theoretical content and actual content must balance, in chemical equivalents, the difference in alkaline cations.

$$(rMg^a + rCa^a) - (rMg^t + rCa^t) = (rNa^t - rK^t) - (rNa^a + rK^a) .$$

Detailed studies have been carried out in many places. The study of Piper et al. (1953) in the Long Beach area (California) is a good reference. The findings are also confirmed through studies in many other areas (see Schoeller, 1956, 1962; Custodio, 1967, 1968, 1976a; Back and Hanshaw, 1965; Lusczynski and Swarzenski, 1966). The changes and mixtures are easily identified in chemical diagrams (see section 6.7). Two examples of calculations are given in tables 6.3 and 6.4. The presence of ion complexes somewhat changes the ionic balance and alters the interpretations, but the calculations are a good approximation to reality.

The alkaline-ion to chloride ratio ((rNa + rK)/rCl or simply rNa/rCl) is also very useful to study salt relationships in coastal areas. The r means that the chemical values are given in meq/l. The numerical value of the ratio is not interesting as its variation along a water flow path. For sea water the ratio varies generally between 0.87 and 0.885. The value for fresh water is a function of chemical processes during recharge, but in many circumstances the value is 1.0 ± 0.1. In granitic areas and especially in aklaline volcanic terrains may attain values as high as 3 or greater.

When salt water displaces fresh water the exchange process is more intense, the alkaline/chloride ratio decreases with respect to the fresh water value and frequently reaches lower values than in sea water about the displacement front, where if fresh water displaces salt water or washes out young marine sediments, the ratio increases and may reach remarkably high values. All this can be easily explained through the hardening or softening processes.

When ground exchange capacity is fully saturated, no more ion exchange occurs, and then the original ratio values are maintained in the fresh or salt water body, but not in the vicinity of the moving front, except if it is stationary or the exchange capacity of the aquifer minerals is very small, as inside the main channels in karstic areas, or in very pure sand or gravel aquifers.

The study of the rNa/rCl ratio gives very useful indications in many studies (Custodio, 1967, 1968; Arad, Kafri and Fleisher, 1975).

Table 6.3 - Example of mixing of fresh and sea water in the ground. It corresponds to the Besós Delta aquifer (Barcelona, Spain). In a confined aquifer with a reducing environment.

Data for the problem (compensated chemical analyses in meq/l)

Ions	$rHCO_3$	rSO_4	rCl	ΣA	r(Na+K)	rCa	rMg	ΣC
Fresh water, f	5.0	3.0	4.0	12.0	4.0	6.0	2.0	12.0
Sea water, S	2.8	68.2	610.0	618.0	538.0	26.8	116.2	681.0
Mixed water	9.0	35.0	425.0	469.0	335.0	42.0	92.0	469.0

Fresh water fraction in the mixture $x = \dfrac{610.0 - 425.0}{610.0 - 4.0} = 0.3053$

Calculated mixture composition $M = M_f \cdot x + M_s(1 - x)$

Ions	$rHCO_3$	rSO_4	rCl	ΣA	r(Na+K)	rCa	rMg	ΣC
Real mixture	9	35	425	469	335	42	92	469
Calculated mixture	3	47	425	475	375	20	80	475
Difference	+6	-12	0	-6	-40	+22	+12	-6

a) $SO_4^=$ is reduced; HCO_3^- increases (sulphate reduction and biological organic matter oxidation)
b) Na^+ disappears; $Ca^{++} + Mg^{++}$ appears (ion exchange)
c) There is a 6 meq/l difference, probably a precipitation of $CaCO_3$.

Figure 6.2 shows the results of the study of the chemical composition of the deltaic semipervious lens separating the two aquifers of the Llobregat delta (see case history no. 1 in chapter 10). Connate sea water trapped in the sediments shows a low rNa/rCl ratio due to the ionic exchange of sodium rich sea water with calcium and magnesium rich river transported sediments. The secular upward flow of fresh water displaces the salt water and the mixed water becomes enriched in Na (lower part) and also in HCO_3^- and $SO_4^=$ as a consequence of ion-exchange and redox reactions. Figure 6.3 shows the ionic exchange produced when fresh water artificially displaces salt water in a sea water intruded aquifer. Another example is presented in figure 6.4 for a volcanic aquifer in Hawaii, in which a Ca-Cl scatter diagram is used. Figure 6.5 corresponds to the saline intrusion in the Wittmund area in the Federal Republic of Germany.

Table 6.4 – Example of mixing of recharge water (secondary treated urban sewage water) with saline native groundwater in the Besós Delta confined aquifer (Barcelona, Spain), with a reducing environment. Data in meq/l. Chemical analyses ionically equilibrated.

Ions		$rHCO_3$	rSO_4	rCl	ΣA	rNa	rK	rCa	rMg	rNH_4	rFe	ΣC
Recharge water		6.0	4.4	15.9	26.3	13.4	0.7	7.2	3.4	1.6	0.0	26.3
Native water		4.2	38.9	460.5	503.6	366.6	2.6	38.0	96.0	0.0	0.4	503.6
1	Real	4.6	26.1	291.9	322.6	241.1	2.0	22.4	56.9	0.0	0.2	322.6
t=0.73 days	Calculated	4.9	25.8	291.9	322.6	232.7	1.9	26.3	60.9	0.6	0.2	322.6
x=0.3791	Difference	-0.3	+0.3	0.0	0.0	+8.4	+0.1	-3.9	-4.0	-0.6	0.0	0.0
2	Real	4.9	20.8	224.6	250.3	190.0	1.6	14.8	43.7	0.0	0.2	250.3
t=1.06 days	Calculated	5.1	20.6	224.6	250.3	179.2	1.6	21.6	46.9	0.8	0.2	250.3
x=0.5306	Difference	-0.2	+0.2	0.0	0.0	+10.8	-0.1	-6.1	-3.5	-1.1	0.0	0.0
3	Real	5.9	9.6	85.5	101.0	79.5	0.9	5.9	14.4	0.2	0.1	101.0
t=2.1 days	Calculated	5.7	9.8	85.5	101.0	68.7	1.0	12.0	17.9	1.3	0.1	101.0
x=0.8435	Difference	+0.2	-0.2	0.0	0.0	+10.8	-0.1	-6.1	-3.5	-1.1	0.0	0.0
4	Real	6.3	4.6	17.0	27.5	21.3	0.7	3.8		1.6	0.1	27.5
t=22 days	Calculated	6.0	4.5	17.0	27.5	14.3	0.7	10.9		1.6	0.0	27.5
x=0.9974	Difference	+0.3	-0.3	0.0	0.0	+7.0	0.0	-7.1		0.0	+0.1	0.0
5	Real	6.3	4.6	22.4	33.3	22.8	0.7	8.0		1.7	0.1	33.3
t=48 days	Calculated	6.0	4.9	22.4	33.3	18.6	0.7	12.4		1.6	0.0	33.3
x=0.9854	Difference	+0.3	-0.3	0.0	0.0	+4.2	0.0	-4.4		+0.1	+0.1	0.0

t = time since start of injection through the recharge well
x = calculated fraction of recharge water through the Cl^- content

Mixed water is sampled at 12 m distance

There is neither solution nor precipitation. Changes in $SO_4^=$ and HCO_3^- do not seem significant. Na^+ is liberated by the aquifer material in exchange for Ca^{++}, Mg^{++} and NH_4^+. Finally, NH_4^+ saturates the exchange capacity.

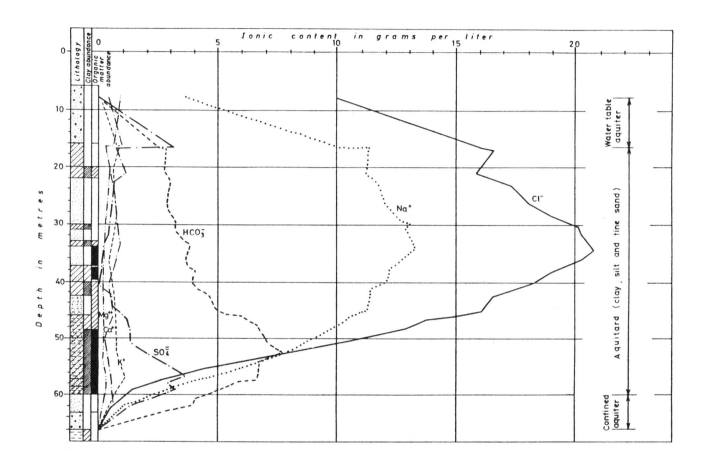

Fig. 6.2 – Vertical distribution of ions in a coastal borehole near the coast in the Llobregat delta (Barcelona, Spain). Since until some years ago the confined aquifer had a higher water head that the water table aquifer, this situation lasting almost a thousand years, there is a slight displacement of water composition. In the aquitard, the water chemical composition has been determined through leaching of the unaltered solid samples with distilled water (after Custodio, Bayó and Peláez, 1971). Connate sea water has a low rNa/rCl ratio due to ionic exchange with continentally generated sediments, but in the lower part, where fresh water mixes with and displaces the salt water, a high value is found.

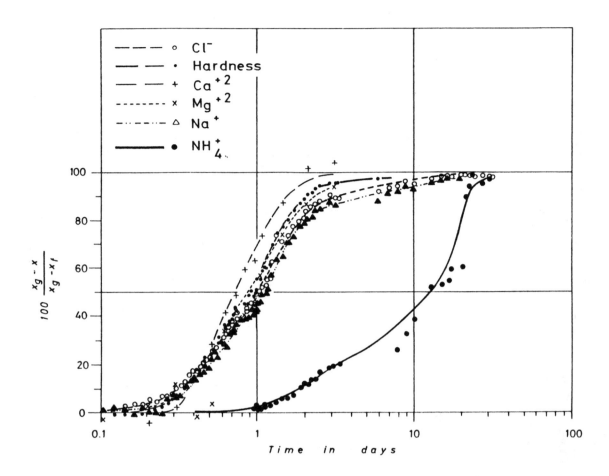

Fig. 6.3 - Normalized breakthrough curves in an observation borehole at 12 m from a fresh water recharge well in a saline aquifer. To normalize the values to 100% fresh water mixture it is calculated $100(x_g-x)/(x_g-x_f)$ in which x_g = concentration in groundwater; x_f = concentration in the injected fresh water; x = concentration in the sample. The Cl^- ion is the reference since it is not altered by the mixing and during the ground passage. Ammonia in the fresh water (it is a secondary treated urban sewage water) is ion exchanged in the formerly NH_4^+ free aquifer material, until it becomes saturated (about 25 g/m³ of aquifer), and its movement is retarded. The other shown ions are diluted by the injected water. In a given time Ca^{++} is at higher percentage than Cl^-; it represents that, since a greater percentage of fresh water is not possible, some Ca^{++} is lost by ionic exchange with the aquifer. The same is true for the Mg^{++} and the Na^+ behaves inversely, since it is released by the aquifer materials (after Custodio, Tourís and Balagué, 1981).

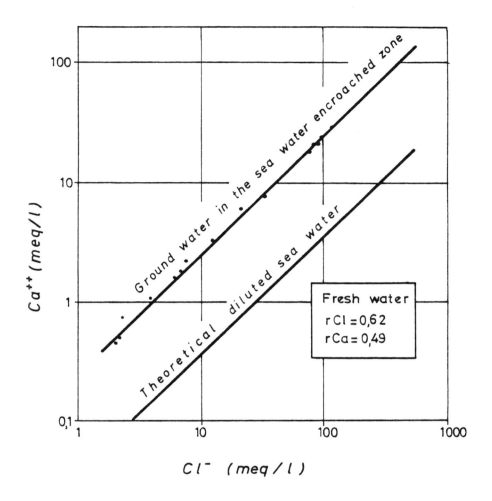

Fig. 6.4 - Ca-Cl scatter diagram. When there is a wide variation in salinity, logarithmic scales are recommended. In the figure there is a clear relationship between rCa and rCl. It corresponds to brackish ground-water in Oahu Island (Hawaii), in a coastal aquifer affected by sea water intrusion (after Mink, 1960). The line representing the expected rCa and rCa values from the simple dilution of sea water with local fresh water is shown. There is an excess of rCa due to Na-Ca exchange in the ground. It indicates that sea water intrusion is progressing.

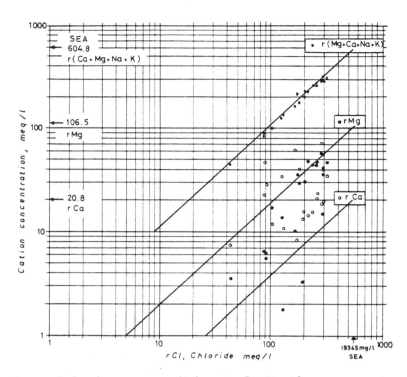

Fig. 6.5 - Behavior of ionic composition of North sea water intrusion in Wittmund area, in western Germany (Hahn, 1975). Total cationic content (rMg + rCa + rNa + rK) responds to the theoretical mixture, but an excess of Ca develops that shows the presence of ionic exchange. Mg is conserved or decreased, sometimes highly decreased, in the ionic exchange process (in that case mainly sediment diagenesis).

6.4   Other chemical modifications

The mixture of calcium carbonate saturated fresh and sea water (sea water is in general slightly oversaturated) is a water generally undersaturated (especially in the 10-20% sea water content range), due to the influence of ionic strength (decrease in effective concentration or activity through the formation of ionic complexes and non ionic compounds). It can be studied through classical chemical equilibrium methods (see Back and Hanshaw, 1965, 1970; Back et al., 1979; Hanshaw and Back, 1979; Plummer and Busenberg, 1982). This is clearly indicated in figure 6.6, for different partial pressures of CO_2. The change of Ca^{++} activity due to the increasing salinity is shown schematically in figure 6.7. Up to 0.3 mmol/1 of $CaCO_3$ can be dissolved in the optimum mixture.

Then, a calcite saturated fresh water, without the addition of more CO_2, after mixing with sea water becomes aggressive and further dissolution takes place, increasing the Ca^{++} and HCO_3^- content. This process of increased rapid dissolution and karstification of some coastal carbonate formations inside the mixing zone was recognized early on by Mandel (1964, 1965) and observed by Schmorak and Mercado (1969).

The observations made in southern Italy (Cotecchia, Tazioli and Tittozzi, 1975a, 1975b; Tazioli and Tittozzi, 1977) shows that the fresh-salt water mixture is aggressive to the calcite until a maximum limit of 9% (5 g/l

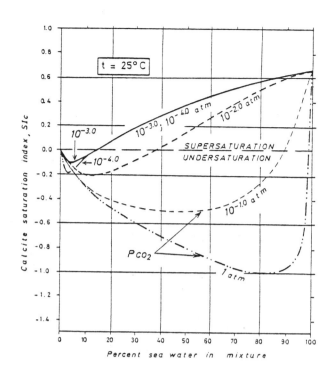

Fig. 6.6 – Saturation index of calcite ($CaCO_3$) in mixtures of sea water and calcite saturated fresh-water, at different CO_2 partial pressures (after Plummer, in Back and Zoelt, 1975). The saturation index is defined SI = log ($\langle CO_3^= \rangle$ $\langle Ca \rangle$ /P_{CaCO_3}) in which $\langle \ \rangle$ is the activity of the ions and P is the solubility product of $CaCO_3$ at the considered temperature. P_{CO_2} is the partial pressure of CO_2 in atm.

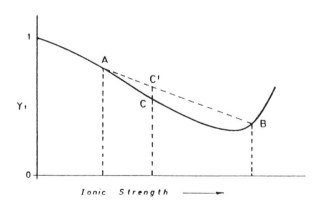

Fig. 6.7 – Change in the calcium activity coefficient when the ionic strength is increased due to the mixing with saline water. The mixture of waters A and B does not produce a calcium activity coefficient C', but a smaller value C, responsible for the increased $CaCO_3$ solubility. The calcium activity coefficient $\gamma Ca \equiv \langle Ca^{++} \rangle / [Ca^{++}]$ in which $\langle \rangle$ indicates the activity or chemical effective concentration and [] the molal concentration.

TDS), even though the CO_2 partial pressure remains constant. In the mixed water of the Apulia region, ion increases of 12.5% for Ca^{++}, 9.2% for Mg and 29.3% for HCO_3^- over theoretical values have been found, (see section 10.4 for additional details, especially in fig. 10.67.) Then, the karstification effects seem more pronounced inside the mixing zone, especially where mixing is accompanied by an appreciable circulation. In a fractured medium, dissolution concentrates in the most fractured zones.

In a fresh water-salt water front, Cotecchia (1977) argues that there is also the possibility of CO_2 migration from fresh water to salt water, thus increasing the salt and brackish water HCO_3^- content, as observed in Southern Italy.

When sea water is displaced by fresh water, the softening process in the mixing zone also increases the capacity to dissolve more calcium carbonate. In the reverse process, that of sea water encroachment, the mixed water can reach the calcium carbonate saturation and then precipitation and clogging may occur.

The picture is still more complicated if sulphate reduction processes take place in organic material rich sediments (see Schbeller, 1956, 1962; Custodio, 1968, 1976a; Hem, 1970) because the pH is changed and CO_2 is generated and incorporated into the water. The calcium carbonate equilibrium is altered and in many cases it becomes dissolved.

All these processes may coincide, complicating the chemical study, although a careful selection of some ionic ratios may be useful for the understanding of the processes. The result is an increase in the bicarbonate content, sometimes to 300-400 ppm in saline water, in contrast with the low concentration in sea water. The calcium ion content generally increases also, but its behavior can be masked by the exchange between Ca^{++} and Mg^{++}, in secondary dolomitization processes in which the rMg/rCa ratio decreases.

Besides the great utility of the rNa/rCl ratio, the rSO$_4$/rCl, rMg/rCa and rCl/rHCO$_3$ ratios are very useful in recognizing sea water in salty or brackish water. In some instances the ratio (rNa+rK+rCl+rSO$_4$)/(rCa+rMg+rHCO$_3$) is also useful because in most fresh waters it is less than 1 and attains 4.2 in sea water. The rSO$_4$/rCl ratio in sea water is invariably 0.10 to 0.11. Old salt water may present frequently greater values, that aid in its identification.

In some cases, fresh, young salt water and old salt water differ clearly in the silica (SiO_2) content, as in some areas in the Netherlands (Engelen and Roebert, 1974; Meinardi, 1976). The SiO_2 (really H_4SiO_4) content is a function of lithology and residence time, and of temperature for deep warm aquifers. So, its use in geochemical studies must be careful.

Figures 6.8 and 6.9 are sketches of the main chemical processes in coastal aquifers, according to the preceding comments.

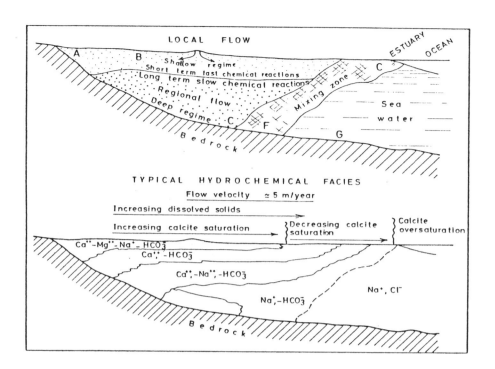

Fig. 6.8 – Hypothetical flow and chemical changes in a big coastal plain, as deduced from studies in the U.S. Atlantic Coastal Plain (Back, 1966). The dominant environments and chemical reactions are:

A – Felspar hydrolysis; clay alteration; pyrite oxidation when there are lagoons, pools and sewage water discharge.

B – Gas generation; ionic exchange; mineral watering.

C – Estuary environment: local and regional sea water encroachment; local and regional sources of organic matter; heavy metal mobilization.

D – Solution and precipitation of carbonates: ionic exchange; sulphate reduction; evaporite solution; peat and lignite decomposition.

E – Mineral alterations; cement deposition; dolomitization.

F – Man-made effects when there is deep injection of waste water.

6.5   Other saline groundwaters in coastal aquifers

As described in section 3.2.13, not all the saline groundwaters in coastal areas are modern sea water. Ancient sea water with a variable degree of modification and dilution or concentration can be present and also non sea related saline waters can be found. Such saline waters are frequent in many areas, and generally occupy the lower part of the coastal formations.

Typical examples are those of the Netherlands (Meinardi, 1974, 1975), some areas of the United States Eastern Coast (Winograd and Farlekas, 1974), some Mediterranean deltas, such as those in Catalonia, in Northeast Spain (Custodio, Bayó and Batista, 1977); they are all related with old sea water.

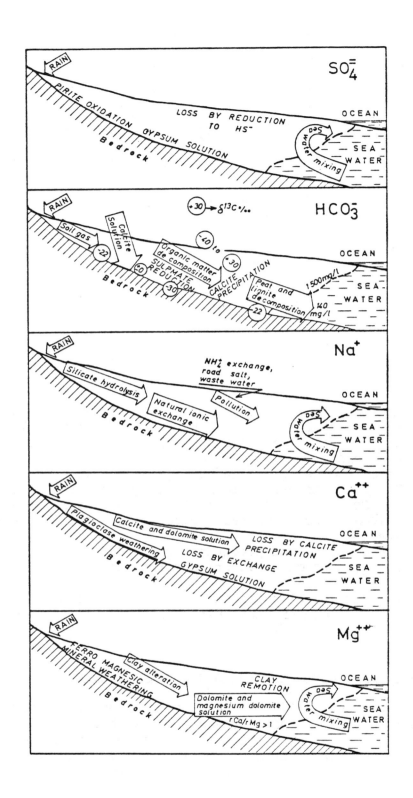

Fig. 6.9 – Main ionic changes in a coastal aquifer in which the processes of figure 6.8 occur.

In some cases, connate sea water or sea water that penetrated in the past, cannot be expelled because there is not enough fresh water head (the land surface is close to sea level or there is a dense superficial drainage system), as it happens in recent deltaic areas (see section 3.3.2). Marine sediments may still withhold their saline water since it is trapped in closed permeable zones or in low permeability formations. Figures 6.10 and 6.11 show the water mixing and chemical behavior in an English limestone coastal aquifer, in which the coastal part contains very old water.

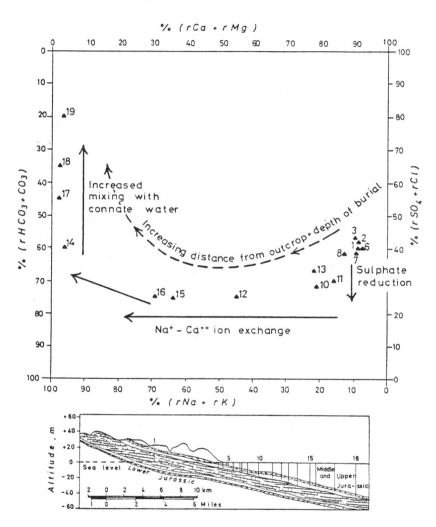

Fig. 6.10 – Square representation of anionic composition versus cationic composition showing the groundwater evolution path along a flow line. The example corresponds to a limestone aquifer in Lincolnshire (U.K.) in which the point numbering correspond to a flow line from the outcrop (points 1 and 2) through the confined part (points 1 to 19). After Lawrence, Lloyd and Marsh (1976).

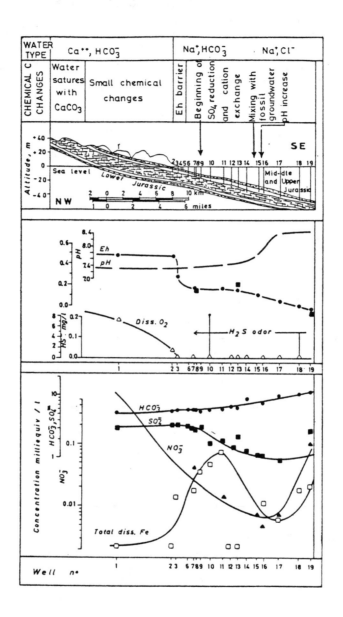

Fig. 6.11 - Groundwater chemical changes along the flow path in the fissured Lincolnshire Jurassic limestones (U.K.), after Edmunds and Lloyd (1979). The typical calcium bicarbonate water suffers a sudden Eh change near the coast and its chemical composition evolve to a sodium bicarbonate water. Finally, the mixing with old salt water transforms it to a sodium chloride water, high in bicarbonate and low in sulphate.

Chemical criteria are generally not enough to distinguish between young and old sea water. Old sea water shows a higher diffusive and dispersive mixing than young sea water, and large bodies of water with a salinity less than that of sea water are frequent. Such dilution is generally accompanied by a softening effect (a decrease in calcium and magnesium ion content) and a parallel increase in sodium.

Salt water generated by evaporites or old sea water, in many instances shows a high rSO_4/rCl value.

In some circumstances, in geopressured areas, a process of natural membrane filtration may lead to bodies of different salinity at both sides of a clay layer acting as a geological membrane. One of these bodies may become more salty than sea water. In these processes the ionic composition can be greatly modified. Since natural membrane processes proceed at a very slow rate, its effects are only important in very old systems, many of them associated with oil and gas deposits, and do not significantly influence fresh sea water conditions in coastal aquifers except for vertical leakages, especially when leaky wells exist.

Maximum theoretical osmotic pressure differential between fresh and marine water can reach 240 m of fresh water column (Wick, 1978). This may create a high hydraulic gradient that favors fresh water penetration into closed salt water bodies, and tend to reduce marine water penetration into confined fresh water aquifers, but the effect in most coastal aquifers probably is not very important.

Non sea related salty waters, such as that related to evaporite salt dissolution near the coast, are generally chemically very different from sea water, and the ionic ratios clearly show it.

In arid coastal areas, brackish groundwater is common, but its origin is mainly climatic. When deep infiltration plus surface runoff is only a very small fraction of precipitation, the water reaching the water table can be highly saline, especially when rain water is slightly contaminated by marine airborne salts. In some coastal areas of Lanzarote and Fuerteventura Islands, in the Canaries, Spain (Custodio, 1978a), groundwater reaches 10 g/l dissolved solids, with more than 5 g/l of Cl^-. These salinities can be explained entirely by the climatic effect. Near the coast a chloride content in rain water between 10 and 40 ppm Cl^- is common. At a few tens of km the content may still be of 8 to 15 ppm (Schoeller, 1962; Custodio, 1976b, 1978b; Meinardi, 1976; Cotecchia, 1977). The salts contributed by the dust are included in these figures. The actual figure depends on the wind direction, its intensity, the agitation of the sea, and land form, etc., and also on the rainfall duration and the previous solid deposition.

In some large aquifers, brackish water can be found near the coast, representing the final end of regional flow systems, in which deep very slow flow in fine porous or microfractured groundwater systems occur. A long and deep run results in slow but continuous ground salt uptake by the water. When water residence mean time in the aquifer is small, almost all the soluble salts are already washed out, but in some systems transit time may reach many thousand years, and the wash out of soluble salts is not yet completely finished, especially if it depends on the contribution of certain substances by the water, such as oxygen (pyrite oxidation), carbonate aggressivity, etc.

A balance of water and salts is generally very useful in order to obtain a good picture of global aquifer behavior, and to confirm some hypothesis about brackish water origin. Arad, Kafri and Fleisher (1975) demonstrate that a brackish source in Israel, supposed to discharge connate water, is really discharging diluted sea water, since present discharge is enough to exhaust all the previously existing connate water several times. Contrarily, in northern Lanzarote Island (Canary Islands, Spain) brackish water has an excess of salinity over that due to the aridity of the climate; this excess is related to water stagnation (Custodio, 1978b), and a groundwater residence time in the ground of several hundred thousand years is assumed.

6.6   Minor and trace constituents

Minor and trace constituents are potential chemical tools for the study of groundwater systems, particularly those near the coast. Unfortunately the natural behavior of many of these minor and trace constituents is not well known, and sampling, sample conservation and analytical problems are not fully solved in practical terms.

Many of the studies involving these constituents have not yielded the desired results or sometimes no valuable practical results, have been obtained from the point of view of identifying salt water origin or interrelationships between different aquifers.

The bromide ion seems very interesting, but it is seldom determined nor is it easily measurable in the presence of the much greater chloride concentrations with a reasonable accuracy. The ratio rCl/rBr in sea water is about 550-600, with only slight variations. The value for continental waters may be very different, generally much greater. Diluted sea water can be easily detected through the ratio decrease (Arad, Kafri and Fleisher, 1975; Custodio, 1978b). The ratio can be clearly smaller for waters associated with marine rocks of organic origin or with evaporite rocks, but residual brines in lagoons with high evaporation rates, brackish phreatic water in dry zones and brackish water in regional flow systems have a much greater ratio (Schoeller, 1956; Piper et al., 1953; Custodio, 1978b). Studies in Apulia (southern Italy) show that along different boreholes with fresh, mixed and sea water, the Br behaves almost identically to Cl. Rain water, due to the nearby origin in the sea, show a similar rBl/rBr ratio to that of the sea water (Tadolini and Tulipano, 1975).

Iodide is also highly characteristic, but is seldom determined. The ratio rCl/rI in sea water is about 130,000 to 500,000, generally much greater than in continental water, since in the sea living organisms fix the I^-. Saline waters originating in evaporite deposits usually have much lower ratios (Schoeller, 1956). In a coastal aquifer the rCl/rI ratio decreases with increasing salinization. In Apulia (Southern Italy) this ratio increases from 110-220 in fresh water (rain has 0.1-0.3 mg/l I in summer and about 1.1 mg/l in fall-winter) to 200,000-300,000 in salt water, sea water showing 0.33-0.55 mg/l to 50 m depth near the coast (Tadolini and Tulipano, 1975). Considering the ratio rBr/rI, in fresh water it is typically less than 25 (usually 0.3 to 0.8) and reaches 200-800 in salty water. Howard and Lloyd (in Lloyd, 1979) make the distinction of present sea water intruding the aquifers in the United Kingdom, from old salt water by means of the rCl/rI ratio. Its value is about 600,000 for present sea water and less than 250,000 for old salt water, the lowest value being 15,000 for diluted old water.

Strontium has a chemistry similar to that of Ca and Mg, but its concentration is small since the strontium content in the ground is small. Strontium sulphate is only slightly soluble, about 60 mg/l in fresh water, but increases with water salinity. The rCa/rSr value in sea water is about 70, and in limestone is much higher, about 1000. In old sea water, since the contact time is very long, the ratio decreases with respect to modern sea water, because the sea water is saturated with respect to the Ca, but it is unsaturated with respect to the Sr (Custodio, 1976a, 1978b; Foster, Parry and Chilton, 1976). The same is true for the ratio of any major cation to Sr.

Though a lot of work dealing with heavy metals has been carried out, the results are not very encouraging at present.

Argon seems a very useful tool because its content depends only on the temperature in the recharging rain. Some salt or brackish water can be differentiated from sea water through its argon content. Sampling and measurement are complicated.

6.7   Chemical mapping and geochemical representations

Salinity distribution in coastal areas is three-dimensional, and poses some difficulties for representation. Generally the salinity is represented by one of the following values: (a) the chloride ion content; (b) total salinity or total dissolved solids; (c) the electrical conductivity at a reference temperature. The chloride is the most often used value.

When enough data is available, the use of vertical profiles or cross-sections are excellent means for depicting the vertical distribution of salinity, as can be seen in figures 6.2 and 6.12 (see chapter 3 for other figures).

These profiles are generally drawn perpendicular to the coast, according to the characteristics of the sea water wedge, but other orientations can be selected if necessary, and also some profiles can be shown together, in the form of parallel sequential sections or in the form of fence diagrams. Figure 6.13 is a small part of a fence diagram of the U.S. Atlantic Coastal Plain.

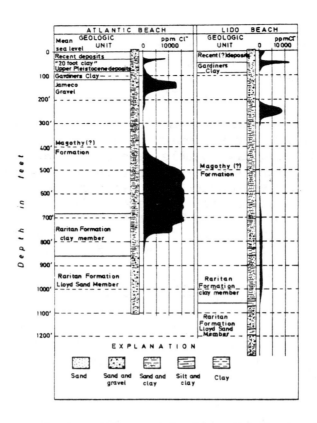

Fig. 6.12 – Columnar sections and chloride distribution curves in two places in Long Island, New York (after Lusczynski and Swarzenski, 1966). Chloride data is from water extracted from cores.

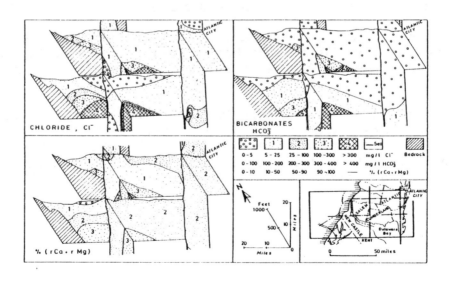

Fig. 6.13 – Chemical cross-sections forming a fence diagram. The figure is a small very simplified part of the study of the U.S. Atlantic Coast (Back, 1966), in which the stratigraphic information is not represented. Brackish water underlies in some areas the young fresh water. Brackish water develops a clear sodium bicarbonate facies.

One another system is the representation in selected points on a map of small vertical logs of the selected salinity parameter versus depth. The best way is to plot the logs just on the point they represent, but if it is too complicated or obscures the map excessively, they can be represented surrounding the map, connected with the respective point by an arrow or other symbol, but the interpretation is more difficult and less straightforward. All these systems allow for the correct representation of single aquifers and also multilayered aquifers or multiaquifer systems. Time variations can be shown.

In many cases, a not so detailed representation is needed or it is not possible since there is not enough data density. Isosalinity maps are constructed, one per aquifer. Different circumstances can be represented such as:

- Penetration of the salt water wedge; the limit of the toe is represented (see fig. 3.44).

- Mean salinity of the water from wells after adopting some criteria to take into account differences in penetration and extraction rates, in order to avoid unrealistic pictures. See figures 6.14 and 6.15, and other figures in chapter 10.

- Depth to salt or brackish water (fig. 6.16).

- Risk of salt or brackish water upconing below the wells.

When the limit between salt and fresh water is to be shown, different criteria can be adopted. In some studies the center of the transition zone or the point of 50% mixing is plotted, but in other studies the maximum salinity acceptable for the water use is selected to define the limit. In some instances two surfaces or lines can be represented, the upper and lower edge of the transition zone. The first one may coincide with the maximum allowable salinity in fresh water and the second one fixed at a certain percentage of marine water, i.e. 90 or 95 percent.

In detailed studies, some chemical values, useful to interpret sea fresh water relationships can be selected, such as the rNa/rCl ratio, the rMg/rCa value, or some others of the previously discussed ones, including those referring to sulphate reduction, or soluble carbon behavior, or some minor elements (see case history no. 1 in chapter 10).

Scatter diagrams, those in which a physical or chemical value is plotted versus another, are sometimes very useful, especially when a high number of data are available. The relationships between different ions or parameters can be established, thus simplifying later surveys, but also the systematic deviations from a theoretical mixture or 'normal' behavior can be easily shown, such as hardening or softening of the water by ion exchange (figs. 6.4 and 6.5). Linear scales can be used, but if the values have a wide range, the use of bilogarithmic paper is recommended.

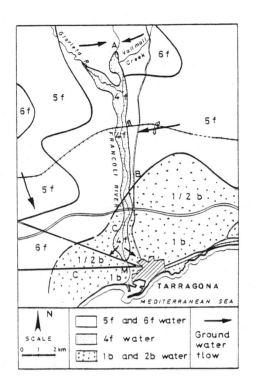

Fig. 6.14 - Simplified map of water type according to the classification given in the text. It corresponds to the lower part of the small Francolí River, in Tarragona (Catalonia, Spain). The geology is complex but a single aquifer can be considered, except in area C, where it becomes confined. The part shown is a coastal area formed by terciary sediments and quaternary outwash, some times flat and sometimes hilly. Local groundwater is of the 5f and 6f type (calcium bicarbonate water, with non dominant sulphate). Groundwater flows toward the river and the sea, but heavy extractions in some areas change the pattern and river water infiltrates. River water has a clearly distinct 4f type, originated upstream, behind the littoral chain. Upstream from A the river is completely effluent. From A to B it continues to be effluent, but the narrow strip with 4f water indicates the effect of irrigation return flows originated from canal derived river water. From B to C there is river water infiltration, but their effect is localized since the wells are close to the river. Downstream C there is a clear river water infiltration, but their influence in the aquifer is masked by the mixing with saline water. Saline water is due to man made sea water intrusion. The 2b type corresponds to slightly contaminated water. The 1b type corresponds to clearly contaminated water, but a normal mixing give a 1a type; the 1b type indicates that in that area there is a Ca increase by cation exchange because the sea intrusion is active. The 4f tongue along the river in the 1b and 2b areas reflect the recharge of the river and represents the upper part of the aquifer. Simplified from a 1979 report prepared by E. Custodio, for the Eastern Pyrenees Water Agency (Barcelona).

Fig. 6.15 - Electrical conductivity, chloride and nitrate maps of the Maresme
coastal strip, just to the northwest of Barcelona (Catalonia, Spain).
About 60 points have been sampled and the interpretation by means of
isolines is given. The aquifer is formed by sand derived from granite
in the coastal chain (indicated by crosses), and becomes silty and
clayish near the shore. The limit shown is an approximation of the
main aquifer border. Wells penetrate a few meters below the water
table aquifer, and near the coast they are scarcely used. Isolines
represent the mean water quality of the upper part of the aquifer,
especially near the coast. Electrical conductivity and chloride show
a similar pattern (chloride is the main contributor to conductivity
near the coast), but the nitrate pattern is different, since it is
derived from intensive agricultural practices and show a high nitrate
pollution in the main irrigated and greenhouse areas between the
towns. Data elaborated by Corominas and Custodio for the Eastern
Pyrenees Water Agency (Barcelona).

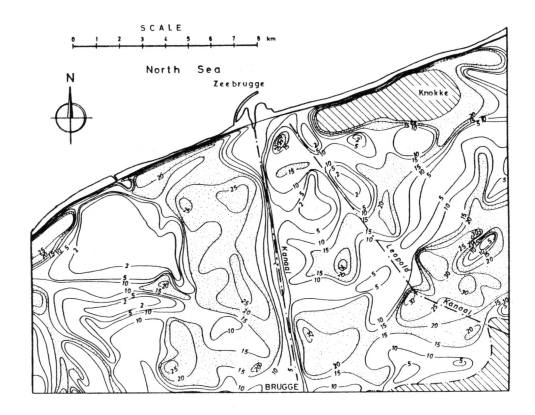

Fig. 6.16 - Map of depth to the salt water interface. It corresponds to a simplified piece of the map of the unconfined aquifer of the Belgian coastal area, prepared by W. de Breuck, G. de Moor, R. Marechal and R. Tavernier, and edited in Brussels in 1974. The interface shown corresponds to the 1500 ppm isosalinity surface. The depth is expressed in meters. In the dashed areas there is no salt water; near the coast they correspond to dunes.

Chemical hydrograms, in which a chemical value is plotted versus time, are very useful to show the evolution and trend of sea water intrusion, and to show the effects of piezometric levels, rainfall, etc., if they are simultaneously plotted (fig. 6.17). After some relationship is pointed out, the study with scatter diagrams or by other graphical or mathematical means is recommended, in order to derive quantitative values. Figures 6.18 and 6.19 show the use of probability plots.

A chemical hydrogram refers to a certain point, generally a well. Except in certain particular circumstances, data from different wells cannot be plotted together because space variations can be important and they are not necessarily simultaneous.

A single well mixes different water layers and the result depends on the discharge, time from start, pumping schedule, piezometric level situation, etc. Thus, in many circumstances the hydrogram is not a smooth curve, and certain smoothing is necessary after correcting the data to a reference situation or simply by judgment.

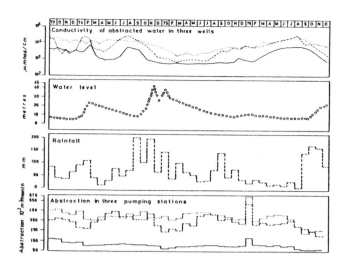

Fig. 6.17 - Conductivity hydrogram of three wells in the coastal area under Brighton, U.K. (after Fleet, Brerenton and Howard, 1978). For comparitive purposes other hydrograms are included. Water conductivity decreases after a rainy period. The highest salinity is attained at the end of the dry period. There is a time lag between rainfall or conductivity changes and groundwater level.

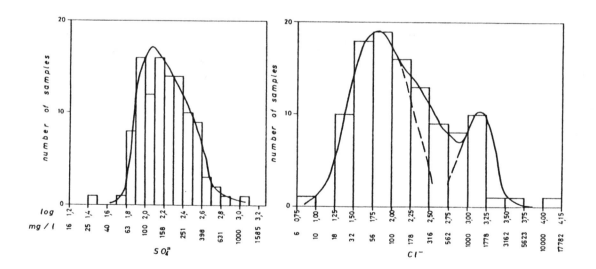

Fig. 6.18 - Frequency distribution of intervals (logarithmic). A bell shaped pattern must appear. The figure shows the frequency distribution of $SO_4^=$ and Cl^- in the Maresme aquifer (fig. 6.15) using 108 groundwater analysis. The sulphate pattern is slightly biased toward the high values, suggesting two origins. The chloride pattern shows clearly that two distributions are mixed, one representing fresh water and one representing groundwater contaminated by sea water.

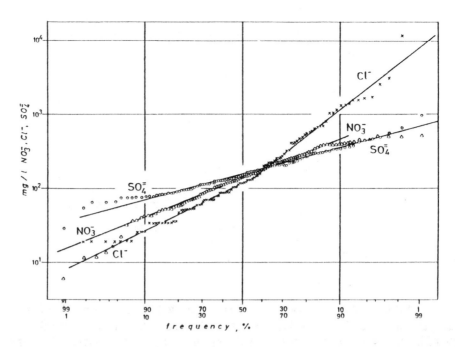

Fig. 6.19 - The same sample of data depicted in figure 6.18 is now plotted in a
cumulative logarithmic probability graph. The $SO_4^=$ distribution
agrees to one distribution but the Cl^- one shows two distinct populations being mixed.

In detailed studies, some chemical diagrams that allow for the simultaneous use of the different fundamental ions are very useful. Some authors
discuss broadly the usefulness of the abundant different chemical diagrams
available (Schoeller, 1962; Hem, 1970; Custodio, 1976b; Catalán, 1969). Only
some of them have a broad utility. They must be easy to be drawn and interpreted.

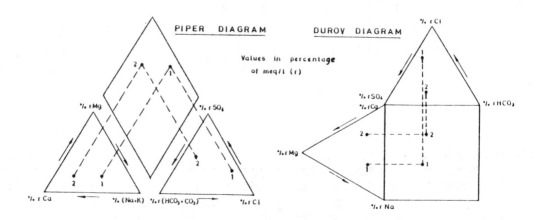

Fig. 6.20 - Triangular chemical diagrams. Piper (Hill-Langelier) and Durov
representations with two ion fields and a conjoint field. The connecting dashed lines are not represented in practical diagrams.

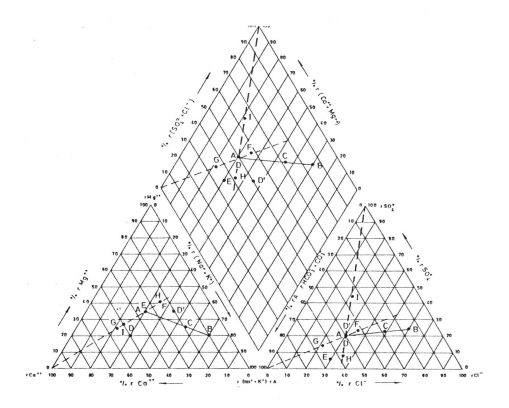

Fig. 6.21 - In a Piper or Durov diagram water modifications in the ground can be observed, especially when the field of points is elongated. Some typical situations are:

(a) C may be a mixture of A and B. C must be in the same system and have an intermediate salinity.

(b) D may be the result of cation exchange. Displacement in the cation diagram parallel to the Mg–Ca side indicates that these are the involved cations, and Ca increases in water (closer to the Ca apex). A simple cation exchange, without other secondary recations, do not change the anion and diamond-shaped diagrams.

(c) D' may be the result of cation exchange, in that case Na–Ca, the Na increasing. There is no change in the anions diagram but since the rCa+rMg change, without changing the anions there is a displacement parallel to the Ca+Mg axis in the diamond-shaped diagram.

(d) E indicates a simple sulphate ion reduction when the decrease in $rSO_4^=$ is compensated the same increase in $rHCO_3$. It is assumed that there is no change in the cation distribution.

(e) F and G indicate simple $CaCO_3$ precipitation and dissolution, respectively.

(f) H and I indicate simple $CaSO_4$ precipitation and dissolution, respectively.

Triangular diagrams, in which anions (Cl, SO_4, HCO_3) and cations (Ca, Mg, Na+K) are represented in percentage of milliequivalents in two separate fields, with a conjoint central field, diamond shaped (Piper and Hill-Langellier diagrams) or squared (Durov), are very useful (fig. 6.20) and allow for the representation of a great number of chemical analyses. Mixtures are easily shown and also ion exchange processes (fig. 6.21). Figures 6.22 and 6.23 correspond to a real example.

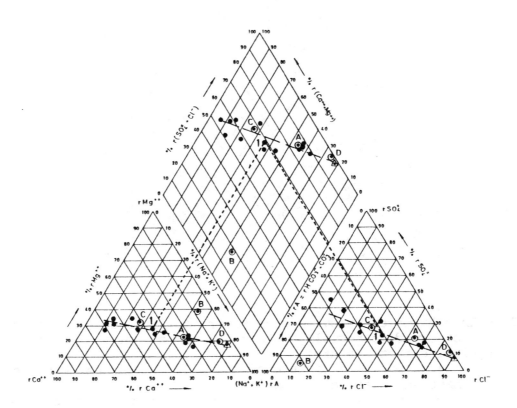

Fig. 6.22 – Piper trilinear diagrams for cations and anions, with a diamond-shaped central diagram. Values in % meq/l. It is indicated how to represent water 1. The dots in the example show that water table waters in the Hospitalet de l'Infant area (Tarragona, Spain) are a mixture of some fresh water and sea water (triangle), since simple mixtures of two extreme waters are represented on the straight connecting them. Other waters from deep wells in the area are also represented. A, C and D have the same probable origin, but B is completely different. The formation yielding water B is not contributing to that area, or that contribution is negligible.

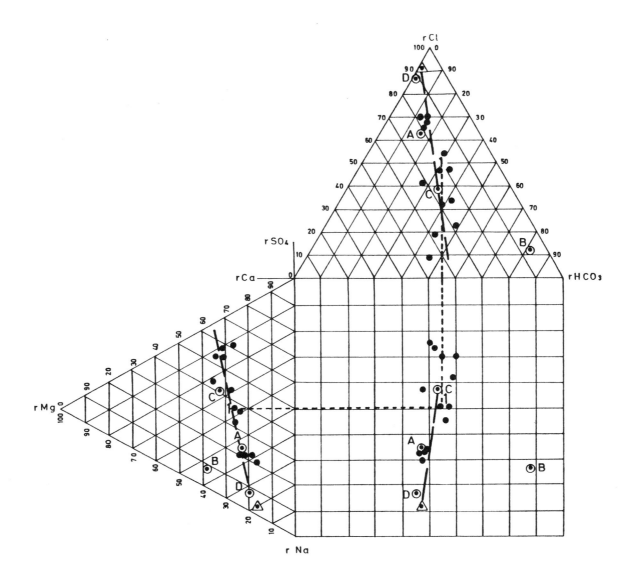

Fig. 6.23 – Durov triangular (trilinear) diagrams for cations and anions, with a square-shaped central diagram. Values in % meq/l. It is indicated how to represent water 1. Hand plotting is somewhat more tiresome than with the Piper diagram, but is equivalent for computer plotting. The same example as in figure 6.22 is shown.

Logarithmic vertical column diagrams (Schoeller-Berkaloff diagrams) only allow for the simultaneous representation of a few analyses, but show the similarities, dissimilarities and evolution of the represented water analysis in a straight form, if they are well chosen and pregrouped with a geographical and areal criteria. Figure 6.24 corresponds to the same points represented in figures 6.22 and 6.23. The ratios rNa/rCl, rMg/rCa and rSO4/rCl are clearly shown and the comparison between different waters is straightforward. The changes in the rNa/rCl ratio are immediately appreciated. Figure 6.25 shows the use of bands, when there is a great quantity of data.

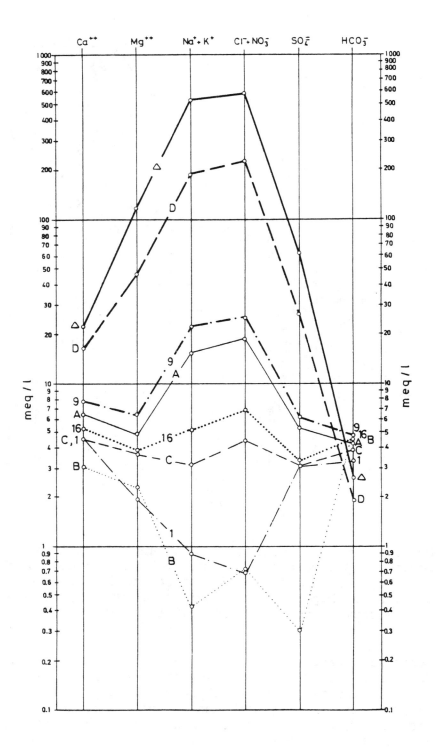

Fig. 6.24 - Logarithmic vertical column representation of some of the coastal
        groundwaters   near Hospitalet de l'Infant (Tarragona, Spain) shown in
        figures 6.22 and 6.23. The waters represent mixtures of local fresh
        water and sea water except B, that corresponds to other aquifer.

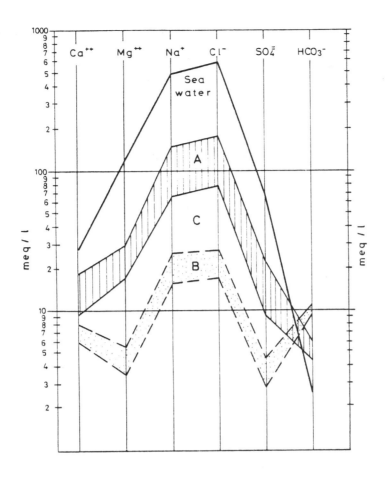

Fig. 6.25 – Logarithmic vertical column diagram of 37 samples taken at different times and places inside a submarine spring (La Falconera, Barcelona, Spain) in the Garraf limestone massif. Zone A corresponds to
samples placed between the outlet and 50 m upstream and zone B to
those between 150 and 200 m of penetration. Mediterranean sea water
is also represented. Zone C has only a few analyses that represent a
mixture of the two extremes. The scarcity of C waters indicates that
B waters are contaminated by sea water in a short gallery tract, and
some large fissures can be expected in it (Custodio and Galofré,
1976).

    Other diagrams are not so useful but some of those that can be
represented in a map are interesting in some circumstances. Probably the best
one is a modified form of the Stiff polygonal diagram in order to place the
ions ordered by solubility (Custodio, 1976a). Three equidistant parallel
lines, drawn horizontally, are divided by a line perpendicular to them. From
this line to the left are represented the cations by a point at a distance por-
portional to the concentration in meq; from that line to the right the anions
are represented in the same way and with the same scale. The different points
are connected by segments and a polygon is obtained. Upwards, the order of
plotting is Ca, Mg and Na (or Na+K), and HCO$_3$ (or HCO$_3$+CO$_3$), SO$_4$ and Cl. The
ratios rMg/rCa and rSO$_4$/rCl are easily shown, but it is not the most

important, the rNa/rCl ratio. These diagrams can be easily drawn on a map. One of the biggest disadvantages is the difficulty to cope with large salinity variations; some diagrams become too small and others too long. This can be overcome using logarithmic scales or changing the scales by a ten factor when necessary, and noting the change by a special drawing. A simplified example is shown in figure 6.26.

Columnar diagrams (Collins diagram) are not so useful, though they have been extensively used (Piper et al., 1953).

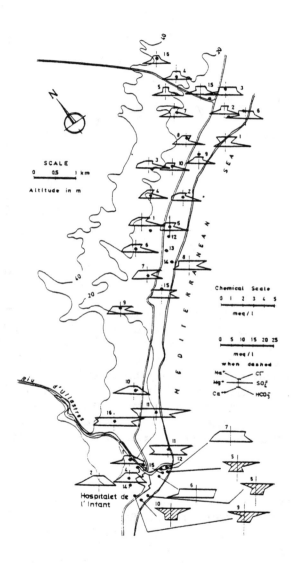

Fig. 6.26 – Geochemical representation of the water chemical composition of the water table aquifer of the South Tarragona Field (Catalonia, Spain) by means of modified Stiff polygonal diagrams (Custodio, 1976a). Brackish and salt water are represented using a different chemical scale. Changes in rMg/rCa; rSO₄/rCl; rSO₄/rHCO₃ are clearly shown, and some water chemical families can be found (East, Center and West).

6.8   Interpretation of results

The main lines of interpreting chemical data to study fresh-salt water relationships have been outlined in the preceding paragraph. This is not a straightforward task and some experience and skill are needed. Other hydrological data must be taken into account, such as river channel form, solid transport, dispersivity, aquifer geometry and properties, piezometric levels, etc. In many circumstances the same chemical situation can be explained in several forms and only the careful study of the other nonchemical data can point out the most probable explanation. Chemical studies are generally cheap and usually yield highly valuable results. It is one of the main tools to check the validity of hypothesis and calculations made by other means, such as the piezometric and hydrodynamical studies.

Unfortunately easy and usable quantitative methods or models to study the chemical behavior in coastal area do not exist, although some progress is expected in the near future. Notwithstanding, quantitative and semiquantitative studies can be done easily and yield useful results. Moreover, chemical balances may aid in evaluating some hypotheses of transient situations. The chloride-alkaline imbalance is one of the most powerful and easy to apply tools, and must be used as much as possible. The determination of Na + K must be recommended when studying coastal areas, though many small laboratories do not have a flame spectrometer and avoid measuring them. They must be measured directly, never by difference.

When mixed water is harder than the theoretical ·value, modern sea water encroachment is probably present. When the mixed water is softer, old sea water or a receding sea water intrusion is involved. If the mixture has a cationic composition practically coinciding with the theoretical value (except for some changes in the Mg^{++} and Ca^{++} values caused by other chemical actions), the sea water wedge is probably in dynamic equilibrium.

Sometimes the situation does not appear in such a clear form, and the nature of the aquifer may not allow for easily identifiable ionic exchanges. Situations in which the rule is reversed are not known.

The study of the chloride pattern is also essential and necessary in order to show the salinity distribution and the possible water movement, especially when data from different years are available.

Also, the study of the rMg/rCa and $rCl/rHCO_3$ ratios is useful to separate a trend to salinization of marine origin from that of evaporation or water reuse or recirculation origin. High salinity with low rMg/rCa values points to a non sea related source of salinity, though the hypothesis must then be verified by other means. When salinity increase is accompanied by a clear increase in total soluble carbon, agricultural practices or residual waters are probably involved, especially when dealing with groundwater.

As described in section 6.5, to understand the origin of the salinity of the fresh water, and especially the chloride content, it is useful to know the atmospheric contribution to salinity. These salts are contributed by the rain or by dry fallout of dust. Airborne salts decrease landwards, especially for sea salts, such as NaCl, but the continental contribution, especially near urban or industrial areas can be important. In an undisturbed system the rNa/rCl ratio in the rainfall, after leaching salts in the dry fallout, often coincides with the values for phreatic water as shown in studies in Apulia (Cotecchia, Tadolini and Tittozzi, 1973), in the Canaries (Custodio, 1974) or near Tarragona.

6.9   Sampling problems

Sampling for chemical analysis in a coastal system is not always an easy task if the samples must represent some situations. Only some general ideas will be presented, since the different sampling methods and devices will be presented in chapter 7. The discussion will be centered about samples taken to determine fundamental ions. The specific procedures to correctly sample, preserve or determine other characteristics must be consulted in standard hydrochemistry books (Rainwater and Thatcher, 1960; Brown, Skougstad and Fishman, 1970; Wood, 1976; Edmunds and Bath, 1976; Everett, 1980). In a general way, the possibility of redox reactions, precipitation, coprecipitation, absorption, or desorption by the bottle walls, gas evolution, etc., must be taken into account, as well as changes in the water chemistry during the analytical process, especially when some values depend on a difference, such as Mg^{++} determined by difference between total hardness and Ca^{++} content.

Generally, one sample is supposed to represent flowing surface water or aquifer water. Thus, a reasonable water renovation rate is necessary in the sampling point and chemical reactions must be absent. By example, a long contact with iron structures or pipes favors the gas evolution and the consequent change in hardness.

In wells or other half-closed structures, not all the water content is renovated. Thus, if a well is to be sampled with a water sampler, it must be lowered to the desired depth inside the screen or open section. The unscreened part of the well may contain water with characteristics different from that of the aquifer, such as mixed water by pumping, water introduced in some tests, surface water or waters from other aquifers that penetrate the well, etc. Vertical mixing by diffusion is a very slow process in small diameter wells (fig. 6.27).

If vertical currents exist in a well, the layers with low water head cannot be sampled because the well is filled with water from the highest head layers. This is a very important fact that must be taken into account to avoid erroneous interpretations or to explain some anomalous situations (see figs. 6.28 and 6.29).

In fissured rocks, water circulation through the rock discontinuities is easier and faster than that in the rock matrix. Water levels and salinity distribution is thus dominated by the system of discontinuities (transmissive system) and the true water chemistry of the rock pore matrix (store rock) cannot be known except by some geophysical logging devices, or by expensive rock sampling. The same situation is true in unconsolidated formations when large permeability variations occur along a borehole.

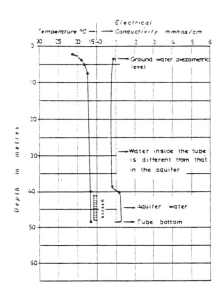

Fig. 6.27 - Temperature and electrical conductivity logs of a 2'' piezometer in the Llobregat delta area. The non-screened part of the piezometer contains a water different from that in the aquifer, introduced six months earlier during a water injection test. Vertical diffusion does not eliminate the introduced water. If a water sampler does not attain the screened portion, the sample does not represent the aquifer water. Convective vertical mixing is hindered when water in the screened portion is more salty, and therefore more dense than water over it.

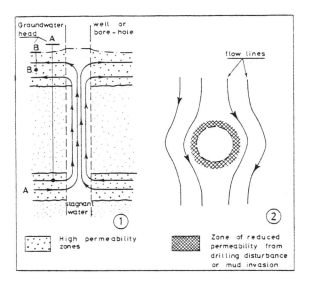

Fig. 6.28 - Problems of sampling in wells and boreholes. In figure 1 the well connects two permeable layers or lenses, A and B, the A with a higher head than B. The well is filled with A water and layer B cannot be sampled. Water below layer A is stagnant and cannot be sampled. To sample layer B a packer must be lowered to isolate it from below, but the method is only effective when there is no flow behind the screen. In figure 2, groundwater flow avoids the borehole if the screen is insufficient, the holes are clogged or the surrounding formation is invaded by drilling mud or clay. Water inside the casing is stagnant or renovates slowly, and the sample may be non-representative.

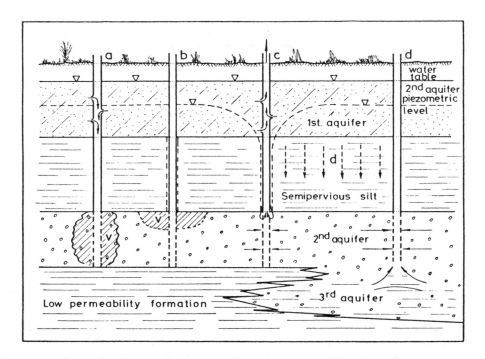

Fig. 6.29 - Problems that may arise in a two aquifer system, when sampling the
deeper one, that has a lower piezometric head. Borehole a is corroded in the first aquifer and its water penetrates through the
borehole into the second aquifer; when the flow velocity in that
aquifer is low, 'thief' sampling gives an erroneous sample, and to
take a pumped water sample one must wait for the elimination of the
extraneous water. Borehole b receives some of the first aquifer
water through the annulus between the hole and the casing, when the
isolation is not enough. Borehole c shows that when pumping in the a
or b situation, first aquifer water may still be a problem. Borehole
d, though isolated from the first aquifer water, gets a mixture of
waters when it is drilled in a place where there is a third aquifer
connected to the second one.

As shown in the case history in chapter 10, the formation separating
the two fresh water aquifers in the Llobregat area contains salt water. The
existence of that salt water could not be found by water sampling, but the
first suspicions about its existence appeared after a geoelectrical survey
showed the existence of low conductivity layers at small depth. In some old
small diameter farm wells, screened in the lower aquifer, but corroded in the
salt water zone, occasional salty water was detected when pumping. When the
well is not used, small quantities of salt water penetrate in the well because
its water head is higher than that of the heavily pumped lower aquifer. When
pumping, at the beginning the fresh water in the upper part of the well was
recovered, but after a short time (two or three minutes) salt water appeared
for a few minutes and afterwards fresh water again because the salt water contribution to the well discharge is very small. The use of a water sampler or a
water electrical conductivity survey would give an erroneous picture of salinity distribution in such a case and the same would occur when sampling by pumping a short time.

One of the most common methods of sampling groundwater is just pumping the well with the installed machinery. This pumping gives a water that is a mixture of different layers, the proportion varying with time. A very short pumping may only produce water stored inside the well, a short pumping produces a mixture of the layers facing the screen and a long pumping produces water that tends to represent a weighed mean composition of the water in the aquifer, and when saline water exists in the lower part, can show a variable degree of salt water upconing. After a long pumping, water leaking from other aquifers through semiconfined layers can also contribute to the sample.

When the well is screened in different aquifers, if differences in water head exist, after a rest period of the pumping, water from the high head layer invades the other layers, the more the longer the rest period. When pumping starts, at the beginning the extracted water represents the high head aquifer, and the contributions of the other layers or aquifers need some time to appear.

Water in uncontaminated rock samples can be studied by:

  - Centrifugation of the sample.

  - Pressing the sample, if it is unconsolidated (Lusczynski, 1961).

  - Extracting the pore water in low permeability unconsolidated materials by dilution with distilled water after thorough mixing to disaggregate the sample. Water salinity and composition can be calculated if the water content in the sample is also determined (Custodio, Bayó and Peláez, 1971). Depending on the dilution water quality, cations are leached differently, because ion exchange phenomena are present, and in detailed studies this must be taken into account (Sayles and Mangelsdorf, 1977). Leaching with ammonia chloride is useful to extract all the adsorbed cations. Figure 6.2 shows the ionic composition of deltaic sediments, obtained by leaching the samples with distilled water. The sediments have acted as a chromatographic column.

6.10   Use of stable isotopes in the study of salt-fresh water
        relationships

The study of the stable isotopes of oxygen and hydrogen can aid in the interpretation of salt-fresh water relationships. The reader is referred to the publications of the International Atomic Energy Agency (IAEA, 1967, 1968, 1970) and other publications. Only some general ideas will be presented.

The proportion of deuterium (D) and hydrogen (protium, H) in water hydrogen, and that of heavy oxygen (^{18}O) and light oxygen (^{16}O) in water oxygen vary according to the water origin, since there is an isotopic fractionation during evaporation, transport and precipitation that depends also on environmental temperature, altitude and season.

The isotopic composition of a 'standard mean ocean water,' SMOW, is taken as a reference and the isotopic variations are measured against it in parts per thousand deviation ($^o/oo$). Thus, local sea water is close to 0 $^o/oo$

values. Continental water is isotopically lighter (D and ^{18}O concentration decreases) than sea water. The mixture of fresh and sea water can be calculated if the sea and the fresh water isotopic composition is known. Also, old sea water can be identified if the isotopic deviations differ considerably from present values in the local sea, thus indicating that the penetration occurred in different climatic conditions (Cotecchia, Tazioli and Magri, 1974).

The main advantage in surface waters is the possibility to identify evaporative processes leading to saline waters, because such evaporative processes alter not only the isotopic deviations, but also the relationships between the two isotopes. In a cartesian plot of D deviations (δD) versus 0-18 deviations (δ^{18}O), meteoric water plots along a meteoric water line, which equation is:

$$\delta D = a\, \delta^{18}O + b$$

a and b being two constants, generally a = 8 and b = 10 for rain from open oceans, if there is no evaporation when falling. When surface evaporation exists, there is a δD and δ^{18}O increase, but since the process is not in equilibrium, the relation does not hold and the evaporation process is pointed out (fig. 6.30). The values of a and b must be established in order to adjust to local situations or to peculiar fresh-brackish water relationships (SPA-15, 1975; Gonfiantini, 1974; Cotecchia, Tazioli and Magri, 1974), especially if atmospheric evaporation occurs during precipitation. In the Mediterranean areas the same b value is found, but b can reach 22.

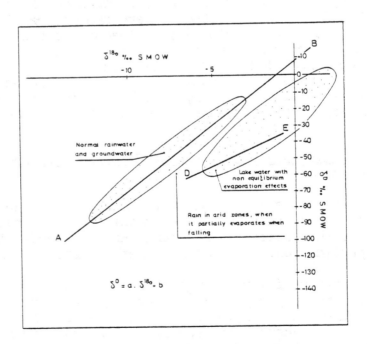

Fig. 6.30 - Relationship between deuterium and oxygen-eighteen in natural waters. When surface evaporation exists, the points representing the water evolution do not follow the normal rainwater line. The normal rainwater line is usually taken as a = 8; b = 10, but it is not always valid, and local a and b values must be determined.

During the infiltration process, isotopic composition is not altered, nor is it in the aquifer under moderate temperature processes. Thus, the origin of brackish water can be studied through the contents in ^{18}O and/or D. Salt water having an isotopic composition different from that of sea water has probably a different origin. If groundwater flow through areas of high temperature, there is an isotopic exchange with the solid material that affects the oxygen isotopic composition. Water becomes heavier in ^{18}O, but isotopic composition of the hydrogen is not modified. Thus, the water origin can be studied and the thermal processes or the mixing with thermal water can be traced back.

Carbon presents two stable isotopes, ^{12}C and ^{13}C. The ^{12}C relative concentration is measured against a special standard of marine limestone, also in per thousand deviation ^{13}C $^o/oo$). Sea water has a $\delta^{13}C$ value close to that of the standard, that is to say, close to zero. After Mook (1970), for sea water at 14^oC 20^oC temperature, $\delta^{13}C$ varies between +1.5 to +2.0 $^o/oo$. Continental water is much lighter (about -13 $^o/oo$ in normal circumstances) due to the plant fractionation effect on the CO_2 carbon ($\delta^{13}C \simeq 25$ $^o/oo$ for most plants) that contributes about one half of the HCO_3^- content in carbonate rich terrains. Thus, intruding sea water is heavy in ^{13}C and salty or brackish water of continental origin is lighter. The complicated chemistry of inorganic carbon and some possible isotopic exchanges between dissolved carbon and carbon in the solid and gaseous phases introduce some uncertainties. Fresh water CO_2 diffuses into salt water and lowers the ^{13}C content (Cotecchia, 1977; Cotecchia, Tazioli and Magri, 1974), but the difference is not fully erased. The ^{13}C content allows, in certain circumstances, the calculation of the mixtures of fresh and salt water, although the relationship is sometimes not linear, due to CO_2 diffusion. In carbonate aquifers the sequence of dissolution-precipitation processes lead to a lowering of the ^{13}C constant, and it is a common phenomenon.

The proportion of stable sulphur isotopes (^{34}S and ^{32}S) in sea water and continental water sulphate is different and also allows for the study of the origin of salty and brackish water, but the possibilities are not yet fully explored, and complicated fractionation effects in redox processes are to be considered.

The $^{32}S/^{34}S$ atomic ratio in sea water sulphate is about 21.8. In sulphates from sediments the range is greater, between 21.7 and 22.1, and in saline domes the range is between 20.8 and 21.9 (Back and Hanshaw, 1965).

6.11 Environmental radioisotopes in the study of salt-fresh groundwater relationships

The most interesting environmental radioisotopes used to study the salt-fresh water relationships in groundwater aquifers are tritium and radiocarbon.

Tritium is a relatively short-lived hydrogen radioisotope (^3H,T). The radioactive half-life is 12.26 years. Natural concentration is highly altered since 1954, after the beginning of the atmospheric thermonuclear tests (hydrogen nuclear bombs). Between 1957 and 1963 great quantities of tritium were introduced into the stratosphere, but after the treaty to cease atmospheric nuclear tests in 1963, only occasionally broken by a few small tests, the atmospheric storage is being depleted through radioactive decay and fallout with the rain. Present values in the Northern Hemisphere are only one hundred of the 1963 peak values, but still five to ten times over the natural values. Concentrations in the Southern Hemisphere are lower due to the fact that most of the tests were carried out in the Northern Hemisphere, and there is a slow interchange between both Hemispheres. Figure 6.31 shows the T content in the rainfall. Generally tritium is not altered by isotopic concentration during infiltration and recharge, except if there is some surface ponding, but since the fraction of precipitation that reaches the aquifer varies along the year, the mean yearly value must be obtained by a proper weighing (fig. 6.32).

Tritium content in recent continental water exceeds always a few ten tritium units (1 TU = 10^{-18} T/H) and is easily identifiable. Deep sea water has almost a zero content since the mean residence time is more than a hundred times the tritium half-life. Mixtures of sea water with small quantities of modern fresh water, with a high tritium content, are easily identifiable. Notwithstanding, the actual situation is more complicated since the upper layers of the sea sometimes have a measurable tritium content, especially in small shallow seas. The correct interpretation needs a careful study of the local circumstances. Electrolytic isotopic concentration allows the easy measurement of 1 or 2 TU. A half liter sample is usually enough, although for salt water a greater volume is recommended due to the difficulty to perform a high quality previous distillation.

Radiocarbon (carbon fourteen, ^{14}C) is a long lived natural carbon radioisotope. The radioactive half-life is about 5700 years. Since this value is comparable to sea water mean residence time, sea water has a ^{14}C close to that of modern organic matter. Thermonuclear bombs have produced large quantities of non natural radiocarbon, but its effect is not so important as in the case of the tritium because there is a high damping effect in the biosphere, and alterations are small and limited to shallow small seas. The effect is an increase in the ^{14}C content (in percentage of modern organic matter content).

The radiocarbon geochemistry is complicated and many uncertainties exist for an accurate water age determination. But qualitative interpretations are easy and allow for the separation of modern sea water (high ^{14}C content, more than 80% of that of modern organic matter) from old sea water in the ground (low ^{14}C content), thus providing a tool for distinguishing between recently encroached active sea water and old entrapped sea water. The migration of modern CO_2 towards old sea water bodies must be taken into account. The ^{13}C content indicates the way to improve age corrections, especially when there is a sequence of dissolution precipitation events, that make a water appear older than it is.

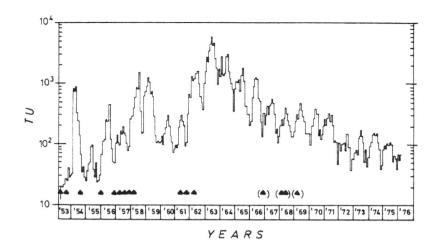

Fig. 6.31 - Tritium concentration in rainfall to Ottawa (Canada), the station with the longest record. Before 1953 the concentration was less than 10 TU. Data as published by the Int. Atomic Energy Agency, Vienna. Data after 1975 is not yet available. The triangles indicate the thermonuclear atmospheric tests. The last four ones were of small intensity and out of the treaty of suppression of atmospheric nuclear tests. Seasonal variations are clear. Values in other places can be obtained through correlation, using the periodic publications of data of the IAEA.

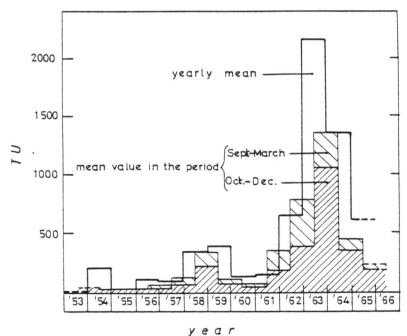

Fig. 6.32 - Tritium concentration in a Central Europe station. It is shown: (a) yearly mean in rainfall; (b) mean value for the wet period of September-March; (c) mean value for the October-December period, the most rainy. The tritium concentration is reduced every time. This is a way to calculate tritium input into the ground. When the rainfall fraction that produces recharge can be calculated, a better weighed mean can be obtained.

-259-

The ^{14}C measurement requires about 3 g of carbon. A 100 to 250 liter water sample is needed, depending on the soluble inorganic carbon content, and must be processed in the field by gas evolution with hydrochloric acid and entrapment in carbon-free alkali, or through direct precipitation by an excess of clean barium hydroxide solution, enough to precipitate also the $SO_4^=$ and to increase the pH.

Further information about the tritium and radiocarbon can be found in IAEA (1967, 1968, 1970), and other publications (Custodio and Llamas, 1976).

Other natural radioisotopes have a much more limited usefulness. Some Italian and French researchers consider the geohydrological interest of natural radon, one of the uranium decay products. It is a gas that dissolves in groundwater. The concentration depends on the rock properties, but also on the water flow velocity. Thus, the movement of water in coastal aquifers can be studied (Cotecchia, 1977; Magri and Tazioli, 1970). Since Rn-222 is a short lived (3.82 days half-life) decay product of the Ra-226, and the Ra-226 (a decay product of U-238) is ubiquitous, the Rn concentration in water increases with flow velocity, but other factors may mask this relationship. Radon sampling is complicated and tiresome, and it needs an in-the-field extraction through degasification or through charcoal absorption.

6.12   Groundwater temperature

Water temperature in the ground depends on many factors but can be related to recharge temperature, flow velocity and depth of circulation, and it is overimposed on the geothermal heat flow. The terrain heat conductivity and heat capacity must be taken into account. But for very shallow aquifers or when surface water recharge is dominant, daily or seasonal surface temperature changes are generally not reflected in groundwater because they dampen out easily, in some meters. Notwithstanding a study of the depth of influence of external temperature variations is interesting in order to avoid errors.

In a coastal aquifer the effect of the sea must be taken into account. The sea absorbs a greater fraction of the solar heat flow than the continent, and thus the mean sea water temperature is about 3°C higher than the mean temperature of the continent. This figure varies from one place to another, but the sea is generally warmer than the continent. Coastal formations up to a depth of some meters are warmer than other formations far from the sea.

Figure 6.33 represents a steady situation solved by Jaeger (1963) in which half the surface of a semi-infinite medium is maintained at a certain temperature (continent) and the other half at a temperature $\Delta\Theta$°C warmer (sea of shallow depth). The solution is:

$$\Theta\ (x,z) = \left(\frac{1}{2} + \frac{1}{\pi}\ \text{arctg}\ \frac{x}{2} \right) \Delta\Theta$$

ΔΘ = increase of temperature over mean continent temperature

x = horizontal distance to the coast line

z = depth.

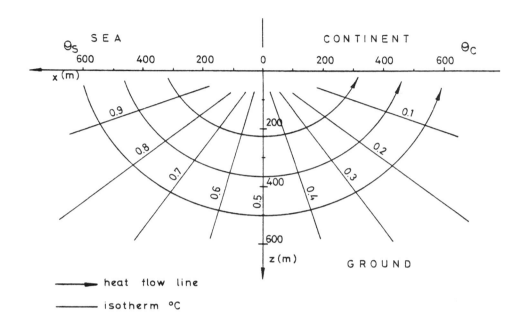

Fig. 6.33 – Steady state heat flow lines and isotherms in an ideal continent limiting with a shallow sea, when the temperature difference between the surface of the continent (Bc) and the sea (Bs) is 1°C. The geothermal heat flow is not considered. The earth heat conductivity is supposed homogeneous and its value does not influence the results.

     The real situation in the limestone Salentine Peninsula, in southern Italy, is shown in figure 6.34. Figure 6.35 shows a similar situation in the Vandellós Massif, in Northeast Spain.

     Generally there is a clear temperature change between groundwater in movement and groundwater almost stagnant. It can be applied to show the transition between active fresh water and slowly moving or stagnant sea water.

     Water temperature is also a useful tool to locate fissures along a borehole, as will be shown in chapter 7.

     In very thick aquifers the geothermal heating of the water, especially when the geothermal gradient is higher than normal, may lead to thermal induced convective water movements that increase the fresh-salt water mixing or the exchange with the ocean (Kohout, 1965), as described in section 3.3.6.

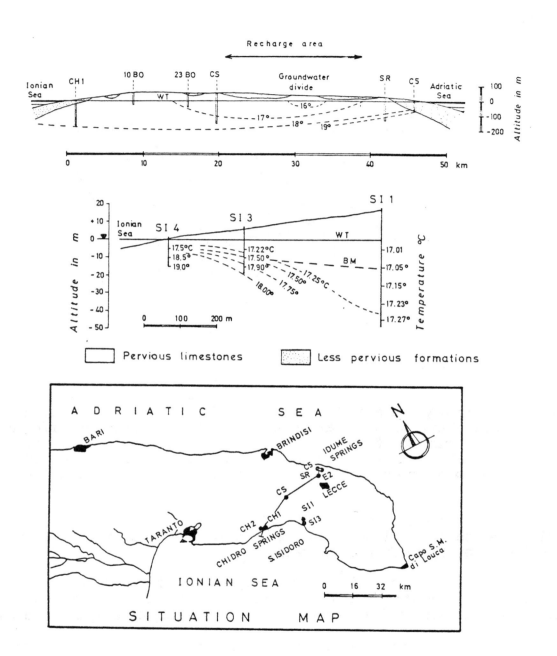

Fig. 6.34 - Groundwater temperature ($^{\circ}$C) in the Salentine Peninsula, in Southern Italy (after Cotecchia, 1977; Carlin, Magri and Mongelli, 1973). WT = water table; BM = base of the mixing zone. The cooling effect of the recharge water is clearly shown, and also the heating effect of the sea.

-262-

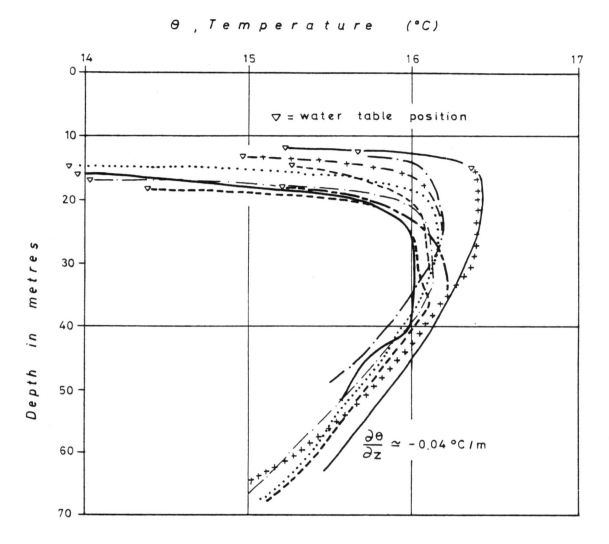

Fig. 6.35 - Temperature logs in some boreholes in the Western parts of Vandellós Nuclear Site (Tarragona, Spain). The logs were performed in winter time. It is a highly permeable alluvial fan limiting with the Mediterranean Sea. A very thick transition zone exists, extending from water table to about 50 m to 100 m depth. The vertical temperature gradient is negative. This anomaly may be explained in two ways: a) a highly active coastal flow system exists, the upper part representing the warming effects of continental ground water and the lower part the cooling effect of landward penetrating sea water, in a dynamic natural system. b) cool continental fresh water discharges preferentially in depth, through the highly karstified bedrock. Other existing data indicates that the second explanation is probably the correct one (Custodio, 1978b).

6.13   References

Arad, A., Kafri, U., Fleisher, E. (1975). The Na'Aman springs, Northern Israel: salinization mechanism of an irregular freshwater-sea water interface. Journal of Hydrology, Vol. 25 (1975), pp. 81-104. Elsevier.

Back, W. (1966). Hydrochemical facies and ground-water flow patterns in Northern part of Atlantic Coastal Plain. U.S. Geological Survey, Professional Paper 498-A. Washington, D.C. 42 pp.

Back, W., Hanshaw, B.B. (1965). Chemical geohydrology. In Advances in Hydroscience, Vol. 2, Ed. Ven te Chow. Academic Press. pp. 49-109.

Back, W., Hanshaw, B.B. (1970). Comparison of chemical hydrology of the carbonate peninsulas of Florida and Yucatan. Journal of Hydrology, Vol. 10, No. 4, June, pp. 330-368.

Back, W., Hanshaw, B.B., Pyle, T.E., Plummer, L.N., Weidie, A.E. (1979). Geochemical significance of groundwater discharge and carbonate solution to the formation of Caleta Xel Ha, Quintana Roo, Mexico. Water Resources Research, Vol. 15, No. 6, pp. 1521-1535.

Back, W., Zoetl, J. (1975). Application of geochemical principles, isotopic methodology, and artificial tracers to karst hydrology. Hydrogeology of Karst Terrains. Ed. A. Burger and L. Dubertret. Paris, International Assoc. of Hydrogeologists, pp. 105-121.

Brown, E., Skougstad, M., Fishman, M. (1970). Methods for collection and analysis of water samples for dissolved minerals and gases. U.S. Geological Survey. Tech. of Water Resources Investigations. Book 5. Chap. A1, 160 pp.

Carlin, F., Magri, G., Mongelli, F. (1973). Temperature delle acque sotterranee della Peninsola Salentina (Groundwater temperature in the Salentine Peninsula). Geologia Applicata e Idrogeologia, Vol. VIII, Part II, pp. 155-198. Bari.

Catalán, J. (1969). Química del agua (Water chemistry). Editorial Blume. Madrid-Barcelona. pp. 320-351.

Cotecchia, V. (1977). Studi e ricerche sulle acque sotterranee e sull'intrusions marina in Puglia (Penisola Salentina). Quaderni dell'IRSA, 20. 466 pp. Rome.

Cotecchia, V., Tadolinia, T., Tittozzi, P. (1973). Precipitazione secche in Puglia e loro influenza sul chimismo delle acque alimentanti la falda sotterranea (Dry fallout in Apullia and its influence on the water chemistry of the groundwater recharge). Geologia Applicata e Idrogeologia. Vol. VIII, Part II, Bari. pp. 253-284.

Cotecchia, V., Tazioli, G.S., Tittozzi, P. (1975a). <u>Geochimica delle acque</u> <u>sotterranee della Penisola Salentina in relazione al rapporti tra le</u> <u>acque di falda, le acque marine sotterranee e il mare.</u> Geologia Applicata e Idrogeologia, Vol. X, Part I, pp. 205-224. Bari.

Cotecchia, V., Tazioli, G.S., Tittozzi, P. (1975b). <u>Geochimica delle acque</u> <u>sotterranee della Penisola Salentina (Italia meridionale) in rela-</u> <u>zione ai processi di dissoluzione carsica in zona satura.</u> Atti III Convegno Internazionale sulle Acque Sotterranee. Palermo.

Cotecchia, V., Tazioli, G.S., Magri, G. (1974). <u>Isotropic measurements in</u> <u>research on seawater ingression in the carbonate aquifer of the</u> <u>Salentine Peninsula, Southern Italy.</u> Isotope Techniques in Groundwa- ter Hydrology 1974. Int. Atomic Energy Agency. Vienna. pp. 445- 463.

Custodio, E. (1967). <u>Études hydrogéochimiques dans le delta du Llobregat, Bar-</u> <u>celona (Espagne)</u> (Hydrogeochemical studies in the Llobregat delta, Barcelona, Spain). General Assembly of Bern. Int. Assoc. Scientific Hydrology. Pub. 62, pp. 135-155.

Custodio, E. (1968). <u>Datación de aguas en el delta del río Llobregat</u> (Water dating in the Llobregat delta). Documentos de Investigación Hidrológica No. 6. Centro de Estudios, Investigación y Aplicaciones del Agua. Barcelona. pp. 205-237.

Custodio, E. (1974). <u>Contribuciones al conocimienta geohidroquímico de la isla</u> <u>de Lanzarote (Islas Canarias, España)</u> (Contributions to the geohydro- chemical knowledge of the Lanzarote Island, Canary Islands, Spain. Int. Symp. Volcanic Terrain Hydrology. CEH-IH-Unesco. Arrecife de Lanzarote. 32 pp.

Custodio, E. (1976a). <u>Hidrogeoquímica</u> (Hydrogeochemistry). In Hidrología Subterránea, Vol. I, Sec. 10. Ed. E. Custodio and M.R. Llamas. Edi- ciones Omega. Barcelona. pp. 1003-1095.

Custodio, E. (1976b). <u>Relaciones agua dulce-agua salada en las regiones cos-</u> <u>teras</u> (Fresh-salt water relationships in coastal areas). Hidrología Subterránea (Ground Water Hydrology). Ed. E. Custodio and M.R. Lla- mas. Ediciones Omega. Barcelona. Vol. II, Section 13, pp. 1313- 1389.

Custodio, E. (1978a). <u>Geohidrología de formaciones e islas volcánicas</u> (Geohy- drology of volcanic lands and islands). Centro de Estudios Hidrográficos e Instituto de Hidrología. Madrid. 303 pp. (see pp. 208-212).

Custodio, E. (1978b). <u>Ensayos para determinar la viabilidad de una excavación</u> <u>profunda en el litoral del macizo de Vandellós (Tarragona, España)</u> (Tests to determine the feasibility of a deep excavation in the Vandellós Massif coastal area, Tarragona, Spain). Int. Symp. on Water in Mining and Underground Works. Granada. Assoc. Nac. Ing. Minas. pp. 85-109.

Custodio, E., Bayó, A., Peláez, M.D. (1971). Geoquímica y datación de aguas para el estudio del movimiento de las aguas subterráneas en el delta del Llobregat (Barcelona) (Geochemistry and water dating for the study of the ground water movement in the Llobregat delta, Barcelona). Primer congreso Hispano-Luso-Americano de Geología Económica, Se. 6, Madrid. pp. 51-80.

Custodio, E., Llamas, M.R. (1976). Hidrología Subterránea (Groundwater Hydrology). Ed. Omega. Barcelona. 2375 pp.

Custodio, E., Galofré, A. (1976). Evolución de la calidad del agua en la surgencia litoral de La Falconera en relación con un gran vertedero de basuras en el macizo de Garraf (Barcelona) (Evolution of the water quality in the Falconera littoral spring in connection with a garbage dump in Garraf massif, Barcelona). II National Assembly of Geodesy and Geophysics, Barcelona 1976. 43 pp.

Custodio, E., Bayó, A., Batista, E. (1977). Sea water encroachment in Catalonia coastal aquifers. Int. Assoc. Hydrogeologists. General Assembly of Birmingham. Vol. XIII, 1. pp. F1-14.

Custodio, E., Tourís, R., Balagué, E. (1981). Behavior of contaminants after injection of treated urban waste water in a well. Proc. Int. Symp. Quality of Groundwater. Noordwijkerhout. Ed. W. van Duijvenbooden, P. Glasbergen and H. van Lelyveld. Studies in Environmental Science. Vol. 17. Elsevier. The Netherlands.

van Dam, J.C. (1977). Determination of horizontal and vertical ground-water flow from piezometric levels observed in groundwater of varied densities. International Hydrological programme. 5th Salt Water Intrusion Meeting. Medmenham, UK. pp 1-19. Also in Delft Progress Report. Civil Engineering, Vol. 3. pp. 19-34.

Edmunds, W.M., Bath, A.H. (1976). Centrifuge extraction and chemical analysis of interstitital water. Environmental Science and Technology. Vol. 10. pp. 467-472.

Edmunds, W.M., Lloyd, J.W. (1979). Application de la geochimie dan les études hydrogéologiques au Royaume-Uni. Bull. BRGM. 2nd Series. Sec. III, No. 3. Paris. pp. 319-333.

Engelen, D.A., Roebert, A.J. (1974). Chemical water types and their distribution in space and time in the Amsterdam dune-water catchment area with artificial recharge. Journal of Hydrology No. 21. pp. 339-356. Elsevier.

Everett, L.G. (1980). Groundwater monitoring. General Electric Co., Schenectady, N.Y. 440 pp.

Fleet, M., Brerenton, N.R., Howard, N.S. (1978). The investigation of saline intrusion into a fissured chalk aquifer on the South Coast of England. Fifth Salt Water Intrusion Meeting. Medmenham, England. International Hydrological Decade.

Foster, S.S.D., Parry, E.L., Chilton, P.J. (1976). <u>Groundwater resource development and saline water intrusion in the Chalk aquifer of North Humberside.</u> Natural Environment Research Council. Institute of Geological Science. U.K. Rep. 76/4. London, 34 pp.

Gilcher, A. (1965). <u>Précis d'hydrologie marine et continentale</u> (Handbook of marine and continental hydrology). Ed. Masson. Paris. 389 pp.

Gonfiantini, R. (1974). <u>Environmental isotope investigation in Canary Islands groundwater.</u> Int. Symp. on Volcanic Terrain Hydrology. Arrecife de Lanzarote. Unesco-Spain.

Hahn, J. (1975). <u>Das Erscheinungsbild der Küstenversalzung im Raume Wittmund, Ostfriesland</u> (The phenomenon of sea-water intrusion on the region of Wittmund-Ostfriesland). Proc. IV Salt Water Intrusion Meeting. Ghent, 1974. Ed. W. de Breuck. IHD. pp. 40-58.

Hanshaw, B.B., Back, W. (1979). <u>Major geochemical processes in the evolution of carbonate-aquifer systems.</u> Journal of Hydrology, Vol. 43 (1979). pp. 287-312. Elsevier.

Hem, J.D. (1970). <u>Study and interpretation of the chemical characteristics of natural waters.</u> U.S. Geological Survey, Water-Supply Paper No. 1473, Washington. 363 pp.

IAEA (1967). <u>Tritium and other environmental isotopes in the hydrological cycle.</u> Int. Atomic Energy Agency. Technical Report Series, No. 73. Vienna. 83 pp.

IAEA (1968). <u>Guidebook on nuclear techniques in hydrology.</u> Int. Atomic Energy Agency. Technical Report Series, No. 91. Vienna. 214 pp.

IAEA (1970). <u>Interpretation of environmental isotope data in hydrology.</u> Int. Atomic Energy Agency. Vienna. 104 pp.

Jaeger, J.C. (1963). <u>Application of the theory of heat conduction to geothermal measurements.</u> Geophysical Monograph Series No. 8. Ed. W.H.K. Lee. Am. Geophysical Union.

Kohout, F.A. (1965). <u>A hypothesis concerning cyclic flow of salt water related to geothermal heating in the Floridan aquifer.</u> Trans. New York Academy of Sciences, Series II, Vol. 28, No. 2, pp. 249-271.

Lawrence, A.R., Lloyd, J.W., Marsch, J.M. (1976). <u>Hydrochemistry and groundwater mixing in part of the Lincolnshire limestone aquifer, England.</u> Ground Water Vol. 14, No. 5. pp. 320-327.

Lloyd, J.W. (1979). <u>Les eaux souterraines salées associeés aux reserves souterraines d'eau douce au Royaume Uni</u> (Salt groundwater associated with fresh groundwater reserves in the United Kingdom). Bull. BRGM. 2nd Series, Sec. III, No. 3. pp. 269-279. Paris.

Lusczynski, N.S. (1961). <u>Filter-press method for extracting water samples for chloride analysis.</u> U.S. Geological Survey Water-Supply Paper 1549-A. Washington.

Lusczynski, N.S., Swarzenski, W.V. (1966). <u>Saltwater encroachment in Southern Nassau and Southeastern Queens Counties, Long Island, New York.</u> U.S. Geological Survey, Water Supply Paper, 1613-F. Washington, 76 pp.

Magri, G., Tazioli, G.S. (1970). <u>Radon in groundwaters of dolomitic and cal-careous aquifer in Apullia (Southern Italy).</u> Isotope Hydrology, 1970, Vienna Symposium. Int. Atomic Energy Agency, Vienna. pp. 815-845.

Mandel, S. (1964). <u>The mechanism of sea-water intrusion into calcareous aquifers.</u> General Assembly of Berkeley. Int. Assoc. Scientific Hydrology. Pub. 64. pp. 127-130.

Mandel, S. (1965). <u>A conceptual model of karstic erosion by groundwater.</u> Proc. Dubrovnik Congress. Int. Assoc. Scientific Hydrology. Unesco, Vol. II. pp. 423-438.

Meinardi, C.R. (1974). <u>The origin of brackish groundwater in the lower parts of the Netherlands.</u> Rijksinstituut voor drinkwatervoorziening. Mededeling 74-6. The Netherlands. 16 pp.

Meinardi, C.R. (1975). <u>Brackish groundwater bodies as a result of geological history and hydrological conditions.</u> Int. Symp. on Brackish Water as a factor in Development. Beer-Sheva. Ben Gurion University of the Negev, Institute for Desert Research, Israel. pp. 25-39.

Meinardi, C.R. (1976). <u>Characteristic examples of the natural groundwater com-position in the Netherlands.</u> Rijkinstituut voor drinkwatervoorzien-ing. Mededeling 76-1. 28 pp.

Mink, J.F. (1960). <u>Some geochemical aspects of sea water intrusion in a coa-stal aquifer.</u> General Assembly of Helsinki. Int. Assoc. Scientific Hydrology. Pub. 52. pp. 424-439.

Mook, W.G. (1970). <u>Stable carbon and oxygen isotopes of natural waters in the Netherlands.</u> Isotope Hydrology 1970. Vienna Symposium. Int. Atomic Energy Agency. Vienna. pp. 163-190.

Piper, A.M., et al. (1953). <u>Natural and contaminated waters in the Long Beach, Santa Ana Area, California.</u> U.S. Geological Survey, Water Supply Paper, No. 1136.

Plummer, L.N., Busenberg, E. (1982). <u>The solubilities of calcite, aragonite and vaterite in CO_2-H_2O solutions between 0 and 90°C, and an evaluation of the aqueous model for the system $CaCO_3$-CO_2-H_2O.</u> Geochimica and Cosmochimica Acta. Vol. 46, pp. 1011-1040. Pergamon Press.

Rainwater, F.H., Thatcher, L.L. (1960). <u>Methods for collection and analysis of water samples.</u> U.S. Geological Survey. Water-Supply Paper, 1454. Washington, D.C. 301 pp.

Sayles, F.L., Mangelsdorf, P.C., Jr. (1977). The equilibration of clay minerals with sea water: exchange reactions. Geochimica and Cosmochimica Acta. Vol. 41, pp. 951-960. Pergamon Press.

Schoeller, H. (1956). Géochimie des eaux souterraines. Application aux eaux des gisements de pétrole (Groundwater geochemistry. Application to oil fields waters). Editions Techniques. Institut Francais du Pétrole. Paris.

Schoeller, H. (1962). Les eaux souterraines (Groundwater). Ed. Masson. Paris.

Schmorak, S., Mercado, A. (1969). Upconing of fresh water-sea water interface below pumping wells: field study. Water Resources Research, 5. pp. 129-1311.

SPA-15 (1975). Estudio científico de los recursos de agua de las Islas Canarias: Informe técnico final (Scientific study of the water resources in the Canary Islands: final technical report). Government of Spain (Public Works Ministry), Unesco-PNUD. 4 vols. Centro de Estudios Hidrográficos. Madrid.

Tadolini, T., Tulipano, L. (1975). La misura del contenuto in cloro, bromo e iodio delle acque sotterranee della penisola Salentina (Italia Meridionale) in rapporto alle acque di mare di invasione continentale (Measurement of chlorine, bromine and iodide content in groundwater from the Salentine peninsula (Southern Italy) in respect to the sea water encroaching the continent). 3rd Convegno Internazionale sulle Acque Sotterranee. Palermo. 8 pp.

Tazioli, G.S., Tittozzi, P. (1977). Evolution of porosity and permeability of coastal carbonate aquifers due to marine pollution on fresh groundwater. Proc. Symp. on Hydrodynamic Diffusion and Dispersion in Porous Media. Pavia. Int. Assoc. for Hydraulic Research, Committee on Flow Through Porous Media. Istituto di Idraulica dell'Università di Pavia. pp. 201-208.

WHO (1971). Normes européennes applicables a l'eau de boisson (European standards for potable water). World Health Organization. 2nd edition. Geneva. 62 pp.

Winograd, I.J., Farlekas, G.M. (1974). Problems in ^{14}C dating of water for aquifers of deltaic origin: an example from New Jersey coastal plain. Isotope Techniques in Ground Water Hydrology, Vol. 2. Vienna Symposium. Int. Atomic Energy Agency. Vienna. pp. 69-93.

Wick, G.L. (1978). Power from salinity gradients. Energy, Vol. 3, pp. 95-100. Pergamon Press.

Wood, W. (1976). Guidelines for collection and field analysis of groundwater samples for selected unstable constituents. U.S. Geological Survey. Tech. of Water Resources Investigations, Book 1, Cap. D.2.

7. Methods of study and survey*

V. Cotecchia with additions of E. Custodio

Contents

7.0   Introduction

Study and survey methods for coastal aquifers do not differ essentially from those applied in other situations. They can be found in standard books and papers dealing with the matter; see Keys and MacCary (1971), Custodio and Llamas (1976), Everett (1980), Sahuquillo (1981), and the classical texts on groundwater hydraulic tests.

---

*Chapter based on the work done by Prof. Vincenzo Cotecchia, Institute of Engineering Geology and Geotechnique, Bari University, Italy, and carried out under the Finalized Project 'Promotion of Environmental Quality' of the Italian National Research Council (IRSA). It has been adapted and rearranged by the coordinator. The paragraphs marked (*) have been added by the latter.

However, the existence of a variable density fluid introduces several peculiarities that impose new needs and methods. Only those relevant to the groundwater salinization problem will be reviewed here. Some of them have been already presented and described in previous chapters, especially in chapter 6, when dealing with chemical sampling, and will not be repeated here.

7.1   General hydrogeological studies

For an exact interpretation of the phenomena which govern the coexistence of freshwaters and saltwaters in coastal aquifers, a general understanding of the hydrogeological situation is needed. This helps to define and acquire data concerning groundwater movement with special reference to the precise identification of geological and structural trends and the distribution of permeability characteristics within the aquifer.

The classical breakdown of geological formations into those 'permeable for porosity' (primary permeability) and those 'permeable for fissuring' (secondary permeability) (Fourmarier, 1958) has been accepted and used by many other authors (Coma, 1972), but it is of no great theoretical or practical interest nowadays. The underlying motives for the subdivision do not really provide a satisfactory generalization of the circumstances when there is any petrological, lithological and tectonic variability involved.

Certainly the kind of data taken in an aquifer will differ depending on the type of aquifer concerned. In this regard the difference in hydrogeological anisotropy found in fissured or karst aquifers on the one hand, and in porous aquifers on the other, will no doubt come to mind. Yet this kind of distinction tends to disappear when, for instance, tectonic dislocations and faults in porous aquifers bring materials of different permeability into direct contact, thus isolating water-bearing levels which were originally in communication with one another.

A hydrogeological study covering many counties in California has revealed the great importance of geological structures as impermeable barriers. In the Owens Valley, for instance, the existence of a fault permits better utilization of the aquifer for the Los Angeles Water Supply than would otherwise be the case (Williams, 1970). In Orange County (CDWR, 1966) the presence of a set of faults controls levels of diverse permeability and locally circumscribes seawater intrusion. As a result of the stratigraphic succession encountered there, it often happens that these aquifers have several superimposed water-bearing levels each with a different salinity, separated by impermeable or semipermeable levels.

(*) Good geological mapping is essential for a correct understanding of the performance of coastal aquifers. The relevance of geology has been pointed out in sections 3.3.1 and 4.4.1 and generally in the chapters 3 and 4. Especially important are the mapping and prediction of changes in permeability and the development or closing of fissures in fractured rocks.

Karst aquifers are far more complex than other kinds of fissured aquifers. Generalization and extrapolation may be impossible. There may be substantial differences between one part of a karst region and another, even when the area involved is small. In coastal karst aquifers these differences concern such matters as the geometric and hydrodynamic attributes of the aquifer, the way recharge and seaward outflow occur, the pattern of subterranean water movement and the chemical properties of the groundwaters connected with the kind of relationship that exists with the seawaters intruding the landmass. These aspects are influenced not only by the degree of fracturing of the carbonate rocks involved, but also by the following three factors:

(a) Marked anisotropy which governs the genetic-evolutive processes, and the distribution and spatial orientation of the karst conduits. Karst conduits develop along predetermined lines dictated by local and regional tectonic elements, the general direction of groundwater flow, and the often discontinuous presence of lithotypes that are not subject to karstification or only slightly so. The selective character of the lines of major karst development may be explained by the fact that the karstogenic role of each tectonic joint or bedding plane depends not so much on the extent to which it is open, but rather on its dip and strike compared with the direction of groundwater flow (Grassi, 1974).

(b) Palaeogeograhic vicissitudes which often affect various parts of a vast region in a different manner. During the course of geological time, geographic vicissitudes may result in changes in the general base level of groundwater movement, thus influencing the processes governing karst cavity development. So it happens not infrequently that several different rock horizons, which are particularly permeable as a result of karst action, may not be in communication with one another owing to the lack of or poor development of tectonic fissuring or to the local absence of rocks subject to karstification. This can produce a somewhat singular hydrogeological environment, characterized by the separation of the karst-aquifer groundwaters: above the main body of water there may be several other water levels, perhaps of considerable thickness, and perhaps having diverse hydrological and chemical properties if they lie at elevations where they are influenced by seawater intrusion.

(c) Effect of terra rossa. Terra rossa not infrequently affects the groundwater system both positively and negatively. This material is produced by the karst process and also regulates its development in some cases. For instance, it tends to block karst conduits, thus reducing permeability and hence slowing down or even halting development there, so that the waters are forced to open up new conduits. It is not uncommon to find well fields where the discharge has fallen by as much as 80 or 90% after being in operation for ten or twenty years.

It is evident from the foregoing that tectonic-structural and statistical analysis of fracturing, performed on drill cores, and of subhorizontal karst conduits, combined with a detailed palaeogeographic appraisal, are essential when studying any karst aquifer thoroughly.

When dealing with coastal springs (see sections 3.3.5 and 3.3.6) it is important to find out everything possible regarding the spring feed area, the infiltration conditions and the structure of the aquifer, especially in the resurgence area.

It is often difficult to plot the limits of the feed area, especially for springs fed by karst aquifers and by fissured aquifers in general. In such cases it is necessary to have recourse to structural analysis, involving subsurface geological investigations and the use of tracers.

Of course, information must also be acquired on the tectonic or geomorphological situations which played a role in development of the springs. In particular in the case of submarine springs it is essential to correlate the physical and chemical characteristics of the aquifer feed with those of the springs and to pay close attention to anthropic action. This clearly requires the performance of investigations in wells drilled onshore.

Also, remote sensing may be very useful for an accurate, rapid inventory of subaerial and submarine coastal springs, as will be described below.

7.2   (*) Inventories

Inventories of wells, water levels, hydrometrical and hydrometrorological data, abstractions, etc., are the cheapest and fastest method to get information about present situation and the only way to know the past evolution. Standard techniques are used, using especially trained personnel. There is a tendency to assign the inventory tasks, that are tedious, boring, tiresome and obscure, to the lowest levels of the team or those just arrived, and this may be a tremendous error, since the inventory is the source of data and guides for the foregoing work.

When dealing with coastal aquifers, special emphasis must be put on the gathering and acquisition of data on:

- water salinity, its variations and the vertical distribution;

- the salt-fresh water interfaces or the mixing zone;

- the accurate distribution of permeable (or fractured) zones and water heads along the bore-holes;

- the existence, importance and variability of coastal springs;

- the sea level and the shore changes, both as a result of tides or other short term changes, or due to a long term evolution (sedimentation, abrasion);

- subsidence in flat unconsolidated areas.

7.3 Observation wells

Many of the traditional methods still appear essential for hydrogeological studies. In particular, observation wells are of undoubted value for the direct acquisition of data on equilibrium conditions affecting groundwaters and intruding seawaters.

Bore-holes and observation wells especially drilled for the study of coastal aquifers run through the entire thickness of the aquifer and penetrate for several dozen meters into the underlying seawaters. They permit useful hydrological checks and investigations to be made, such as: natural radioactivity of the soils; fluctuations in groundwater level; saline and thermal stratification of groundwaters; changes in grondwater-seawater interface; direction and velocity of groundwater flow; vertical currents (using artificial radioactive tracers); radon and CO_2 content of water; and isotope content. They also enable vertical changes in the zone of dispersion and variations in the salinity of the groundwaters to be monitored and related to recharge by rainfall on the one hand and extraction for beneficial use on the other.

During drilling operations and when the observation well is complete, particular hydrogeological conditions may be encountered which may falsify the data collected from the desired levels if provision is not made to cope with these. Since the final completion of the wells must ensure that the aquifer is not disturbed, the casing must be installed only after the hydraulic head has been ascertained at all points in the well, since the aquifer may consist of a series of water levels each with a different hydraulic head owing to vertical variations in permeability. Under such circumstances, the drilling of the well creates an artificial means of communication, which results in vertical currents being generated in the water column, running from levels with the greatest head to those with the smallest.

The existence of such currents, even relatively small ones, renders the collected data imprecise or reduces their significance (see section 6.9), since they tend to even-out the chemical and physical properties of the waters in the well. It is thus necessary, in these cases, to restore the original conditions in the aquifer by isolating those vertical sections in the well where preferential water movements occur. This involves the use of 'cells' of various lengths. These cells can be created initially by temporary means, which enable the local hydrogeological situation to be investigated before completing the well permanently by cementation.

Temporary isolation (Cotecchia, 1977) is achieved by using pneumatic packers, mounted on metal or PVC pipe, the whole being fixed to the end of a blind piezometric column which runs up to ground level. The packers are inflated from the surface by means of compressed air (which is delivered via small-bore rubber lines) so that they adhere closely to the sides of the borehole. If the walls of the bore are such that a perfect seal cannot be achieved with a single packer, several can be installed (fig. 7.1).

The use of temporary packers enables accurate hydrological information to be collected even from wells which were not designed and completed specifically for research work. The temporary isolation stage is often essential to acquire the data needed for the final design of wells to be used as permanent monitoring and measuring stations.

For permanent isolation (Carlin and Tadolini, 1969; Cotecchia, 1977) cells of various lengths can be created, cell diameter being close to that of the bore when hard rock is involved or smaller when loose rocks are encountered. The cells are perforated (perforations accounting for about 15% of the total area) so as to permit the passage of groundwaters. They are isolated from one another by cement plugs and are serviced from ground level by 50 mm diameter piezometers, down which measuring equipment is lowered. PVC pipe is used generally for the cells and the piezometers, since it stands up to the corrosive action of brackish water better than steel.

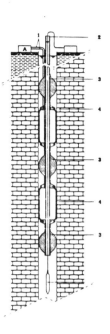

Fig. 7.1 - Arrangement for isolating lengths of borehole (A: compressed air; 1: compressed air lines; 2: piezometer; 3: entering devices; pneumatic packers). After Tazioli (1973).

There is a tapered metal shoe at the bottom of the cell to assist descent down the hole, while at the top there is a rubber-gasketed metal plate for connecting the piezometer. The plate also supports the layer of gravel which is installed to prevent the cell being filled with the cement which is positioned to ensure isolation (figs. 7.2 and 7.3).

In some cases it is possible to avoid the piezometers of lower cells passing through those above, by placing the cells side by side, when the borehole diameter is large enough to permit this.

To ensure that cells are not blocked by the cement plugs positioned between them, a 1.50 m thick layer of gravel is placed above them. The grading of the gravel decreases from 10 mm to 0.1 mm going upwards (fig. 7.4). The layer is dropped into place, so the waters themselves ensure further grading as the pieces fall into position. When selecting the amount and size of gravel to be used, account must be taken of the dimensions of the fissures and cavities encountered in the rock, as well as the volume of the length of hole to be packed. A careful check must be made of the thickness of the gravel layer.

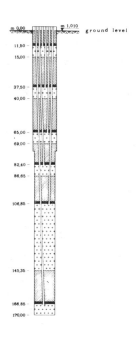

Fig. 7.2 - Arrangement of cell in borehole completed in fissured rock   (Cotecchia, 1977).

Fig. 7.3 - Section of a cell and plan view of connecting plate. 1: piezometer of cell 2; 2: piezometer union; 3: piezometer passing through from cell 1 below; 4: metal plate to hold rubber gaskets; 5: rubber gaskets; 6: cell/piezometer connecting head; 7: cell-mouth for introduction of measuring instruments; 8: PVC cell; 9: metal shoe of cell.   On the right, connecting plate and cell showing perforations (Carlin and Tadolini, 1969).

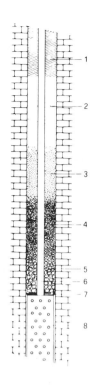

Fig. 7.4 - Arrangement of cell in borehole completed in dolomitic limestones.
1: cement plug; 2: medium-fine sand (0.1-0.5 mm); 3: medium-coarse
sand (0.5-5 mm); 4: fine gravel (5-10 mm); 5: gravel (10-25 mm); 6:
piezometer; 7: connecting plate with rubber gaskets; 8: perforated
cell. (Carlin and Tadolini, 1969).

        The cement plugs between the cells are gravitated into position
through 25 mm diameter pipes. Cementation is performed in several stages so
that a check can be made on possible losses of grout through cracks in the
rock. Once the wall has been cemented to the planned height, the cell is
positioned above the plug (Carlin and Tadolini, 1969; Cotecchia et al., 1974).

        Well completion design (number of cells, their length and position)
is usually decided case by case, to suit the technical characteristics of the
well and the aims to be achieved. The number of wells and their location will
depend on the hydrogeological characteristics of the area to be studied.

        However, when it is wished to study the overall behavior of ground-
waters floating on seawaters, care must be taken to ensure that the observation wells are not sited in areas where there are cones of depression caused
by operating wells. It is therefore very important to distinguish between
observation wells needed to study the cone of depression caused by drawdown or
the wedge of intruded seawater beneath the well, and observation wells
designed to check on the overall aspects of the groundwater regimen. The
former must be sited around the well, generally using the same criteria as
adopted for piezometers; their number, mutual spacing and depth depend on
aquifer permeability, anisotropy, static level of water above sea level and
the amount of money available.

The use of observation wells to investigate hydrodynamic phenomena around a well is always very costly. The wells are very deep, since they have to penetrate into the seawater, so they must be wisely sited to permit a saving on numbers.

As just noted, the observation wells used to check on the overall hydrodynamic conditions of the groundwaters should be sited away from wedges of intruded seawater and cones of depression caused by pumping. Here, too, the cost is considerable, so as many checks as possible should be made in each well and the maximum attention must be given to ensuring the most suitable location, taking account of geological factors and the distribution of production wells in the area.

Since the cost of a well depends on its depth, whenever possible the observation wells should be sited where ground elevation is lowest. The cost of a network of observation wells should be in line with the importance of the problems involved and the gravity of the hydrogeological situation to be checked.

A concrete idea in this regard can be gained from consideration of a 500 km^2 area of the Salento Peninsula (Apulia) which is covered by a network of piezometers, a score or so of which are observation wells in the true sense of the word, i.e. they are drilled to a depth of 700 or 800 m to check on the zone of dispersion (see chapter 10).

7.4   Salinity logging

(*) The most usual method for in-situ measurement of water salinity is the conductivity-meter method, that involves the measurement of water electrical conductivity (or its inverse, the electrical resistivity), which depends essentially on salinity but which also varies with water temperature and percentage of ions. In sodium-chloride dominant waters this last factor only has a small influence.

(*) The instrumentation consists of:

- a leakproof probe containing the electrodes and in many instances also a temperature sensor (thermistor or platinum resistance);

- a cable connecting the probe to the measuring device, generally with 3 or 4 conductors and a steel cable to give strength and stiffness, attached to a drum and a depth measuring device;

- a conductance (or resistance) measuring device based on the principle of the Kohlraush (alternating current Wheatstone) bridge, with manual or electronic zeroing.

They are portable, battery-powered and some models are commercially available. Figure 7.5 shows the scheme for water level, temperature and salinity probes.

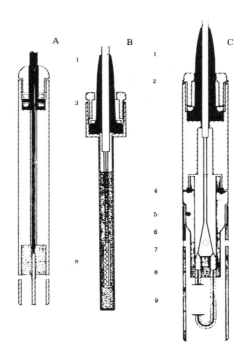

Fig. 7.5 — Probes for measuring: (A) groundwater level; (B) temperature and (C) salinity. 1: power cable, 2: grommet for sealing cables; 3: copper mesh; 4: rubber ring; 5: housing and PVC sheath; 6: pitch compound; 7: 100-ohm Ni resistance; 8: epoxy resin; 9: platinum plated platinum discs (Cotecchia, 1977).

The salinity of the waters sampled is ascertained by reference to calibration curves. Having obtained the resistivity of the unknown sample at ambient temperature (R_t), the resistivity at 25°C is calculated by applying the formula $R_{25} = (R_t - R_C) \cdot (1 - \alpha t)$, where α = temperature factor (= 0.025) and R_C is the resistance of the electrode cable.

The calibration curve is obtained by plotting the resistivity (R_{25}) and salinity values of each sample solution on a log scale and then interpolating.

Temperature correction must be applied for all resistivity values measured in situ, so the temperature of the water must be recorded at each relevant point.

Multichannel self-recording conductivity meters which operate with the same measuring cells as above are used to check on the way the salt concentrations of surface and deep well waters very with time. The recorded values are transformed into mg/l total salinity using the reference curve procedure.

This method of salinity measurement has the advantage of being very practical and reasonably accurate, though it has some drawbacks, not the least of which is the polarization of the electrodes of the salinometer. This causes a 'drift' in the measurements owing to an increase in apparent resistivity for the same salt concentration in the water. Thus, the electrodes must be replated with platinum every so often, and the calibration curves must be checked and, if necessary, replotted for each logging operation. For the above reasons the usual conductivity meter methods are not suitable for making easy continuous measurements of salinity in deep wells.

A less common device for water salinity measurements is the neutron probe (Cotecchia and Pirastru, 1970), that measures mainly the water in the formation surrounding the bore-hole, except for high diameter wells, in which water inside is preferently measured. This method of measurement is based on the property possessed by chlorine to capture thermal neutrons. The neutrons emitted by the probe source are thermalized by the water, whose chlorine content is to be determined. The difference in the capture of thermal neutrons exercised by waters containing different amounts of chlorine can be followed fairly closely by a thermal neutron counter (Magri and Pirastru, 1968; Keys, 1966; Keys and MacCary, 1971), which is placed in the water together with a fast-neutron source (fig. 7.6).

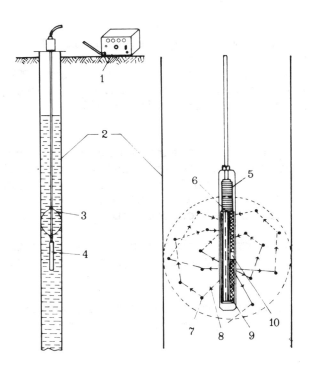

Fig. 7.6 - On left, arrangement of equipment for neutron-probe measurements of chlorine content of borehole waters; on right, diagram of neutron probe illustrating neutron slow-down and scattering. 1: scaler; 2: perforated casing; 3: centering device; 4: probe; 5: pulse preamplifier; 6: boron trifluoride counter; 7: atoms; 8: neutrons; 9: lead shield; 10: Am-Be source. (Magri and Pirastru, 1968).

Owing to the presence of elements other than chlorine in the water, not all the thermal neutron capture in excess of that caused by pure water can be attributed to chlorine alone. The breakdown generally accepted is 98.5 percent as a result of capture by chlorine and a relatively constant 1.5 percent as a result of other elements present in the water.

It should be pointed out that boreholes of over 200 mm diameter are needed in order to be able to use the neutron probe for the type of investigation described, owing to interference caused by the rock walls and the well casing.

This method has been widely used to study seawater intrusion of the Apulian aquifer (see chapter 10) and to measure fluctuations of the seawater-freshwater interface. The neutron probe was calibrated by three different procedures based on theoretical considerations, the chloride ion content of the water being correlated with the corresponding counts. In figure 7.7 is shown the neutron probe calibration curve utilized in Apulia. There is clearly a good agreement among the three methods for plotting the probe calibration curve.

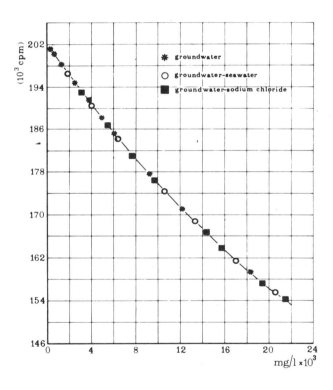

Fig. 7.7 - Neutron probe calibration curve for measuring chloride ion content of waters. The probe was calibrated by mixing fresh water of known chemical composition with seawater and with sodium chloride, respectively. Note the good agreement (Magri and Pirastru, 1968).

The probe used for chlorine measurement is quite similar to that commonly utilized for determining the natural water content of soils. The essential feature is that it must be watertight even at high hydrostatic pressures. It was built and tested by the Laboratory of Hydrogeology of the Engineering Geology and Geotechnique Institute of Bari. This probe has an Am-Be source and a helium-3 proportional counter clad with a lead and cadmium shield (Cotecchia and Pirastru, 1970).

7.5 Temperature logging

Like chemical composition and natural isotope content, temperature constitutes an effective environmental tracer for studying groundwater origin and movement in general, but it is even more useful where seawater intrusion is concerned as described in section 6.12.

When hydrogeological conditions are favorable, examination of temperature trends in wells enables very valuable information to be acquired on the location of recharge areas, rate of renewal of groundwaters and the dispersion of seawater in fresh groundwaters.

Portable instruments are used to measure groundwater temperature. The probes have a Ni resistance (100 ohm at $0^{\circ}C$) housed in a stainless steel tube and connected to the meter by three-core cable (fig. 7.5).

Before and after each series of measurements the equipment is checked by means of a mercury thermometer having $1/100^{\circ}C$ divisions accurate to between -0.02 and $+0.03^{\circ}C$ in the 9 to 20° range.

Though there exists the possibility of error due to the instrument not being perfectly horizontal, imperfect calibration, self-heating of the thermometric resistances, etc., it is considered that the temperature data collected in this manner are correct to within $\pm0.1^{\circ}C$.

(*) Platinum-resistance thermometers are also widely used, especially in geothermal prospecting. They are reliable, inexpensive, and very compact measurement devices. In some circumstances a precision of $\pm0.01^{\circ}C$ can be attained, but to get reliable data the probe must be operated carefully, in an undisturbed bore-hole, measuring when lowering the probe.

(*) An improvement is the differential temperature log (Keys and MacCary, 1971) in which the temperature difference between two sensors separated by a given distance is determined. Using high sensitivity and accurate sensors a log which is very sensitive to temperature changes is obtained. It is easier to interpret and the contacts are clearly shown. Usually this device is standard in geophysical logging vans. In fissured rocks they are very useful for the location of active discontinuities (Monkhouse and Fleet, 1975).

7.6   (*) <u>Representativity of bore-hole measurements</u>

Generally, salinity and temperature logs from the water inside a bore-hole are taken as representative of the water in the nearby aquifer. If there are vertical flows along the bore-hole or piezometer, including small ones, the stratification is altered and the log no longer represents the aquifer. Such vertical flows are very common (near the coast, near pumping wells, when there are more than one aquifer, near recharge zones) and neglecting them may lead to erroneous conclusions. A bore-hole may present tracts with temperature or salinity completely changed, and the interfaces only represent the depths where water gets in or gets out (see section 6.9). Near pumping wells the fall in fresh water head in an observation bore-hole penetrating to salt water, is accompanied by a great rise in the salt water, according to the BGH principle. It does not represent the slow behavior of the aquifer (Rushton, 1980). Figure 7.8 shows how the conductivity logs do not clearly show or do not show at all the salinity in the chalk of Brighton (UK), deduced from electrical logging. In that area, changes in the interface inside the observation bore-holes have been observed and sometimes an 86 m change from high to low tide has been measured (Monkhouse and Fleet, 1975), which evidently does not represent the aquifer, but the hydraulic interaction among fissures, interconnected by the bore-hole. Persistently repeated lows and highs in the water conductivity only represent the effect of fissures, that can carry fresh or salt water, different from that in the chalk pores.

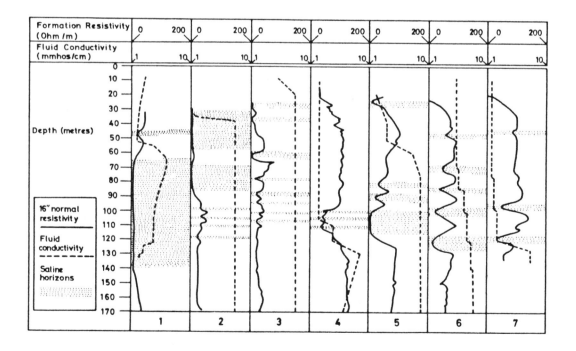

Fig. 7.8 - Resistivity and conductivity logs from 7 boreholes in the Brighton area, U.K. (after Fleet, Brerenton and Howard, 1978). Fluid conductivity logs do not represent the aquifer vertical distribution of salinity. Water circulates mainly through fissures and the higher potential ones condition the water conductivity, especially in boreholes 2 and 3.

All this shows that in fissured rocks, bore-holes must be used with caution as salinity control devices.

In order to properly measure the salinity at a particular point in an aquifer and also to measure the pressure head in terms of the water that exists at that point in the aquifer, there is no substitute for a fully-cased piezometer terminated by a very small screen or short length of open hole. Also, there must be no annular passageway between the casing and the rock wall. Otherwise, the potentials are inadvertently short-circuited, giving rise to false pressure-head readings and false data on the salinity of the groundwater. Even worse than giving erroneous information, however, an open borehole can provide an easy path for saline water to contaminate shallow parts of the aquifer.

7.7 Groundwater sampling

(*) According to Kohout and Hoy (1963), there is no such thing as a bad water sample, only badly collected samples. It may be defined as a water sample that yields erroneous or incomplete information of the position and distribution of salt water in the aquifer. Generally, a badly collected water sample cannot be distinguished from a properly collected sample. Confidence, then, rests on how and by what method the sample is collected.

Though it is possible to use commercially available bottles for sampling groundwaters for chemical analysis, many of these suffer from drawbacks, such as limitations on the depth at which they can be used, well diameter, etc. It is thus preferable to prepare suitable bottles which can also be used to sample waters via small-bore piezometers. One such bottle is illustrated in figure 7.9. The springs act independently on the closing discs ensuring a perfect seal, except when the sample is being taken. This kind of bottle is fitted with valves controlled by a pair of messengers or by compressed air.

(*) A detailed study of sampling devices can be found in Everett (1980). When selecting a sampling device the desired goals must be brought to mind. Salinity and especially chloride are unalterable, so crude sampling devices are enough, provided the samples are taken in a downward direction and pertubation in the water column is as low as possible. But when easily alterable ions or components are involved (Fe^{++}, NH_4^+, gases, ...) contact with air must be avoided, and also temperature changes. See section 6.9 for other comments and details.

7.8 (*) Bore-hole geophysical logging

Bore-hole geophysical logs, including the nuclear ones, are very useful in coastal studies. The method of interpretation does not differ for the general ones (Keys and MacCary, 1971), but resistivity is very sensitive to salty groundwater in the ground. Then, it has been widely used, when possible, for the determination of the interface or mixing zone (figs. 7.10, 7.11 and 7.12). The bore-hole must be uncased.

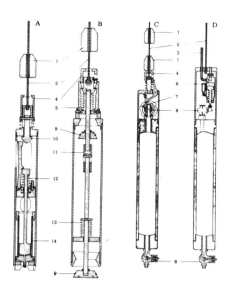

Fig. 7.9 – Water sampling equipment for boreholes. From left to right: (A) mechanically-controlled syringe, (B) mechanically-controlled bottle, (C) PVC bottle with messenger-controlled valve, (D) PVC bottle with air-controlled valve. 1: messengers; 2: steel cables; 3: compressed air line; 4: release devices; 5: spring for closing upper disc; 6: air ram; 7: spring for opening and closing valve; 8: valves; 9: rubber rings; 10: release pin; 11: collar for altering rod length; 12: syringe control spring; 13: spring for closing upper disc; 14: glass syringe. (Tazioli, 1973).

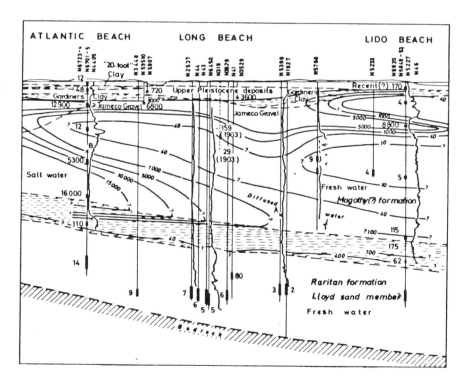

Fig. 7.10 – Cross-section along the south coast of Long Island, New York, showing the vertical salinity distribution, as deduced from electric logs of bore-holes after completion (Lusczynski and Swarzenski, 1966).

-285-

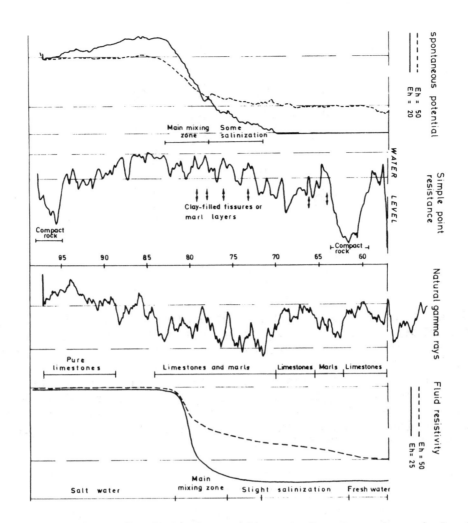

Fig. 7.11 – Geophysical downhole logs of an exploratory bore-hole in the fissured limestone of the Garraf Massif, near Castelldefels (Barcelona). The conjoint use of spontaneous potential, simple electrode resistance, natural gamma rays and fluid resistivity is shown. The progressive compactness and limestone dominance of the rock makes the resistance log not enough clear, but the mixing zone is more clear in the fluid resistivity and spontaneous potential log. A radioactive tracer test shows that only a few very small fissures exist under the water table, that do not reflect in the spontaneous potential log.

The method is also useful in fissured rocks, with a high storage, low permeability matrix, as the chalk (Fleet, Brerenton and Howard, 1978).

The use of nuclear logging (neutron-neutron for porosity, gamma-gamma for density) can be useful to determine total porosity or rocks and perhaps to locate cavities and the most fractured levels. Caliper and sonic logs are also very useful in respect to the last aspects, but they have the drawback that the bore-hole must be uncased, which is not necessary for nuclear logs.

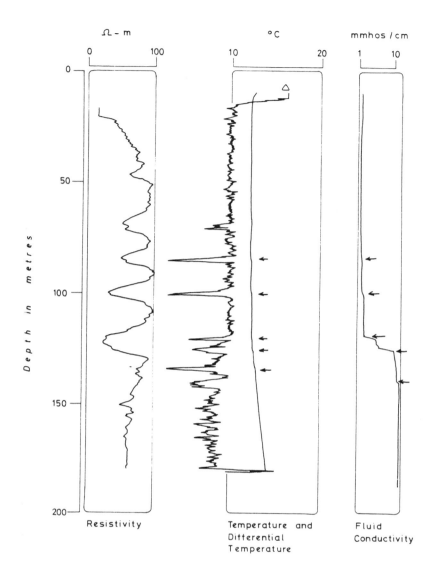

Fig. 7.12 - Irregularities in temperature and water conductivity logs in fractured rocks show the situation of main fractures. The use of differential temperature is very clear in this respect. The shown example corresponds to a coastal borehole near Brighton, UK (after Fleet, Brerenton and Howard, 1978).

Conventional devices are used, from the portable ones (spontaneous potential, simple point resistance and natural gamma rays) to the more complete ones, installed in a van.

Resistivity logs can be applied in screened, PVC lined piezometers in order to follow the time changes in the measured resistance, as shown in figure 7.13.

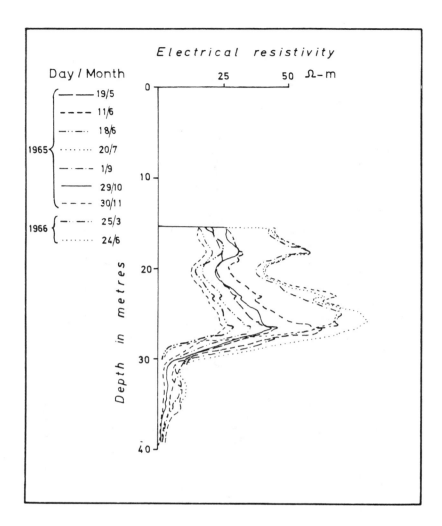

Fig. 7.13 - Resistivity logs in a coastal bore-hole, showing the time variations. Below 30 m there is an oscillation of water salinity according to the recharge. Different subaquifers exist (after Debuisson
and Mousu, 1967).

Permanently installed multiple electrodes in a bore-hole (filled or
unfilled with sand), measured with a disposition similar to a long normal
resistivity device or other configuration used in geoelectrical protecting has
been used in Holland (van Dam, 1976b) and in Sweden (Leander, 1977) to follow
the advancement and movement of salinity in the aquifer. The terminal electrodes are reunited in a cap that can be periodically monitored, selecting
those best fitted to the desired depth.

Geoelectrical logging, when using an appropriate dispositive such as
the long normal one (simple point electrical logging only gives resistance),
gives ground resistivity ρg. It is related to water resistivity ρw by the
formation factor, F (Archie, 1942): F = $\rho g / \rho w$. F must be defined for a given
temperature (generally 25°C) and depends on the lithology. In many instances
F = m^{-2}; m = saturated porosity (García Yagüe in Custodio and Llamas, 1976).

7.9   Limits and utility of geophysical investigations

Useful information on subsurface structure, lithology, trend of contacts, outline of the hydrogeological situation, and quantity and quality of stored waters can be provided by seismic and electric geophysical prospecting when used to complement exploratory investigations of aquifers affected by seawater intrusion. The electrical method is particularly useful, because the surfaces of separation of different types of ground can be identified in the subsurface on the basis of resistivity differences and the geometry of saline zones can be delimited (Lloyd et al., 1977). Electrical prospecting (see standard books on geophysics applied to hydrogeology, such as Orellana, 1972; Astier, 1971; García Yagüe in Custodio and Llamas, 1976) or geoelectrical sounding permits identification of the interface because of the resistivity change that occurs at the passage from freshwater to saltwater. In effect, seawater contamination of fresh groundwater is indicated by decreasing resistivity values as the water comes to have virtually the same salinity as that of the sea. In the case of perched aquifers or of those situated below sea level the hydrogeological situation can be ascertained by interpreting differences in resistivities that occur between permeable and impermeable lithofacies under dry or saturated conditions.

In the case of non-clayey homogeneous aquifers, rock resistivity has resulted proportional to water resistivity, so that there is a sharp decrease in resistivity at the passage from the zone outside the aquifer to freshwater zone and from this to the saltwater zone. However, resisitivity changes registered are not rough, as the former passage is subdued by the capillary zone and the latter by the dispersion zone. Therefore, in this case (homogeneous soil) there are three electrically different 'layers:' zone outside the aquifer, freshwater zone and saltwater zone) with transition zones (capillary zone and dispersion zone). Generally speaking, the zone of dispersion makes the geoelectrical method more difficult to be applied, for the existence of a multiple layered system with a non-constant resistivity layer.

However, specific studies (Mosetti, 1961; van Dam and Meulenkamp, 1967; van Dam, 1976a) have shown the existence of a sharp limit between fresh water and salt water, corresponding to an isohaline above which resistivity is uniformly high.

Yet, if porosity or salinity distribution vary locally, the electrical discontinuity does not coincide with the isohaline.

It follows, therefore, that in the case of porous rock, if the salt concentration varies within a given section of thickness H, the corresponding resistivity measured (ρ) varies in a section that is only a small fraction of thickness H. So when the geoelectrical method is used to locate the interface, though there is a broad band where the salinity varies, the zone in which the resistivity varies is very small and it causes little disturbance to interpretation of the electrical sounding. This is shown very clearly in figure 7.14 in which the resistivity (ρ) trend is indicated for a porous rock on the basis of a given trend of salt concentration C, determined by reference to the laws of diffusion.

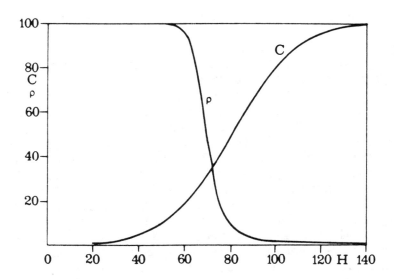

Fig. 7.14 - Trend with depth (H) of resistivity (ρ) of a porous rock imbued with water, relating to salt content (C) variations of the imbuing water (Mosetti, 1961).

Figures 7.15 and 7.16 show two typical resistivity curves obtained in a calcareous formation at the contact between freshwater near the surface and saltwater in depth. These curves are found when the overburden has a lower resistivity than that of the limestones imbued with freshwater (fig. 7.15) and when the outcropping limestones are dry for a certain stretch, or are overlied by materials having a higher resistivity (fig. 7.16).

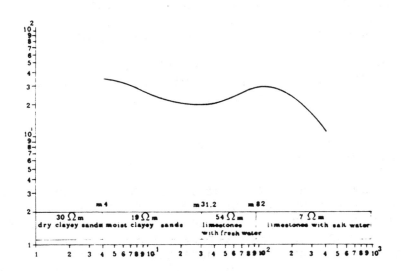

Fig. 7.15 - Resistivity curve for a limestone imbued with fresh water near the surface and with salt water in depth, and with an overburden having a low resistivity (Mosetti, 1961).

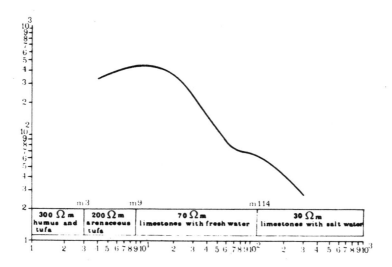

Fig. 7.16 - Resistivity curve for a calcareous formation in the same situation of figure 7.15, but with an overburden having high resistivity (Mosetti, 1961).

When a log diagram resistivity profile is obtained comparing the values of half the electrode spacing with the apparent resistivity measured; mathematical interpretation is made by comparing the resistivity profile obtained with theoretical calibration curves.

On the basis of data from groundwater samples previously drawn in the area under examination, it is possible to arrive at rating curves (fig. 7.17) for the conversion of resistivity data into the chloride content of the groundwaters (van Dam and Meulenkamp, 1967).

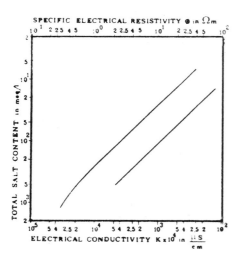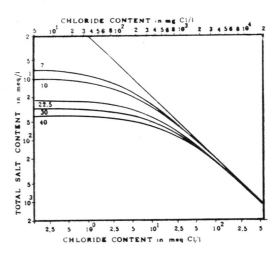

Fig. 7.17 - Relationship between chloride content, total salt content, electrical conductivity and specific electric resistivity for diluted sea water (van Dam and Meulenkamp, 1967).

Reliability of data obtained from resistivity soundings that have been interpreted through standard curves already available can be checked by comparing them with resistivity curves calculated by a computer (Cnudde, 1977).

Resistivity methods do not give information about groundwater movement, recharge, hydrogeological constants and about the existence of thin layers with low hydraulic conductivity which can be instead very important as to hydrogeological problems (van Dam and Meulenkamp, 1967). The depth to the water can be influenced by the capillary rise in fine materials.

A factor to be considered is the extension of the investigation area because electrical sounding gives reliable information for a zone whose area is at least equal to investigation depth. So, if at the bottom of a well there is a strong raising at the contact between fresh and salt water, but limited to a narrow area, said raising may not be pointed out through the geoelectrical method. This was for instance the case of some wells drilled in limestone which was very permeable vertically.

(*) One of the main deficiencies with the geoelectrical method is the impossibility of properly distinguishing a clay containing fresh or brackish water from a sea water saturated sand. Also, it is difficult to detect fine clay layers, due to the supression principle (van Dam, 1976a), when the clay resistivity is about one-third or half the sand resistivity. One must accept the case in which the salinity is greater over than below the layer in question. This is an unstable situation in which a clay layer must be present in order to maintain such a situation, and thus this layer is known indirectly, though the thickness cannot be known. The clay layer becomes invisible when there is fresh water over and salty water below.

(*) Geoelectrical prospecting has been used as a common tool for the determination of the depth to the mixing zone (Gorhan, 1976; Arora and Bose, 1981; Ginzburg and Levanon, 1976) and is used in many areas such as the Netherlands (Boekelman, 1979; Leenen, 1980) and in islands (see section 3.3.7).

It can be used from time to time to know the salinity evolution (van Dam, 1976; see also case history no. 6 in chapter 10).

(*) The Schlumberger arrangement is the most common one. In order to diminish the effects of electrically non-horizontal layers (e.g., a steep fresh-salt water interface) the sounding are placed in a line as much as possible perpendicular to the expected slope of the interface. For small electrode spacings, considerable changes in apparent specific resistivity values can be noticed, due to the effect of nonhomogeneities in the upper layers.

(*) Figures 7.18 and 7.19 show the results of two surveys in the Netherlands. Figure 7.20 shows the depth to the top of the mixing zone along a N-S profile in Belgium. Figure 7.21 corresponds to a section crossing the Groot Mijdrech polder in Holland, and shows the mixing zone and the upward discharge of salt water.

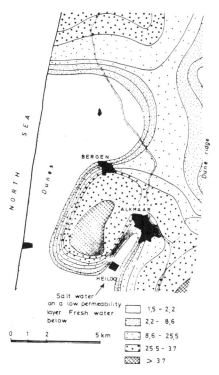

Fig. 7.18 - Results of a geoelectrical prospecting in the surroundings of Alk-
maar (the Netherlands) reflecting the ground resistivity value at
15 m below mean sea level (van Dam, 1976b). Under the dunes and the
sand ridges there is fresh water, but salty water is present in the
depressed areas.

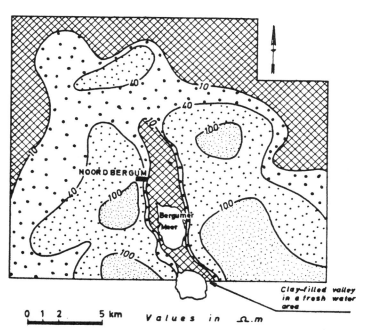

Fig. 7.19 - Electrical resistivity at a depth of 60 m below land surface in
the vicinity of Noordbergum, the Netherlands (van Dam, 1976b) showing the greater salinity below the depressed areas.

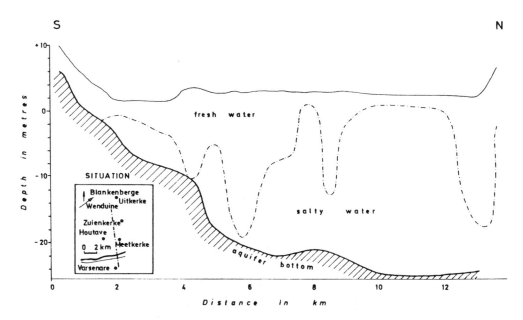

Fig. 7.20 - North-South section through the coastal aquifer of Belgium, showing the depth to the top of the mixing zone (a rather sharp one), as determined by resistivity sounding (de Breuck, 1975).

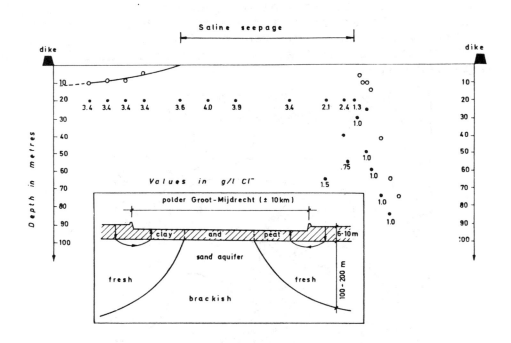

Fig. 7.21 - Cross-section (W-E) through the central part of the Groot Mijdrecht polder in the Netherlands (Leenen, 1980), obtained through electrical sounding. The results transformed in chloride content are shown. There is a rather sharp interface between fresh and brackish water and brackish water discharges by vertical seepage into the drained polder.

(*) The electrical walking method, in which the electrodes are moved along a line maintaining a predetermined separation, is useful for a rapid mapping using apparent resistivity values. Several maps for different AB (electrode specing) can be easily drawn, thus giving a tridimensional picture.

(*) Another electrical method is the electromagnetic one, that every day seems more promising due to the possibility of rapid surveys (Arora and Bose, 1981; Mülern and Ericksson, 1981), especially by the electrical walking method. The salt water body acts as the in the ground conductor. Rather long emittor-receptor distances are needed, between 30 and 100 m for interfaces not more than a few tens of meters deep. The method is less interesting for greater depths.

(*) Geoelectrical methods have also been used to study the sediments on the sea floor (Bogoslovskiy and Ogil'vi, 1973) using a bottom dispositive. Also areal, spontaneous potential can be used.

Another geophysical method which sometimes works to study hydrogeological situations is the seismic refraction method, which particularly in fissured rocks and in karst rock masses is useful for revealing the marked anisotropy which characterizes these formations. In karstified carbonate lithofacies, very considerable variations in the velocity of longitudinal elastic waves may be found. Sometimes the variations occur gradually both vertically and horizontally and sometimes they occur suddenly owing to the marked karstification of the medium concerned. The values may be extremely low when the behavior of the karstified rock mass is much the same as that of a loose, unconsolidated soil; or they may be considerably higher when the rock is not very fractured or karstified. Consequently seismic surveying is used to characterize karstified rocks in situ and to identify the amount of karstification present, on the basis of the velocities of the longitudinal waves registered.

7.10   Use of artificial tracers

Artificial radioactive tracers used in hydrogeology consist of water-soluble substances whose molecules contain a radioactive atom that emits beta or gamma radiation. The use of such tracers is widespread, because of the ease with which they can be detected in water. There is a slight preference for gamma type tracers because their concentration can be measured in-situ by simple equipment such as Geiger-Muller counters or scintillation counters, pulse meters, scalers and recorders, which are, of course, very convenient. With beta tracers, instead, laboratory determinations using liquid-phase scintillation equipment are required.

Bromine-82 and iodine-131 are very useful in coastal aquifers, since the same stable elements, present naturally in the waters, serve to carry along the radioactive isotopes that are injected. Which of the two tracers to use depends on the length of the experiment, because their half-lives are 1.5 and 8 days, respectively. They are generally used with a high quantity of a non-radioactive isotope in order to minimize retention.

Sodium-24 would have the same advantages, but its use is very limited owing to the danger involved in the high-energy gamma radiation produced.

In some particular experiments of average duration, chromium-51 complexed with EDTA gives satisfactory results. Its half-life is 27.8 days and it is hardly fixed at all by argillaceous terrains.

In the case of measurements to be made in wells whose waters are immediately destined for domestic consumption, it is preferable for stable artificial tracers to be either dyes (fluorescein, rodamine, methylene blue, etc.) or strong electrolytes or particular salts whose molecules contain atoms with a large capture cross-section for thermal neutrons.

Measurement of groundwater flow velocities are of great importance in hydrogeological investigations, since this parameter provides indications on aquifer permeability and transmissivity, and, consequently, of the discharges involved. The single-borehole tracer-dilution method is the most common way of measuring the velocity of groundwater flow; this is based on the relationship that exists between the velocity with which an injected tracer is diluted and the velocity of flow of the water.

(*) There are different techniques, from the more reliable and also more complicated and expensive ones (Drost et al., 1968; Halevy et al., 1966; Tazioli, 1973, 1976) to the simple ones (Plata, 1972; Baonza, Plata and Piles, 1970; Custodio and Llamas, 1976, chapter 12.3; Custodio, 1977), that get a semiquantitative answer in exchange of rapidity and reduction in equipment.

A given quantity of gamma-emitter tracer is injected into the well at the desired level and the labelled water eventually leaves the well in a exponentially decreasing way, the time required depending on the velocity of groundwater flow and well diameter.

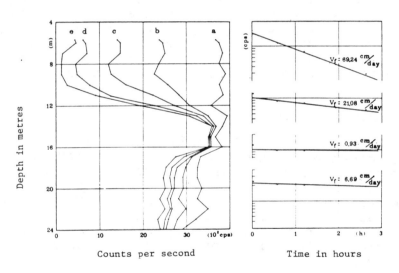

Fig. 7.22 - Velocity of groundwater flow measured in a borehole penetrating the groundwaters (5-15 m) and the intruding seawaters (15-24 m). The diagram on the left shows the variation of tracer activity with depth and time. The straight lines indicate the activity values measured from the time of tracer injection, namely at 0.03, 0.57, 1.20, 1.82 and 2.62 hours respectively (a), (b), (c), (d) and (e). The rate of dilution of the tracer at different depths is plotted on the semilog diagram on the right; the slopes of the lines are proportional to the velocity of groundwater flow. In this borehole, the groundwaters and the seawaters are both in movement, while the interface is practically stationary. Depths are measured from ground level (Tazioli, 1973).

Figure 7.22 shows diagrams of measurements made in the limestone dolomite aquifer of the Salento Peninsula, where the groundwaters float on seawaters that have intruded the land-mass. As can be seen from the diagrams on the left, the different velocities of groundwater flow at various depths in the aquifer have a very marked effect on tracer dilution. In this case, the intruding seawaters are also endowed with some degree of mobility. The lines illustrating the effect of time on dilution trends at given depths are shown on the right. The flow velocities can be calculated readily by their angular coefficient.

(*) Figures 7.23 and 7.24 show two examples performed with the simplified Plata method. Combining the results on several bore-holes it is possible to depict the permeability distribution in the aquifer, as shown in figure 7.25.

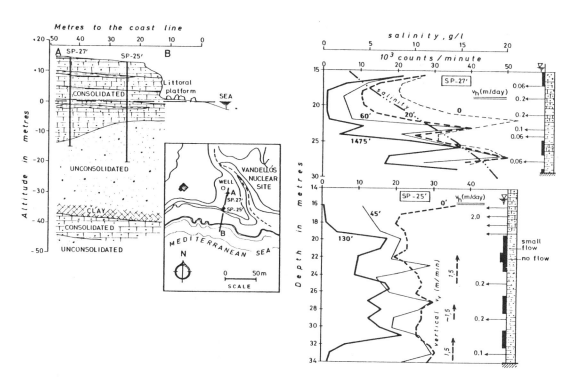

Fig. 7.23 - Study of horizontal groundwater flow velocity by means of the borehole dilution method after tracing with I-131 the whole piezometric column (Spanish method). The permeability stratification is easily shown. When testing borehole SP-25', a 250 l/s pumpage was initiated in a 30 m distant well; after 50 minutes the measurements are altered by the nearby pumping. A small vertical upward flow develops, because the most pervious zone is just below the water table. In absence of pumpage only horizontal flow exists. The mixing zone is thick and extend until the water table, in that coarse alluvial fan, containing unconsolidated materials and highly cemented layers. The consolidated parts contain washed out layers and open vertical joints (Custodio, 1978a).

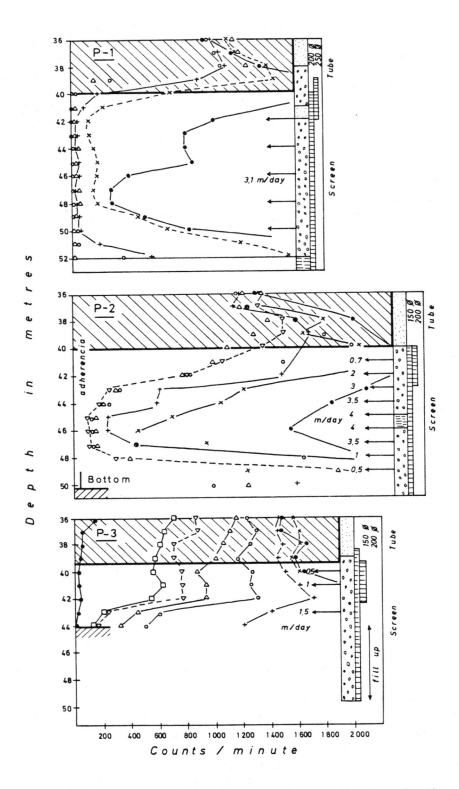

Fig. 7.24 – Measurement of horizontal water flow velocity in the Besós delta confined aquifer (Barcelona, Spain), that is sea water intruded. The borehole dilution method is applied after tracing the whole piezometric water column with I-131 (Custodio, Suárez and Galofré, 1976).

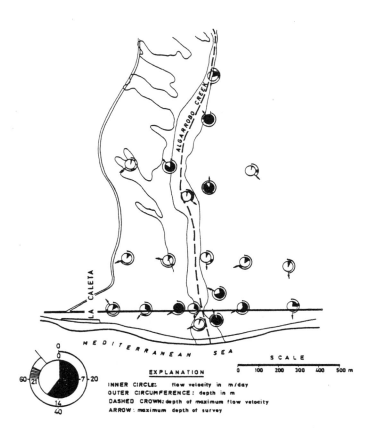

INNER CIRCLE: flow velocity in m/day
OUTER CIRCUMFERENCE: depth in m
DASHED CROWN: depth of maximum flow velocity
ARROW: maximum depth of survey

Fig. 7.25 - Groundwater flow velocity around a coastal creek near Malaga
(southern Spain). The flow velocity and the most permeable zone are
shown. Each piezometer represents a local circumstance. The study
of all the results give the regional picture (Baonza, Plata and
Escolano, 1970).

Determination of the presence and magnitude of vertical currents
provides pointers on interchanges between different aquifers or different levels of the same aquifer. Information on the presence of such currents is
essential when wells have to be completed in such a manner as to ensure temporary or permanent isolation of given water levels for the acquisition of
correct data on hydrogeological parameters (Tazioli, 1976).

Vertical currents in wells are determined by injecting the tracer at
the point where knowledge of the stratigraphy indicates such currents might
exist, and by following the movement of the 'cloud' by a Gieger-Muller or a
scintillation counter. Figure 7.26 indicates the trend of the tracer cloud as
it moves downwards in a well drilled in alluvial deposits.

The most precise information is obtained by recording the passage of
the radioactive cloud by means of a series of detectors installed at fixed
points in the borehole, and by determining the average velocity of the vertical current between two successive points, using the 'peak-to-peak' method.

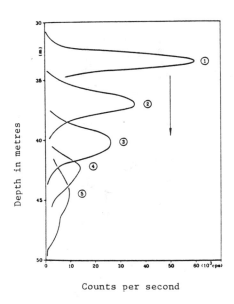

Fig. 7.26 - Measurement of vertical flow in a bore-hole by means of tracers.

The choice of method depends, of course, on the hydrogeological conditions encountered and the type of investigations involved. The following points may be made regarding the two methods:

- the peak-to-peak method enables average velocities to be measured in wells with a fair degree of precision, but it involves the use of a large number of counters to give a detailed picture of the distribution of velocities in the column of water. However, it does not provide a correct evaluation of such dilutions as may leave the vertical discharge unaltered;

- the total-count method offers the possibility of ascertaining whether there are any horizontal components between two measuring points. For instance, if there were an equal inflow and outflow, the total discharge would remain unchanged, but there would obviously be a decrease in the total count, N, proportional to the dilution of the tracer that occurs. This is, therefore, a very useful method to supplement the information provided by the first one.

The radioactive tracers best suited to this type of measurement are iodine-131 and bromine-82. A stable tracer successfully used for hydrogeological investigations in alluvial formations is cadmium chloride in an alcohol solution.

A special device may be used to inject radioactive tracers into wells, namely a syringe with electrical or mechanical control from the surface. This reduces the radiation hazard faced by those engaged on the investigation, as it takes only a few seconds to load the syringe.

(*) In the simplified method (Spanish method) vertical currents are clearly visible and are easy to measure from the progressive washout of the bore-hole column. The entry and exit zones are thus identified.

An estimate of the direction of groundwater flow often contributes greatly to understanding particular situations. For instance, in those parts of the Apulian coast where the groundwaters flow freely to the sea, it has been found that there is a periodic reversal of the direction of flow owing to oscillations in sea level. In some cases it has been observed that the seawaters which intrude into the land-mass move inland at high tide and seawards at low tide.

The direction in which maximum activity occurs is measured by a collimated scintillation probe (Tazioli, 1976). The orientation of the probe in the well can be changed from the surface, either by means of rods or by remote controls (Mairhofer, 1963; Borowczyk et al., 1965; Drost et al., 1968).

When velocities are high, it is preferable to use tracers that are fixed by the ground, but when they are lower, iodine-131 and bromine-82 also give satisfactory results.

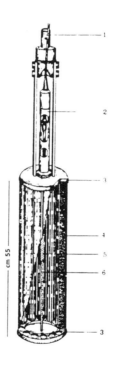

Fig. 7.27 - Equipment for measuring direction of groundwater flow. 1: rod coupling device; 2: electromagnetically-controlled syringe for tracer injection; 3: aluminum discs to carry tubes; 4: perforated stainless steel tubes filled with granular activated carbon; 5: small tube with fine holes and cover of closely-woven nylon; 6: tracer injection tube. The equipment can be used in different diameter boreholes by substituting the aluminum discs with others that can carry more or less tubes, to suit the case (Tazioli, 1973).

As an alternative to the above method it is possible to use an annular array of perforated tubes filled with granular activated carbon which is a good adsorbent of gases and of many radioactive tracers and dyes, including ^{51}Cr-EDTA, ^{131}I and fluorescein. In this case the tracer is injected by an electromagnetically-controlled syringe into the middle of the array; a small tube with fine holes and a cover of closely-woven nylon slows down the release of the tracer (fig. 7.27). After a sufficient length of time, which may vary from a few hours to several days, depending on the velocity of groundwater flow, the equipment is pulled out of the well and the activity of the individual tubes is measured by a gamma scintillation counter. The flow direction is indicated by the tubes with the greatest activity.

The apparatus is oriented in the well by a set of aluminum tubes when depths do not exceed 100 m. Where greater depths are involved, the direction can be measured by lowering the apparatus on a steel cable and then photographing the position of a magnetic needle by means of a flash (fig. 7.28).

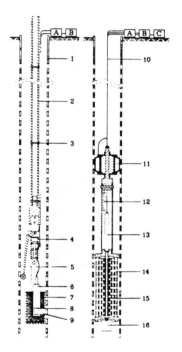

Fig. 7.28 - Arrangement for measuring direction of groundwater flow. On the left: collimated probe direction measuring device; on the right: granular activated carbon tube measuring device. A: scalers; B: compressed air; C: power source for electromechanically-operated syringe; 1: borehole casing; 2: hollow aluminum rods; 3: tapered connection; 4: air ram for moving probe off center; 5: lever for moving probe; 6: scintillation counter; 7: lead shield; 8: NaI (Tl) crystal measuring 25 x 38 mm; 9: window; 10: steel cable: 11; pneumatic packer; 12: GM counter; 13: electromechanically-controlled syringe for tracer injection; 14: array of tubes filled with granular activated carbon; 15: tracer injection tube; 16: box containing direction-indicator. (Tazioli, 1973).

The use of this apparatus is particularly indicated when high groundwater flow velocities are involved, since directional measurements with the collimated counter are difficult, if not impossible, under such conditions (Tazioli, 1976; Cotecchia, 1977).

(*) The measurement of the aquifer effective thickness (aquifer thickness times dynamic porosity) can be determined through tracer transfer from a bore-hole to a pumping well (Custodio and Llamas, 1976, chapter 12.3; Custodio, 1977; Zuber, 1974). Figures 7.29 and 7.30 show two examples.

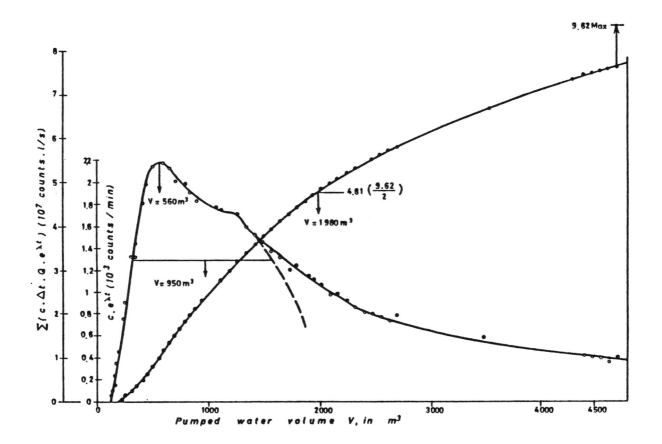

Fig. 7.29 - Measurement of effective porosity (m) injecting a tracer (I-131) near a pumping well. The shown experience corresponds to the highly permeable coastal alluvial fan in Western Vandellós Nuclear Site (Tarragona, Spain). The well can be considered a fully penetrating one, since it attains a locally continuous clayish layer. Pumpage rate reached 260 l/s, but the discharge was changed during the test and the pump stopped two times. Recovered water volume is used instead of pumping time. The injection bore-hole is 11 m far. The form of the breakthrough curve indicates a heterogeneous formation with preferential paths. The most probable value of b · m (aquifer thickness times effective porosity) is 4.4 m and effective porosity can be taken as 0.13. Intrinsic dispersivity is 2.9 m (Custodio, 1978b).

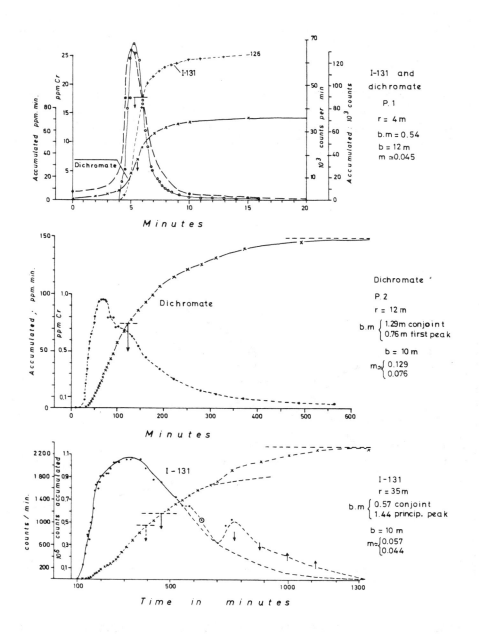

Fig. 7.30 – Measurement of effective porosity (m) injecting a tracer near a pumping well. The shown experiences correspond to an experimental treated-sewage water recharge well near the coast, in the sea water intruded Besós confined aquifer near Barcelona, Spain (Custodio, Suárez and Galofre, 1976). The well is fully penetrating and abstraction is 80 l/s. The experience has been performed in three piezometers, 4, 12 and 35 m far, using I-131 and sodium dichromate as tracers. The b · m (aquifer thickness times the effective porosity) value is calculated. The flow is not exactly radial around the well and then the calculated values must be corrected. The porosity values are smaller than expected for a coarse gravel aquifer. Probably not all the aquifer thickness is permeable.

-304-

7.11   <u>Identification and monitoring of zone of dispersion</u>

Salinity and temperature logging performed periodically in a network of observation wells provide a suitable way of identifying the zone of dispersion and of keeping check on the way it changes with time.

Studies carried out so far on seawater intrusion using these methods have led to the recognition of certain laws which govern temporal changes in the zone of dispersion (Cotecchia et al., 1974; Cotecchia, 1977).

In the first place there is a relationship between the thickness of the zone of dispersion and the distance from the sea. The thickness of the zone, in itself, depends largely on the permeability of the aquifer. The thinnest zones occur in rocks that are not very permeable and which anyway have few fractures, especially vertical ones. Observation wells drilled in fractured limestones near the coast have encountered dispersion zones no more than a few meters thick at most, while the same kind of wells in fractured limestones inland have revealed that the transition from fresh groundwaters to the underlying seawaters occurs gradually the result being that the zone of dispersion is several dozen meters thick. Here, again, the thickness depends on rock permeability and on the orientation of tectonic discontinuities.

It is apparent that measurement of the fluctuations in the static level in observation wells does not constitute a suitable way of estimating the amount of recharge or of outflows which occur from the aquifer. This is because the changes in groundwater levels caused by the direct and indirect effect of variations in atmospheric pressure and by periodic and aperiodic fluctuations in sea level mask those actually caused by recharge and outflow (fig. 7.31); Magri and Troisi (1969) and Cotecchia (1977) provide more details in this regard. Recharge and outflow, in fact, are reflected not so much in changes in the level of the water table (or piezometric surface) but rather by fluctuations of the interface. In other words, the magnitude of recharge and outflows is given by the variation in the thickness of the groundwaters measured from the level of the water table (or piezometric surface) to the top of the zone of dispersion.

Figure 7.32 illustrates the trend of the top of the zone of dispersion in some observation wells located on the Salento Peninsula, for the September 1968-October 1970 period. It is apparent from comparison of the diagrams for the various observation wells that there is also a relationship between the amplitude of the oscillations in the zone of dispersion and the distance from the coast: the further the distance inland the greater the oscillations.

Recharge and extraction are obviously major factors having a bearing on movement of the zone of dispersion. On the Salento Peninsula it has been possible to relate alternating wet and dry periods with oscillations of the interface. Sometimes there is a lag of as much as three months between the inflow of rainfall of some magnitude and the lowering of the top of the zone of dispersion. Similar findings have been reported from other parts of the world (see chapters 3 and 4).

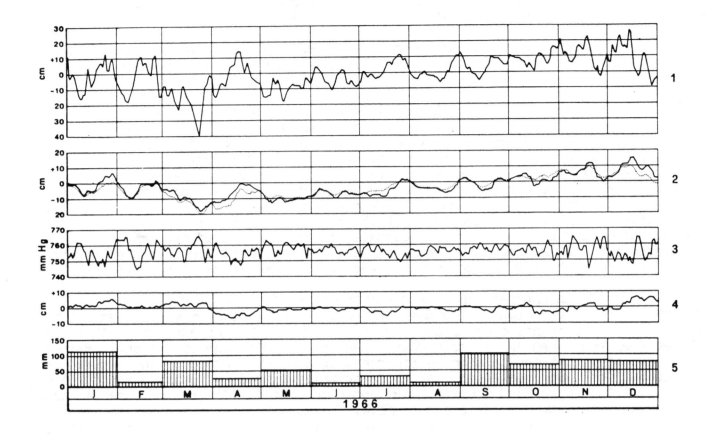

Fig. 7.31 – Relation between aperiodic fluctuations of sea (diagram 1), atmospheric pressure (diagram 3), mean monthly rainfall (diagram 5) and changes in ground water level (unbroken line in diagram 2) at a well. The dotted line in diagram 2 shows the calculated curve that most closely approximates to the changes in ground water levels in the well; attenuation = 1.4 days$^{1/2}$. Comparison of the two curves in diagram 2 clearly illustrates the influence of sea level fluctuations on ground water levels. The differences between the two curves in diagram 2 are shown in diagram 4 which thus represents the changes in ground water level that are 'not influenced' by sea level fluctuations. It is apparent from comparison of diagrams 3 and 4 that atmospheric pressure has virtually no direct influence on water table levels, while comparison of diagrams 4 and 5 similarly indicates that inflows from autumn-winter rainfall, outflows to the sea and abstraction during the summer have no appreciable influence. The relationship between atmospheric pressure and non-periodic fluctuations of the sea emerges clearly from a comparison of diagrams 1 and 3 (Cotecchia, 1974).

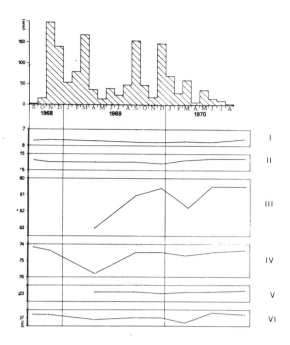

Fig. 7.32 – Fluctuation of the top of the dispersion zone measured in six wells of Apulia, starting from September 1968. Depths (m) measured below water table or piezometric surface. Total monthly rainfall (mm) shown in histogram form (Tadolini and Tulipano, 1970).

The most recent investigations made in Apulia pointed out that the intense water drafts from the aquifers of the region have resulted in a tendency of the seawater to rise. This rising tendency, which can be visualized through the rise of the 40 g/l isohaline, leads to an increase in the average salt content of the groundwaters; this fact is clear from the diagrams in figure 7.33, which shows the behavior of the transition zone with time in some observation wells since 1974.

The theoretical depths at which seawater is encountered in each well is also reported. This depth is calculated by applying the Ghyben-Herzberg relation, except that here the real densities of all the water in the aquifer are considered, namely, the overlying fresh water, that of the transition zone and the underlying sea water. It will be noted that, as a general rule, the two depths -- the theoretical and the experimental depths -- are very different from one another (Tadolini and Tulipano, 1979).

By means of the salinity and temperature distribution in a bore-hole it is possible to derive the density log and from it, with pure static equilibrium conditions of the groundwaters on the sea waters, establish the theoretical head, h_t, of the groundwaters at sea level. The difference $\Delta h = h_t - h_r$, between the theoretical and the actual head, provides a clear guide as to the extent of the nonequilibrium of the groundwaters.

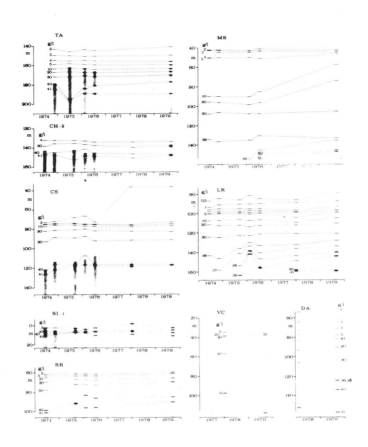

Fig. 7.33 – Variations in the time of the trend of salinity stratification inside the transition zone. The grey bands represent the theoretical elevation of the saltwater (Tadolini and Tulipano, 1979).

In the Salento Peninsula all the h_t values calculated in this way are higher than the real head values h_r measured in each observation well considered. The lowest differences occur near the coast, while the greatest ones are found in the innermost parts of the peninsula. The higher the difference the thicker will be the zone of dispersion, since the recharge and type of water movement also influence dispersion (Tadolini and Tulipano, 1977).

7.12   (*) Remote sensing

The specific application of remote sensing to coastal aquifers is the rapid survey of coastal springs, using a thermal-infrared scanning device installed in an airplane. Great advances have been made recently in the accuracy (commonly 0.2°C, but can be less than 0.1°C) in the magnetic recording methods and in the interpretation of results.

For the survey of coastal springs use is made of multispectral radiometers capable of acquiring and storing information coming from the earth's surface as radiation with wavelength in the spectral window between 3 and 5 µm, and 8 and 14 µm. The system is based essentially on the distribution of the surface temperature of the area surveyed. In the specific case of seaward outflows of groundwaters, this method reveals the thermal anomalies produced in the sea by freshwaters which, as will be appreciated, are usually at a different temperature from those of the sea.

The flight must be carried out when the sun does not influence the measurements, and the earth is cooled by the night. Then, better flight time is during 2 to 3 hours at dawn, although the use of the longest wavelength window avoids the sun's influence. A cloud- and fog-free day must be selected, with a low tide, calm sea, and when the temperature difference between spring and sea water is maximal. It thus follows that only a few days a year are available for an optimum survey. The fly-path of the airplane must be carefully traced and measurements of the soil and sea temperature must be carried out, directly or through a calibrated radiometer.

The technique has been applied in many different areas, with variable results (Guglielminetti et al., 1975; Brerenton and Dowwing, 1975; Davies, 1973; Custodio, 1978a, pp 233-234; Paredes, 1974).

The results, though interesting and useful, are not completely satisfactory since:

- shore-springs are easily detected but are already known and easily identifiable by other means;

- submarine springs are not detected but for those having a significant discharge, greater the deeper the outlet. According to Davis, a 130 l/s spring is poorly recognized when discharge is at 1 m depth, when the sea has moderate waves;

- sea bottom irregularities, submarine rocks, changes in the color of bottom sediments (different heat absorption), continental discharges, sea upwellings, vortices, etc., produce thermal anomalies that can be easily mistaken as groundwater discharges.

After the survey, a careful study of the anomalies must be carried out in order to eliminate interfering effects, and this needs a good knowledge of the coast, and experience.

Figure 7.34 shows a flow-chart for performing a thermal-infrared survey.

Recently, airborne electromagnetic resistivity-depth mapping has been considered, using a helicopter that trails the emitter-receiver device on a long cable. It is a 0.5 m diameter, 10 m long cylinder, generating an electromagnetic field close to 900 hz. The flight is at a few tens of meters over ground level (Sengpiel and Meiser, 1979). The method is still in its earliest stages, though it seems promising for flat low lying areas, with the interface only a few meters deep, as is the case of sand islands and bars.

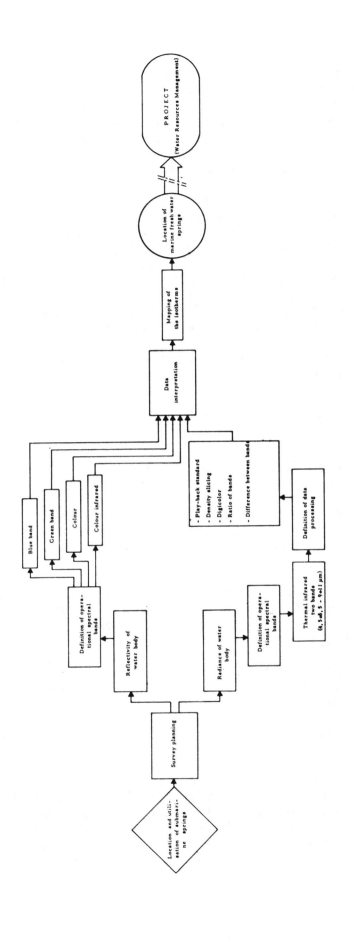

Fig. 7.34 – Flow chart of operating sequences in a general project whose goal is the location of submarine fresh water springs (Guglielminetti et al., 1975).

7.13   References

Arora, C.L., Bose, R.N. (1981). <u>Demarcation of fresh- and saline-water zones using electrical methods (Abohar area, Ferozepur District, Punjab)</u>. Journal of Hydrology, 49 (1981), pp. 75-86. Elsevier.

Astier, J.L. (1971). <u>Géophysique appliquée a l'hydrogéologie</u> (Geophysics applied to hydrogeology). Ed. Masson, Paris. Also: Paraninfo, Madrid.

Baonza, E., Plata, A., Piles, E. (1970). <u>Aplicación de la técnica del pozo único mediante el marcado de toda la columna piezométrica</u> (Application of the single well technique by tracing the whole piezometric column). Isotope Hydrology, 1970. Vienna Symposium Int. Atomic Energy Agency. Vienna. pp. 690-711.

Baonza, E., Plata, A., Escolano, A. (1970). <u>Empleo de isótopos radioactivos para la medida de la velocidad de filtración de aguas subterráneas por el método de pozo único</u> (Use of radioactive isotopes for the groundwater filtration velocity measurement, by the single well method). Documentos de Investigación Hidrológica, No. 8. Centro de Estudios Investigación y Aplicaciones del Agua. Barcelona, pp. 41-61.

Boekelman, R.H. (1979). <u>Geo-electrical survey in the polder 'Groot Mijdrecht.'</u> VI Salt Water Intrusion Meeting. Hannover 1979. Geologisches Jahrbuch. 1981. Hannover, pp. 241-253.

Bogoslovskiy, V.A., Ogil'vi, A.A. (1973). <u>Potential of geophysical methods for studying fresh-water discharges in the coastal zones of seas.</u> Soviet Hydrology: Selected Papers. Vol. 1, pp. 51-56.

Borowczyk, M., Grabczak, J., Zuber, A. (1965). <u>Radioisotope measurements of grondwater flow direction by the single-well method.</u> Nukleonika, Vol. 10, pp. 19-28.

Brerenton, N.R., Dowwing, R.A. (1975). <u>Some applications of thermal infra-red linescan in water resources studies.</u> Water Services, March 1975, 6 pp. London.

de Breuck, N. (1975). <u>The evolution of the coastal aquifer of Belgium.</u> Proc. IV Salt Water Intrusion Meeting. Ghent, 1974. IHD. pp. 158-172.

Carlin, F., Tadolini, T. (1969). <u>Soluzione tecnica adottata per la sistemazione di un pozzo perforato per studi idrogeologici.</u> Geologia Applicata e Idrogeologia, Vol. IV, pp. 65-92. Bari.

CDWR (1966). <u>Santa Ana Gap salinity barrier, Orange County.</u> Bull. 147-1. California Department of Water Resources. 178 pp.

Cnudde, J.P. (1977). <u>Interpretation of resistivity soundings in areas with saline groundwater.</u> Proceedings Fifth Salt Water Intrusion Meeting, Medmenham. IHP. pp. 158-164.

Coma, J.R. (1972). <u>Mapa hidrogeológico nacional</u> (National hydrologic map). Mem. Inst. Geol. y Min. de España. Vol. 81. Madrid.

Cotecchia, V. (1974). <u>The huge aquifer and the marine intrusion into the fissured and karst mesozoic limestones of Apulia (Southern Italy): recent studies and investigations by employing modern methodologies.</u> Colloque géologie de l'ingénieur, pp. 291-312, Liege.

Cottechia, V. (1977). <u>Studies and investigations on Apulian groundwaters and intruding seawaters (Salento Peninsula).</u> Quaderni dell'IRSA 20, 466 pp. Rome.

Cotecchia, V., Pirastru, E. (1970). <u>An epithermal neutron probe for measuring the water content of soils.</u> Geologia Applicata e Idrogeologia, Vol. V, pp. 135-157. Bari.

Cotecchia, V., Tadolini, T., Tulipano, L. (1974). <u>The results of researches carried out on diffusion zone between fresh water and sea water intruding the land ass of Salentine Peninsula (Southern Italy).</u> Proceedings International Symposium on Hydrology of Volcanic Rocks, Lanzarote, Canary Islands, Spain.

Custodio, E. (1977). <u>Utilización de radioisótopos en Cataluña para solucionar problemas de ingeniería hidráulica subterránea</u> (Radioisotope use in Catalonia to solve ground hydraulic problems). Jornada Técnica sobre la Industria Nuclear en Cataluña. Feria Internacional de Barcelona, Sector Tecno-Transfer, and Sociedad Nuclear Española. pp. 158-207.

Custodio, E. (1978a). <u>Geohidrología de terrenos e islas volcánicas</u> (Geohydrology of islands and volcanic terreins). Instituto de Hidrología. Centro de Estudios Hidrográficos. Madrid. 303 pp.

Custodio, E. (1978b). <u>Ensayos para determinar la viabilidad de una excavación profunda en el litoral del macizo de Vandellós (Tarragona, España)</u> (Tests to determine the feasibility of a deep excavation in the Vandellós massif littoral (Tarragona, Spain)). Int. Symposium on Water in Mining and Underground Works. Granada, Spain. Vol. I, pp. 85-109.

Custodio, E., Suárez, M., Galofré, A. (1976). <u>Ensayos para el análisis de la recarga de aguas residuales tratadas en el delta del Besós</u> (Tests to study the feasibility of recharge with treated sewage water in the Besós delta). II Asamblea Nacional de Geodesia y Geofísica. Sección de Ciencias Hidrológicas. Barcelona, Instituto Geográfico y Catastral. Madrid. pp. 1893-1936.

Custodio, E., Llamas, M.R. (1976). <u>Hidrología Subterránea.</u> Ed Omega. Barcelona. 2 Vols. 2375 pp.

van Dam, J.C. (1976a). <u>Partial depletion of saline groundwater by seepage.</u> Journal of Hydrology, Vol. 29, No. 3/4, pp. 315-339. Elsevier.

van Dam, J.C. (1976b). <u>Possibilities and limitations of the resistivity method of geoelectrical prospecting in the solution of geohydrological problems.</u> Geoexploration, 14 (1976). pp. 179-183. Elsevier.

van Dam, J.C., Meulenkamp, J.J. (1967). <u>Some results of the geo-electrical resistivity method in ground water investigations in the Netherlands.</u> Geophysical Prospecting, Vol. XIII, No. 1, pp. 37-65.

Davies, M.C. (1973). <u>A thermal infra-red lineascan survey along the Sussex coast.</u> Water and Water Engineering, Vol. 77, pp. 382-386.

Debuisson, J., Mousu, H. (1967). <u>Une étude experimentale de l'intrusion des euax marines dans une nappe cotiere du Sénégal sous l'effect de l'exploitation</u> (An experimental study of the marine water intrusion in a coastal aquifer of the Senegal under exploitation effect). Artificial Recharge and Management of Aquifers. Haifa Symposium. Int. Assoc. Scientific Hydrology. Pub. 72, pp. 15-44.

Drost, W., Flotz, D., Koch, A., Moser, H., Neumaier, F., Rauert, W. (1968). <u>Point dilution methods of investigating ground water flow by means of radioisotopes.</u> Water Resources Research, Vol. 4, No. 1, pp. 125-146.

Everett, L.G. (1980). <u>Groundwater monitoring.</u> General Electric Co. Schenectady, N.Y. 440 pp.

Fleet, M., Brerenton, N.R., Howard, N.S. (1978). <u>The investigation of saline intrusion into a fissured chalk aquifer.</u> Fifth Salt Water Intrusion Meeting, Medmenham, IHO, England. 1977. pp. 137-157.

Fourmarier, P. (1958). <u>Hydrogéologie.</u> Paris. Masson, 294 pp.

Ginzburg, A., Levanon, A. (1976). <u>Determination of a salt-water interface by electric resistivity depth soundings.</u> Hydrological Sciences Bulletin, XXI, 4, 12/1976, pp. 561-568.

Gorhan, H.L. (1976). <u>The determination of the saline-fresh water interface by resistivity soundings.</u> Bull. Assoc. Engineering Geologists, Vol. XIII, No. 3, pp. 163-176.

Grassi, D. (1974). <u>Il carsismo della Murgia (Puglia) e sua influenza sull'idrogeologia della regione.</u> Geologia Applicata e Idrogeologia, Vol. IX, pp. 119-160. Bari.

Guglielminetti, M., Boltri, R., Marino, C.M. (1975). <u>Remote sensing techniques applied to the study of fresh water springs in coastal areas of Southern Italy.</u> Proceedings Tenth International Symposium on Remote Sensing of Environment, pp. 1297-1309. Ann Arbor, Michigan.

Halevy, E., et al. (1966). <u>Borehole dilution techniques: a critical review.</u> Isotopes in Hydrology, Vienna Symposium. Int. Atomic Energy Agency. Vienna. pp. 531-564.

Keys, W.S. (1966). The application of radiation logs to groundwater hydrology. Isotopes in Hydrology. Int. Atmoic Energy Agency. Vienna Symposium. (Pub. 1967). Vienna. pp. 477-486.

Keys, W.S., MacCary, L.M. (1971). Application of borehole geophysics to water-resources investigations. Techniques of Water-Resources Investigations of the United States Geological Survey. Book 2, Collection of Environmental Data, Chapter E 1, 126 pp. Washington.

Kohout, F.A., Hoy, N.D. (1963). Some aspects of sampling salty groundwater in coastal aquifers. Ground Water, Vol. 1, No. 1.

Leander, B. (1977). Study of anticipated saline intrusion into a limestone aquifer in southern Sweden. Proceedings Fifth Salt Water Intrusion Meeting, pp. 108-113. Medmenham, UK.

Leenen, J.D. (1980). Results of a geo-electrical survey to the depth of the fresh water-salt water interface in the polder Groot Mijdrecht. Research on Possible Changes in the Distribution of Saline Seepage in the Netherlands. Committee for Hydrological Research, TNO. Proc. and Information No. 26, pp. 124-139.

Lloyd, J.W., Rushton, K.R., Taylor, H.R., Barker, R.D., Howard, K.W.F. (1977). Saline groundwater studies in the chalk of northern Lincolnshire. Proceedings Fifth Salt Water Intrusion Meeting, pp. 89-97. Medmenham, UK.

Lusczynski, N.S., Swarzenski, W.V. (1966). Saltwater encroachment in Southern Nassau and Southeastern Queens Counties, Long Island, New York. U.S. Geological Survey Water-Supply Paper 1613-F. Washington. 76 pp.

Magri, G., Pirastru, E. (1968). La misura diretta del contenuto di cloro nelle acque sotterranee mediante determinazione della cattura di neutroni termici. La Ricerca Scientifica, 49. pp. 195-206. Rome, CNR.

Magri, G., Troisi, S. (1969). Sull'influenza delle fluttuazioni di specchi d'acqua sui livelli delle falde costiere: applicazioni allo studio della circolazione idrica sotterranea nella Penisola Salentina. Geología Applicata e Idrogeologia. Vol. IV, pp. 25-42. Bari.

Mairhofer, J. (1963). Bestimmung der Stromungsrichtung des Groundwassers in einem einzigen Bohrloch mit hilfe radioaktiver Elemente. Atompraxis, Vol. 9, pp. 2-24.

Monkhouse, R.A., Fleet, M. (1975). A geophysical investigation of saline water in the chalk of the South coast of England. Quarterly Journal of Engineering Geology, London. Vol. 8, pp. 291-302.

Mosetti, F. (1961). Un'applicazione del sondaggio geoelettrico: evidenziazione della zona di contatto tra acqua dolce e acqua salata in formazioni calcaree. Boll. di Geofisica Teorica e Applicata, Vol. III, No. 12, pp. 307-313.

Mülern, C.F., Ericksson, L. (1981). <u>Testing VLF-resistivity measurements in order to locate saline groundwater.</u> VII Sea Water Intrusion Meeting. Uppsala, Sveriges Geologiska Undersökning. Rapporter och Meddelanden No. 27. Uppsala. pp. 91-100.

Orellana, E. (1972). <u>Prospección geoeléctrica en corriente continua</u> (Geoelectrical prospecting in direct current). Biblioteca Técnica Philips, Paraninfo. Madrid. 523 pp.

Paredes, J. (1974). <u>Desarrollo della termografía infrarroja aplicada a la hidrología</u> (Development of infrared thermography applied to hydrology). Inst. Symp. on Volcanic Terrein Hydrology, Arrecife de Lanzarote. Spain-Unesco.

Plata, A. (1972). <u>Isótopos en hidrología</u> (Isotopes in hydrology). Ed. Alhambra. Madrid. 328 pp.

Sahuquillo, A. (1981). <u>Métodos de estudio para la detección y control de la contaminación de aguas subterráneas: situación actual y aplicación futura</u> (Study methods for the detection and control of groundwater pollution: present situation and future application). Jornadas sobre Análisis y Evolución de la Contaminación de Aguas Subterráneas en España. Curso Internacional de Hidrología Subterránea. Barcelona (1982). General Report 5.

Sengpiel, K.P., Meiser, P. (1979). <u>Locating the freshwater-saltwater interface on the island of Spiekroog by airborne EM resistivity-depth mapping.</u> VI Sea Water Intrusion Meeting. Hannover, 1979. Geologisches Jahrbuch, Hannover, 1981. pp. 255-271.

Tadolini, T., Tulipano, L. (1970). <u>Primi resultati delle ricerche sulla zona di diffusione della 'falda profonda' della Penisola Salentina (Puglia).</u> Atti I Convengno Internazionale Sulle Acque Sotterranee, Palermo.

Tadolini, T., Tulipano, L. (1977). <u>The conditions of the dynamic equilibrium of ground water as related to encroaching sea water.</u> Proceeding Symposium on Hydrodynamic Diffusion and Dispersion in Porous Media. pp. 173-185. Pavia, IAHR.

Tadolini, T., Tulipano, L. (1979). <u>The evolution of fresh water-salt water equilibrium in connection with drafts from the coastal carbonate and karstic aquifer of the Salentine Peninsula (Southern Italy).</u> Sixth Salt Water Intrusion Meeting, Hannover. Geologisches Jahrbuch, 1981, Hannover.

Tazioli, G.S. (1973). <u>Metodologie e techniche radioisotopiche in idrogeologia.</u> Geologia Applicata e Idrogeologia. Vol. VIII, Part II, pp. 209-230. Bari.

Tazioli, G.S. (1976). <u>Metodologie e techniche radioisotopiche in idrogeologia.</u> Atti Seminario su Falde Soterranee e Trattamento della Acque, pp. 42-61. Bari. Ente Irrigazione.

Williams, J.R. (1970). <u>Ground water in the permafrost regions of Alaska.</u>
    United States Geological Survey, Prof. Paper 696.

Zuber, A. (1974). <u>Theoretical possibilities of the two-well pulse method.</u>
    Isotope Technique in Groundwater Hydrology. Vienna Symposium, 1974.
    Int. Atomic Energy Agency. Vol. II, pp. 277-294.

8. Prediction methods

E. Custodio

Contents

8.0   Introduction

Forecasting the future evolution of a coastal aquifer when man influences the groundwater flow is a difficult task, since most of the existing experience deals with the study of present situations and the adjustment of methods to explain it from observations made at best during a short time relative to the slow modifications taking place. The complication of the fresh-salt water mixture and the increased influence of nonhomogeneities in the mixing zone work against the availability of enough well documented case studies to allow for the testing of forecasting methods, both the simpler and the most sophisticated ones.

Furthermore, a great part of the available studies deal with natural or slightly perturbed situations, and they do not allow for a sound calibration of the methods in order to be confident of their ability to predict with an acceptable degree of accuracy.

It is necessary to stress here the need of more and well planned pilot studies in order to get the necessary information, with special emphasis on already deeply altered systems in which the evolution due to man's activities can be followed up.

There are three levels of prediction:

- based on case studies, when the similitude can be reasonably established. This is one of the goals of presenting case histories in chapter 10;

- based on calculation methods, especially the most simple ones;

- based on more or less sophisticated analogical or numerical models.

These prediction methods rest on the concepts and explanations presented in the preceding chapters.

8.1   Forecasting based on case studies

8.1.1   General considerations

Groundwater flow and fresh-salt groundwater relationships depend on many factors, with a great incidence of local situations. It can be said that no fully similar situations can be found. Fortunately, a good understanding of a particular situation can point out the dominant factors on which one may establish the desired similitudes.

It is dangerous to make forecasts of the behavior of a coastal aquifer by a simple extrapolation of an apparently similar case, except if a carefully established similitude exists, taking into account lithology, spacial distribution of permeability and porosity, groundwater flow pattern and variability, coastal and sea bottom conditions, sea water oscillations, recharge, and hydrological history of the zone. Then, a good knowledge of the system in consideration is the first goal to be accomplished.

Small differences in aquifer characteristics, sometimes difficult to know or evaluate, such as anisotropy, existence of clay lenses, small discontinuities, etc., produce significant changes in the salt-fresh water relationships, especially during non-steady situations, which are not only the most interesting, but those which ask for a better forecasting.

To these natural difficulties, differences in exploitation works, abstraction patterns, total withdrawal, etc., add new complications for an easy and reasonable forecasting based on case studies.

However, some actual cases will be shortly described in order to point out some typical situations. Unfortunately there is not a broad spectrum nor a worldwide coverage of examples. Some areas will be in detail. It does not mean that other areas are less known or less important or are devoid of well studied cases. It is only a question of personal knowledge of some areas, or more accessible data at the moment of writing.

The same classification used in section 3.3 will be used here. In many aspects there are no essential differences between the different groups, but it is the easiest method of organizing the presentation. Since in some cases the references consist mainly of internal reports, no reference will be made to them. In chapter 10 more references will be given at the end of the different case histories.

The reader will find some duplication when comparing this section with other chapters, mainly 3, 4 and 6, but it is unavoidable in order to present a full picture. In those chapters can be found the relevant bibliographical references.

A sufficient geological and hydrogeological knowledge is assumed. When establishing the similitude, the hydroclimatic conditions and the recharge must be considered in every case.

8.1.2 Deltas and coastal alluvial formations

The following aspects must be considered:

- The existence of a two or more layered system, of a fine sand, silt, loam or clay intermediate lens, of a variable sedimentation according to the formation stages, and of the possible presence of a more pervious deep layer, in some areas, corresponding to the old terraces and alluvial cones, that can be in a more easy relationship with the sea bottom than do other deep permeable formations;

- the continuity of the semipervious covers and intermediate lenses, especially in the coast and seaward. They may thin out;

- the presence of natural, recent or old salt or brackish water, in reduced or extensive water bodies;

- the hydraulic possibility of fresh water circulation in deep permeable formations, according to existing land and groundwater table slopes;

- the land use, and water return flows, especially in irrigated areas that existed, are under exploitation or are being planned;

- the possible losses of canals and ditches and the salt-fresh water relationships in open channels;

- the existing groundwater abstraction pattern and the effects on the water balance and on groundwater heads. The distance of wells to the coast, their depth and construction method are important considerations to be accounted for.

Residual, recent or old, salt and brackish water is very often encountered, sometimes forming extensive water bodies, or occupying areas of variable size. This salty or brackish water can move toward the water abstraction works and to the drainage systems established to reclaim these generally low lying areas, especially when salt water underlies the area.

A lot of experience exists in the Netherlands, which is formed mainly by the combined Rhine and Meuse river deltas, both from the point of view of low land reclamation (polderization) and fresh groundwater exploitation in the dune belts. Advantage is taken, as much as possible, of the existence of interbedded clay layers and lenses that impede or retard the upward flow of deep saline water and limit the salt contamination of the fresh water when the water works are correctly calculated and set. The conservation of the low permeability layers is important, and when destroyed, they must be reconstructed using suitable low permeability materials or impervious sheets. The destruction of the upper semipermeable materials in building foundations or to exploit sands, impairs the salinization problems.

The sand dunes and ridges favor the creation of fresh water bodies, but the exploitation must be done carefully when there is saline water below or in the surroundings. The saline water upconing below wells may be noticeable after a few days of pumping if the drawdown or penetration is excessive.

The lateral movement of the saline water to carefully constructed and operated wells, ditches or drains is slow and follows the shrink of the fresh water body. The salinization occurs if a new safe equilibrium situation is not reached. Only a part of the local recharge can be exploited permanently, but, in some cases, water mining can solve temporal problems. When the interface movement is great, about some ten meters per year, dispersion is important and salinization occurs faster than expected, but the water salinity increases slowly.

In some deltas, fresh ground water is seldom used, especially when a network of irrigation canals exist, although fresh groundwater can be an important source of potable water. In some of these areas, in the early days of land occupation, irrigation was initiated by means of shallow wells constructed randomly in the search for fresh water accumulations. Fresh water is encountered in or near shallow wells. In these areas, along the irrigation canals and below the rice fields existing in many areas, fresh groundwater bodies have been growing, contributing to some flushing of the salt water, but the drainage systems often impede the development of large fresh water bodies.

Along the main river channels the situation depends on the river water salinity variations. Frequently these areas are intermittently flooded and a fresh water body forms, but in some instances, when the soil permeability is low, lagoons and swamps form, and when evaporation is intense, saline water bodies can be formed, which contribute to the groundwater contamination.

In estuaries, where mixing is important, the surface brackish water can penetrate the ground through some intermediate more exploited layers, thus creating a wedge that splits the fresh ground water body into an upper layer and a lower layer, as reported in some areas along the River Thames in the U.K., in the River Garonne, in western France, or in India.

In many circumstances the delta covers the old river valley or a river estuary that existed during the last glacial age, when the sea level was about 80 to 90 m lower than today. Depending on the sediment source areas, basin characteristics and river slope near the coast, fine sand, sand and gravels were deposited, filling the channel and valley bottom, and afterwards covered by finer materials deposited while the sea level went up, flooding the coastal areas. Thus, confined or semiconfined aquifers were formed, which are sometimes very important sources of fresh water, recharged by water infiltrating through the river bed upstream.

The presence of fresh, brackish or salt water in these confined or semiconfined aquifers depends on the land altitude. When the water is initially fresh and the well discharge can be high due to the good transmissivity conditions, a fast development generally occurs in such areas (intensive irrigation, settlement of high water demand industries, pumping centers to supply areas outside the basin, etc.), and the piezometric water levels easily fall below sea level in spite of the induced river recharge, especially when the wells are close to the coast. Then, a slow process of sea water intrusion starts in some areas. The inlet can be the main buried channel, directly of through the overlying formations if they have enough vertical permeability, or by means of some ill-constructed or abandoned wells. In order to avoid these situations, a careful control on the abstraction rates is required, as well as proper location and construction of the wells.

In the small Besòs delta (10 km^2, just northeast of Barcelona, in Catalonia, Spain) a serious salinization developed after about 5 years of intense exploitation (100% of the river basin resources). In the Llobregat delta (80 km^2, southwest of Barcelona) salinization of the deep aquifer was noticed after 10 years of exploitation (20% of the river basin resources) and after 20 years only one third of the wells are affected (see case history 1 in chapter 10). In the small Tordera delta (10 km^2, Catalonia, Spain), after five years of mild exploitation (10% of the river basin resources) no sea water encroachment has been encountered and some boreholes along the coast continued to flow, but after 10 years the first salinization problems appeared and coastal boreholes ceased to flow. In all these cases, the location of the wells and the center of mass of the pumpage has a great influence in the sea water intrusion, and also the river infiltration and its preservation has a major influence. The closer the deep wells (to exploit the confined aquifer) to the coast the larger the risk of a fast sea water contamination.

In larger and flatter deltaic areas in many instances the deep aquifers contain salt water, but perhaps in some circumstances old entrapped fresh water can be found. This is not the case when the deep aquifers discharge large groundwater basins, as in the area near Venice and in the Po river delta, in Italy; there is fresh water in the deep aquifers.

Small rivers and creeks create small alluvial plains. Some interbedded clay and silt layers often split the formation into more than one layer, though the separations are sometimes of only local significance. There exists an easy connection with the sea.

Permeability of alluvium depend on many circumstances. Sometimes it is almost an aquitard, but in many instances highly transmissive strips form. Since wells are then highly productive, there is a tendency to overpump them, especially during the irrigation period, or during the summer in touristic resorts. In extreme cases sea water contamination can be produced in a short time, perhaps in a few months, but the aquifer recovers in some way during the following rainy period, in which groundwater abstraction is reduced.

When the clay lenses effectively delay the sea water intrusion, an intense overdraft in summer can be performed in the lower parts without excessive risk of sea water intrusion, with water levels well below sea level, if during the rest of the year water levels return for some months to high positions. Thus, the coastal aquifer can be used as a local storage reservoir. The protection of the clay lenses is essential and wells must be carefully constructed in order to impede vertical through-flow, and a distance of more than 1 km from the coast free of wells or drainages is recommended. Such an aquifer is operated in the Sant Feliu de Guixols-Platja d'Aro area, on the Costa Brava (Girona, Spain), and after 10 years no salinization problems have occurred, in spite of the very fast salinization of the other coastal aquifers of the region. After the construction of new wells closer to the coast, salinization problems appeared.

In such small coastal alluvial formations, the substratum frequently plays an important role. When it is pervious, it may be a preferential and fast path for salinization through upconing or lateral movement.

Very small highly pervious coastal alluvial formations often do not store fresh water and frequently brackish water dominates. Only upstream seasonal exploitation of fresh water can be carried out if a low permeability layer occurs about or over sea level. This is especially true in the lower part of the intermittent Mediterranean creeks, and in many high islands (the Canaries, Madeira, etc.).

8.1.3   Coastal plains

The following aspects must be considered:

- surface drainage, existence of internal marshy or lagoon areas, and evaporation-evapotranspiration rate;

- presence of dune belts that receive recharge and may impair land drainage. Also the existence of other permeable ridges must be considered, such as ice-pushed sands;

- nature of the shore line and presence of coastal islands, sand bars, and shallow sea water areas;

- presence of shallow bedrock and its permeability, and the existence of nonhomogeneities and clay layers;

- previous existence of salt or brackish water, according to the recent geological history and former land use and water exploitation pattern;

- distance to the shore, penetration, construction and exploitation of wells.

In many instances more than one aquifer or subaquifer can be found at a place, each one showing a different water head. Sea water contamination is encountered or proceeds differently in every one of the layers. Forecasting based on apparently analogous situations is very difficult, but in general the simultaneous tapping of various levels by the same well must be avoided as much as possible, and each one of the layers must be surveyed independently, as done in the Los Angeles coastal aquifers and other Californian areas, or the coastal plains of Israel (see case histories in section 10.3).

The great extent and the small water gradient in those aquifers make the lateral movement of the salt water a very slow process, but when salt water underlies the well area, salt water upconing can take place easily if low permeability lenses or layers are absent. The salt water upconing depends on many factors; apparently similar wells can yield water of very different salinity. The presence of nonhomogeneities plays an important role, and also the pumping schedule and the discharge.

The possible existence of deep saline water must be always taken into account. The geological history of the area must be studied and can explain many situations. When extensive horizontal low permeability layers exist, deep saline water is not a serious salinization danger.

In the small coastal plains the conditions are similar to that in the larger ones, but natural or induced sea water penetration can reach the whole width of the plain in different areas. Changes in aquifer transmissivity, aquifer thickness, characteristics of the sediments near the coast, groundwater recharge, etc., can produce important variations along the coast.

Sometimes the movement of the mixing zone due to the tides is noticeable and movements of some tens of meters can be measured from one year to another due only to variations in natural recharge, as studies in a small coastal plain in Digha, India (Goswami, 1968). In such small plains, changes in the coastal line has noticeable effects when they are flat, as in Digha, where a backward movement of the beach is reported to be about 50m in 2 years, or in the Llobregat area, near the river mouth, with about 100 m in 5 years.

Concentrated exploitations located on or near towns or irrigated areas frequently induce localized sea water encroachments, but if water abstracted is not too saline due to mixing, and the industry can use it, a continuous pumping of this water protects inland areas.

Sometimes the inland movement of the sea water may follow preferential paths, such as in the Palma Plain (Isle of Majorca, Spain) where the main paths are located in pervious young tertiary calcarenites bordering the plain, while the central part has some protection due to a lower permeability and a groundwater flow increased by the leakage from the town water supply network. In that case, deeper aquifers contain salty water or are more easily sea water intruded. Some reported salt water contamination problems in some supply wells far from the coast were corrected simply by cementing up the lower part of the wells that reached the deep aquifers.

In other areas, a thick sequence of sediments exists, including different clay lenses, continuous or discontinuous, that retard effectively the vertical groundwater movement. When these deep layers outcrop or are recharged in areas of enough high elevation, fresh water is encountered under flowing conditions, such as in the Olinda-Goiana area (fig. 8.1) just north of Recife, Brazil (400 m depth, 14 m water head), where a direct contact with

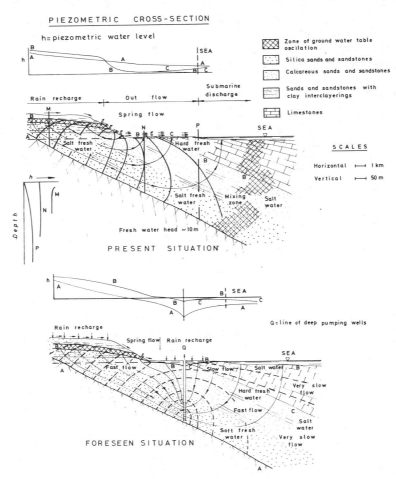

Fig. 8.1 – The upper figure shows the natural flow pattern in a cross-section perpendicular to the coast in the coastal aquifer of Olinda-Goiana, toward the north of Recife (Brazil). The vertical scale is greatly exaggerated in order to consider the pronounced permeability anisotropy of the medium due to clay interlayerings. The fresh water heads in deep wells near the coast in non exploited areas reach 14 m over mean sea level, enough to overcome 400 m of salt water column, according to the BGH formula (minimum head is 400/40 = 10 m). Discharge into the sea is through vertical flow, a very slow process. Ascending water changes from soft water to hard water due to the dissolution of carbonates in the upper sediments. The lower figure shows the situation expected when the exploitation by deep wells will start. Salinization is supposed a very slow process (after Custodio, 1975, in Custodio and Llamas, 1976, pp 2262-2263).

the sea is not probable or is too far. Then, deep wells are recommended, carefully cemented in order to avoid water vertical movement along the annulus between the borehole and the tube well, and also to prevent corrosion openings in upper saline layers or in reducing water environments. Lateral movement of deep salty water will be slow and the contamination produced is expected to be small. Reported cases of salt water contamination correspond mainly to defective well construction or wells placed where the elevation of the recharge area was not enough to create an extensive deep fresh water body (Custodio, et al., 1977).

The permeability and characteristics of the bedrock must be taken into account because, when permeable and open to the sea it can be a source of saline water through upconing or lateral movement.

Similar situations are frequent in small coastal plains in which the pervious formations are deep enough to contain bottom salt water. In many areas with aquifers in chalk, calcarenites, fissured limestones, coarse alluvial deposits, etc., such as the South of England, the aquifers of the southeast and southwest of the Island of Majorca, the south of the Tarragona Province, some areas in the volcanic formations of the Canaries, etc. Some of them will be mentioned below. The slow lateral movement of the fresh-salt water interface does not allow an easy forecasting based on observations. The dispersive effects may play an important role, as indicated in the Tarragona Plain case, where a 30 m/year salt water front advancement has been measured for a 0.7 to 0.9 reduction in groundwater flow toward the sea, and up to 60 m/year in the penetration of the mixing zone top (100 ppm Cl^-).

In the Mar del Plata plains (Argentina) a sea water intrusion of 100 to 300 m/year, depending on the area, has been reported. It represents the speed of the brackish water front reaching the well bottoms. The local groundwater table is below sea level (Pedriel, 1977).

In the coastal plain between the Dradere and Soueire wadis, in western Morocco, the exploitation of about 0.5 times the total recharge is expected to move the salt water wedge to a new equilibrium situation between 1 to 3 km inland (deduced from Bonnet and Sauty, 1975), the true position widely varying according to the rainfall.

When recharge depends on river infiltration, especially on the flood water infiltration in piedmont areas, the construction of dams may change the situation, generally impairing it, but not always. Generally it is difficult to separate the effect of the dam or of a river water diversion from the effect of dry years and the effect of an increase in the aquifer exploitation.

8.1.4   Hard rocks

The following aspects must be considered:

- orientation of fissures in the space, that is to say, not only the orientation on a map, but also their indication. Other necessary data are the penetration below sea level, the opening or filling degree and the way they are connected with the sea;

- fracture density;

- nature of the rock matrix, porous or compact;

- relationship between fissure water and pore water.

Non karstic hard rocks such as granites, volcanics, sandstones, etc., in most cases present a dominant fissure permeability, depending on local and regional tectonics and also on the tensions created when the rock is brought to the surface by erosive processes (unloading) and on the effect of weathering.

The generally small void coefficient or porosity associated with large fissures implies a fast movement of the water, and consequently a rapid salt water encroachment that favors the salinization of the abstracted water in a short time, especially when the well penetration is great and the water level drawdown is noticeable.

Generally, coastal fissured rocks must be avoided as much as possible when they are in direct contact with the sea, especially when fissures intersect the coast or they are deep seated. They also contribute to the easier salinization of the water exploited in unconsolidated formations lying on or bordered by these rocks, as in many situations in the Canary Islands (Spain), where volcanics dominate, or in the Mar del Plata plains (Argentina), where old fissured sandstones exist.

In volcanic formations the complicated vertical sequence of materials often divides the aquifer into local subaquifers, through which different movements of the salt water occur. A careful construction of the wells, avoiding some layers that contain saline water or are prone to be sea water contaminated, can aid in retarding or avoiding undesirable situations.

8.1.5   Special situations in karstic formations

The following aspects must be considered, in addition to those given for hard rocks in the preceding section:

- characteristics and depth of karstic conduits;

- relationships between the sea and the karstic conduits;

- nature, orientation, density and distribution of fractures and fissures intersecting the karstic conduits;

- in confined karst, the permeability characteristics of the cover.

In carbonate formations the situation is close to that described for the rocky non karstic coastal areas, but it is frequently magnified by the enlargement of fissures and development of underground channels by solution processes.

Water flow inside these karstic fissures and channels can be very fast from a groundwater point of view, and the exploitation must be very carefully done, if feasible at all, because sea water contamination can be produced in hours or in days in areas far from the coast. Tapping such a karstic channel is not always a good idea in a coastal area since it is an easy way for salt water encroachment, and sometimes small fissures are preferable in order to limit salinization problems.

In many situations the rock is almost impervious near the coast, except near the main karstic channels (Garraf massif, south of Barcelona, Catalonia, Spain), where avoiding sea water contamination is very difficult. A well that intersects a small karstic cavity 7 km from the sea gets salt contaminated water within a few hours, if the pump discharge is not carefully controlled. The production must be greatly reduced in summer time.

In other areas, where a penetrant salt water body exists, the floating fresh water can be best exploited by means of skimming galleries or drains, excavated or drilled from the ground surface or placed at the bottom of large diameter wells.

Confined fissured and karstified limestones, when the cavities are free from sediments and other clogging materials, generally present better and easier conditions for exploitation, since the overlying sediments impede a direct contact with the sea bottom. But the impermeable nature of the cover must be well established. In many instances it only delays the sea water penetration.

The soft porous chalk formations are a special case, well documented through studies in some coastal areas in the U.K., mainly on the South Downs (Monkhouse and Fleet, 1975; Fleet, Berenton and Howard, 1975; Nutbrown, 1977). The chalk can store large quantities of fresh water in the pores, but is has very small permeability, except when fissured. Fissures occur mainly in the upper part, up to a depth of a few tens of meters. The salt water moves much faster through the fissures than through the non fissured porous matrix. Thus, the coastal wells exploited during the summer become salt water contaminated through the fissures, but they recover when the pumpage stops. The abstraction of salt water in those wells aids to protect other wells placed inland, during the high water demand period. The temporal salt water advancement through fissures is not very dangerous if it lasts a short time. The most fractured zones must be avoided as much as possible in order to delay the salinization in the coastal wells and to protect permanently other inland wells. Since chalk permeability reduces downwards and the rock is almost impervious at 100 m depth, the risk of salt water upconing is greatly reduced.

8.1.6   Small pervious islands

A.   Rocky small oceanic islands

In addition to previous considerations, the following must be taken into account:

- in small flat islands, the relationships between water table, groundwater quality and vegetation;

- the generally great mixing zone thickness;

- the effect on the fresh water of the permeability variations and also of differences in effective sea and lagoon levels;

- the minimum exploitable fresh water lens thickness.

The situation on rocky small oceanic islands is similar to that in rocky coastal areas. In the very permeable areas, a fresh water body of variable thickness floats on salt water, and in many cases the mixing zone is rather thick, thus reducing the volume of usable fresh water, and posing serious problems of fresh water abstraction. Skimming wells or non penetrant galleries are needed, and the areas where the fresh water lens is thicker than 10 meters must be selected. The safe yield is only a small fraction of total recharge.

Frequently these small islands are of volcanic origin or are formed of coral reefs, frequently on the top of submarine volcanic cones.

In the volcanic Canary Islands, the exploitation is generally carried out through wells fitted with bottom galleries. The increasing demand of fresh water has started a slow but continuous process of sea water intrusion. In some areas, wells close to the coast, generally in the bottom of the steep creeks, have been abandoned and new wells have been excavated further inland, yielding much more expensive water. The process may be slow, and some years are needed for a given situation to worsen noticeably. In some areas a steady situation has been reached after stabilization of the abstraction. In other areas, the exploitation has ceased, but the recovery is very slow or at an almost imperceptible pace. An exploitation of 20 to 30 percent of local recharge can be sustained, though some wells must be relocated after some time.

On the more permeable Hierro Island (Canary Islands, Spain), the exploitation of more than half the total resources of El Golfo coastal areas has not produced severe adverse results, even a few years later. A salinity increase has been noticed in the farthest wells and the wells closer to the sea are now abandoned. These wells just reach the deep water table and are designed to avoid upconing problems. However, in the Azores Islands (Portugal) fresh water floats on salt water and this creates difficult problems for the exploitation of fresh water in the coast with normally drilled wells. Many of the salinity problems encountered on the Lanzarote and Fuerteventura Islands (Canary Islands, Spain) are due to climatic effects, but in areas with young lavas, sea water penetrates deeply, and no fresh water can be exploited.

In the Hawaiian Islands, skimming galleries excavated in the low permeability materials in the coastal plains yield permanently fresh water. Below these materials a thick pervious volcanic formation is exploited by means of deep wells. Some salt water intrusion has occurred slowly. In the area where deep salt groundwater exists, the mixing zone expands toward the partially penetrating wells, the lower boundary being almost steady (Todd and Meyer, 1971).

In the islands with recent (quaternary or upper tertiary) coral reefs, important permeability variations can be expected. The situation differs from pure or oceanic coral reefs, in which no other rocks exist except sand dunes, and rocky islands with old rocks partially or totally surrounded by a frange of coral reefs. Talus deposits, generally less pervious, and other frequently associated rocks such as calcarenites (biocalcarenites and eolianites) play an important role.

In oceanic coral reefs the total recharge and permeability variations control the extent and exploitability of the small, tinny fresh water lenses, and also the tidal effect on dispersion.

In the Bahamas, high permeability cavernous limestones are covered by low permeability limestones (Mather and Buckley, 1973). Groundwater exploitation is difficult but can be better accomplished where the less permeable beach deposits occur. The cavernous limestones contain salt or brackish water, and the mixing is high due to the increased tidal effect by the greater permeability. In the Caymans, a model study (Chidley and Lloyd, 1977) also show the important effect of total recharge and permeability distribution.

In the Tarawa atoll (Gilbert and Ellice Islands, Pacific Ocean), in spite of the high rainfall (1800 m/year), the small size of the islands surrounding the atoll central lagoon makes difficult the development of exploitable fresh groundwater lenses (Mather, 1977). Some fresh water can be found where on the coral limestone and boulders surface (at about sea level) there are dune and beach sands. Though some salinity increase is unavoidable when exploitation starts, skimming galleries can be permanently used where there is more than 6 m of fresh water. The galleries perform better than dug wells. The excavation of the sand for construction purposes reduces significantly the fresh water resources.

On Bermuda, in the Atlantic Ocean, the coral reef calcarenites that form the island show important lateral variations of permeability (Vacher, 1978). The island is divided along its length into two strips, one of which is about 14 times as permeable as the other. The less permeable one is the younger (karstification and dolomitization is less developed) and it faces the ocean side of the big atoll. The main fresh water lenses are contained in the less pervious formation where the mixing zone is also thinner.

The southern part of the Island of Menorca (Spain) is formed by a quaternary flange coral reef leaning to the old outcropping bedrock of the island. The old relief is covered by later tertiary calcarenites and marls which are covered by the coral reef talus deposits and on the top the pervious coral reef limestones. The risk of sea water intrusion depends on the position of this top coral reef limestone with respect to the mean sea level. It explains the different penetration of the sea water in different pumped areas of the island. Where toward the sea the most permeable formations of the reef are over sea level or completely eroded, the wells are reasonably protected against sea water encroachment. However, the characteristics of the old limestones in the bedrock must be considered because they also contain pervious limestones of Jurassic age, in direct connection with the sea.

Similar conditions exist in the other Balearic Islands, and also on Malta and Cyprus. On Cyprus, in the Morphou area, the heavy exploitation has produced a continuous water table drawdown of 0.3 to 0.4 m/year, reaching 4 m below sea level at about 4 km from the coast (Dijon, 1978, 1982). A first calculation indicates that total groundwater abstraction doubles the recharge, and the salt water encroaches at a rate of 30 m/year. On Malta the water table barely attains 1 m of elevation over mean sea level at the center of the 246 km^2 island, where a fresh water lens of a maximum thickness of 15 m exists. Fresh groundwater is only exploited where there is more than 7 m of fresh water thickness. The exploitation by means of skimming galleries excavated at the bottom of deep shafts allow for the permanent extraction of reasonably fresh water and permits the control of the salinity by modification of the water level inside the galleries. They have been operated with success since the beginning of this century, after some perched aquifers were drained or yielded insufficient water. The use of drilled wells does not allow a careful exploitation. After some months or a few years, the water becomes brackish and badly alters the shape of the fresh water lens. In such a case, the wells are not a good solution for a durable groundwater exploitation.

On small islands a fresh water lens does not develop or is too tinny and unstable to be used at all.

As a general rule, wells must be as far from the coast as possible.

B. **Small islands formed by unconsolidated materials**

Small islands formed by unconsolidated materials are frequent in low lying coastal areas and near the mouths of the rivers, sometimes among the different branches of the river in a delta. Generally they are sandy formations. The situations encountered are similar to many of those already described, and in some areas fresh water is scarce and difficult to get if salt water contamination is to be avoided. Salt water upconing takes place within hours or a few days when no protective clay lenses are present. Skimming wells and drainage trenches are recommended. The groundwater abstraction reduces the size of the fresh water lens that shrinks slowly. Only a small part of total recharge can be put into beneficial use.

Studies conducted in the Saloum Islands, in a deltaic area near the mouth of the Gambia River, show that in the islands having less than 2 m altitude over mean sea level, no exploitable fresh water can be found, and at least 2 to 3 m of elevation is needed to get a fresh water lens of 8 to 10 m thickness. The situation is worse in elongated or indented islands. Wells must be placed far from the coast, frequently where there is more sand. Here the fresh water lens thickness is not limited by the available recharge, but by the ground elevation, island size, dispersive effects, and drainage of the soil zone.

When such small islands are placed in a brackish or salty water area, the saline water can penetrate through preferential layers, especially those more pumped, then isolating a bottom fresh water body from an upper fresh water body.

In bigger islands, the situation is closer to that existing in continental coasts. A good example of such an island is Long Island (New York), formed mainly by glacial and fluvio-glacial deposits. Heavy pumpage in densely populated areas has caused sea water intrusion problems, but in other areas the groundwater exploitation proceeds satisfactorily, though the fresh water body shrinks according to the reduced fresh groundwater flow available at the coast. The high water table in some areas of the island frees them from bottom salt water and the wells can penetrate deeply into the ground (Cohen, Franke and Foxworthy, 1969).

8.1.7   Notes on similitude

In the way that a correspondence is established between a prototype and a physical model (see section 5.3) it is possible to establish similitude ratios for two real situations that follow the same differential equation with the same kind of boundary conditions.

No attempt to establish such easily derivable ratios is known because there is any control on the natural characteristics, and a real similitude is only a rare chance. It is better to rely on calculation formulae, that allow for more freedom in the comparison when they respond reasonably to reality and the governing parameters are well determined.

8.2   Prediction based on calculation methods

8.2.1   General considerations

The basis of calculation methods is given in section 5.2. Now some applications will be given here, with emphasis on the simple formulae, ready for direct application, with a comment on the introduced errors. Most developments deal with a sharp interface situation and, unfortunately, many real situations present a wide mixing zone. Though in steady state situations the predicted sharp interface is in many instances somewhere inside the mixing zone, from a practical point of view the upper limit of the mixing zone is the relevant data looked for. This upper limit is very difficult to predict, but since many calculation methods use the Badon Ghyben-Herzberg principle coupled with the Dupuit-Forchheimer approximations:

- horizontal flow

- constant velocity along a vertical

- water head gradient coinciding with water table slope and a stationary salt water body,

the predicted interface is in most cases too high and then it is in the security side and closer to the top of the mixing zone.

Problems dealing with a moving interface are much more difficult than those dealing with a steady interface, but in many instances they are the most interesting ones. So some approximate calculation methods will be given.

The formula to predict the saltwater wedge position will be preceded by the calculation methods for the upconing process, in which a steady horizontal sharp interface will be assumed.

The effect of tides and other head changes have been considered in section 3.1.7 and will not be discussed anew.

8.2.2   Prediction of depth to the interface

The most used formula to predict the depth to the interface is the Badon Ghyben-Herzberg one (see section 3.1.2). It must be used with caution because it is assumed that no vertical water flow components exist or hydrostatic conditions prevail, with the salt water potential coinciding with mean sea level. A sharp contact between fresh and salt water or that the mixing zone thickness is only a small fraction of total saturated or flow thickness is also assumed.

Many papers mention that the BGH formula is not usable at all in the case studies they describe, including citing examples in which, where the water table is below sea level, the interface is well below. The existence of a dynamic unsteady system in which the vertical flow is effectively retarded by the stratification or by less pervious lenses (or in which the fresh water potential increases rapidly downwards) can explain it, but the result is that the BGH formula cannot be easily used, and substantial corrections must be introduced, such as those presented in section 3.1. In many instances the corrections only give a way to properly use the formula. Most of the examples that show that the formula does not work use incorrect input data.

It is very frequent that in situations in which dynamic effects dominate (transient situations after exploitation starts, variable pumping, variable recharge, transition from a dry period to a wet one or the converse), the BGH cannot be applied without great corrections, in order to forecast the depth to the interface. These corrections need at least two piezometric surfaces, one of fresh water and another of point water heads in salt or brackish water, defined with close observation point boreholes in order to avoid the effects of vertical flows. Then the Hubbert formula (section 3.1.3) is suitable. But, in most cases, the required information is not available.

In order to define the fresh water body, especially in islands and areas where salt water underlays the fresh water, the top of the transition zone must be predicted. In some cases, when dynamic effects are not very important, the BGH can be used, but with a reduced α value, in agreement with some local observations. Values of α between 15 and 30 are mentioned. It seems also that the true mixing zone thickness is smaller than the thickness observed in fully screened boreholes (de Breuck, 1978).

In dynamic situations, the determination of horizontal and vertical groundwater flow is needed in order to interpret the flow pattern and to forecast the future changes in salinity (see section 3.1.6 and also van Dam, 1977). Density difference distributions have a dominant effect since water movement against such a field imposes new gravitational forces besides the viscous forces (Bond, 1973).

8.2.3   Prediction of upconing below pumping wells

In coastal aquifers, where salt water underlays fresh water, partially penetrant wells are constructed in order to avoid as much salt water as possible. These wells are sometimes called skimming wells. They were discussed in chapter 4.

When such a well is pumped, the reduced head towards the well causes an upconing or mounding of the interface under the well. In order to predict the maximum fresh water discharge that can be obtained from a skimming well without entrainment of salt water, it is necessary to know how the underlying brine is going to upcone beneath the well in response to pumping.

The two fluids are miscible and they tend to mix at their contact. Fresh water and salt water are separated by a zone of dispersion with density decreasing with elevation. Ideally, any theory concerning flow in such a situation should be developed using an equation of flow which includes the effect of hydrodynamic dispersion at the contact of the two fluids. But such a treatment is difficult from the practical point of view, and simplifications are introduced. Generally a sharp fresh-salt water interface is assumed, without mixing, and salt water is considered at rest.

The earliest approximate solution to the problem of upconing beneath wells was presented by Muskat and Wyckoff (1935, see also Muskat, 1937). The problem considered was that of brine coning in response to pumping in the overlying oil zone in a confined reservoir. Muskat and Wyckoff obtained a steady state solution assuming that the upconing of brine did not perturb the potential distribution in the oil zone. Muskat's model can be derived as a linearized approximation based on small perturbations (Bear and Dagan, 1964; Bear, 1972). Vertical components can be taken into account. More simple results can be obtained through the application of the horizontal flow pattern assumption (Dupuit-Forchheimer). In a confined aquifer the upconing is similar to the drawdown in a water table aquifer, or better to the drawdown in a confined aquifer in which an area surrounding the well is overpumped until becoming depressed below the upper confining layer (Streltsova and Kashef, 1974).

The great areal extent of the cone relative to the vertical dimensions explains that the Dupuit-Forchheimer approximations give good results. But near and below the well, vertical components cannot be ignored, and the critical discharges and drawdowns are underestimated.

For a given freshwater thickness and well penetration there is a critical well discharge (and a critical well drawdown) for avoiding direct salt water contamination; a greater discharge or drawdown produces an unstable cone, due to the fact that upward drag forces overcome the gravity segregation forces for the heavier salt water, and salt water reaches the well bottom. Regardless of the well geometry and the aquifer and fluid properties, the highest stable cone can never rise as high as the bottom of the well screen.

A stable cone must be flat below the well. A cusped cone is an unstable situation.

The flows along the interface are:

fresh water (f): $\quad q_f = - \dfrac{k_o \gamma_f}{\mu_f} \dfrac{dh_f}{ds}$; $\quad \dfrac{dh_f}{ds} = - \dfrac{\mu_f}{k_o \gamma_f} q_f$

$$\text{salt water (s):} \quad q_s = - \frac{k_o \gamma_s}{\mu_s} \frac{dh_s}{ds} \quad ; \quad \frac{dh_s}{ds} = - \frac{\mu_s}{k_o \gamma_s} q_s$$

s = differential length along the interface

k_o = intrinsic permeability

γ = specific weight

μ = dynamic viscosity

h = head on the interface

subscript s = salt water

subscript f = fresh water.

The pressure equilibrium on the interface at depth z leads to:

$$z = \frac{\gamma_s}{\gamma_s - \gamma_f} h_s - \frac{\gamma_f}{\gamma_s - \gamma_f} h_f$$

and differentiating along the interface of slope α:

$$\frac{dz}{ds} = \sin \alpha = \frac{\gamma_s}{\gamma_s - \gamma_f} \frac{dh_s}{ds} - \frac{\gamma_f}{\gamma_s - \gamma_f} \frac{dh_f}{ds} = \frac{1}{k_o(\gamma_s - \gamma_f)} (\mu_f q_f - \mu_s q_s) .$$

For a static salt water $q_s = 0$ and $\sin \alpha = \dfrac{\mu_f}{k_o(\gamma_s - \gamma_s)} q_f \leq 1$. Then, for a stable cone $q_f \leq \dfrac{k_o(\gamma_s - \gamma_f)}{\mu_f}$. Higher values of q_f imply a salt water flow and consequently an unstable situation.

Bear and Dagan (1964) and Dagan and Bear (1968) (see also Bear, 1972, pp. 539; 1979, pp. 425-433) obtained solutions for the time-dependent interface upconing using the method of small perturbations, when only relatively small interface rises are produced (less than 1/3 d; d = distance from the point well opening of well bottom to the initial horizontal, sharp interface, see fig. 8.2) and water thickness and well penetration are great in respect to d. The interface elevation over the initial horizontal interface is:

$$\zeta(r,t) = \frac{\alpha Q}{2\pi k_h d} \left((1 + \bar{r}^2)^{-1/2} - [(1 + \bar{t})^2 + \bar{r}^2]^{-1/2} \right)$$

$\bar{r}$ = dimensionless radial distance = $\dfrac{r}{d} \sqrt{k_v/k_h}$

$\bar{t}$ = dimensionless time = $\dfrac{k_v t}{2\alpha m d}$

r = horizontal radial distance to the well vertical

t = time since pumping started

Q = constant well discharge

k_h, k_v = permeability for fresh water, h = horizontal; v = vertical;
$\alpha = \rho_f/(\rho_s - \rho_f)$; ρ = density; s = salt; f = fresh water.

When r = 0 (well vertical):

$$\xi(t) = \frac{\alpha Q}{2\pi k_h d} \left[1 - \left(\frac{1}{1 + \bar{t}} \right) \right].$$

The final cone elevation is (t → ∞)

$$\xi(r)_{max} = \frac{\alpha Q}{2\pi k_h d} (1 + \bar{r}^2)^{1/2} \quad ; \text{ under the well } \xi_{max} = \frac{\alpha Q}{2\pi k_h d}$$

valid for $\xi_{max} < d_c$ = critical elevation < (0.4 to 0.6)d

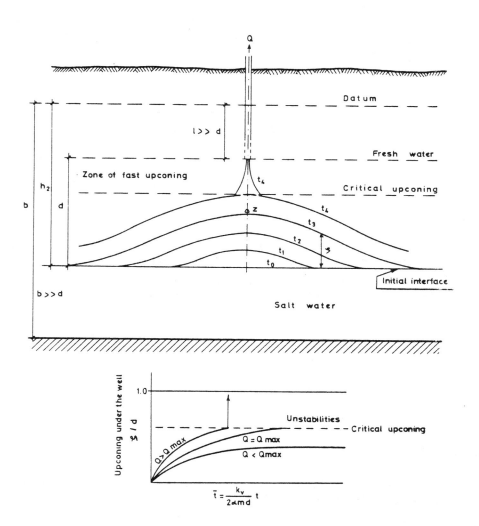

Fig. 8.2 - Upconing below a well at different times. The upper illustration
assumes that well discharge is greater than the critical value.

The formulations are acceptable according to some experiments in the laboratory and in the field (Schmorak and Mercado, 1969). The upconing mean velocity below the well can be easily derived:

$$\frac{\xi}{t} = AQ - B\xi; \qquad A, B = \text{constants}$$

It is proportional to the well discharge and, for a given well discharge, it decreases the greater the elevation of the cone. For the calculation of the critical discharge a ξ_{max} of 1/3 d to 1/4 d is recommended, in order to be on the security side.

A well discharging less than the critical value does not receive salt water, but can be affected to some extent by the dispersed brackish water.

When pumping ceases, the saltwater cone drops. Since one deals with linearized solutions, the residual cone elevation is:

$$\xi(r,t) = \frac{Q}{2\pi k_h d} \left[(1 + \bar{t})^2 + \bar{r}^2) \right]^{-1/2} - \left[(1 + \bar{\tau})^2 + \bar{r}^2) \right]^{1/2}$$

and under the well ($\bar{r} = 0$)

$$\xi(t) = \frac{\alpha Q}{2\pi k_h d} \quad \frac{1}{1 + \bar{t}} - \frac{1}{1 + \bar{\tau}}$$

in which

$\bar{t}$ = dimensionless time for the time since the start of pumping

$\bar{\tau}$ = dimensionless time for the time since the stop of pumping.

Since the up and down interface movement increases dispersion, after repeated pumping and rest periods of the well the mixing zone can grow thicker, so the well gets an increasing degree of pollution. It increases the greater the discharge and the more frequent the start-stop sequences.

A graphical method has been proposed by Miroshnikov (1973) using the experience in oil exploitations. Graphs in figure 8.3, taken from Efros (1963), are valid for a thick salt water layer.

The different values are:

λ = screen length in fresh water

b = fresh water thickness

R = radius of influence (R $\simeq$ 100 to 500 m for a water table aquifer; R $\simeq$ 300 to 1000 m for a confined aquifer)

x = anisotropy = $\sqrt{k_h/k_v}$

k = permeability, h = horizontal; v = vertical

$a = \rho_f/(\rho_s - \rho_f)$; ρ = density; s = salt; f = fresh water.

Graphs A or B yield Q after calculating $\bar{\lambda}$ and $\bar{b}$

$$\bar{\lambda} = x\lambda/R \qquad \bar{b} = xb/R$$

$$Q = \text{critical well discharge} = \frac{k_h}{ax^2} R^2 \bar{Q}$$

Graph C yields

$$\Delta h = \text{critical well drawdown} = \frac{1}{aX} R\Delta\bar{h}$$

For a two layer aquifer, 1 the upper one and 2 the lower one,
$b = b_1 + b_2 \cdot k_1/k_2$; $\lambda = \lambda_1 + \lambda_2 \cdot k_1/k_2$ if well penetrates the two aquifers.
$\lambda = \lambda_1$ if well only penetrates the upper one.

If $k_1 > k_2$, the critical discharge is increased.

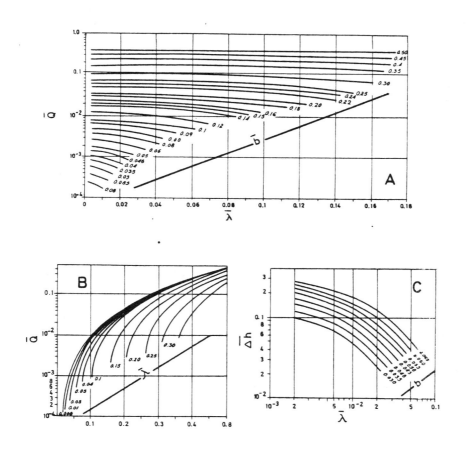

Fig. 8.3 – Curves for upconing calculation (after Efros, 1963, in Miroshnikov, 1973), using dimensionless values.

Sahni (1973a, 1973b) and Chandler and McWhorter (1975) have elaborated numerical solutions taking into account the existence of vertical
flows, especially under and near the well. The Bear and Dagan formulations
yield acceptable results. The length of the well screen has only a small
effect (Haubold, 1975). Pinder and Page (1976) calculate the local upconings
in an island by numerical methods.

Literature is scarce on prediction methods for saltwater upconing
under wells, that consider the mixing zone. A useful method for practical
application is the method of moving fronts (Bruggeman, 1975). It neglects the
differences in density that originate from the differences in salinity, and
thus the flow problem is reduced to a single phase system with one simple
fluid, marked by different concentrations of dissolved solids(see chapter 5).

A suitable solution for the head pattern created by the well or
wellfield is chosen. The flow paths and the water fronts are determined by
numerically solving the differential equations by means of a computer, starting from an arbitrary initial salt distribution (Obdam, 1979). To consider
the effect of differences in density, that may considerably influence the
groundwater flow, the vertical and horizontal velocities due to differences in
density must be computed.

The fresh groundwater displacements in vertical and horizontal
directions are calculated for a timestep Δt by the computer program, and then,
different extra displacements are added for the mixed and salt water bodies.
First, vertical and horizontal salinity gradient velocities are considered,
and afterwards the vertical displacement due to the density difference (Obdam,
1979).

After calculation of the new position of the followed water particle, a new calculation step can be started. In general, after some calculation steps the density gradient must be adjusted to the altered width of the
transition zone due to the gradient velocities.

The method presents some additional problems. One of them is the
problem of shifting the streamlines due to the retardation of saline of brackish groundwater as compared to fresh water. The effective depth is then progressively changed. Another problem derives from the fact that particles from
the lower part of the aquifer are retarded with respect to fresh water particles and thus the abstraction that initially is assumed equally distributed
over the well screen must be redistributed in such a way that the abstraction
of the upper part of the well screen increases whereas that of the lower part
decreases. The vertical movement of salt groundwater particles may decrease
to zero after some time, when equilibrium is attained.

If

ρ = density

μ = dynamic viscosity

v = flow velocity

k_o = intrinsic permeability

γ = $\rho_f / (\rho_s - \rho_t)$

h = water head

z = vertical distance fro the datum

v = vertical, h = horizontal

s = salt, f = fresh water.

The following can be derived (Obdam, 1979):

vertical velocity in salt water $v_{vs} = v_{vf} \dfrac{\mu_f}{\mu_s} - \dfrac{k_o v_f}{\alpha} \dfrac{\mu_f}{\mu_s}$

horizontal salt groundwater velocity $v_{hs} = v_{hf} \dfrac{\mu_f}{\mu_s}$

increase in vertical velocity due to a vertical density gradient =

$- k_{o_z} \dfrac{h - z}{\rho} \dfrac{\partial \rho}{\partial z}$

increase in horizontal velocity due to a horizontal density gradient
$= - k_{o_h} \dfrac{h - z}{\rho} \dfrac{\partial \rho}{\partial z}$.

It has been observed that in many instances, when a well above salt or brackish water starts pumping, after a period from some hours to some days, in which the well yields fresh water, the salinity of the water increases very fast, sometimes following an exponential pattern, but after some time the pace of salinity augmentation decreases, and the curve tends to a horizontal asymptote or top value of the water salinity. This evolution can be described roughly by a logistic curve:

$$\frac{C_{max}}{C} = 1 + \frac{C_{max} - C_o}{C_o} e^{-kt}$$

in which

C, Cmax, C_o = water salinity (actual, top, initial values)

t = time since the salinization initiates

k = constant that varies from case to case.

For small t: $C \simeq C_o e^{kt}$ which shows an exponential evolution.

In some circumstances observed during pumping tests has been a logarithmic evolution of the chloride content, eg. in the south of Tarragona Plain, and in Denmark (Ambo and Haman, 1974), after some time.

These evolutions follow a law:

$$C = A \log Bt; \qquad A, B \text{ constants}$$

If the constant A can be assumed proportional to the well discharge Q (in fact the chloride concentration changes clearly with the Q), comparing the former equation with the Jacob drawdown equation:

$$s_p = \frac{2.3Q}{4\pi T} \log \frac{2.25\ Tt}{r_p^2\ S}$$

s_p = drawdown in a well of effective radius r_p at time t after the start of pumping at constant discharge

T = transmissivity

S = storage coefficient.

Eliminating the time between two equations:

$$C = \frac{4\pi T\ As_p}{2.3\ Q} + A \log \frac{r_p^2\ S\ B}{2.25\ T} = D\ \frac{s_p}{Q} + E; \quad D, E = \text{constants} .$$

Then, for a constant discharge, the chloride concentration increases proportionally to the increasing well drawdown.

The top or maximum salinity depends on the well characteristics (penetration, diameter) and on the well discharge, besides the aquifer characteristics. For a given well in a given aquifer, each discharge can be associated with a top or maximum value of the salinity. This top value of the salinity can change from season to season and from year to year, according to recharge and the global effect of the aquifer exploitation. In a certain area, when no new wells are added nor the pumping pattern changed, after some years of exploitation it is possible to gather enough data to establish the relationships between discharge, salinity and rainfall. This allows rough predictions of the water salinity to be expected in a given situation when the salinization is due to salt water upconing. When there is an unbalance in the aquifer that slowly produces a general sea water encroachment, such rough prediction cannot be easily done.

Some authors (Rodriguez-Gavela and Iglesias, 1976; Iglesias and Rodriguez-Gavela, 1978, for some areas on Majorca) have found that the relationship between top salinity and discharge is linear for a given well if the salinity is not too high (such linearity is impossible for high salinity because there is a maximum value, that of the sea water). That relationship is of the form $C = C_0 + AQ$ in which C is top water salinity for discharge Q, C_0 is the water salinity for $Q = 0$ and A is a constant. Such a relationship can be obtained easily with step drawdown pumping tests with 3 to 5 steps long enough to allow for the determination of the C value for the Q of the step.

In a small area, according to those authors, other wells with similar characteristics show the same A value, though the C_0 value can be different. If a value of C is known for a given Q, then it is possible to calculate the discharge for a given top salinity (determined after the limits for irrigation, supply, etc).

In other areas such a linear relationship does not hold. After a study by Baeza (1960, see also Custodio and Llamas, 1976, pp. 1370-1372), the plotting of Q (C - C_0) versus Q must yield a straight line of equation Q (C - C_0) = ξ (Q - η). Then, the relationship between C and Q is approximately:

$$C = \xi(1 - \frac{\xi}{Q}) + C_0;$$

ξ = slope of the straight of C - C_0 versus Q - η

η = constant.

For a very high discharge C tends to a maximum attainable value of $\xi + C_0$. The formula cannot be used for small Q values.

8.2.4   Salt water ridges under drains

Under a horizontal drain, trench, trough or gallery abstracting fresh water, a salt water mound or ridge forms. The problem has been studied by Bear and Dagan (1964), Strack (1972, 1973). A critical salt water elevation exists, corresponding to a critical discharge, over which the salt water mound is unstable (takes a cusp form) and salt water reaches the drain.

The Muskat approximation can be used. For a drain in a thick aquifer, far from the top and the bottom (Bear, 1979):

$$\xi = \frac{\alpha q}{2\pi k} \ln \frac{d^2 + x_0^2}{d^2 - \xi^2} \qquad \text{for} \qquad \xi/x_0 < 1/3$$

α = $\gamma_f/(\gamma_s - \gamma_f)$ γ = specific weight, s = salt, f = fresh water

q = discharge per unit drain length

k = permeability of the isotropic aquifer

d = vertical distance from the horizontal drain to the initial horizontal interface

ξ = mound elevation under the drain

x_0 = distance to the mound limit.

The critical q value is for $\dfrac{\xi}{d^2 + \xi^2} = \dfrac{nk}{\alpha q}$.

For a semi-infinite aquifer, in which the drain is on the top:

$$\xi = \frac{\gamma q}{2\pi k} \ln \frac{Ch \frac{nx_o}{d} + 1}{Ch \frac{n\xi}{d} + 1} ,$$

though this last formula may introduce rather large errors with respect to an exact solution (Bear and Dagan, 1962).

The critical q value is for $\dfrac{\sin\frac{n\xi}{d}}{Ch \frac{n\xi}{d} + 1} = \dfrac{2kd}{\alpha q}$.

As described in the previous paragraph dealing with upconing below wells, the Dupuit-Forchheimer approximation yields acceptable results except near and below the drain.

For very thick aquifers, with the drain at a distance d over the initial horizontal interface, the following solutions are obtained:

Confined aquifer: $b^2 - h^2 = \frac{\alpha q}{k} (x_o - x)$

b   = initial fresh water thickness

x_o = distance of influence

h   = fresh water thickness at distance x

Water table aquifer (Bear, 1979, pp 421):

$$\frac{q}{2k} (x_o + x) = \frac{1}{\alpha^2} \left[[\alpha b - (1 + \alpha)d] (d - h_2) + \frac{1}{2} (1 + \alpha) (d^2 - h_2^2) \right]$$

b   = initial fresh water thickness

h_2 = fresh water thickness below the drain plane at distance x.

The transient mound can be determined by (Bear and Dagan, 1964; Dagan and Bear, 1968):

$$\xi(x,t) = \frac{\alpha q}{\pi \sqrt{k_h k_v}} \int_0^\infty \frac{1}{\lambda} \frac{Ch[\lambda(b - d)]}{Sh\lambda b} \left[1 - \exp\left(\frac{- \lambda k_v}{\alpha m(Cth\lambda b + Cth\lambda b')} \right) t \right] \cdot$$

$$\cdot \cos\left(\lambda x \sqrt{\frac{k_v}{k_h}} \right) d\lambda$$

and for a very thick aquifer:

$$\zeta(x,t) = \frac{\alpha q}{2\pi\sqrt{k_h k_v}} \ln \frac{\left(\frac{k_v}{k_h}\,x\right)^2 + \left(\frac{k_v t}{2m\alpha} + d\right)^2}{\left(\frac{k_v}{k_h}\,x\right)^2 + d^2}$$

k = permeability; h = horizontal; v = vertical

λ = dummy integration variable

t = time

x = distance

b = initial freshwater thickness (confined in the top)

b' = initial saltwater thickness (confined in the bottom)

d = altitude of the drain above the initial interface

m = porosity

Ch, Sh, Cth = hyperbolic cosine, sine and cotangent.

The decay of the upmounded interface can be obtained by superposition, e.g. by subtracting the solution for τ (time since the stop of pumping) from the solution for t (total time since the start of pumping). For a very thick aquifer:

$$\zeta'(x,t) = \frac{\alpha q}{2\pi\sqrt{k_h k_v}} \ln \frac{\left(\frac{k_v}{k_h}\,x\right)^2 + \left(\frac{k_v t}{2m\alpha} + d\right)^2}{\left(\frac{k_v}{k_h}\,x\right)^2 + \left(\frac{k_v \tau}{2m\alpha} + d\right)^2}$$

When there is seaward flow, the decaying interface can be moved accordingly. Seaward flow distorts the mound, but this effect is negligible up to 30° interface slope (Bear, 1979, pp 432).

The mounding effect by two parallel drains on the top of a confined aquifer has been studied by Mishra, Madhav and Subramanya (1973) by using the inversion of the hodograph and the Schwarz-Christoffel transformation.

Ackermann and Chang (1971) give solutions to the effect of pumping fresh water from drains where the fresh water aquifer was bounded on its lower surface by a stationary body of salt water and on its upper surface by a horizontal plane having a constant piezometric head (eg. the bottom of a lagoon or basin). The drains consist of a series of line sinks spaced at periodic intervals, inside the fresh water region. The solution is obtained by methods of conformal mapping in vertical planes normal to the drains. A graph for aid in the calculations is given.

8.2.5   Prediction of salt water penetration under steady state

A.   Water table or confined aquifer

The salt water wedge penetration in a homogeneous horizontal water table aquifer can be easily derived for stationary salt water and a sharp interface, if the BGH principle and the Dupuit-Forchheimer approximations are applied.

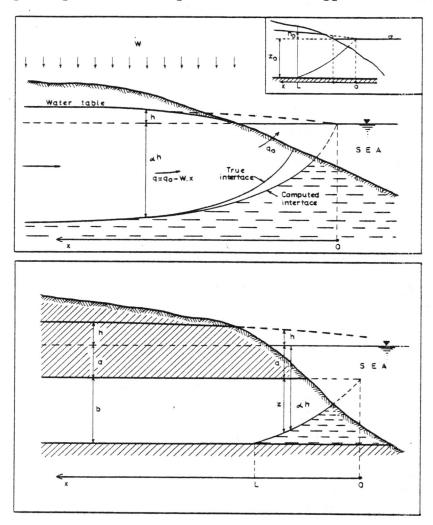

Fig. 8.4 - Salt water wedge in a recharged water table aquifer and in a confined one.

For a rectilinear coast receiving a uniform flow q_0 (per unit length) it can be established at point x from the coast (Santing, 1963; Custodio and Llamas, 1976, pp 1355) in a water table aquifer (fig. 8.4):

$$q_0 - W_x = k(h + \alpha h) \frac{dh}{dx}$$

W = areal recharge

h = fresh water head over mean sea level

k = permeability

$a = \rho_f / (\rho_s - \rho_f)$; ρ = density, s = salt, f = fresh water.

It results that

$$h^2 = \frac{2q_o x - Wx^2}{k(1 + a)} \; ; \quad z = \alpha h$$

z = depth to the interface.

If recharge is negligible $h^2 = \frac{2q_o x}{k(1 + a)}$; $z = \alpha h$.

The saltwater wedge toe penetration, L, can be easily derived for a horizontal aquifer bottom at depth z_o below mean sea level.

$$L = \frac{q_o}{W} - \sqrt{\frac{q_o^2}{W^2} - \frac{(\alpha + 1)k}{\alpha^2 W} z_o^2}$$

That for $\frac{(\alpha + 1)kW}{\alpha^2 q_o^2} \ll 1$ can be approximated by

$$L \simeq \frac{(\alpha + 1)k z_o^2}{2\alpha^2 q_o} \; .$$

For a confined aquifer in similar conditions (fig. 8.4), since W = 0:

$$q_o = k(\alpha h - a) \frac{dh}{dx}$$

a = depth below sea level of aquifer top.

It results that:

$$(\alpha h - a)^2 = \frac{2\alpha q_o x}{k} \; ; \quad z = \alpha h \; .$$

The penetration of the water wedge is:

$$L = \frac{k b^2}{2\alpha q_o}$$

b = aquifer thickness.

It must be recalled that x is measured from the aquifer outcrop (top of aquifer).

These formulae, though based on very simple assumptions, are useful for first calculations, and generally yield depths to the interface (when there is rapid transmission) and salt water wedge penetration in the security side.

Several authors have studied the validity by different methods. Kashef and Safar (1975) have introduced some improvements by considering a linear variation of fresh water head along a vertical.

More exact solutions have to consider vertical flows. Glover (1959) solved that problem by means of the complex potential for a confined aquifer of infinite thickness with the top just at sea level, and with a shallow flat sea bottom (fig. 8.5).

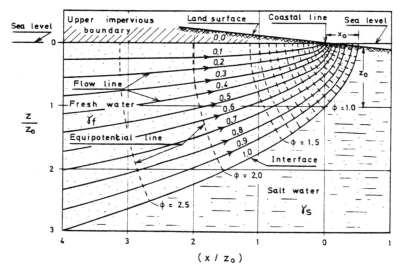

(x / z_0)

Fig. 8.5 – Exact Glover's (1959) solution for a fresh water body flowing on a stationary salt water body with a sharp interface. It is a homogeneous and isotropic aquifer of infinite thickness, confined just at sea level, with a horizontal outflow face just at sea level. Total fresh water flow is q_0 and 10 flow tubes are shown. If $\alpha = (\gamma_s - \gamma_f)/\gamma_f$; γ = specific weight; s = salt water, f = fresh water; the fresh water head is $h = \phi z_0/\alpha = \phi q_0/k$. ϕ = figure on the corresponding equipotential line and z_0 represents the depth to the interface in the coastal line and $x_0 = z_0/2$ is the fresh water outflow width. x represents the distance to the coastal line and z the depth under the mean sea level.

A potential function $\phi^2 = \dfrac{q_0}{\alpha k}\left(x + \sqrt{x^2 + z^2}\right)$ and a streamline function $\psi^2 = \dfrac{q_0}{\alpha k}\left(-x + \sqrt{x^2 + z^2}\right)$ can be defined, where:

x = horizontal distance from the coast, positive landward

z = vertical distance from mean sea level downwards.

The interface equation is:

$$z^2 = \frac{2q_0 \alpha x}{k} + \frac{q_0^2 \alpha^2}{k^2} .$$

That differs from that previously found (a = 0) in the term $\frac{q_0^2 \alpha^2}{k^2}$.

The simpler formula is a good approximation when

$$\frac{2q_0 \alpha x}{k} \gg \frac{q_0^2 \alpha^2}{k^2} \qquad \text{i.e.} \qquad x \gg \frac{q_0 \alpha}{k}$$

or

$$z^2 \gg \frac{q_0^2 \alpha^2}{k^2} \qquad \text{i.e.} \qquad z \gg \frac{q_0 \alpha}{k} .$$

Then, the saltwater wedge toe position is correctly predicted when:

depth of aquifer bottom, $z_b \gg \frac{q_0 \alpha}{k}$, say $z_b \geq 8 \frac{\alpha q_0}{k}$

(Bear, Zaslavsky and Irmay, 1969).

From Glover's formula it can be deduced that:

x_0 = width of fresh water outlet on the ocean flow = $\frac{q_0 \alpha}{2k}$

z_0 = depth of interface at the coastline = $\frac{q_0 \alpha}{k}$

h_0 = fresh water head at z_0 = $\frac{q_0}{k}$.

When the contact with the sea is a vertical outflow face, after Henry (1959), $z_0 = 0.741 \frac{q_0 \alpha}{k}$.

The x_0, z_0 and h_0 values can be used to improve the simple calculations using them as boundary conditions at the coast, instead of $x_0 = z_0 = h_0 = 0$. In a flat sea bottom it suffices to start the distances from x_0 seaward. It improves the forecastings close to the coast, but to calculate the saltwater wedge penetration the formulae without correction are better.

In a similar to way to Glover's formula, Verruijt (1968) calculates for a non recharged water table aquifer:

$$z^2 = \frac{2q_0 x}{k} \frac{\alpha^2}{\alpha + 1} + \frac{q_0^2}{k^2} \alpha^2 \frac{\alpha - 1}{\alpha + 1} .$$

It admits the same discussion as above.

It results that the saltwater toe is well defined if:

$$z_b \gg \frac{q_0 \alpha}{k} \sqrt{\frac{\alpha - 1}{\alpha + 1}}$$

$$x_0 = \frac{q_0}{2k}\left(\alpha - 1\right)$$

$$z_0 = \frac{q_0 \alpha}{k} \sqrt{\frac{\alpha - 1}{\alpha + 1}}$$

$$h_0 = \frac{q_0}{k} \sqrt{\frac{\alpha - 1}{\alpha + 1}} .$$

After Rumer and Harleman (1963), for a confined aquifer limiting through a vertical surface with the sea, the interface equation is:

$$(z - a)^2 = 2 Ax + 0.55 A^2 \quad ; \quad A = \frac{q_0 \alpha}{k(1 + \alpha)}$$

when x starts in the vertical outflow face.

The formerly obtained solution

$$(z - a)^2 = \frac{2\alpha q_0 x}{k}$$

differs in the term $0.55 A^2$.

The fresh water thickness at the outlet face (x = 0) is:

$$(z - a)_0 = 0.741 \frac{q_0 \alpha}{k(1 + \alpha)}$$

a value very close to that of Henry (1959).

Van der Veer (1977b) has solved the two-dimensional flow in a vertical plane of a water table coastal aquifer, with uniform recharge and sharp interface, with salt water in steady state and in movement. It results that the case with salt water in movement reduces to the steady case when the α value ($\alpha = \rho_f / (\rho_s - \rho_f)$; ρ = density; s = salt; f = fresh water) is substituted by

$$\alpha' = \alpha \left(1 + \frac{q_s}{q_f + Wl_e} \frac{\rho_s}{\rho_f}\right)$$

q_s = salt water flow (positive landward and negative seaward)

q_f = fresh water outflow (positive seaward)

W = recharge

le = distance from the coast to the seaward limit of freshwater flow in a shallow sea (fig. 8.6).

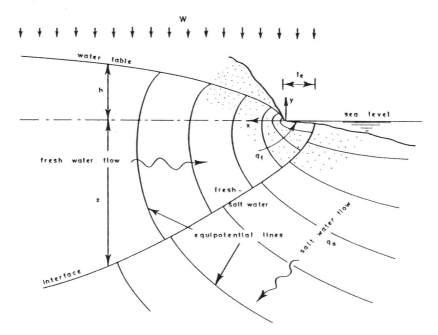

Fig. 8.6 - Schematization of steady fresh water and salt water flow in a water table aquifer with uniform recharge.

The solutions are:

$$\text{Water table } h^2 = \left(\frac{W}{k_f} x^2 - 2 \frac{q_f + Wl_e}{k_f} x \right) \frac{1 + \frac{W}{k_f} a'}{1 + a'}$$

$$+ \left(\frac{q_f + Wl_e}{k_f} \right)^2 \frac{a' - 1 - \frac{Wa'}{k_f}}{(1 + a')(1 - \frac{W}{k_f})}$$

$$\text{Interface depth } z^2 = \frac{\frac{W}{k_f} x^2 - 2 \frac{q_f + Wl_e}{k_f} x}{(1 + \frac{Wa'}{k_f})(1 + a')} a'^2$$

$$le = \frac{q + Wl_e}{W} \left[1 - \sqrt{1 - \frac{W}{k_f} \frac{a' - 1 - \frac{Wa'}{k_f}}{(1 - \frac{W}{k_f})(1 + \frac{Wa'}{k_f})}} \right]$$

-349-

x = distance from the coast, landwards

k_f = permeability to fresh water.

It results that for stationary salt water, the simple calculation with horizontal flow is generally very accurate and it is exact when there is no precipitation.

The salt water movement greatly influences the values of h and z (fig. 8.7).

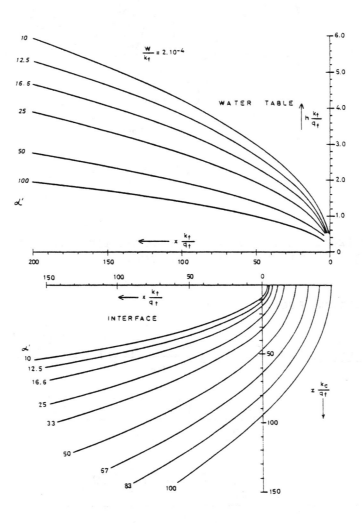

Fig. 8.7 - Water table and depth to the interface in a homogeneous coastal water table aquifer, with recharge, under variable sea water flow conditions $\alpha' = \alpha \left(1 + \dfrac{q_s}{q_f} \dfrac{\rho_s}{\rho_f}\right)$.

In the special case of no salt water flow with constant negative recharge (constant evapotranspiration or surface outflow) in such a way that at the coast $q_f = 0$, the water table and the interface are straight lines defined by:

$$h^2 = x^2 \left(\frac{W}{k_f} \frac{1 + \frac{Wa}{k_f}}{1 + a} \right) \qquad z^2 = x^2 \frac{a^2 W/k}{(1 + \frac{Wa}{k_f})(1 + a)}$$

with

$$W = -\frac{k}{2a} \left(1 + \frac{4a(1 + a)}{i^2} \right)$$

i = slope of the water table.

Panigrahi et al. (1980) has solved numerically a similar problem to that of van der Veer without recharge, for a limited, anisotropic aquifer in which at the upstream boundary a uniform flow is imposed. The distance to the boundary, x_B, can be neglected when:

$$\frac{x_B}{h_b} \sqrt{k_v/k_h} \geq 1000$$

h_B = water level at the boundary

k = permeability, v = vertical, h = horizontal.

For a confined aquifer of finite thickness different authors have presented some solutions (Henry, 1964; Bear, 1972, pp 547-557). They are rather complicated but the following conclusions can be derived when the assumption of a sharp interface is valid:

- When $L > z_o$, the solution for an infinite thickness aquifer can be applied without excessive error. The greater differences appear near the toe, but they are acceptable;

- for an aquifer limited landwards, the solution for semi-infinite aquifers can be applied if the toe does not close to the inner boundary;

- in spite of the approximations involved in the Dupuit-Forchheimer assumptions, the results they yield are accurate enough for practical pur-poses.

The situation of an aquifer confined at the coast and recharged upstream in a water table or semiconfined portion can be easily solved by cou-pling the two solutions at the boundary between the two regions. On that boundary the depth to the interface (or the freshwater head) must be the same. Let L_c = length of the confined coastal area, wholly affected by the salt water wedge, and L_n = length of the recharged portion affected by the salt water wedge. It is assumed that the confining layer is at sea level and that the recharged portion is of constant thickness (semiconfined).

In the recharged part:

$$z^2 = \frac{a}{k}\left[zq_0\,(x - x_0) - W(x - x_0)^2\right]$$

x_0 = ficticious distance of $z = 0$ in that part

x = distance from the outlet. q_0 = ficticious freshwater outlet.

In the confined part:

$$z^2 = \frac{2aq_c x}{k}$$

q_c = water that is poured into the sea water entering the confined area = $q_0 - Wx_0$.

At $x = L_c$ the two values must coincide. Then:

$$W(L_c - x_0)^2 - 2\,x_0\,(W \cdot L_c - q_0) = 0 \ .$$

That allows for the calculation of x_0.

Simple solutions for flow in different circumstances of static or moving salt water under steady conditions are presented by Brillant and de Cazenove (1975).

B. Semiconfined aquifer

For a semiconfined aquifer below the sea or a lake under the following circumstances:

$$\alpha = \rho_f/(\rho_s - \rho_f) \qquad \rho = \text{density; s = salt; f = freshwater}$$

P = head of the sea (transformed into fresh water head) or the lake water (on the upper face of the aquitard)

h_f = fresh water head in the aquifer

h_s = salt water head in the aquifer = 0 (reference level)

H = fresh water thickness in the aquifer, over the salt water

a = depth of the aquifer top

b' = aquitard thickness of vertical permeability k'

c = hydraulic resistance of aquitard = b'/k

k = aquifer permeability.

The differential equation is (van Dam, 1975):

$$kc \, H \frac{d^2 H}{dx^2} + kc \left(\frac{dH}{dx}\right)^2 - H - a - \alpha P = 0$$

without any general solution.

An approximate solution can be found by the introduction of:

$\overline{H}$ = mean value of H over a certain reach.

The differential equation is now:

$$kc \, H \frac{dH}{dx} - (\overline{H} + a - \alpha P) x + c = 0 \qquad c = \text{constant} .$$

The integration domain is divided in a certain number of reaches and the equation is solved successively from one extreme to another.

The method has been applied to the study of the fresh water flow and the interface depth in an elongated polder area isolated from other areas. The polder area presents two different levels so as fresh water flows from the high level polder to the low level one (van Dam, 1975, 1976; van Dam and ten Hoorn, 1977), and the results are considered acceptable.

The approximate solution for a two water level, elongated and isolated polder case (fig. 8.8) is:

depth to the interface:
$$z^2 = \frac{\overline{H} + (1 + \alpha) \, a - \alpha P}{kc} x^2 - \frac{z q_o \alpha x}{k} + H_o^2$$

fresh water flow
$$q = - \frac{\overline{H} + (1 + \alpha) \, a - \alpha P}{\alpha c} x + q_o$$

taking
$$\overline{H} = \frac{H + H_o}{2}$$

The q_o and H_o values are of the fresh water flow and the interface depth is at the beginning of the integration element.

Final solutions are:

$$H = \frac{x^2}{4kc} + \left(H_o^2 + \frac{x^2}{2kc} H_o - \frac{2 q_o \alpha x}{k} + \frac{x4}{16 k^2 c^2} + \frac{x^2}{kc} [(1 + \alpha) \, a - \alpha P] \right)^{1/2}$$

$$q = q_o - \frac{1/2(H + H_o) + (1 + \alpha) \, a - \alpha P}{\alpha c} x .$$

When starting with $q_o = 0$ on one side one must finish with $q = 0$ on the opposite side. Different trials lead to the right H_o value. The solution appears very sensitive to small changes in the value of $\hat{a}$, which depends on the salt water head (fig. 8.9). The conditions to find acceptable solutions are described in van Dam (1975, 1976).

The method can be applied to a set of different water levels in the polder area (fig. 8.9).

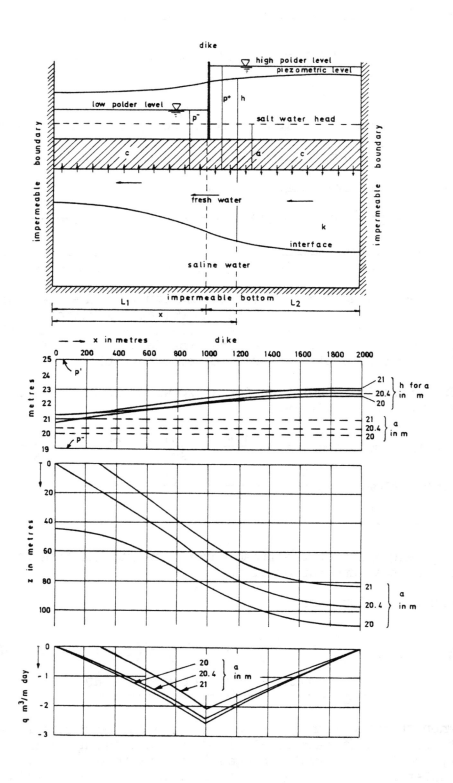

Fig. 8.8 - Isolated elongated polder with two water levels. Effect of the salt water head on the fresh water head, depth to the interface and fresh water flow (after van Dam, 1975, 1976).

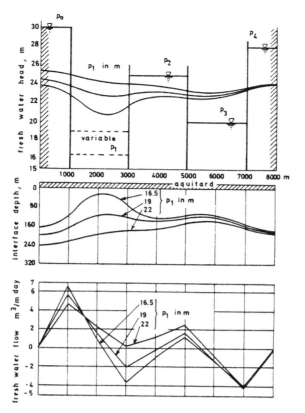

Fig. 8.9 - Isolated elongated polder with four water levels. Effect of one
water level changes in section 2 on the ground fresh water head,
depth to the interface and fresh water flow. Calculated for $\alpha = 50$,
$k = 25$ m/day, $c = 1000$ days (after van Dam and ten Hoorn, 1977).

New solution techniques have been developed (van Dam, 1979, 1981);
ten Hoorn, 1979; van Dam and Sikkema, 1982; Sikkema and van Dam, 1982).

A closely related problem was treated by Venhuizen (1975) for a dune
belt in Holland over a semipervious layer, when a fresh water lens forms.

For the case of a circular lake creating a radial-symmetric flow
instead of a plane flow, under the same circumstances the following differential equation is obtained:

$$kc \left[rH \frac{d^2H}{dr^2} + r\left(\frac{dH}{dr}\right)^2 + H \ \left(\frac{dH}{dr}\right) \right] - r[H + a - \alpha P] = 0$$

r = radial distance

that also has no general solution. With the introduction of a mean value $\bar{H}$
over a certain reach it is possible to resolve successively the equation:

$$H \frac{dH}{dr} - \frac{a + \bar{H} - \alpha P}{2kc} r + \frac{C}{r} = 0 \qquad c = \text{constant} .$$

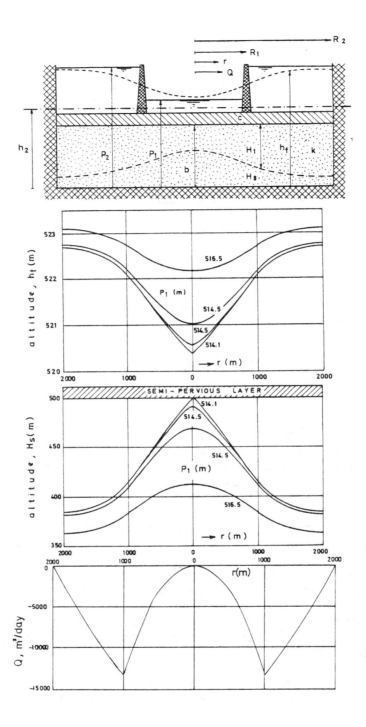

Fig. 8.10 - Isolated circular polder with two concentric water levels. Effect of the water level changes in the inner part on the fresh water head and the depth to the interface. R_1 = 1000 m; R_2 = 2000 m; b = 500 m; h_S = 520 m; c = 1000 days; k = 25 m^2/day; P_e = 525 m; a = 50. For P_1 = 514.1 m the salt water reaches the semipervious layer. The lower illustration shows the fresh water flow for one of the situations (after Molenkamp, 1980).

If at $r = R_0$ the fresh water flow is $Q = Q_0$ and $H = H_0$, they (van der Molen in van Dam, 1975):

$$H^2 = H_0^2 + \frac{a + \bar{H} - \alpha P}{kc}\left(\frac{r^2 - R_0^2}{2} + R_0^2 \ln \frac{R_0}{r}\right) + \frac{\alpha Q_0}{\pi k} \ln \frac{R_0}{r}$$

$$Q = Q_0 + \pi \frac{a + \bar{H} - \alpha P}{\alpha c}(R_0^2 - r^2) \ .$$

It can represent the situation of a circular island with a semiconfined aquifer.

An improvement of the method has been applied to an isolated polder containing two concentric water levels (Molenkamp, 1980) using a solution method called APSOM. Figure 8.10 shows an example.

C. Layered aquifers

Often a coastal aquifer is divided by impervious or semipervious layers of small thickness into different subaquifers, as shown in figure 8.11 for a two layered system.

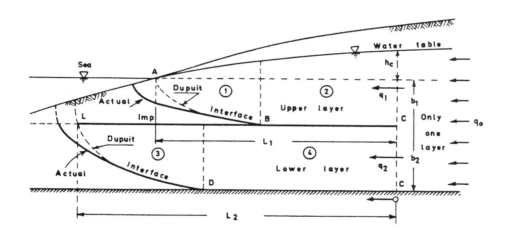

Fig. 8.11 - Two-layer aquifer separated by a semipervious sheet. Formation of two interfaces.

The problem for two layers separated by an impervious sheet has been considered under steady state conditions by some researchers (Bear, 1979, pp 396; Collins and Gelhar, 1971). Several regions must be considered according to the position of the salt water wedges. Collins and Gelhar (1971) consider the existence of vertical flow components, reunited in a correction term. Numerical solutions are needed. Results are only approximate when compared to a Hele-Shaw model. Bear (1972) gives the solution (see fig. 8.11 for definitions).

Flow in the upper layer $q_1 = \dfrac{T_1}{L_1} (h_c - b_1/2a)$

Flow in the lower layer $q_2 = \dfrac{T_2}{L_2} (h_2 - b_2/2a - b_1/2a)$.

Water table elevation over mean sea at the entry section:

$$h_c = \frac{\dfrac{T_2\,b_2}{2L_2 a} + b_1 \dfrac{\dfrac{T_1}{2L_1} - \dfrac{T_2}{L_2}}{a} + q_o}{\dfrac{T_1}{L_1} + \dfrac{T_2}{L_2}}$$

T = transmissivity

b = thickness

$a = \rho_f/(\rho_s - \rho_f)$; ρ = density, s = salt, f = fresh water

L = length of the aquifer until the end of the impermeable sheet

1 = upper aquifer

2 = lower aquifer.

Salt water penetration increases with total thickness $b_1 + b_2$, with permeability k, and with decreasing the fresh water q_o. The increase of b_1/b_2 produces a slow increase in q_1/q_2. The lower interface is relatively longer than the upper one.

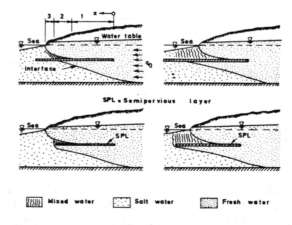

Fig. 8.12 – Two-layer aquifer separated by a semipervious sheet. Formation of two interfaces. Upflowing fresh groundwater from the lower aquifer mixes with the salt water in the upper one. Different situations are possible according to the seaward extension of the semipervious sheet and the position of the lower salt water wedge in respect to the upper one.

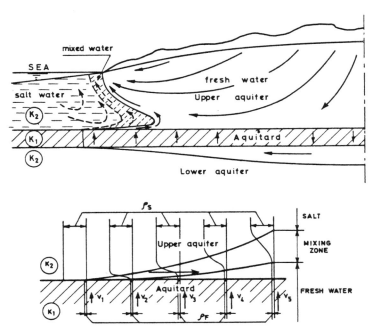

Fig. 8.13 - Mixing of water at the lower part of the upper salt water wedge in
a two layer aquifer separated by a semipervious sheet (aquitard).
Vertical density currents appear. The lower illustration shows the
density logs. The upward seeping velocities increase from v_1 v_5
(after ten Hoorn, 1981).

The case of a semipervious sheet has been studied by Mualem and Bear
(1974) by using the Dupuit-Forchheimer approximations (fig. 8.12). The
introduction of a mean value of the fresh water thickness allows for the
linearization of the equations. Experimental results with a Hele-Shaw model
to test the validity of the equations seem to agree rather well, with deviations less than 8%. According to the Rumer and Shiau (1968) work, the interface, similar to a streamline, is refracted upon passing from one layer to the
next. This effect and the problem of the lower fresh water being discharged
upward through the upper salt water wedge has been studied in detail by ten
Hoorn (1981). In the upper salt water wedge an inversion in density may
occur, and unstable density gradients arise (fig. 8.13).

8.2.6   <u>Steady salt water wedge with abstraction of fresh water</u>

A.   <u>Drains parallel to the coast</u>

It is possible to use the formulae of paragraph 8.2.5-A to study the
steady effect of a drain parallel to the coast subjected to a constant
discharge q_d (per unit length), when a sharp interface and only horizontal
flow can be assumed (fig. 8.14). Then partial penetration effects are
neglected.

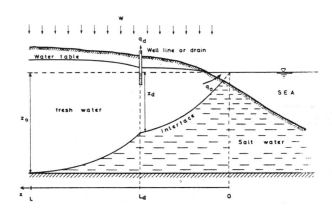

Fig. 8.14 - Drain or well-line parallel to the coast in a water-table aquifer
with uniform recharge, abstracting fresh water.

For a drain at distance L_d from the coast and over the salt water
wedge, the interface depth can be predicted using the mentioned formulations
in two areas:

(a) from the saltwater toe (at distance L) to the drain, with natural
flow (increased by recharge);

(b) from the drain seaward, with natural flow reaching the drain reduced
by the drain abstraction (increased by recharge).

Both solutions must give the same z for the interface at $x = L_d$, and
this condition makes the link between the two equations.

Let q_o be the natural discharge at the coast in a water table
aquifer:

$$\text{Area a)} \quad z^2 = \frac{2(q_o - Wx')(x - x') - W(x - x')^2}{k} \cdot \frac{a^2}{1 + a}$$

x' = distance from the coast to be determined where $z = 0$ in absence of the
drain. The value $q_o - Wx'$ is to discount the recharge from x' to the sea.

$$\text{Area b)} \quad z^2 = \frac{2(q_o - q_d) x - Wx^2}{k} \cdot \frac{a^2}{1 + a} \cdot$$

At $x = L_d$ both z values must coincide. Then:

$$x' = \frac{q_o}{W} \left[1 - \sqrt{1 - \frac{2WL_d q_d}{q_o^2}} \right] \simeq L_d \frac{q_d}{q_o} \qquad \text{for} \qquad \frac{2WL_d q_d}{q_o^2} \ll 1 \, .$$

Then the z values are fully determined.

Let q_o be the constant natural discharge of a confined aquifer:

Area a) $(z - a)^2 = \dfrac{2\alpha q_o (x - x')}{k}$

Area b) $(z - a)^2 = \dfrac{2\alpha (q_o - q_b)x}{k}$.

At $x = L_d$ both z values must coincide. Then $x' = L_d \dfrac{q_d}{q_o}$ and the z values are fully determined.

The salt water wedge penetration is now L for $z = z_o$ in area a:

$$L = \frac{kb^2}{2\alpha q_o} + L_d \frac{q_d}{q_o} .$$

The value $L_d \dfrac{q_d}{q_o}$ represents the increase in penetration, as it does approximately in the water table aquifer situation.

When the density differences can be neglected, salinization is avoided if some fresh water flow at the coast line remains:

$$q < T \cdot i_o$$

T = mean aquifer transmissivity

i_o = natural groundwater gradient.

When $q > T \cdot i_o$ the salt water front approaches the water intake and reaches it after a time:

$$t = \frac{m_o b d_o}{q - T i_o}$$

b = mean aquifer thickness

d_o = distance from the drain to the coast.

B.   Effect of wells on the salt water wedge penetration

When differences in density can be neglected, some easy calculations can be made assuming a sharp straight contact between fresh and salt water.

In an extensive aquifer without natural flow, it can be shown (Babushkin and Goldberg, 1967) that for a well or group of close wells abstracting a flow Q at a distance d_o to the salt water body (the sea or a lake or a tidal estuary), when there is not saltwater wedge formation:

$Q < 2\pi T \cdot i \cdot d_o$: salt water does not penetrate since a fresh water outflow remains (the downstream stagnant point is between the well and the boundary);

$Q < 2\pi T \cdot i \cdot d_o$: salt water penetrates continuously and finally will reach the well;

T = aquifer transmissivity

i = natural fresh water gradient.

That time is:

$$t \simeq \frac{mb}{Ti} \left(\frac{Q}{2\pi Ti} \ln \frac{Q}{Q - 2\pi Tid_o} - d_o \right)$$

m = effective porosity

b = aquifer thickness.

When Q is large and i very gentle, the following approximation of pure radial flow can be applied:

$$t \simeq \frac{\pi d_o^2 bm}{Q} .$$

The evolution of abstracted water salinity, after the saline front reaches the well in a radial flow system, is given by (Custodio and Llamas, 1976, pp. 1369):

$$C = C_o + \frac{C_s - C_o}{\pi} \text{ arc cos } \sqrt{t_o/t}$$

in which

C, C_o, C_s = water salinity (actual, initial, of the salt water)

t = time since the start of the pump

t_o = time at which salinization starts = $\pi mbd_o^2/Q < t$

Q = constant well discharge

m = aquifer porosity

b = aquifer saturated thickness

d = distance from the well to the initial plane of separation of the two water bodies.

After a very fast increase in salinity, the salinity trend is to a top value of $1/2 (C_o + C_s)$.

In real situations, that very fast increase is preceded by a slow salinity increase due to the dispersive effects, that can be dominant in many circumstances. The top value can vary from a fraction of sea water salinity when there is enough fresh water flow to the sea in the aquifer, to almost pure sea water when the effect of the sea (positive barrier) or other wells dominate.

    In the case of essentially steady, horizontal fresh water flow, in
which there is now flow in the salt water zone, Strack (1976) has developed a
technique for determining the shape and position of the interface.

    For a single well located at distance x_W from the rectilinear coast,
pumping at a constant rate Q_W superimposed on a uniform flow q (discharge per
unit width through the entire thickness of the aquifer) starting from very far
(fig. 8.15), the equation of the interface toe is (Strack, 1976; Bear, 1979,
pp. 403):

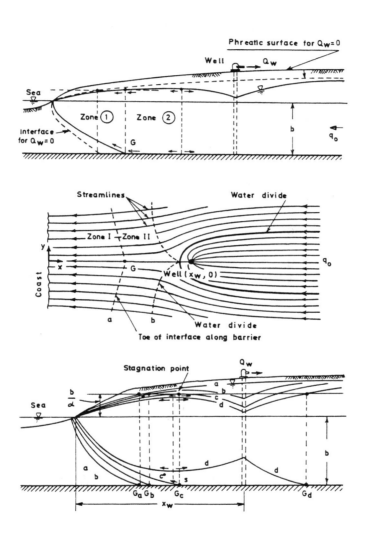

Fig. 8.15 - Well near the coast. S is the stagnation point and G is the
        closest interface toe.   If G is seaward of S no salinization of
        wellwater is produced when a sharp interface can be assumed.   The
        lower illustration shows the displacement of point G from $Q_W = 0$
        (curve a) to high well discharge (curve d). Curve c corresponds to
        the critical condition in which G coincides with point S.

-363-

$$\frac{1}{2}(1+a)\frac{b^2}{a^2} = \frac{q}{k}x + \frac{Q_W}{4\pi k}\ln\frac{(x-x_W)^2 + y^2}{(x+x_W)^2 + y^2}$$

b = freshwater thickness below mean sea level

k = permeability (supposed homogeneous and isotropic)

x = distance from the coast line

y = distance to the perpendicular line from the well to the coast

$a = \rho_f/(\rho_s - \rho_f)$ ρ = density, s = salt, f = fresh water.

BGH conditions and Dupuit-Forchheimer approximations are assumed. In order to assure that the interface toe is to be arrested at some distance seaward of the well, a continuous fresh water head above b/a must be maintained between the well and the sea, although in the well surroundings the head may be smaller than b/a; or inclusive below sea level (fig. 8.15).

There are two significant points along the line perpendicular to the sea passing through the well (fig. 8.15):

- point G: water head is b/a;

- point S: the stagnation point on the water divide created by the well on the uniform natural flow. Landward of S the flow is towards the well and seaward of S it is towards the sea. On point S there is no flow:

$$x_S = x_W - \frac{Q_W}{2\pi q}$$

for constant water thickness.

$$x_S = x_W \sqrt{1 - \frac{Q_W}{\pi q x_W}}$$

for a water table aquifer.

For low Q_W values, point G remains seaward of S and the salt water wedge is arrested.

As Q_W increases, point G approaches point S and when it is attained a critical unstable situation arises. Any further pumping increase will produce an increased water table drawdown, resulting in a rapid advance of the interface with the toe landward of the well, until a new equilibrium is reached (fig. 8.15). Then, for the well not being subjected to sea water intrusion (direct or through upconing), there is a maximum well discharge at which points G and S coincide.

The Strack method is easily amenable for a programmable hand calculator (Alvarez, Doblas and Iglesias, 1981).

Figure 8.16 shows different cross-sections of situations in coastal, partially penetrating wells, when they are attained by the salt water wedge.

The upconing problem discussed in section 8.2.3 is compounded with the fresh water circulation above the interface. Kashef and Smith (1975) simply impose a well solution under radial flow to the natural aquifer flow.

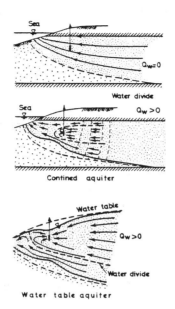

Fig. 8.16 – Formation of water divides in a vertical cross-section normal to the sea through a partially penetrating well. The heavy solid line represents the actual interface and the water table, and the heavy interrupted line the water divide. The light interrupted line represents the interface and the water table for $Q_W = 0$. Point A is the stagnation point.

A similar treatment to that of Strack has been proposed by Goldberg (1973) without taking into account the density differences. Thus the critical situation is when point S reaches the shoreline or the salt water boundary. As shown earlier it works when $Q > \pi Tid_0$. Then the length of coastline through which salt water penetrates is:

$$2y_0 = 2d_0 \sqrt{\frac{Q}{\pi Tid_0} - 1}$$

and the maximum salinity of pumped water is:

$$C_{max} = C_0 + \frac{C_1 - C_0}{\pi} \text{ arctg } \frac{2\sqrt{\beta - d_0^2}}{\left| \beta - 2d_0^2 \right|} : \qquad \beta = \frac{Qd_0}{\pi Ti}$$

C_0 = freshwater salinity

C_1 = sea or salt water salinity.

First arrival of salt water to the well is at time:

$$t_o = \frac{m}{k \cdot i} \left[\frac{d_o - x_s^2}{|x_s|} \text{arctg} \frac{d_o}{|x_s|} - d \right]$$

x_s = distance from the stagnation point to the coast line

$$x_s^2 = d^2 - \frac{Q d_o}{\pi T i_o}$$

k   = permeability

and the maximum salinity value is attained at time:

$$t_{lim} = \frac{2 \pi m d_o^2 b}{Q} \left[1 + \left(\frac{2 d_o^2 - \beta}{2 \sqrt{\beta - d_o^2}} \right)^2 \right] \cdot$$

$$\left[1 - \left(\frac{2 d_o^2 - \beta}{2 \sqrt{\beta - d_o^2}} \right)^2 \text{arcsec} \left[1 + \left(\frac{2 d_o^2 - \beta}{2 \sqrt{\beta - d_o^2}} \right)^2 \right]^{-1/2} \right]$$

When $\frac{Q}{\pi b d_o} > 0.03 \, k_i$ then: $t_o = \frac{2 \pi m d_o^2 b}{3 Q}$

t (for a given c) $= \frac{2 \pi m d_o^2 b}{Q} \cdot$

$$\left[1 - \left(\frac{C - C_o}{C_1 - C_o} \text{cotg} \left(\pi \frac{C - C_o}{C_1 - C_o} \right) \right) \text{cosec}^2 \left(\pi \frac{C - C_o}{C_1 - C_o} \right) \right] \cdot$$

In the case of an infinite array of wells parallel to the coast, above the salt water wedge, the following solutions are obtained (Bear and Dagan, 1963; Bear, 1979, pp 424):

$$b^2 - h^2(x,y) = \frac{2aq - Q_w/2}{2ak} (L_1 - x) + \frac{aQ_w}{2\pi k} \left[\frac{\pi L_1}{a} - \ln 2 \left(\text{Ch} \frac{\pi x}{a} - \cos \frac{\pi y}{a} \right) \right]$$

$$h^2(x,y) - h_s^2 = \frac{2aq - Q_w/2}{\alpha ak} (L_2 - x) - \frac{\alpha Q_w}{2\pi k} \left[\frac{\pi L_2}{a} - \ln 2 \left(\text{Ch} \frac{\pi x}{a} - \cos \frac{\pi y}{a} \right) \right]$$

b   = saturated thickness

a   = half-distance between two contiguous wells

h(x,y) = fresh water head in the x,y plane (only horizontal flow is assumed) q   = natural flow per unit width

Q_W = well discharge

k   = permeability

α = $\rho_f/(\rho_s - \rho_f)$; ρ = density; s = salt; f = fresh water

L_2 = distance from wells to the coast

L_1 = distance from wells to the nearest landward saltwater toe.

Figure 8.17 represents the interface in that case.

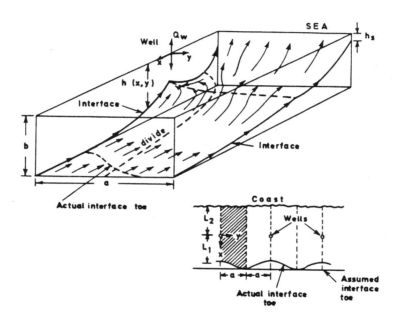

Fig. 8.17 - Infinite array of equally spaced wells parallel to the coast, when they are on the salt water wedge. The upper illustration represents the half space associated with a well, according to the lower illustration (after Bear and Dagan, 1963).

Such an array can be represented with enough accuracy by a drain extracting the same water quantity, except near the wells. The difference between the array and a drain is negligible at distances from the well line greater than the well semispacing.

Kishi and Fukuo (1977) deal with a fan-shaped confined aquifer in which an abstraction area is placed.

8.2.7 Prediction of the movement of the salt-fresh water interface

When the equilibrium situation of a coastal aquifer is altered as a consequence of changes in water abstraction or recharge, the interface or the mixing zone moves to a new equilibrium configuration. This movement is done generally at a slow pace and mixing increases. Most treatments, in order to simplify the solutions, assume a sharp interface.

Density differences must be taken into account. Some solutions for a homogeneous fluid, given in some of the preceding paragraphs, are only rough estimates or are valid only for fresh-brackish water systems.

For the two-dimensional movement in a vertical plane perpendicular to the coast, Bear and Dagan (1964) got an approximate solution assuming that in the transient phase the interface can be described by quasi-steady solutions.

The natural flow q_i on the salt water wedge toe is changed to q_i' due to upstream alterations. If:

q = fresh water flow on the salt water wedge (per unit width) (Function of time);

q_o = fresh water outflow to the sea. (Function of time); then the following solutions are obtained for a confined aquifer:

(a) q at distance x from the sea is proportional to the fresh water thickness:

$$\frac{6\alpha t}{mkb^3} = \frac{1}{q_i'^2} \ln \frac{q_o}{q_i} - \frac{1}{q_i}\left(\frac{1}{q_o} - \frac{1}{q_i}\right) - \frac{1}{q_i'^2} \ln \frac{q_i' - q_o}{q_i' - q_i}$$

b = aquifer thickness

k = permeability

m = porosity

$\alpha = \rho_f/(\rho_s - \rho_f)$; ρ = density; s = salt; f = fresh water

t = time since the change was produced.

It is valid when $q_i' > a_i$, that is to say, when the salt water wedge retreats, and especially for $q_o > q_i'/2$.

(b) q at distance x from the sea decreases with fresh water thickness faster than in the former situation, with a coefficient factor c. In that case the interface adopts a sigma-form (fig. 8.18), with an inflection point at depth:

$$z_B = \frac{b}{1 + \sqrt{c(1 - q_i'/q_o)}} .$$

-368-

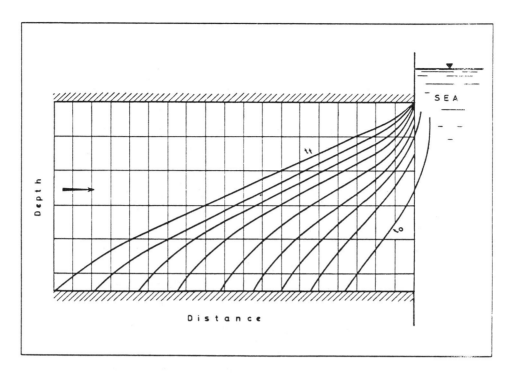

Fig. 8.18 - Evolution of interface position in a confined aquifer when fresh water flow is reduced upstream. The results are taken from an experience made by Bear and Dagan (1964) with the help of a Hele-Shaw model. t_O represents the initial steady interface and t_f the final steady interface. Some intermediate positions are shown.

The best c value is c ≃ 0.1 according to Hele-Shaw model tests. Actually the deviations from the parabolic form are only important near the salt water toe.

Figure 8.19 presents the results for a penetrant salt water wedge and q_O being still important. For the case when $q'_i = 0$ (all the natural flow is intercepted):

$$\frac{q_i}{q_O} = \sqrt{\frac{14.3\alpha t q_i^2}{mkb^3} + 1} \; ; \quad L^2(t) = \frac{\beta kbt}{\alpha m} + L_O^2$$

L_O = initial salt water wedge length

$L(t)$ = salt water wedge length at time t

β = coefficient, which value varies between 1 and 3 according to different studies. Bear and Dagan (1964) obtain $\beta = 3$ for case (a) and $\beta = 1.75$ for case (b); Rumer and Harleman (1963) obtain $\beta = 1$.

In that case, the salt water wedge toe advances with a velocity v:

$$1/v = 2 \sqrt{\beta At + A^2 L_O^2} \; ; \quad A = \frac{m}{kb(1 + \alpha)} \; .$$

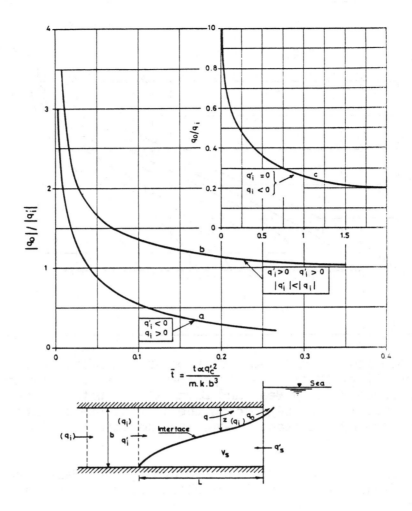

Fig. 8.19 – Curves to compute the freshwater outflow to the sea (q_0) with moving interface, after Bear and Dagan (1963, 1964). See the text for the definition of the variables. The volume of the salt water body per unit length is $V_S = mkb^3/(6\alpha q_0)$.

The calculations are also valuable for a water table aquifer, far from the coast, when z is measured from the water table. It is also valuable for a sloping aquifer. Vappicha and Naggaraja (1976) also use the method of successive steady states in order to determine the transient profile of an interface in a coastal aquifer for different boundary conditions at the salt water wedge toe vertical, with the aquifer bottom horizontal or sloping. They use the steady fresh water thickness below mean sea level, z, at distance x from the coast, given by:

$$x = (1 + \alpha) \left[\frac{kz^2}{2\alpha^2 |q|} - 0.26 \frac{|q|}{k} \right]$$

-370-

$|q|$ = fresh water flow at x, per unit length (absolute value)

k = permeability for water table aquifer with a vertical sea outlet.

New calculation improvements by the use of boundary integral equation solutions are due to Liu et al. (1981).

Rumer and Harleman (1963), from a series of Hele-Shaw viscous fluid models, deduced that

$$v = v_o e^{-\lambda t}$$

v = salt water wedge toe velocity after time t of the change in fresh water flow

v_o = initial salt water wedge toe velocity

λ = constant function of the density difference and the permeability, but with the form not determined.

The method of analytical complex functions with degrees of freedom (van der Veer, 1976, 1978) has been used to solve different two-dimensional problems related to semiconfined aquifers in polderlands. The degrees of freedom are used to make the solution satisfy the boundary conditions at a number of points of the boundary of a subregion of constant properties of the ground and the fluid (bounded element). An exact solution is obtained for any non-steady flow pattern within an approximate boundary, because the solution is made to satisfy the boundary conditions at a number of points of the boundary, and within that boundary the flow is described by analytical methods. Relatively large steps in time may be used. An application to a real case is given by Atwater (1980), for the Groot-Mijdrech polder in Holland, in which the interface reaches the drained polder bottom. From a vertical interface depth of 50 m, it raises to the polder bottom in about 5 years, at the same time that the interface in the high water table area drops to about 80 m due to the decreasing salt water head. From about 7 years onwards the salt water outflow at the polder bottom decreases steadily, with decreasing salt water head, and the upward salt water flow is negligible after a few centuries.

For a two-layer aquifer, Bear and Kapuler (1981) give a numerical solution for the case where exists a fine impervious sheet separating them.

8.2.8   Prediction of salt water thickness on small pervious islands

On small pervious islands a fresh water lens forms, floating on sea water. Generally a thick transition zone develops and simple formulations, based on a sharp interface, are only a rough approximation. Only in homogeneous sand islands in well recharged areas present a relatively sharp interface.

In some instances the freshwater thickness until the top of the mixing zone can be obtained by an empirical α factor, but it is not sure that it can be used under changing circumstances.

On a small circular island, at distance r from the center. (Dupuit-Forchheimer approximations are used):

$$\text{recharge} = \pi r^2 W = 2\pi r k \, (1 + \alpha) \, h \, \frac{dh}{dr}$$

it results:

$$h^2 = \frac{W}{2k \, (1 + \alpha)} \, (R^2 - r^2) \; ; \qquad h^2_{max} = \frac{WR^2}{2k \, (1 + \alpha)} \; ; \qquad z = \alpha h$$

h = freshwater head

z = interface depth

k = permeability

R = effective island radius

W = recharge, assumed uniform and constant

$\alpha = \rho_f / (\rho_s - \rho_f)$; ρ = density; s = salt; f = fresh water.

The Dupuit-Forchheimer approximation produces good results when common values of W are used (Henry, 1964).

For an elongated island or a sand bar of width 2l:

$$\text{'in+1.0i'ti-1.0iW} \cdot x = k \, (1 + \alpha) \, h \, \frac{dh}{dr} \; .$$

It results that:

$$h^2 = \frac{W}{k \, (1 + \alpha)} \, x^2 \; ; \qquad h^2_{max} = \frac{Wl^2}{k \, (1 + \alpha)} \; ; \qquad z = \alpha h$$

x = distance from the coast.

The exact solution is due to Henry (1964) and shows that the above approximate formulation is acceptable when W is moderate, and the assumption of a sharp interface is reasonable.

When the island is not homogeneous but has an upper layer of thickness b_1 and permeability k_1, and a lower one also affected by the fresh water of respective values b_2 and k_2, Fetter (1972a) obtains:

$$h^2 \, (k_1 + \alpha k_2) + h(b_1 k_1 + b_2 k_2) = x^2$$

equivalent to a homogeneous elongated island of permeability

$$\bar{k} = \frac{k_1(b_1 + h) + k_2(\alpha h - b_1)}{h(1 + \alpha)} \; .$$

The k values are weighed by the fresh water saturated thickness in every situation.

When a homogeneous circular island is subjected to the discharge Q of fresh water, from a concentric circular canal at radius d (or from a set of wells along that circumference), the following solutions are obtained for the interface depth:

Inside the canal $0 \leq r \leq d$

$$z^2 = \frac{\frac{W}{2}(R^2 - r^2) - \frac{Q}{\pi}\ln\frac{R}{d}}{(1 + \alpha)\,k}\,\alpha^2$$

Outside the canal $d \leq r \leq R$

$$z^2 = \frac{\frac{W}{2}(R^2 - r^2) - \frac{Q}{\pi}\ln\frac{R}{r}}{(1 + \alpha)\,k}\,\alpha^2\;.$$

For the transient buildup and depletion of water in circular islands, due to recharge and evaporation, Basak (1982) has found the following solution:

$$p(\bar{r},\tau) = (1 - \bar{r}^2) - 8\sum_{n=1}^{\infty}\frac{J_0(\alpha_n x)}{\alpha_n^3 J_1(\alpha_n)}\,e^{-\alpha_n^2\tau}$$

$$p(0,\tau) = 1 - 8\sum_{n=1}^{\infty}\frac{e^{-\alpha_n^2\tau}}{\alpha_n^3 J_1(\alpha_n)} \quad \text{in the center of the island}$$

$$p = \frac{h^2 - b^2}{\mu \cdot b^2}\;;\quad h = b\sqrt{1 + \mu}\;;\quad \mu = \frac{W}{2k}\left(\frac{R}{b}\right)^2\;;\quad \text{for recharge events,}$$

$$p = \frac{b^2 - h^2}{\mu \cdot b^2}\;;\quad h = b\sqrt{1 - \mu}\;;\quad \mu = \frac{W}{2k}\left(\frac{R}{b}\right)^2\;;\quad \text{for evaporation, and}$$

W $\quad$ = constant recharge or evaporation rate

b $\quad$ = depth to the aquifer bottom from mean sea level

h $\quad$ = water table height over mean sea level

k $\quad$ = permeability (assumed homogeneous)

R $\quad$ = island radius

r $\quad$ = distance from the island center

$\bar{r}$ $\quad$ = r/R

τ $\quad$ = kbt/mR^2

t $\quad$ = time since start of the event at which h = 0

m $\quad$ = porosity

J_0, J_1 = Bessel functions

α_n = roots of $J_O(x) = 0$

n	1	2	3	4	5	6	7	8	9
α_n	2.401	5.520	8.653	11.791	14.930	18.071	21.071	21.211	27.493

$$J_O(x) \approx 1 - \frac{x^2}{2^2} + \frac{x^4}{2^2 \cdot 4^2} + \frac{x^6}{2^2 \cdot 4^2 \cdot 6^2} + \ldots$$

$$J_1(x) \approx \frac{d}{dx} J_O(x) = - \left[-\frac{2x}{2^2} + \frac{4x^3}{2^2 \cdot 4^2} - \frac{6x^5}{2^2 \cdot 4^2 \cdot 6^2} + \ldots \right].$$

The greater the μ value the higher or the lower the water table. For $\mu = 1$ in steady state ($t = \infty$) a lineal water table is obtained for evaporation conditions.

For $\tau = 0.4$, a situation at 90% of the steady state is attained.

8.2.9 Formation of freshwater bodies by injection

Formation and depletion of fresh water bodies in salt water aquifers by fresh water recharge or injection has been studied by Hantush (1968). It shows that the interface problem can be treated as a water table with fresh water flow along a line 1, being:

$$q_e = -\frac{1}{2}(1 + \alpha) k \frac{\partial H^2}{\partial \rho}$$

q_e = flow velocity

α = $\rho_f/(\rho_s - \rho_f)$; ρ = density; s = salt; f = fresh water

k = permeability

l = flow path

H = fresh water thickness.

Solutions in different situations use different well or drain functions already developed for other calculations (Hantush, 1964; 1967; Carslaw and Jaeger, 1959).

For an injection well far from the aquifer boundaries:

$$H^2 = A_1 \cdot S(\tau, \rho) \simeq A_1 W(\mu) \qquad \text{for } t > 30\ r_w^2/\overline{\vartheta}$$

$$A_1 = \frac{Q\alpha^2}{2\pi(1 + \alpha)k}\ ; \qquad \tau = \frac{\overline{\vartheta}_1 t}{r_w^2}\ ; \qquad \rho = \frac{r}{r_w}\ ; \qquad \overline{\vartheta} = \frac{k\overline{H}}{\alpha \cdot m}$$

Q = well flow rate

t = time since start of injection

r = distance from the well

r_w = well radius

m = porosity

$\bar{H}$ = mean fresh water thickness

$S(\tau, 1)$ = function tabulated in Hantush (1964)

$W(\mu)$ = confined aquifer well function as shown in any standard book $= \int_u^\infty \frac{1}{e}^{-u} du$, where $u = \frac{r^2 m}{4k\bar{H}t}$.

When the well is near the coast:

$$H^2 = A_1(S(\tau,\rho) - S(\tau,\rho')) \simeq A_1(W(u) - W(u')) \text{ for } t > 30\ r_w^2/\bar{\mathbb{V}}$$

$$\rho' = r'/r_w \ ; \qquad u' = r'^2/4\bar{\mathbb{V}}t$$

r' = distance to the image well (symmetrical respect the coast line).

Since now a portion of the recharged water seeps to the sea, the part of the well injection flow that effectively goes to storage is:

$$Q_r = Q\ \mathrm{erfc}\ \frac{x_o}{\sqrt{4\bar{\mathbb{V}}t}}$$

x_o = distance from the well to the coast

$$\mathrm{erfc}(x) = 1 - \mathrm{erf}(x) = 1 - \frac{2}{\sqrt{\pi}} \int_o^x e^{-x^2} dx.$$

The total fresh water volume in storage up to time t is:

$$V_r = 4Qt\ \mathrm{i^2erfc}\ \frac{x_o}{\sqrt{4\bar{\mathbb{V}}t}}$$

$\mathrm{i^2erfc}$ = second repeated integral of the error function (see Carslaw and Jaeger, 1959).

For an injection drain parallel to the coast, far from the aquifer boundaries:

$$H^2 = A_2\ \sqrt{4\bar{\mathbb{V}}t}\ \mathrm{i^1erfc}\ \frac{(x)}{\sqrt{4\bar{\mathbb{V}}t}}\ ; \qquad A_2 = \frac{qa^2}{(1+a)k}$$

q = injection flow rate per unit width

x = distance to the drain

$\underset{ierfc}{1}$ = first repeated integral of the error function.

When the drain is near the coast, at distance x_o:

$$H^2 = A_2 \sqrt{4\bar{\textit{v}}t} \left[\underset{ierf}{1} \frac{(x)}{\sqrt{4\bar{\textit{v}}t}} - \underset{ierfc}{1} \frac{2x_o + x}{\sqrt{4\bar{\textit{v}}t}} \right]$$

$$H^2(t \to \infty) = 2A_2(x_o + x) \text{ for } -x_o < x \le 0$$

$$= 2A_2x_o \qquad \text{for } 0 \le x .$$

The flow that goes into storage is:

$$q_r = q \text{ erfc } \frac{x_o}{\sqrt{4\bar{\textit{v}}t}}$$

and the fresh water volume until time t is:

$$V_r = 4qt \underset{ierfc}{1} \frac{x_o}{\sqrt{4\bar{\textit{v}}t}} .$$

Other solutions can be found in Hantush (1968). All these solutions depend on $\bar{\textit{v}} = \frac{k\bar{H}}{\textit{am}}$ and $\bar{H}$. The mean value of the fresh water thickness must be calculated beforehand. It needs a stepwise calculation, as described by Hantush (1968).

A more elaborate solution is presented by Gelhar, Wilson and Miller (1972), but it is not ready for practical applications.

Glazunov (1967) studied the case of a saline aquifer with a central pumping well with four radially distributed fresh water recharge wells, when piston flow without density effects can be assumed.

With the four wells operating simultaneously, the time at which a distance r_i is obtained is given by:

$$t = -\frac{\pi m T}{4Q_r - Q_p} \left[r^2 - r_i^2 - 4 \frac{Q_r}{Q_p} \phi \left(\text{arctg } \frac{r^2}{\phi} - \text{arctg } \frac{r_i^2}{\phi} \right) \right]$$

if $Q_r/Q_p < 1/4$

m = effective porosity

T = transmissivity

Q = well flow; r = recharge; p = pumping; all recharge wells inject the same volume rate

r = distance to the recharge wells

r_i = distance to the freshwater front (the two boundaries) along the four perpendicular axis containing the recharge wells.

$$\varphi = r^2 \left(4 \frac{Q_r}{Q_p} - 1 \right)^{-1/2}.$$

The arrival to the pumping well is at:

$$t = \frac{\pi m r^2 \varphi_i T}{4Q_r - Q_p} \qquad \varphi_i = \frac{4Q_r/Q_p}{\sqrt{4Q_r/Q_p - 1}} \ \text{arctg} \ \sqrt{4Q_r/Q_p - 1} \ .$$

Formulae for the case that the central well stops are also given.

In similar situations Grodzensky (1967) studied the formation of fresh groundwater lenses from leaking canals and pits, taking into account density differences, but assuming a constant permeability, a sharp interface and only vertical flow, in a thick salt water body.

For infiltration pits with a constant recharge rate Q:

Distance to the boundary of the lens = $a(t) = \left(\dfrac{8Qkt^2}{\pi m^2 \alpha} \right)^{1/4}$

Water table elevation $h = \sqrt{\dfrac{Q}{2\pi kd}} \left(1 - \dfrac{r^2}{a^2(t)} \right)$

r = radial distance

$\alpha = \rho_f/(\rho_s - \rho_f)$; ρ = density; s = salt; f = fresh water.

When the recharge flow decreases according to $Q(t) = Q_0 \, e^{-\lambda t}$:

$$a(t) = \left(\frac{16 k Q_0}{m^2 \pi \lambda^2 \alpha} (\lambda t + e^{-\lambda t} - 1) \right)^{1/4}$$

$$h(r = 0) = \left(\frac{Q_0}{4\pi k \alpha} \right)^{1/4} \frac{1 - e^{-\lambda t}}{\sqrt{\lambda t + e^{-\lambda t} - 1}} \ .$$

For infiltration canals, with a constant recharge per unit length, q:

$$a(t) = \left(\frac{9qkt^2}{2m^2 \alpha} \right)^{1/2}$$

$$h = \frac{3qt}{ma(t)(1 + \alpha)} \left(1 - \frac{x^2}{a^2(t)} \right)$$

x = distance to the leaking canal.

When the recharge flow decreases according to $q(t) = q_0 e^{-\lambda t}$:

$$a(t) = \left(\frac{9q_0 k}{m^2 \lambda^2 \alpha} (\lambda t + e^{-\lambda t} - 1) \right)^{1/3}$$

$$h(x = 0) = (1 - e^{-\lambda t}) \left(\frac{3q_0^2 \lambda}{8mk\alpha^2 (\lambda t + e^{-\lambda t} - 1)} \right)^{1/3} .$$

8.2.10   Prediction of dispersion

Though mixing or dispersion in the contact between fresh and salt water was analyzed by Wentworth as early as 1948, under the hypothesis of a rinsing action due to tides, the only analytical solution available until present is that of Henry (1964), using stream and concentration functions, solved by the Galerkin's method applied on the Fourier representation of the two above mentioned functions. The solution is for a vertical rectangular cross-section in a homogeneous medium. It is complicated and is not amenable to practical uses without truncation of the series and numerical calculation. It is used as a reference to test model solutions. Henry's solution reproduces the salt water and mixed water flow, so as the sigma form of the isoconcentration lines found in the field.

An approximate solution is due to Gelhar, Wilson and Miller (1972), but it is complicated for practical purposes. The solutions have been studied with a pie-shaped horizontal radial flow model, consisting of a 15-degree sector, filled with uniform plastic beads mixed with epoxy resin. Dispersion effects tend to delay the change in tilting of the interface.

Rumer and Harleman (1963) obtained an approximate solution for the simplified equation:

$$\overline{u(x)} \frac{\partial c}{\partial x} = D(x) \frac{\partial^2 c}{\partial z^2}$$

x   = coordinate parallel to the interface (close to the horizontal)

z   = coordinate across the interface (close to the vertical), from the aquifer top (confined) downwards

c   = salt concentration in water

D   = transverse dispersion coefficient at point x

$\overline{u(x)}$ = mean value of water velocity along the interface = one-half of the

q   = fresh water flow per unit length

m   = effective porosity

z_0 = fresh water thickness.

      The following approximate solution is obtained, when it is assumed that the limits of the transition zone will not touch either the top or the bottom of the aquifer:

$$\frac{c}{c_s} = \frac{1}{2} \, erfc \, \frac{z_0 - z}{\left[\int_0^L dx (D(x)/\overline{u(x)}) \right]^{1/2}}$$

c_s = sea water salinity.

$$erfc(x) = 1 - erf(x) = 1 - \frac{2}{\sqrt{\pi}} \int_0^X e^{-x^2} dx$$

      Near the ocean the interface cannot be considered close to the horizontal, so that the solution is not valid there.

      In a steady interface, since concentration of salts has only a significant variation across it, it can be written (Hunt, 1979):

$$D \frac{\partial^2 c}{\partial z^2} = \frac{\omega}{m} \frac{\partial c}{\partial z}$$

c = salt concentration in water (ground assumed not reactive)

z = vertical coordinate, assumed approximately perpendicular to the interface

D = transverse dispersion coefficient assumed independent of z

m = effective porosity

ω = $- W (1 + z/b)$ = vertical velocity assumed linear from the bottom ($\omega = 0$) to the water table ($\omega = -W$)

W = recharge rate

b = aquifer thickness

At z = - b; c = c_s (sea water concentration).

      The water table is a barrier to the dispersive process.

      The solution is:

$$\frac{c(z)}{c_s} = 1 - \frac{\sqrt{\frac{\pi \varepsilon}{2}} \exp \frac{\varepsilon}{2} \, erf \left[\left(1 + \frac{z}{b} \right) \sqrt{\frac{\varepsilon}{2}} \right]}{1 + \sqrt{\frac{\pi \varepsilon}{2}} \exp \frac{\varepsilon}{2} \, erf \sqrt{\frac{\varepsilon}{2}}} \, ; \qquad \varepsilon = \frac{Wb}{mD}$$

ε is a dimensionless value similar to the Peclet number. The function

$$\text{erf}(x) = \frac{2}{\sqrt{\pi}} \int_0^x e^{-x^2} dx \ .$$

The $c(z)/c_s$ values decrease when W increases. For $\varepsilon < 10$ there is fresh water at the water table, but for greater values only brackish water is found in it.

The situation of stationary salt water below horizontally flowing fresh water, the assumed situation for deep salt and brackish salt water in the Netherlands, has been considered by Verruijt (1971) and Meinardi (1974, 1975). The initial sharp contact is progressively diluted by dispersion in the upper moving layer.

If

x = horizontal distance following the fresh water flow, starting at the inner boundary

z = elevation over the initial interface

it results for a steady supply of salt (a quasisteady solution):

$$\frac{c - c_1}{c_o - c_1} = \text{erfc}\left(\frac{Z}{2\sqrt{X}}\right) - \frac{V}{\sqrt{\pi X}} \exp\left(-\frac{Z^2}{4X}\right)$$

$$Z = \frac{z}{\sqrt{\lambda(\lambda + 2\mu)}} \ ; \qquad X = \frac{x}{\lambda + 2\mu} \ ; \qquad V = \alpha v \sqrt{\frac{\lambda}{\lambda + z}}$$

c   = actual concentration

c_o = sea water concentration

c_1 = fresh water concentration

λ, μ = constants related to v and D, with an order of magnitude equal to the nonhomogeneity dimensions, d (dimension L).

$$\lambda + 2\mu \simeq d \ ; \qquad \lambda = d/8$$

v = fresh water flow velocity (L/T)

D = transverse dispersivity (L^2/T)

α = resistance coefficient to vertical transfer of solutes (T/L), defined from:

$$D \frac{dc}{dz} = \frac{1}{\alpha}(c - c_o)$$

V, X, Z are dimensionless.

The solution is valid for $x \gg 1$ and $x \gg V^2$.

For increasing X:

$$\frac{c - c_1}{c_o - c_1} = \text{erfc} \frac{z}{2\sqrt{X}} \ .$$

For $Z = 0$ (on the initial sharp contact):

$$\frac{c - c_1}{c_o - c_1} = 1 - \frac{V}{\sqrt{\pi X}} \ .$$

In the Netherland's situation, $d = 2$ meters results.

If the fresh water body is also stationary, the only driving force for mixing is molecular diffusion. In that case:

$$\frac{c - c_1}{c_o - c_1} = \text{erf} \frac{z}{2\sqrt{D_m t}}$$

D_m = molecular diffusivity (L^2/T)

t = time (T).

8.3 Prediction methods by means of models

Models to make predictions of coastal aquifer behavior are mainly of the numerical type. They were described in chapter 5.

Most of the models deal with known present situations and try to reproduce the observed situation. There are few cases in which an evolution can be reproduced, since well documented cases are scarce, a special observation network is needed and salt-fresh water relationships change at a slow pace. Little experience exists on the follow-up of predictions.

In many situations, in spite of the lack of an adequate calibration of the models, simple or complicated ones, models are very useful to know the influence of different effects and to allow for the calculation of extreme possible situations.

To make forecasts, a set of logical assumptions on abstraction rates and locations, and recharge patterns in space and time, must be made. When such assumptions are clearly different from that used for the model adjustment, predictions must be done carefully, if it is possible.

One of the common problems is the prediction of the saline encroachment under a maintained or increased abstraction rate under mean recharge conditions, in a large aquifer, in which water movement is slow and fresh water mean residence time is of many years.

One other common problem is the prediction of saline encroachment under certain constant or variable abstraction rates in small aquifers, in which fresh water mean residence time is of a few years. In such situations, salt-fresh water relationships depend heavily on abstraction rates and on the recharge events. There is a special interest in the study of the ability of the aquifer to sustain a given exploitation in high demand periods or under dry conditions. These dry conditions are elected on a 10, 20 or 50 year return period, and are obtained from the hydrometrical records. Thus, they represent real events under a given probability of occurrence.

The model is usually chosen to ensure the attainment of specific objectives and also to suit the accessibility of equations and cost. Establishment of the field to be investigated is important, because the problems connected with the applicability of the model adopted vary with the size of the field.

Aquifer behavior has already been discussed. In other instances the interest focuses on the operation of a well near the coast or above a salt water interface. Yet whether one wishes to study the behavior of the aquifer as a whole or the way an individual pumping well operates, the view of the problem is never total because in the first case parameterization of the dynamic pressures connected with the intruding wedge of seawater is missing, and in the second the consequences of the pumping on the behavior of the zone of dispersion are equally lacking. This has great repercussions, especially in the areas where groundwaters are being pumped most intensively, where the aquifer lacks equilibrium and so the overall view of the hydrodynamic situation can be derived only from symbiosis of the global model and operation of the individual well.

However, to get reliable answers it is advisable to study simple cases, dividing the global vision of the phenomenon from the partial vision thereof.

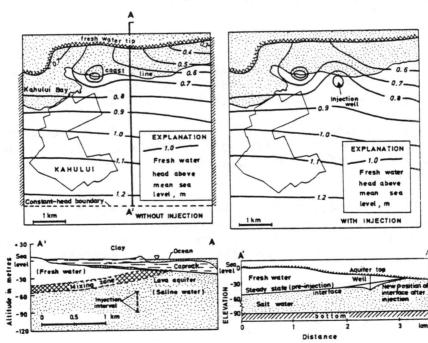

Fig. 8.20 - Prediction of the behavior of the fresh water injected in well, inside the salt water body and close to some wells for cooling an electric facility, near Kahului, Maui, Hawaii (Mercer, Larson and Faust, 1981). The basaltic aquifer is semiconfined in the coast under the 'caprock' formation and some clay layers.

Mercer, Larson and Faust (1981) have applied a sharp interface model to the semiconfined basaltic aquifer near Kahului, Maui, Hawaii, to predict the effect of injecting treated sewage fresh water into the salt water body (fig. 8.20). A simpler model was used to predict the results of different exploitation alternatives in the plain between the rivers Dradere and Sueire, in northwest Morocco (Bonnet and Sauty, 1975; Bonnet and Carlier, 1974); the model was adjusted to reproduce the natural situation, and then used to predict salt water movement and reductions in river flow (figs. 8.21 and 8.22), under three year-long dry periods, with recurrence times of 2, 10 and 40 years.

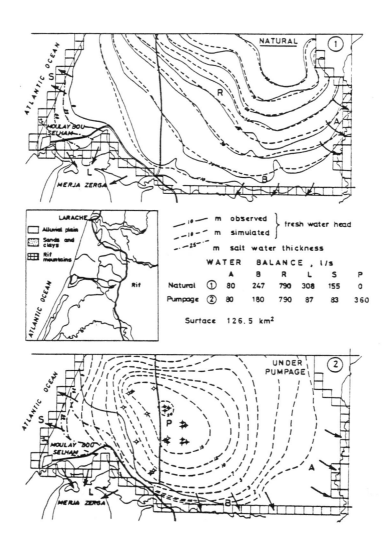

Fig. 8.21 – Predicted effect of the proposed abstraction plan on the salt water wedge for the shown well discharge, after three years, with rainfall recurrence (R) of 2 and 40 years, and the effect on the part of the Dradere River discharge coming from the right side (after Bonnet and Sauty, 1975). The years are hydraulic ones, beginning in October.

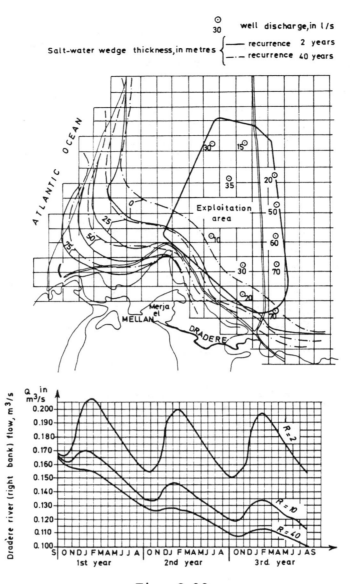

well discharge, in l/s
Salt-water wedge thickness, in metres { —— recurrence 2 years
                                        —.— recurrence 40 years

Fig. 8.22

The interesting and difficult situation in the Hermosillo coastal aquifer (Sonora, Mexico) has been the subject of several studies, the latest being that of Andrews (1981), applying a finite element model to simulate the progress of the salinity in the 2- and 3-layer aquifer. In Apulia (southern Italy), studies on a discretized flow model have provided important results on the evolution of the water table as a result of pumping of fresh water and salt water. The application of this model to a 600 km^2 area required the discretization of 16,000 meshes, each with 200-m sides (Troisi, 1978).

The problem of salt water seepage in polderlands, besides the analytical calculation methods, are being studied with models. Pereboom (1980) applies the finite difference method to a vertical cross-section, using linearized equations, and Schoneveld (1980) solves one and two dimensional cases by means of finite elements.

Fully mixed water (salt transport) groundwater models have been less used due to the lack of an efficient tool and also of scarce data for a right calibration. The attempts of Lee and Cheng (1974), Segol and Pinder (1976) and Pinder (1973) were mentioned in section 5.3.3, and the references can be found in the chapter 5 reference list.

Different prediction models have been applied to oceanic islands. Chidley and Lloyd (1977) use an $\alpha = \rho_f / (\rho_s - \rho_f)$ value of 20, instead of the normal 40 for the fresh water lenses in Grand Cayman Island. It is an experimental value obtained to define the top of the mixing zone, derived from a geoelectrical survey. A maximum of about 12 m of fresh water exists, which can support several consecutive dry years. Under heavy exploitation the fresh water lens breaks down in a few months. The best point for extraction is the center of the island, where the lens is more stable, but only a fraction of recharge can be exploited permanently. A similar model was applied to Tarawa Island (Lloyd et al. 1980), also under natural conditions.

Anderson (1976) solves the situation in a two-layered island by means of finite differences. Since the method used, only considers the existence of horizontal flow as most models do, a simultaneous vertical movement of the interface when the water table changes is implicit. This is not actually true, since the needed wide movements are impossible and then vertical flows cannot be neglected. The assumption of a delayed interface response, adjusted during the calibration process, seems to yield satisfactory results for the interface depth, though it introduces appreciable balance errors.

When dealing with fissured aquifers it must be taken into account that:

- infiltration of rainwaters into fissured rocks and the flow of groundwaters are usually of a random and variable nature;

- flow tends to follow the joint system (diaclases) rather than the minor fractures (leptoclases);

- between one fracture and the next the rock is either dry or encloses motionless waters;

- certain zones or rock horizons which are unfissured or poorly fissured act as aquiclude levels; flow velocity varies from one conduit to another and from one point to another in the same conduit.

Owing to the presence of karst solution processes in carbonate rocks, the development of fractures into conduits is complex and, over the course of time, results in substantial changes in the whole underground flow system. The situation becomes even more complicated in cases where groundwaters in massive rocks float on seawaters that have intruded the landmass.

Physical models have been used mainly for research and laboratory tests, but seldom to solve real situations in coastal aquifers. One of the few existing examples correspond to the west coast of Florida (Christensen and Evans, 1975) and has been used to predict in an easily understandable form the effect of abstractions. It is a vertical Hele-Shaw model. To study the possible salt water pollution of coastal aquifers in western France after oil exploitation, Jeanson and Dufort (1970) made a series of tests in a sand model (glass filled tank). Jones and Memon (1977) have applied Hele-Shaw models to study the optimal pumping regime in chalk and sandstone aquifers in the United Kingdom; the effect of low permeability interlayerings has been studied comparing it to the homogeneous situation.

In order to study fresh water storage in a saline water aquifer by means of recharge and discharge drains, Haitjema (1977) used a Hele-Shaw model to test the validity of other calculation methods.

8.4   References

Ackermann, N.L., Chang, Y.Y. (1971). Salt water interface during ground-water pumping. Proc. Am. Soc. Civil Engineers, J. Hydraulics Division. HY 2 pp. 223-232.

Alvarez, C., Doblas, G., Iglesias, A. (1981). Aspecto hidrodinámico de la intrusión marina (Hydrodinamical aspects of sea water intrusion). Jornadas sobre Análisis y Evolución de la Contaminación de las Aguas Subterráneas en España. Barcelona. Curso Internacional de Hidrología Subterránea. Barcelona. Vol. I, pp. 507-523.

Ambo, K., Haman, K. (1974). The fresh-salt water relationships in a white chalk water-table aquifer at Alborg, Denmark. IV Sea Water Intrusion Meeting, Ghent. Ed. W. de Breuck, 1975. IWD. pp. 141-157.

Anderson, M.P. (1976). Unsteady groundwater flow beneath strip oceanic islands. Water Resources Research, Vol. 12, No. r, pp. 640-644. Washington.

Andrews, R.W. (1981). Salt-water intrusion in the Costa de Hermosillo, Mexico: a numerical analysis of water management synopsis. Ground Water, Vol. 19, No. 6. pp. 635-647.

Babushkin, V.D., Golberg, V.M. (1967). Hydrogeological investigations and estimation of fresh ground water resources in coastal areas. Artificial Recharge and Management of Aquifers. IASH. Simposium Haifa. Pub. 72, 1967, pp. 383-389.

Baeza, H. (1960). Pozos de captación subterránea próximos a la costa (Groundwater captation wells near the coast). VII Interamerican Sanitary Engineering Congress. Montevideo. Also in: Intrusión Marina (Sea Water Intrusion). Ed. S. Arocha Ravelo. Universidad Central de Venezuela. Facultad de Ingeniería.

Basak, P. (1982). Groundwater buildup and depletion in islands during monsoon and summer. Journal of Hydrology, Vol. 56 (182). pp. 265-275. Elsevier.

Bear, J. (1972). Dynamics of fluids in porous media. American Elseiver Publishing Co. Inc., New York, 764 pp.

Bear, J. (1979). Hydraulics of groundwater. McGraw Hill, New York, 567 pp.

Bear, J., Dagan, G. (1962-1966). The transition zone between fresh and salt water in coastal aquifers. Technic Research and Development Foundation. Haifa, Israel: 1962. Progress report no. 1. The steady interface between two immiscible fluids in a two-dimensional field of flow. 125 pp; 1963. Progress report no. 2. A steady flow to an array of wells above the interface, approximate solution for a moving interface; 1964. Progress report no. 3. The unsteady interface below a coastal collector; 1966. Progress report no. 4. Increasing the yield of a coastal collector by means of special operation techniques; 1966. Progress report no. 5. The transition zone at the rising interface below the collector.

Bear, J., Dagan, G. (1963). Intercepting fresh water above the interface in a coastal aquifer. Int. Assoc. Scientific Hydrology, General Assembly Barkeley. Pub. 64 (1964). pp. 154-181.

Bear, J., Dagan, G. (1964). Moving interface in coastal aquifers. Proc. American Society of Civil Engineers, Jornal of the Hydraulics Division, HY 4, Vol. 90, 1964. pp. 193-215.

Bear, J., Zaslavsky, D., Irmay, S. (1969). Physical principles of water percolation and seepage. Arid Zone Research. Unesco. 465 pp.

Bear, J., Kapuler, I. (1981). A numerical solution for the movement of an interface in a layered coastal aquifer. Journal of Hydrology, Vol. 50 (1981). pp. 273-298. Elsevier.

Bond, D.C. (1973). Deduction of flow patterns in variable-density aquifers from pressure and water-level observations. Symp. on Underground Waste Management and Artificial Recharge. New Orleans. Am. Assoc. Petrol. Geologists-United States Geological Survey, Int. Assoc. Scientific Hydrology, pp. 357-378.

Bonnet, M., Carlier, P. (1974). Étude par modeles du dispositiv de captage et consignes d'exploitation optimales d'une nappe littorale en communication avec la mer: le bassin du Dradere-Souerie (Model study of the abstraction works and optimal exploitation rules of a coastal aquifer communicating with the sea: the Dradere-Souerie basin). Bull. BRGM, 2nd Series, Sec. III, No. 1. Paris. pp. 125-135.

Bonnet, M., Sauty, J.P. (1975). Un modele simplifié pour la simulation des nappes avec intrusion saline (A simplified model for the simulation of sea water intruded aquifers). Proc. Bratislava Symp. Sep. 1975. Int. Assoc. Scientific Hydrology, Pub. 115, pp. 45-56.

de Breuck, W. (1978). Groundwater conditions and water supply in the coastal region of Belgium. Seminar on Selected Water Problems in Islands and Coastal Areas with special regard to Desalination and Groundwater. Malta U.N. Economic Comm. Europe. WATER/SEM. 5/R.18. 8 pp.

Brillant, J., de Cazenove, E. (1975). Le modele du terrain stratifié en hydraulique souterraine: application a l'eau douce au-dessus d'eau salée (Stratified terrain model in hydraulics: application to fresh water on salt water). Hydrological Sciences Bull., XX, 2, 6. pp. 233-247.

Bruggeman, G.A. (1975). Analytical treatment of moving fronts in two- and three-dimensional groundwater flow. IV Sea Water Intrusion Meeting. Ghent. Ed. W. de Breuck. Ghent. IHD. pp. 59-84.

Carslaw, H., Jaeger, J.C. (1959). Conduction of heat in solids. Oxford Univ. Press, London, 1959.

Chandler, R.L., McWhorter, D.B. (1975). Upconing of the salt water-fresh water interface beneath a pumping well. Ground Water, Vol. 13, No. 4. pp. 354-359.

Chidley, T.R.E., Lloyd, J.W. (1977). A mathematical model study of fresh-water lenses. Ground Water, Vol. 15, No. 3. pp. 215-222.

Christensen, B.A., Evans, A.J., Jr. (1975). Salt water encroachment in coastal aquifers evaluated by physical models. Water for Human Needs. Proc. II World Congress on Water Resources. Vol. III, New Dehli. Int. Water Resources Assoc. pp. 299-312.

Cohen, Franke, Foxworthy (1969). An atlas of Long Island's water resources. New York Water Resources Commission, Bulletin 62. State of New York.

Collins, M.A., Gelhar, L.W. (1971). Seawater intrusion in layered aquifers. Water Resources Research, Vol. 7, No. 4, pp. 971-979. Washington.

Custodio, E., Llamas, M.R. (1976). Hidrología Subterránea (Groundwater hydrology). Ed. Omega. Barcelona. 2375 pp. 2 Vols.

Custodio, Cruz, Bráz, Jardim, Peixoto (1977). Estudo sobre os perigos de intrucao marinha no aquifero Beberibe (Study on the danger of marine water intrusion in the Beberibe aquifer). Revista de Geociencias. Sociedade Brasiliera de Geologia. Vol. 7, No. 3, Sep. pp. 239-255.

Dagan, G., Bear, J. (1968). Solving the problem of local interface upconing in a coastal aquifer by the method of small perturbations. Journal of the Int. Assoc. Hydr. Research No. 1, Vol. 6, pp. 15-44.

van Dam, J.C. (1975). Fresh water-salt water relationships. IV Sea Water Intrusion Meeting. Ghent. Ed. W. de Breuck. Ghent. IHD. pp. 12-29.

van Dam, J.C. (1975-1976). Partial depletion of saline groundwater by seepage. IV Sea Water Intrusion Meeting. Ghent. Ed. W. de Breuck, Ghent. IHD. pp 107-140. Also in Jornal of Hydrology. Vol. 29 (1976). pp 315-339. Elsevier.

van Dam, J.C. (1977). Determination of horizontal and vertical groundwater flow from piezometric levels observed in groundwater of varied densities. Delft Progress Report Vol. 3. pp 19-34.

van Dam, J.C. (1979). <u>The shape of the fresh-water/salt-water interface in a semi-confined aquifer.</u> VI Salt Water Intrusion Meeting. Hannover. 1979. Geologisches Jahrbuck, 1981. Hannover. pp 149-157.

van Dam, J.C. (1981). <u>Analysis of the possible shapes of the fresh water-salt water interface in a semiconfined aquifer with axial-symmetric boundary conditions.</u> VI Salt Water Intrusion Meeting. Uppsala. Sveriges Geologiska Undersökning. Raporter och Meddelanden No. 27. pp 220-230.

van Dam, J.C., ten Hoorn, W.H.C. (1977). <u>Effects of urbanization on the distribution of fresh and saline groundwater in the Netherlands.</u> Symp. Effects of Urbanization and Industrialization on the Hydrological Regime on Water Quality. Amsterdam. Int. Assoc. Scientific Hydrology. Pub. 123. pp 488-499.

van Dam, J.C., Sikkema, P.C. (1982). <u>Approximate solution of the problem of the shape of the interface in a semiconfined aquifer.</u> Journal of Hydrology, 56 '1982). pp 221-237. Elsevier.

Day, P.R. (1956). <u>Dispersion of a moving salt-water boundary advancing through saturated sand.</u> Trans. Am. Geophys. Union, Vol. 37. pp 595-601.

Dijon, R. (1978). <u>A review of United Nations water resources in coastal areas and islands.</u> Seminar on Selected Water Problems in Islands and Coastal Areas with Special Regard to Desalination and Groundwater Delta. U.N. Economic Commission for Europe. WATER/SEM.5/R.52. 13 pp.

Dijon, R. (1982). <u>Utilisation rationnelle des resources en eau dans les zones cotieres: quelques considérations tirées des activités des Nations Unies en ce domaine</u> (Rational use of water resources in coastal areas: some considerations from the United Nations activities in this field). IV International Conference on Water Resources Planning and Management. Marseille. CEMPE. Vol. 1. 9 pp.

Efros, D.A. (1963). <u>Research on nonhomogeneous system filtration</u> (in Russian). Gostoptejizdat. Leningrad.

Fetter, C.W. (1972). <u>Position of the saline water interface beneath oceanic islands.</u> Water Resour. Res. 8 (5). pp 1307-1315.

Fetter, C.W., Jr. (1972). <u>Position of the saline water interface beneath oceanic islands.</u> Water Resources Research Vol. 8, No. 5. pp 1307-1315. Washington.

Fleet, M., Berenton, N.R., Howard, M.S. (1978). <u>The investigation of saline intrusion into a fissured chalk aquifer on the South Coast of England.</u> Fifth Salt Water Intrusion Meeting. Medmenhann, England. IHD. pp 137-157.

Gelhar, L.W., Wilson, J.L., Miller, J.S. (1972). <u>Gravitational and dispensive mixing in aquifers.</u> Proc. Am. Soc. Civil Engineering. J. Hydraulics Division. H 412. pp 2135-2153. Washington.

Glazunov, I.S. (1967). <u>Artificial formation of fresh ground water lenses by means of wells.</u> Symp. on Artificial Recharge and Management of Aquifers. Haifa, 1967. Int. Assoc. Scientific Hydrology. Pub. 72. Gentbrugge. pp 237-242.

Glover, R.E. (1959). <u>The pattern of fresh water flow in a coastal aquifer.</u> Journal of Geophysical Research. Vol. 64, No. 4, 1959. pp 457-459. Also in: Sea Water in Coastal Aquifers. U.S. Geological Survey Water-Supply. Paper No. 1613-C, 1964. Washington.

Goldberg, V.M. (1973). <u>The movement of fresh and salt water towards a water intake in the coastal areas.</u> Int. Symp. on Development of Ground Water Resources. Madras. Council of Scientific and Industrial Research. India. pp 4.11-4.22.

Goswami, A.B. (1968). <u>A study of salt water encroachment in the coastal aquifer at Digha, Midnapore District, West Bengal, India.</u> Bull. Int. Assoc. Scientific Hydrology, XIII, No. 3. pp 77-87.

Grodzensky, V.D. (1967). <u>Formation of fresh ground water lenses as a result of percolation from canals and pits.</u> Symp. on Artificial Recharge and Management of Aquifers. Haifa, 1967. Int. Assoc. Scientific Hydrology. Pub. 72. Gentbrugge. pp 360-364.

Haitjema, H.H. (1977). <u>Dynamic storage of freshwater in a saline aquifer.</u> V Salt Water Intrusion Meeting. Medmenham, England. IHD. pp 20-37.

Hantush, M.S. (1964). <u>Hydraulics of wells.</u> Advances in Hydroscience. Ed. V.T. Chow. Academic Press, New York and London.

Hantush, M.S. (1967). <u>Growth and decay of ground water mounds in response to uniform percolation.</u> Water Resources Research. Vol. 3, No. 1, first quarter. pp 227-234.

Hantush, M.S. (1968). <u>Unsteady movement of fresh water in thick unconfined saline aquifers.</u> Bull. Intern. Assoc. of Sci. Hydrology. Vol. 13, No. 2. pp 40-60.

Harris, W.H. (1967). <u>Stratification of fresh and salt water on barrier islands as a result of differences in sediment permeability.</u> Water Resources Res., Vol. 3, No. 1.

Haubold, R.G. (1975). <u>Approximation for steady interface beneath a well pumping fresh ater overlaying salt water.</u> Ground Water. Vol. 13, No. 3. pp 254-259.

Henry, H.R. (1959, 1964). <u>Interfaces between salt-water and fresh-water in coastal aquifers.</u> Sea Water in Coastal Aquifers. U.S. Geological Survey Water-Supply Paper No. 1613-C, Washington. pp C35/C70.

Henry, H.R. (1964). <u>Effects of dispersion on salt encroachment in coastal aquifers.</u> Sea Water in Coastal Aquifers. U.S. Geological Survey Water-Supply Paper No. 1613C, Washington. pp C70/C82.

ten Hoorn, W.H.C. (1979). Some calculations concerning the fresh water/salt water interface in the subsoil. VI Salt Water Intrusion Meeting. Hannover, 1979. Geologisches Jahrbuck, 1981. Hannover. pp 177-204.

ten Hoorn, W.H.C. (1981). The shape of a freshwater lens in the case of two aquifers separated by a semipervious layer. VII Salt Water Intrusion Meeting. Uppsala. Sveriges Geologiska Undersökning. Repporter och Meddelanden No. 27. pp 249-261.

Hunt, B.W. (1979). An analysis of the groundwater resources of Tongatapu Island, Kingdom of Tonga. Journal of Hydrology, Vol. 40 (1979). pp 185-196.

Iglesias, A., Rodriguez-Gavela, W. (1978). Pumping tests in high permeability coastal aquifers with sea water intrusion problems. Seminar on Selected Water Problems in Islands and Coastal Areas with Special Regard to Desalination and Groundwater. Malta. U.N. Economic Comm. Europe. WATER/SEM.5/R.14. 5 pp.

Jeanson, B., Dufort, J. (1970). Étude sur modele physique des conditions de pollution des nappes cotieres par l'eau salée lors de la production (Study by a physical model of coastal aquifer salt water pollution problems after production). Bull. BRGM, 2nd Series, Sec. III, No. 3. pp 99-148. Paris.

Jones, G.P., Memon, B.A. (1977). The use of Hele-Shaw models to determine optimal pumping regime in thick coastal aquifers in Britain. V Salt Water Intrusion Meeting. Medmenham, England. IHP. pp 60-71.

Kashef, A.A.I., Smith, J.C. (1975). Expansion of salt-water zone due to well discharge. Water Resources Bull. 11 (6). pp 1107-1120.

Kashef, A.I., Safar, M.M. (1975). Comparative study of fresh-salt water interfaces using finite element and simple approaches. Water Resources Bulletin, American Water Resources Association, Vol. II, No. 4. pp 651-665.

Kishi, Y., Fukuo, Y. (1977). Studies on salinization of groundwater, I: theoretical consideration on the three-dimensional movement of the salt water interface caused by the pumpage of confined groundwater in fan-shaped alluvium. Journal of Hydrology, Vol. 35 (1977). pp 1-29. Elsevier.

Liu, P.L.F., Cheng, A.H.D., Ligget, J.A., Lee, J.H. (1981). Boundary integral equation solutions to moving interface between two fluids in porous media. Water Resources Research, Vol. 17, No. 5. pp 1445-1452. Washington.

Lloyd, J.W., Miles, J.C., Chessman, G.R., Bugg, S.F. (1980). A ground water resources study of a Pacific ocean atoll, Tarawa, Gilbert Islands. Water Resources Bulletin, Vol. 16, No. 4. pp 646-653.

Mather, J.D. (1977). <u>Saline intrusion and ground water development on a</u> <u>Pacific atoll.</u> Fifth Sea Water Intrusion Meeting. Medmenham, England. Int. Hydrological Programme. pp 127-135.

Mather, J.D., Buckley, D.K. (1973). <u>Tidal fluctuations and ground water con-</u> <u>ditions in the Bahamian Archipelago.</u> First Int. Conf. on Ground Water Planning. Palermo.

Meinardi, C.R. (1974). <u>The origin of brackish ground water in the lower parts</u> <u>of the Netherlands.</u> Rijksinstituut voor drinkwatervoorziening. Mededeling 74.6. The Netherlands. 16 pp.

Meinardi, C.R. (1975). <u>Brackish groundwater bodies as a result of geological</u> <u>history and hydrological conditions.</u> Symposium on Brackish Water as a Factor in Development. Beer-Sheva, Israel. Also in: Rijksinstituut voor drinkwatervoorziening. The Netherlands. 22 pp.

Mercer, J.W., Larson, S.P., Faust, C.R. (1981). <u>Simulation of salt-water</u> <u>interface motion.</u> Ground Water, Vol. 18, No. 4. pp 374-385.

Miroshnikov, Y. (1973). <u>Gasto límite del agua dulce en los pozos iperfectos</u> <u>del litoral</u> (Fresh water critical discharge in coastal partially penetrant wells). Voluntad Hidráulica. X No. 27. pp 26-34. La Habana.

Mishra, G.C., Madhay, M.R., Subramanya, K. (1973). <u>Salt-water intrusion due</u> <u>to pumping by two drains in a coastal aquifer.</u> Proc. Int. Symp. on Development of Ground Water Resources. Madras. Council of Scientific and Industrial Research, India. Vol. 2. pp IV-9 - IV-15.

Molenkamp, G.L. (1980). <u>Some results obtained with an analytical solution in</u> <u>a radial symmetric profile.</u> Research on Possible Changes in the Distribution of Saline Seepage in The Netherlands. Committee for Hydrological Research, TNO. Proceedings and Informations, No. 26. pp 77-101.

Monkhouse, R.A., Fleet, M. (1975). <u>A geophysical investigation of saline</u> <u>water in the chalk of the South coast of England.</u> Quarterly Journal of Engineering Geology. London. Vol. 8. pp 291-302.

Mualem, Y., Bear, J. (1974). <u>The shape of the interface in steady flow in a</u> <u>stratified aquifer.</u> Water Resources Research, Vol. 10, No. 6. pp 1207-1215.

Muskat, M. (1937, 1946). <u>The flow of homogeneous fluids through porous media.</u> J.W. Edward Inc. Ann Arbor. pp 480-506.

Muskat, M., Wyckoff, R.D. (1935). <u>An approximate theory of water coning in</u> <u>oil production.</u> Trans. Am. Institute Mining, Metallurgical Petroleum Engineerig. Vol. 114. pp 144-163.

Nutbrown, D.A. (1977). <u>Aquifer management in the context of saline intrusion.</u> Fifth Salt Water Intrusion Meeting, Medmenham, England. Int. Hydrological Programme. pp 78-87.

Obdam, A.N.M. (1979). <u>Calculation of the salinity process of partially penetrating wells in a semi-confined anisotropic aquifer.</u> VI Salt Water Intrusion Meeting, Hannover, 1979. Geologisches Jahrbuch, 1981. Hannover. pp 159–175.

Panigrahi, B.K., Das Gupta, A., Arbhabhirama, A. (1980). <u>Approximation for salt-water intrusion in unconfined coastal aquifer.</u> Ground Water, Vol. 18, No. 2. pp 147–151.

Pedriel, A. (1977). <u>Invasión salina en acuíferos costeros</u> (Sea water encroachment in coastal aquifers). Argentina's National Committee for the United Nations Water Conference. Mar del Plata. Confagua C 13/3. 19 pp.

Pereboom, D. (1980). <u>Some results obtained with a finite difference method.</u> Research on Possible Changes in the Distribution of Saline Seepage in the Netherlands. Committee for Hydrological Research TNO. Proc. and Informations, No. 26. The Hague. pp 50–76.

Pinder, G.F., Page, R.H. (1976). <u>Finite element simulation of salt water intrusion on the South Fork of Long Island.</u> Int. Conf. on Finite Elements in Water Resources, Princeton, N.J. July, Part II. 18 pp.

Rodriguez-Gavela, W., Iglesias, A. (1976). <u>Método de ensayo en acuíferos costeros de alta permeabilidad salinizados por intrusión marina</u> (Test method for high permeability aquifers sea water contaminated). Tecniterrae, III No. 13; August-September. Madrid. pp 55–60.

Rumer, R.R., Harleman, D.R.F. (1963). <u>Intruded sea-water wedge in porous media.</u> Proc. ASCE. Journal of the Hydraulics Division. HY 6. pp 193–219.

Rumer, R.R., Shiau, J.C. (1968). <u>Salt water interface in a layered coastal aquifer.</u> Water Resources Research 4 (6). pp 1235–1247.

Santing, G. (1963). <u>Salt water-fresh water relationships.</u> Chap. 10, The Development of Ground Water Resources with special reference to Deltaic Areas, Trans. Reg. Seminar Develop. Groundwater Resour. Spec. Ref. Deltaic Areas, April 24-May 8, 1962. U.N. Pub. 64. H.F. 5, Economic Commission for Asia ad the Far East and UNESCO (ESCAFE). New York: Water Resources Series No. 39.

Schmorak, S., Mercado (1969). <u>Upconing of fresh water-sea water interface below pumping wells: field study.</u> Water Resources Research, 5 (6). pp 1290–1311.

Schoneveld, J. (1980). <u>The finite element method in fresh saline groundwater.</u> Research on the Possible Changes in the Distribution of Saline Seepage in the Netherlands. Committee for Hydrological Research. TNO. Proc. and Informations, No. 26. The Hague. pp 102–111.

Shani, B.M. (1973). <u>Physics of brine coning beneath skimming wells.</u> Ground Water, Vol. 11, No. 1. pp 19–24.

Shani, B.M. (1973). _Skimming of fresh water afloat upon salt water._ Int. Symp. on Development of Ground Water Resources. Madras. Council of Scientific and Industrial Research. India. pp IV-31/IV-42.

Sikkema, P.C., van Dam, J.C. (1982). _Analytical formulae for the shape of the interface in a semi-confined aquifer._ Journal of Hydrology 56 (1982). pp 201-220. Elsevier.

Strack, O.D.L. (1972). _Some cases of interface flow towards drains._ J. Eng. Math., 6 (2): 175-191.

Strack, O.D.L. (1973). _Many valuedness encountered in groundwater flow._ Thesis, Delft University of Technology, Delft.

Strack, O.D.L. (1976). _A single-potential solution for regional interface problems in coastal aquifers._ Water Resources Research, 12 (6). pp 1161-1174.

Streltsova, T.D., Kashef, A.A.I. (1974). _Critical state of salt-water upconing beneath artesian discharge wells._ Water Resources Bull., Am. Water Res. Assoc. 10, No. 5. pp 995-1008.

Todd, D.K. (1959). _Groundwater hydrology._ John Wiley and Sons. 336 pp.

Todd, D.K., Meyer, C.F. (1971). _Hydrology and geology of the Honolulu aquifer._ Proc. Am. Soc. Civil Engineers, J. Hydraulics Division, HY 2, Feb. Washington. pp 233-256.

Troisi, S. (1978). _Modelli d'inquinamento marino di falde acquifere costiere_ (Model of coastal aquifer marine pollution). Atti covegno su metodologie numeiche per la soluzione di equazioni differenziali dell'idrologia e dell'idraulica, Bressanone, Trento.

Vacher, H.L. (1978). _Hydrogeology of Bermuda: significance of an across-the-island variation in permeability._ Journal of Hydrology. Vol. 39, Amsterdam. pp 207-226.

Vappicha, V.N., Naggaraja, S.H. (1976). _An approximate solution for the transient interface in a coastal aquifer._ Journal of Hydraulics 31 (1976). pp 161-173. Elsevier.

van der Veer, P. (1976). _Calculation method for two-dimensional groundwater flow._ Delft Progress Report 2. pp 35-49. Delft.

van der Veer, P. (1977). _The pattern of fresh and saltwater flow in a coastal aquifer._ Civil Engineering. Delft Progress Report 2. pp 137-142. Delft.

van der Veer, P. (1977). _Analytical solution for a two-fluid flow in a coastal aquifer involving a phreatic surface with precipitation._ Journal of Hydrology, 35 (1977). pp 271-278. Elsevier.

van der Veer, P. (1977). _Fresn and salt groundwater flow in a coastal aquifer._ V Salt Water Intrusion Meeting. Medmenham. IHP. pp 46-59.

van der Veer, P. (1977). <u>Numerical calculation of the behavior in time of an interface between two moving fluids in a polder aquifer.</u> V Salt Water Intrusion Meeting. Medmenham. IHP. pp 38-45.

van der Veer, P. (1978). <u>Calculation methods for two-dimensional groundwater flow.</u> Ph.D. Thesis. Delft. Rijkswaterstaat Communication No. 28 (1978). The Hague.

Venhuizen, K.D. (1975). <u>The shape of the fresh-water pocket under the dune water catchment area of Amsterdam.</u> IV Salt Water Intrusion Meeting. Ghent. Ed. W. de Breuck, Ghent IHD. pp 179-201.

Verruijt, A. (1968). <u>A note on the Ghyben-Herzberg formula.</u> Bull. Int. Assoc. Scientific Hydrology. XIII, 4-12, 1968. pp 43-45.

Verruijt, A. (1971). <u>Steady dispersion across an interface in a porous medium.</u> Journal of Hydrology. Vol. 14 (1971). Elsevier.

Wentworth, C.K. (1948). <u>Growth of the Ghyben-Herzberg transition zone under a rinsing hypothesis.</u> Trans. Am. Geophysical Union. Vol. 29, No. 1. pp 97-98.

9. Methods to control and combat saltwater intrusion

E. Custodio

Contents

9.0   Introduction

As explained in chapter 4, groundwater exploitation in coastal aquifers reduces the fresh water seepage into the sea or other coastal features such as lagoons, estuaries and channels. The generally long delayed response of the interface or mixing zone produces a false security feeling for the sustained exploitations that exceed the safe yield of the system, especially in large aquifers, but on the other side it allows the use of aquifer fresh water storage to meet point demands or to allow for the economic development of an area for several years.

The main principles are presented in chapters 3 and 4, and chapter 5 presents the calculation methods. Here the general concepts and ideas to control and combat saltwater intrusion are presented, the calculation methods being an application of those presented in chapter 8.

When dealing with saltwater intrusion and contamination of aquifers, the main objective is the conservation of groundwater quality in the abstraction work (well, gallery, ditch, trench, etc.), from lateral saltwater encroachment as well as from upconing when saltwater occupies the lower part of the aquifer.

The exploitation of a coastal aquifer implies consideration of:
- how to develop a coastal aquifer
- how to prevent salinization
- methods to remedy and stop sea water intrusion
- methods to maintain an existing exploitation

9.1 General considerations to prevent sea water intrusion

Some rules to prevent sea water intrusion are:

- total annual abstraction from the aquifer must be less than total recharge. The smaller the coastal strip in which salinization is accepted, the less the safe yield of the aquifer.

- concentrated abstractions must be avoided as much as possible, especially near the coast.

- when fresh water floats on salt water, abstraction works must limit their discharge and penetration in the aquifer, and the drawdown must be as small as possible.

- protective horizontal impervious or low permeability layers must be looked for and preserved in order to limit sea water upconing.

- when salt water exists under the well, discharge must be less than the critical value. It is not clear whether continuous or intermittent pumpage is preferable in order to avoid dispersion. Tidal induced fluctuations or lack of regulation capacity may impose other exploitation schedules.

- a carefully installed and operated water level and depth-salinity control network must exist, and an annual or biannual report must be prepared to show salinity changes and trends. The observation of abstracted water salinity is not enough, and some years without adverse effects do not necessarily signify that the operation is safe.

- aquifer recharge sources must be protected as much as possible.

- a sustained regional groundwater drawdown below sea level is a continuous risk of sea water intrusion, including for confined coastal aquifers, except when the aquifer is fully isolated from the sea, and the wells do not destroy such isolation.

- prevention can be forever or for an economical time period. This changes the protective measures to be undertaken.

- in coastal areas, in order to reduce and extend as much as possible the effective drawdown around abstraction areas, horizontal impervious or semipervious layers, placed over the salt water must be located and used, if they exit.

- when salt water can be expected in the lower part of the aquifer, horizontal stratification and reduced penetration of the well are favorable factors in sea water encroachment prevention. Vertical permeable discontinuities, such as faults and open joints, must be avoided as much as possible. This is especially important in hard rock aquifers. In low permeability old volcanics, dikes increase vertical permeability and sea water penetration is favored if they are perpendicular to the coast, but they aid in prevention if they are parallel to the shore line.

- well construction in coastal areas must be carefully carried out in order to conserve protective layers and to prevent vertical flow from one aquifer to another. Special specifications must be included in drilling contracts in order to be sure that the annulus between the tube well and the borehole well is sealed, especially in front of the less pervious layers. All this must be applied also to exploratory boreholes, piezometers and other control works.

- when a well or borehole is abandoned, it must be filled up with grout or cement or clay, in such a way as to prevent any vertical circulation of salt water, including after the well casing becomes corroded or broken. It requires special administrative regulations.

- in areas with a wide tidal range, when highly permeable terrains occur, pumped water salinity many change according to the tidal stage. A careful pumping and rest schedule, coupled with a regulating small reservoir, can aid in improving water quality, concentrating the abstraction when ground water salinity is low. Something similar can be done in littoral springs and fractures influenced by the tidal stage, including when partially flooded at floodtide.

9.2 Construction and operation of abstraction works

The most common groundwater abstraction work is the well. When no salt or brackish water exists, a normal well is used. When salty water underlays fresh water, there is a danger of salt water upconing. The pumping rate and penetration must be limited. Some simple calculations methods of salt water upconing have been given in chapter 8.

The development of a thick transition zone under the well, especially when no seaward flow exists, is one of the main sources of salinization of the abstracted water.

A well drilled just to sea level is not necessarily protected against salinization because, since brackish water is lighter than sea water, it may reach the well bottom. Generally this only occur when the discharge is high or when the fresh water thickness is very small, but in the latter case the well penetrates only a few centimeters, and only a small discharge is possible, except if a fissure is intersected in hardrock, or a fan of horizontal drains are drilled inside the well at sea level.

If enough fresh water flow exists, the well can penetrate below sea level, but the discharge must be carefully controlled in order to maintain a small drawdown, that is to say less than the piezometric altitude over mean sea level. This drawdown is that existing in the outer part of the well, that is to say, after subtracting the well losses.

In order to get a higher discharge per well without excessive salinization, the small drawdown must be distributed over a surface as great as possible. This can be attained by constructing horizontal drains or galleries inside the well, just at sea level. A large diameter well or shaft is needed.

In homogeneous islands, the best solution from a theoretical point of view is a peripheral drain or array of wells placed midway between the center and the coast, but in mountainous islands some other less efficient solutions are preferable.

In unconsolidated materials, such as beach sands, modern radial drain wells, fitted with 20 to 50 m drains 100 to 200 mm in diameter, can be constructed, using some of the existing commercial methods. But the high cost of such a well may preclude its construction from an economic point of view, especially if the discharge must be kept low to avoid salinization.

In hardrock, well development by means of explosives, hydrofracturing or acid treatment must be carried out, but some care is needed to avoid an increase in vertical permeability or the enlargement of more penetrating fissures. If the well development or stimulation guarantees the enlargement of only horizontal fissures, it is highly recommended. The advice of a specialist is desirable.

Galleries are also drilled to catch coastal fresh water. In order to attain the sea level from ground surface, a sloping initial part of the gallery exists, as done in some areas of the Hawaiian Islands. The galleries just skim the water table or penetrate only a few decimeters. To control water salinity, weirs and sluices can be installed. Access to the gallery can also be had through a shaft, as mentioned above.

A well fitted with bottom galleries or drains, and a gallery finishing in a well, are water abstraction works responding to similar principles.

When only a gallery is drilled, it can be oriented in two ways. In order to catch as much groundwater flow as possible, the gallery must be parallel to the coast. But if an improvement in water quality is the goal, it must be perpendicular to the coast in a landward direction.

On Malta, where only a thin fresh water lens floats on salt water, a shaft is excavated to sea level, and then a radial set of galleries is completed, some of them of more than a kilometer length. The bottom of the galleries is at sea level or penetrates a few decimeters under sea level. As a consequence of water withdrawal, brackish water can reach the bottom. In order to maintain an acceptable upper salinization limit, the water level inside the galleries is controlled by means of a weir placed near the entry. Water is collected at the shaft bottom and pumped out. Since these abstraction works are placed near the center of the island a high water elevation is needed.

In the Canary Islands, a 2.5 to 3m diameter shaft is also excavated in the volcanic materials, and horizontal galleries are then excavated at sea level, mostly in a landward direction, since they are placed in narrow coastal plains or creek bottoms. At present the galleries have been changed for drilled horizontal 2 in. to 3 in. diameter boreholes with a length between 50 to a few hundred meters (400 m is a maximum). The drilling machine, electrically driven, is placed at the well bottom and a small cave is excavated at the opposite side in order to facilitate the drilling operations.

In elevated, rough coastal areas, the location of the gallery entry or access well depends on the topography. Sometimes it may be placed near the shore, where no fresh water can be obtained. One solution is to excavate a long horizontal gallery far enough from the sea to be able to find exploitable fresh water. In this case, if the groundwater table is high enough, fresh water can be obtained by gravity. One other solution is to begin the gallery in the mountain slope, well above sea level, and when penetration is sufficient, excavate a well at the gallery bottom, in which a pump is installed. If necessary, the well can be fitted with bottom galleries or drains, but usually it is too expensive since the work must be done under difficult conditions. One other possibility is to drill small diameter (3 in. to 8 in.) vertical boreholes and to extract the water with an air lift pump or, if the depth to the water table is small, to use a suction pump connected to all the tubes. Figure 9.1 shows schematically some of the possibilities mentioned.

When the depth to the water table is small, trenches are better than galleries and horizontal drains. These trenches may be open works, but in order to protect water quality, a perforated pipe or tube is often colocated in the bottom, surrounded by appropriate permeable material, and then the trench is refilled with the excavated earth, with an impermeable upper cover if necessary.

In order to collect the fresh water flowing into the sea after performing the task of maintaining the interface position, an interceptor drain can be installed along the shore line (fig. 9.2). The water will always have some salt contamination. The installation and operation of such an abstraction work needs great care and the cost of the water is high. Several proposals and studies have been carried out in Israel (Bear and Dagan, 1964; Kahana, 1964; Shechter and Schwartz, 1970).

Fresh water littoral springs can be tapped by standard methods, but attempts to increase the flow by deepening the outlet increase water salinization, and the works that elevate the resurgence level may reduce or stop the discharge. The development work can be improved if a collector drain is installed at the right altitude.

When water flows through a fissure in the rock, separated from the sea by low permeability sediments, these protective sediments must be carefully conserved and improved.

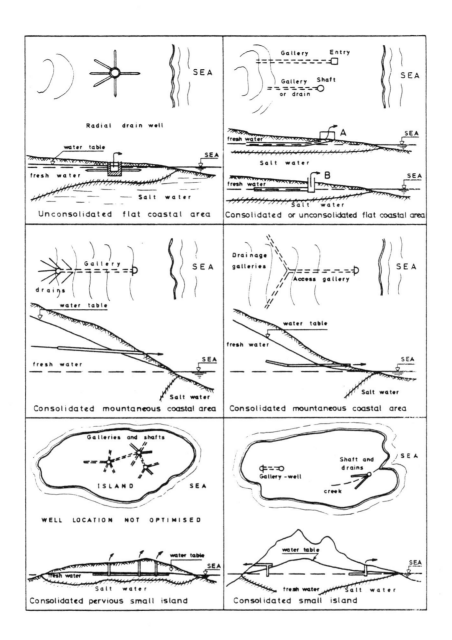

Fig. 9.1 – Schematic representation of several coastal situations exploited by means of special works such as radial wells, galleries, shafts and a combination of them. They are based on real situations in the Canary, Hawaii and Malta islands.

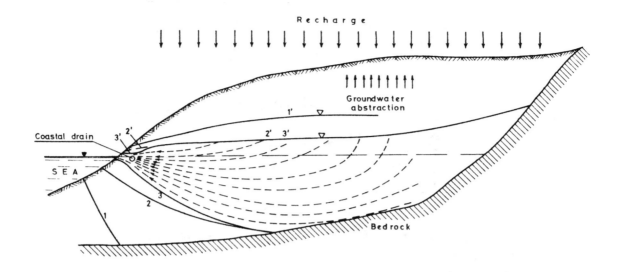

Fig. 9.2 – Coastal drain to intercept the fresh water discharging to the sea after maintaining a certain interface situation. 1' and 1 are respectively the water table and the interface in natural conditions. The new equilibrium after a certain exploitation (less than the recharge) is represented by water table 2' and interface 2. The coastal drain alters the groundwater flow near the coast and water table changes to 3' and the interface raises up to 3. Some mixing of waters is unavoidable and the intercepted water will be slightly brackish, so much the more important is the percentage of intercepted flow (after Bear and Dagan, 1964; Kahana, 1964).

9.3   Exploitation of coastal springs

Submarine fresh or brackish springs are very difficult to tap in spite of numerous attempts having been made in many parts of the world, sometimes involving the constructing of ingenious equipment (fig. 9.3). Direct abstraction presents serious problems, because the influence of sea water must be avoided as much as possible, constructing enclosures to isolate the outlet from the sea (fig. 9.4). If pumping is carried out, a small drawdown can easily cause sea water contamination through the existing open fissures, and when a small level increase is allowed, the fresh water frequently finds another outlet. When an attempt is successful, as in the case of a well-defined submarine exit, the preservation of the water work during severe storms may be very difficult. There are curious descriptions of the provision of water to cities or ships (including submarines) from these submarine springs in war time, but the quantities involved are relatively small and possibly the water obtained was slightly brackish.

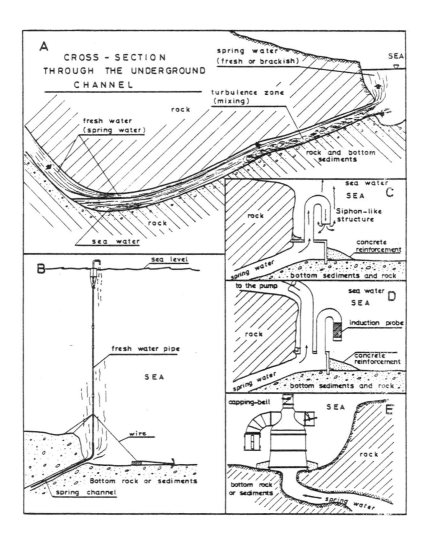

Fig. 9.3 - Possible methods to abstract fresh water from submarine springs (after Stefanon, 1973a; 1973b). (A) shows the general phenomenon: the spring water exits through the upper part of the channel, leaving space for the sea water to enter the mouth and to descend to the lowest part; some of the sea water is dragged out by turbulence and mixing with fresh water. (B) shows a dispositive to protect some of the outflowing fresh water from being sea water contaminated. (C) shows a siphon-like structure to avoid the saline contamination at the spring mouth; if the structure is correctly designed, sea water will be unable to ascend the outer descending part of the tube. (D) shows an abstraction structure with a siphon to control sea water-fresh water interface by means of an induction probe. (E) shows a capping bell as placed in the outlet of Citrello spring, in Taranto, southern Italy; the bell permits an easy connection with a pump and the siphon allows for the control of the salt-fresh water interface. It is supposed that a unique outlet exists without satellite fissures. When they exist, the fresh water abstraction may be impossible.

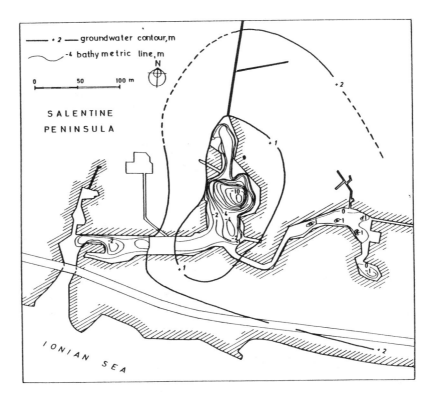

Fig. 9.4 - The Chidro spring, in the Salentine Peninsula (Italy). The main outlet is inland and connected with the sea by means of a natural canal. Daming this canal has been proposed in order to isolate the direct surface effect of the sea (Cotecchia 1976a). The illustration shows: (a) sluice dam, (b) conduit, (c) reservoir.

The same is applicable to littoral caverns and underground channels. Attempts to pump fresh water (usually it is slightly brackish), inclusive at great distance from the sea, usually fail because salinity increases very fast. A horizontal cavern at sea level is like a coastal river, and a layer of salt water exists in its bottom. If the channel runs below sea level, the fresh water head must be enough to overcome the equivalent fresh water head corresponding to the sea at the outlet depth. Thus, as described in section 3.3, most of these channels discharge or the water is diffused through small fractures. These fractures act as a way for sea water penetration in low discharge periods and are the main way of contamination when any significant pumping is attempted. Some small abstractions can be sustained under favorable circumstances, but the high investments generally do not pay for the small quantity of fresh or slightly brackish water recoverable.

The attempts to dam the spring outlet near the sea do not produce the desired effects because other minor exit ways exist or can develop, and the dam may be destroyed easily in one of the peak discharges typical in karst areas, except if a weir or automatic gates are provided, thus greatly complicating and overrating the work, if feasible at all. A dam inside the underground channel, sufficiently far from the coast, is very expensive and must provide an overflow system for high discharge periods. It can only be done when the channel is visitable by divers and an access well to reach from ground surface to the desired site must be constructed. Such a work has been recently finished in Port Miou (fig. 9.5), in the French Mediterranean coast (Potié, 1973; Potié and Ricour, 1978). The underground channel is under sea level, and a salt layer penetrates deeply. The dam has been constructed in such a form that upstream salt water could be expelled through under-the-dam outlet tubes when raising the water level upstream. When the salt water was completely expelled, the dam was finished (fig. 9.6). Total fresh water out-flow is about $2m^3$/s but only $0.5 \ m^3$/s are to be recovered by the Marseille Water Works. Though the project is not fully finished, first attempts to pump fresh water have failed, and only brackish water was obtained, possibly due to the existence of small fissures that carry salt water. Anticipated cost of water is rather high, though not excessive in that area.

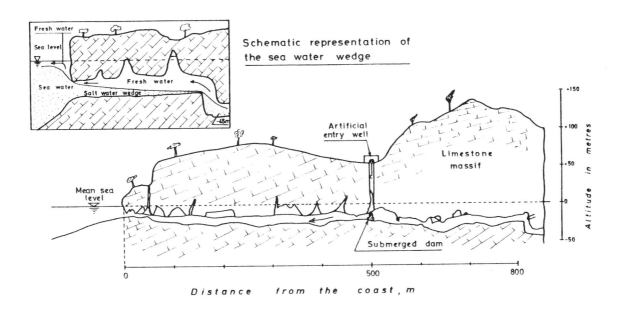

Fig. 9.5 - The channel of the Port Miou (Cassis, near Marseille, France) submarine fresh water spring, after Potié (1973). The channel has been
explored by divers to 850m from the sea outlet. At 500m from the
coast a underground submerged dam has been placed (see fig. 9.6).

9.4   Methods to improve or remedy sea water intruded aquifers

Remedying a sea water encroached aquifer is a very difficult task. Not only must intruded sea water be expelled and substituted by fresh water, but also trapped salts in closed or halfclosed pores in the ground must be washed out. This calls for a high quantity of fresh water. The process is very expensive and takes a long time, longer than the salinization time, usually many years. In many circumstances, in a human time scale, the sea water encroached part of an aquifer must be considered an irreversible situation.

       Most of the methods described below are passive ones, in the sense they do not actively deal with the sea water intruded part of the aquifer.

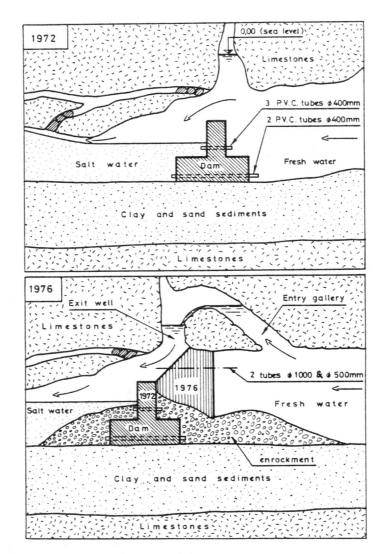

Fig. 9.6 - Scheme of the dam constructed inside the Port Miou submarine spring
(Cassis, near Marseille, France), at 500m from the sea outlet (after
Potié and Ricour, 1978). The first phase was to drain out sea water
existing upstream and to prepare the site. In the final phase an
overelevation of fresh water have been created and a spill-weir was
constructed, taking advantage of rock forms. The comportment under
abstraction is not yet known. The dam has been built through an
artificial access well and with the aid of a special team of divers.

9.4.1   Abstraction reduction

A first possibility to remedy an existing situation is to reduce abstraction,
especially in the most impaired areas and near the coast. The importance of
water abstraction reduction depends on a reappraisal of the aquifer safe yield
based on global balances and, if possible, with the aid of a model. Historical records of the hydrological variables involved are needed, especially
those related to the interface movement. Problems related to salt water
upconing must be separated in order to know if salinization is due to salt
water penetration or to incorrect construction and operation of water
abstraction works.

A permanent landward groundwater gradient in the coast is a sure warning that an overdraft exists in a water table aquifer, though in confined aquifers it does not necessarily mean a close danger of sea water intrusion.

In aquifers in which a significant part of the recharge is obtained through induced river infiltration or leakage from other aquifers of surface fresh water bodies, a reduction in abstraction is not fully effective in diminishing sea water intrusion because fresh water recharge may decrease at the same time. In this case and when pumping is too close to the coast, a relocation of water abstraction works is an attractive alternative in order to maintain fresh water recharge and to reduce local excessive drawdown near the coast.

The problems involved in that situation are: (a) the economic loss of abandoning existing investments; (b) the establishment of new and probably long water transportation canals and pipes; (c) generally a higher energy consumption since the new wells will usually be in areas with deeper water levels; and (d) the need to convince people or organizations to accept such a solution and to enforce it by special regulations.

A simple reduction of total abstraction is not always an easy task. A special regulation must be enforced or people and organizations must be convinced of the need of the groundwater savings. A water district or some kind of user's organization can be a good solution. A careful survey of distribution networks often produces an important reduction in fresh water losses. This is important when the served area is outside the aquifer, but not so important from the aquifer point of view if lost water returns to it. The same can be said of agricultural uses. Domestic water use is difficult to be reduced, but warnings about the problems associated with wasting water and the presentation of benefits and practice of water conservation may produce positive results. Also, an increase in water price when water use exceeds certain limits can yield positive results, though they are not spectacular, but they may create social complaints.

9.4.2   Abstraction substitution

In order to get an important groundwater abstraction reduction, important socioeconomic changes have to be introduced in the area. This is something difficult, frequently undesirable, and may create economic and social problems. A dramatic abstraction reduction must be linked with new water sources to substitute the suppressed groundwater abstractions.

If some water uses tolerate brackish or salt water, some sea water contaminated wells can be devoted to such uses, thus helping the protection of other wells, but a special sewage network must be needed to take this water without affecting the sewage treatment plants and the nearby aquifers.

9.4.3   Artificial recharge

The aquifer fresh water balance can be improved through artificial recharge, if enough water is available. The question about the direct use of that water to supply demand or its utilization for aquifer recharge immediately arises. The answer depends on many circumstances, such as the duration and time in which that water is available, the place where it is, the water quality and the need for treatment, the water transportation works available, the existing storage facilities, the feasibility of artificial recharge and the distance from the place where water is, etc. Artificial recharge is a means to reach certain objectives and not an objective in itself.

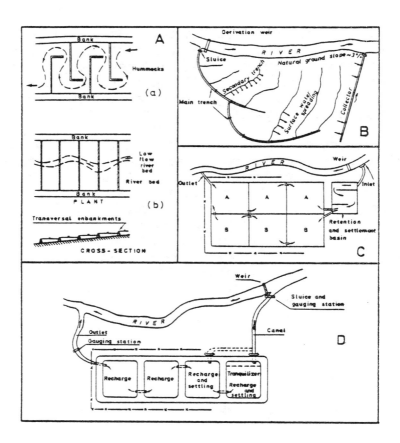

Fig. 9.7 - Different methods of artificial recharge in or near a water stream. Recharged water may restore or increase ground water recharge, and aid in the control of sea water intrusion. (A) Recharge in the river bed; (a) is useful when recharge is only a fraction of the river flow; (b) is useful when all the river discharge is infiltrated or the dams are fitted with overspill structures. (B) Recharge by means of canals and ditches in a river alluvial plain or in an alluvial fan. (C) Recharge through a system of lateral basins. (D) Recharge through a single set of basins.

The sources of water for artificial recharge vary according to local circumstances, and also with the possibility to introduce that water into the ground. Possible sources, when available, are river water (fig. 9.7), flood water (fig. 9.8), imported water, treated or raw sewage water (fig. 9.9 and 9.10), cooling water, etc. Water may be recharged in the river channel, or in other surface locations, including flood control structures, or through wells. A long experience exists in southern California, the Netherlands, Israel, etc. (see chapter 10), and is under study in other areas such as Sicily, Catalonia, Majorca and Tunis, (Bensalah et al., 1975). A recent review of artificial recharge methods can be found in Custodio (1980).

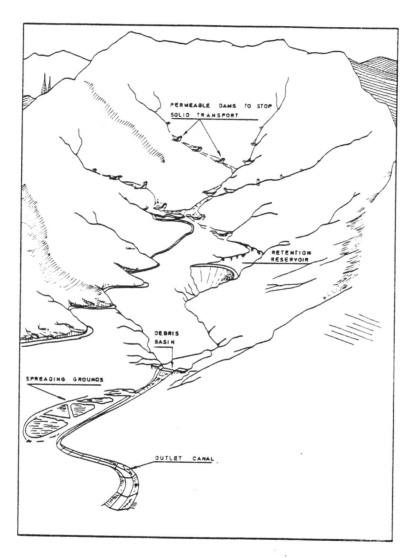

Fig. 9.8 - Headwater basin management to control floods as applied near Los Angeles, California. Runoff is damped in the creek erosion control reservoir. Water released downstream, is clarified in a settling basin and then spread in lateral grounds in order to increase groundwater recharge in the alluvial fan.

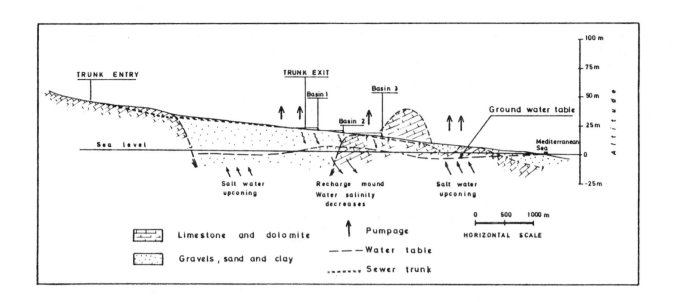

Fig. 9.9 - Hydrogeological cross-section of the Sitges-Sant Pere de Ribes
plain, along the Vilafranca Creek, south of Barcelona (Spain). The
creek carries sewage water directly discharged in it, 20 km
upstream. In the area a reasonable partial selfdepuration has taken
place and this water was recharged temporarily by means of small
earth dams, that were rebuilt after the floods. This recharge
improved water salinity in an area affected heavily by salt water
upconing (after Custodio Suárez, and Galofré, 1977). The flood was
highly effective in maintaining the infiltration capacity. The
method was applied for about 2.5 years.

The smaller the infiltration surface, the greater are the recharge
problems. Then, infiltration by surface spreading is much easier than well
recharge, but surface recharge needs a large area and it can only be done if
low permeability layers between the surface and the water table do not exist.
Water flow through the unsaturated zone favors water autodepuration and protects the aquifer from certain pollutants. In this respect, surface recharge,
when possible, is superior to well recharge.

Generally, artificial recharge is expensive and an economic study
must be undertaken to know the real benefits. Artificial recharge feasibility
depends on the specific aquifer characteristics, and thus experience from one
area cannot easily be transferred to another area. Careful preliminary tests
must be carried out in order to find the right recharge system, the best water
pretreatment or quality standards and the most correct operation and maintai-
nance of the facilities.

Artificial recharge must be studied together with abstraction in order to minimize sea water intrusion and fresh water losses to the sea. An aquifer simulation model is very useful in this respect and it allows for correct planning in order to avoid local disequilibria. Such planning needs legal power or public consent to enforce it. Many artificial recharge projects are unfeasible due to some kind of legal problem (property of the water, distribution of costs and benefits, etc.). Sometimes subtle legal considerations must be involved. The State of California has made substantial progress in such directions.

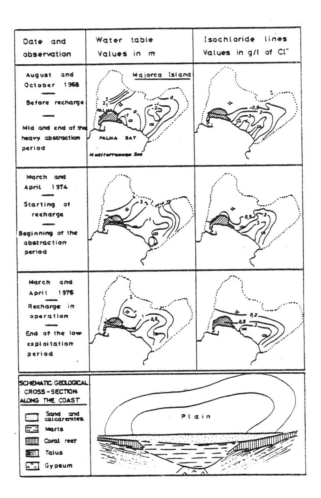

Fig. 9.10 - Changes in water table elevation and groundwater salinity as a consequence of treated sewage water recharge through wells in the clastic limestone aquifer of the Llano de Palma (Majorca, Balearic Islands, Spain). The general improvement is the combined result of the recharge and a tight control on new wells (after Iglesias and Porras, 1978). Water is used exclusively for irrigation. The schematic geological cross-section is a personal communication from Barón and Bayó (1979).

9.4.4   Well correction

From another point of view, if salinization is caused by leaky wells and boreholes, it is necessary to repair them. It supposes recasing of the well, cementing certain zones, isolating a part of it, etc. It is not an easy task and sometimes the best thing is just fill up the well in such a way as to seal the salty horizons.

Detection and location of leaky wells and boreholes is generally very difficult. A record of the salinity changes during the first minutes of pumping is generally very useful, as also are studies of vertical water circulation inside suspected wells by means of highly sensible current meters of by means of tracers, generally radioactive. When enough points of chemical control exit, a localized salinity source can be found through inspection of the isosalinity lines pattern, but such a situation seldom occurs clearly.

Old abandoned wells may become a future problem, especially when they penetrate various aquifers. Many of these wells just disappear when there is a land use change, without any backfilling. They may create future problems, very difficult to correct. Well abandoning must be strictly surveyed.

9.5   Methods to maintain the existing aquifer exploitation

When the reduction of groundwater abstractions is not a desirable or feasible alternative, and sea water is encroaching the aquifer, two main solutions exist. One is to increase aquifer recharge, as commented in the foregoing paragraph, and one another is to create barriers against sea water penetration. This 1st alternative will be explained below, in a qualitative form. Quantitative methods can be easily developed from the calculation methods presented in chapter 8. Most of the methods described must be considered active ones.

9.5.1   Physical barriers

An obvious sea water barrier, though not practical, is a sufficiently impermeable wall along the coast, penetrating the whole aquifer thickness. Certainly this does not solve overpumping, but it allows to abstract all the aquifer recharge and in the case of a water table aquifer, the used storage capacity increases because greater water table oscillations can be applied.

Such a barrier can be built in unconsolidated materials with sheet-piles, or filling up deep trenches with clay, cement, concrete or asphalt. The costs are very high. Only small penetrations can be practically attained. It is generally better, in consolidated or unconsolidated materials, to reduce the ground permeability by pressure injection of cement, bentonite, bituminous substances or some special chemicals such as silica-gel, calcium acrylate or some expansive substances, by means of close spaced boreholes along the coast, 2 to 4m apart, generally in two or three alternating rows. The effectiveness of the operations needs a careful control of the works. In highly permeable formations it is difficult to achieve a substantial permeability reduction, though some new substances seem very effective. The attainable depth is also small and generally 30 m is a practical limit.

The main inconveniences are:

- very high cost.

- limitation in the penetration attainable, through a partially penetrating barrier already contributes to reduce fresh water outflow and sea water penetration.

- difficulties in dealing with high permeability layers.

- possible high maintenance costs when ground movement or siesmic shocks are frequent. If not, the maintenance cost of a well constructed physical barrier can be very low.

No examples of these barriers can be mentioned, and the envisaged projects have been abandoned after the feasibility study and cost-benefit evaluation. Perhaps it is feasible in small coastal alluvial formations to meet short term demands when the water price is very high.

An appreciable reduction in permeability can be achieved by air injection into the saturated zone through some rows of boreholes fitted with short screens. The air is taken in place and neither uptake nor disposal systems for the fluid is needed. Only small pilot experiments are known (Roberts, 1967).

9.5.2   Injection hydraulic barriers

Probably the most effective and cheap barrier is a hydraulic barrier, of which several good examples exist, mainly in California (Bruington and Sears, 1965; Bruington, 1972). A hydraulic barrier can be built up by recharging fresh water along the cost or by pumping sea water from the ground, or by a combination of both methods.

If fresh water is recharged along the coast in such a form as to maintain in every one of the aquifers a fresh water head that in any point is higher than that needed to balance the salt water head, sea water intrusion is impeded.

Since the fresh water head inside a salt water body increases with depth, the deeper the aquifer the greater must be the fresh water head elevation to be created.

In water table aquifers, without low permeability layers between the ground surface and the water table, the hydraulic recharge barrier can be created by coastal leaking canals, trenches or infiltration fields, if the ground surface is at an altitude over sea level enough to allow the creation of a sufficiently high fresh water elevation (fig. 9.11).

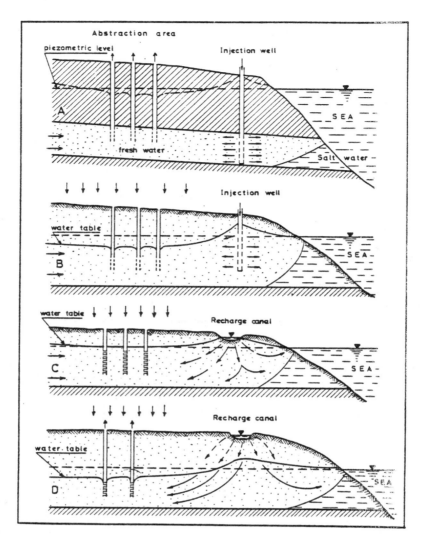

Fig. 9.11 - Different types of hydraulic recharge barriers. (A) By means of wells in a confined aquifer. (B) By means of wells in a water table aquifer; ground elevation is enough to avoid land surface logging by injected water. (C) By means of a recharge canal in hydraulic connection with the aquifer. (D) By means of a recharge canal separated from the water table by an unsaturated zone; infiltration is not influenced by water table depth.

These surface recharge facilities are used in the Amsterdam dune field. In urbanized areas they pose certain problems such as lack of enough space, interference with roads and streets, and perhaps sanitary nuisances, and moreover the cost of the land is generally too high.

One other alternative is the use of injection wells, in one or two lines, creating a fresh water injection barrier. Well distance is a compromise between the investment and maintenance costs and the injection water needs. Injection water flow increases with well spacing, because the mean fresh water elevation is higher in order to guarantee the minimum elevation in the mid-point between the wells.

In confined aquifers or when a low permeability layer exists close to the surface of the ground, the injection well is the only solution (fig. 9.11). A different well system must be constructed for every one of the involved aquifers in order to attain in every one of them the needed piezometric head with the right recharge inflow. In Los Angeles (California), in order to avoid wells of different penetration, a single well is sometimes used to inject water in the multiaquifer system, separating the different screens with grout and recharging differently the various aquifers with the aid of packers that isolate the water injection pipes (fig. 9.12). Kashef (1976) presents some calculation methods in ideal conditions. These can be derived easily from classical well hydraulics and from the methods explained in chapter 5.

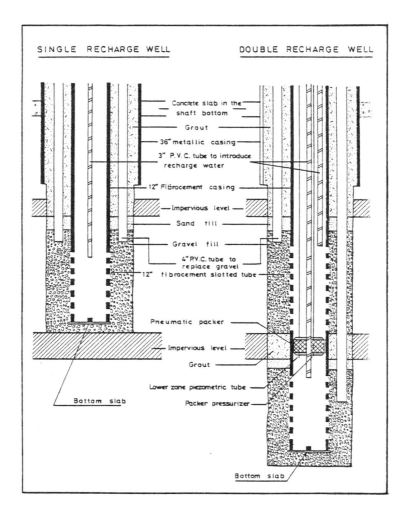

Fig. 9.12 – Schematic profiles of a single well and a double well for groundwater recharge as used in the Alamitos sea water intrusion barrier (California). In order to effectively control the sea water intrusion a different fresh water head must be reached in every one of the sublayers and aquifers, and to avoid an excessive water recharge flow, the injection in one layer must be separated from the other layers.

Wells have the advantage of using less ground surface, but space for the pipes, connections, well heads, etc., must be provided, and also to carry out the periodical well cleanings.

A hydraulic injection barrier is costly because wells and fixtures are expensive, but also water is more expensive because water must be clean in order to avoid clogging the wells within a short time. Injected water is usually of potable quality, though studies are being carried out to determine the feasibility of using treated sewage water for injection (Bargman, Adrian and Tillman, 1974; Cohen and Durfor, 1966; Custodio, Suárez and Galofré, 1976, Shuval, 1977; Custodio, Tourís and Balagué, 1981). Different experiments around the world have been reviewed in Custodio (1980).

Water must be introduced through a submerged pipe in order to avoid air-entraining. Entrained air reduces local transmissivity sharply, and in confined aquifers it may cause damaging explosions. Wells must be cleaned and redeveloped periodically. In the West Coast Basin Barrier Project (Los Angeles, California) well cleaning is carried out with a one to two year interval. The injection pipes are removed and a drilling rig is mounted. The cleaning can be done by installing a pump and pumping the well intermittently, until capacity is restored as far as possible. The treatment can be aided by the use of chemicals (polyphosphates, hydrochloric acid, sulphamic acid, chlorine, etc.), depending on the nature of the clogging substance. The chemicals used must be the right ones, not only because they are expensive, but also because poor selection or application may seriously damage the well. Bailing and surge-plunge can be also applied, but generally their use is limited to severely damaged wells. If the operation is correct, pumping is enough to restore well capacity.

In some situations the pumped water during the clean-up operations is a great nuisance and their disposal is a major problem, when not in urban areas. Pumping by air lift can be used, isolating short lengths of screens with the aid of packers. The small quantity of abstracted water is temporarily stored and settled in a big drum, and the clean water is then slowly disposed of into the sewage system.

According to local experience, the facilities existing in the Barcelona area include a permanently installed pump in the recharge wells, with a daily to fortnightly cleaning for 10 to 15 minutes (Custodio, Isamat and Miralles, 1979). In an experimental recharge well, to inject treated sewage water in a salt water aquifer, a daily cleaning was the most effective way to conserve well capacity, with more distant periods of overchlorination to destroy organic matter (Custodio, Suárez and Galofré, 1976; Custodio, Tourís and Balagué, 1981; Custodio, 1981). The well design is based on the Llobregat recharge wells shown in figure 9.13.

An effective injection or recharge barrier necessarily supposes a certain outflow to the sea, that in steady state depends on the interface penetration, and consequently on the distance from the coast to the recharge line. The closer this recharge line to the aquifer sea outlet, the greater the fresh water flowing into the sea.

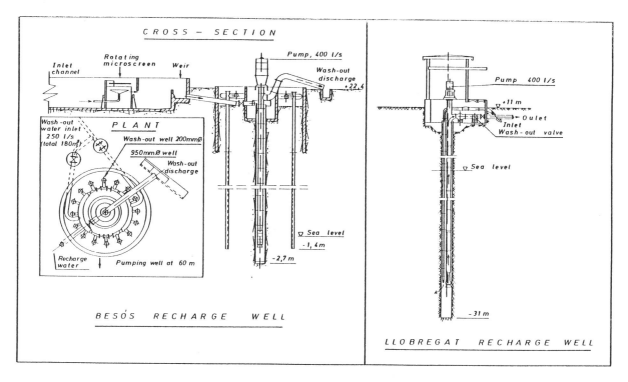

Fig. 9.13 - Two methods of well recharge used near Barcelona by the Sociedad
General de Aguas de Barcelona. The Besós wells are special ones
with backwashing tubes functioning when the cleaning pump is
started; slightly dirty water is introduced. The Llobregat wells
are normal wells fitted with a pump to clear periodically the well;
potable quality water is recharged (after Custodio, Isamat and
Miralles, 1979).

The percentage of the recharged fresh water that is lost to the sea
depends on the water abstraction in the aquifer and the mean water level on
it. Really, the most important question is not the percentage of water loss
but the increase in total water resources in the aquifer system and the benefit of an increased ground water reservoir capacity.

When water loss is suspected to be high, the recharge can be carried
out with fresh water of inferior quality, such as slightly brackish water,
treated sewage water, etc., if the recharge facilities admit such a water and
the effect on the natural aquifer water, is acceptable. If it is not acceptable, the sea water intrusion problem may be exchanged for a pollution problem.

When a recharge barrier is established on an already sea-water-
intruded area, a part of the salt or brackish water is trapped behind the barrier (fig. 9.14). This is a source of salinization that may last for many
years unless special measures are implemented in order to extract this water
or to prevent the upconing. The upconing danger decreases with the decreasing
salt water potential.

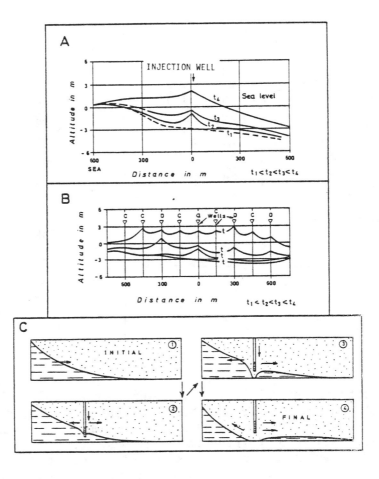

Fig. 9.14 - Evolution of water levels and the salt water wedge in a coastal area after an injection barrier starts operating, as observed in the Los Angeles West Coastal Basin Barrier (after Todd, 1959). (A) Section normal to the sea, showing the water level evolution after a recharge well was established. (B) Section following the barrier; (a) is the first well, followed by (b) and finally by wells (c). (C) shows how the sea water wedge is split in two by the injection barrier, leaving an entrapped salt water body landwards; transient situations are shown; most of the injected water flows landward and only the flow needed to maintain the salt water wedge position is lost to the sea.

Recharge water can be abstracted from the same aquifer, along a well line landward from the recharge one. The abstraction energy is thus used to fight sea water intrusion. Since energy is expensive, a careful economic analysis is needed.

The use of two lines of wells, and especially the case of a injection and an abstraction well has been studied by Sheahan (1977), as a proposal to a Palo Alto (California) barrier. For a given recharge-discharge flow, there is a critical distance between the two wells in order to stop sea water intrusion. This distance decreases as the number of doublets (pairs of wells) increase. This system allows for the use of bad quality injection fresh water because the part flowing landwards is abstracted by the pumping wells, thus avoiding landward pollution problems. The problem has been treated and solved analytically by Vandenberg (1975).

When planning a recharge barrier, several questions must be posed and answered carefully, because the experience and realizations in one site, such as California, are not necessarily valid for other sites from a practical and economical point of view. Some of these questions are:

- how much water is needed to operate an effective barrier in steady state?

- how much water is needed to create the barrier from an existing situation and how much time is needed to attain the steady state?

- if the needed water is available, which is the best use: (a) injection; (b) direct use and subsequent groundwater abstraction reduction?

- is the available water quality suitable to the chosen recharge method, and if not, what water pretreatment and treatment are needed?

- is the selected recharge or injection method feasible, and if so, what maintenance problems will it pose?

- what is the operational life of the barrier facilities?

- does the cost of barrier maintenance and operation justify the benefits expected?

- what is the cost of the protected fresh water?

The answer to some of these questions frequently deceives, because a barrier, if feasible, is in many circumstances a luxury or an overdone technique. Simple but detailed calculations are needed in order to foresee the piezometric level evolution and sometimes a model is highly desirable. A pilot plant is highly recommended in order to make a good choice of recharge facility and to get a tested operation manual. Things are generally more complex than expected.

In areas with great drawdowns it is better to begin with the recharge near that area in order to restore the water table aquifer storage and then study the feasibility of complementary actions to preserve the aquifer.

9.5.3   Pumping hydraulic barriers

The interception of salt water when flowing landwards is also a protection method. The most simple method to intercept salt water is by means of a line of coastal wells screened in the lower part of the aquifer to be protected. Salt water is pumped out (fig. 9.15), and returned to the sea. The discharge and closeness of the wells must be enough to avoid salt water penetration between them, and depends on aquifer hydraulic parameters, distance to the coast, aquifer depth and water level situation in the aquifer.

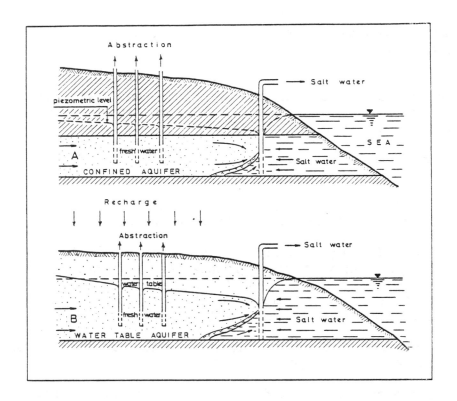

Fig. 9.15 – Sea water intrusion control by means of a pumping barrier or trough. Some fresh water is lost, mixed with the abstracted sea water. The salt water wedge penetrates beyond the well line, especially in the mid-line between the wells.

The abstraction wells take salt water and also fresh water, and then some fresh water from the aquifer is lost, thus impairing the fresh water balance. Since the wells are placed in the continent, the strip between them and the sea becomes completely salty. Moreover, a certain penetration of the salt water in the form of a scalloped wedge beyond the well line further reduces the area of the aquifer effectively protected.

Such a pumping barrier or pumping trough needs a significant investment in wells, salt water resistant screens, casings and fittings, pumps and electrical facilities and salty water disposal pipes or canals; and the cost of the energy to pump out the water is high. In compensation, no fresh water for injection has to be purchased. A pure extraction (pumping barrier) has been experimented with in the Oxnard basin, in California (Coe, 1972).

Since the fresh water balance of the aquifer is maintained when not impaired, in certain cases the barrier is only effective if some reduction in fresh water abstraction is carried out. In some instances the pumped salty water can be used for cooling in specially designed facilities.

A pumping barrier is seldom justified as a permanent situation, but it is a very effective method for reducing an existing sea water intrusion, depleting the encroached sea water. Wells are constructed inside the sea water intruded area. When a partial restoration of the aquifer is achieved, it is better to change to other protective method, such as a recharge barrier or a abstraction reduction or artificial recharge landwards.

For such a transitory situation, though it can last for some years, cheaper wells and installations are needed, and some of the existing wells, instead of being abandoned when the water becomes salty, can be used as salt water pumping wells, if adequate disposal of the water can be carried out.

When industry accepts salt or brackish water for its purposes, it acts involuntarily as an imperfect sea water pumping barrier. Such was the situation in the Besós area (figure 9.16).

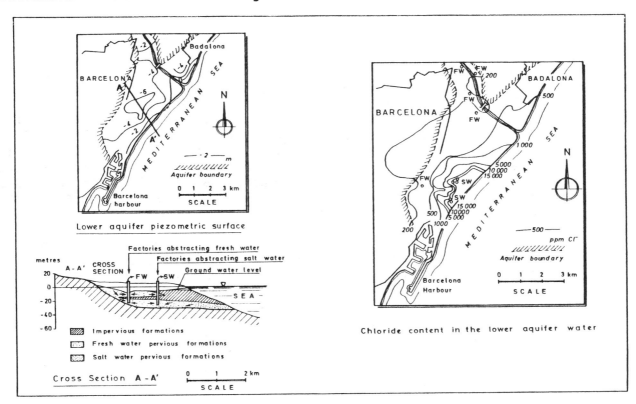

Fig. 9.16 - Sea water intrusion in the Besós delta lower aquifer. Near the coast salt water wells (SW) protect landward fresh water wells (FW). Salt water is used mainly for cooling purposes. Many of the salt water wells have been given up recently, and the fresh water wells are in danger of salinization.

It is presently also the situation in the eastern part of the Llobregat delta, near Barcelona, where the abstraction of brackish water in one industrial area protects one another landward, but the progressive closing of the saline wells is accelerating the salinization of those wells further inland.

In some areas of California (Orange County) a combination of coastal pumping barrier and a parallel injection barrier exists. A simple injection barrier is not feasible because the ground has not enough elevation to allow enough water build-up around the recharge wells in the water table aquifer. Injected water, with a logical separation of the wells, will flow out of the ground. Then, to maintain an effective injection barrier without logging the ground, the salt water head is depressed by a salt water pumping barrier between the injection barrier and the coast.

Part of the injected water flows to the pumping wells and is abstracted in greater quantity than if the pumping barrier were not there, but the systems work.

The aquifer dissolved salts balance must be considered in order to avoid an excessive recirculation of water (it can be important in groundwater irrigated areas), that may lead to a progressive total dissolved solids increase. A certain degree of water renovation must be assured.

9.6   Active control of upconing under a freshwater well

In order to prevent salt water upconing in a pumping well, the construction of a second well at the same place, tapping the salt water, has been proposed. A careful control of fresh and salt water discharge can maintain the salt-fresh water interface at a convenient position between the two screens. The existence of an intermediate semipermeable layer is highly favorable. Some theoretical studies exist (Babushkin, 1963a, 1982), some of them referring to a single well with two screens, one in the fresh water and another in the salt water, but in this case, the interface control is very difficult and small operation failures lead to fresh water contamination or loss of fresh water through the deep pump. The main advantage is that only one well is needed.

In spite of the solution's attraction, only occasional examples exist, generally related to experiments done by universities or as part of international projects. An example in Pakistan and one another in Indonesia, now abandoned, were cited in the United Nations Economic Commission for Europe Seminar held in Malta in June 1978, to study some 'Selected Water Problems in Islands and Coastal Areas with special regard to Desalination and Groundwater'. The main drawback is the cost of the second well, the second pump and the energy, the great quantity of salt water to be abstracted, and the cost and problems caused by the safe water disposal. Babushkin (1982) mentions that the system is being used in the USSR-Turkmenia.

In order to eliminate the second well, the single well must be used, with two screens and two pumps, but placing a packer between them in order to isolate the upper and lower parts. If axle driven pumps are used, the same axle may be used for the two pumps, but with a special tow placed in the packer.

The flow of the pumps must be regulated so that the flow boundary separating the flow to each one of the pumps remains over the fresh-salt water interface. Let Q be the well discharge, λ be the screen length in an aquifer of thickness b, c is the distance from the top of the screen to the static water table (fig. 9.17), with (s) salt water and (f) fresh water. After Babushkin (1963, 1982), the well discharges, and the depth z to the flow boundary from the initial water table, when density differences can be neglected are related by:

$$\frac{\mu_f}{\lambda_f} + \frac{\mu_s}{\lambda_s} \frac{Q_s}{Q_f} + \frac{Q_s + Q_f}{bQ_f} \left[\frac{1}{2b-z} - \frac{1}{b+z} \right] = 0$$

$$\mu_f = \frac{1}{2-c_f} + \frac{1}{2-c_f+\lambda_f} + \frac{1}{z+c_f+\lambda_f} - \frac{1}{z+c_f}$$

$$\mu_s = \frac{1}{c_s-z} - \frac{1}{c_s-\lambda_s-z} + \frac{1}{c_s+\lambda_s+z} - \frac{1}{c_s+z}$$

More detailed theoretical studies have been carried out (Wolanski and Wooding, 1973), considering the dispersion phenomena. Also Sugio and Ueda (1973) deal with the saline water head depletion by sucking it by deep drains. The abstraction of salt water by a central well in a small circular island has been studied by Molenkamp (1980); the water table is slightly depressed, but the salt water head and the interface are greatly lowered around the well.

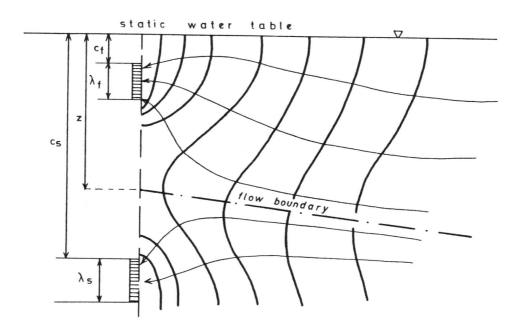

Fig. 9.17 - Flow to two screens at different depths when density differences are neglected.

9.7   <u>Use of coastal saline aquifers to store fresh water and to dispose of waste water</u>

In some flat coastal areas the topography, the high surface permeability, the intensity of land use or the high evaporation rate do not allow for, nor make attractive, the surface storage of water. Fresh water can be stored, under certain circumstances, in the ground, when there is salt or brackish water. These salt water aquifers - saltaquifers or salaquifers - have been studied in order to get theoretical and practical experience of the feasibility of the fresh water storage, from the point of view of recovery or the chemical reactions involved.

Near Miami (Florida) the highly pervious and porous deep limestone aquifer (boulder zone) which contains brackish and salt water, receives fully treated sewage water (García-Bengochea, et al., 1973; García-Bengochea, 1973). The primary goal is water disposal, but if a stable fresh water storage develops, it may be useful in the coming years. In St. Petersburg (Tampa, Florida) surface run-off water is recharged to the aquifer (Kaufman, 1973).

In order to obtain effective storage, a moderate dispersivity is required and the native water must be almost stagnant in order to avoid dragging the injected fresh water. Dispersion is enhanced by the presence of heterogeneities and also by the gravity segregation of light fresh water inside heavier salt water. In some studies in the Besós area (Barcelona) the fresh water body was found to be unstable.

Some real or simulated experiments in flowing aquifers show fresh water recoveries higher than 25%, and increases with the number of operating cycles (Kimbler, 1970; Kimbler, Kazmann and Whitehead, 1973; Kazmann, Kimbler and Whitehead, 1974; Khan, 1980). This recovery is impaired when there is a delay between the injection and the pumping. The storage seem feasible (Mouler, 1970, Brown and Silvey, 1973a, Singh and Murty, 1980, Larson and Papadopulos, 1977, Schuurmans and van der Akker, 1981).

Recovery is inversely proportional to the permeability, so that better storage can be achieved in low permeability formations (Esmail and Kimbler, 1967), although in them the flows are small, except if the saturated thickness is great, but in that case the density segregation effects are enhanced.

In section 8.2.10 some comments are made on calculation methods. The problem of gravitational and dispersive mixing has been studied by Gelhar, Wilson and Miller (1972), and by Peters (1981). The preeexisting groundwater movement can be controlled by means of bounding wells (Whitehead and Langhettee, 1978).

In some instances the injection of fresh water dramatically alters the permeability near the well screen due to clay defloculation by sodium rich mixed water in contact interfaces (Brown and Silvey, 1977; Edworthy and Downing, 1979; Nightingale and Bianchi, 1977). The pretreatment of the well by injecting a calcium-rich water (e.g., with $CaCl_2$ incorporated) seems effective in controlling that permeability reduction. One possible alternative is the use of trivalent aluminum compounds.

It has been observed (Brown and Silvey, 1973a) that when a core formerly saturated with salt or brackish water is washed with fresh water, the fresh water may become turbid due to the dragging of clay particles, which are dispersed and migrate, and thus may produce a reduction in permeability.

9.8 Combatting sea water salinization through surface water

Salt water penetration through a river mouth towards the inner part of an estuary, not only impairs the river quality, but also may contaminate the aquifer water through induced recharge.

In many situations, especially when the exploitation is small, the aquifer discharges fresh water into the estuary, thus preventing salt water penetration, and a salt water wedge may be formed. The principles are the same as those applied to the sea, but since the weight of the water column is reduced by the existence of the upper fresh water layer, the penetration is less important in the estuary. When the aquifer is exploited the groundwater discharge is reduced until the flow is reversed, locally or regionally. Then, bottom saline water and mixed brackish water can penetrate.

To preclude this effect, pumpage must be placed as far as possible from the river or estuary bank and controlled in order to conserve some groundwater discharge. In many cases such a situation is neither practical nor desirable, because the aquifer regulating capacity is not fully used and it is not possible to take advantage of the water distribution properties of the aquifer. It is much better to preclude salt water penetration into the estuary applying corrective measures to it, such as submerged dams or mobile sluices. The same is true for littoral channels, ditches and drains.

Dealing with salt or brackish water lagoons, contamination presents the same characteristics as for sea water in a coastal formation, although it is localized in the lagoon surroundings. Brackish water has a density between that of fresh water and salt water, and then, the salt water wedge is less penetrant. When the lagoons are elongated parallel to the coast line, the fresh water flow may preclude lagoon water penetration, especially if it is brackish. Water abstraction near these lagoons can reverse the flow and lagoon water can penetrate the ground. One solution is to reduce groundwater abstraction and to avoid pumping wells close to the lagoon. However if possible, it is better to reduce the lagoon salinity.

In polderlands, such as Holland, the lowlands reclamation produce the upward saline seepage described in chapter 4. Though it is possible to pump out the saline of brackish water below the semipervious polder bottom layer, it is costly due to the energy consumption and the evacuation pipe needed. The best way to cope with this problem is to drain the saline water with shallow ditches, jointly with infiltrated fresh water, and then to dilute the drained water with surface water, since it is available in that case.

In the Dutch case, there are two lines of polders. The salt and brackish water flow to the closer polder and the sea line reduces the salt water potential in the second line, thus aiding in the decrease of the salt production in it.

9.9   Alternatives to developing coastal aquifers

Development of coastal aquifers from a water management point of view, needs the consideration of some desirable aquifer policies and the avoidance of adverse effects. The definition of aquifer safe yield cannot be established if these policies and effects are not taken into account.

Aquifer exploitation reduces fresh water discharge into the sea and consequently increases the salt water wedge penetration, although the inland movement is slow and a long time may be needed to attain the new stationary position, generally with a thicker transition zone.

The abstraction of the whole aquifer recharge certainly produces a full encroachment of sea water into the aquifer. When the wells are placed far from the coast, in a place where the bedrock or aquifer bottom is above sea level, the pumpage can be maintained but fresh water recharged in the encroached part of the aquifer is lost. The regulating capacity of the underground reservoir is highly reduced, thus impairing the possibility of peak supply or seasonal regulation. When the coastal part of the aquifer is confined, such a loss of regulation capacity is not so important, since that capacity corresponds to the areas landward.

The abstraction of a part of the groundwater flow also produces a landward movement of the salt water. The fresh water that existed in the salt encroached portion of the aquifer is lost to the sea during the transient phase, and thus an important one-time fresh water reserve is wasted without any direct benefit.

One other important drawback of the alternative to exploit an important fraction of total recharge is that all abstraction works existing in the encroached area must be progressively abandoned, and since the aquifer fresh water distribution properties are lost, a surface network of canals and pipes must be constructed to carry the water to the existing demand points, or these demand points must be moved to other locations near the new wells. All this must be carefully evaluated from an economical, sociological and political point of view.

The exploitation of preexisting or specially constructed wells until they yield salty water, allows for a greater beneficial use of the one time fresh ground water reserve. Perhaps more than 25 to 50% of this one-time reserve must be exploited if the water abstraction works are correctly placed and operated. A simulation model can be highly useful. The attainable degree of recovery is a function of the admissible water cost and also of legal and administrative constraints.

Legal problems may preclude such an alternative if established fresh water rights are to be protected or conserved, depending on the country status of the property. Much legislation allows for the expropriation of existing water rights if a public interest exists, but it may be too expensive in some circumstances. Since the actual aquifer recharge is difficult to know accurately, especially when river induced recharge or lateral inflow is present, in large aquifers, or in coastal confined aquifers the true abstraction to recharge ratio is not well known, and may change due to human activities (urbanization, change in agricultural practices, river management, river increased pollution, etc.). Careful observations over a long period must be introduced to know the right evolution and to select the desired development alternative, if possible with the aid of a simulation model.

Another alternative is to mine fresh water from the aquifer, and when depleted (one part of the coastal aquifer becomes sea water intruded, and other parts become dry or with water levels too deep to justify economical abstraction) to just abandon it, looking for new sources of fresh water, such as the development of a new aquifer, the direct use of water from a local river or water transportation from other basins by means of a canal. Then, the new supply system finds an already established demand. Thus, the water economy is highly improved. However, such an alternative may not be socially nor legally acceptable, especially when fresh water and natural reservoirs are scarce. Storage in a local aquifer has sometimes an important stategical value and reduces the risk of water shortages in the event of accidents or pollution of the other water sources or facilities. This is especially important in densely populated coastal areas.

One other alternative or policy, on the other hand, is to avoid sea water penetration as much as possible. If the special measures presented in the preceeding sections are not undertaken, it means that only a small fraction of the recharge can be put into beneficial use, but existing wells can be conserved and a full use of the aquifer water transportation capacity is possible. This can be important in areas with a very dispersed small demand. Overpumping in the short term is admissible only if abstraction is greatly reduced during the rest of the year, so that the yearly recharge largely exceeds the annual pumped volume. This is a very important utilization scheme in coastal tourist or agricultural zones, where a high demand exists during two or three summer months, and falls almost to zero in the others. However, careful control is needed to be sure that the interface position oscillates about a safe central position without excessive dispersion.

9.10 Plan for groundwater exploitation in a coastal aquifer

Management techniques applied to coastal aquifers are one of the tools to control sea water intrusion. Since it is a science and technology different from that of the present monograph, the reader is referred to specialized literature. Some recent papers will be described below. Different calculation methods and models are used as a tool to furnish situations which are treated in different ways, from pure tabulation or comparison of ratios, to more sophisticated linear and dynamic programming. It must be said that many of the mathematically sophisticated methods are frequently more academic than practical, and they lack the validation of solving real situations. Management and planning need the consideration of a complicated set of social and political restrictions or constraints besides the pure technoeconomic considerations.

Auriol, Bonnet and Vandenbeusch (1978) consider the available resources and corresponding pumping field design of a coastal aquifer in Morocco, with a network of control points where the drawdown must be kept below certain limiting values in order to reduce the salinization danger. The objective function to be maximinized is the total discharge of the wells. It is done through a classical linear programming method, with a finite difference model to compute the coefficients of influence.

The short term operation of coastal groundwater basins need some hydrological operating rule for the annual pumpage. It consists on a fixed part and a variable part which is proportional to the prevailing actual storage of fresh water. This rule is a function of the physical characteristics of the basin, its groundwater balance and design variables, and furthermore on the natural replenishment, which is a statistical variable. Such a problem has been analyzed by Bachmat (1976). Short range operations, such as the annual pumpage, require that the probability of a failure, which may result in an irreversible damage to the water resources or to the water consumers (agriculture, population or industry), be as small as possible. Taking into account the general caution of decision makers, it seems appropriate to have a separate evaluation of the annual exploitable yield, which depends primarily on the physical characteristics. Treatments considering economical restrictions are considered by other authors, such as Cummings (1971) and Cummings and McFarland (1974), and the references contained in them.

9.11 References

Auriol, J., Bonnet, M., Vandenbeusch, M. (1978). Optimization of irrigation pumping networks by simulation on mathematical models and linear programming. Sem. on Selected Water Problems in Islands and Coastal Areas, with special emphasis on Dealinization and Groundwater. Malta. U.N. Econ. Comm. Europe (Annexes). 15 pp.

Babushkin, V.D. (1963). Ekspluatatsiya lins bez primeneniya merpo zaschie ot podsasyvania solenykh vod snizu. (Exploitation of water lenses without applying the protective measures from salt water entrainment upwards). M., Izd-vo AN USSR, pp. 95-106.

Babushkin, V.D. (1963). Methods of exploiting and evaluating the resources of fresh water lenses. The Development of Ground Water Resources with Special Reference to Deltaic Areas. United Nations, Water Resources Series no. 24. ECAPE, pp. 188-191.

Babushkin, V.D.; Goldberg, V.M. (1967) Hydrogeological investigations and estimation of fresh groundwater resources in coastal areas. Artificial Recharge and Management of Aquifers. Haifa Symposium. Int. Assoc. Scientific Hydrology. Pub. 72, pp. 383-389.

Bachmat, Y. (1976) Annual operation of a coastal groundwater basin at a prescribed reliability level. Journal of Hydrology, 31 (1976). pp. 97-118. Elsevier.

Bargman, R.D.; Adrian, U.N.; Tillman, D.C. (1974) Water reclamation in Los Angeles. Am. Soc. Civil Engineers, Journal Environmental Engineering Division. E.E.G. Washington, pp. 939-955.

Bear, J.; Dagan, G. (1964) Intercepting fresh water above the interface in a coastal aquifer. General Assembly of Berkeley, 1963. Int. Assoc. Scientific Hydrology. Pub. 64, pp. 154-181.

Bear, J. (1972) Dynamics of fluids in porous media. Am. Elsevier Environmental Science Series. No. 4. p. 764.

Bensalah, D.; Besbes, M.; de Marsily, G.; Mouillard, L.; Zebidi, H. (1975) Alimentation artificielle par puits pour la regeneration et al conservation de l'aquifere cotier de Teboulba, Tunisie. (Well artificial recharge for the restoration and conservation of the Teboulba coastal aquifer, Tunisia). 3rd Int. Symp. on Groundwater. Palermo. 4 pp.

Brown, R. F.; Silvey, W.D.; (1973) <u>Underground storage and retrieval of fresh water from a brackish-water aquifer.</u> Underground Waste Management and Artificial Recharge: Vol. 1, New Orleans Symp., Int. Assoc. Scientific Hydrology - American Geophysical Union, pp. 349-414.

Brown, D.L.; Silvey, W.D. (1973) <u>Underground waste management and artificial recharge.</u> II Int. Symp. on Underground Waste Management and Artificial Recharge, New Orleans. AAPG - USGS - IASH. Vol. 1, pp. 379-419.

Brown, D.L.; Silvey, W.D. (1977) <u>Artificial recharge to a fresh-water sensitive brackish-water and aquifer, Norfolk, Virginia.</u> U.S. Geological Survey, Prof. Paper 939. 54 pp. Washington.

Bruington, A.E.; Seares, F.D. (1965) <u>Operating a sea water barrier project.</u> Proc. Am. Soc. Civil Engineers, Journal Irrigation and Drainage Division. Vol. 91, IR1. pp. 117-140.

Bruington, A.E. (1969) <u>Control of sea-water intrusion in a ground-water aquifer.</u> Ground Water. Vol. 7, No. 3, pp. 9-15.

Bruington, A.E. (1972) <u>Salt water intrusion into aquifers.</u> Water Resources Bulletin. Vol. 8, No. 1, pp. 150-160.

Charmonman, Cartens, May (1976) <u>A fresh-water canal as a barrier to salt-water intrusion.</u> Artificial Recharge and Management of Aquifers. Haifa Symposium. Int. Assoc. Scientific Hydrology Pub. 72; pp. 374-382.

Coe, J.J. (1972) <u>Sea water intrusion extraction barrier.</u> Am. Soc. Civil Engineers, J. Irrigation and Drainage Div. IR 3, pp. 387-403.

Cohen, P.; Durfor, C.N. (1966) <u>Design and construction of a unique injection well on Long Island, New York.</u> U.S. Geological Survey, Prof. Paper 550 D, pp. D253-D257. Washington.

Cohen, P.; Durfor, C.N. (1966) <u>Artificial recharge experiments utilizing renovated sewage plant effluent: a feasibility study at Bay Park, New York, USA.</u> Haifa Symposium. Int. Assoc. Scientific Hydrology-UNESCO. Pub. 70, pp. 193-197.

Cummings, R.G. (1971) <u>Optimum exploitation of groundwater reserves with salt water intrusion.</u> Water Resources Research, Vol. 7, No. 6, pp. 1415-1424. Washington.

Cummings, R. G.; McFarland, J.W. (1974) <u>Groundwater management and salinity control.</u> Water Resources Research. Vol 10, No. 5. pp. 909-915. Washington.

Custodio, E.; Suárez, M.; Galofré, A. (1976) <u>Ensayos para el análisis de la recarga de aguas residuales en el delta del Besós.</u> (Tests for the study of waste water recharge in the Besós Delta). II Asamblea Nacional de Geodesia y Geofísica. Barcelona. Instituto Geográfico y Catastral, Madrid. pp. 1983-1936.

Custodio, E.; Isamat, F.J.; Miralles, J.M. (1979) <u>Twenty five years of</u>

groundwater recharge in Barcelona (Spain). International Symposium on Groundwater Recharge. Dortmund. May. 10 pps.

Custodio, E. (1980) Recarga artificial de acuiferos: avances y realizaciones. (Aquifer artificial recharge: progress and achievements). Contribution to the Bilateral Project USA-Spain. 'Water Conjunctive Use in Complex Surface-Groundwater System) (to be published). 214 pgs.

Custodio, E; Tourís, R.; Balagué, S. (1981) Behaviour of contaminants after injection of treated urban waste water in a well. International Symposium on Quality of Groundwater. Noordwickerhout (Amsterdam). Studies in Environmental Sciences, Vol. 17. Elsevier, pp. 395-401.

Custodio, E. (1981) Método de calculo de las mezclas de agua resultante de la recarga artificial con aguas residuales tratadas en el acuifero cautivo del delta del Besós. (Calculation method for the resulting mixtures from the treated waste water artificial recharge in the confined aquifer of the Besós delta). IV Asamblea Nacional de Geodesia y Geofísica. Zaragoza, 1981. Instituto Geográfico Nacional. 18 pgs.

Edworthy, K.J.; Downing, R.A., (1979): Artificial recharge and its relevance in Britain. The Institution of Water Engineers and Scientists, Vol. 33, March, London, pp. 151-172.

Esmail, O.J.; Kimbler, O.K. (1967) Investigation of the technical feasibility of storing fresh water in saline aquifers. Water Resources Research, Vol. 3, No. 3, pp. 683-695.

García-Bengochea, J.I., et al. (1973) Artificial recharge of treated waste waters and rainfall runoff into deep saline - aquifers of Peninsula of Florida. II Int. Symp. Underground Waste Management and Artificial Recharge, New Orleans. Am. Assoc. Petroleum Geologists - USGS - IASH, Vol. 1, pp. 505-525.

García-Bengochea, J.I. et al. (1973) Recharge of treated wastewaters and rainfall runoff into deep saline aquifers of South Florida. USA. Atti. 2 Convergo Internazionales sulle - Acque Sotterranee. Palermo. ESA/AIH/AIRH. pp. 687-700.

Gelhard, L.W.; Wilson, J.L.; Miller, J.S. (1972) Gravitational and dispersive mixing in aquifers. Proc. Am. Soc. Civil Engineering. J. Hydraulics Division. HY 12. pp 2135-2153. Washington.

Iglesias, A.; Porras, J. (1978) Re-use of treated sewage for sea water intrusion control in Llano de Palma (Balearic Islands). Seminar on Selected Water Problems in Islands and Coastal Areas with special regard to Desalinization and Groundwater. Malta. U.N. Economic Commission for Europe. Paper SEM5/R13 8 pgs.

Kahana, M.S.Y. (1964) Coastal groundwater collectors as a means of intensifying exploitation of groundwater. General Assembly of Berkeley. Int. Assoc. Scientific Hydrology. Pub. 64, pp. 182-193.

Kashef, A.A.I. (1976) Control of salt-water intrusion by recharge wells. Am. Soc. Civil Engineers. J. Irrigation and Drainage Div. IR 4, pp. 445-457.

Kaufman, M.I. (1973) <u>Subsurface wastewater injection, Florida.</u> Am. Soc. Civil Engineers. Journal Irrigation and Drainage Division. IR 1. Washington, pp. 53-70.

Kazmann, R.G.; Kimbler, O.K.; Whitehead, W.R. (1974) <u>Management of waste fluids in salaquifers.</u> Am. Soc. Civil Engineers, J. Irrigation and Drainage Div., IR 2, pp. 413-424. Washington

Kahana, M.S.Y. (1964) <u>Coastal groundwater collectors as a means of intensifying exploitation of groundwater.</u> IASH. Aseamblea General de Berkeley. Pub. 64. pp. 182-193.

Khan, I.A. (1980) <u>Waste water disposal through a coastal aquifer.</u> Water Resources Research, Vol. 16, No. 4, pp. 608-614.

Kimbler, O.K. (1970) <u>Fluid model studies of the storage of freshwater in saline aquifers.</u> Water Resources Research, Vol. 6, No. 5, pp. 1522-1527.

Kimbler, O.K.; Kazmann, R.G.; Whitehead, W.R. (1973) <u>Saline aquifers: future storage reservoir for fresh water?</u> Underground Waste Management and Artificial Recharge, New Orleans. AAPG, USGS. IAHS, Vol. 1, pp. 192-203.

Larson, S.P.; Papadopulos, S.S. (1977) <u>Simulation of wastewater injection into a coastal aquifer system near Kahului, Maui, Hawaii.</u> Proc. Hydraulics in the Coastal Zone. Am. Soc. Civil Engineers. College Station,Texas, pp. 107-116.

Molenkamp, G.L. (1980) <u>Some results obtained with an analytical solution in a radial symmetric profile.</u> Research on Possible Changes in the Distribution of Saline Seepage in the Netherlands. Committee for Hydrological Research, TNO. Proceedings and Information, No. 28. The Hague. pp. 77-101.

Mouler, E.A. (1970) <u>Freshwater bubbles: a possibility for using saline aquifers to store water.</u> Water Resources Research, Vol. 6, No. 5. Octubre. pp. 1528-1531.

Nightingale, H.I.; Bianchi, W.C. (1977) <u>Groundwater turbidity resulting from recharge.</u> Ground Water, Vol. 15, No. 2, pp. 146-152.

Nutbrown, D.A. (1977) <u>Aquifer management in the context of saline intrusion.</u> Fifth Salt Water Intrusion Meeting, Medmenham, England. Int. Hydrological Programme. pp. 78-87.

Peters, J.H. (1981) <u>Application of vortex distributions in modelling the storage of fresh water in saline aquifers.</u> VII Salt Water Intrusion Meeting, Uppsala. Sveriges Geologiska Undersokning, Rapporter och Meddelanden No. 27, Uppsala. pp. 162-170.

Potié, L. (1973) <u>Études et captage de résurgences d'eau douce sous-marines.</u> (Study and captation of fresh water submarine springs). Atti. 2 Convegno Internazionale sulle Acque Sotterranee. Palermo. ESA-IAH-IAHR. pp. 603-620.

Potié, L.; Ricour, M.J. (1978) Étude et captage d'eau douce dans un milieu fissuré ou karstique situé en bordure de mer. (Study and captation of fresh water in a fissured or karstic medium placed at the sea shore). Seminar on Selected Water Problems in Islands and Costal Areas with Special Regard to Desalinization and Ground Water. Malta U.N. Economic Commission for Europe. Paper SEM5/R48.

Roberts, G.D. (1967) Use of air to influence ground-water movement. Artificial Recharge and Management of Aquifers. Int. Assoc. Scientific Hydrology. Symposium of Haifa. Pub. 72, pp. 390-398.

Schuurmans, R.A.; van der Akker, C. (1981) Artificial removal of intruded saline water in a deep aquifer. VII Salt Water Intrusion Meeting. Uppsala. Sveriges Geologiska Undersokning. Rapporter och Meddelanden, No. 27. Uppsala. pp. 239-246.

Sheahan, N.I. (1977) Injection/extraction well system - a unique sea water intrusion barrier. Ground Water, Vol. 15, No. 1. pp. 32-50.

Shechter, M.; Schwartz, J. (1970) Optimal planning of a coastal collector. Water Resources Research, Vol. , No. 4, pp. 1017-1024.

Singh, S.P.; Murty, V.V.N. (1980) Storage of freshwater in saline aquifers. Am. Soc. Civil Engineers, J. Irrigation and Drainage Div. IR 2, pp. 93-104. Washington.

Stefanon, A. (1973a) Evaluation and capture of submarine springs. Atti 2 Convegno Internazionalle sulle Acque Sotterranee, Palermo. ESA-IAH-IAHR. pp. 579-590.

Stefanon, A. (1973b) Ulteriori osservazione sulla polla di Rovereto e sulla altre sorgenti sottomarine della Mortola (Riviera di Ponente). (Last observations about the Rovereto sea spring and about other submarine springs of Mortola). Riviera di Ponente. Atti. 2 Convegno Internazionale sulle Acqua Sotterranee Palermo. ESA - IAH - IAHR. pp. 591-601.

Shuval, H.I. (1977) Water renovation and reuse. Academic Press. Inc. 463 pgs.

Sugio, S.; Ueda, T. (1973) Analysis of fresh-salt water interface in aquifer during salt water draining. Proc. Int. Symp. on Development of Ground Water Resources. Madras. Council of Scientific and Industrial Research. India. Vol. 12. pp. IV-1-IV-8.

Todd, D.K. (1959). Ground Water Hydrology. John Wiley and Sons, Inc. 361 p.

Vandenberg, A. (1975) Simultaneous pumping of fresh and salt water from a coastal aquifer. Journal of Hydrology. Vol. 24. pp. 37-43. Amsterdam.

Whitehead, W.R.; Langhetree, E.J. (1978) Use of bounding wells to counteract the effects of preexisting groundwater movement. Water Resources Research, Vol. 14, No. 2, pp. 273-280.

Wolanski, E.J.; Wooding, R.A. (1973) <u>Steady flow to sink pair symmetrically situated above and below a horizontal diffusing interface.</u> Water Resources Research, Vol. 9, No. 2, pp. 415-425.

10. Case histories

Contents

10.1   Introduction

A number of case studies on groundwater salinization as a consequence of man's intervention in coastal areas are presented below. A wide and complete coverage of the many different possible situations has not been possible since the available space is limited, and detailed studies where besides the general description and the present situation, the calculation methods with a follow-up of the forecasts and the results of the management measures are included, are scarce.

     Inquiries sent to the IHP National Committees and different organizations have not yielded the expected results, and some of the case studies have been rejected since they did not cover the objectives.   However, the information contained in them has been used in the previous chapters.

     The case histories are of two types: a) a few in which the subject is dealt with in some detail; and b) short reports to outline the subject, avoiding the details.

     They have been classified as:

          --Deltas and alluvial aquifers
          --Coastal plains
          --Carbonate rocks
          --Islands
          --Salt balance studies

     This is rather nonhomogeneous classification, and the limits between the items are not well defined, but it is consistent with Chapter 3.

     The geographical coverage is unbalanced in spite of an effort to get examples from all over the world. This is partially corrected in the previous chapters. There is the feeling that in spite of the existence of a large number of coastal and island studies, few of them deal with a detailed follow-up of man's influence.

     The case histories are reproduced from the authors' papers, with only minor changes to coordinate them. They are thought to represent the authors' ideas and the way they emphasize the different aspects involved.

10.2   Deltas and alluvial aquifers

Case history no. 1: Sea-water intrusion in the Llobregat delta, near Barcelona (Catalonia, Spain)*

Geographical location

The Llobregat delta is a a medium-sized quaternary formation located at the southwest edge of Barcelona (the capital of Spain's Catalonia), as shown in Figure 10.1 Barcelona and its metropolitan area, facing the Mediterranean Sea, is a densely populated area of about 3.5 million inhabitants.

Important industrial areas are located around Barcelona, some of them on the Llobregat delta (car and truck factories, artificial textiles, paper mills, industrial ceramics, asbestos, etc.), and intensively irrigated agricultural zones exist, though urban and industrial settlements are displacing them.

Since the water demand is high, there is an intense exploitation of the Llobregat river water, both through surface and underground abstraction works (fig. 10.1).

Though small, the Llobregat basin is the most extensive coastal basin from the French border to the Ebro delta. Its area of 5000 km^2 ,and irregularly distributed rainfall throughout the year, yield a highly variable discharge averaging about 20 m^3/s. Floods may reach peak discharges of a few thousand m^3/s, and during periods of drought the discharge can be as low as 4 m^3/s.

Headwater surface reservoirs in the few places available have corrected this situation somewhat, but the Llobregat delta and low valley aquifers are still the most important and efficient water-storage reservoirs. Total water volume is about twice the yearly groundwater demand. It has a very small water mean residence time in respect to most aquifers.

Geology and hydrogeology

The Llobregat delta and the lower valley boundaries are clearly defined since the 80 km^2 alluvial plain is surrounded by mountains and the sea. The upstream limit of the valley is a narrow, through which the groundwater exchanges can be considered as negligible. The mountains can be regarded as formed by impervious materials, represented by schists, marls, compact limestones and clayish sandstones and conglomerates.

---

*Prepared by E. Custodio, Eastern Pyrenees Water Authority and Barcelona Polytechnical University, International Groundwater Course.

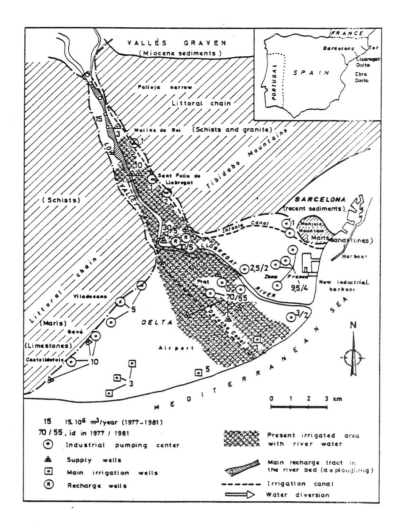

Fig. 10.1 - Situation and groundwater exploitation map. River water is the main water recharge source, directly in the channel (natural or artificially favored by periodic ploughing), through canal losses, return irrigation flows, artificial recharge by means of wells and sewage water infiltration. The small creeks from the littoral chain also contribute some fresh water. Abstractions are carried out mainly through high-discharge deep wells, open in fluviatile gravels. In the delta, most of the wells correspond to the deep aquifer. The figures represent annual water volumes in 1977 and/or 1981.

Figure 10.2 shows some hydrogeological cross-sections of the alluvial formations. The lower valley deposits are an accumulation of coarse gravels and sands, in direct connection with the river bed, with minor silt interlayerings.

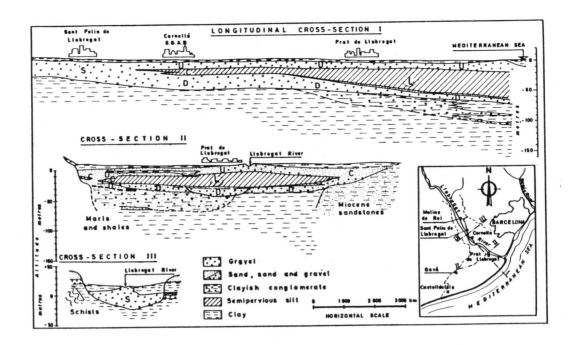

Fig. 10.2 - Typical hydrogeological cross-sections of the lower Llobregat valley and delta unconsolidated formations. U = upper delta aquifer,
that can be considered as a water table one. D = deep delta confined and leaky aquifer; DD indicates the most permeable areas. S =
single lower valley aquifer. L = clay, silt and fine sand semipervious intermediate lens. C = connection between the two aquifers,
the vertical permeability being much less than the horizontal one.

At the mouth of the lower valley, the water table aquifer splits
into two aquifers, an upper water table aquifer and a deep confined aquifer,
separated by a low permeability lens. This clay, silt and fine sand lens
thickens towards the sea, where it reaches a maximum thickness of about 50
meters. There the clay frequency is greater, some layers of peat are present,
and some methane gas if found.

This lens may be regarded as an aquitard whose vertical permeability
varies from a negligible value near the central coastal zone (almost impervious) to a high value at the valley mouth and near the delta boundaries, where
the two aquifers are clearly connected or no separation exists at all. The
hydraulic resistance (b'/k') varies from less than 1,000 days to more than
100,000 days.

Near the delta boundaries, the situation may be more complicated in
detail, as shown in Figure 10.3. In these areas, lagoon, marsh and beach conditions occurred alternatively during the sediment built up, jointly with
alluvial influences from local creeks and sometimes from the main river.

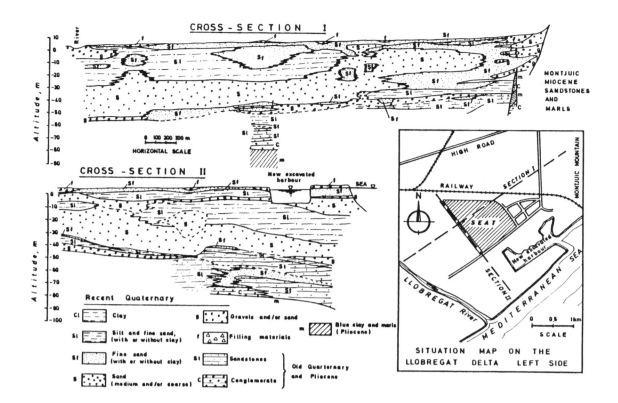

Fig. 10.3 – Simplified lithological cross-sections of the formations of the left part of the Llobregat delta (Zona Franca). The main delta clay and silt lens changes to a complex of layers of silt, fine sands and sands, with a low but not negligible vertical permeability. The deep aquifer is not always well defined, and in some areas it reduces to sands or is almost inexistent.

The upper aquifer discharges directly into the sea through a sandy bottom, except the eastern part, where at present, the sea floor is dominantly muddy.

The coarse highly pervious gravel and sand sediments of the deep aquifer concentrate in a strip parallel to the river, but displaced westwards, with a lobe extending towards the eastern border, without reaching the sea. Sea deep aquifer connections are poorly known. It is assumed that the main formation (estuary deposits) outcrops on the sea floor some 4 km offshore, below some 110 m of water. Probably the effective thickness and the permeability decreases sharply towards the outlet.

The deep aquifer lies on blue-clay Pliocene deposits, which can attain more than 700 m thickness. Near the coast some clayish conglomerate lenses appear, but they may be regarded as relatively impervious ones, and of small extension.

The geographic delta is a relatively young formation because in Roman times the Montjuic Mountain was an island. The shore was almost 2 km inland, as shown by some archaeological discoveries. In the Middle Ages, the Barcelona harbour was protected by the western side of Montjuic Mountain, some 1.5 km inland from present shoreline. The present harbour, on the other side, was built when the old one filled up with sand. Increased solid transport from the rivers was probably caused by intensive deforestation and inadequate agricultural practices which lead to an intense land erosion.

Water abstraction

The main abstraction points are shown in figure 10.1 Most of the wells are deep tube wells, exploiting mainly the deep delta aquifer, where it exists. Total figures in 10^6 m^3/year, are:

Area	1977	1981	Aquifer
Delta's western limit	15	15	semideep (1)
Right side of the delta	82	65	mainly from the deep one
Left side of the delta (Zona Franca)	13	7	mainly from the deep or semideep (1)
Mouth of the valley	30	5	semideep (1) (2)
Valley	17	17	single, water table
TOTAL	157	109	

(1) in direct connection with the upper one.

(2) variable abstractions, in accordance with river water availability. Maximum installed pumping capacity 120 x 10^6 m^3/year. Artificial recharge from 0 to 12 x 10^6 m^3/year is an average figure over the last ten years.

Total abstraction has been steady from 1965 to 1977, but the center of mass has moved from the valley mouth towards the Prat area, closer to the sea, since annual abstractions for supply have decreased and industrial pumpage has increased. At present (1982) total abstraction has been reduced to about 100 x 10^6 m^3/year, in part due to better water use in industries, but also to the world economic crisis and the replacement of salted-up wells by connections to the water mains.

Groundwater flow

In natural steady state, before the exploitation started, the valley aquifer was in equilibrium with the river. The river recharged the aquifer in the upper part and discharged it in the lower one. The upper delta aquifer received its recharge mainly from rainfall and lateral run-off infiltration, and it was drained by the lower tract of the river and the sea, where there were marshes and fresh and brackish water lagoons. Figure 10.4 schematizes the former and present situations.

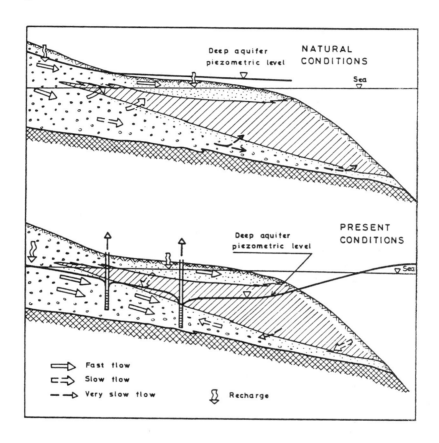

Fig. 10.4 - Sketch of the flow pattern in the central cross-section of the Llobregat delta under natural and present conditions.

The deep confined aquifer was fed from the valley, mainly from infiltrated river water. Since leakage to the sea was small and leakage towards the upper aquifer was almost negligible, the circulation through the more permeable formations was sluggish. Piezometric water levels were about n 6 to 8 m over mean sea level (Santa Maria and Marín, 1910). Considering the existing piezometric gradient, it was enough to allow for fresh water discharge at the assumed undersea outlet, according to the BHG principle.

As shown in Figure 10.5 the clay lens covering the deep aquifer still contains connate sea-water, trapped between 5,000 and 10,000 years ago. Therefore, vertical upward flow can be taken as negligible. Only in marginal areas where vertical permeability is much higher, has the saline water been completely flushed out. The existence of such a interlayering of salt water, has in earlier times given root to incorrect interpretations of geoelectrical surveys. Only after its existence was discovered could the existing data be corrected.

In spite of the existence of some important pumping centers, in 1960 the piezometric levels of the deep aquifer along the coast were still over mean sea level, at least during part of the year. In 1965 the piezometric water levels were below sea level over the whole delta, and they have gone down ever since. This is not caused by a preferential use of the groundwater reserves, since annual abstraction is of the same order of magnitude as the usable stored water, as previously mentioned. The main causes of this downward trend of piezometric levels are:

--Progressive displacement of the abstraction center of mass from the valley mouth to the central delta area.

--Progressive deterioration of river water infiltration. At present the river remains perched over the water table. Then, river infiltration is not regulated by the water table position, and can only be increased by artificial recharge activities, applied from time to time (Custodio, SuaArez, Isamat and Miralles, 1977; Custodio, 1978). Total river infiltration decreases steadily owing to an increase in water-suspended solids, a decrease in intensity and frequency of floods and changes in the river bed permeability through gravel mining. River bank improvements also reduce the recharge capacity during floods.

--A sequence of preferently dry years in which the storage of the valley water table aquifer has been half emptied. The resulting low piezometric levels allow for the penetration of water from other sources such as the sea and the delta upper aquifer in marginal areas, in order to compensate for the decrease in river infiltration and the depletion of water storage, and a reduction in abstractions in areas where the saturated thickness is not enough. The use of the one time reserve in the sea front represents only 0.2 per cent of total abstraction (Custodio, 1982). Figure 10.6 represents a piezometric map of the area, corresponding to a typical situation in 1971. River and aquifer water levels coincide at the upstream end. Downstream, the river is perched over the groundwater table up to Prat de Llobregat, where it receives water from the upper delta aquifer. The deep aquifer piezometric levels are below sea level, presenting a huge drawdown cone in the central-eastern part, that extends seawards. The concentration of contour lines in the eastern part is the result of a lower transmisivity and the recharge from the upper aquifer and the sea (total abstraction in this area was only seven per cent of the total abstraction at that time).

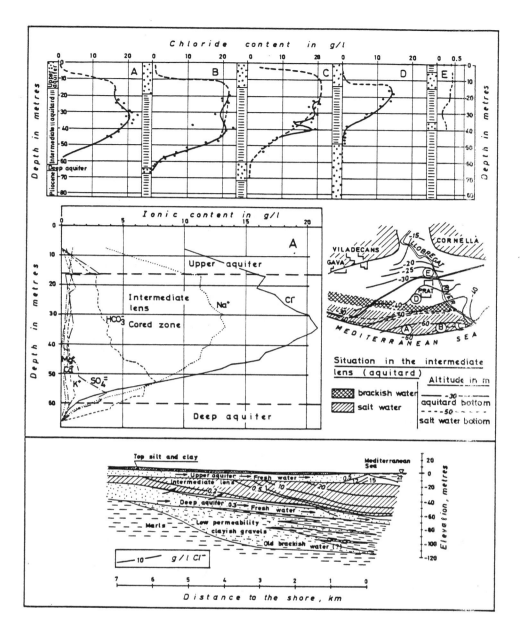

Fig. 10.5 - Results of the study of the pore-water salinity of the intermediate clay, silt and fine sand lens. Logs A, B and C show that formation sea water remains in the sediments and only the lower part has
been replaced by fresh water; a typical dispersion front develops.
In D salt water is partially flushed out and in E only fresh water
is found due to the greater vertical permeability. The detail of
log A shows the behavior of the main ions; it can be seen that in
the lower part there is a sodium deficit caused by ion exchange during the upward displacement; the increase in HCO_3^- is due to the
presence of peat and organic matter, and the $SO_4^=$ probably comes from
the oxidation of sulphides during the dilution process. These logs
allow for the correct interpretation of geophysical data. The
results concerning the salt water bottom and the distribution inside
the lens is shown in the enclosed situation map and cross-section.

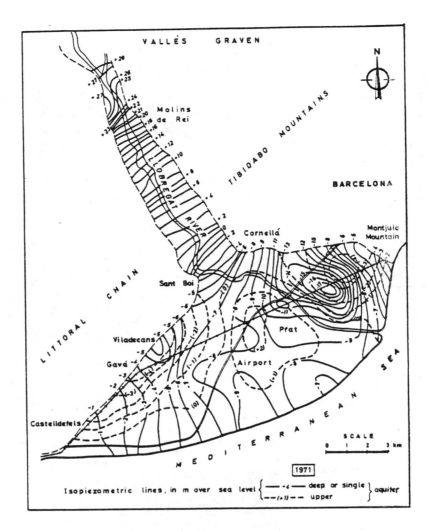

Fig. 10.6 - Isopiezometric map of the Llobregat's lower valley and delta aquifers in a typical situation in 1971. In the whole deep delta aquifer, water levels are below sea level; a regional drawdown cone is present in the center-eastern part.

In the central coastal part, a small elevation in the piezometric level coincides with the area of higher transmisivity and shows the effect of some kind of connection with the sea. There is a steeper gradient towards the sea outcrop, directly or through a more conductive top layer. The east-west groundwater movement in the deep aquifer is negligible since transmisivity in the western area is small.

In the central part of the delta upper aquifer, groundwater levels are over sea level because recharge from rainfall, canal losses and return irrigation water are high. This water mound spreads towards the river and the sea and also toward the western delta boundary, where water is transferred from the upper to the deep aquifer.

A similar situation existed in the upper aquifer on the left side of the delta until 1970. Afterwards, irrigation with river water was suppressed in this area, and intensive industrial settlements, with paved areas and intense land occupation took place. Then, recharge was greatly decreased. Seepage towards the deep aquifer through the boundary areas creates a wide zone, with water levels below sea level. It is prone to sea water intrusion. This situation has potentially worsened with the inland excavation of an extension of the industrial harbor.

Figure 10.7 shows two detailed situations in the central-eastern zone, one on May 1973 and another from May 1977. The increase in seaward water gradients is clearly shown. Figure 10.8 shows the situation in the upper aquifer in the same months. The situation has not changed too much, but for a decrease in the elevation of the mound on the right side, as a result of a sequence of predominantly dry years.

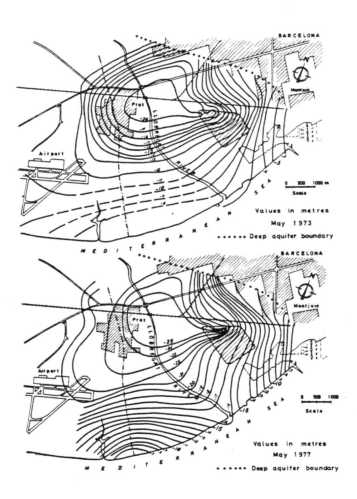

Fig. 10.7 - Piezometric maps of the eastern deep delta aquifer in May 1972 (end of a wet period). The whole zone (Puerto Franco and Prat) is under sea level. Annual abstraction is of the same order of magnitude of groundwater reserves.

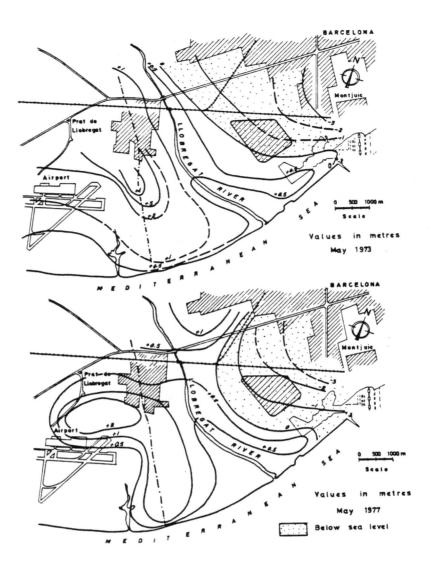

Fig. 10.8 - Piezometric maps of the eastern upper delta aquifer in May 1972 (end of a wet period) and in May 1977 (semidry period). The eastern border is under sea level due to the downward leakage of water towards the deep aquifer. The direct exploitation of this aquifer can be regarded as negligible.

Figure 10.9 shows the groundwater level evolution in the valley and deep delta aquifers between 1967 and mid-1977. Groundwater levels decreased sharply after the 1968-1972 preferently wet period, in which an excessive groundwater development in the delta occurred. In 1977 the storage in the valley aquifer, the main underground reservoir, was almost depleted. Piezometer A-11'-d does not descend as much as the others because it reflects the influence of the sea open boundary.

Different studies have been carried out in order to understand the groundwater movement in the area from a qualitative and quantitative point of view (MOP, 1966; Custodio, 1967, 1968, 1982b; Marqúes, 1975; VilarAo, 1967; Vilaró and Martín Arnáiz, 1968; Llamas and Vilaró, 1967; Custodio, Bayó and Peláez, 1971).

-446-

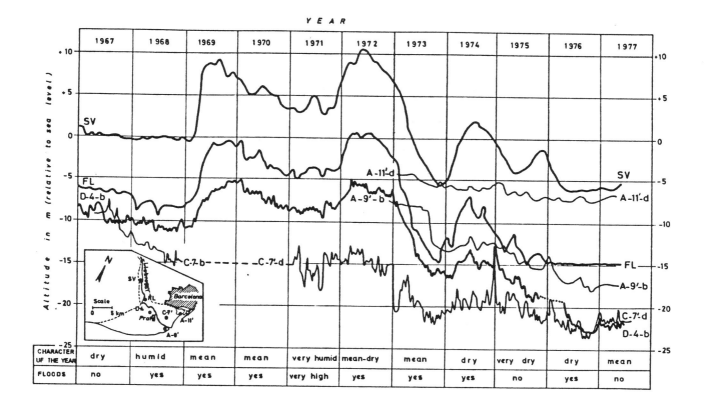

Fig. 10.9 – Evolution of groundwater levels in the valley and deep delta aquifers. The hydraulic character of the shown years is given. Water levels show a clear decrease after the 1969–1972 predominantly wet period, during which new important groundwater developments took place in the delta. Total abstraction was maintained since the pumpage in the valley mouth was reduced with the construction of a 80 km long canal to supply Barcelona from outside the Llobregat basin. Annual abstraction is of the same order of magnitude of total groundwater reserves.

In 1965, a dense network of observation bore-holes was established by the Eastern Pyrenees Water Authority. Some observation bore-holes have existed in the valley aquifer since 1944.

Figure 10.10 shows the natural radioisotope content of the deep delta aquifer water. Data are adjusted to the year 1973. Recent waters from the river only fill the inner part of the delta up to the main pumping centers. Infiltration in the river or through canals and irrigated lands, account for about 60 to 75 per cent of total recharge, depending on the year.

Along the coast the water tritium content is zero because it is old fresh water, now flowing landwards or still. The situation is clearer in the less permeable materials of the deep aquifers below the river mouth area.

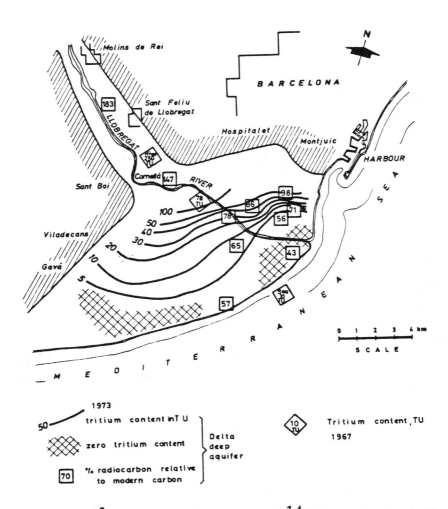

Fig. 10.10 – Tritium (T,$^3H_1$) and radio-carbon ($^{14}C_6$) content of the Llobregat delta deep aquifer water. Values are referred to 1973. Tritium values are given in tritium units (TU); 1 TU = 10 30^{-18} T/H. Radiocarbon values values are given in percentage of radiocarbon content relative to modern carbon. According with local experience, present infiltration values varies between 65 to 70 per cent; higher values indicates nuclear-bomb radiocarbon. Up to Prat de Llobregat, water renovation is very rapid because the aquifer is highly transmissive and the abstraction very important. Toward the sea there is a mixture of new and old water, and near the sea very old water is found, representing the recharge under undisturbed conditions.

The radiocarbon content shows the same facts. Up to the 30-50 tritium units (TU) line, radiocarbon from atmospheric nuclear test was found. Along the 10 TU line the radiocarbon content just shows recent water without contamination from nuclear tests. Along the coast, the radiocarbon content is clearly below that of recent non-contaminated groundwater. Maximum water ages are from 3,000 to 4,000 years in the less permeable sand formations. No data is available on the two areas through which sea water intrusion is supposed to proceed.

Water between the 50 and 100 TU lines, in 1973, corresponds to rainfall and river water infiltrated in 1962, and water in the valley mouth is less than one year old. Transit time between these two places 6 km apart is about 11 years.

A similar figure is obtained when the changes in the chloride content in the river water are compared with the changes observed in the Prat well water, as shown in Figure 10.11. The great increase in chloride content in river water is a consequence of salt and potash mining activities upstream. Recent river water is easily identifiable by its chloride content and chemical composition (Custodio, 1968), and their underground movement can be studied. Figure 10.12 shows the zones of the aquifers filled with the chloride-polluted river water.

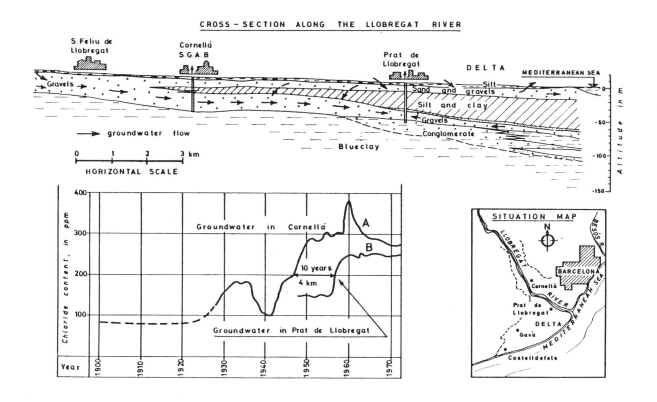

CROSS – SECTION ALONG THE LLOBREGAT RIVER

Fig. 10.11 - Longitudinal cross-section of the Llobregat's lower valley and delta showing the groundwater flow and a chart of the chloride variation in two well sites along the flow lines, about 4 km far. A ten year delay exists. Curve A shows the chloride evolution in a well near Cornellá, that reflects the damped chloride variation in the river with a 9 to 12 months delay. Curve B correspond to a well in Prat de Llobregat; abstracted water is a mixture of the water coming through Cornellá, and some of the less saline delta old water.

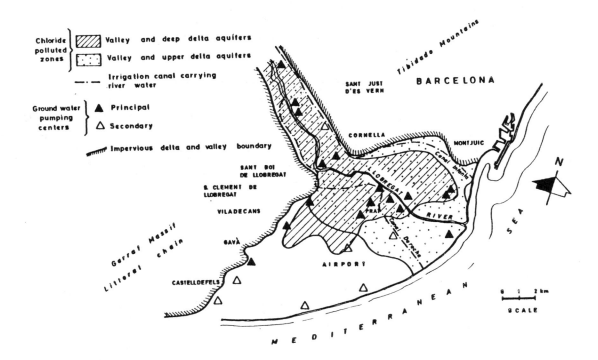

Fig. 10.12 - Areas in the Llobregat lower valley and delta influenced by the high chloride pollution of the river. Chloride pollution in the upper delta aquifer is through canal losses and irrigation. In the deep delta aquifer it is through induced recharge in the valley caused by the intense abstraction. The river receives residual brines from the potash mines upstream. This salinization must not be confused with that produced by sea water admixture.

Groundwater salinity

Since the river crosses areas where evaporite salts (mainly sodium chloride and gypsum) outcrop, the natural background in the lower Llobregat is about 80 to 120 ppm Cl. This is the chlorinity of the old water referred to before and now found in the central part of the delta. But as shown in figure 10.13, in some areas near the coast, especially in the western area, much higher values are found, resulting from a mixing of this water with old entrapped sea water, in an unfinished process of sea water wash-out. It is clearly shown by the alkaline-ion to chloride, and the magnesium to calcium ratios (fig. 10.14) (Custodio, 1968; Custodio, Bayó and Peláez, 1971; Custodio, Cacho, Peláez and García, 1976), that show the cation exchanges taking place. Areas with high values correspond to slowly flowing waters.

The two other saline zones will be discussed below, because they represent modern sea water intrusion. Higher values landward represent river related young water or water concentrated by evaporation through irrigation and reaching the deep aquifer by seepage through the upper aquifer.

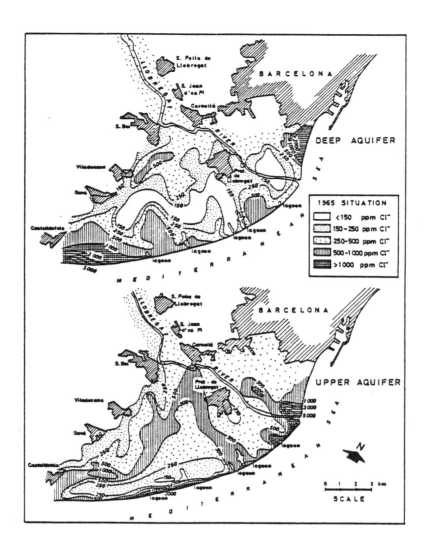

Fig. 10.13 - Chloride content pattern in the deep and upper Llobregat's delta
aquifers (after Custodio, 1971). The pattern is influenced by old
river water, new river water contaminated with residual brines,
local water, old sea water, new sea water encroaching the aquifers
and irrigation return flows.

In the upper aquifer, the chemical composition of the water is variable, since different sources exist: rainfall infiltration, lateral run-off
infiltration, canal water infiltration, irrigation return flows and used water
infiltration. The angled strip area of more than 500 ppm Cl on the right side
of the delta (fig. 10.13) represents water concentrated by evaporation,
directly from the ground when the water table is shallow or after irrigation
with groundwater. On the western side there is mixing with old sea water due
to pumping. Some saline penetrations along the coast represent the effect of
coastal lagoons and marshes. The saline zone existing just at the left of the
river is due to a higher permeability area, reduced recharge, waste infiltration and some residual sea water. The low chlorinity water existing near the
coast in the central-western part is mainly rainwater infiltrated in the dune
belt existing there, floating on more saline water.

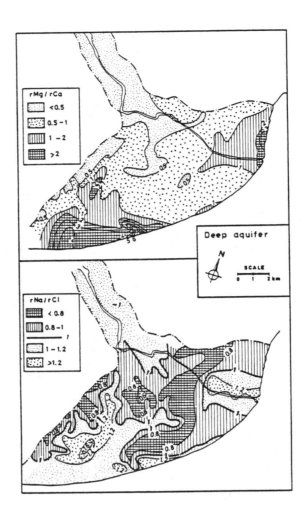

Fig. 10.14 - Chemical characterisics of groundwater in the deep aquifer as deduced from the rMg/rCa and rNa/rCl ratios. The increase in the rMg/rCa ratio is due to the mixing with sea water, but near the river mouth it is due to Ca^{++} exchange and precipitation. The areas with rNa/rCl greater than 1 (in that case the recharge water has a ratio close to 1) represent recent water from the river or groundwater affected by sea water intrusion; when that ratio is clearly less than 1, old waters in a low permeability portion of the aquifer are involved, both fresh and brackish water.

The chemical composition of the saline water trapped in the semipervious intermediate layer is also shown in figure 10.5. The Na deficit in the central part corresponds to the ionic exchange between sea water and the sediments transported by the river. The Na excess in the lower part shows that historically an upward flow (now reversed) was occurring, since the new fresh water interchanges ionically with the lens materials. The chemical characteristics in the semipervious formations has been obtained by extracting undisturbed cores. In the laboratory they were either dispersed in distilled water and the resulting chemical composition determined, or vacuum distilled for tritium measurements.

Sea water encroachment

The present water flow pattern in the central and eastern part of the deep aquifer of the Llobregat delta, deduced from the piezometric maps and hydro-chemical studies, is as shown in figure 10.15.

Groundwater arriving from the valley is distributed to the main pumping centers, and some recharge is added from the upper aquifer along the east boundary. At the same time, sea water encroaches through two main areas.

The first one is located between the river mouth and the airport, coinciding with the deep old river channel (formed under a previous estuarine situation), which is supposed to be the main outcrop of the deep aquifer on the sea floor. This penetration was suggested by the 1965 chloride map and was fully developed in 1977, as shown in figure 10.16. Unfortunately, the saline water, at present only a mixture of fresh water with some sea water, advances through an elongated narrow area devoid of observation wells. Dispersion is very high, as expected in such an unsteady process. Break-through is concentrated in privileged portions of the aquifer.

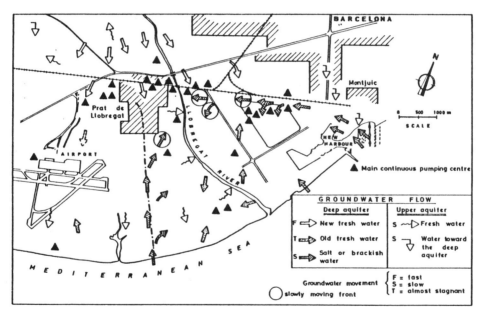

Fig. 10.15 - Groundwater flow pattern in the eastern Llobregat delta aquifers in 1977. Fresh water comes from the river, through infiltration in the valley (deep aquifer) or through canal losses and irrigation return flows (upper aquifer). Non-renewable old fresh water flows towards the pumping centers and is replaced by new fresh water or sea water. Sea water penetrates through the deep aquifer and moves towards the pumping centers, being mixed with fresh water. When the symbol is encircled it indicates the tendency, and only a slight salinization existed in 1977, with seasonal fluctuations according with recharge or changes in the pumping pattern. Since some wells extract brackish or saline water, a further penetration is hindered, although the concentrations seaward continue to increase.

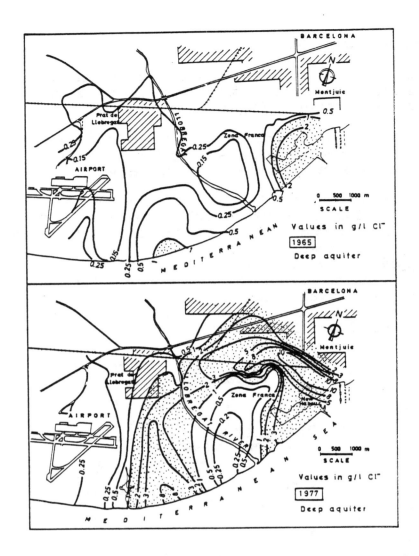

Fig. 10.16 - Chloride content pattern in the eastern Llobregat delta deep aquifer in 1965 and 1977. The two sea water encroachment areas are clearly shown, and also the effect of sea water abstraction in the Zona Franca area (eastern sector), that cuts the salt water penetration, thus protecting areas closer to Prat de Llobregat.

The second one is located in the eastern boundary. Salinization proceeds mainly downwards near the coast, since in this area a thick sequence of sand formations prevails, and sea water is only hindered by a scarcely effective muddy sea floor. The flow follows the shortest path to the main industrial wells in the Zona Franca area and towards the highly permeable deep aquifer lobe extending from the valley mouth up to those wells. Sea water is diluted by the inflow from the upper aquifer and by mixing with fresh water. The penetration was clearly indicated in 1965 and well developed in 1977 (fig. 10.16).

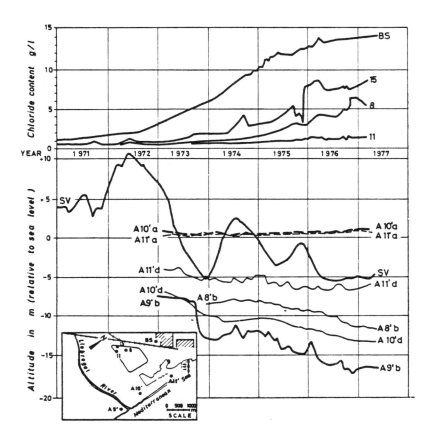

Fig. 10.17 - Salinity increase in four wells in the Zona Franca area (Eastern Llobregat delta) and water level trend in the deep aquifer. Piezometer SV is in the river lower valley and represents the main area of recharge. BS, 8, 11 and 15 are pumping wells in the deep aquifer. A-10', A-11', A-8', and A-9' are piezometer sites, the a indicating the upper aquifer, and the b and d deep layers.

Figure 10.17 reproduces the piezometric level trends in some of the observation bore-holes in the central-eastern area, and also shows the salinity evolution in some of the wells near the main pumping center in the Zona Franca. Well BS is in the path of the sea water encroachment and the salinization is clearly developed. Wells 15 and 8 show the same trend but less developed, in spite of being in the main pumping center; they are placed in the boundary of the above mentioned more permeable lobe and an intense hydrodynamic mixing takes place in them between diluted sea water and river infiltrated water coming from the valley. Well 11 only shows a slight salinization because it is placed outside the lobe, and extracts preferently old water, slowly draining from a deep sandy formation around the river mouth. The salinization process was accelerated in 1972 when the groundwater levels went down during the predominantly dry period that followed.

Figure 10.18 shows the detailed piezometric and chloride map in the surroundings of the main pumping center in the Zona Franca area.

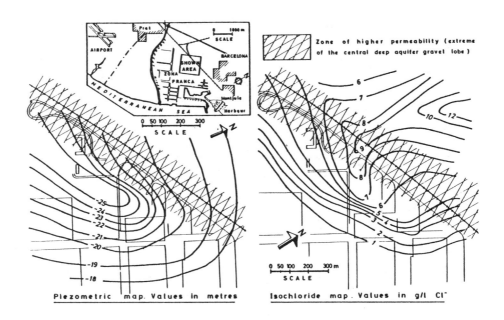

Fig. 10.18 - Detailed piezometric and isochloride maps of the deep delta
aquifer in the surroundings of the main pumping center in the Zona
Franca area. There are 12 active industrial pumping wells, with a
discharge between 15 and 40 1/s per well. The high permeability
zone in the boundary of the well zone is shown. The isochloride
lines show the diversion of incoming sea water towards these wells.

An important fact is the contribution of old fresh water stored in
less permeable sand formations, without replenishment of new fresh water.

Another important fact is the barrier effect of these pumpings,
which prevent the salty water reaching the wells around Prat de Llobregat, but
for a small fraction. Until 1976, generally there was a slight but positive
water gradient from Prat toward the Zona Franca, but after that year the water
gradient was reversed most of the time (increased pumpage in Prat and
decreased pumpage in the Zona Franca area), thus allowing the movement of part
of the intruded sea water towards Prat. Wells near that area pump fresh water
with a slight admixture of salt water, that sharply increases when the wells
in the Zona Franca stop for some time. Chemical diagrams agree with the
existence of this sea water intrusion (fig. 10.19) in the commented areas.

The present advancement of the central intrusion is also indirectly
controlled by some wells that get brackish water.

Between the two main encroachment areas exists old salty water in
less permeable formations. The upper ground water varies from slightly salty
to sea water, depending on the local circumstances, but the underlying fine
sand formation contain old fresh water with only a slight sea water contamination. Although salinity increases downward, in the deep aquifer sublayers the
salinity can increase up or downwards, depending on local circumstances. Figure 10.16 shows that probably some sea water intrusion exists now in this
area, but it is of minor importance.

Until now, the excavation of the harbor has not produced adverse effects since water levels in the upper aquifer are sufficiently over sea level (tidal range can be neglected since it is less than 0.3 m), but may be another way of contamination in the long term since water recharge has been greatly reduced after land occupation.

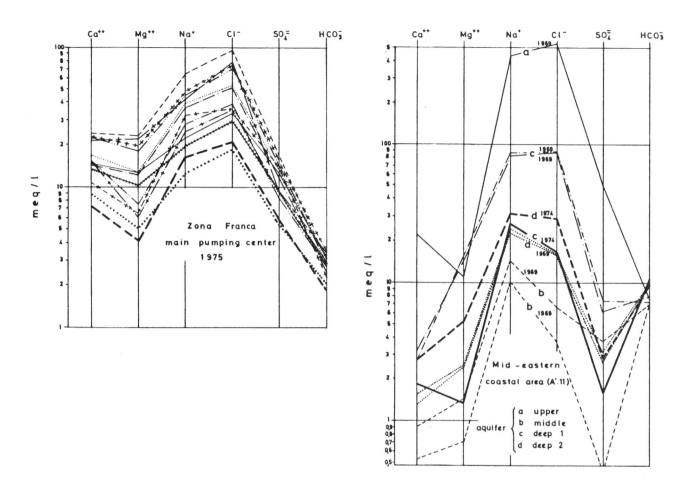

Fig. 10.19 - Logarithmic vertical column chemical diagrams of groundwater of the Zona Franca area. In the wells of the main pumping center, the sea water intrusion is well established with positive chloride-alkaline ion unbalance ratios. In the Mid-Eastern coastal area the upper aquifers are sea water contaminated after some years. In the deep aquifers, the highly negative chloride-alkaline ion unbalance ratio indicates that in 1969 the flushing of old sea water still was predominant although at present it is reversed. In the middle aquifer, flushing is dominant. Studies carried out with radioactive tracers show that level c recharges level d. Both c and d aquifers receive sea water contamination, but it is more intense through level c.

The percentage of origins of water recharge to the main deep aquifer of the Zona Franca are:

Year	1965	1970	1973	1975	1977
% water from the valley	24	51	53	50	19
% water from old water in the SW	8	4	4	4	6
% water from old water and upper aquifer in the NE	16	12	13	13	19
% sea water	52	33	30	33	76

and the calculated sea water encroachment:

	1965	1970	1973	1975	1977
$10^6 m^3$/year of sea water pumped out	0.01	0.07	0.19	1.00	1.70
$10^6 m^3$/year of sea water entering through the through the E boundary	1.3	1.7	2.2	3.6	3.9
m/year of salt or brackish water encroachment					
-from the sea to the main pumping center in the Zona Franca	270	360	450	550	820
-from the main pumping center in the Zona Franca toward the main pumping center in Prat	0	0	0	0	500

In the western part of the delta, sea water intrusion also takes place, induced by the abstractions along the boundary. Salinity is now increasing. The salinity originates in deep old sea water. This water moves through the deep formations until it appears in the wells in the area where the two aquifers communicate. A first study of well water salinity shows that salinity decreases seaward, but this is due to the fact that most of the wells in this area are shallow or intermediate ones, not reaching the deep formations except at the boundary.

Prediction of sea water intrusion

In order to study the groundwater flow quantitatively and to forecast future situations, a groundwater mathematical model was derived and completed in 1971. A two-layer finite difference model was selected, using irregular polygons in lieu of a regular rectangular net, in order to follow the characteristics of permeability distribution and piezometric gradients with a minimum of equations (REPO, 1971; Cuena and Custodio 1971; Custodio, Cuena and Bayó, 1971; Vilaró and Custodio, 1973; Custodio 1982a; Cacho, Custodio, García, 1977). It permitted the model to run on small computers. Figure 10.20 shows the grid and some results of the model calibration.

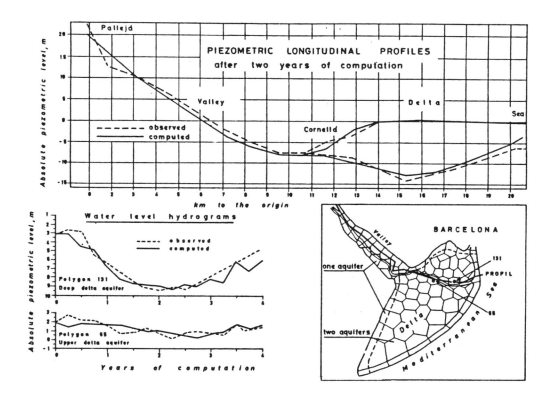

Fig. 10.20 - Results of the calibration of the Llobregat model of the lower valley and delta aquifers. Sea water encroachment is calculated after evaluation of sea-aquifer water exchanges.

The permeability values near the coast vary between 500 and 1,000 m^2/day in the deep aquifer, slightly higher in the upper one. Vertical permeability of the lens in the delta was between 0.005 and 0.001 m/day, and somewhat smaller, about 0.0005 along the coast in the right delta side.

One of the major difficulties for the model were the sea boundary conditions. In the upper aquifer the nodes were placed at the shore and the water level fixed to zero, without the BHG correction. The error is small since the upper-aquifer bottom is only 10 to 15 m below sea level.

Since the characteristics of the deep aquifer under the sea were unknown, it was closed by an impervious boundary, introducing a connection with the sea, proportional to the vertical water gradient, and adjusting the coefficients in the calibration runs.

The adjustment of the model showed 0.5 x 10^6 m^3/year of sea water encroachment in 1971. In a dry year, the predicted quantity is 1.10 x 10^6 m^3/year, and an increase of pumping in Prat of 15 x 10^6 m^3/year will increase the sea water intrusion to 4 x 10^6 m^3/year. These figures are somewhat lower than that calculated from a chemical balance, but they are of the same order of magnitude.

The model does not intend to predict the saline water front movement, but some positions were calculated by hand and they agree roughly with observations. The model predicted the sea water encroachment through the right delta side, at that time not fully recognized.

Administrative actions

In spite of the serious sea water encroachment in the Llobregat delta deep aquifer, only timid administrative actions have been undertaken. The main explanation is the private character of groundwater according to the old Spanish Water Law (first written in 1866, promulgated in 1878).

Water protection is the matter for the well owners and until recently they have not been aware of the problem, in spite of its seriousness.

The Public Administration through the Eastern Pyrenees Water Authority and the Public Works Geological Service, has carried out some detailed studies since 1965 and operates a dense observation network. A shortage of manpower and economic resources, and insufficient legal support has prevented more complete studies and actions to be undertaken.

That Authority, in an effort to reduce the problem, has gained some administrative control of the whole Llobregat delta, using some possibilities of the Water Law, although groundwater continue to be private. The argument that groundwater abstraction diverts public river water from its natural course, though weak, has allowed the promotion of a User's Association that intends to take care of the problem, and the first results appear in a reduction of total abstraction and on a strict control of new wells.

The lack of an adequate land planning is also one of the factors leading to the difficult present situation. Present actions to redress the situation must accept established situations.

Costs and solutions

Only rough estimations of the direct cost of the salinization problem are available. The figures refer to the substitution of well water for treated river water. Present total cost of well water is about 1 to 2 ptas/ m^3, depending on elevation and well discharge (150 ptas $\sim$ \$ 1 U.S.). The price of treated river water, distributed to the saline areas, will be around 25 to 45 ptas/ m^3, This is an excessive increase for the industries with a high water demand. For the artificial textiles and paper mills this accounts for about 300,000 to 600,000 ptas increase per worker and per year, and for the car factories about 20,000 to 40,000 ptas/worker/year or about 1,500 ptas per car. The last figures are not significant, but not the first ones.

In a few years time, there will not be enough regulated water in the river, and no space exists for new reservoirs to replace the lost storage capacity of the aquifers. This compels the consideration of the construction of a new transportation water canal from the Ebro river (a 150 km long canal with a 300 m initial elevation, with acute political and administrative problems, and possibly an excessively long construction period) or sewage water reuse. The cost of water from these doubtful solutions, to substitute for the non useful salty water, including water treatment distribution, will be at least 40 ptas/ m^3 for the canal water or about 25 ptas/ m^3 for the reclaimed sewage water. The canal will cost about 3 x 10^9 ptas and sewagewater treatment and transportation facilities about 6 x 10^9 ptas.

The preceeding figures justify the interest in solving the sea water intrusion problem. Different simultaneous actions are foreseen:

1. Reduction of total abstraction. Several of the main industries are taking serious steps in this direction. It is not an easy task because the present plant-layout impedes efficient water recycling without major modifications. A 50 per cent reduction in water demand is foreseen. The displacement of the industries to other areas will cause tremendous social problems. No new industrial wells will be allowed except for small ones. Some of the groundwater agricultural demand will be supplied with treated sewage water, coupled to artificial recharge. The assumed cost of demand reduction is about 2 to 5 ptas/ m^3.

2. Temporarily pumping of salt water in the more effected areas, until other more definitive measures can be applied. The cost may be around 2 to 3 ptas/ m^3 of total available water.

3. Improving river water recharge in the lower valley by surface artificial recharge practices in the river bed. This will probably be the most effective means to combat sea water intrusion through a general increase in groundwater levels. If the water table in the low valley aquifer can be maintained near the river bottom, piezometric levels in the delta deep aquifer will be increased by 10 m, thus reducing present sea water encroachment rate to 1/3 and to at least 1/10 if total abstraction is reduced by 50 per cent. The cost may be about 0.5 to 1.5 ptas/ m^3 of abstracted water. The efficiency of the method needs detailed pilot tests. Present artificial recharge is not enough. Coastal fresh water injection barriers do not appear neither effective nor cheaper, although some connector wells to drain the excess water from the upper aquifer (now lost to the sea) must be useful and cheap, though only a small water quantity is available.

All these actions need a legal and administrative framework that allows for the necessary management, good operation and adequate economical support.

From a regional water management point of view, the Llobregat lower valley and delta aquifers must be used in such a way that their regulating capacity would be at maximum, without forgetting the transmissive properties. This implies that a more effective use of river water must be developed to supply industry, giving to the aquifers the role of providing water for human consumption and for agriculture. It is also an important backup system for the river.

Acknowledgements

The author is indebted to the Eastern Pyrenees Water Agency, the Prat de Llobregat Municipality and the SEAT factory for permitting the use of the data obtained for them. The studies were initiated in 1965 by M.R. Llamas and followed by F. Vilaró as chief of the working team on the Eastern Pyrenees. Some of the data also come from reports made by students of the International Groundwater Course. The observations and conclusions do not represent any official statement, but the ideas of the author.

References

Cacho, F., Custodio, E., García, J.L. (1977). Modelling the aquifers of the Llobregat delta (Barcelona, Spain). Int. Assoc. Hydrogeologists. General Assembly of Birmingham, Vol. XIII-1, pp. E 12-24.

Cuena, J., Custodio, E. (1971). Construction and adjustment of a two layer mathematical model of the Llobregat delta. Mathematical Models in Hydrology, Proc. of the Warsaw Symposium, IASH-Unesco-WMO. Vol. 2 (published 1974), 62 pp. 950-964.

Custodio, E. (1967). Études hydrogéochimiques dans le delta du Llobregat, Barcelona (Espagne). General Assembly of Bern, Internat. Assoc. Scientific Hydrology, Pub. 62 pp. 135-155.

Custodio, E. (1968). Datación de aguas en el delta del rio Llobregat (Water dating in the Llobregat delta). Documentos de Investigación Hidrológica no. 6, Centro de Estudios, Investigación y Aplicaciones del Agua, Barcelona, pp. 205-237.

Custodio, E. (1978). Artificial recharge in the coastal aquifers near Barcelona (Spain). Seminar on Selected Water Problems in Islands and Coastal Areas, with special regard to Desalination and Groundwater, United Nations, Economic Commission for Europe, Malta, Water Sem. 5/R.8, 10 pp.

Custodio, E. (1982a). Model of the aquifers in the Llobregat delta (Catalonia, Spain). Groundwater Models, Case History 2, Unesco, Studies and Reports in Hydrology no. 34, Paris, pp. 39-51.

Custodio, E. (1982b). Sea water encroachment in the Llobregat and Besós areas, near Barcelona (Catalonia, Spain). Intruded and Relict Groundwater of Marine Origin, VII Sea Water Intrusion Meeting, SWIM, Uppsala, Sveriges Geologiska Undersokning, Repporter och Meddelanden 27, pp. 120-152.

Custodio, E., Bayó, A., Peláez, M.D. (1971). Geoquímica y datación de aguas para el estudio del movimiento de las aguas subterráneas en el delta del Llobregat (Barcelona). (Geochemistry and water dating for the study of the groundwater movement in the Llobregat delta, Barcelona), Primer Congreso Hispano-Luso-Americano de Geología Económica, Sec. 6, Madrid-Lisboa, pp. 51-80.

Custodio, E., Cuena, J., Bayó, A. (1971). Planteamiento, ejecución y utilización de un modelo matemático de dos capas para los acuíferos del delta del Llobregat (Barcelona). (Establishment, completion and utilisation of a two-layer mathematical model of the Llobregat delta aquifers, Barcelona), Primer Simposio Hispano-Luso-Americano de Geológia Ecónomica, Madrid-Lisboa, Vol. III, paper E. 3-17, pp. 171-198.

Custodio, E., Cacho, F., Peláez, M.D., García, J.L. (1976). Problemática de la intrusión marina en los acuíferos del delta del Llobregat. (Sea water encroachment problems in the Llobregat delta aquifers), II National Assembly of Geodesy and Geophysics, Barcelona, Instituto Geografico y Catastral, Madrid, pp. 21-3-2129.

Custodio, E., Suárez, M., Isamat, F.J., Miralles, J.M. (1977). Combined use of surface and groundwater in Barcelona Metropolitan Area (Spain). Internat. Assoc. Hydrogeologists, General Assembly of Birmingham, Vol. XIII.1, pp. c.14-27.

Llamas, M.R., Vilaró, F. (1967). Die rolle der grundwasser speicher bei der wasserversorgung von Barcelona. (The role of the groundwaters in the supply of Barcelona), Des Gas-und Wasserfach, Wasser-Abwasser, Vol. 34, no. 15, pp. 945-953.

Marqués, M.A. (1975). Las formaciones cuaternarias del delta del Llobregat. (The quaternary formations of the Llobregat delta), Acta Geologica Hipánica, Vol. X, pp. 21-28.

MOP (1966). Estudio de los recursos hidráulicos totales de las cuencas de los rios Besós y Bajo Llobregat, 2° informe. (Study of the total water resources of the Besos and Low Llobregat rivers, 2nd report), Comisaria de Aguas del Pirineo Oriental y Servicio Geologico de Obras Publicas, Barcelona, 4 vols.

Santa Maria, L., Marín, A. (1910). Estudios hidrológicos en la cuenca del rio Llobregat. (Hydrological studies in the Llobregat basin), Boletin de la Comisión del Mapa Geológico in Espana, Madrid, pp. 31-52.

REPO (1971). Construcción, ajuste y utilización de un modelo matematico de los acuíferos del Bajo Llobregat. (Construction, adjustment and utilization of a mathematical model of the Low Llobregat aquifers), Estudio de los Recursos Hidráulicos Totales del Pirineo Oriental, Comisaria de Aguas del Pirineo Oriental y Servicio Geológico de Obras Públicas, Edes, Barcelona, 1 Vol, 130 pp.

Vilaró, F. (1967). Balance del aprovechamiento actual del Bajo Llobregat. (Balance of the present water use of the Low Llobregat), Documentos de Investigación Hidrológica no. 2, Barcelona Symposium, Centro de Estudios, Investigación y Aplicaciones del Agua, Barcelona, pp. 155-169.

Vilaró, F., Custodio, E. (1973). Data aquisition and methodology for a simulation model of the Llobregat delta (Barcelona, Spain). Symposium on Design of Water Resources Projects with Inadequate Data, Unesco-WMO-IASH, Madrid, Studies and Reports in Hydrology No. 16, Vol. 1, pp. 581-598.

Vilaró, F., Martín Arnáiz, M. (1968). Balance hídrico del Llobregat. (Water balance of the Llobregat), Seminario de Balances Hidricos, FAO-IGME, Madrid.

Case history no. 2: Fresh water extraction and salt water encroachment in the Amsterdam dune water catchment area*

Introduction

The dune-water catchment area of the Amsterdam Water Supply Board is situated along the Dutch North Sea coast, south of the city of Haarlem. Water withdrawal in this area, some 36 km^2, started as early as 1853, by the simple method of draining a system of open canals, dug for the purpose. By this type of development, water was extracted from the upper phreatic aquifer. It was not until many years later that the presence of a vast stock of semi-confined water of excellent quality was discovered deeper in the subsurface.

In the catchment area, the subsurface at a greater depth is saturated with salt water. The fresh water is limited to a fresh-water pocket, or lens, under the dunes. Since 1903, water has been extracted from the lower subsurface by a system of wells.

The volume of water withdrawal in the Amsterdam catchment area has been gradually stepped up.

Annual water withdrawal in million m^3 are:

Year	Aquifer		Total
	Upper	Lower	
1900	9	--	9
1925	14	6	20
1956	10	21	31
1970	57	7	24

The upper aquifer in 1970 includes
$52 \times 10^6 m^3$ of river water
artificially recharged.

The only natural source of replenishment for the whole system is effective precipitation, which, for the entire catchment area, is no more than 13 million m^3 annually. Consequently, the system has been overdrawn for more than 25 years.

In order to achieve a more intensive exploitation of the whole catchment area, the upper aquifer is now artificially recharged with water from the River Rhine, a process which started in 1957 (Biemond, 1957).

This brought the annual capacity up to 83 million m^3. At the same time, water extraction from the lower aquifer was virtually stopped, for a number of reasons, one of them being that an increasing number of wells had been contaminated with salt water. There remains, however, a vast stock of high quality groundwater, and possible methods for its development are being studied.

----

*Contributed by A.J. Roebert, City of Amsterdam Water Supply Board.

Geology

The conditions for fresh water development in the Amsterdam catchment area are largely determined by its geological situation. The geological build-up of the area can be derived from a large number of scattered boreholes, 35 of which go down to depths of over 80 m - O.D. Many of them have been turned into observations wells for level and quality checks of the groundwater. For the deeper boreholes, annual water analyses are being made and a number of recent bores have permanent electrode systems for groundwater salinity inspection (Walter, 1967).

Figure 10.21 shows the stratigraphic and hydrological sequence of the subsurface. Most important, from a geohydrological point of view, is the clay-layer located at a depth of 18 m - O.D., from now on referred to as clay-layer. Quite often, this clay-layer fails to show up in geological logs, but its presence is indicated by a general resistance to vertical waterflow at this level throughout the area. Several bores show loam or clay-layers at various depths between 60 m and 90 m - O.D. Especially in the northern part of the catchment area, these layers divide the lower aquifer into two sub-aquifers. In the following paragraphs, it will be shown that these layers, from now on referred to as loam-layer, are of major importance, locally, to the rate of salt water contamination in the extraction wells.

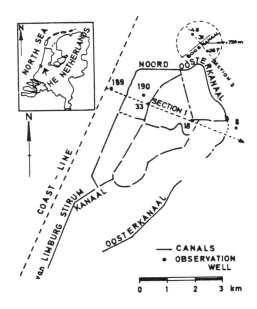

Fig. 10.21 - Stratigraphy and hydrology of the subsurface. T is the transmissivity and c is the aquitard hydraulic sensitivity.

Hydrological situation

The clay-layer divides the subsurface into an upper and a lower aquifer. The lower aquifer's semi-pervious base is located at 160 m - O.D. (fig. 10.22). Due to their effective separation, both aquifers have their own flow regimen. In some places, the difference in head is several meters, with a current average, for the whole area, of 2.25 m. In 1957, the year which ended a long period of intensive extraction from the lower aquifer, the watershed is fairly close to the sea coast, so that relatively little fresh water is lost to the sea. Most of the water infiltrating through the clay-layer flows to the land side. Part of it is directly recovered in wells and another portion adds to the stock of water in the fresh water lens.

In salt water, conditions are different. The boundary conditions for the salt water flow below the fresh water lens are, to the west of the catchment area, mean sea level of 0.15 m - O.D. and to the east, the Haarlemmermeer-polder level of 5.75 m - O.D. The seepage flow, caused by the low level of the Haarlemmermeer-polder--a reclaimed tract--is creating a serious salt water intrusion problem in the polder's many ditches.

The hydrological constants of the catchment area have been established through water balances and numerous pumping tests (Huisman, 1954). Figure 10.21 shows the average rates of transmissivity (kb) of the aquifers and resistance (c) of the semi-pervious layers. These constants appear to differ widely throughout the area.

The recharge of the lower aquifer from the upper aquifer varies with the difference in head on either side of the clay-layer. The current recharge volume is about 10 million m^3 annually, and annual extraction from the lower aquifer averages some 4 million m^3. Frequent readings show that, after decades of overdraft, the stock of water in the fresh water lens has been on the increase since 1957.

In the southern region of the extraction area, the fresh water lens under the dunes is strictly separated from the underlying salt water by an interface of no more than 5 m thickness. This sharp interface is 'washed clean' by fresh water flowing along it, the effect of which outstrips that of interfacial diffusion. In areas where the loam-layer is well-developed, the original stock of salt water is hardly, if at all, displaced by fresh water. In figure 10.22, this stock is indicated as 'residual brackish water.' Figure 10.22 is based on hundreds of groundwater analyses, carried out since 1903. It shows the area in cross-section, perpendicular to the coastline. This section is marked 'section 1' in figure 10.23. In the western part of this cross-section, it will be seen that, owing to groundwater extraction between 25 m and 35 m - O.D., the original sharp fresh water/salt water interface has extended into a transition zone of some 50 m thickness. An example of this phenomenon will be discussed in detail later.

Formation of the fresh water lens

The formation of the Older Dunes (fig. 10.22) started about 4000 years ago, when a coastal strip, covering the site of the present catchment area and the dunes east of it, began to build up gradually to a level above its surroundings. The formation proceeded in several stages and resulted in a series of barriers running parallel to the coast. The oldest barriers are those lying further inland (Jelgersma and Van Regteren Altena, 1969). In their final stage, the Older Dunes covered a strip at least 8 km wide. It is generally assumed that the Older Dunes were rather low, much lower, at any rate, than the Younger Dunes, some of which are as high as 40 m + O.D.

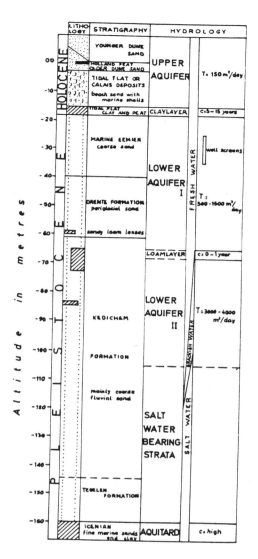

Fig. 10.22 – Hydrogeological cross-section. The trace is shown in fig. 10.21.

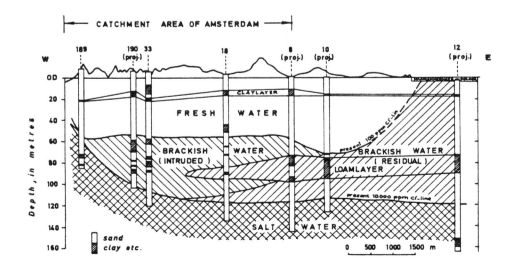

Fig. 10.23 – Situation map of the catchment area.

Prior to the formation of the Older Dunes, the landscape was flat, proof of which can be found in the marine tidal flat and beach deposits. The entire subsoil was saturated with salt water. Precipitation could effect no more than superficial desalinization, because the higher density (ρ) of the subsurface water prevented fresh water from penetrating deeply into the subsoil. Salt water (ρ_s = 1020 kg/m^3) can only be displaced by fresh water (ρ_f = 1000 kg/m^3) if sufficient fresh water has accumulated to provide a certain overpressure. Accordingly, it was only after the first of the Older Dunes had formed, some 4000 years ago, that precipitation began to build up a body of fresh water, according to the Badon Ghyben-Herzberg principle.

In practice, the maximum recorded depth of the interface between the fresh water and the underlying salt water is between 120 m and 130 m - O.D. The interface's lowest point is located halfway under the Older Dunes. The Younger Dunes, formed after A.D. 1200 are much higher. They constitute a strip no more than 4 km wide, covering the western part of the Older Dunes complex. Consequently, the eastern boundary of the Younger Dunes no doubt had some additional effect on the shape of the fresh water lens. At any rate, new boundary conditions were introduced with the reclamation of the Haarlemmermeer-polder, in 1850. As a result of this intervention in natural conditions and of water winning from the lower aquifer, which started in 1903, a major change has also begun in the thickness of the interface. This process will be discussed in more detail in the following paragraphs.

Fresh water stocks

Any computation of groundwater stocks in water bearing strata is essentially deceptive. The very word 'stock' seems to imply the possibility of consumption, because stocks are usually open to some kind of use. The vast reserves of groundwater found to be present by such computations foster the belief that there is no need to worry about future supplies.

For the Amsterdam catchment area, however, this kind of computation is quite relevant and, for several reasons, even interesting. Firstly, because the area is a hydrological unit, and, secondly, because the available data make it possible to calculate the stocks available at two different points in time, separated by a period of no less than 60 years. The volume of water extracted during that period constitutes a considerable portion of the total stock. A comparison, therefore, of the fresh water volume present at both points in time, will produce an interesting picture of the dune area's water balance. Around 1910, the catchment area contained 23 observation wells reaching down into the salt water zone. At the time of their drilling, a few years earlier, a large number of samples was drawn from temporary piezometers, placed at various depths. From the analyzed samples, the original position of the fresh water/salt water interface can be determined with a fair degree of accuracy. Since 1910, the position of the interface has been determined from the readings of 35 observation wells and the results of a geo-electrical research project, carried out by the Ground Water Survey, T.N.O. (Van Dongen, 1969).

Figure 10.24 was drawn on the basis of these data, to show the position of the 100 ppm isochlor, as it was in 1910 and 1970.

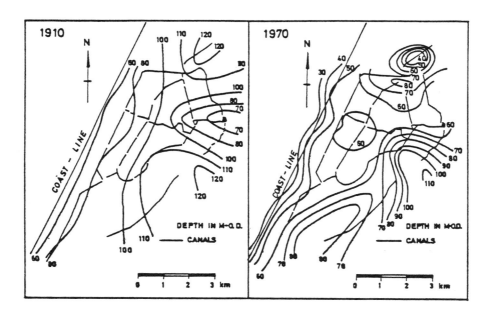

Fig. 10.24 – Contour map of the 100 mg/l isochlor in 1910 and in 1970.

The Boogkanaal constitutes the northern most part of the catchment area (fig. 10.23). Owing to its relatively low water level of 1.75 m – O.D., the canal attracts water from the upper aquifer. Next to the waterline, 20 wells have been drilled at distances of 50 m, with screens in the lower aquifer. Due to the canal's particular low level, the wells are of the artesian type, each supplying some 10 m³/h. The Boogkanaal deep water extraction system has been in operation since the start of water withdrawal from the lower aquifer, in 1903. Between 1903 and 1970, a total of over 313 billion m³ has been extracted here, in a fairly continuous process. In the Boogkanaal area, the loam-layer is almost entirely absent. The 100 ppm isochlor, originally found at 120 m – O.D., has gradually risen to 25 m – O.D. in the center of the row of wells, at the site of observation well 31 (fig. 10.25). The fact that the elevation is not due to a local upconing of brackish water is proved by analyses of water from boreholes 48 and 257, where a similar rise of the 100 ppm isochlor has been found. The rise observed at 257 was stronger than at 48, which is explained by several factors. One of them is the water extraction from the lower aquifer along the Noordoosterkanaal at a distance of 500 m from the Boogkanaal, which was started in 1948. Another factor is the water extraction, in the same area, by the Water Supply Board of the nearby village of Zandvoort. The original direction of groundwater flow is also playing a part.

Figure 10.26 shows the situation in 1970. Near bore 31 the 100 ppm isochlor has moved upward some 95 m, and that the 10,000 ppm isochlor has risen about 40 m based on the assumption that the transition zone was originally a sharp interface. The elevation velocity of the 100 mg/l isochlor is quite constant. At the Boogkanaal, it is 1.4m/year, and at 500 m distance it averages 1 m/year.

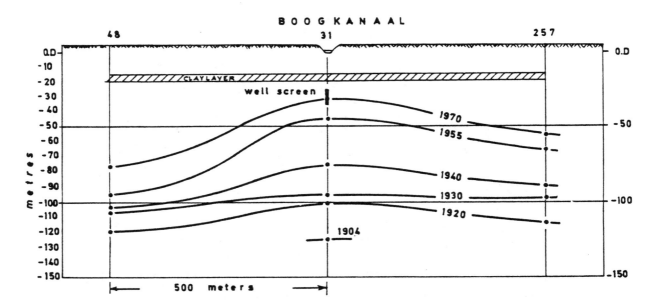

Fig. 10.25 – Rise of the 100 mg/l isochlor. Cross-section perpendicular to the Boogkanaal, following section 2 in fig. 10.21.

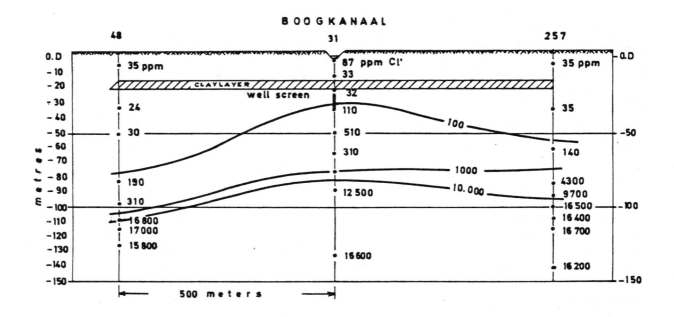

Fig. 10.26 – The hydrological situation in 1970. Cross-section perpendicular to the Boogkanaal, showing the 10^2, 10^3 and 10^4 mg/l isochlors, following section 2 in fig. 10.23.

On the basis of this information, we can work out a schematic water balance for an area with a radius of 750 m around the center of the Boogkanaal (fig. 10.23). For this area, the water balance of the lower aquifer, to the extent that it is saturated with water containing up to 100 mg/l Cl is:

$$Q = D - Dm + Fi - Fo$$

in which

Q = the volume of extracted groundwater;
D = depletion of fresh ground water stock (< 100 mg/l Cl);
Dm = that portion of D mixing with salt water, thus enlarging the brackish dispersion zone;
R = recharge of the lower aquifer through the clay-layer;
Fi = horizontal inflow;
Fo = horizontal outflow.

Extraction (Q) = 2 million m^3/year. Depletion (D) is computed as follows: Elevation velocity of the 100 mg/l isochlor is put at 1 m/year. For a porosity of 0.4, D equals 700,000 m^3/year. Recharge (R) is computed from the difference in head on either side the clay-layer and the resistance of the clay-layer is found to be 200,000 m^3/year. Fi = 2 million m^3/year. Fo = 400,000 m^3/year. The value thus found for Dm is 500,000 m^3/year. From this schematic water balance it is evident that there is little direct recharge into the lower aquifer, due to high resistance of the clay-layer in and around the Boogkanaal area.

This favors the rise of salt and brackish water. Owing to the low rate of recharge, deep water extraction along the Boogkanaal tends to deplete the available stock. Water extracted from the lower aquifer in the Boogkanaal wells now has an average Cl concentration of 95 mg/l.

Figure 10.25 shows that, within a few years, deep water extraction from the Boogkanaal will have to be stopped on account of the increased Cl concentration. From the water balance it is also clear that depletion of the fresh water stock entails a perhaps even greater loss of fresh water through mixing with salt water. But this particular point still calls for more detailed research.

Salt water contamination of the wells

From figures 10.22 and 10.26 it is clear that practically throughout the catchment area fresh water is found to a depth of at least 60 m – O.D. As the wells are screened between 25 m and 35 m – O.D., there are at least 25 meters of fresh water between the screens and the underlying salt water zone. There is, however, a vertical waterflow which accounts for most of the salt water intrusion in the wells. Due to the sharp drop in head in the wells, narrow cones of brackish water are drawn up to the well screens from the underlying dispersion zone. In some cases, the cones rise from brackish zones situated as much as 50 m below the screens. In case of upconing, the Cl ion concentration in the bottom section of the well screen is always higher than that in the top section. The process of upconing is discussed in an interesting article by Huisman (1954). As in 1954, a good mathematical explanation for this phenomenon has not yet been found.

Pennick (1914) was the first to draw attention to salt water contamination of the extraction wells in the Amsterdam catchment area. The process took on more serious proportions in the forties and fifties, when water extraction from the lower aquifer was greatly intensified.

Original dune water has about 30 mg/l C1. A well that has been contaminated with salt water during a period of intensive extraction will again produce original dune water after some time of rest. If extraction is resumed, the wells will be re-contaminated after some time, but experience in this field is only fragmentary. In one particular case, however, (the Barnaart-Schusterkanaal) it was found that the wells after a ten year rest, still showed no trace of contamination six months after extraction has been resumed. The total number of wells is about 502.

Salt water encroachment in 1956/57 ended a long period of intensive extraction from the lower aquifer. The importance of the loam-layer for the rate of salt water contamination of the wells is clear. This layer is most effective in the northeastern part of the catchment area, and it appears that in this very region no salt water contamination of the wells has been found, despite intensive exploitation. In most other places, wells appeared to be contaminated, even if the 100 mg/l isochlor hardly ever reached as high as the bottom of the well screens. Contamination in these places is caused by upconing of brackish water.

Conclusion

The clay layer is of key importance, because it separates the upper aquifer from the lower aquifer. Owing to this effective separation, the lower aquifer is barely affected by the artificial infiltration of Rhine water into the upper aquifer. However, in the lower aquifer salt water encroachment may increase because of the high resistance of the clay-layer. Salt water encroachment in the lower aquifer springs from two different sources;

1. The rise of the fresh water/salt water interface, and its extension into a dispersion zone.

2. The local upconing of brackish water under individual wells.

All available data from the lower aquifer indicate that, apart from some recharge through the clay-layer withdrawal from this level would mean depletion of the aquifer. It will be impossible to develop all of the 850 million m^3/year of fresh groundwater still present in the lower aquifer of the extraction site.

One of the additional problems created by the elevation of the salt water level is its activation of salt groundwater seepage flow from the sea to the Haarlemmermeer-polder. During extraction periods when the head under the dune catchment area is low, seepage flow to the polder is limited, but after extraction is discontinued, the seepage flow continues under the catchment area towards the polder.

However, the present rate of salt water encroachment does not imply that deep water extraction should be stopped altogether. The Amsterdam Water Supply Board is now using the lower aquifer as a reserve stock for periods when the quality of Rhine water is particularly poor for artificial recharge. During such periods, good quality drinking water may be obtained by a process of mixing infiltrated river water with water from the lower aquifer. In general, deep water extraction will continue to serve as a source of water supply in emergency situations.

References

Biemond, C. (1957). Dune water flow and replenishment in the catchment area of the Amsterdam water supply. J.I.W.E., Vol. II, No. 2, March.

Dongen, P.G. van (1969). Geo-electrisch onderzoek duinwaterwinplaats Amsterdam. Intern. Rapport 44, Dienst Grondwaterverkenning T.N.O.

Huisman, L. (1954). La formation de cones d'eau saumatre. UGGI Assemblée Générale de Rome 1954, Comptes Rendues at Rapports pp. 146-150.

Jelgersma, S., van Regteren Altena, J.F. (1969). Geological history of the coastal dunes in the western Netherlands. Geologie en Minjnbouw, Vol. 48, pp. 335-342.

Pennink, J.M.K. (1914). Verzoutingsrapport. Stadsdrukkerij Amsterdam.

Walter, F. (1967). Elektrische boorgatmetingen. Water, 50, 2, pp. 25-32.

10.3   Coastal plains

A wide range of different situations are included, having the common feature that a coastal plain is formed, different from a delta area.

Case history no. 3: Protection of a coastal aquifer against sea water intrusion: Case study of an artificial fresh water barrier in the Tel Aviv area*

Introduction

The municipal area of Tel Aviv-Yafo** covers a strip of land 3 to 6 km wide and 10 km in length, along the Mediterranean coast of Israel (fig. 10.27). It forms the nucleus of an urban complex consisting of six municipalities extending over an area of approximately 170 km^2, lying along a 13.4 km long shoreline. Tel-Aviv which in 1948 had a population of about 250,000, today contains over one million inhabitants.

The region in which the Tel-Aviv Metropolitan area is situated is one of coastal dunes, low sandstone ridges and flat plains covered with sandy loams and clays. The Yarqon River, a coastal stream fed mainly by springs rising at the foot of the Judean Hills, spills into the sea near Tel-Aviv's present northern border; its estuary has for some years been completely filled by sea water, since practically the whole of its fresh water flow is intercepted in the foothill region to supply water for irrigation and for municipal use.

Within the Tel-Aviv Metropolitan area the town of Tel-Aviv has the longest record of groundwater exploitation, the surrounding towns having developed more recently and reached their present extent only during the last two decades. Tel-Aviv's present water consumption amounts to 47×20^6 m^3 (million cubic meters) per year, of which 25×10^6 m^3 are expended for domestic consumption and 7×10^6 m^3 supply industrial demands. About 15×10^6 m^3 is accounted for in public uses and water losses.

Today, Tel-Aviv obtains about 43×10^6 m^3 per year, or 91 per cent of its water requirements, from wells exploiting a limestone aquifer tapped in the foothill region; about $1.5 - 2.0 \times 10^6$ m^3 per year, or 4 per cent of the demand is supplied from Tel-Aviv municipality wells exploiting a sand-sandstone aquifer underlying the coastal plain, and a further 2×10^6 m^3 per year are pumped from the same aquifer by private wells located within the municipal area.

---

*Prepared by Samuel H. Aberbach and Z.L. Shiftan. Tahal, Tel-Aviv, Israel.

**Tel-Aviv was founded in 1909 as a suburb of the ancient town of Yafo (Jaffa).

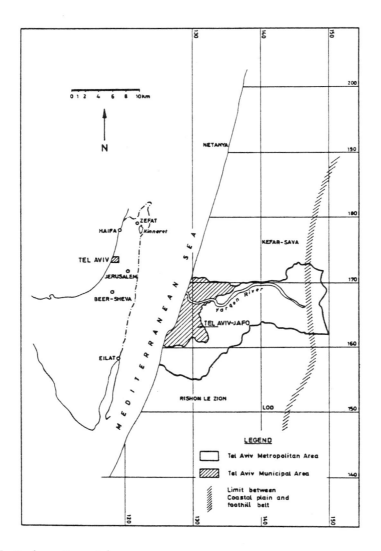

Fig. 10.27 - Tel-Aviv: location map.

        Until 1957, most of the water consumed in Tel-Aviv was pumped
locally from the coastal plain aquifer. However, a critical situation
developed in the mid-fifties when withdrawals from this aquifer rose, in a
matter of four years, from 6×10^6 m^3 55×10^6 m^3. In 1958, when water from
an outside source became available, the pumpage from the municipal wells was
gradually reduced to its present rate, which has remained fairly stable since
1973.

Geology and climate

The Mediterranean Coastal Plain in the Tel-Aviv region is built up by a
sequence of calcareous sandstones and sands, partly of shallow marine, partly
of terrestrial origin, interbedded with red sandy loams, and clays. This
sequence is about 160 m thick near the shore line, and narrows to about 120 m
thick at the eastern limit of the Greater Tel-Aviv region, wedging out to a
thickness of a few tens of meters about 16 km inland. The eastward (inland)

-475-

reduction of thickness is accompanied by a progressive substitution of the calcareous sandstones by unconsolidated sands and loams (see fig. 10.28). This sand-sandstone-loam sequence is of Plio-Pleistocene age: it contains the Coastal Plain aquifer underlying the entire Mediterranean shore of Israel.

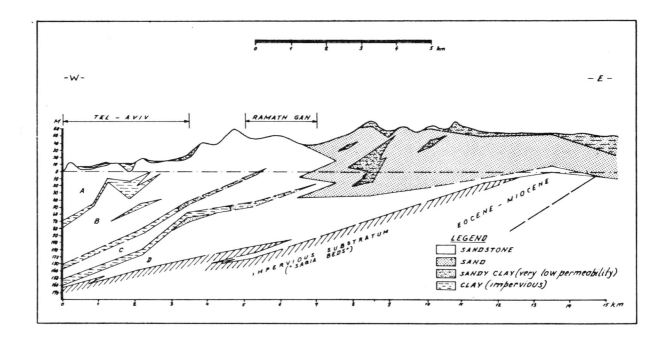

Fig. 10.28 - Tel-Aviv Region: geological cross-section along the strip number 31.

        The Plio-Pleistocene sequence is underlain by sequences of sandy shales and shales of marine origin and Mio-Pleistocene age, many hundreds of meters thick, which are to be regarded as the impervious substratum of the Coastal Plain aquifer in the Tel-Aviv region.   Further east, the Plio-Pleistocene sequence overlies older Tertiary sediments, which are also non-aquiferous.

        As shown in the section (fig. 10.28) the Plio-Pleistocene aquifer is subdivided in the Greater Tel-Aviv region into four sub-aquifers, identified with four prominent sandstone wedges (sub-aquifers A, B, C and D) which are separated by loam and clay beds. Some loam or clay lenses are included in the four main sandstone units.

        The contact between the Mio-Pliocene impervious substratum and Plio-Pleistocene aquiferous sequence inclines from east to west at a gradient of about one per cent. The loam and clay beds separating the sandstone and sand units show gradients of 2 to 2.5 per cent. Both the Plio-Pleistocene aquiferous sequence and the impervious substratum continue west of the coast-line, below the sea bed.

Climate is of the Mediterranean type with warm summers and mild winters. The rainy season corresponds to the winter months of October through March. Average annual rainfall (1921 to 1950) is 532 mm with considerable variations from year to year. Within the last 30 years, there have been 9 years in which annual rainfall exceeded 700 mm and 5 years in which annual rainfall was less than 300 mm.

Description of the problem and the influence of man

The need to supply Tel-Aviv with water from external sources arose because groundwater withdrawals from the Coastal Plain aquifer in the Tel-Aviv area and surroundings had by 1957 greatly exceeded this aquifer's sustained yield. Withdrawals in the greater Tel-Aviv area amounted, in that year, to 106 x 10^6 m^3, while the sustained yield was estimated at only about 18 x 10^6 m^3. Of the total amounts pumped, abstraction by Tel-Aviv municipality wells amounted to 55 x 10^6 m^3/year. Fifty to sixty-five per cent of these intensive withdrawals were pumped from wells less than 3 km away from the coast. Groundwater levels declined continuously from an average of 3 m over mean sea level in 1935 to about 8 m below mean sea level in 1957, at distances of 1.5 to 2.0 km from the coast (see figs. 10.29 and 10.30). This decline in water levels brought about an intrusion of saline water into the aquifer, which manifested itself through a gradual deterioration of the water quality in 23 out of 60 municipal wells (see fig. 10.31).

It was quite obvious therefore that the demands of the rapidly growing city could never be met exclusively by the original source, that is, the part of the Coastal Plain aquifer underlying the Tel-Aviv municipal area.

Neither could the Coastal Plain aquifer underlying adjoining area be considered as a source for Tel-Aviv, because in all of these areas, local abstractions had also outgrown the sustained yield. Yet, at the same time it was realized that a city like Tel-Aviv could not be left without a reliable source of locally pumped water to meet possible emergency situations, and that some municipal wells of sufficient pumping capacity would therefore have to be maintained. Taking this into consideration, it became imperative in the late 1950s, in view of the dangerous decline in water levels and the noticeable penetration of sea water into the aquifer, to halt with all haste the advance of sea water intrusion and rebuild water levels through artificial recharge of the aquifer. The quantities of water required for this purpose could only come from a source outside the Tel-Aviv area.

The possibility of obtaining the necessary water became feasible with the completion of the National Water Carrier (Jordan-Negev pipeline). The most suitable period for putting a recharge venture into effect was the time immediately following the completion of the Carrier, because at that time sufficient amounts of surplus water were still available during the wet winter seasons.

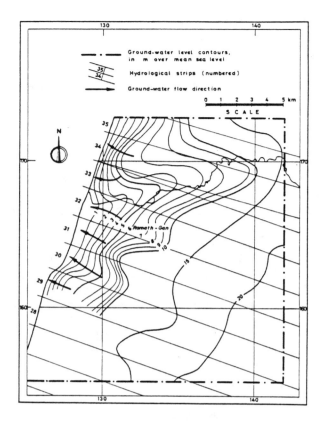

Fig.10.29 – Tel-Aviv Region: groundwater table contour map. Average groundwater levels 1933-1935.

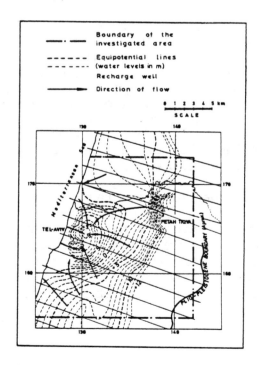

Fig. 10.30 – Tel-Aviv Region: groundwater contour map in Tel Aviv area in autumn 1957.

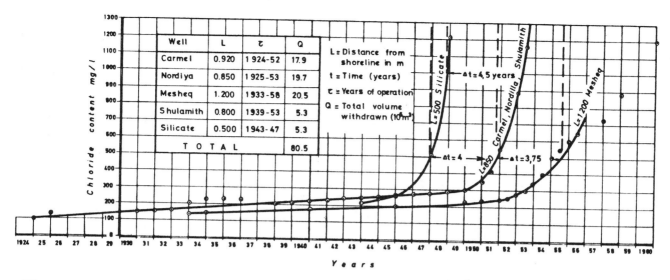

Well	L	τ	Q
Carmel	0.920	1924-52	17.9
Nordiya	0.850	1925-53	19.7
Mesheq	1.200	1933-58	20.5
Shulamith	0.800	1939-53	5.3
Silicate	0.500	1943-47	5.3
T O T A L			80.5

L = Distance from shoreline in m
t = Time (years)
τ = Years of operation
Q = Total volume withdrawn $(10^6 m^3)$

Fig. 10.31 - Tel-Aviv Region: trend of salinity in three selected municipal wells (1924-1956).

Field data collection

The Coastal Plain aquifer including the part corresponding to the Tel-Aviv area is covered by a dense network of observation wells, spaced at distances of less than 2 km apart. Water levels in the observation wells are observed monthly to construct annual well hydrographs. Groundwater contour maps are prepared twice a year to represent the maximum and minimum position of the water table. In the Tel-Aviv area, water level observations started in 1933 and about 70 observation wells were operative in 1957.

Water samples for the monitoring of water quality are taken from pumping wells, normally twice a year.

All water used in Israel has been metered since 1957, including water used in the Tel-Aviv area. Withdrawals prior to 1957 were computed by correlation with electrical power consumption, for which records were available for all wells equipped with electrical motors. The hydraulic properties of the aquiferous formations were defined on the basis of the results of aquifer tests (drawdown, recovery, interference). With these data, it was possible to draw up an approximate groundwater balance for the area.

For the purpose of verifying the extent of penetration of sea water, about 15 observation wells of 2-inch diameter, some with more than one string of observation pipes, were installed in the various sub-aquifers in the Tel-Aviv region. These wells were located mostly east (inland) of polluted pumping wells. Salinity profiles in these observation wells were measured by a conductivity bridge and an electrode cell lowered into the well. Salinity was determined on the basis of the calibration of the electrode cell by immersion into solutions with different salt concentration.

The rate of advance of the sea water in the aquifer could be inferred only from past salinity records of pumping wells and the ascent of the fresh water/salt water interface in the observation wells.

The depth of this interface was also observed in two observation wells located near the coast, equipped with 6 separate 2-inch diameter pipes for the various sub-aquifers, so that piezometric levels and salinities could be measured independently for each sub-aquifer.

Abandoned production wells were pumped for two to four hours prior to sampling, to ensure that the salinity of the samples taken from these wells be representative of the salinity in the aquifer.

The above data collection system has provided since the late 1950s a fairly clear picture of the hydrologic conditions in the Tel-Aviv area. It was further improved in 1965, when additional water was made available from the Jordan-Negev Project.

Methods of investigation

In order to protect the remaining fresh water wells of the municipality from sea water intrusion, it was decided to create a fresh water barrier to stem the further advance of the sea water front. Water levels were to be built up by introducing fresh water into various sub-aquifers by means of recharge wells. Recharge was to be effected during the rainy winter months, from October to April, when irrigation demands were lowest and consequently surplus water would be available from the Jordan-Negev pipeline.

A vertical Hele-Shaw model was used for the hydrological investigations related to the planning of the fresh water barrier. The area was divided into five strips each 2 km wide and 14-16 km long, perpendicular to the coast. The specific geological subsurface section along each strip, as known from logs of boreholes and observation wells, was reproduced on the model, and tests were conducted separately for each strip. The Hele-Shaw model was selected for this investigation mainly because it was at that time the only device capable of simulating sea water intrusion into multiple-layered aquifers.

The original intention was that after building up the groundwater table to the desired level, annual amounts to be injected should be determined by the need to balance the increasing annual groundwater overdraft drawn through the Tel-Aviv wells. This overdraft was estimated to be $10-14 \times 10^6$ m^3 per year, taking into account withdrawals by the municipality wells, forecast in accordance with the engineering and demand situation.

The scheme proposed, on the basis of the results of the model studies, involved operations of artificial recharge intended both to build up a fresh water barrier and to fill up a groundwater depression centered, at that time, east of the Tel-Aviv municipal area, within the boundaries of the municipality of Ramat Gan.

To create the fresh water barrier 22×10^6 m^3 per year were to be recharged into the various sub-aquifers through injection wells located along a line 8 km long, at a distance of 1.5 to 2.5 km from the seashore. Recharge operations were to be performed during the months November-April only.

The distance of the barrier from the coast was determined with a view to site all injection wells east (inland) of the farthest point of penetration of the sea water front. The distribution of the amounts to be recharged through the different wells was designed to counterbalance the existing deficit in storage and the current overdraft in the western part of each of the 2 km wide strips of the aquifer.

A second problem to be alleviated through recharge operations was that of the above mentioned groundwater table depression centered in the Ramat Gan area, east of the Tel Aviv municipal area, and 5 km from the coast. This depression, with water levels at elevations of -2 to -3 m relative to msl, had developed as a consequence of concentrated pumping by private and municipal wells in Ramat Gan, and was now diverting water from the aquifer underlying the Tel-Aviv area. It was, therefore, necessary to build up the water table in this depression in order to assure the efficient functioning of the projected fresh water barrier in the adjoining Tel-Aviv area.

The Ramat Gan municipality rejected a proposal to reduce abstractions from the aquifer and to have part of is demand supplied from outside sources; it opted for the alternative of having the aquifer recharged and continuing to pump its own wells in order to satisfy existing demands.

Consequently, recharge wells were drilled in this area with the intention of injecting 8 to 12 x 10^6 m^3 per year into the aquifer, during the rainy season. After the build up of water levels in the depression, recharge rates were to be reduced.

The proposed scheme was to be carried out in two stages:

First stage: Formation by artificial recharge of a hydrological barrier to halt the advance of the sea water/fresh water interface, while a water level depression persists east (inland) of the barrier. The artificially recharged water was intended in part to serve to maintain the necessary outflow to the sea, and in part to counterbalance withdrawals east of the crest of the barrier.

Second stage: Keeping the sea water/fresh water interface stationary, while rebuilding water levels in the area of the water table depression. The quantities of water artificially recharged during this stage were to be sufficient to maintain the hydrological barrier and counterbalance pumpage in its vicinity, and also fill up the depression and counterbalance excess pumpage in its area.

Comparison between predictions and the resulting situation

Recharge operations for the creation of the fresh water barrier started in December 1964, in eleven wells located south of the Yarkon River. Five new recharge wells were at that time still under construction, and became operative only in February-March of 1965, that is, one or two months before the end of the recharge season.

In some of the wells, water was injected through the pump columns, while in others the pumping equipment had been removed, and water was introduced through a special recharge pipe reaching below the water table.

The target of recharging the aquifer during the 1964/65 season along the fresh water barrier line with 18 x 10^6 m^3 was not achieved, and actual recharge amounted to only 6.3 x 10^6 m^3. Another 0.8 x 10^6 m^3 were injected in the Ramat Gan groundwater depression area.

The discrepancy between the planned and actual amounts recharged was due to the smaller than expected number of operating hours (40 to 80 per cent of the expected number of hours per well) during which water for recharge was available and also to the delay in the completion of five new wells. In addition, a decline of the specific recharge rates for individual wells were only 35 to 75 per cent of the planned rates.

Another constraint on recharge capacities was due to the fact that all the new wells had to be located in subsurface concrete boxes, and two meters of strainer pipe had to be cut from each well. Thus, the permissible pressure build up was reduced and consequently also the recharge capacity.

As a result, the total capacity of recharge was only 2,656 m^3/h instead of the expected 5,120 m^3/h.

On the other hand, total withdrawals from the aquifer declined in the summer of 1965 due to much reduced pumping from the municipality wells located south of the Yarqon River and also from the wells of the neighboring municipalities of Givatayim and Benei Berak, where withdrawals were reduced from 11 x 10^6 m^3 6 x 10^6 m^3.

The result was a pronounced recovery of the water table along the barrier line. There, water levels had risen 2.5 to 3.5 m by April 1965, as compared to a rise of only 0.2 to 1.0 m in areas not affected by the recharge operations. At distances of one to two kilometers from the coast, spring (end of rainy season) water levels reached the levels that were to be maintained as average levels in the aquifer almost everywhere (fig 10.32).

After the termination of the recharge season in April 1965, water levels declined again in subsequent months at the rate of 0.2 to 0.3 meters per month.

Meanwhile, a danger zone persisted in Strip No. 31, where water samples from observation wells indicated that recharge had so far no effect on the salinity of the groundwater at the base of the aquifer, indicating a continued salt water encroachment. But at almost all other observation points along the fresh water barrier, the recharged water had reached the bottom of the aquifer, halting, for the time being, further sea water encroachment.

It was expected that during the second recharge season--the winter of 1965/66--about 5.6 x 10^6 m^3 would be injected along the fresh water barrier line, and about 20 x 10^6 m^3 in the area of the water table depression east of Tel-Aviv. However, the actual recharge again fell short of expectations, because eight new recharge wells in the water table depression area were not yet operative. In addition the supply of water for recharge was irregular, because the winter of 1965/66 was relatively dry, and much water from the National Water Carrier had to be allocated to irrigation.

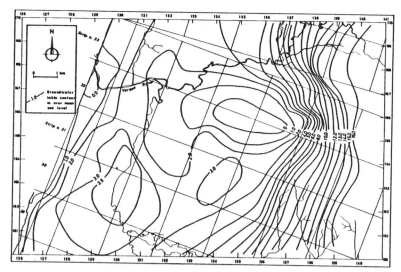

Fig. 10.32 - Tel-Aviv Region: groundwater table contour map, June 1967.

As a result, only 3 x 10^6 m^3 were injected along the barrier, and another 3 x 10^6 m^3 in the water table depression area. The rise of water levels was therefore only slight--0.6 m along the barrier and 0.75 m in the water table depression area. In general, water levels in wells west of the barrier were lower at the end of the wet season of 1965/66 than at the end of the wet season of 1964/65, although they were, of course, higher than at the beginning of the recharge operation. Chlorine salinity along the barrier, at the base of aquifer B into which most of the water was introduced, was lower than the chlorine salinity of the recharge water (240 to 250 ppm), with the exception of the segment of the barrier located in Strip No. 31, where chlorine salinity still exceeded 1,000 ppm.

The third recharge season started in October 1966 and ended in mid-May 1967. There was, however, a prolonged interruption lasting from 3 March to 4 April. A total of 18.8 x 10^6 m^3 was recharged through 29 wells, subdivided as indicated in the following table.

				Recharge capacity (m^3/h)	
Area	Planned recharge (10^6 m^3)	Actual recharge (10^6 m^3)	No. of wells	Planned	Actual
Fresh water barrier	8.6	6.3	16	2,880	1,990
Water table depression area	12.0	11.5	9	3,990	2,730
North of Yarqon River	4.1	1.0	4	1,380	335

At the end of the 1966/67 recharge season, water levels along the fresh water barrier equalled those recorded at the end of the 1964/65 season, and were around +3.5 m msl. An improvement was also noted in the northern part of the area where levels rose to +2 m msl, as compared with +0.5 m msl at the beginning of the season. Salt water intrusion was halted there too.

Since 1968, production of water from the Tel-Aviv municipality wells has declined to 1.4 to 2.0 x 10^6 m^3 per year. Recharge continued at an annual rate of five to eight x 10^6 m^3 in the water table depression area. Leakage of water from the municipal distribution and sewerage system, estimated at between five to six 10^6 m^3 per year, constitutes an additional continuous groundwater increment.

Artificial recharge in the fresh water barrier zone was terminated in 1968/69, which was a year of high natural replenishment.

Today, water levels in the southern and central part of the Tel-Aviv municipal area (Strips 29 to 31) are still significantly higher than prior to the 1964-1968 recharge operations. In the northern part, too, the situation of the water levels improved considerably.

A problematic situation still exists in Strip 32 just south of the Yarqon River, as a result of continued high pumpage northeast of Tel-Aviv, and the gradual reduction of artificial recharge into the water table depression area.

Monitoring operations are jeopardized by the clogging of part of the observation wells and the destruction of some of them as a result of construction works.

The pumpage from the municipal wells in the course of the last decade is only about half the volume previously recharged through these wells. As the chloride salinity of the recharged water was slightly higher than that of the fresh water of the aquifer, no conclusion should be drawn from the present groundwater salinity as to the possible course of a salinization process, because the water pumped today is a mixture of original aquifer and recharge water.

Present water levels, although much improved in comparison with pre-recharge times, are still not sufficient to bring the advance of the salt water front to a complete standstill. But the advance has certainly been slowed down.

In conclusion it can be said that the main result of the artificial recharge operation and the creation of a fresh water barrier was the conservation of a sizeable reserve of good quality groundwater in the local aquifer and of a corresponding pumping capacity that can cope with the city's water demands in any emergency.

Case history no. 4: Combatting sea water intrusion in Los Angeles County, California*

Introduction

This section acquaints the reader with the aspect of the salt/fresh water balance in coastal zones, as affected by inland groundwater exploitation, known as 'sea water intrusion.' First, the problem is described in general terms: what it is, how it occurs, and the potential result if it continues. Then, a location in Los Angeles County, California where it has been encountered and for which information is more complete than in others is discussed in detail. The details include a description of the method selected for counteraction, a description of facilities employed, results of the construction, costs for construction and operation, and benefits due to the construction.

Sea water intrusion

Sea water intrusion is defined as that condition in which sea water invades fresh water-bearing aquifers. Necessarily, aquifers so affected have hydraulic continuity with the ocean. Typically, the aquifer is replenished with fresh water at inland points above sea level so that the hydraulic gradient slopes toward the ocean, although a local deviation becomes a more pronounced 'trough' when extraction rates are raised to meet higher demands in supply or when droughts lower replenishment rates. This hydraulic trough can and does deepen to the extent that groundwater elevations are drawn down below sea level, so that the hydraulic gradient reverses and flow proceeds landward from the ocean. When this happens, sea water intrusion has begun. This invasion constitutes a problem when either the aquifer itself is in direct use in a water supply system or when the aquifer instead serves as a conduit through which sea water may migrate to another aquifer which is in use in a water supply system. Under either circumstance, the following results can be expected: contamination (therefore wastage) of fresh water in storage; occupation (loss) of potential storage space leading to possible need for substitute storage and distribution facilities; loss of funds invested in the water supply system; and possible increases in the cost of obtaining water because of the need to develop an alternate source of water to replace local water which cannot be utilized.

The West Coast Basin Barrier project

The West Coast Basin, located as shown in figure 10.33 is a natural underground basin, bordered on the west by Santa Monica Bay, on the south by the

---

Palos Verdes Hills and San Pedro Bay, on the east by the Newport-Inglewood Uplift, and on the north by the Ballona escarpment. The West Coast Basin is about 16 miles (26 km) long and 9 miles (14.5 km) wide, covering an area of approximately 144 square miles (370 km^2). Based on a figure appearing in a report published by the State of California (1957), Department of Water Resources, the Basin contained about 22,000,000 acre feet (27 x 10^9 m^3) of water in 1960.

The Basin is subject to intrusion from both Santa Monica Bay on the west and San Pedro Bay on the south. The discussion following deals principally with the former—intrusion from the west. A separate project is in operation to protect against intrusion from San Pedro Bay.

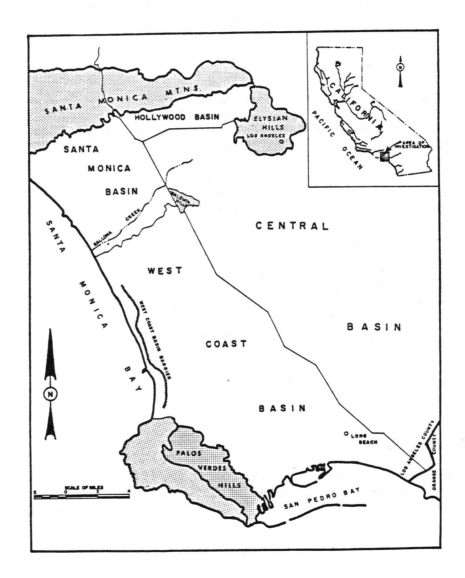

Fig. 10.33 - Location map of the Los Angeles West Coast Basin.

Geologically speaking, there are three aquifers parallel to the coast and a fourth intersecting the alignment. The aquifers as a whole are narrow at the north, thicken, become thin again toward the middle, and thicken again greatly in the southerly part before ending in bedrock at the south boundary. The principal aquifer ('Silverado') extends the full length of the reach, is accompanied by one other shallow aquifer (the '200-Foot Sand') in the north and central reaches and a third ('Lower San Pedro') deeper aquifer runs from the center to the south. The upper separator would be continuous but for the aquifer ('Gardena') which intersects the alignment, causing a sub-terranean canyon. The lower separator is continuous. Overlying the whole area at the surface the foregoing is depicted in figure 10.34.

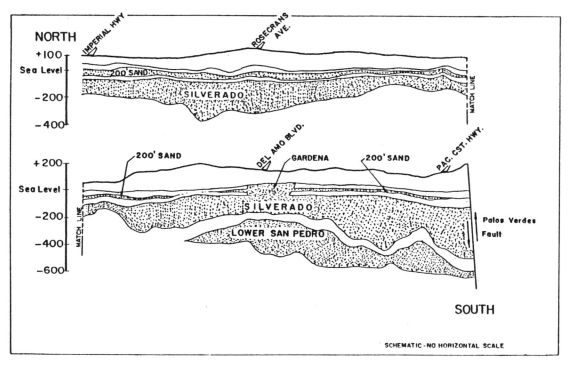

Fig. 10.34 - Geological cross-section along the saltwater intrusion control barrier alignment in the West Coast Basin.

The shallowest aquifer, the 200-Foot Sand, in the north and center is up to 60 feet (18 m) thick and consists of fine to coarse sand with 5 to 30 per cent gravel. The upper separator is from 0 to 150 feet (0 to 45 m) thick and consists of fine sand, silty sand, clayey sand and silty clays. The Silverado aquifer averages 100 feet (30 m) in thickness, with a maximum of 150 feet (45 m), and consists of granitic sands and gravelly sand with silty or clayey lenses grading down to fine silty sands with some clay. The lower separator is 30 to 200 feet (9 to 60 m) thick and consists of fine to very fine sand and silty sand. The Lower San Pedro aquifer ranges from 20 to 180 feet (6 to 55 m) in thickness and consists of coarse sands and gravels. The aquifer which intersects the alignment is 4,500 feet (1400 m) wide and locally incised into the top of the principal aquifer (Silverado) to a depth of approximately 120 feet (36 m).

-487-

A regular program of chemically analyzing groundwater samples began in the 1930s. At the outset the samples were taken primarily from producing water wells. Chemical analyses of the samples taken showed 'an alarming increase in saline concentrations' by the late 1930's (State of California, 1957). There followed studies and experimental tests to determine a feasible method for preventing sea water intrusion. One test resulted in the construction of 12 recharge wells, 36 observation wells and 1,100 feet (330 m) of water supply pipeline. A report dated February 1961 (LAFCD, 1961) contained detail of investigations of the location and control of sea water intrusion along the county's western coastline. Data pertaining to groundwater elevations and chloride concentrations obtained from observation wells, presented in the form of groundwater contour maps and isochlor maps, provided a basis for the evaluation of changes in the hydraulic gradient and movement of the intruding sea water. Examples of groundwater contour and isochlor maps are included as figures 10.35 and 10.36. Groundwater contour maps and isochlor maps remain most useful tools for identifying and evaluating suspected intrusion problems. In preparing maps, consideration should be given to adjusting groundwater elevations to reflect varying densities of the waters samples, otherwise significant errors may result in interpretation (Angus, 1977).

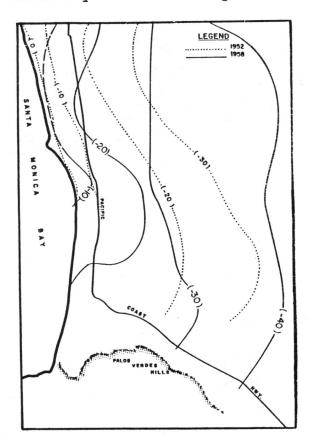

Fig. 10.35 - Groundwater level contours of the Silverado aquifer.

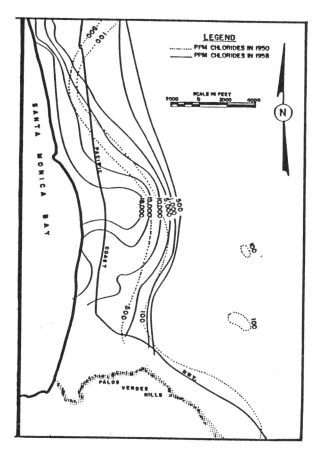

Fig. 10.36 - Groundwater isochloride contours of the Silverado aquifer.

Several methods have been studied and in some instances applied to prevent sea water intrusion. These include increasing the replenishment rates, decreasing the withdrawal rates, constructing an impermeable wall, creating a fresh water barrier between the sea and the basin, developing a trough between the sea and the basin by pumping, and a combination of the last two. The method employed in the West Coast Basin Barrier Project is of the fresh water barrier type, also known as the 'pressure ridge' type. In this method fresh water is injected into the aquifer by means of water 'recharge' or 'injection' wells. The mound so formed may be an actual water mound in an unconfined aquifer, or a piezometric mound if the aquifer is confined. The wells are located so as to form a mound transverse to the path of intrusion. The objective is to bring a pressure due to the fresh water to bear at the bottom of the aquifer which is equal to or slightly higher than the pressure imposed at the same point by the sea water. Then the height of fresh water required must be higher, due to the difference in specific weight between the two kinds of water. If the specific weight of sea water is 2.5 per cent higher than fresh water, then the height required for the fresh water mound must be the same percentage higher to reach a balance. For example, the height required to equalize pressure at a point 300 feet (90 m) below sea level will be 307.5 feet (92.95 m) and the protective elevation required is +7.5 feet (2.25 m).

Facilities required for a barrier of this type include recharge wells, observation wells, and water supply pipeline. Conditions may also warrant the addition of chlorinating equipment, a means of reducing the pressure in the water supplied, and pipelines for disposing of water pumped in maintenance operations. The recharge wells utilized in the West Coast Basin Barrier Project have, for the most part, 12-inch-I.D. (305 mm) asbestos-cement casings extending to depths varying between 135 and 760 feet (41 and 230 m) below ground suface. The observation wells are of 4-inch-I.D. (100 mm) plastic casing ranging in depth between 20 and 850 feet (6 and 260 m). They are located both seaward and landward of the barrier, as well as along the barrier alignment itself.

The total length of the recharge (barrier) line is 9 miles (14.5 km). It consists of 103 recharge wells, 98 observation wells, and 75,000 feet (23 km) of water supply pipeline. In addition, there are a pressure-reducing station, chlorination facilities, and water disposal pipelines.

The groundwater monitoring program now consists of sampling approximately 230 wells. Most of these wells have been drilled for the specific purpose of groundwater monitoring; the remainder are abandoned extraction wells. Each well is sampled in the spring of the year (for chloride content and water surface elevation), and many are sampled again in the fall. Nearly half (40%) of the wells are situated directly on the barrier alignment. The off-line wells are distributed generally at distances of 500, 1,000 and 2,000 feet (150, 300 and 600 m) on either side of the barrier, with the majority of them on the landward side.

An arbitrary standard has been set that an effective barrier and satisfactory conditions exist when the chloride concentrations of the aquifer along the barrier alignment are equal to the chloride concentrations of the injected fresh water and there is a seaward hydraulic gradient on the seaward side practically free of sea water intrusion. The Silverado aquifer is nearly so. There is a reach of about 2,000 feet (1600 m) at the south end where the results of most recent construction have yet to take effect, and there are three other reaches where the possibility of intrusion remains. Intrusion has been slowed down in the Lower San Pedro zone but not halted. Figures 10.37 and 10.38 show the configuration for key isochlors in the aquifers as they were in the fall of 1976. The injection capacity is being increased with the addition of new wells and it is presumed that this will result in protective hydraulic elevations.

Costs of the barrier project

Costs of the barrier project include the following: fixed assets construction, operation and maintenance, purchase of water, and engineering. These are listed below as either lump sums or as annual costs where appropriate:

1. Fixed assets construction, including rights of way, contractor's bid price, inspection, contract administration, etc. (lump sum) - $10,200,000

2. Operation and maintenance and engineering (annual) $600,000

3. Purchase of water (current annual cost based on water price of $58 per acre-foot; 0.45¢ per m^3) $2,300,000

It should be noted that all of the value of the water purchased is not lost. In fact, less than 10 per cent is 'wasted,' exiting on the seaward side. The balance, worth at least $2,100,000 per year, moves landward of the barrier toward the pumping field to be eventually utilized by consumers.

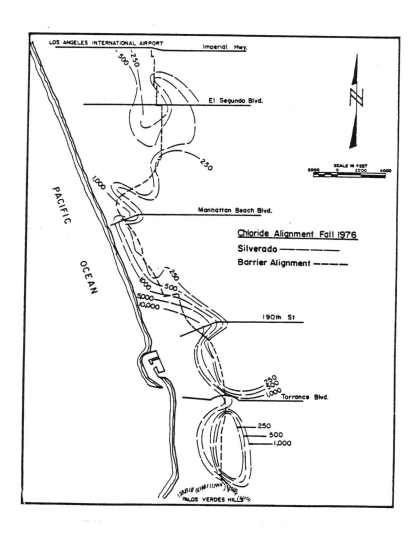

Fig. 10.37 - Configuration for key isochlors in the Silverado aquifer in the Fall of 1976.

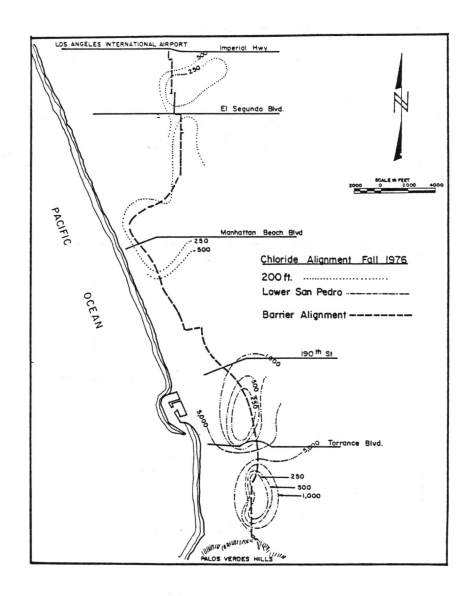

Fig. 10.38 - Configuration for key isochlors in the Lower San Pedro aquifer in the Fall of 1976.

In evaluating benefits, an earlier report previously cited (LAFCD, 1961) indicated that preserving storage capacity alone is worth $6,000,000 annually. This was on the premise that 'if the groundwater basin is allowed to become completely intruded with sea water, surface delivery of water currently pumped will be required and surface storage to provide for water demand peaks must be constructed.' The $6,000,000 consisted of the costs for capital construction, purchase of right of way, operation and maintenance, and purchase of water. It did not account for the loss of water in storage, the loss of annual amounts of replenishment from local sources, nor for the loss on investments represented by the facilities in use for pumping the groundwater.

References

Angus, J.S. (1977). _Evaluation of a barrier against sea water intrusion._ Proc. 15th Annual Hydraulics Div. Speciality Conference in Hydraulics in the Coastal Zone. Am. Soc. Civil Engineers, pp. 178-189.

LAFCD (1961). _Report on required facilities for replenishing and protecting ground water reserves in the Central and West Coast ground water barriers._ Part I, Los Angeles County Flood Control District, February, 1981.

State of California (1957). _Sea water intrusion in California._ Bull. No. 63, appendix B, Department of Water Resources, Division of Resources Planning, State of California, pp. 27, March, 1957.

State of California (1957). _Inventory of coastal ground water basins._ Bull. No. 63-5, Department of Water Resources, State of California, pp. 315.

Case history no. 5: Saline intrusion in the Mar del Plata aquifer (Argentina): present day situation. Studies and measures undertaken*

Geographical situation and geological features

The City of Mar del Plata is located in the Province of Buenos Aires, Argentina Republic. It has an area of 50 km^2 and part of it is built on the last counterforts of the Tandilia highlands (formed by paleozoic quartzites) and the rest on terrains belonging to the Quaternary sedimentary cover (fig. 10.39).

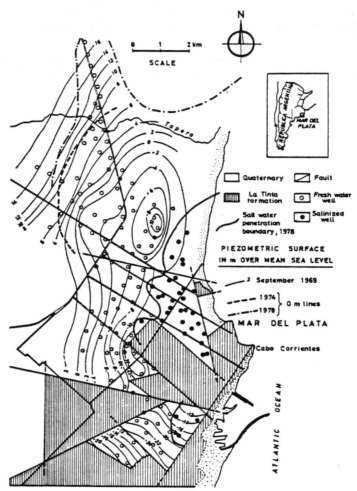

Fig. 10.39 - Sea water intrusion at Mar del Plata aquifer. The figure shows the piezometric map of the area in 1976 and the change in the cero piezometric water level in 1977 and 1978. The limit of salt water contamination is also shown.

---

*Prepared by Valerio Ferrante (Obras Sanitarias de la Nación) and Mario Hernández (La Plata National University). Contributed by Adolfo Pedriel, Obras Sanitarias de la Nación, Gerencia Regional Pampeana, Mar del Plata, Argentina.

It presents a relief reflecting the structure of blocks of the paleozoic quarzites. Out of these rocky outcrops, one finds the terrains belonging to the Quaternary sedimentary cover of eolic origin. These pervious sediments are formed by silt and fine sands, whose thickness approaches a hundred meters and lies, in some cases, on an aquitard of pelites, which serve as a roof to marine sandstones of the same age, and in others directly upon the paleozoic rocks (Groeber, 1954).

The region, having a moderate climate and a rainfall of about 900 mm per year, lacks substantial surface water resources, and therefore the Quaternary aquifer is the only source of water. The water is aquired by means of tube wells which yield about 80 to 120 m^3/hour.

Description of the problem

Geohydrologically speaking, it is a region which shows a surplus in the water balance, a direct recharge and a very reduced recharge zone. Therefore, the local supply depends exclusively on the surplus of the natural water cycle.

Since 1913 the enterprise 'Obras Sanitarias de la Nacion' has been supplying water through exploitation of the aquifers by means of tube wells. As a result of this intensive and punctual exploitation, the aquifer piezometric levels became negative in relation to the sea level. This inversion of the water gradient has produced an east-west intrusion of saline water, from the sea toward the continent (Ruiz Huidobro, 1971; Ruiz Huidobro and Tofalo, 1975a, 1975b).

At the present time, most of the urban area has negative piezometric levels.

Since the year 1943, there is a process of salinization which still continues. At present there are 33 wells reached by the progressive salinization. Those recently abandoned are at about 2,000 m from the coast.

In the following example the chemical composition of the water may be seen, in its natural state (analysis 1) and once the well has been salinized (analysis 2).

The speed of advancement of the saaline front starts at about 50-100 meters per year, according to the areas, a speed which nowadays tends to increase due to increased demand (Pedriel, 1977).

The consumption has reached 70 x 10^6 m^3 per year and, due to the demographic and development growth, the plans for the expansion of the Enterprise 'Obras Sanitarias de la Nacion', losses of water and plans for new water using plants, have produced a basic diagnostic type study. It is to measure the local hydrological phenomenon, and to simulate possible solutions based on surveys of the extraction and the transportation of water from distant areas within the same groundwater basin.

Well O.S.N. No. 50	Analysis 1 (15 Oct 1948)	Analysis 2 (20 Aug 1967)
Color	2	1
Turbidity	0.3	2.3
Smell	---	---
pH	7.6	7.7
Residuum to 105°C	860 mg/l	2.25 mg/l
Total hardness	160	690
Bicarbonate alkalinity in $CaCO_3$	570	390
Chlorides	118	970
Sulfates	33	18
Nitrates	17	8
Nitrites	0.05	0.01
Ammonium	0.05	0.05
Silica	54	86
Calcium	40	152
Magnesium	14	72
Sodium and potassium	283	501
Fluorine	0.5	0.7
Vanadium	0	---
Arsenic	0.04	---

Present day studies

The planned acquisition of country data began in 1977, in the context of the above mentioned study, in an area of 1800 km^2, which is approximately the area of the basin. Five types of data sets are recognized:

1. Replacing of original piezometric information, and the collection of samples for chemical analysis, at 620 points;

2. Periodic operation (monthly and bi-monthly) of a piezometric network of 170 stations.

3. Periodical operation of hydrochemical sampling in 158 stations of the piezometric network mentioned above;

4. Shallow groundwater and rain water sampling to measure the isotope content (stable, tritium and radiocarbon);

5. Operation of river gauging stations (now being installed).

At present it is not possible to make predictions since the diagnosis of the problem has only recently been finished. This has been carried out in collaboration with the Hydrogeology Department of the La Plata National University, and a series of interim and final reports are available (González and Hernández, 1975).

Administrative actions

The administrative actions carried out by the entreprise 'Obras Sanitarias de la Nacion' include measures intended for the control of the private extractions through the installation of water meters in all the industrial water wells, placed mostly out of the enterprise limits, but within the groundwater basin. Also planned is the installation of meters to cover not only the small and medium consumers, who already have their consumption measured, but also city houses and buildings.

On the other hand, the enterprise has carried out, through agreements with research institutions, several studies of the saline intrusion in the aquifer, the last of which has, as a main aim, after the diagnosis stage ends, the description of an analytical mathematical model which will serve as a basis to the prediction.

Cost of the problem

Regarding the cost of water supply which the enterprise must develop, together with attacking the problem of saline intrusion, it can be said that in a 35 year term, 33 water wells had to be taken out of service, and replaced by the same number, whose price, including electrical, mechanical and hydraulic facilities, amounted to US $1,000,000 each.

The relative cost of these possible solutions will become clear once the alternatives based on the study and economy of the necessary works for each case have been established.

References

González, N., Hernádez, M.D. (1975). _Metodología para el estudio de acuíferos costeros; su importancia económica._ (Methodology for the study of coast aquifer; its economic importance), 2nd Ibero-American Congress of Economic Geology, T.1, section 3, Buenos Aires, pp. 417-434.

Groeber, P. (1954). _Geology and hydrogeology of Mar del Plata connected with the problem of provision of current water to the urban zone._ Rev. Municipal Museum 1, (2), Mar del Plata, pp. 5-25.

Ruiz Huidobro, O.J. (1971). _La intrusión de agua de mar en el acuífero de Mar del Plata._ (The sea water intrusion in the Mar del Plata aquifer), Primer Congreso Hispano-Luso-Americano de Geología Económica, Vol. 2, Sec. 3, Instituto Geológico y Minero de Espana, Madrid-Lisboa, pp. 845-858.

Ruiz Huidobro, O.J., Tofalo, O.R. (1975a). _La intrusión de agua del Mar en acuíferos litorales: su control en Mar del Plata_ (Sea water intrusion in coastal aquifers: its control in Mar del Plata), VI Congreso Geológico Argentino, Bahía Blanca.

Ruiz Huidobro, O.J., Tofalo, O.R. (1975b). _La administración de agua subterránea en acuíferos litorales,_ (Groundwater administration in littoral aquifers), Segundo Congreso Ibero-Americano de Geología Económica, Vol. I, Buenos Aires, pp. 541-559.

Pedriel, A. (1977). <u>Invasión salina en acuíferos costeros,</u> (Saline invasion in coastal aquifers), National Comm. for the United Nations Conference on Water, CONFAGUA, Mar del Plata, c 13/3, March, 1977, pp. 17.

<u>Case history no. 6: The Rifá area in the Tarragona Plain, Catalonia, Spain*</u>

<u>Geographical location</u>

The Tarragona Plain is a part of Catalonia which extends along the coast from the city of Tarragona, some 250 km south of the Spanish-French border, up to the place where the Catalanides Mountains (western mountaineous system of the Catalan coastal chain) reach the Mediterranean sea, some 35 km toward the south (fig. 10.40).

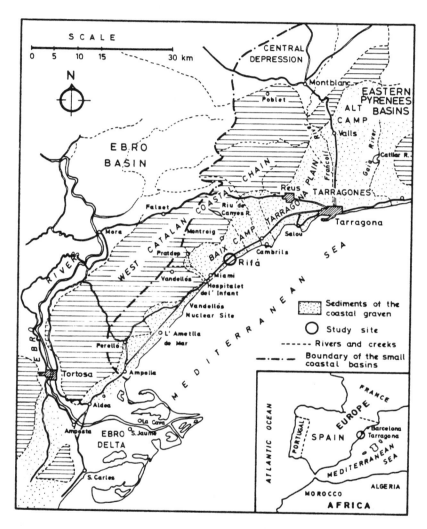

Fig. 10.40 – General situation map of the Tarragona Plains (Baix Camp, Alt Camp and Tarragonés). The coastal graven, the West Catalan Coastal Chain and the Ebro delta are shown. The encircled area corresponds to the study area.

---

*Prepared by E. Custodio, Eastern Pyrenees Water Authority and Barcelona Polytechnic University, Barcelona.

General outline of the problem

The area is dominantly agricultural (olive, potatoes, vegetables, beans) with specialized crops in the NE (hazel nuts, fruits and wine). The main towns have a well developed and rapidly expanding industrial belt (petrol chemistry, oil refining, machinery, chemicals, food processing). In the south, a 500 MW nuclear plant was completed in 1972 and a 1000 MW new one is under construction.

A population of about 200,000 inhabitants, an important tourist belt, industry and an expanding irrigated agriculture, generates a water demand that exceeds local resources, and the small water imports from basins outside the area are not enough. The groundwater reserves are used, with the related problems of a continuous drawdown in the water table and sea water intrusion along the coast. This is common in the NE part, and more local in the less developed SW part, where the problem is complicated by the existence of deeply penetrating natural sea water and the presence of some saline groundwater originated in Triassic formations (Custodio, Bayó and Ortí, 1971; Ortí, 1970; Custodio, 1976).

As an example, only the situation in the Rifá area, in the SW part, will be presented. The problems near Tarragona, the biggest and more complex ones, involving two aquifers and deep limestones, are not considered here.

General outline of the hydrology of the Tarragona Plain

The Tarragona Plain consists of deep gravel filled with continental and marine semi-consolidated sediments. The gravel extends from NE to SW, where it sinks under the sea. The NW border is a mountainous belt that from NE toward SW is formed by limestones, schists, granite and finally limestones, dolomites and marls. It is a reasonably impervious groundwater boundary.

Well developed quaternary, moderately to highly permeable alluvial fans and piedmont deposits form an almost continuous belt along the mountain foot, extending till the sea in the SW part. These previous sediments can attain a thickness of more than 200 m. Groundwater levels are generally deep, sometimes more than 100 meters in the inner parts.

No permanent surface water flows exist in the Plain, except the Francoli river, near Tarragona. Permanent or intermittent flows from the mountainous belt rapidly infiltrate when reaching the alluvial fans. Only very brief flows exist, coinciding with intense rainfalls of more than 50 mm/day. Water losses along the creek (barranco) channels are noticeable (Bayó, Doménech and Custodio, 1976).

Groundwater recharge depends on rainfall infiltration in the Plain (20 to 150 mm/year; mean value 80 mm/year) and runoff infiltration or contribution from the mountains (about the same figures).

In the SW part, the basins are small and available groundwater flow is about 1.2×10^6 m^3/year/km of shoreline, perhaps to 1.5×10^6 m^3/year/km in the limestone coastal formations that close the Plain (Custodio and Martín Arnáiz, 1976).

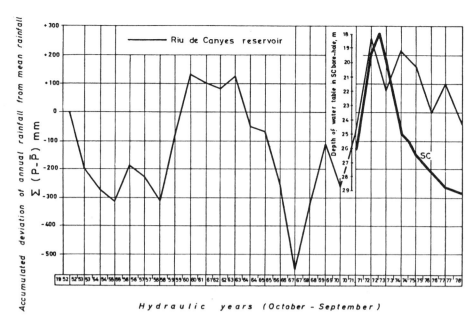

Fig. 10.41 – Accumulated deviation of annual rainfall, P, from mean annual rainfall, P̄ , in the 1952-1978 period. The figure shows $\Sigma(P-\bar{P})$, and the groundwater level variation in a control borehole (SC), between the Rifa and Pixerota creeks, in Montroig, at 2300 m from the sea, in the middle of the alluvial fan formations of the South Tarragona Plain. Mean rainfall in the Riu-de-Canyes reservoir, near Montroig town, is 565.3 mm/year.

Figure 10.41 shows the accumulated deviation of annual rainfall in the piedmont zone. After a long period of drought (1964-1967), a clearly wet period developed between 1967 and 1972, when the groundwater observation network was established. From 1972 to the end of 1978 a sequence of moderately dry years dominated. The groundwater table closely follows this evolution, and from early 1973 until the present, the extraordinary high levels of 1972 have receded continuously, with more than 10 meters drawdown in the center of the southern part.

The Rifá coastal area (Montroig, Tarragona)

The Rifá coastal area is located around the mouth of the Rifá creek and is formed by beach and eolian deposits, partly overlying the extreme of the well developed Rifá alluvial fan. Figure 10.42 shows the geological cross-sections of the area.

The aquifer decreases in transmissivity from the interior, about 2500 m^2/day, to about 500 m^2/day near the beach. Saturated thickness is about 25 m. Though in detail two or three pervious layers exist, in practice it behaves as a single aquifer, without meaningful vertical water flows. Only small differences in ionic composition can be found between top and bottom groundwater, showing the influence of local recharge and irrigation return water.

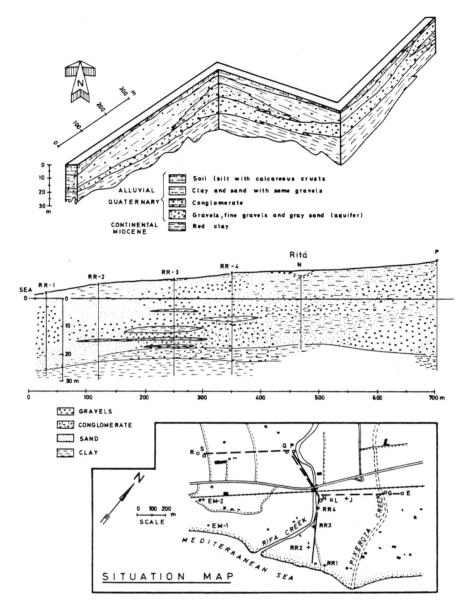

Fig. 10.42 - Geological cross-section of the low Rifá area. The situation of the main wells and observation boreholes is shown. The permeability of the alluvial fan and river deposits decreases toward the sea.

Groundwater flow is calculated to be about 1.0 to 1.3 million m^3/year (mean) per km of seashore, and represents the deep rainfall infiltration in the plain and the runoff of the mountain boundary.

Until 1970 groundwater exploitation was mainly for irrigation and farm use. Since then it has increased somewhat in the zone considered, since the tourist settlement has taken former agricultural wells. It amounts to about 0.2 million m^3/year/km.

Since 1970, eight wells have been put into operation to supply a nuclear plant, abstracting 1.2 million m^3/year, or about a total of 0.8 million m^3/year/km, reducing significantly the fresh water flow toward the sea, but still leaving some outflow. Since the maintenance of a constant fresh water supply is essential, exploitation has been carefully controlled, and two lines of observational bore-holes have been established, at right angles to the coast, in addition to other observational wells around the pumping wells.

The combined result of this exploitation and the natural groundwater level recession has been a drawdown in this area of about 0.1 to 0.2 m/year up to 1979, depending on the distance to the shore. Figure 10.43 shows the piezometry in the west Montroig plain, and in the area under consideration. Near the coast the groundwater flow is almost normal to the shoreline.

Between 1972 and 1978 the groundwater gradients have decreased from 0.008 to 0.004, without significantly changing the aquifer transmissivity.

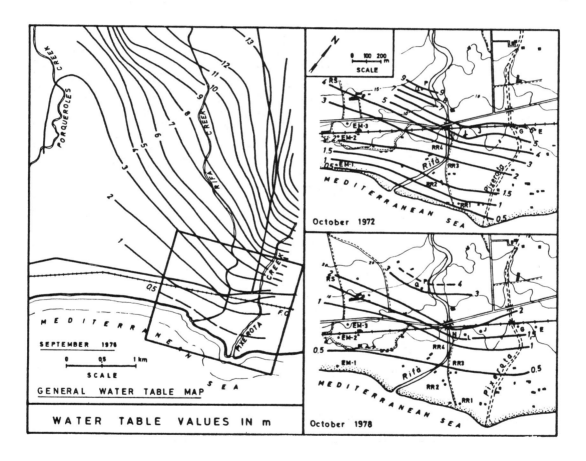

Fig. 10.43 - General water table table map of the West Montroig Area and detaild situation in the low Rifá area in October 1972 (end of the wet period) and October 1978 (semi-dry period). Intensive exploitation began in 1970.

Sea water intrusion in the Rifá coastal area

The groundwater salinity, measured through the chloride content is shown in figure 10.44 The background chloride content is about 30 ppm, slightly higher in irrigated areas (to 60 ppm). In 1968, at the end of the preceding dry period, only near the coast was noticed a slight increase in the chloride content, to about 90 ppm, the salt water penetration being almost negligible. In 1972, at the end of the wet period, salinity near the coast was higher, extending locally toward the P Q wells, the most heavily exploited ones, though the S well is also intensively pumped.

At the end of the 1978 summer, the same pattern was found, with very high salinity values near the coast, and the saline tongue rooted at the left side of the Rifá creek mouth, but without reaching the wells.

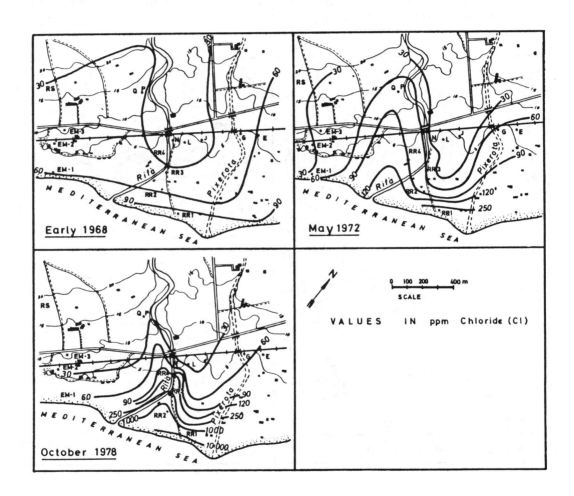

Fig. 10.44 - Isochloride maps of the Low Rifá area in early 1968 (before intensive exploitation at the end of a dry period), May 1972 (end of the wet period) and October 1978 (semi-dry period).

The apparent electrical resistivity of the ground, obtained through a surface survey, has not changed from 1970 to 1978, except at the sea shore, where a sharp increase appeared. Figure 10.45 shows the isoresistivity maps for current electrode separations AB = 50 and 100 m. The existence of a conductive clay layer under the pervious materials and the high dispersion of the incoming salt water does not favor the geoelectrical survey as the best method for early salt water intrusion detection, except for a dense, and therefore costly net of geoelectrical soundings.

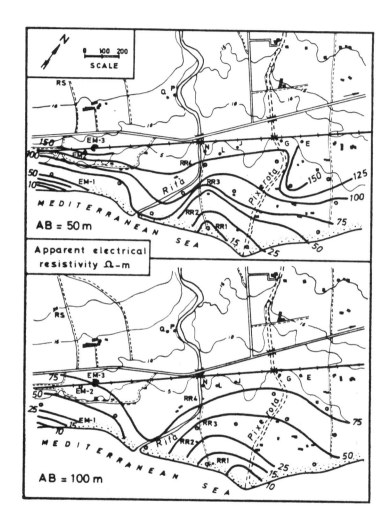

Fig. 10.45 - Electrical apparent isoresistivity maps (August 1978) at two different current electrode distances (AB = 50 m; AB = 100 m). Sea water encroachment is only slightly visible near the Rifá Creek mouth. A more dense network of geoelectrical points is needed, but it is expensive and also it is difficult to find places to make the measures correctly. The circles show the places where the geoelectrical measures have been carried out (Schlumberger dispositive), up to AB = 300 m.

As shown in figure 10.46, periodic chemical analysis of bore-hole samples, and also of the wells, clearly uncover the slight sea water containa-tion process. It is shown by the water chloride content, but also by the alkaline-ion/chloride ratio, initially and naturally greater than 1. It decreases and finally gets smaller than 1. It reaches values smaller than that of sea water, when the sea water intrusion is well established. Thus, the sea water intrusion process is clearly defined, in site of the small chloride increase.

The slight sea water contamination reaches the closest-to-the wells bore-hole (RR-4). It probably also reaches some of the wells, but is not noticeable because the abstracted water is a mixture of this slightly saline water with a much greater quantity of non-contaminated water, due to the hydrodynamic effect of the flow pattern around the wells.

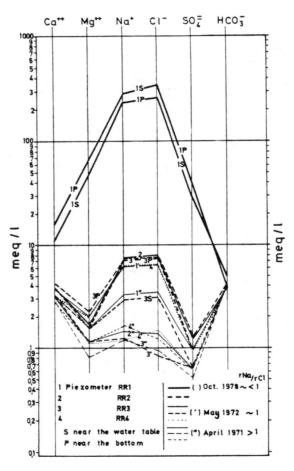

Fig. 10.46 - Ionic composition of groundwater taken from the Rifá piezometer line (RR1 through RR4) in three times. The tendency to salinization is clear through the increase in Cl$^-$ and Na$^+$, but also by the cation exchange process (mixed water has less Na$^+$ than the theoreti-cal mixtures), as shown by the rNa/rCl. Native waters have a predominantly greater than 1 value, that changes into less than 1, smaller than that of sea water.

Periodic logging of the electrical conductivity of the bore-hole water with a simple submersible conductivity cell have been very useful. Since salinity changes have been very slight in the different bore-holes, except in the closer-to-the shore (RR-1, at 25 m), only in this one significant results are obtained, as shown in figure 10.47. No vertical through-flows are to be expected. The progressive salinization can be explained also by the progressive abrasion of the coast.

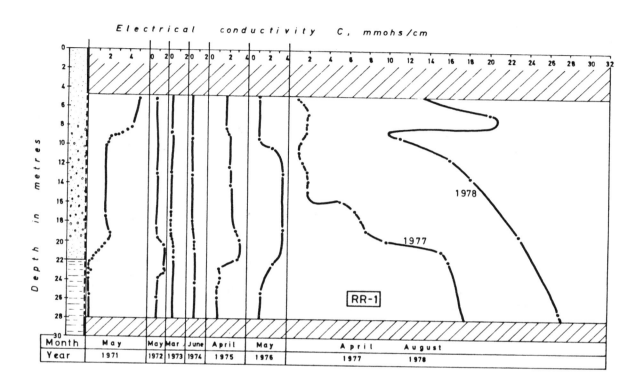

Fig. 10.47 - Water electrical conductivity logs of the RR1 piezometer. The piezometer is near the shore (15 m). The high salinity values near the top in 1971 and 1978 are due to the effect of salt water infiltrated during sea storms. At present the piezometer is taken out by the coast recession.

In 1971, a slight sea water contamination was noticed in the bore-hole RR-1, but in the following years it disappeared as a consequence of the higher groundwater flow after the wet period. From 1975 onwards, the salinization grew more intense, and in 1977 the salt water wedge clearly appeared. In 1978 most of the bore-hole was filled with water close to sea water after a heavy storm. The logs show also the effect of aquifer nonhomogeneities.

Forecasting

Rough interface calculations with simple formulae based on the BGH principle, such as those presented in chapter 5, do not differ too much from observations. The salt water wedge is advancing at a 30 m/year speed and the interface presents a 0.15 slope. No dispersion studies have been undertaken until now.

Simple calculations of salt water penetration using the piezometric maps agree reasonably well with observations. The isosalinity lines are moved according to the groundwater flow velocity pattern, as obtained from the permeability, water gradient and porosity values. Predictions over a short time are good, but for long-term forecasting the dispersion must be considered. If not considered, the results are probably on the safe side, that is to say, they give a pessimistic picture of the situation.

Under present conditions, the water supply can be maintained without noticeable sea water contamination for a minimum of 3 to 4 years. However, a wet period will enlarge the useful life of the exploitation, if the groundwater abstraction is not increased in the west Montroig area.

Management measures to control the sea water intrusion

It is very difficult to fight and correct the salinization process, since no water is available to substitute present abstractions, to increase recharge or to feed a water injection barrier. Furthermore, the Water Law impedes any action from the Public Administration, since groundwater is a private good. Voluntary Users Associations may be formed in order to agree on a control of the abstractions and location of the wells, but such an agreement is very difficult between farmers and the other water users, especially when abstracted water will be used outside the Municipal territory.

A new well line has been drilled farther from the sea in order to have a new, though more costly, water supply source. Local authorities have denied the permission for pump and pipeline installations.

Then the measures suggested to control the sea water intrusion reduces to trying to develop new fresh water sources in other areas, limit or reduce present day abstraction rates and persuade local authorities not to allow new abstractions without careful studies.

Costs

The cost of the water at the local pumping station, including the capital costs of the investment in wells, machinery, pipes, land aquisition, and energy cost, is about 5 ptas/m^3 (150 ptas $\sim$ \$1 U.S.), or about 10 ptas/m^3 at the nuclear plant, at a distance of 17 km, when a 25-year exploitation period is considered.

If these wells become sea water contaminated and the new wells 4 km landward are allowed, the pumpage of the water from 100 m depth and the other costs, over a 25-year exploitation period will give a water cost of about 15 ptas/m^3 at the distribution reservoir or about 20 ptas/m^3 at the nuclear plant. Really, the exploitation of both exploitation areas will be 25 years. If the Rifá exploitation becomes too salty in 4 years and 75 per cent of the abstraction must be transferred to the new wells, the cost of the water over the real life-time will be about 20 ptas/m^3 at the distribution reservoir or about 25 ptas/m^3 at the nuclear plant. The cost of sea water intrusion is at least 80 million ptas for a 1.2 million m^3/year supply, if the alternative solution is allowed.

References

Bayó, A., Doménech, J., Custodio, E. (1976). Estudio geológico del Macizo de Vandellós para definir sus características hidrogeológicas. (Geological study of the Vandellós mass if to define its hydrogeological characteristics). Simposio Nacional de Hidrogeología, Valencia, Grupo de Trabajo de Hidrogeología de la Asociación de Geólogos Espanoles, pp. 89-107.

Custodio, E. (1976). Estudio de la salinización de las aguas subterráneas en la región litoral entre Ametlla de Mar y Montroig (Tarragona). (Study of water salinization at the coastal area between Ametlla de Mar and Montroig (Tarragona)), Simposio Nacional de Hidrogeología, Valencia, Grupo de Trabajo de Hidrogeología de la Asociación de Geólogos Espanoles, pp. 984-1006.

Custodio, E., Bayó, A. Ortí, F. (1971). Características geológicas, hidrogeológicas y geoquímicas de los acuíferos costeros entre Cambrils y L'Ametlla de Mar (Tarragona). (Geological, hydrogeological and geochemical characteristics of coastal aquifers between Cambrils and L'Ametlla de Mar), Primer Congreso Hispano-Luso-Americano de Geología Económica, Sección 3, Tomo 1, Madrid-Lisboa, pp. 147-170.

Custodio, E., Martín Arnáiz, M. (1976). Métodos de balance de agua subterránea en el área de Vandellós. (Groundwater balance methods in the Vandellós area), Simposio Nacional de Hidrogeología, Valencia, Grupo de Trabajo de Hidrogeología de la Asociación de Geólogos Espanoles, pp. 1262-1290.

Ortí, F. (1970). Notas acerca de la prospección hidrogeológica realizada para el abastecimiento de la Central Nuclear de Vandellós (Tarragona). (Notes on the hydrogeological survey for the supply of the Vandellós Nuclear Plant (Tarragona)), Instituto de Investigaciones Geológicas de la Diputación Provincial, Universidad de Barcelona, Vol. XXIV, Barcelona, Spain. pp. 77-78.

Case history no. 7: Sea water encroachment in East Var (French Riviera)*

The exploitation of the water resources of the Bas-Argens and the Mole and Giscle aquifer is confronted by sea water encroachment arising from the particular hydrogeological conditions of these coastal aquifers.

Hydrogeological characteristics

The water bearing strata consist of materials of fluviomarine origin that filled in the overdeepening of the micaceous and gneissic bedrock during the Flandrian transgression.

(a) __Bas-Argens aquifer:__ It is split into an upper, superficial bed and a deeper bed to some extent isolated by clayey and alluvial layers.

Superficial bed: Under the clay-sand surface silts, it is mainly made up of red to gray and fine to coarse sands, sometimes with stoney or clayey seams or pebbles. It is 5 to 25 m deep.

Deep bed: Consisting of a substantial thickness of coarse sands and gravel with stones that are often round. It extends from a depth of 25 m down to 80 to 130 m.

The distribution of the alluvial and clayey horizons that separate the superficial and deep beds is not uniform, and local connections between the two are likely.

The upper groundwater deposit is fed and drained by the River Argens whose bed is already at sea level, 5 km from its mouth.

(b)__Giscle and Mole aquifer__: The aquifer's deposits are split into two main zones:

—one occupies the broad part of the plain from the coast and was fed by fluviomarine sediments. The borings in it extract from a sandy-clayey site, intersected by rough channels of fluviatile origin which act as a drain for the whole aquifer.

—the second zone, characterized exclusively by alluvial deposits, extends upstream in the Giscle and Mole valleys, and is made up of coarse sands, pebbles, and gravel which represent the normal prolongation of the downstream fluviatile channels.

---

*Prepared by J. Chales and J.-F. Clavel. Compagnie Générale des Eaux; Régie du Syndicat des Communes de la Banlieue de Paris pour les Eaux (France).

The salt water front

Within a pervious material, fresh water and salt water meet due to diffusion caused by the differences in the NaCl concentration in the bevel-shaped sea water front. The brackish water, because of its greater density, settles in the lower part of the aquifer (fig. 10.48).

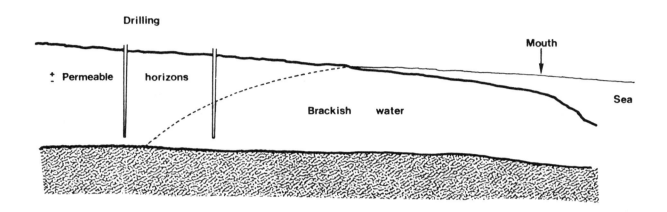

Fig. 10.48 - Schematic position of salt water front in river axis.

The general groundwater flow in the aquifer towards its natural discharge point establishes an equilibrium which in the absence of other perturbances is mainly subject to the variations in the groundwater's transit velocity.

The salt water front can be compared to a tongue stretching under the fresh water. It advances towards the land interior in periods of groundwater deficit, and, under the weight of the load, tends to be pressed back towards the coast during rainy periods. These fluctuations and the diffusion phenomena give rise to a transition zone of brackish water.

The Argens aquifer: The superficial bed is highly exposed to the phenomena of salinity because during low flow periods (the river's flowrate can fall to 1.5 m/s) sea water penetrates the Argens.

The deep bed, whose salinity is very old but is not excessive, also seems subject to the influence of marine waters acting through preferential advances in the pebble layers and against the bedrock, as well as through communications with the upper bed.

Giscle and Mole aquifers: The salt penetrates through the river channel and also from the sea front through permeable horizons.

Evolution of the salt front

Any modification of the flow regimen or of the position of the 'source of NaC1' changes the fresh water-salt water equilibrium. Developments are represented by isosalinity curves (500 mg/l, 1000 mg/l, etc.) (fig. 10.49).

(a) **Modification of sea front**: The destruction of the offshore bar results:

-from the urbanization (Port Grimaud, Marine de Cogolin) with development inland in initially marshy areas with basins in direct communication with the sea; and

-from the exploitation of sand pits or the removing of materials resulting hydrogeologically in a substantial increase in the permeability of the area in question, which brought about an inland advance of several hundred meters.

Moreover, the geometry of the saline penetration detected by geophysics and continuous measurements clearly shows that sea water contaminates the aquifers by pushing upstream into waterways. The rivers' slopes are small and in summer the low flows are too small to keep the salt water downstream.

(b) **Modification of groundwater flow**: The sinkings of the groundwater table caused by drillings and abstractions obviously change the hydraulic gradient. This phenomenon is well illustrated by the behavior of the Giscle and Mole aquifers, which is better known than that of the Argens aquifers because they have been under close study longer.

These resources are furnished by:

-a flow through the alluvia (13,000 m^3/day in years of normal rainfall);

-reserves stocked in the alluvial bed and normally reconstituted during the rainy season.

From the month of September through the end of May, less than the groundwater flow is pumped. The surplus moving through the aquifers flows into the sea and may even contribute to flooding of the lower plain in winter.

From the month of June through the month of August, the total output of pumping is greater than the groundwater flow, and the necessary surplus is extracted from reserves whose available volume is assessed at 600,000 m^3 (the effective porosity of the materials is on the order of 2 per cent). This volume represents the maximum and as for this value, the piezometric surface is lowered over 3/4 of the aquifer's capacity. The cone of depression in this case spreads rapidly for a small increase in the volume of freed water.

Every summer the fresh water flow from upstream of the valleys is abstracted through pumping, and thus no longer compensates the drainage of the coastal aquifer. This drainage is marked in piezometry by the upward development of the inland sea water curve.

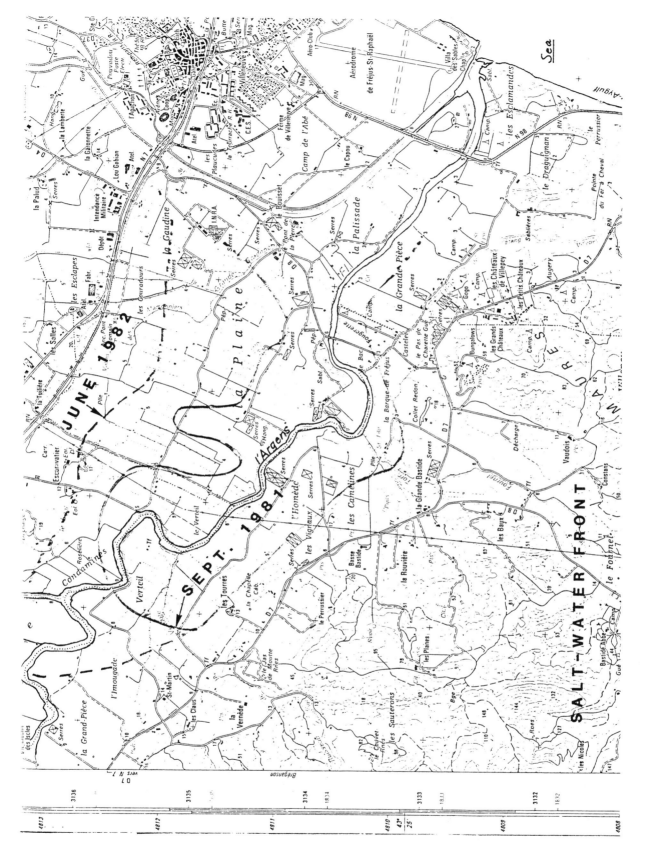

Fig. 10.49 – Isosalinity map of the superficial aquifer of the Bas Argeus. The 500 mg/l line is taken as the salt water front.

Finally, the position of the salt water front at a given time is a direct reflection of the state of the aquifer's reserves, conditioned by the concurrence of the extraction rate and the natural recharge.

Means employed

(a) Following the evolution

(i) Salinity maps

The results of analyses of water samples in the structures, as they are carried out every year, are conditioned by:

-the depth of the soundings which, for the most part, do not reach all the way through the alluvial replenishment. The possible presence of salt at a depth greater than the base of the drilling is therefore not detectable.

-the state of these piezometers which, relatively old, can be subject to localized clogging and contain water that is not representative of the surrounding groundwater.

-the distribution of the monitoring points remaining usable which constitute a relatively wide-meshed network which inevitably involves some extrapolation in the interpretation of the measurements.

So the representations of sea water encroachment given by the salinity maps are only a reflection of the real position of the sea water wall. Geophysics has moreover shown the existence of alluvial invasion by salt which had remained unknown. This occurs at too great a depth with respect to the structures or outside of the monitoring network's mesh. But the establishment of the maps each year before and after the period of maximum groundwater extraction, enables us to follow the invasion's evolution and seasonal fluctuations.

(ii) Geophysics

The method consists of measuring the resistivity of the ground at different depths at a given point. The correlations between the ground sections given by the different electrical soundings allow to reconstitute profiles and to know the three-dimensional distribution of the facies. The resistivity of a given horizon depends on its porosity, i.e., on its nature, and on the conductivity of the water impregnating it, i.e., on the water's mineral load.

A soil that is resistant because it has little clay and is impregnated with fresh water will become conducting if it is invaded by salt water. The method can therefore be used to catch sight of sea water encroachment. However, the differentiation between the gravelly levels saturated with salt water and naturally conducting clayey horizons can be difficult. Moreover, the electric method is sensitive to relatively high salt contents in the impregnating water, and the definition of the brackish water fringe that sets up between the sea water and the fresh water is more uncertain.

(b)   Management of pumping

Knowledge of the groundwater's behavior allows the water supplier, after a campaign of measurements carried out before the summer period, to adapt the scheduled extractions to the aquifer's recharge flow (plus the 600,000 m^3 reserve).

This recharge flow can be related to the pluviometry of the preceding 30 months through statistical adjustment with a mathematical model. The physical evolution can be followed by a survey after the summer.

The communities have escaped the restraints imposed on the volumes that can be extracted without a danger of irreversible deterioration of water quality, by using outside resources.

Means to be employed in the future

(a)   Technique

Studies of anti-salt dams have been launched. These structures are intended:

-to improve the replenishment of fresh water by the set-up of a sill in the rivers (rock filling or concrete structures with a spillway designed to let flood water flows pass);

-to set up an impervious screen in depth (injections, molded barrier).

These projects are scheduled for completion in the coming years.

(b)   Administration

(i)   Controlling the soil and development projects

Development projects liable to modify either the position of sea water, the drainage of the plains (flood control), or the permeability of the ground (sand and gravel pits), must integrate a concern for protection of groundwater against salt.

(ii)   Controlling pumping

We have seen that the communities using the groundwater resources for public water supply have provided themselves through their water supply enterprises with the means of managing abstractions. But there also exist many private drillings (possibly for irrigation) which still remain to be registered amid which are devoid of any rational management.

10.4   Carbonate rocks

The specific characteristics of fractured and karstified carbonate rocks present some peculiarities that are treated here. Small carbonate rock islands are considered in the following section.

Case history no. 8: Salt-fresh water relationships in the carbonate formations of Apulia (southern Italy)*

Apulia (fig 10.50) lies on the eastern side of the peninsula of Italy. It extends from the Adriatic to the Ionian seas which pass beneath the entire region and are in direct communication with each other.

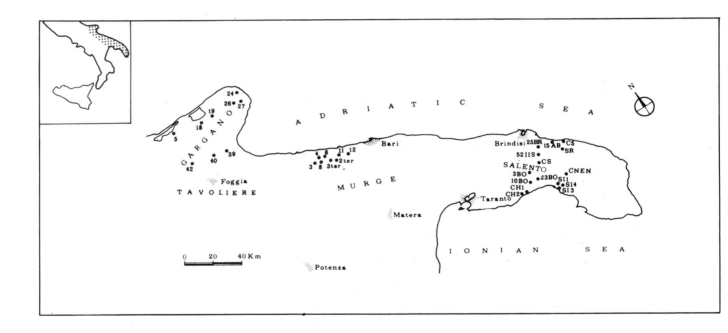

Fig. 10.50 - Map of Apulia (southern Italy) and location of the observation wells.

The climate of Apulia is essentially Mediterranean, with the main rains in autumn-winter; these provide far more recharge to the aquifers than do the spring-summer rains (see table). Rainfall increases with elevation, especially when the mountains rise at a short distance from the sea (Cotecchia and Magri, 1966).

---

* Prepared by Vincenzo Cotecchia, Institute of Engineering Geology and Geotechnique, Bari University, Italy.

Place	J	F	M	A	M	J	J	A	S	O	N	D
Lecce	75	60	57	45	33	25	6	19	41	77	100	93
Bari	58	49	46	35	28	20	9	22	44	64	75	76
Gioia Del Colle	63	45	53	48	42	37	12	26	45	58	90	75
Foggia	44	37	37	35	34	31	14	23	49	41	55	54
Vieste	67	48	41	32	27	20	14	19	48	50	71	89
S. Marco in Lamis	114	93	87	66	59	50	34	36	61	93	117	136

It is possible to recognize four distinct hydrogeological units in Apulia: Gargano, Tavolierre, Murge and Salento.

Owing to the geological, morphological, structural and climatic diversities characterizing the four units, groundwater movement in each occurs in quite a different manner; the result is that problems which may be of prime importance in one area may not arise at all in another. This is the case, for instance, where sea water intrusion is concerned. While this is particularly serious in the Salento peninsula, it is of little or no importance in the innermost parts of the Murge and the Tavoliere. It is natural, therefore, that the numerous basic research topics in the various areas should also be diverse, though the final aim remains that of ascertaining everything about the fundamental parameters for resource planning.

Palaeogeography

For a proper understanding of the hydrogeological aspects of the Apulian aquifer it is necessary to consider the past changes that have occurred in the level of the sea, influencing and creating the potential of the present-day groundwater reserves.

Particularly significant in this regard has been the study of relative movements of the sea and land mass over the last 200,000 years during the Tyrrhenian and Holocene (Cotecchia and Magri, 1967; Cotecchia et al. 1969). It is especially important to remember that since the last maximum retreat of the sea, which occurred some 14,000 years ago, its level has risen an average of some 100 m as a result of the Flandrian transgression which is still under way (fig. 10.51). This rise in sea level has decreased the distance between the Ionian and Adriatic by about one-third what it used to be, and, of course, the thickness of the body of fresh and brackish groundwaters has thus been reduced in a like manner (fig. 10.52). Consequently, in order to compensate for the big reduction in the volume of groundwaters there has been a rise in the level of underlying sea waters and more marked intrusion of salt waters during the Flandrian (Cotecchia et al. 1974a).

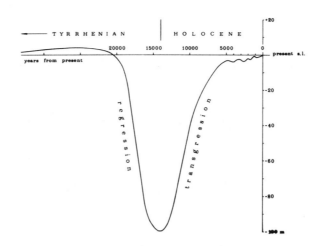

Fig. 10.51 – Schematic diagram of Apulian boundaries during Lower Eocene and during the Pre-Flandrian regression (Cotecchia, 1974), and variation of sea level in the Gulf of Taranto during Tyrrhenian and Holocene (Cotecchia et al., 1971a).

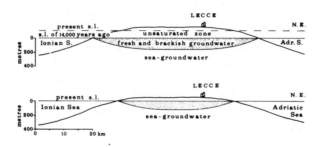

Fig. 10.52 – Schematic sections through the Salento Peninsula, showing thickness and extent of fresh and brackish groundwaters at the present time (bottom) and at the climax of the last retreat of the sea (top) (Cotecchia et al., 1974a).

This has given rise to a whole chain of geochemical changes relating to the migration of sea water during the course of time, and the alternation of saturated and unsaturated states in the rock mass. Evolving states of karst have thus been produced, the knowledge of which is essential in order to understand the aquifer properly from the resource-development point of view.

Geology

As is apparent from figure 10.53, the framework of the mountains (Gargano) and hills (Murge and Serre of Salento) is formed of a Jurassic-Cretaceous limestone-dolomite series partly covered by Miocene sandstone around Lecce and on the western fringes of the Gargano, and by Quaternary formations especially on the Tavoliere and the Salento peninsula.

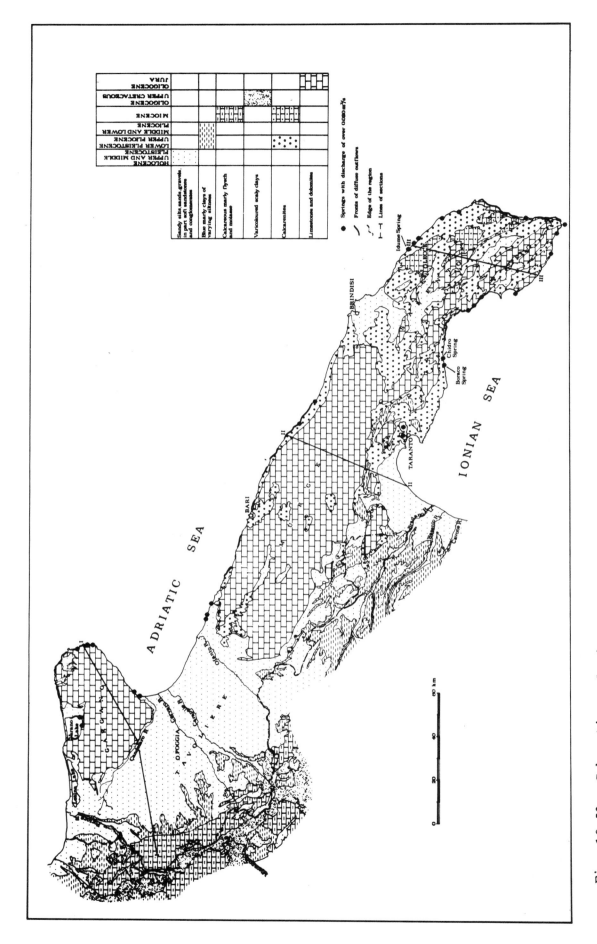

Fig. 10.53 – Schematic geological map with hydrogeological orientation of Apulia.

The carbonate complex is well bedded and about 9000 m thick, while the Mio-Plio-Quaternary cover is never more than 100 m thick (fig. 10.54).

The attitude is generally subhorizontal and the tectonic structure is fairly simple.

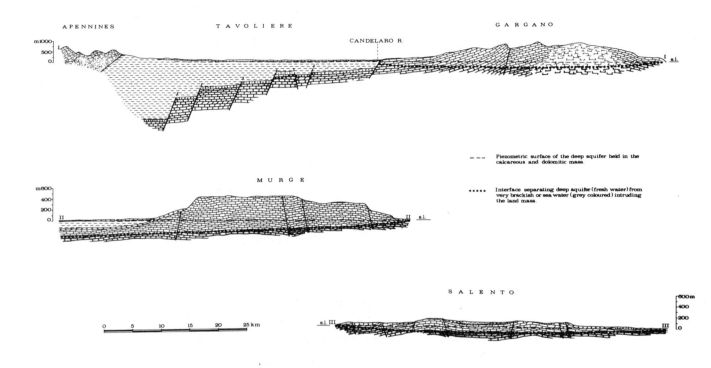

Fig. 10.54 - Schematic geological sections through the four hydrogeological units of Apulia (Gargano, Tavoliere, Murge and Salento). Section lines and legend are indicated in Figure 10.4.4.

Structure

The Fossa Brandanica (Brandano Trough) is the structural element joining the Apulia-Gargano region to the Apennines. The structural elements rising from there are the Gargano headland and the Murge hills.

The structure of the Gargano and the Murge is the direct result of a succession of tectonic phases which started in Upper Cretaceous times and continued to the late Quaternary. Taken as a whole the Gargano has a horst structure, within which are minor folds mainly with Apennine (NNW-SSE), Antiapennine (NNE-SSW) and Gargano (E-W) trends. There are also faults which split up the horst into secondary blocks, giving rise to variously oriented monoclines. The Candelaro fault, which follows the course of the Candelaro river, provides a clean break between the Gargano headland and the low-lying plains of the Tavoliere, thus creating a characteristic geological, hydrological and orographic unit.

The carbonate deposits of the Murge also form a monocline affected by folds and dissected by faults. The monocline itself is bounded by tension faults which separate it from the Gargano and Salento carbonate heights (Martinis, 1970), as well as from the carbonate deposits which form the substratum of the Adriatic basin and the Fossa Brandanica.

On the Salento peninsula, tension faults have given rise to a block structure, while folds have produced lines of ridges. There is a very clear relationship here between structure and landscape, which is particularly characterized by the three lines of hills, known locally as 'serre', that converge on the Cape of Santa Maria di Leuca, partially enclosing basins, mainly of an endoreic nature.

The hills on the Salento peninsula coincide with structural 'highs' (horsts). They rise a few dozen meters above the elevation of the surrounding plains which represent the structural 'lows' (grabens), mostly filled with Neogene and Quaternary transgressive deposits.

Structural maps have been plotted for the whole of Apulia. Figure 10.55 shows the map of faults and lineaments of non-anthropogenic origin for the Salento peninsula, derived by interpretation of satellite imagery and photos (Guerricchio and Zezza, 1979).

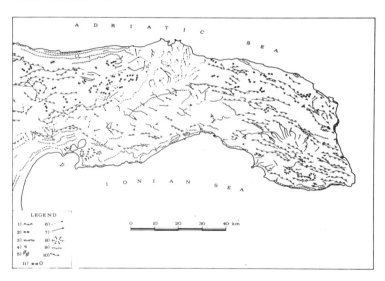

Fig. 10.55 - Map of the morphological evidences of neotectonics in the Salento Peninsula. 1: Fault slope; 2: Fault incision; 3: Flexure slope; 4: Counter-slopes with respect to the main crest or located on secondary watersheds; 5: Watercourses transversal to morphological-structural ridges; 6: River-bed trunks with generally rectilinear or anomalous trend; 7: Paleo-river-beds and relative diversions; 8: Areas with centripetal hydrography; 9: Edges of alluvial and marine terraces; 10: Canyon; 11: Lines of dolines (Guerricchio and Zezza, 1979).

Hydrogeological setting

The Mesozoic carbonate rocks forming the geological basement of the region are markedly affected by fracturing and karst dissolution phenomena, which have created a large groundwater reservoir.

It should be clearly understood that when speaking of groundwaters, reference is being made only to those contained in the Mesozoic carbonate rocks, permeable as a result of fissuring and karstification, thus forming what is known as the 'deep' aquifer. No reference is made to any shallow aquifers which may occur in the permeable post-Cretaceous formations in the study area. In any case the potential of these aquifers is usually small and they rarely constitute a water resource suitable for large-scale development.

Also absent from the ensuing treatise is any reference to the deep aquifer in the Tavoliere, since this lies at great depth in the Cretaceous limestones overlain by Pliocene-Calabrian clays and yellow sands that are encountered up to 1000 m below ground level. The waters of this aquifer are confined and owing to the great depth at which they often occur they are generally so brackish that they cannot be used for any common purposes.

The first time seawater was found in the Tavoliere was in 1952 near San Marco in Lamis when water with a salinity of around 42000 mg/l was discovered in the Cretaceous limestones beneath 800 m of Calabria clays. The presence of H_2S due to bacterial reduction of the $SO_4^=$ using the organic matter present in some sedimentary rocks was also ascertained. A similar discovery was made in a well at Gaudiano (Lavello) 60 km inland, where seawater was encountered in the limestones at a depth of 1400 m (Cotecchia, 1955).

Owing to the great depth at which the Tavoliere deep aquifer occurs, the groundwaters that are found in the Quaternary sediments, running virtually without any break from the Apennines to the sea in the flattest part of the Tavoliere, are of notable practical importance since they lie at a shallow depth, are easy to tap, are quite common and have good quality (Cotecchia and Ippolito, 1958).

In virtually all parts of the region the deep aquifer faults on seawater which intrudes the land-mass. Equilibrium between the two types of water is regulated not only by the different density of the waters but also by dynamic factors concerning the way the waters move to reach their natural points of emergence.

At the contact between the two waters there is a zone of dispersion, the thickness of which ranges from a few dozen meters in the areas farthest inland to a few decimeters along the shore (Cotecchia et al. 1974b).

Because the groundwaters float on the seawaters, their base level is sea level. The manner in which the balance of the aquifer is maintained through recharge, flow and seaward discharge depends essentially on the vertical and horizontal permeability of the aquifer rocks.

Though there is only one aquifer system in the Mesozoic rocks of Apulia, the overall hydrogeological characteristics differ quite considerably from one area to another. For instance, high storage capacity is a general feature of the Salento aquifer, but not of the Murge, where, owing to the complex karst environment and tectonic fracturing recognized at depth, the deep karst aquifer has very specific attributes and requisites, that result in very singular flow characteristics. As the aquifer is bounded at the top by virtually impermeable rocks and as its overall permeability is often relatively low (compared with that in the Salento peninsula), the waters generally move under confined conditions with high hydraulic heads, not infrequently at considerable depths below sea level. The geometric configuration is very irregular and, as stated above, the storage capacity is comparatively low (Grassi, 1973; Grassi and Tadolini, 1974).

In the Gargano, instead, the hydrogeological situation is very similar to that on the Salento peninsula, since in both cases there is a single groundwater body floating on intruding seawaters. As regards relationships between the main mass of groundwaters and the seawaters, the Gargano behaves almost like an island.

The fault which follows the line of the Candelaro river brings the main Gargano aquifer into communication with the deep aquifer of the Tavoliere.

It is also important to mention the relationship involving groundwater flow from the karst rocks of the Murge to those of the Salento peninsula, the influence of which is felt as far east as Lecce.

Karst forms and tectonic fracturing

The distribution and mode of development of common surface and subsurface karst forms which are common everywhere, especially in the Salento area, are directly related to the carbonate nature of the basement, the tectonic setting and the changes that have occurred in shorelines, although there are many other factors which play a role in the development of karstification.

One of these is the marked anisotropy which regulates the genetic-evolutionary processes connected with the distribution and spacial orientation of the karst conduits (Grassi et al. 1977). These follow pre-established lines imposed by the local and regional tectonic features, the general direction of groundwater flow, and the possible and often discontinuous occurrence of lithotypes that are affected by karstification, to a negligible extent at best and sometimes not at all. The selective nature of the lines of major karstification is explained to some extent by the fact that the karst-forming role of each tectonic joint or bedding plane depends not so much on the extent to which it is open, as on the way it is inclined and oriented compared with the direction of subsurface flow.

On the Salento peninsula, comparison of the density of fracture places on given orientations with the lines of development of the karst conduits, indicates that there exists a relationship between underground karst and the more intensely fractured zones. However, for a given degree of fracturing, the preferential directions of development are influenced by the state of the joints themselves (open, filled, closed, etc.), by the type of bedding and by the relationship between bedding and jointing.

The karst cavities follow preferential and not random lines of development (Zezza, 1975). Here, the intersection of the joints and bedding planes results in the Cretaceous limestones being subdivided into blocks ranging from a few cubic decimeters to several cubic meters in size, the longest side running parallel to the fracture planes.

In the neighboring Murge region, statistical analysis (mainly on cores from a large number of water wells, some as much as 750 m deep) indicates that as a whole the Mesozoic rocks there are affected by relatively infrequent, often discontinuous fracturing, especially at depths where the deep aquifer groundwaters are found on the neighboring Salento peninsula (Grassi, 1974). Here, too, they follow the regional and local structural trends.

Figure 10.56 (Grassi, 1974) serves to emphasize the close relationship between structure and karst development. In this regard the Castellana karst caverns are of decided interest. The caverns developed as the result of a system of subvertical faults which provided the easiest flow paths for groundwaters (Grassi, 1974). The cave system is over 3000 m long and runs to a depth of 70 m below ground level at the lowest point so far explored (Zezza, 1975).

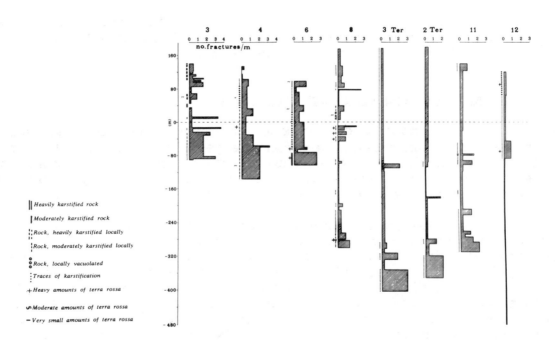

Fig. 10.56 - Histograms of fracture frequency, calculated from cores sampled from the most representative boreholes (Fig. 10.54) in the Murge. Symbols near each histogram show the state of rock karstification and the presence of 'terra rossa' in joints and karst cavities (Grassi et al., 1977).

Karst solution phenomena are of considerable importance in the Gargano, too. This is especially true of the central and western parts, where the Cretaceous and Jurassic limestones and dolomites are fissured and karstified at depth and on the surface, as evidenced by the extensive plateaus and dolines absolutely devoid of any surface drainage network whatsoever (Cotecchia and Magri, 1966).

The presence of areas of absorption is certainly a factor of particular interest in the Murge and especially in the Salento peninsula, where such areas have all the characteristics of well-defined endorreic basins. These are centers of karst activity in the true sense of the word, there being subterranean forms of considerable vertical extent (swallow holes of various dimensions, natural wells, etc.), exhibiting typically isogravitational karst land forms.

In this context, in an area where the groundwaters float on the seawaters intruding the land-mass, the retreat of the sea, of course, leads to rejuvenation of the karst cycle. The groundwaters which issue forth at sea level and which, during their flow towards the sea cause more or less energetic dissolution of the limestones, thus come to encounter different conditions and so they start to move in relation to the new karst base level. It therefore seems reasonable to move in relation to the new karst base level. It therefore seems reasonable to assume that the concentration of karst conduits on given successive horizons is directly linked with the lowering of the groundwater base level as a result of relative movements between sea and land.

To sum up, the movements in question have given rise to polycyclic karst. They have repeatedly slowed down cavity formation, favored the accumulation of 'terra rossa', disrupted the unitarian nature of the karst drainage system, caused precocious fossilization and complex superimposition situations in the karst landforms, etc. The result is that nowadays, down a given vertical section in the Mesozoic series, it is possible to find systems of karst conduits which are extremely well-developed in some places and are barely discernable in others, often being confined to well-defined rock horizons or intervals which can sometimes be correlated both among themselves and with old shorelines (these correlations are under study at the moment).

A further point in this regard is that, with the uplifting of the spring zone, many karst conduits, abandoned by the groundwaters even by late Tyrrhenian times, have started to work under pressure, as is also borne out of the submarine karst risings recognized especially in the southeastern Murge.

Springs

The conditions under which the groundwaters issue forth near the shore are closely linked with the geological nature of the rocks outcropping along the coast and, of course, with the degree and type of permeability. Indeed, the main lines of flow occur where permeability is good over a wide area. When these flows reach the coast they give rise to large springs or spring complexes. At the present time these spring waters are lost to the sea, not as yet being harnessed for beneficial use, though this could be done. The use of infrared techniques in Apulia has enabled numerous submarine and subaerial springs to be located, some visible and some not. At times it has also been possible to estimate the size of the discharges (Cassa per il Mezzogiorno, 1974; Guglielminetti et al. 1975; Tulipano, 1976). For instance, on the Salento peninsula it has been estimated that the total seaward outflow is certainly in excess of 25 to 30 m^3/s. These waters are already decidedly contaminated by intruded seawaters, and the salinity is rarely less than 2500/mg/1.

The biggest springs in Apulia have been studied in detail, mainly with a view of harnessing them for beneficial use. This is precisely the case, for instance, as regards the Chidro spring (figs. 10.57 and 10.58), which has an average seaward discharge of 2.4 m^3/s and a salinity of around 3500 mg/1 (Cotecchia et al. 1973a), as well as the 2.4 m^3/s Boranco spring and the submarine springs of the Mar Piccolo in Taranto (fig. 10.59) known locally as 'citri,' which have a discharge of 1.5 m^3/s and a salinity ranging from 3500 to 12000 mg/1 (Cotecchia, 1977a).

Diffuse outflow occurs frequently around the coasts of Apulia. The groundwaters, which are unconfined in these areas, drain seawards along extensive fronts. Though discharges from individual springs are relatively small, the overall outflow is certainly considerable. This type of seaward discharge is characteristic of much of the coastline of the Salento peninsula (especially on the Ionian side). It is also typical of the Gargano (Cotecchia and Magri, 1966), especially on the southeastern shores of Lake Lesina, where the overall average discharge is estimated to be 1.14 m^3/s. The salinity ranges from a minimum of 1400 mg/1 to a maximum of 6400 mg/1.

Outflows along the Adriatic coast of the region, however, are smaller. For instance, in the Murge the discharge of the Fiume Grande, Fiume Piccolo and Morello springs are of the order of 0.35 to 0.70 m^3/s. The exception as regards size of discharge occurs in the case of the Idume spring in Lecce (Tadolini et al. 1971), with around 1.2 m^3/s.

Data collected

One of the most salient facts to have emerged from the studies and investigations conducted so far is that the hydrogeological behavior and the geometric and hydrodynamic properties of the aquifer and hence the groundwater flow schemes differ substantially in the Gargano, the Murge and the Salento peninsula, despite the fact that in most of the region the karst aquifer constitutes a single, continuous system, often underlain by seawaters.

Along with the natural diversities that characterize the various units, there is also a marked difference as regards data that can be acquired or which are already available. Thus, while there are not many data available for the Murge or the Gargano, there is a wealth of information on the Salento peninsula.

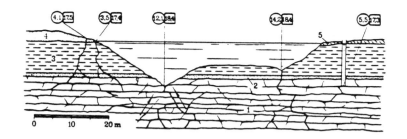

Fig. 10.57 - Schematic hydrogeological section through the Chidro Spring basin. Radon contents (10^{-10} Ci/1) indicated in circles and temperatues ($^{\circ}$C) in squares. 1: Upper Cretaceous limestones and dolomitic limestones; 2: Calabrian bioclastic limestones and calcarenies; 3: Calabrian clays and sandy clays; 4: Tyrrhenian calcarenies; 5: Marshy alluvial deposits of the Holocene (Cotecchia et al., 1973a).

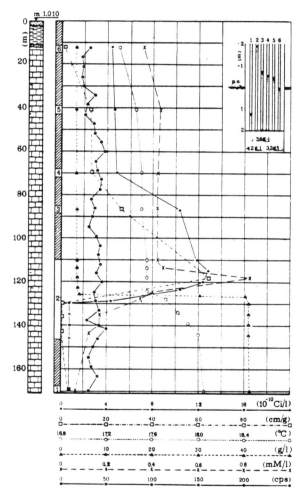

Fig. 10.58 - Average values over five—year period of radon content (Ci/1), velocity (cm/g=cm/day), temperature ($^{\circ}$C), salt content (g/1), free CO_2 (mM/1) and natural radioactivity of rock (cps) in six cells of well CH1 (Fig. 10.54), drilled near Chidro Spring. The hydraulic head of the groundwaters, related to ground level, is shown in the small diagram (Cotecchia et al., 1973a).

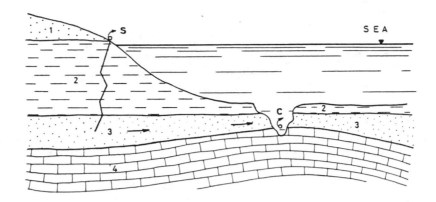

Fig. 10.59 - Schematic geological section through a 'citro' in the Mar Piccolo
(Taranto). 1: Generally coarse, compact calcarenites, ranging from
poorly to slightly permeable through porosity and fissuring
(Tyrrhenian-Calabrian); 2: Clay and clayey marls with frequent sand
interbeds, practically impermeable (Calabrian); 3: Fine, very compact calcarenies, not very permeable (Upper Pliocene); 4: Limestones
and dolomitic limestones, very permeable through fissuring and karstification (Senonian-Turonian) (cotecchia, 1977a).

The main types of investigations performed to date are: geological
surveys; statistical surveys of tectonic fracturing and karst forms; well
inventory and measurement of groundwater levels; hydraulic tests; temperature
and salinity logging; in-situ measurements of groundwater flow rates and of
vertical currents in wells by means of radioisotope probes; and sampling of
groundwaters for chemical and isotopic analysis. From the data acquired by
means of these investigations it has been possible to obtain a very good picture of aquifer properties.

Hydraulic tests

Information on the way groundwater movement occurs in Apulia has been obtained
from short-term and long-term discharge tests performed on wells. For example, by plotting specific discharge maps for the Salento peninsula and the
Murge, it has been possible to outline areas where large quantities of groundwaters can be tapped with only small amounts of drawdown and hence with little
likelihood of increasing aquifer salinity. Specific discharge (discharge per
unit of drawdown) on the Salento peninsula can range from less than one l/s/m
to over 70 l/s/m, with maximum values usually between 100 and 200 l/s/m.

In the Murge, except for a few small coastal areas, the specific
discharge remains below 0.5 l/s/m, with discharges that do not exceed 10 l/s,
while drawdown is often greater than 50 m.

Plotting of the water table or piezometric surface of the deep
aquifer has provided important information about its conformation and groundwater movement. For instance, the group of water table contours between 7 m
and 3 m above mean sea level indicates the hydrogeological boundary between
the aquifer system in the Murge and that in the Salento area. This group of

contours, which indicates a fairly high hydraulic gradient (0.0006), provides a visual picture of the outflow of groundwaters from the Murge heights--where hydraulic heads not infrequently exceed 80 m over sea level to the Salento aquifer system. Considering the hydraulic gradient on the Murge-Salento border, the length of the front through which outflow occurs and the estimated flow velocity, it is calculated that the amount of recharge received by the peninsula aquifer in this manner does not exceed 8 to 10 m^3/s.

The greater overall permeability of the Salento carbonate aquifer than that of the Murge is demonstrated by the lower hydraulic gradients, which are generally around (0.00025), with maximum hydraulic head of 5 m over sea level, against about 0.004 to 0.005. In the Gargano, too, hydraulic gradients are quite low, owing to the very permeable nature of most of the limestone-dolomite terrains of the headland at the level of the groundwater table or piezometric surface, as the case may be.

Throughout the region the conformation of the water table is influenced by the irregular distribution of aquifer permeability properties. The longest drainage fronts and the largest individual coastal springs invariably exert influence on the shape of the water table. Concentrated outflows generally cause narrow depressions in the water table contour plots, thus indicating preferential lines of flow. Diffuse outflows, on the other hand, tend to result in some increases in the distance between the contours on a vast scale; in other words they cause a marked decrease in the hydraulic gradient.

Discrete flow models have been used in Apulia to study the changes in the water table as a result of extraction (Benedini et al. 1972,; Pinder, 1973; Troisi, 1978). Covering an area of 600 km^2, they involved discretization of 16000 meshes with 200 m sides.

A more complete picture of the mobility of the waters in the Apulian aquifer has been obtained by studying the amount of attenuation (Magri and Troisi, 1969), that occurs in the case of the periodic and aperiodic oscillations in sea level transmitted inland and affecting the groundwaters (fig. 10.60).

Salinity

One of the specific properties of the waters of the deep Apulian aquifer is their salt content and spatial distribution. As the aquifer is recharged by the infiltration of atmospheric waters, the lowest possible concentration of salts in the groundwaters must be the same as that in the recharge waters. Studies made in this regard on the Salento peninsula show that the average dissolved solids content of the recharge waters is around 500 mg/l. This is because the rainwaters which infiltrate during the autumn-winter period dissolve and carry into the aquifer the salts deposited on the ground both by dry fallout and by spring-summer rainwaters which can be considered to evaporate completely (Cotecchia et al. 1971b; 1973b).

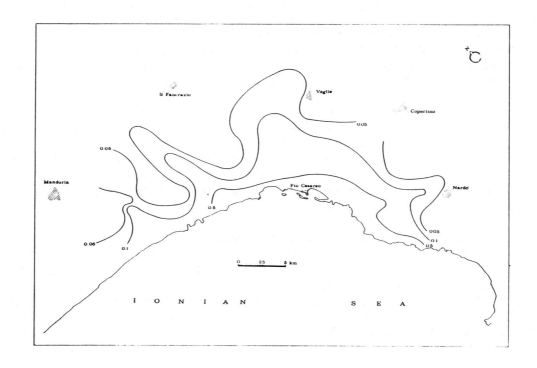

Fig. 10.60 - Map of attenuation values for a coastal strip of the Salento Peninsula.

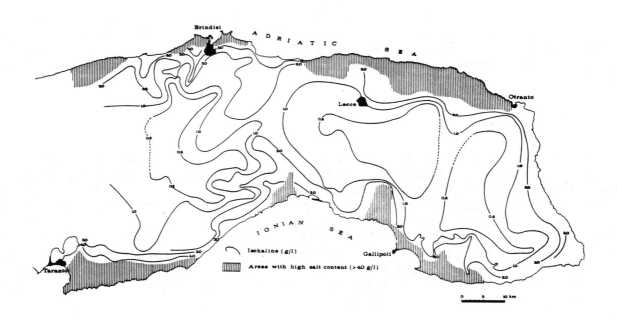

Fig. 10.61 - Groundwater salinities in the Salento Peninsula (Cotecchia, 1977b).

On the basis of the information obtained from figure 10.61 regarding the Salento peninsula, it is possible to assess the state of contamination of the groundwaters by the seawaters that intrude the land mass. It is evident that along vast stretches of the areas closest to the shore there are waters whose salinity exceeds 4000 mg/1, which is too high for them to be harnessed directly for beneficial use. This is the situation that is encountered around Taranto, where the contaminated zone extends inland for some 4 km, and at the tip of the peninsula where similar contamination occurs, the limit being the 5000 mg/1 isohaline in this case.

In general, contamination is likely to increase in all parts of the peninsula, owning to the uncontrolled extraction of groundwaters (Tadolini and Tulipano, 1977b). This idea is borne out also by comparison of the results of salinity logging performed on the same observation wells at different periods.

There is a different situation in the Murge area, where the salinity of the groundwaters is generally low, usually less than 1000 mg/1 and often below 500 mg/1, while the Cl$^-$ content ranges from 40 to 300-400 mg/1. However, along a 4-5 km wide coastal strip, more intense fracturing and subterranean karst cavities, which are very well developed in some places, permit greater freedom of movement to and from the land mass; this results in the groundwater having higher salinity there, with values in the 3000-18000 mg/1 range and a Cl$^-$ content of 9000 mg/1 at the most.

In the Gargano, both along the Candelaro valley to the west and along the coasts, where the main aquifer comes in contact with the sea, there is a fringe of brackish groundwaters (Cotecchia and Magri, 1966).

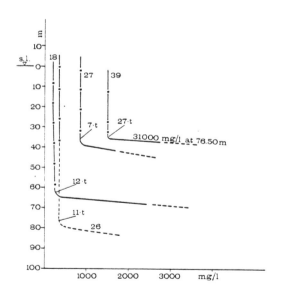

Fig. 10.62 - Salt content variations with depth in the waters of some wells (see Fig. 10.4.1) of the Gargano. t = static level referred to sea level.

An odd situation, certainly attributable to the presence of ground-water currents in tectonic discontinuities, has been encountered in some Gargano wells (fig. 10.62) where contamination by seawaters is evidenced by constant, relatively high salinity from the surface of the groundwater body downwards.

Examination of the distribution of salinity in the groundwaters of the whole of Apulia reveals the existence of a theoretical line running through Brindisi and Taranto, signaling the inflow of fresher waters from the Murge system to the Salento peninsula system, thus creating a vast area where the salinity is lower than 500 mg/1. This groundwater inflow is also clearly marked by the higher values of the Ca^{++}/Mg^{++} values, indicating that the waters have been in the aquifer an extremely long time and have taken part in significant dolomitization processes.

An important relationship has been discovered between groundwater flow-lines and salinity. It is generally observed that the major flow-lines occur in areas where--for a given distance from the coast--groundwater salinity is lower; the large inflows of fresh recharge hinder the intrusion of seawaters at depth. As a corollary, salinity is high in areas where flow is lower.

Data on saline stratification have been acquired by salinity logging in unpumped wells. The logs were run to ascertain the spatial boundaries of the aquifer, to establish the actual elevation of the fresh water-salt water interface and to study the dynamic behavior of the zone of dispersion (Tadolini and Tulipano, 1977a).

Dynamic behavior is influenced by the periodic recharge of the aquifer, the distance from the sea, the trend in water-table levels, and the direct and indirect effect of variations in barometric pressure. It is felt in a different manner from the bottom to the top of the zone of dispersion, and the 'hysteresis' varies from one part of the aquifer to another. Salinity at the top of the zone of dispersion is about 4000-5000 mg/1, and increases quite rapidly and regularly with depth, to 41000-42000 mg/1, which is typical of seawater.

Generally speaking, it can be considered that throughout the region the depth below sea level at which the top of the zone of dispersion occurs is equal to about thirty times the hydraulic head.

Temperature

In the Apulian carbonates the study of groundwater temperatures has proved very useful for identifying saltwaters at the bottom of the groundwater body, especially when the contact between these two kinds of water occurs at a considerable depth below sea level, and hence it is often very difficult to use direct methods of investigation such as observation wells to accurately pinpoint the position of the zone of dispersion.

This is the case, for instance, in the Murge karst, where hydraulic heads may be very high at times (up to 200 m over sea level), and consequently the zone of dispersion occurs at a considerable depth, to several thousand meters below sea level (Cotecchia et al. 1978).

The investigations have shown that the zone of transition between the mobile groundwaters and the intruding seawaters (which may be considered as stationary) is marked by a temperature increase. For instance, in the Salento peninsula, there is reason to believe that the $18^{\circ}C$ isotherm roughly marks the contact between fresh groundwaters and the brackish waters forming the zone of dispersion.

Analysis of temperature distribution and observation of temperature gradients also enables better use to be made of the information that has been acquired so far on the position of the most important flow-lines. Moreover this approach provides additional information on the distribution of groundwater flows in different levels at various depths in the aquifer.

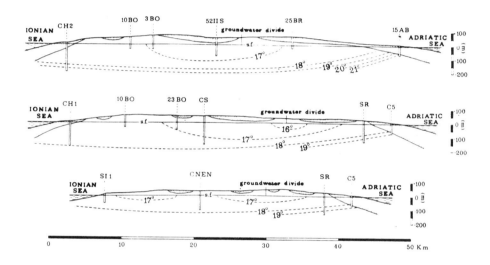

Fig. 10.63 - Schematic geological sections showing trend of groundwater isotherms in the Salento Peninsula. In blank: Cretaceous limestones and dolomites containing the aquifer; stippled: Mio-Plio-Quaternary formations (calcarenities and/or clays), usually slightly permeable or virtually impermeable; s.f.: Water table or piezometric surface; broken lines: Isotherms ($^{\circ}C$). Wells are located in Figure 10.50 (Carlin et al., 1973).

Figure 10.63 indicates the significant isotherms of schematic sections of the Salento peninsula (Carlin et al. 1973). It is interesting to note that along the coastal strip the isotherms have a concave form as a result of the influence of the sea and of the heat extracted from the geothermal flux by infiltrating waters and groundwater flows. The greater the depression, the greater the amount of heat absorbed. This happens actually where direct recharge is highest (in the subterranean watershed area) and where the groundwaters are the most mobile (near the areas of major seaward outflows). In this regard, the downswing of the isotherms at the subterranean watershed and the big seaward outflow from the Chidro spring is evident from figure 10.63 (Chidro spring is shown on the left hand side of the first two sections).

Examination of the temperatures measured at various seasons in three wells (fig. 10.64) drilled in the San Isidoro area (Ionian coast of the Salento) at 600, 220 and 18 m from the shore, shows that going seawards there is a rise in the average groundwater isotherm value (December 1967 - September 1969; nine measurements). This phenomenon is also enhanced by the effect stemming from the length of time the waters have been in the ground. It is apparent that there is heat flow from the sea, at least to a depth of 20 m below sea level, which decreases going inland.

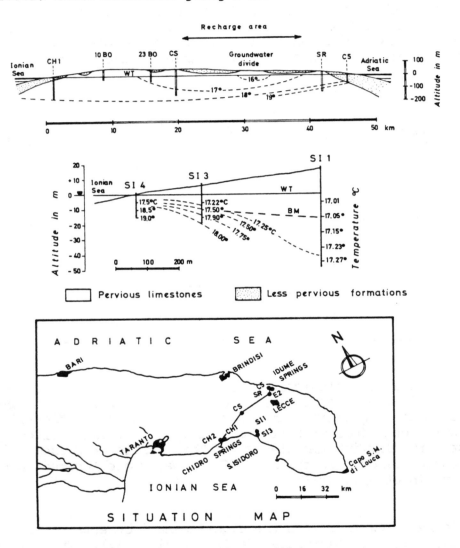

Fig. 10.64 - Mean groundwater isotherm along a section at right angles to the shore in the S. Isidoro area (Salento Peninsula), indicating a flow of heat from the sea to the land (Carlin et al., 1973).

The acquisition of data on the distribution of temperature on the waters of the deep aquifer, both at the water table and at various depths, has also provided much important information on the main recharge areas. For instance, the minimum temperatures encountered in the Murge-Salento border area, even less than 15°C, indicate that here the inflow of waters from the Murge is felt most decidedly, these being colder waters that evidently infiltrated at higher elevations.

Figure 10.65 shows the trend of temperatures in observation wells and the relevant distance from the sea in the Gargano. Here considerable temperature differences have been noted even between parts of the aquifer fairly close together. For instance, there is a 7°C temperature difference between the waters of wells 39 and 40 which are only 3.5 km apart.

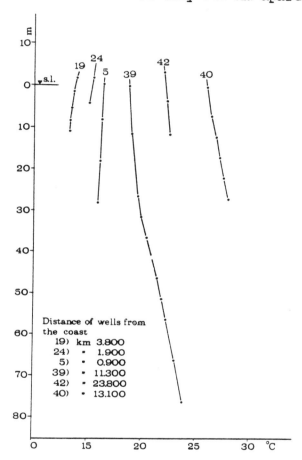

Fig. 10.65 - Variations of temperature with depth in the waters of some wells (fig. 10.50) located at different distance from the coast in the Gargano (Cotecchia and Magri, 1966).

Such temperature differences may well initiate very considerable convection currents in the groundwaters floating on the intruding seawaters, especially where preferential flow-paths exist, thus leading to the mixing of groundwaters of different salinities.

It is a known fact that groundwater temperatures which are significantly higher than the mean annual air temperature may be the result of exothermic reactions (oxidation of pyrite and oil deposits, hydration of anhydrite,
etc.). However, the temperature increases observed in the groundwaters of the
western Gargano (20 to 26°C compared with a mean annual air temperature of
14.4°C) are too great to have been caused by exothermic reactions; it is quite
likely, instead, that such temperatures may be attributable to high geothermal
gradients (Cotecchia and Magri, 1966). This idea is borne out by the high
geothermal gradient measured in the waters of wells 39, 40 and 42, all located
near the Candelaro fault (fig. 10.65).

A high geothermal gradient in limestones and dolomites that usually
have a low gradient may be due to the existence of magmatic masses that are
cooling at relatively shallow depth. In point of fact, outcrops of basic
igneous rocks are known at Punta delle Pietre Nere, in Lake Lesina, and
Masseria San Giovanni in Pane, in Apricena (Cotecchia and Canitano, 1954).

Water chemistry

The freshwaters at the top of the Gargano and Salento deep aquifers and the
confined waters in the isolated levels in many parts of the Murge are of the
calcium bicarbonate type, while the waters present in the coastal strips and
in the bottom part of the deep aquifer are of the sodium chloride type.

The intruding seawaters have average HCO_3^- concentrations similar to
those of ordinary seawaters, but the free CO_2, Ca^{++}, Cl^- and $SO_4^=$ concentrations are decidedly higher, while those of Mg^{++} are somewhat lower (fig.
10.66).

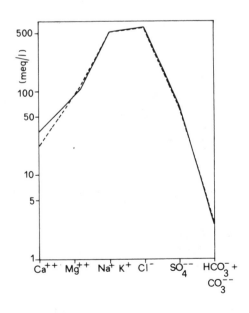

Fig. 10.66 – Average chemical composition of the brackish groundwaters of the
Salento Peninsula (solid line) and of Ionian and Adriatic Seas (dotted line) (Cotecchia et al., 1975a).

Studies of the chemical composition of the groundwaters have revealed the influence of contamination by seawaters on carbonate rock dissolution processes and hence on the variations in permeability of the water-bearing medium. If the quantity of waters of marine origin mixed with fresh waters does not exceed 9 per cent, the water becomes aggressive, while the partial pressure of the CO_2 remains constant, so the values of Ca^{++}, Mg^{++} and HCO_3^- measured in waters contaminated with seawater are generally much higher than those resulting from the stoichiometric calculation of the mix (Cotecchia et al. 1975a; 1975b; Tazioli and Tittozzi, 1977). In the Salento peninsula the average increases recorded are 12.5 per cent for Ca^{++}, 9.2 percent for Mg^{++} and 29.3 per cent for HCO_3^- (fig. 10.67).

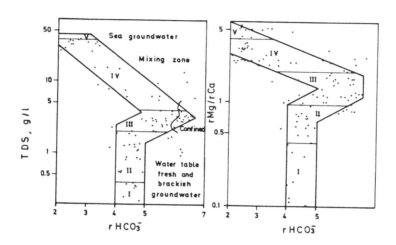

Fig. 10.67 - Variation of HCO_3^- concentrations as a function of the total solids content in groundwaters of the Salento Peninsula (Cotecchia et al., 1975a).

The Ca^{++} saturation values of the groundwaters generally point to supersaturation in the shallowest levels of the aquifer uncontaminated by seawaters and to undersaturation in the waters with salinity of between 1000 and 4000 mg/l. The lowest undersaturation values usually occur in levels where groundwater movement is most active.

The study of characteristic ratios is of particularly importance in characterizng the waters of the Apulian aquifer. For instance, variations of the Mg^{++}/Ca^{++} ratio in groundwaters enables a check to be made on the double exchange phenomena involving groundwaters and limestone in the secondary dolomitization process, which lead to an increase in the Ca^{++} content of groundwaters and a decrease in the amount of Mg^{++} (Cotecchia and Magri, 1966).

Analysis of the salt content and the chloride content, plus consideration of the trend of the Cl^-/I^- and Br^-/I^- characteristic ratios with depth, provides an important assessment of the situation regarding the extent and depth of the zone of dispersion and also the maximum change in level of the top of the zone of dispersion (Tadolini and Tulipano, 1975).

Radioactive tracer investigations

Widespread use has been made of artificial radioactive tracers in the study of groundwater movement in Apulia in order to identify the most useful water bearing levels. These tracers are particularly useful for measuring groundwater flow rates, for detecting vertical currents, for ascertaining direction of flow and for establishing the amount of seawater intrusion of the land mass (Carlin et al. 1968; Tazioli, 1973; 1976; 1977).

The investigations have revealed marked differences in the method of groundwater flow in the various areas studied, owing to the lithological differences and seawater intrusion.

By way of example, the flow velocities ascertained in a small part of the Murge coast north of Bari vary decidedly from place to place, owing to the nonhomogeneous nature of the aquifers and the irregular distribution of hydraulic heads. The average flow velocities range from 2 to 600 cm/day.

The values recorded on the Salento peninsula average around 1.5 cm/day some 10 km inland but are as high as 600 cm/day at about 250 m from the shore. Higher values have been found in a shallow Miocene calcarenite aquifer.

Figure 10.68 illustrates the flow velocity trends of groundwaters and intruding seawaters in a schematic section of the Salento peninsula from the Ionian to the Adriatic. It is also evident from figure 10.68 that exchanges with intruding seawaters extend for several kilometers inland (Cotecchia et al. 1975a; Tazioli, 1977).

Figure 10.69 illustrates a situation that occurs frequently in the Murge, near Bari. In this case a difference in hydraulic head between various water bearing levels of the aquifer separated by impervious rock causes a descending current from a depth of 125 m to 400 m (Grassi et al. 1977; Tazioli, 1977).

In the Chidro Spring area the groundwaters are confined by a bed of Calabrian clay (fig. 10.70). The difference in hydraulic head between the bottom and the top of the aquifer constitutes a very adverse fact here, and to some extent explains the widespread contamination of the groundwaters by seawaters in this area (Cotecchia et al. 1973a; Tazioli, 1977), taking account also of the high permeability of the aquifer owing to karst fracturing.

Natural isotopes have also been used to investigate the hydrogeological situation in Apulia. These include ^{14}C, ^{13}C, ^{3}H, ^{18}O and Rn. They have provided some very useful information on the relationships existing between the groundwaters and the seawaters, as well as on the methods by which the groundwaters are recharged and renewed.

For instance, along those stretches of the coast where there is unimpeded seaward flow, the ^{14}C and ^{13}C concentrations decrease going inland, while in areas where the groundwaters are isolated from the sea by impervious rocks and in those parts of the aquifer farthest from the sea, the ^{14}C concentrations are virtually zero, while the ^{13}C values are more or less midway between those of the seawater and the groundwater (Cotecchia et al. 1974a).

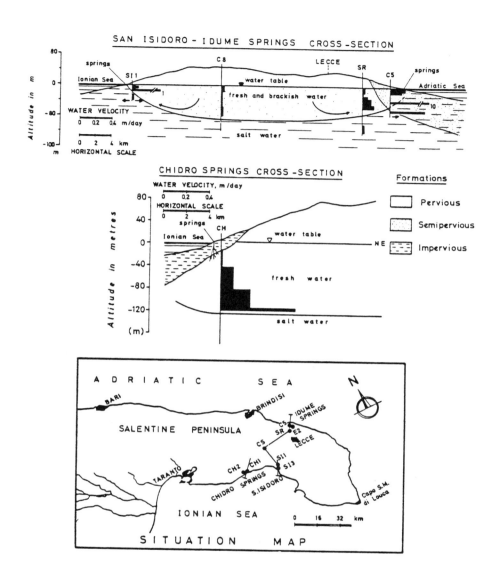

Fig. 10.68 - Schematic cross-section of the Salento Peninsula showing groundwater velocity trend measured in wells reaching the sea-
groundwaters. 1: Mio-Plio-Quaternary formations (calcarenites
and/or clays); 2: Cretaceous limestones and dolomites, which constitute the aquifer (Cotecchia et al., 1975a).

The natural ^{3}H contents measured in various water bearing levels in
the Murge around Bari, where, as stated above, the waters are confined, have
provided indications on the time the waters stay in the aquifer. Tritium
values of virtually zero measured in the deepest level of the aquifer indicate
that the waters have been in the subsurface for certainly more than 25 years,
while those measured in the shallower levels are similar to those for rainfall, thus indicating active groundwater movement, as also borne out by evi-
dence provided by artificial radioactive tracers (Grassi et al. 1977).

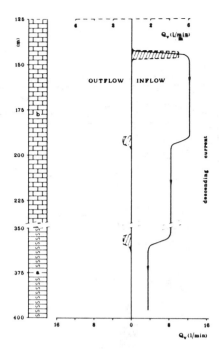

Fig. 10.69 - Downward current in a borehole sunk into the Murge (near Bari), 8 km away from the sea, in Cretaceous marly dolomites (a) and marly limestones (b), with occasionally interbedded small clay lenses. Depths are referred to ground level (Tazioli, 1977).

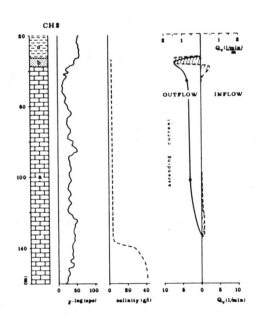

Fig. 10.70 - Natural radioactivity of the rocks (γ - log), vertical currents and salinity measured in borehole CH2 (Fig. 10.54), 1 km away from the sea, in the Chidro Spring area. Depths are referred to ground level (a: Cretaceous limestones and dolomites; b: Calcarenites; c: Calabrian clays) (Tazioli, 1977).

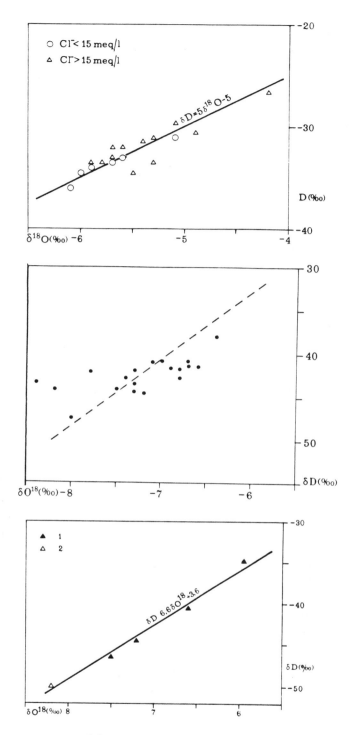

Fig. 10.71 - Relation between δ¹⁸O and δD values of fresh and brackish ground-
waters: in the Salento Peninsula (Cotecchia et al., 1974a), in the
Murge (Grassi et al., 1977) and in the Gargano (1: Deep aquifer; 2:
Perched aquifer) (Cotecchia, 1977a).

Analysis of stable hydrogen and oxygen isotopes (fig. 10.71) has provided information on the location of the main recharge areas and on the way recharge occurs (diffuse or concentrated inflows, surface runoff, etc.). In the case of the Gargano, for instance, it may be observed that recharge is generally from high ground and that inflow is rapid. The groundwaters of the Murge and the Salento peninsula, instead, are recharged partly by local rainfall (at an elevation only slightly above mean sea level) and partly by rainwaters which infiltrate farther inland on the high ground of the Murge. The slope of the $\delta D - \delta^{18}O$ curve indicates marked evaporation prior to infiltration in the case of the latter (Grassi et al. 1977).

References

Benedini, M., Giuliano, S., Troisi, S. (1972). Alcune considerazioni sulla tratatazione matematica del problems del moto in acquiferi fessurati. Geologia Applicata e Idrogeologia, vol. VII, pp. 75-100, Bari.

Carlin, F., Dai Pra', O, Magri, G. (1968). Segnalazione di polle-inghiottitoi marini lungo la costa ionica della Penisola Salentina. Quaderni della 'Ricerca Scientifica, 49, pp. 205-212, IRSA, Roma.

Carlin, F., Magri, G, Moncelli, F. (1973). Temperatura delle acque sotterranee della Penisola Salentina. Geologia Applicata e Idrogeologia, vol. VIII, part II, pp. 155-198, Bari.

Cassa per il Mezzogiorno: Idrotecneco, SpA; Rossi, SrP. (1974). Rilievo aereo multispettrale-Puglia, Rapporto Interno.

Cotecchia, V., Canitano, A. (1954). Sull'affioramento delle 'pietre nere' al lago di Lesina. Boll. Soc. Geol. It., vol. LXXIII, pp. 1-16.

Cotecchia, V. (1955). Influenza dell'acqua marina sulle falde acquifere in zone costiere, con particolare riferimento alle ricerche d'acqua sotterranea in Puglia. Geotechnica, 3 pp. 1-24.

Cotecchia, V., Ippolito, F. (1958). Gli aspetti geoidrologici del Tavoliere. In: Indagine sulle acque sotterranee del Tavoliere-Puglia. pp 10.23, Cassa per il Mezzogiorno, doc. 2.

Cotecchia, V., Magri, G. (1966). Idrogeologia del Gargano. Geologia Applicata e Idrogeologia, vol. I, pp. 1-86, Bari.

Cotecchia, V., Magri, G. (1967). Gli spostamenti delle linee di costa quaternarie del mare Ionio fra Capo Spulico e Taranto. Geologia Applicata e Idrogeologia, vol. II, pp. 1-34, Bari.

Cotecchia, V., Dai Pra', G., Magri, G. (1969). Oscillazioni tirreniane e oloceniche del livello mare nel golfo di Taranto, corredate da datazioni col metodo del radiocarbonio. Geologia Applicata e Idrogeologia, vol. IV, pp. 93-148, Bari.

Cotecchia, V., Dai Pra', G., Magri, G. (1971a). Morfogensi litorale olocenica

tra Capo Spulico e Taranto nella prospettiva delle protezione cos-
tiera. Geologia Applicata e Idrogeologia, vol. VI, pp. 65-78, Bari.

Cotecchia, V., Tadolini, T., Tittozzi, P. (1971b). Influenza del chimismo
delle piogge sulle acque sotterranee della Puglia. Geologia Applicata e Idrogeologia, vol. VI, pp. 175-196, Bari.

Cotecchia, V., Tadolini, T, Tazioli, G.S., Tulipano, L. (1973a). Studio idro-
geologico della zona della sorgente Chidro (Taranto). (Atti II Convegno Internazionale sulle Acque Sotterranee, Palermo.

Cotecchia, V., Tadolini, T., Tittozzi, P. (1973b). Precipitazioni secche in
Puglia e loro influenza sul chimismo delle acque alimentanti la
falta sotterranea. Geologia Applicata e Idrogeologia, vol. VIII,
part II, pp. 253-284, Bari

Cotecchia, V. (1974). The huge aquifer and the marine intrusion into the fissured and karst meszoic limestones of Apulia (Southern Italy).
recent studies and investigations by employing modern methodologies.
Colloque geologie de l'ingenieur, pp. 291-312, Liege.

Cotecchia, V., Magri, G., Tazioli, G.S. (1974a). Isotopic measurements in
researches on seawater ingression in carbonate aquifer of the Salentine Peninsula, Southern Italy. Proceedings symposium isotope techniques in groundwater hydrology, vol. I, pp. 443-463, IAEA, Vienna.

Cotecchia, V., Tadolini, T., Tulipano, L. (1974b). The results of researches
carried out on diffusion zone between fresh water and sea water
intruding the land mass of Salentine Peninsula Southern Italy).
Proceedings international symposium on hydrology of volcanic rocks,
Lanzarote, Canary Islands, Spain.

Cotecchia, V., Tazioli, G.S., Tittozzi, P. (1975a). Geochimica delle acque
sotterranee della Penisola Salentina in relazione ai rapporti tra le
acque di falda, le acque marine sotterranee e il mare. Geologia
Applicata e Idrogeologia, vol. X, part I, pp. 205-224.

Cotecchia, V., Tazioli, G.S., Tittozzi, P. (1975b). Geochimica delle acque
sotterranee della Penisola Salentina (Italia meridionale) in relazione ai processi di dissoluzione carsica in zona satura. Atti III
convegno internazionale sulle acque sotterranee, Palermo.

Cotecchia, V. (1977a). Studi e ricerche sulle acque sotterranee e
sull'intrusione marina in Puglia (Penisola Salentina). Quaderni
dell'IRSA, 20, 466 pp., Roma.

Cotecchia, V. (1977b). Direct and laboratory observations of the mixing
phenomena of fresh and salt water in coastal groundwater, particular
case of fractured media. Proceedings IAHR symposium on hydrodynamic
diffusion and dispersion in porous media, pp. 489-524, Pavia.

Cotecchia, V., Tadolini, T., Tulipano, L. (1978). Ground water temperature in
the Murgia karst aquifer (Puglia, Southern Italy). Proceedings
international symposium on karst hydrology, Budapest.

Grassi, D. (1973). <u>Fondamentali aspetti dell'idrogeologia carsica della Murgia (Puglia), con particolare riferimento al versante adriatico,</u> Geologia Applicata e Idrogeologia, vol. VIII, part II, pp. 285-3313, Bari.

Grassi, D. (1974). <u>Il carsismo della Murgia (Puglia) e sua influenza sull'idrogeologia della regione,</u> Geologia Applicata e Idrogeologia, vol. IX, pp. 119-160, Bari.

Grassi, D., Tadolini, T. (1974). <u>L'acquifero carsico della Murgia Nord-occidentale, Puglia</u> , Geologia Applicata e Idrogeologia, vol. IX, pp. 39-58, Bari.

Grassi, D., Tadolini, T., Tazioli, G.S., Tulipano, L. (1977). <u>Ricerche sull'anisotropia dei caratteri idrogeologici delle rocce carbonatiche mesozoiche della Murgia Nord-occidentale,</u> Geologia Applicata e Idrogeologia, vol. XII, part I, pp. 187-213, Bari.

Guerricchio, A., Zezza, F. (1979). <u>Evidenze morfologiche di neotettonica della Puglia, in: ENEL,</u> Carta degli elementi di neotettonica del territorio italiano, Firenze (in press).

Guglielminetti, M., Boltri, R., Marino, C.M. (1975). <u>Remote sensing techniques applied to the study of fresh water springs in coastal areas of Southern Italy,</u> Proceedings tenth international symposium on remote sensing of environment, pp. 1297-1309, Ann Arbor, Michigan.

Magri, G., Troisi, S. (1969). <u>Sull'influenza delle fluttuazioni di specchi d'acqua sui livelli delle falde costiere, applicazioni allo studio della circolazione idrica sotterranea nella Penisola Salentina,</u> Geologia Applicata e Idrogeologia, vol. IV, pp. 25-42, Bari.

Martinis, B. (1970). <u>Osservazioni sulla struttura di S. Giorgio Jonico (Taranto),</u> Rend. Cl. Sc. Fis. Mat., S.8, Acc. Naz. Lincei, Roma.

Pinder, G.F. (1973). <u>A Galerkin-finite element simulation of groundwater contamination on Long Island, New York,</u> Water Resources Research, vol. 9, no. 6, pp. 1657-1689.

Tadolini, T, Tazioli, G.S., Tulipano, L. (1971). <u>Idrogeologia della zona delle sorgenti Idume (Lecce),</u> Geologia Applicata e Idrogeologia, vol. VI, pp. 41-64, Bari.

Tadolini, T., Tulipano, L. (1975). <u>La misura del contenuto di cloro, bromo e iodio delle acque sotterranee della Penisola Salentina (Italia meridionale) in rapporto alle acque di mare di invasione continentale,</u> Atti III convegno internazionale sulle acque sotterranee, Palermo.

Tadolini, T., Tulipano, L. (1977a). <u>Identification by means of discharge tests of water-bearing layers in fractured and karstic aquifers through the analysis of the chemico-physical properties of pumped waters,</u> Proceedings IAHR symposium on hydrodynamic diffusion and dispersion in porous media, pp. 159-171, Pavia.

Tadolini, T., Tulipano, L. 1977b). The conditions of the dynamic equilibrium of ground water as related to encroaching sea water, Proceedings IAHR symposium on hydrodynamic diffusion and dispersion in porous media, pp. 173-185, Pavia.

Tazioli, G.S. (1973). Metodologie e tecniche radioisotopiche in idrogeologia, Geologia Applicata e Idrogeologia, vol. VIII, part II, pp. 209-230, Bari.

Tazioli, G.S. (1976). Gli isotopi ambientali nelle ricerche idrogeologiche, Atti seminario su falde sotterranee e trattamento delle acque, pp. 63-69, Ente Irrigazione, Bari.

Tazioli, G.S. (1977). Groundwater circulation in the coastal carbonate aquifers of Apulia, Proceedings IAHR symposium on hydrodynamic diffusion and dispersion in porous media, pp. 187-199, Pavia.

Tazioli, G.S., Tittozzi, P. (1977). Evolution of porosity and permeability of coastal carbonate aquifers due to marine pollution on fresh ground water, Proceedings IAHR symposium on hydrodynamic diffusion and dispersion in porous media, pp. 201-208, Pavia.

Troisi, S. (1978). Modelli d'inquinamento marino di falde acquifere costiere, Atti convegno su metodologie numeriche per la soluzione di equazioni differenziali dell'idrologia e dell'idraulica, Bressanone, Trento.

Tulipano, L. (1976). Cenni su alcune techniche del remote sensing ed applicazioni in idrogeologia, Atti seminario su falde sotterranee e trattamento delle acque, pp. 35-41, Ente Irrigazione, Bari.

Zezza, F. (1975). Le facies carbonatiche della Puglia e il fenomeno carsico ipogeo, Geologia Applicata e Idrogeologia, vol. IX, part I, pp. 1-54, Bari.

Case history no. 9: Saline intrusion in the chalk near Brighton, U.K.*

Introduction

Over 50 per cent of the groundwater abstraction in England is from chalk. This aquifer is a soft, fine-grained, fissured, white limestone that crops out over extensive areas in eastern and southern England and forms a considerable part of the coast line in these areas. At a number of localities where large volumes of water are abstracted, saline intrusion has occurred. One of these localities is along part of the south coast of England.

General Description

The chalk forms the coast line in southern England for some 90 km to the west of Eastbourne. The aquifer's outcrop is about 10 km wide and it has the form of a northward facing escarpment with the dip-slope falling towards the coast from maximum elevations of about 230 meters above sea level. The outcrop is dissected into units by several rivers that cross it from north to south (fig. 10.72). One of these units, lying between the Rivers Adur and Ouse and referred to as the Brighton Unit, is the subject of a detailed groundwater study. This is now being extended into adjacent units particularly the Worthing Unit which lies to the immediate west of the Brighton Unit. The coastal region of the Brighton Unit is subject to saline intrusion and the objectives of the study are to determine the extent to which the fresh water resources of the unit can be developed without inducing undesirable saline intrusion and, in particular, the extent to which the resources can be temporarily over-developed in a drought that has a frequency of occurrence of 1 in 50 years, the usual design criterion in Britain. The results of the study will be applied to the entire chalk outcrop.

The chalk attains a thickness of over 300 m but groundwater flow is essentially through fissures and the thickness through which significant flow occurs is limited to at most the upper 100 m. The specific yield is typically 1 per cent and the transmissivity exceeds 2500 m^2/d in the main valleys but declines to less than 100 ^{2}/d below the high ground where fissures are not well-developed. The average annual infiltration into the Brighton Unit is 87.3 million m^3 and some 28 million m^3 are abstracted each year from 11 pumping stations, each usually comprising two or more wells which generally yield at least 5000 m^3/d.

Description of the problem

In 1949, during a very dry summer, saline water locally penetrated up to 2.6 km inland along fissures in the chalk and contaminated public supply wells. As a result of this experience the pumping regime from the unit as a whole was

---

*Prepared by R.A. Downing, Central Water Planning Unit, Reading, U.K.

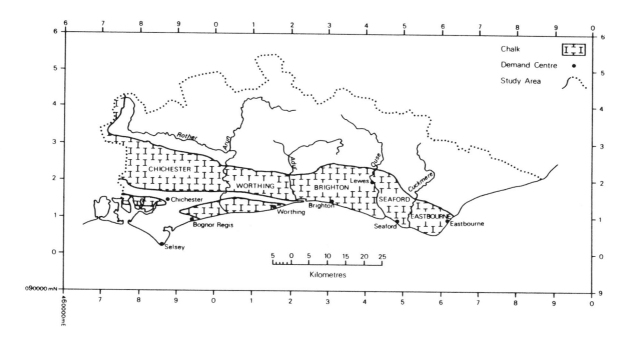

Fig. 10.72 - The Chalk outcrop showing the main groundwater units.

modified in an attempt to control the extent of saline intrusion. The wells were classified into two groups referred to as 'storage' and 'leakage' stations. The storage stations are more remote from the coast and the leakage stations are near the coast or tidal rivers. Leakage stations intercept natural groundwater flow before it enters the sea and are pumped during the winter when groundwater levels and natural groundwater discharge from the aquifer are high. As the chloride content rises in the summer, abstraction from the leakage stations is reduced and the storage stations are used to a greater extent to draw on the large volume of groundwater stored in areas more remote from the coast (Warren, 1964). This approach has increased the volume of water stored in the aquifer as a whole and considerably increased the annual volume of water that can be abstracted from individual wells.

Field data collection

As the demand for groundwater increased, more detailed studies of the form of the saline intrusion were started in 1971 (Anon., 1972, 1975). Groups of three observation boreholes were drilled along lines extending inland from the coast at intervals of 2 to 3 km between groups, to monitor the movement of saline water.

Geophysical logging, in the form of resistivity, fluid conductivity and differential temperature profiles confirmed that the saline water intrudes along the fissures and that the chloride content in the fissures exceeds that in the pores of the chalk's matrix. The velocity of the saline intrusion front depends on the extent and interconnection of the fissure system; at some locations it is rapid and at others relatively slow as shown in figures 10.73, 10.74 and 10.75 (Monkhouse and Fleet, 1975, Fleet et al. 1978).

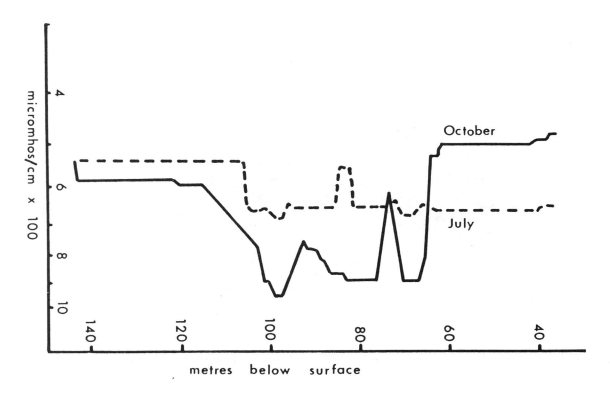

Fig. 10.73 - Fluid conductivity logs in Sompting No. 3 borehole showing the change from July (broken line) to October 1973 due to saline intrusion along fissures (after Monkhouse and Fleet, 1975).

Prediction and resulting situation

Further development of the groundwater resources of the chalk will require additional wells at sites remote from the coast (that is additional storage stations) and these wells will have to provide supplies during an extended drought. Model studies have suggested that because of the low permeability of the chalk below the higher ground, pumping from inland sites is likely to lower water levels preferentially towards the coast and thereby induce saline intrusion. During an extended drought the reduction in storage could be critical (Nutbrown et al. 1975).

Extrapolation in detail of model results to field conditions in a fissured aquifer such as the chalk is unreliable and, therefore, the response to pumping will have to be measured during pumping tests. New wells are being drilled at inland sites and these wells, together with existing inland wells, will be tested in groups over periods of several months to assess the effect on groundwater levels, the response of the saline interface and the rate of recession of the interface after pumping stops.

Currently the study is being extended into the Worthing Unit which lies to the west of the Brighton Unit. In both units 42 observation wells have been drilled including 22 along the coast to monitor the saline interface. Eleven new production sites have also been or will be drilled in both units.

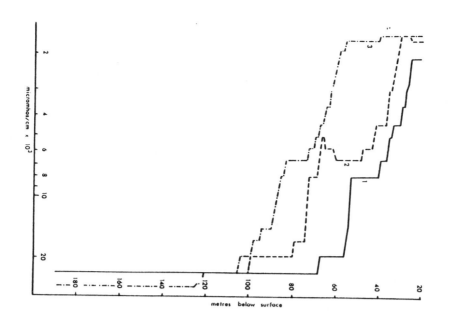

Fig. 10.74 - Fluid conductivity logs in a coastal observation borehole from high tide (1) through mid-tide (2) to low tide (3). (After Monkhouse and Fleet, 1975).

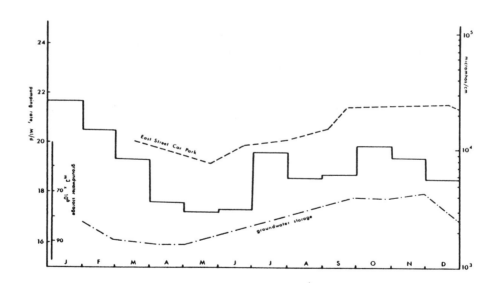

Fig. 10.75 - Variation in fluid conductivity in the East Street Car Park borehole in 1972, related to changes in pumping rate and volume of groundwater storage above mean sea level. (After Monkhouse and Fleet, 1975).

Costs

As mentioned previously, the overall objectives of the study are to determine the reliable yield of the chalk and the optimum method of developing the resources bearing in mind the risk of saline intrusion both with increasing abstraction and under drought conditions. The total cost to meet these objectives in both the Brighton and Worthing Units is about 600,000 pounds sterling of which 70,000 pounds is the cost of observation boreholes to monitor the movement of the saline interface.

The study is now the responsibility of the Southern Water Authority, but it is supervised and directed by committees which include representatives of the Central Water Planning Unit and the Water Research Center.

References

Anonymous, (1972, 1975). South Downs Groundwater Project, First and Second Progress Reports, Water Resources Board and Sussex River Authority.

Fleet, M., Brereton, N.R. and Howard, N.S. (1978). The investigation of saline intrusion into a fissured Chalk aquifer, Fifth Salt Water Intrusion Meeting, Medmenham, England, 1977.

Monkhouse, R.A., and Fleet, M. (1975). A geophysical investigation of saline water in the Chalk of the south coast of England, Q. Jl Engng Geol. 8, pp. 291-302.

Nutbrown, D.A., Downing, R.A. and Monkhouse, R.A. (1975). The use of a digital model in the management of the Chalk aquifer in the South Downs, England , J. Hydrol. 27, pp. 127-142.

Warren, S.C. (1964). Chemical aspects of controlled pumping and automation, Proc. Soc. Wat. Treat. Exam., 13, pp. 7-11.

Case history no. 10: Exploitation of open coastal aquifers in Cuba*

General geographical and geological aspects

The island of Cuba is located approximately between latitudes 19° and 22° north, and at longitudes 74° and 85° west (fig. 10.76).

From east to west Cuba has a length of 1200 km and its maximum width does not exceed 145 km; in some places its minimum width is 40 km. The average temperature in the coldest month, January, is 20°C and in the hottest one, August (and sometimes, July) is 29°C or little more. Maximum rainfall is in summer and minimum in winter.

Because of its geographical situation Cuba receives a great amount of heat, about 170-180 kilocalories/cm kilocalories/cm² yearly. The relative air humidity is rather high during the year and it has an average of about 80 per cent.

The territory is covered by carbonate rocks where limestones prevail and karstic processes have been developed. About 65 per cent of the territory is covered by those rocks (Rodriguez and Trian, 1980). In 1971 it was reported that 27 per cent of the hydraulic complex studies were constructed on karstic areas, which meant at that time an impressive figure (Shwaletski and Iturralde, 1971).

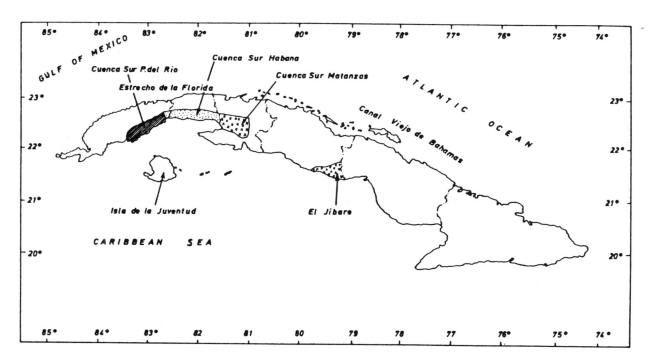

Fig. 10.76 - Geographic situation of Cuba. Water basin mentioned.

Prepared by Arturo Gonzáles-Báez, Water Planning Department, Hydroeconomic Institute, La Habana, Cuba.

Cuban karstic formations are developed mainly in carbonate, carbonate terrigenous, carbonate metamorphic and terrigenous carbonate rocks.

Groundwaters are located principally in Miocene strata where consequently the major withdrawals are made for agricultural, industrial and domestic supplies.

The specific yields recorded in these Miocene formations fluctuate very much and values from one l/s/m to over 1000 l/s/m are recorded depending on karst development. Most coastal zones of open basins have the highest specific yields but this should not be taken as a general rule. The coefficient of transmissivity ranges from 1000 m^2/day to over 40000 m^2/day.

The storage coefficient, the vital element in the determination of groundwater resources for exploitation purposes, changes considerably 0.06 to 0.12 and over this being, to a certain extent, a matter of discussion.

Man's influence on aquifer formations

Negative aspects

Cuban coastal basins have been affected by sea water intrusion which has changed groundwater natural conditions. An intensive groundwater exploitation along with some successive periods of more or less long drought have caused a drawdown of groundwater with sea water intrusion into inland, e.g., 14 km inland in the so-called south basin of La Habana (Dverak, 1972).

The most affected areas of our country are located in the former provinces of Pinar del Río, La Habana, Las Villas and, in a lesser degree, in Matanzas and the southern coastal areas of Isla de la Juventud.

In the 1948-1950 period a zone of rice crop was established to the east of Alonso Rojas town, which belonged, at that time, to Consolación del Sur municipality in Pinar del Río province. Rice cultivation was developed in this area and irrigation using groundwater was applied. As a result of such extractions and as a consequence of a lack of knowledge about aquifer capacities, withdrawals higher than water table capacities and feedings were made. In less than 5 years, such extractions caused a large cone of water-table depression and, consequently, sea water intrusion up to 20 km inland. This resulted in high soil and aquifer salinity because irrigation had continued, in spite of the fact that the salt content of the water had increased considerably. In fact, rice crops were lost due to the occurrence of withering in rice fields (Lapshin, 1969).

In Jíbaro area in Sancti Spiritus, former province of Las Villas, something similar happened, but the hazard was avoided when wells stopped pumping (Lapshin, 1969).

Because of the drainage in coastal zones, the construction of canals and excessive withdrawals of fresh water, the groundwater level was drawn down and groundwater leaks to the ocean were also reduced in the south basin of La Habana. The dynamic balance of fresh and sea waters was altered and strong salt water intrusion up to 14 km inland occurred. In this area, 15 km from the coast brackish water continues penetrating inland to such a degree that at 50 m depth from the mean sea level, water with 12-14 g/1 of chloride were recorded (Dverak, 1972). According to available data in the 1954-1969 period sea water level increased at a rate of 1.5 - 1.9 m/year and later it was reduced to 0.5 m/year. For instance, in the TS-9 observation point in the south basin of La Habana where, in 1954, at 38 m depth below the mean sea level, fresh water had only 30 mg/1 of chloride. After 10 years (1964) brackish water with 17 g/1 of chloride was found, and in 1968 sea water had already reached that point (Dverak, 1972).

In the south basin of Matanzas, sea water intrusion has also occurred although to a less degree than in the other basins. This basin is similar to the ones mentioned above. It is an open basin, i.e., its waters are closely related to sea water but its distinctive characteristic is that Zapata Swamp represents a barrier which protects, to a certain extent, the basin against highly mineralized water intrusion from the Caribbean Sea (fig. 10.77). The main crop irrigated with groundwater in this basin is citrus fruits, very sensitive to salinity. Their maximum permissible value of chloride is 140 mg/1. In the basin important karstic depressions exist, which play an important role in the recharge of water table. Thus in La Carraca, where Palmilla River loses its waters, the estimated water volume entering the karstic depression for a 26-hour flood and with 25 per cent of probability is 36.3×10^6 m^3. Generally, rainfall water is lost in karstic depressions.

Excessive withdrawals which a part of this basin experienced, along with intensive agricultural activity, timber harvesting in small woods, an artificial drainage of perimeter zones in cultivated areas, and the total or partial filling of sinkholes or caves as a result of agricultural activities, were the main causes of the hydrochemical unbalance occurred in the southern part of this underground basin. The withdrawals made in many pumping stations located on wells in this part of the basin resulted in a groundwater drawdown below the mean sea level. This caused large cones of water-table depression, a distortion of groundwater flow direction and a mineralized water front, both surface and sub-surface. A study of the vertical changing movement of mineralized water was made using water samplers and different geophysical methods. All the affected zone was accurately determined.

Corrective measures taken and their effects

In the south basin of Pinar del Rio the following corrective measures were taken:

    - To stop pumping for 12 years in 100 percent of wells;

    - To artifically recharge the underground basin through the building of canals to collect surface run-off, with recharge wells coordinated with their slopes -El Roblar, San Diego and San Cristóbal canals.

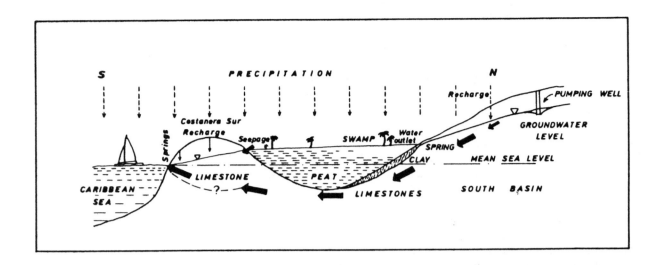

Fig. 10.77 - Position of Matanzas Southern Basin in relation with the Caribbean Sea and the Zapata swamp.

Before re-starting the exploitation of this basin, the following steps were made:

- To determine the occurrence of mineralized water through the use of water samplers in the existing wells and in the specific network of observation points established for this purpose;

- To re-assess the basin exploitable groundwater resources taking into account the available information of groundwater flow and data of groundwater exploitation;

- To determine the safe yield of withdrawal in individual wells according to local geological conditions, the occurrence of mineralized waters, the hydrogeological parameters determined in each well pumping test and the situation of the static water level from the mean sea level.

The use of stored surface water helps to improve local conditions, mainly in the reclamation of soils affected by mineralized waters.

In the south basin of La Habana withdrawals were stopped after the triumph of the Revolution, in 1959, to prevent the situation from worsening. In the last 20 years many measures have been taken to protect this basin against salinity. Among them, we may mention the following:

- To close wells with high mineralization contents;

- To decrease or to stop (totally or partially) pumping yields of wells containing over 200 mg/1 of chloride;

- To avoid pumping which may reduce the groundwater level below +0.60 m (taking the mean sea level as a reference point);

- To constantly and systematically observe static and pumping water levels and groundwater quality using soundings, stage gaging stations and water samplers;

- To strictly control groundwater extractions;

- To re-assess the basin groundwater resources for exploitation purposes.

In El Jibaro area the same measures were taken as in the Southern basin of La Habana.

A thorough hydrogeological study was made in the Southern basin of Matanzas because of its economical importance, to accurately determine the real exploitable groundwater resources of the area. In the central part of the territory, where water withdrawals are very intensive, a systematic, continuous and effective control is made. Well exploitation parameters similar to the above mentioned have been established to prevent groundwater level from a drawdown below the mean sea level.

In this basin the most important well geophysical studies in the country and additional works using water samplers in places for vertical hydrochemical control were made. These works allowed us to accurately define the position of the surface of soluble salts containing one g/l and 145-240 mg/l of chloride, which limit the use of water in citrus fruit irrigation.

In the above mentioned cases, exceptional conditions of withdrawal have been established in the zones most affected by salt intrusion and excessive groundwater drawdown was prevented.

The large resources used in these works have been counterbalanced with a constant and guaranteed development of the citrus fruit cultivation plan. Among other works made we may mention:

- Artificial recharge projects in 6 zones of the underground basin and the implementation of almost 60 per cent of the projected works for zone 1;

- The closing of the drainage canal located in the southern part of the zone with the resulting recovery of the natural ground water level;

- The establishment of a safe pumping water level for individual wells and well battery, below which projects of new groundwater intakes or the exploitation of the present ones are prohibited depending on the locations of such intakes in the area.

Present and future corrective measures will guarantee an optimal exploitation of natural resources and the recovery of those affected by man's activity.

Other information

Many researchers have made studies of Cuban coastal basins, and at present much experience has been gained. Initially, the design of well fields was carried out on open coastal aquifers based on the criterion of a natural linear or Darcian flow, but recently the criterion of non-linear flow and the calculation method established by Diosdado Pérez Franco, Professor of the Faculty of Construction of the University of Havana, have been considered. Both criteria are being applied in our country and their results are closely observed.

In the determination of the mineralized water vertical movement, the BGH principles have been followed with acceptable results, generally speaking.

The characteristics of karstic formations, their heterogeneity and anisotropy and the occurrence of a non-linear flow in specific conditions of water circulation do not permit a simple application of the common methods of calculation. This hinders the calculation and makes the determination of the optimal yield of exploitation in a basin more difficult. Recently serious works have been started, directed towards applying mathematical models to studies of linear or non-linear non-stationary flow in aquifers subjected to pumpings and recharges. This will allow calculations to be made and a comparison between the reality and the forecast.

In small areas, estimates of exploitation forecastings have been made based on groundwater flow observation, and real groundwater exploitation, and according to the real situation, calculations are acceptable.

Calculations of exploitation of groundwater resources and natural storaged water have been made applying methods used in the USSR.

References

Rodriguez, G., Trian, D. K.(1980). _Experiencias de las investigaciones geofísicas en zonas cársicas de Cuba,_ (Experiences of geophysical investigations on karstic zones of Cuba), _Voluntad Hidráulica_ Technical Journal No. 52-53, Year XVII, 1980.

Shwaletski, E., Iturralde, M. (1971). _Estudio ingeniero-geológico del carso cubano_ (Engineering-geological study of Cuban karst), _Serie Espeleológoca y Carsológica_ No. 31, Academia de Cinencias de Cuba, 1971.

Dverak, L. (1972). _Intrusión salina en la Cuenca Sur_ (Salt-Water intrusion in the south basin). _Voluntad Hidráulica_ Journal No. 24, Year X, 1972.

Lapshin, N. N. (1969). _Salinización de las planicies costeras_ (Salinization of coastal plains), _Voluntad Hidráulica_ Journal No. 17, 1969.

<u>Case history no. 11: The Augusta's coastal aquifers (eastern Sicily, Italy)</u>*

Along the eastern coast of Sicily (Italy), in the stretch corresponding to the Augusta bay, during the last twenty years many big chemical and oil industries have been located and the hydrogeological balance has broken down to such an extent that the basic features of subterranean waters of the area have changed.

The worst symptom of the situation is given by the static level of the water-bearing stratum which, during recent years, has subsided so much that in certain spots its lowering has exceeded 100 meters. A consequence of this lowering, which has brought the static and even more the dynamic level to a negative value, is the intrusion of sea water in the water-bearing strata.

In the area three aquifers, each upon the other one, which show quite different characteristics both from the hydraulic and the supply point of view.

Tectonics, which in differnt periods has been very active in the area, both with extending and compressing actions, have remarkably complicated the position of the various formations, and have often put in contact, by faults, layers which differ among them as for their age. The extending tectonic movements have gone along with a violent volcanic activity which has provoked the presence, among the sedimentary materials, of big layers of volcanic materials.

The stratigraphic succession which can be identified in the area, once simplified, from the superficial layer towards down, is the following:

1. Recent and terrace alluvium
       (Aquifer I)
2. Pleistocene sands and calcareous sandstones
3. Pleistocene clays
4. Plio-Pleistocene calcareous sandstones
       (Aquifer II)
5. Plio-Pleistocene volcanic rocks
6. Upper miocene limestones alternating with calcareous sandstones and marls
7. Upper miocene and miocene volcanics rocks
       (Aquifer III)
8. Oligo-miocene limestones

The first aquifer consist of alluvium, sands and Pleistocene calcareous sandstones. It is not very interesting because it is barely fed and because it is drained by the rivers which pass through it. Its bed is made of Pleistocene greyblue clays.

_____

*Prepared by Aurelio Aureli, Prof., University of Catania, Italy.

The second aquifer consists of Plio-Pleistocene calcareous sand-stones and by the volcanics rocks of the same epoch. It shows some interesting features, but its characteristics are not yet entirely known. Its bed consists of alternate and clay-like tuffs, or of the most marly fraction of the alternation limestone-marl of Upper Miocene.

The third aquifer, the most important, consists of Oligocene-Miocene limestones.

Tectonics have had a quite important influence on the relationships of the three aquifers. The numerous faults which can be observed often put in contact different aquifers.

In the imaginary section in fig. 10.78 are shown some possible relationships between the different formations.

Pleistocene clays are distributed along all the coast line which surrounds the Augusta bay, fig. 10.79, and by their wedge or lens structure, which stretches itself underneath the sea level, constitute a water-tight barrier which separates the sea-waters from the lower permeable structures, thus hindering or stopping the intrusion of sea water in the lower aquifers. The distribution of clays, as it is shown in fig. 10.79, is nevertheless limited, and southwards and northwards the permeable terrains constituting the lower aquifers are directly in contact with the sea.

Because of a series of lucky circumstances, some of them fortuitous, some others purposely obtained, most wells exploiting this area are placed where the Pleistocene clays are. This fact is of paramount importance in understanding the hydrogeological situation which has arisen through the settling of big industrial plants and the consequent indiscriminate exploitation of the water-bearing strata.

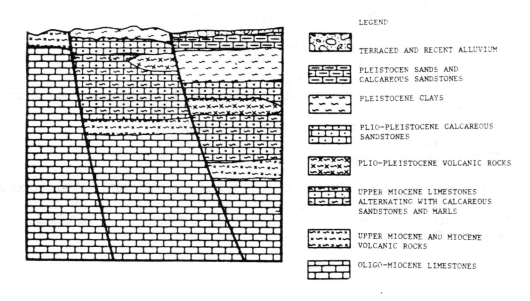

LEGEND

TERRACED AND RECENT ALLUVIUM

PLEISTOCEN SANDS AND CALCAREOUS SANDSTONES

PLEISTOCENE CLAYS

PLIO-PLEISTOCENE CALCAREOUS SANDSTONES

PLIO-PLEISTOCENE VOLCANIC ROCKS

UPPER MIOCENE LIMESTONES ALTERNATING WITH CALCAREOUS SANDSTONES AND MARLS

UPPER MIOCENE AND MIOCENE VOLCANIC ROCKS

OLIGO-MIOCENE LIMESTONES

Fig. 10.78 - Geological cross-sections of the Augusta Plains sediments.

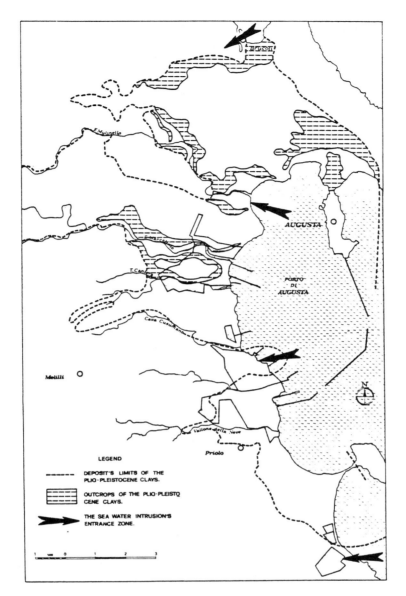

Fig. 10.79 - Situation map of Augusta, in western Sicily, between Catania (N) and Siracusa (S), showing the main sea water inflow areas and the limits of the overlying coastal clay deposits that confine and protect the central part of the deep, highly exploited aquifer.

The three aquifers are fed in three different ways:

(a) through the infiltration of rain water into the superficial permeable structures, the waters being partly drained by the local rivers,

(b) through the infiltration, in some particular areas, of the local rivers,

(c) through a deep feeding in limestones from neighbouring or distant areas.

In 1961, when industrial plants began to be built, they took a census of the existing wells, permitting the drawing of a map of the piezometric level. This map is reproduced in fig. 10.80.

In 1961 there were only 32 wells and the piezometric level was always over the sea level, with an almost constant gradient.

In 1981, we had the situation shown in fig. 10.81. The observed wells amounted to 109.

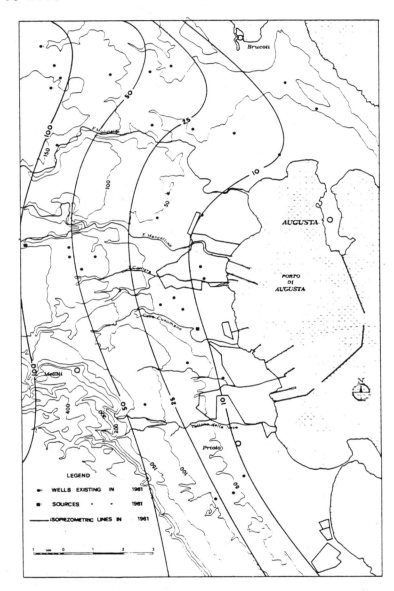

Fig. 10.80 - Isopiezometric map in 1961, close to the natural situation. Values in meters over mean sea level.

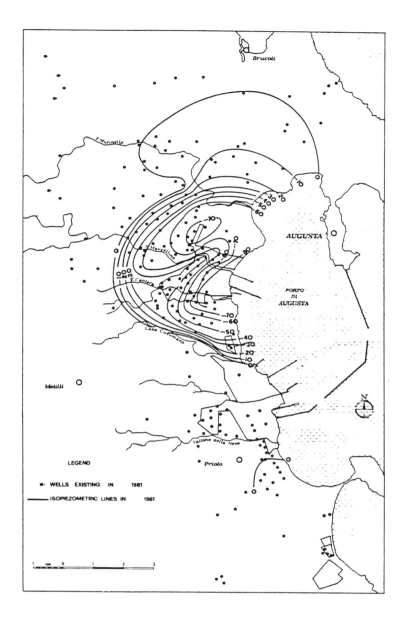

Fig. 10.81 - Isopiezometric map in 1981. The deep drawdown cone is clearly shown. Values in meters over (the negatives below) sea level.

The static piezometric level shows a lowering of about 100 meters, and absolute depths sometimes below -80 m. The dynamic level has shown a peak value of -130 meters below sea level.

As it can be seen in figure 10.81, the aquifer has come to a situation in which there is a funnel with a large piezometric gradient, and which attracts all waters circulating in the three aquifers.

In the region, the first aquifer, the superficial one, has no water. The intermediate aquifer shows strange phenomena in different places: in some places it becomes rapidly exhausted, in some other places it maintains a certain supply. The lower aquifer, the one in limestone, presents different supply conditions when a spot is near or far from fault zones, or in the presence of karst-conduits. Both the intermediate aquifer and the lower one, which originally were confined and showed artersian conditions, today are to be considered almost everywhere as free aquifers, as the piezometric level has gone below the impermeable layer which constitutes their roof.

The general data obtained by inquiries are the following:

-zones where the water-bearing stratum is naturally fed 136 km^2

-efficacious infiltration 175 mm

-average volume and annual infiltration 23.8 x 10^{6}m^3

-volume coming from the rivers or from the deep circulation 30.0 x 10^{6}m^3

-comprehensive volume of the natural feeding 53.8 x 10^{6}m^3

-volume abstracted at the present time 64.0 ~x~10^6 m^3

-annual volume abstracted from the reserve at the present time 10.2 ~ x~10^6 m^3

During the last twenty years increase in exploitation has been constant, and we may consider 102 x 10^{6}m^3 as the total volume which has been withdrawn from the reserve during this period.

The most dangerous effect of this situation is the call phenomenon which the piezometric depression imposes on the waters circulating in the neighboring areas, and in particular towards the sea water along the coast line. This phenomenon is very well pointed out by the increase of the chloride content which has been observed in some wells.

In 1961, the analysis which were carried out showed that in all wells the chloride contents was always below to 50 mg/l. The situation observed in 1981 was very different. In fig. 10.82 the chloride content in well waters is shown.

In the area where the Pleistocene clays are present, an area which coincides with the spots where the lowering of the piezometric level has reached its highest value, the percentage of chloride contained in the waters is still very low. One can observe a big increase of chlorides in the waters of the wells on the northern and on the southern sides of this area, corresponding to permeable terrains which are in direct contact with the sea.

The peak values of chloride in the water of some wells, at the present time, are of about 5460 mg/l.

The study of the situation has been brought about by a campaign of research lasting more than six years, and which has consisted of very detailed geological, geophysical and hydrogeochemical observations.

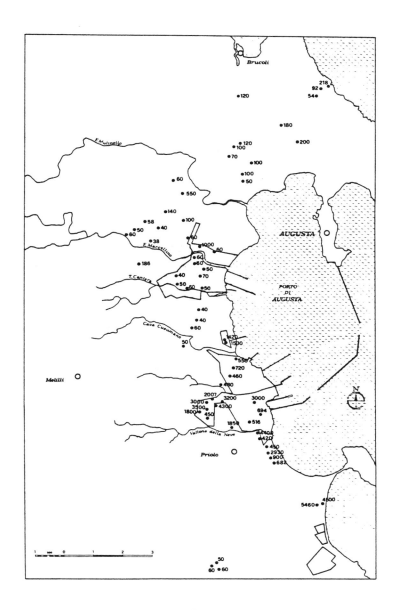

Fig. 10.82 - Map showing the chloride-ion concentration in deep wells, in mg/l, in 1981.

All results obtained have allowed us to build up a multistratum, square meshed mathematical model, variable in dimensions, according to the method of finite differences.

This has enabled us to compare the results obtained with the data obtained through the classical calculations of hydrology, the periodical checks of supply, and exploitation following variations in piezometric levels and chloride contents. The checks still go on through the measurement, each month, of the piezometric levels and the chloride contents in 97 wells.

Besides, there are now 26 groundwater level recorders for a permanent check of piezometric variations, and three salinometers in order to follow any development in the chloride contents of water (fig. 10.83).

The sea water intrusion has created very grave problems in the zone. It is sufficient to remember, in particular, that many wells are or were used both by the inhabitants of Augusta and Priolo as drinking water, and by the big industrial plants. These plants, for many of their specific production processes need good quality water.

The increase in salinity has made it necessary to put out of service many wells, and the authorities have been obliged to plan the construction of a new aqueduct for the towns and settlements of the area. This aqueduct will be supplied with superficial waters coming from another basin: waters which must first beforehand be treated in a plant to clarify them and make them drinkable.

The construction costs of this new aqueduct and the future costs of management are very high, especially if compared with the ones we had when exploiting the wells.

Some of the industries have been obliged to modify their production processes, or they have ceased using the water of the wells and have purchased water in other zones, obviously with much higher costs.

To face the situation they have now come to, and in order to ensure in all cases the water supply, they have designed, and to a large extent brought about, some important works; their cost, for the Italian community, has proved to be considerable.

These works include the creation of a large artificial basin which will collect the waters of the Simeto River, which flows on the North of the quoted area; the creation of transportation and feeding pipes; and the creation of plants for lifting, transporting, collecting and distributing the waters of another river, the Ciane, which flows in the South. In addition, it is planned to bring the water-bearing stratum gradually back to its original condition through the artificial recharge of these strata through 13 injection wells, using waters coming from the above quoted plants for making the waters clear and drinkable.

The first results obtained, which will be checked by means of a new mathematical model, are pretty encouraging, since they have indicated both the progressive lowering of the piezometric levels and the stabilization of the value of the chloride content. At least, this is happening in the central area where the quoted cone of piezometric depression is placed. One must wait to see how the waters will behave in the northern and southern areas, where the increasing salinity from sea water intrusion has been the greatest and the most dangerous problem.

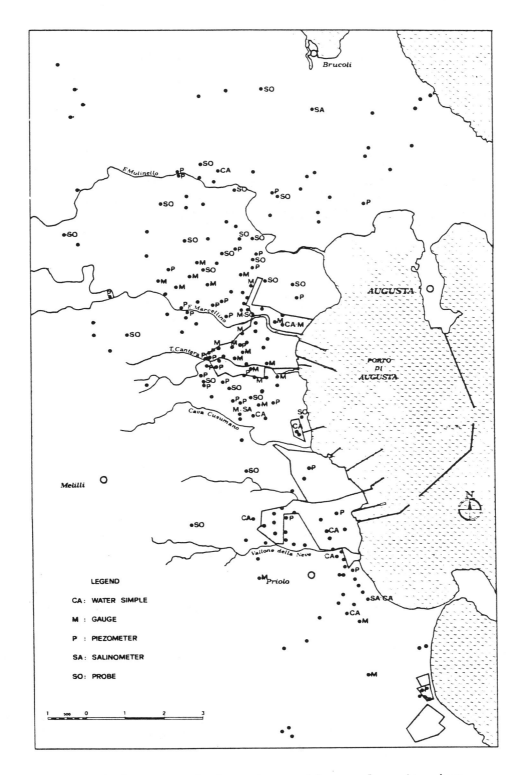

Fig. 10.83 - Network for groundwater observation and monitoring.

10.5   Islands

Case history no. 12: Sea water intrusion in coral reef islands: Devonshire Lens, Bermuda*

Introduction

Bermuda (see fig. 10.84) is a small group of limestone islands in the western North Atlantic at approximately 31°N and 65°W. Some 1000 km to the west is Cape Hatteras, N.C., U.S.A., the nearest point of land. The Bermuda Islands number more than 300 and total to 56 km^2. About 80 per cent of the landmass is in a single island. In this main island occurs three of Bermuda's five fresh water lenses. The largest and easily the most important of these is Devonshire Lens (fig. 10.84).

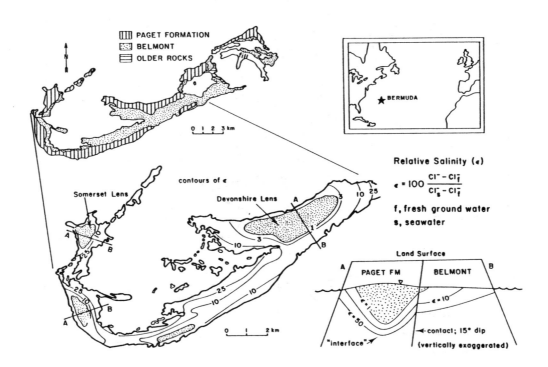

Fig. 10.84 - Summary of the hydrogeology and occurrence of fresh groundwater in Bermuda.

Bermuda is an affluent British Colony with about 60,000 permanent residents. Tourism is the major industry and draws about a half million visitors per year, mostly from North America.

---

* Prepared by H.L. Vacher and J.F. Ayers, Department of Geology, Washington State University, Pullman, Washington, U.S.A.

The water supply is mostly from roof-top catchments and basement cisterns as is common on Caribbean-type islands. There are a few desalination plants of various types and sizes. Groundwater withdrawals by water suppliers are almost exclusively from Devonshire Lens and amount to about 3000 m³/day, on the average. These withdrawals are predominantly to support tourism and are not returned to Devonshire Lens. There are a few thousand household wells scattered throughout Bermuda. These withdrawals are largely for flushing water and swimming pools and are returned (minus consumptive losses) via the cesspits at about the points of withdrawal.

The question of interest is 'To what extent have the extractions affected the configuration of Devonshire Lens?' Unfortunately, development preceded research, so there is no documentation of prior conditions which could be compared to present ones. Nevertheless, the question can be answered, because a map of pristine conditions can, in fact, be drawn from the knowledge of recharge and hydraulic conductivity of Bermuda. In this way, the effect on the lens of other man-related activities can also be assessed.

Hydrogeology of Bermuda

Bermuda is a limestone-capped volcanic seamount. The top of the volcanics is tens of meters beneath the lenses. The limestones are Pleistocene biocalcarenites (popularly, but mistakenly, known as coral), deposited as shoreline dunes and associated sediments in response to glacioeustatic sea-level changes (Bretz, 1960; Land, et al. 1967; Vacher, 1973).

Relative-age relationships of the eolianites reflect accretion of younger limestones around the periphery of the island mass. The youngest formation, the Paget, occurs along the external shoreline (fig. 10.84). The Belmont, in general, borders the inshore sounds and reaches. Permeability of these rocks (in the present-day saturated zone) increases as a function of their age. Thus in most of Bermuda, there is an across-the-island increase in permeability, from one shoreline to the opposite shoreline (Vacher, 1978a). Hydraulic conductivities are approximately: Upper Paget, 30 m/day; Lower Paget, 90 m/day; Belmont, 1000 m/day (Vacher and Ayers, in press). Older limestones are notably cavernous and outcrop over small areas.

Marshes occur in many places along the Paget-Belmont contact. They represent inter-eolianite topographic lows that have been filled by peat during the Holocene sea-level (and water-table) rise. These hydrogeologic units are steep-sided plugs of low-permeability muck extending downward through the lenses.

Recharge in Bermuda is about 350 mm/yr (Vacher and Ayers, in press), or about 25 per cent of the rainfall. Recharge occurs mainly during the winter (Nov.-Apr.), and there is a soil-water deficit in the summer (Plummer, et al. 1976). In the marshes, recharge is considerably less, because, among other reasons, potential evapotranspiration does not exceed actual evapotranspiration during the summer, whereas it does in the non-marshy areas (Vacher, 1974).

The configuration of the water table closely reflects the across-the-island variation in permeability (Vacher, 1978a). Because of the Badon-Ghyben-Herzberg relationship there is a similar geologic control on the depth of the freshwater-saltwater interface below the water table—or the thickness of the BGH lens. As seen in cross-island sections (fig. 10.84), the BGH lenses are relatively inflated in the Paget sectors of the saturated zone. In other words, the Paget rocks act as dams to the shoreward groundwater flow. In contrast, the more solution-altered, and thus more permeable, Belmont sectors act as drains.

There is no interface between the fresh groundwater and underlying seawater (fig. 10.84). Instead, there is a transition zone in which salinity grades from that of the (unmixed) fresh groundwater to that of (undiluted) seawater. The variation with depth is described by an error function with the mid-point corresponding to the position of the interface that would be present if there were no mixing. As shown in the cross section in fig. 10.84, the transition zones are rather large, so that the freshwater lenses are significantly smaller than the BGH lenses.

The thickness of the transition zones is related to the amplitude of water-table fluctuations (Vacher, 1978a). These fluctuations are due largely to changes in sea-level—both tidal and non-tidal (Vacher, 1978b). Thus the magnitude of the water-table fluctuations diminishes inland, at a rate depending on the permeability of the rocks. Therefore the water-table fluctuations are of greater amplitude, and the transition zones are of greater thickness, in the Belmont than in the Paget sectors of the island (Vacher, 1978a). Thus the location of fresh-water lenses is also geologically controlled.

Models: Pristine vs present Devonshire Lens

Many flow problems in oceanic lenses can be treated effectively by combining Darcy's Law, the equation of continuity, the Dupuit assumptions, and the Badon-Ghyben-Herzberg Principle (Bear, 1972, p. 561). For unsteady flow, the relationships generate the extended Boussinesq problem (Collins, 1976; Anderson, 1976). The usefulness of the Ghyben-Herzberg-Dupuit formulation is shown for Bermuda by Vacher (1978a): The cross-sectional variation of thickness of Devonshire Lens, in minimally developed areas, can be described closely from application of Ghyben-Herzberg-Dupuit methodologies to an infinite-strip island composed of two segments, one 14 times as permeable as the other. The current effort in Bermuda is to extend the methodologies to treat islands of irregular shape and to treat, also, unsteady flow. Some results are shown in figs. 10.85 and 10.86 (from Ayers, Ph.D. dissertation, Washington State University, in preparation).

Figure 10.85 shows the results for Somerset Island, where there is a small freshwater lens that is largely undeveloped. The fit for 1976 conditions was obtained by using the values of hydraulic conductivity given above and by adjusting monthly recharge values. The contours on the large map represent the 1976 averages as generated by the model. As shown in the figure, these results agree closely with the 1976 water-table elevations measured at the five observation wells in Somerset. There is good agreement, also, for individual months, as illustrated for two wells in the table. The sum of the twelve monthly recharges, found during the tuning of the results of the model to the prototype, is 330 mm, close to the value of annual recharge found in other ways (Vacher and Ayers, in press).

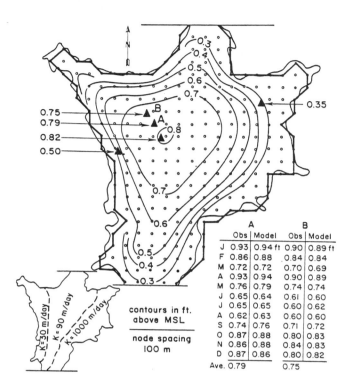

	A		B	
	Obs	Model	Obs	Model
J	0.93	0.94 ft	0.90	0.89 ft
F	0.86	0.88	.0.84	0.84
M	0.72	0.72	0.70	0.69
A	0.93	0.94	0.90	0.89
M	0.76	0.79	0.74	0.74
J	0.65	0.64	0.61	0.60
J	0.65	0.65	0.60	0.62
A	0.62	0.63	0.60	0.60
S	0.74	0.76	0.71	0.72
O	0.87	0.88	0.80	0.83
N	0.86	0.88	0.84	0.83
D	0.87	0.86	0.80	0.82
Ave.	0.79		0.75	

contours in ft. above MSL

node spacing 100 m

Fig. 10.85 - Water table of Somerset Lens in 1976. Contours are from computer model and show the annual mean. Monthly values (relative to monthly mean sea level) are in table for two representative wells. Triangles denote observation wells.

Devonshire Lens is considerably more complicated than the small, undeveloped Somerset Lens. The observed 1975 configuration of the water-table is shown in part A of fig. 10.86. This map is based on semi-weekly measurements at the 36 indicated sites.

A good fit to the observed maps and hydrographs was obtained by taking account of the distribution of Paget and Belmont formations and their hydraulic conductivities; the location and pumping schedule of the various extraction sites; hydraulic conductivity of the marsh muck within the Belmont terrain; the presence of the canal; and, as at Somerset, a schedule of monthly recharges. In addition to these 'regional' recharges, it was necessary to find recharge schedules for local areas, or groups of nodes: the marshes; the vicinity of Hamilton (Bermuda's business district which is sewered and lies to the south and east of the canal); and Bermuda's refuse-disposal area (which lies to the north of Hamilton in a reclaimed marsh). Recharge schedules that result from the trial-and-error fitting are reasonable: for example, the 1975 'regional' sum is 38 cm and for the marshes, 6 cm.

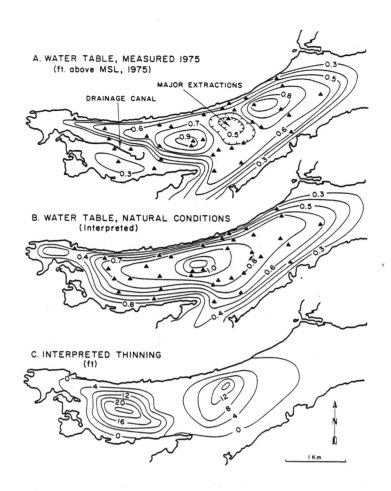

Fig. 10.86 - Devonshire Lens, 1975. A) Water table as measured in 1975: A drainage canal and a pumping area create groundwater level draw-downs. (B) Interpreted water table under natural conditions. (C) Thinning of the fresh water lens. Values are in feet.

Part B of fig. 10.86 shows the result obtained when the model for Devonshire Lens was run again with only natural parameters--that is, with the regional and marsh recharge schedules and the various hydraulic conductivi-ties; and without the extractions, drainage canal, and other man-related features. Thus, fig. B is the author's interpretation of pristine Devonshire Lens--the water-table configuration that would have been present in 1975 if there were no modifications due to man.

The effects of man on the configuration of Devonshire Lens can thus be visualized by comparing parts A and B of fig. 10.86. Part C of fig. 10.86 portrays the difference (B minus A) multiplied by 41, the BGH factor. Thus, this figure illustrates the extent that Devonshire Lens has been thinned--by extractions in the eastern part and urban development in the western part.

References

Anderson, M.P. (1976). <u>Unsteady groundwater flow beneath strip oceanic islands</u>, Research, Vol. 12, pp. 640-644.

Bear, J. (1972). <u>Dynamics of fluids in porous media</u>, Am. Elsevier Environmental Science Series, New York, 764 pp.

Bretz, J.H. (1960). <u>Bermuda: partially drowned, late mature, Pleistocene karst</u>, Geological Society of American Bulletin, v. 71, pp. 1729-1754. abort

Collins, M.A. (1976). <u>The extended Boussinesq problem</u>, Water Resources Research, Vol. 12, pp. 54-56.

Land, L.S., Mackenzie, F.T., Gould, S.J. (1967). <u>Pleistocent karst</u>, Geological Society of America Bulletin, v. 78, pp 993-1006.

Plummer, L.N., Vacher, H.L., Mackenzie, F.T., Bricker, O.P., Land, L.S., (1976). <u>Hydrogeochemistry for Bermuda: a case history of groundwater diagenesis of biocalcarenites</u>, Geological Society of America Bulletin, v. 87, pp. 1301-1316.

Vacher, H.L. (1973). <u>Coastal dunes of Younger Bermuda</u> in Coates, D.R. (ed.), Coastal Geomorphology: Binghamton, N.Y., State University of New York at Binghamton, Publications in Geomorphology, pp. 355-391.

Vacher, H.L. (1974). <u>Groundwater hydrology of Bermuda Government of Bermuda</u>, Public Works Department, Hamilton, p. 87.

Vacher, H.L. (1978a). <u>Hydrogeology of Bermuda: significance of an across-the-island variation in permeability</u>, Journal of Hydrology, v. 39, pp. 207-226, Amsterdam.

Vacher, H.L. (1978b). <u>Hydrology of small oceanic islands: influence of atmospheric pressure on the water-table</u>, Groundwater, v. 16, pp. 417-423.

Vacher, H.L., Ayers, J.F. (in press). <u>Hydrology of small oceanic islands: utility of an estimate of recharge inferred from the chloride concentration of the freshwater lenses</u>. Journal of Hydrology.

Case history no. 13: Determination of the fresh water pocket under Mactan Island, The Philippines*

Objective of the study

In the coming years industrial and domestic demands of freshwater are expected to increase on Mactan Island. The present situation of water supply, both in terms of quantity and quality, seems inadequate to cope with the future needs. The main problem is the progressive salinization of the groundwater, due to rather local overpumping. In order to make sound decisions regarding the positioning and allowable pumping rates (safe yields) of wells, knowledge of the present groundwater regime is a prerequisite.

This study concerns primarily the detection of the extent of the fresh water lens. Special attention is paid to the tidal effect on the groundwater table and its significance for the fresh water-saline water interface. The study was carried out between November 1978 and February 1979 as part of a cooperation between Delft University of Technology (Section of Hydrology and Water Resources) and the University of San Carlos (Water Resources Center) in Cebu.

Description of the study area

Mactan Island is part of Cebu Province which is situated in the central part of the Philippines (fig. 10.87). Its total area is about 35 km^2 and its population amounts to some 80,000 inhabitants. The study area is restricted to the central and northern part of the island (area about 25 km^2).

Climate and hydrology. Mactan has a climate classified as dry sub-humid, as based on Thornthwaite's moisture index. Average annual precipitation is 1440 mm. Average annual evapotranspiration is some 1100 mm (based on Penman E = 0.8 E$_0$: 1086 mm/year, based on Turc-Langbein: 1105 mm/year). Roughly speaking, groundwater recharge (about 1.6 mm/day) occurs only from June to December, due to (not very distinctive) wet and dry seasons. Surface runoff is negligible.

Geology. In geologic terms, Mactan Island can be described as a recent build-up of Carcar Limestone which is mainly composed of coralline limestone with irregular bodies and interbeds of marl, marly silts and chalky limestone, occasionally dense and fractured, often powdered and generally porous. The interface with the underlying Cansi vulcanites is estimated at 800 to 1000 meters depth. Outcrops of the Carcar Limestone show all over the island. In general, only a thin layer of top soil (some decimeters) is present.

---

*Prepared by Hans R. Vermeulen, Delft University of Technology, The Netherlands.

Next to numerous minor ones, one big active fault zone, extending in a north-south direction from coast to coast, appears to be of major importance. It acts as an underground barrier and so divides the groundwater regime into two independent parts, as is shown in the resulting maps.

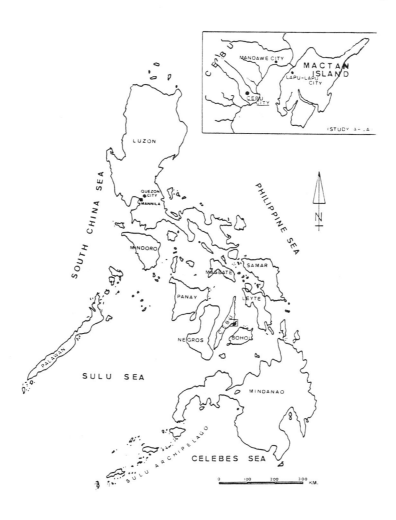

Fig. 10.87 - Situation of Mactan Island.

There are numerous sinkholes in the study area. In general, both permeability and infiltration capacity are high.

Topography and vegetation. The topographic relief of Mactan Island is low. Maximum elevation is about 30 meters. The remainder of the island is below 15 meters and the most part of this lies below 6 meters.

Vegetal cover is thin or even absent in the major part of the island. Where present, trees are mostly well spaced. Agriculture is applied on all possible sites, but is not substantial. Off the roads, the terrain is hardly accessible, unless by foot.

Further data. Besides meteorologic data, some findings from an exploratory well, located in the center of the island, a tentative report on the groundwater resources of Mactan Airbase from 1966, and an air-photo mosaic of the study area (scale 1:5,000) were available. From the mosaic very useful information regarding topographic and geologic features has been obtained. It also served as a basis for the 1 to 10,000 maps that had to be compiled for this study.

Geo-electrical soundings

Regarding the available knowledge of the geology of the island, it was considered worthwhile to try vertical geo-electric soundings (VES), in spite of the acknowledged possibility of failure due to geological inhomogeneities, tidal effects, etc.

In principle VES is a method to determine by measurements at the surface the underground sequence of layers in terms of electrical resistance.

The applied method consists of four electrodes in a line arrangement (fig. 10.88). The two outer electrodes are current electrodes (CE) which drive the current through the subsoil, where the inner electrodes are used as potential electrodes (PE).

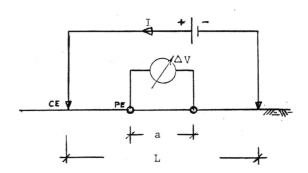

Fig. 10.88 - Four-electrodes in line arrangement.

The current I and the drop in potential ΔV are measured for a series of values of L and a. The resistivities (R) of the adherent subsoil bodies bounded by the equipotential faces can be computed (Ohm's law: $R = \Delta V/I$).

The specific resistivity of the (complex) medium ρ then can be computed from $\rho = KR$, where K is a geometrical factor which depends only on electrode spacings (L and a).

Plotting ρ versus L/2 (fig. 10.89) gives a field graph that can be compared with synthetic graphs calculated for known subsoil profiles. Proper matching with one of these so-called standard curves gives the profile sought in terms of electrical properties.

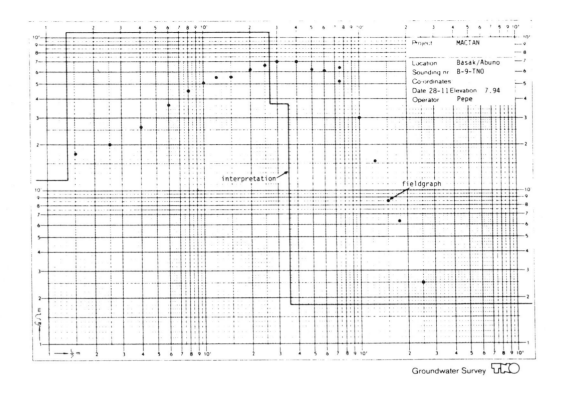

Groundwater Survey TNO

Fig. 10.89 - Geoelectrical sounding.

Next a second phase of interpretation is necessary to 'translate' the layers found with their specific resistivities and depths into hydro-geological strata. Here other information about the underground, e.g., obtained from one or two bore-hole investigations, is indispensable.

For more extensive information about the method, its applicability and limitations the reader is referred to the literature cited in this case study.

In this study a total of 35 sites were selected and surveyed with respect to mean sea level. For the soundings several types of instruments were used. Both Wenner and Schlumberger arrangements of electrodes were applied. A preliminary interpretation of the obtained fieldgraphs was done with three layer standard curves. Final interpretation occurred by matching with eight layer standard curves computed on a programmable pocket calculator. Unfortunately unique interpretations could only be obtained for a handful of soundings. In general the result was not conclusive enough because of observed equivalency of interpretations and relatively poor fits. This may underline the general warning against the application of geo-electrical sound-ings in karstified areas.

It was decided to use the findings exclusively to check the results to be obtained from an extensive shallow well survey.

Well survey

Since the entire population of Mactan Island relies on shallow wells for
drinking water supply, there are numerous wells scattered all over the area.
Most are private open wells, some tens are government wells with better per-
formances. Apart from two electrically pumped wells of modest capacity, all
are operated with buckets or handpumps. In this survey, 91 open wells were
selected for monitoring and further analysis of water levels and salinity
(fig. 10.90). A number of these wells, located in the eastern and northeastern part of the island, had been abandonned because of too high chlorinity
(> 900 ppm Cl⁻). The other wells, with fair to good quality in terms of chlorinity although with sometimes excessive hardness, were still used. A major
problem in determining the water levels was caused by the propagation of the
twice a day tide. Its amplitude being only about one meter, the influence on
the island groundwater levels is nevertheless substantial, due to the high
permeability of the limestone and the numerous fissures and underground channels. In order to establish the mean water level in each well, the levels in
22 wells roughly located in four cross-sections almost perpendicular to the
coastline were monitored simultaneously for 12 hours.

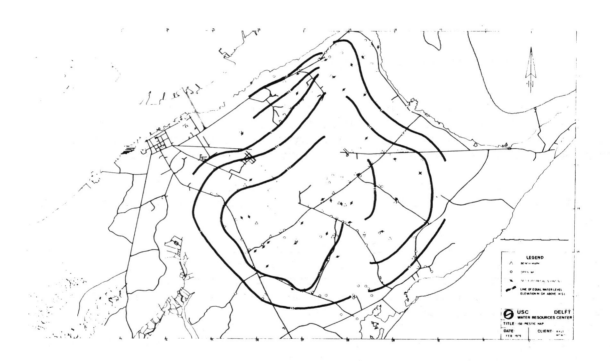

Fig. 10.90 - Isopiestic map.

From comparison with the total graph recorded at Dolphin Island in
the open sea, lag times and amplitudes could be derived. The isochronal map
in figure 10.91 shows a picture of the lag times, and the positions of the
cross-sectional lines 1 to 4.

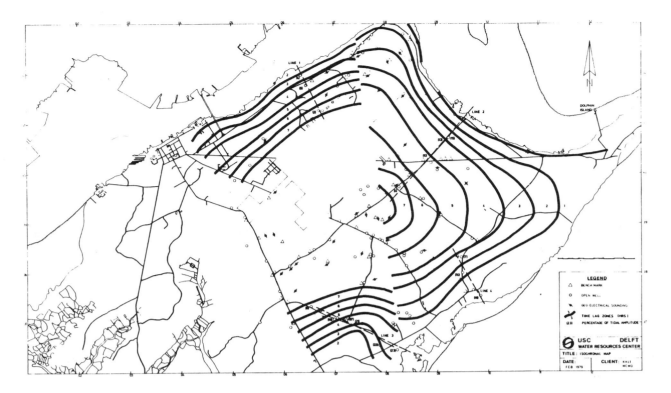

Fig. 10.91 - Isochronal map.

All wells have been levelled with a relatively high degree of accuracy. Control levelling showed deviations nowhere bigger than four millimeters.

Bench marks erected for the levelling were made permanent immediately. This may avoid a lot of work for eventual future activities.

After levelling and further elaborations of the measurements an isopiestic map (fig. 10.90) was obtained by contouring. It shows average water table levels with respect to mean sea level. The above mentioned major fault is clearly reflected.

Care was taken that no substantial withdrawals from the wells under observation occurred prior to the readings, so as to avoid spurious results.

When tidal and seasonal influences are minor, a rather sharp fresh-saline water interface can be expected. According to the Badon-Ghyben-Herzberg principle, under stationary conditions for every place $z = \alpha h$, where z is the depth of the fresh-salt water interface below mean sea level, h is the groundwater level and $\alpha = (\rho_s - \rho_f)/\rho_f$, ρ_s, ρ_f being the specific densities of salt and fresh water respectively (refer to section 3.2).

Here α appeared to be 0.025, meaning that $z = 40\ h$. Since h could be taken from the isopiestic map, a fictitious fresh-saline water interface could be derived. Note that the accuracy in h appears to be of utmost importance for the magnitude of z. Subsequently, the influence of the tide and the seasonal variation in net groundwater recharge have been introduced.

Based on some deductions made from observed qualities in several wells, an indication obtained from the chloride log of the exploratory well and a tentative contemplation of the dynamic flow processes involved, a procedure to convert the fictitious sharp fresh-saline water interface zone was developed.

Since both horizontal and vertical groundwater flow will cause dispersion of salt, the obtained lag times were taken to constitute the most important factor for conversion.

The effect of seasonal fluctuation appeared of less importance, but nevertheless was considered to cause a mixing zone of 0.4 times the thickness of the fresh water lens of which half would be above the fictitious interface and the other half below. This could be particularly derived from the chloride-log of the exploratory well, where the tidal influence was negligible and yet such a mixing zone was present.

At places with zero lag time any (imaginary) fresh water body was considered to be brackish. At places with time lags of seven hours and up, only the seasonal effect was considered, since in these places the relative tidal amplitude is less than about two per cent. In between zero and seven hours time lag, a linear function has been adopted (fig. 10.92).

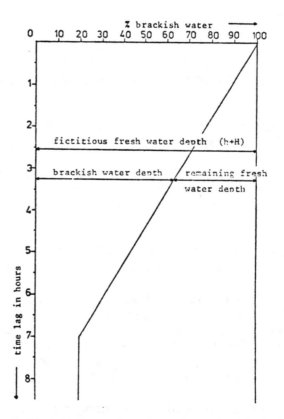

Fig. 10.92 – Division of fictitious fresh water depth into brackish and fresh water due to tidal and seasonal fluctuations.

Basically this is not correct, a kind of logarithmic function would be more appropriate, following leading theories. However, because of the nonhomogeneity of the aquifer and the lack of more data this simplification was considered satisfactory. The resulting fresh-brackish and brackish-saline interfaces are shown in figures. 10.93 and 10.94.

Conclusions

Some major conclusions that can be drawn from the results are:

-Extraction of groundwater should only be done by hand-pumping or lightly powered electrical pumps, thus limiting the draw-down of the water table. Here one has to bear in mind that a steady draw-down of about 10 centimeters will induce an up-coning of the fictitious salt-fresh interface of 4 meters. In many areas of the island the inherent rise of the brackish water would already be catastrophic.

-The spacing between the extraction wells must be chosen very carefully, since the total draw down of the water table in a point will be close to the sum of the individual draw downs in that point as induced by all wells in the surroundings.

-Because of the recharge occurring only during the wet season, the fresh water body at the end of the dry season will be smaller than the one found at the end of the wet season. Moreover, the computed wet season recharge of 1,6 mm per day is only a long period average. Climatic deviations from the average may also affect the shape and thickness of the lens.

-More checks on the actual lens should be made. Especially regular monitoring of the fresh - brackish interface would be useful. To this end one could benefit from the results of so called 'permanent electrode systems'. These electrode systems consist basically of a multi strand special cable which is lowered into a borehole (of even small diameter). Onto this cable a number of electrodes are attached in pairs at various depths, each pair forming an observation point. By means of a simple earth sensitivity meter or more elaborate equipment the electrical formation resistivity at the location of an observation point can be determined. From this resistivity the chloride content of the water and especially the variations thereof can be deduced. For further information one is referred to Walter (1972).

-A proposed sewerage system for domestic sewage must be discouraged, since the net recharge of the fresh water lens would so be severely diminished. This can be shown as follows: the amount of fresh water disposed of via the brackish water zone is estimated at 50% of the groundwater recharge. The remaining 50% will be lost for consumption due to malpositioning of the wells. With the present population only some 50 liters per capita per day would be available.

However, from in situ observations a return flow of about 60% is estimated, thus leading to a net mean possible consumption of 125 liters per head per day as follows from the water balance:

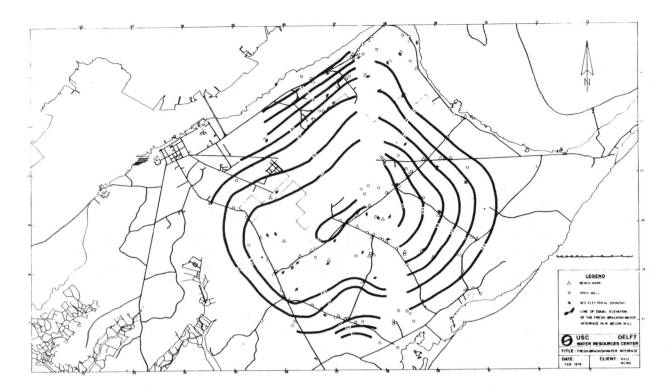

Fig. 10.93 - Fresh-brackish salt water interface.

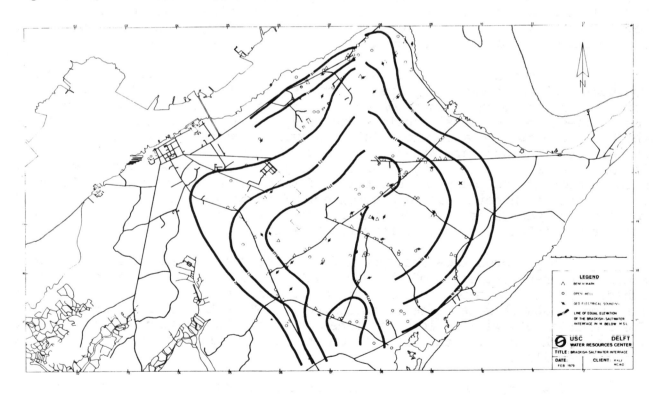

Fig. 10.94 - Fresh-brackish salt water interface.

Natural Recharge + 0.6 Consumption = Consumption $(50 + 0.6 \, C = C \rightarrow C = 125)$

Of course, special precautions have to be taken that sewage water is disposed of at locations well away from the wells in order to avoid bacteriological contamination of the drinking water. In this respect the need for proper locating of the wells is emphasized.

Acknowledgements

This study was carried out as a partial fulfillment of a contract between Local Water Utilities Administration (LWUA, Manila) and Kampsax-Kruger Lahmeyer International (KKLI, Copenhagen, Frankfurt) as their consultants.

The field work and parts of the interpretation were executed by graduate students from Delft University of Technology and staff of the Water Resources Center (WRC) of the University of San Carlos in Cebu.

The Metropolitan Cebu Water District (MCWD) and Weather Bureau PAGASA have been helpful with providing some basic data and clearances.

I am grateful to all those who contributed to this study. For the full report the reader is referred to, 'Geohydrological Survey, Mactan Island.'

References

Geohydrological Survey Mactan Island, University of San Carlos, Water Resources Center, TH Delft Cebu-City, the Philippines.

Walter, F. (1972). The application of permanent electrode systems for groundwater salinity inspection, Salt Water Intrusion Meeting, Copenhagen, June. TNO-DGV, Delft, The Netherlands.

10.6   Salt balances, surface-groundwater

Discharge of groundwater in coastal areas, concentrated or diffuse, can alter the coastal water salinity. The study of such discharges can be done through salt balances.

Case history no. 14: Aquifer-estuary fresh-salt water balance, Miami, Florida*

Introduction

In the course of research studies conducted by the U.S. Geological Survey on the problem of salt-water encroachment into the Biscayne aquifer in 1958, water samples were collected along a line extending from the village of Cutler, Florida to Fowey Rocks (fig. 10.95). The data (fig. 10.99) were sparse but they indicated that seaward-flowing fresh groundwater diluted Biscayne Bay to a distance greater than two miles from shore. Thus, conversely,

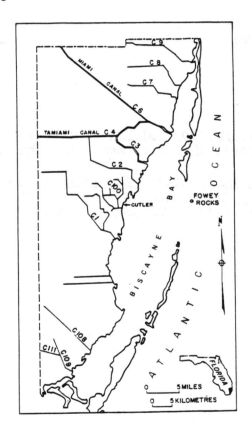

Fig. 10.95 - Map of Miami area showing drainage canals and locations referred to in the text.

---

* Prepared by Francis A. Kohout, U.S. Geological Survey, Woods Hole, Massachusetts 02543, U.S.A.

high salinity water that intrudes into the deep part of the aquifer from the sea floor must necessarily originate beyond two miles from the shore. The subject matter places quantitative limits on the mutual interrelationships between groundwater flow in a coastal aquifer and the salinity of a contiguous bay or estuary.

2. The Biscayne aquifer

Municipal water supplies of southeastern Florida are drawn from the Biscayne aquifer. A section of this shallow water-table aquifer through the Miami area is shown in fig. 10.96. The aquifer consists of high permeable solution-riddled limestone that thins from a maximum thickness of 200 feet (61 m) near the coast to a featheredge 40 miles (64 km) west of Miami. A thick section of clay, marl, and sand of relatively low permeability forms the base for the Biscayne aquifer.

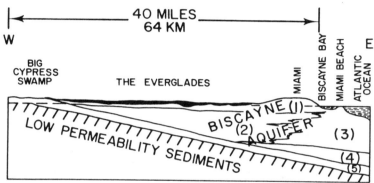

Fig. 10.96 - Generalized west-east geologic section through Miami, Florida showing water-bearing formations of the Biscayne aquifer. The Everglades are underlain by peat and black organic soils.

Between 1909 and 1930, drainage canals were constructed westward through the Miami area to reclaim low-lying land for urban and agricultural development (fig. 10.95). The canals lowered water levels about six feet (1.8 meters) in the Everglades. Sea water encroached into the Biscayne aquifer, and several municipal well fields were abandoned prior to 1945, when control dams began to be constructed. The control dams help maintain relatively high fresh-water levels near the shoreline and also prevent salt water from moving directly inland in the canals during the dry season.

Special attention is directed to Canal C-100 (fig. 10.95), commonly called Cutler Drain. This canal was completed during the course of the investigation and Biscayne Bay, adjacent to the Cutler area, began to be influenced by this new fresh-water outlet in the latter stages of the investigation. Prior to September 1963 (see gate opening graph, fig. 10.100), the canal was either too short to be an effective drainage canal or the control dam was closed.

<u>Cyclic flow of salt water in the Biscayne aquifer</u>

Research investigations in the coastal part of the Biscayne aquifer showed that the salt front had become dynamically stable seaward of the position computed according to the Badon-Ghyben-Herzberg (BGH) principle (see section 3.2; Cooper, 1959; Henry, 1959; Kohout, 1960a, 1960b). In part, the discrepancy related to the fact that the interface between the two fluids was not sharp. Figure 10.97 is a cross section of the zone of diffusion which is the gradational contact between fresh water (16 parts per million chloride in Miami) and sea water (about 19,000 ppm). The isochlors are based on water samples from individual, fully-cased wells, whose bottoms are indicated by the black dots in the cross section. The wells are set up in stations at various distances from the coast and their termini serve as points for collecting water samples and for measuring pressure heads at isolated depths in the aquifer.

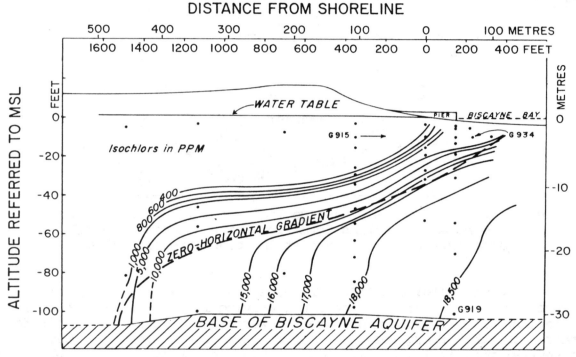

Fig. 10.97 - Cross section through the Cutler area, Miami, showing the zone of diffusion, 18 September, 1958. The dots indicate the termini of fully-cased wells.

The blunt-nosed shape of the isochlor pattern is the characteristic configuration throughout the Miami area. This shape results from the lower boundary, because no salt can diffuse upward across the impermeable base of the Biscayne aquifer. As the dispersion of salt along the base of the aquifer can take place only in a horizontal direction, the isochlors must approach the base of the aquifer vertically to satisfy the boundary condition.

It was concluded, both mathematically and by field observation, that when the fresh-water head was low, sea water flowed inland from the floor of the sea through the lower part of the aquifer into the zone of diffusion, then upward and back to the sea through the upper part of the aquifer (Cooper et al., 1964). Flow throughout the aquifer is determinable from horizontal gradients derived from diagrams that show the distribution of equivalent fresh-water head in both fresh- and salt-water regions of the flow diagram of figure 10.98 represents the average conditions that existed on 18 September, 1958. The landward part of the flowlines representing the cyclic flow of sea water may be traced by following the path of flow lines that start below the zero-horizontal gradient line in figure 10.98. Though the seaward extremity of these flow lines is not shown, it may be assumed that they originate at the bottom of Biscayne Bay at some unknown distance offshore from the view of the cross section. By comparison of chloride content in the bay with that in the aquifer, this report throws light on the minimum distance offshore at which the flow lines originate.

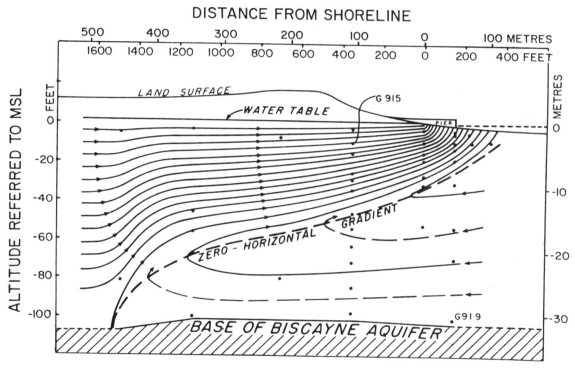

Fig. 10.98 - Cross section through the Cutler area, Miami, showing the flow pattern of fresh and salt water for a low-head condition. The dots indicate the termini of fully-cased wells.

Dilution of Biscayne Bay by ground-water discharge

A. The 1958 chlorinity data

In 1958, water samples were collected at the bottom of Biscayne Bay on a line extending from the Cutler area toward Fowey Rocks (fig. 10.95). At this time, the nearest canal to the Cutler area was about 4 miles away and this suggested that the observed dilution of the bay, at least near shore, related more to ground-water discharge than to the outflow from any canal. Also, due to the very high permeability of the limestone, rainfall percolates very rapidly to the water table and direct runoff from the shoreline is practically unknown except during flood times when the water table itself rises above land surface.

The fluctuations of chlorinity at sampling stations B1 to B6 (fig. 10.99) are erratic between 13,000 and 19,000 ppm chloride because of the interaction of time, seasonal rainfall, and fresh-water runoff. However, the arithmetic averages at the right of figure 10.99 show a consistent trend getting saltier seaward with bay-sample B6 at 2 miles from shore averaging only 17,500 ppm. The graph of well G919 (fig. 10.99) located near the base of the aquifer (see location, fig. 10.97) has small fluctuation and averages 18,300 ppm. At Fowey Rocks, the chlorinity was about 19,800 ppm. Based on these sparse data, it was suspected that the salt water intruding into the deep part of the aquifer at well G919 (fig. 10.98) would have to originate at some location between sampling station B6, two miles from shore, and Fowey Rocks, 12 miles from shore. Also, because Canal C-100 (fig. 10.95) did not exit in 1958, it was suspected that the seaward chlorinity gradient in the bay water was related to the gradual seaward flushing of the fresh ground water by tidal action.

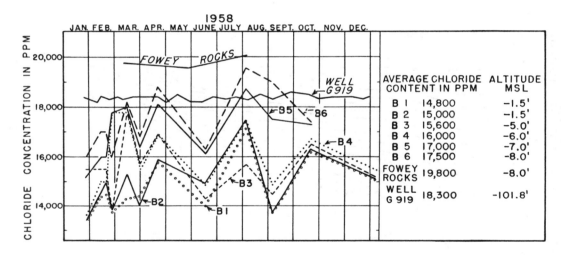

Fig. 10.99 - Fluctuations of chlorinity in samples collected at the bottom of Biscayne Bay offshore from the Cutler area at Miami, Florida, 1958. The location of stations is shown in the insert map of fig. 10.101; Stations B1 and B2 are the same as 1 and 2.

B. Chlorinity in Biscayne Bay, 1963-65.

A sampling program was initiated to improve the 1958 chlorinity profile in Biscayne Bay. In this way, the fresh water itself, though not unique to ground water, would serve as an indicator of dilution.

In connection with biological studies to appraise the effect of construction of the City of Miami sewage treatment plant in 1956, Moore et al. (1955) and McNulty (1961) showed that maximum tidal fluctuation of salinity occurred opposite the mouth of the Miami Canal (fig. 10.95); in intercanal areas, the fluctuations were small. A complete seasonal cycle for surface salinity near Chicken Key, slightly north of Stations 4 and 5 (insert map, fig. 10.101) is given by Woodmansee (1958, p. 248) for the year 1948. The equivalent surface chloride content during that hurricane year ranged from a high of about 19.2 ppt (parts per thousand) in March to a low of about 8 ppt in October.

Figure 10.100 shows the chlorinity in samples collected at the bottom of Biscayne Bay in 1963-65 (see location of stations, fig. 10.102). Station 1 is located in the intertidal zone and the chlorinity varies severely depending on the stage of the tide at the time of sample collection; i.e., the chlorinity is lowest near low tide when the quantity of ground-water discharge is greatest, but rises to high values when flooded by the rising tide. The water at stations 2 and 3 is about 0.5 and 1.5 feet (0.15 and 0.45 m) deep at the lowest tide level. At high tide, the bay water covers all stations and there may be a slight reversal of head so that near shore, the bay water may intrude slightly into the aquifer before being flushed out during the falling tide.

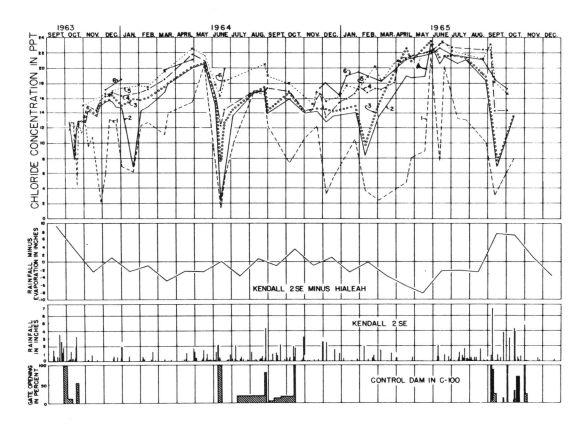

Fig. 10.100 - Graph showing fluctuation of chlorinity in Biscayne Bay related to rainfall, control-dam operation, and the excess or deficiency of rainfall over evaporation, 1963-65. The location of stations is shown in the insert map of Fig. 10.101.

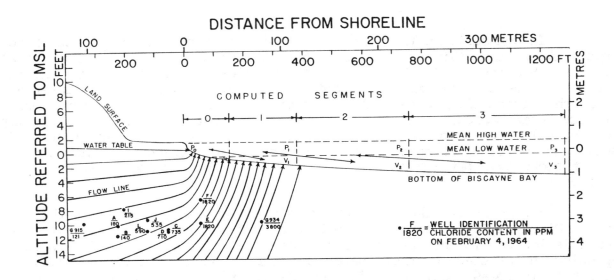

Fig. 10.101 - Graph of the observed mean chlorinity profile in Biscayne Bay offshore from Cutler (1963-65) compared with the computed profile for steady-state groundwater discharge along the shoreline.

The fluctuations o chlorinity are seasonal and correlate reasonably well with the R-E curve (rainfall minus evaporation), which is obtained by comparing rainfall at Kendall 2SE, two miles north of the Cutler site, with evaporation data for the Hialeah station.

In the spring months of 1964 and 1965, the evaporation is greater than rainfall (R-E curve falls below the zero line) and the chlorinity increases to more than 22 ppt (about 3 ppt greater than normal sea water). Under these conditions, the most seaward sampling station (6) has lower chlorinity than those at moderate distance from shore (4 and 5) because sea water of constant chlorinity moves inland into Biscayne Bay from the Florida Straits to supply the evaporative demand. Closer to shore the samples reflect dilution mainly by ground-water outflow because salinity control dams are usually closed under such conditions (gate opening graph, fig. 10.100). In Spring 1965, however, ground-water discharge was apparently reduced to such a low value that samples collected at high tide (even at Station 1) had chloride contents above 21 ppt. This also coincides with the time that strong southeasterly winds packed large quantities of Sargassum weed against the shoreline.

Because of high water and in preparation for Hurricane Flora, which eventually stalled over Cuba, the stop-log gates in the old C-100 control dam were removed on 26 September, 1963. The less dense fresh water formed a fan-shaped lens as it spread seaward over the more dense salt water in the bay. Thus, the hydrologic regimen of Biscayne Bay has changed from one of ground-water outflow as the main dilutant near Cutler (chlorinity data, fig. 10.99) to one of surface- and ground-water outflow combined. It is almost axiomatic that this part of the bay must now undergo much greater fresh-water outbursts and more severe fluctuation of salinity than existed prior to 1963. Although this change has taken place, it is not without merit that the effect of ground-water discharge alone be considered as a factor in the offshore chlorinity profile of Biscayne Bay. These calculations, disregarding direct rainfall, evaporation, and surface-water outflow, will be made in the following section.

Computed and observed chlorinity gradient in Biscayne Bay

A. Computing scheme

The general scheme will be to compute the ground-water discharge into Biscayne Bay from a strip of the aquifer one unit wide. Then, assuming that this ground-water discharge is flushed perpendicularly seaward from the shoreline by tidal action, the salinity profile will be computed for a one-unit wide strip of the bay along the section line shown in the inset map of figure 10.101. The line starts 1600 feet inland from the shoreline for the ground-water computations and extends about 3.5 miles (5.6 km) seaward from the shoreline for the bay salinity computations. The computations assume that along-shore currents are negligible.

B. Computing ground-water discharge

The transmissibility of the Biscayne aquifer at Cutler was determined by pump and tidal fluctuation tests (Ferris et al., 1962, pp. 93–103) to be about 3,000,000 gpd/ft (gallons per day per foot), or about 37,250 m^2/day. Since the aquifer thickness is 105 ft (32 m), the permeability is

$$K = (3,000,000 \text{ gpd/ft})/(105 \text{ ft}) = 28,500 \text{ gpd/ft}^2, \text{ or}$$

$$(37,250 \frac{m^2}{day})/(32 \text{ m}) = 1160 \text{ m/day}$$

A modified form of Darcy's law takes the form:

$$Q = k \cdot i \cdot A$$

where: Q = discharge, k = permeability, i = hydraulic gradient, A = the cross sectional area taken perpendicular to the direction of flow. Coherent units must be used (gallons, day and feet, or m^3, day and m).

Taking the three uppermost flow tubes at a distance of 1600 feet (488 m) inland from the shoreline in figure 10.98, the average flow-tube thickness is 6.6 feet (2.01 m), the permeability is 28,500 gpd/ft^2 (1160 m/day), and the hydraulic gradient in this region is about 0.3 foot in 300 feet or 0.001, as obtained from figure in Cooper et al., 1964. All computations are based on a unit width of section of one foot (or one meter).

$$Q = 28{,}500 \text{ gpd/ft}^2 \times \frac{0.3 \text{ ft}}{300 \text{ ft}} \times 6.6 \text{ ft.} \times 1 \text{ ft}$$

$$= 188 \text{ gpd/flow tube} = 25 \text{ ft}^3/\text{day/flow tube 1 foot wide}$$

$$(2.33^3/\text{day/flow tube 1 m wide})$$

In figure 10.98, the seaward flow of water at the shoreline is represented by 16 flow tubes, of which 14 fresh-water tubes originate inland and 2 sea-water tubes originate at the floor of the sea. Because the method of constructing the flow diagram required that the flow through all tubes be maintained constant and equal to each other, the total discharge is obtained by multiplying the single-tube value by 16:

$$Q \text{ (16 tubes)} = 188 \text{ gpd} \times 16 = 3008 \text{ gpd} =$$

$$402 \text{ ft}^3/\text{day in a one-foot wide strip} =$$

$$(37.3 \text{ m}^3/\text{day in a one-meter wide strip})$$

The seaward flushing of this discharge is related to a tidal period of about 12.5 hours (Sverdrup et al., 1942, Table 70). Therefore,

$$Q \text{ (tide cycle)} = 402 \text{ ft}^3/\text{day} \times \frac{12.5}{24} =$$

$$210 \text{ ft}^3/\text{tide cycle in a one-foot wide-strip}$$

$$(19.5 \text{ m}^3/\text{tide cycle in a one-meter wide strip})$$

Due to the cyclic flow of salt water, the discharge at the shoreline is not completely fresh, but computations indicate that the average water would contain about 1500 ppm chloride.

C. Computing the Bay salinity profile

The method for determining the salinity gradient related to ground-water discharge in Biscayne Bay is adapted from a computing procedure developed by Bostwick H. Ketchum (1951a, 1951b) for tidal flushing of a river estuary. The general idea of Ketchum's method is that on each tide cycle a volume of fresh river water equivalent to the river discharge enters the estuary and moves seaward. However, the distance the volume can travel on each tide cycle is limited by the average excursion of a particle of water during that tide cycle. This might be clarified by comparing it with the classic tidal prism theory in which it was assumed that the entire volume of water from high tide to low tide was lost to the ocean on a falling tide and was replaced by a fresh supply of ocean water on a rising tide. In Biscayne Bay, for example, tidal currents would have to carry fresh ground-water discharge from the shoreline 15 miles seaward to the Florida Straits in the 6 hours from high to low tide. This would represent an average velocity of 2.5 miles per hour (4 km/h) and such velocities are not observed except in tidal channels between the offshore shoals and keys. Ketchum's theory allows for an accumulation of fresh water in the bay because it recognizes that the distance a particle of water can move on a tidal excursion is limited by the geometry of the bay.

An important element of the technique is the volumetric segmentation of the bay (fig. 10.102). The first segment is defined as having an intertidal volume (P_0) equal to the ground-water discharge. The underlying assumption is that ground-water discharge, or runoff (R_{gw}) during a tidal cycle is sufficient to provide the observed rise in water level from low tide to high tide. Once the size of this segment is established, the next seaward segment is defined so that its low-tide volume equals the high-tide volume of the preceding landward segment. This segmentation is carried as far seaward as desired, and by connecting the centers of mass of the segments, it is seen that the average tidal excursions increase in the seaward direction.

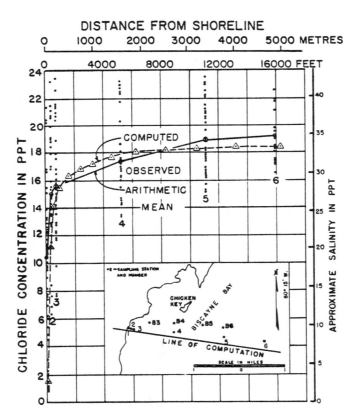

Fig. 10.102 – Section through the Cutler area showing subdivision of Biscayne Bay into volume segments, average tidal excursion of a water particle, and characteristics of groundwater discharge through the bay bottom.

-591-

The logic of the technique (modified from Ketchum, 1951b) can be obtained from the following considerations (fig. 10.102):

$$P_O = R_{gw} \text{ where } R_{gw} = \text{ground-water runoff}$$

$$V_1 = V_O + P_O$$

$$V_2 = V_1 + P_1 = V_O + P_O + P_1$$

$$V_3 = V_2 + P_2 + = V_1 + P_1 + P_2 + = V_O + P_O + P_1 + P_2$$

$$V_N = V_O + \sum_O^{n-1} P_i$$

$$V_n = V_O + R_{gw} + \sum_1^{n-1} P_i$$

where P_i is the intertidal volume (from low to high tide) of the ith segment of the tidal prism.

Allowing the water to push inland as though a piston were displacing it, the amount of water that must pass a particular segment boundary on a rising tide would be equal to the full volume of the tidal prism in all landward segments. For example, the quantity of water that would push inland past the left-hand low-tide boundary of segment 3 would be equal to the high-tide volume of segment 2 but also, because of the method of defining the segments, it would be equal to the total low-tide to high-tide volume of segments 1 and 2. A volume of fresh ground water (R_{gw}) enters the bay on each tide cycle and moves one segment seaward on each subsequent tide cycle, but since these volumes of fresh water are being mixed with larger volumes of ocean water, the concentration of the bay water gradually increases in the seaward direction. Ketchum (1951a, pp. 200-202) states:

'If it is assumed that the water present in each of the volume segments is completely mixed at high tide, the proportion of water removed by the ebbing tide is given by the ratio between the local intertidal volume (that part of the tidal prism within each volume segment) and the local high tide volume. This is defined as an exchange ratio, r, having the value:

$$r_n = \frac{P_n}{P_n + V_n}$$

in which P_n is the intertidal volume and V_n is the low tide volume of the nth segment.

The river water present in each segment is made up of varying proportions of water that arrived at the location under consideration during a series of tidal cycles. Using the tidal exchange ratio, the proportion of river water of various tidal ages removed during each cycle, and the proportion left behind........can be represented by a mathematical series.'

Modifying Ketchum's terminology: the total volume, Q_n of ground water accumulated within any volume segment, n, of the bay at high tide after an infinite number of tide cycles approaches the limit:

$$A_n = \frac{R_{gw}}{r_n}$$

The percentage of fresh ground water in each segment is obtained by dividing the accumulated ground water in any segment by the volume of that segment at high tide:

$$\% \text{ fresh water} = \frac{Q_n}{P_n + V_n}$$

The average chloride content of the ground-water discharge is about 1.5 ppt (fig. 10.102) and this water mixed with 19 ppt sea water is proportioned according to respective percentages to obtain the calculated chlorinity profile extending offshore from the Cutler site. The various computations are summarized in the table.

D. <u>Results of computations</u>

The upper part of the flow diagram of figure 10.98 is reproduced in figure 10.102. The profile of the bay bottom and, hence, the volume computations for the 1-foot wide strip of the bay, are obtained from U. S. Coast and Geodetic Survey Chart 848. It is noted that ground water discharges into the first several segments rather than into the volume assigned in the first segment. As a result, the computed concentrations in these first several segments can be expected to compare poorly with observed data.

The results of the computations related to distance from the shoreline are plotted in figure 10.101. The dark dots are the observed chlorinity data (fluctuation graph, fig. 10.100) for the six sampling stations, 1963-65; a line is passed through the arithmetic average of these points. Near shore, the ground-water discharge does not enter the bay as a lump as the manner of computing assumed, and the computed curve indicates there should be much fresher water near shore than is actually observed. Farther from shore, the computed curve rises above the observed line and then falls below it beyond about 8,000 feet (2440 m). The agreement is fairly good in spite of the fact

Summary of computations for chlorinity profile in Biscayne Bay related to steady-state ground-water discharge of 210 ft^3/tidal cycle per lineal foot of shoreline

Segment	Distance from high tide mark (ft)	Length of segment (ft)	Local volumes			$r_n = \dfrac{P_n}{P_n + V_n}$	$Q_n = \dfrac{R_{gw}}{r_n}$ (ft^3)	Percent ground water $\dfrac{Q_n}{P_n + V_n}$	Percent sea water	Calculated Chlorinity (ppm)
			V_n (ft^3)	P_n (ft^3)	$P_n + V_n$ (ft^3)					
0	150	150	0	210	210	.956	210	100.000	0	1,500
1	380	230	210	470	680	.691	304	44.70	55.30	11,200
2	755	375	680	745	1,425	.523	402	28.20	71.80	14,100
3	1,280	525	1,425	1,050	2,475	.424	495	20.00	80.00	15,500
4	1,980	700	2,475	1,375	3,850	.357	588	15.30	84.70	16,350
5	2,830	850	3,850	1,700	5,550	.306	686	12.40	87.60	16,850
6	3,820	990	5,550	2,050	7,600	.270	778	10.20	89.80	17,200
7	5,220	1,400	7,600	2,800	10,400	.269	780	7.50	92.50	17,700
8	7,220	2,000	10,400	3,800	14,200	.267	786	5.54	94.46	18,030
9	9,250	2,030	14,200	4,200	18,400	.228	921	5.00	95.00	18,130
10	11,750	2,500	18,400	4,800	23,200	.207	1,014	4.37	95.63	18,250
11	14,650	2,900	23,200	6,000	29,200	.205	1,024	3.50	96.50	18,400
12	18,000	3,350	29,200	6,800	36,000	.189	1,111	3.09	96.91	18,460

that direct rainfall and evaporation are not included in the computations. Evaporation, for example, caused a seasonal rise in bay chlorinity in the spring of 1965, to greater than 22 ppt (fig. 10.100) If included, the effect of evaporation would be to shift the computed curves upward toward higher chlorinity by a variable amount; direct rainfall would tend to shift the curve downward.

Conclusions

The correlation of the computed curve with 1958 data (fig. 10.99) and the arithmetic mean of the observed data in 1963-65 (fig. 10.101) indicates that ground-water discharge contributed significantly to the offshore chlorinity of Biscayne Bay. The computed and observed curves pass through a chlorinity value of 18,300 ppm, the average chlorinity in well G919 (figs. 10.98 and 10.99), enters through the floor of the bay on its flow path into the deep part of the aquifer during salt-water intrusion. The maximum length, of course, is about 12 miles (19.4 km) from shore, at the point where the aquifer is truncated vertically by the channel of the Florida Straits.

Thus, a mutual relationship exists between the waters of Biscayne Bay and the Biscayne aquifer. The seaward flow of relatively fresh ground water dilutes the bay water to a distance greater than two miles (3.2 km) from shore and, conversely, the high salinity water that intrudes into the deep part of the aquifer must necessarily originate at a distance greater than two miles (3.2 km) from shore.

Acknowledgements

My friend Leo Heindl, the late Executive Secretary of the U. S. National Committee on Scientific Hydrology, International Hydrological Programme, Unesco, encouraged the submission of this paper and I wish to dedicate it to his memory.

References

Cooper, H. H., Jr., 1959. A hypothesis concerning the dynamic balance of fresh water and salt water in a coastal aquifer: Jour. Geophys. Research, v. 64, no. 4, pp. 461-467.

Cooper, H. H., Jr., F. A. Kohout, H. R. Henry, R. E. Glover, 1964. Sea water in coastal aquifers: U. S. Geol. Survey Water-Supply Paper 1613-C.

Ferris, J. G., D. B. Knowles, R. H. Brown, R. W. Stallman, 1962. Theory of aquifer tests. U. S. Geol. Survey Water-Supply Paper 1536-E.

Henry, H.R., 1959. Salt intrusion into fresh-water aquifers: Jour. Geophys. Research , v. 64, no. 11, pp. 1911-1919.

Ketchum, B.H., 1951a. The flushing of tidal estuaries: J. Fed. Sewage and Industrial Wastes Assoc., v. 23, no. 2, pp. 198-208.

Ketchum, B.H., 1951b. <u>The exchanges of fresh and salt waters in tidal estuaries</u>: J. Mar. Res., v. 10, no. 1, pp. 18-38.

Kohout, F.A., 1960a. <u>Cyclic flow of salt water in the Biscayne aquifer of southeastern Florida</u>: Jour. Geophys. Research, v. 65, no. 7, pp. 2133-2141.

Kohout, F.A., 1960b. <u>Flow pattern of fresh water and salt water Biscayne aquifer of the Miami area, Florida</u>: Internat. Assoc. Sci. Hydrol., Comm. Subter. Waters Pub. 52, pp. 440-448.

McNulty, J., 1961. <u>Ecological effects of sewage pollution in Biscayne Bay, Florida</u>: Sediments and distribution of benthic and fouling macro-organisms: Bull. Mar. Sci. Gulf and Caribbean, v. 11, no. 3, pp. 394-447.

Moore, H.B., Hela, I., Reynolds, S., McNulty, J.K., Miller S., Carpenter, Jr., 1955. <u>Report on preliminary studies of pollution in Biscayne Bay</u>: Univ. of Miami Marine Laboratory Progress Report No. 55-3, 79 p.

Sverdrup, H.V., Johnson, M.W. Fleming, R.H., 1942. <u>The Oceans</u>: Prentice-Hall, Inc., Englewood Cliffs, New Jersey.

Woodmansee, A., 1958. <u>The seasonal distribution of zooplankton off Chicken Key in Biscayne Bay, Florida</u>: Ecology, v. 39, no. 2.